Springer Studies in the History of Economic Thought

This series offers an outlet for research in the history of economic thought. It features scholarly studies on important theoretical developments and great economic thinkers that have contributed to the evolution of the economic discipline.

Springer Studies in the History of Economic Thought (SSHET) welcomes proposals for research monographs, edited volumes, textbooks and handbooks from a variety of disciplines that seek to study the history of economic thinking and help to arrive at a better understanding of modern economics. Relevant topics include, but are not limited to, various schools of thought, important pioneers and thinkers, ancient and medieval economic thought, mercantilism, cameralism and physiocracy, classical and neoclassical economics, historical, institutional and evolutionary economics, socialism and Marxism, Keynesian, Sraffian and Austrian economics, econometrics and mathematical studies as well as economic methodology and the link between economic history and history of economic thought.

All titles in this series are peer-reviewed.

For further information on the series and to submit a proposal for consideration, please contact Johannes Glaeser (Senior Editor Economics) Johannes.glaeser@springer.com.

Pierangelo Garegnani

Capital Theory, the Surplus Approach, and Effective Demand

An Alternative Framework for the Analysis of Value, Distribution and Output Levels

Springer

Pierangelo Garegnani
Roma Tre University
Rome, Italy

Edited by
Roberto Ciccone
Department of Economics
Roma Tre University
Rome, Italy

ISSN 2662-6098 ISSN 2662-6101 (electronic)
Springer Studies in the History of Economic Thought
ISBN 978-3-031-23645-7 ISBN 978-3-031-23643-3 (eBook)
https://doi.org/10.1007/978-3-031-23643-3

This Springer imprint is published by the registered company Springer Nature Switzerland AG
The registered company address is: Gewerbestrasse 11, 6330 Cham, Switzerland

Editorial Preface

This collection of works by Pierangelo Garegnani is the result of a project that was planned by the author for a long time and which, through a thoughtful itinerary that extended to the last period of his life, he had brought to a nearly conclusive stage, as witnessed by the lucid and exhaustive introduction with which Garegnani illustrates the contents of the collection and provides some conceptual premises. However, due to various circumstances, the publication of the volume did not take place with the author alive. In the years following his death in 2011, the realisation of the project was a commitment that Garegnani's wife, Mrs Luisa, took on with great dedication, more recently considering asking for my help in this regard. And, as a pupil and intellectual debtor of Garegnani's, I could only be grateful for such a task.

The volume opens with the Ph.D. thesis that Garegnani discussed in 1958 in Cambridge, and which had not been published in English until now (a consistent part of its contents appeared in 1960 in Italian as *Il capitale nelle teorie della distribuzione*). As can be deduced from notes and provisional drafts, the choice of the further materials to be included in the edition, given also the expected size of the volume, was made from a larger group of works, and then proceeded with successive exclusions that we can guess were sometimes troubled. The composition of the selection that Garegnani finally arrived at seems to indicate that the criterion followed was that of favouring works that—starting with the Ph.D. thesis—expound central elements of the theoretical system he reconstructed and developed, compared to writings that constitute applications of that system in relatively specific spheres. We can presume that in this second category he placed comments and rejoinders to positions of other scholars: an indirect confirmation seems to come from the fact that in the two contributions of that type included nevertheless in the collection we find, along with the discussion of the works (respectively by Samuelson and Blaug) taken into consideration, the reaffirmation of fundamental aspects of Garegnani's conceptual framework.

With regard to the thesis, the text published here differs from the version that was submitted to the examining committee due to the presence of Appendix E, concerning 'The theory of capital in Pareto'. In its final form, the Appendix is evidently the result of an elaboration little posterior to the presentation of the thesis, since it is the translation of the corresponding Appendix in the aforementioned 1960 Italian book, largely drawn from the dissertation. By including it in this edition of the latter, Garegnani shows that he understood that Appendix as a proper integration of the contents of the thesis.

Making the material ready for publication required some substantial editorial work, which consisted primarily of revising the electronic transcription of the Ph.D. thesis (in original typewritten), for which I had the meticulous assistance of Mrs. Luisa Garegnani. Misprints present in some of the collected papers, as previously published, were also corrected. The bibliographical references were in turn subject to integrations and, in some cases, amendments concerning the works or pages cited. Most of these adjustments were made silently, while interventions deemed to be explicit are commented on by editor's notes. The latter is also the form used in the few cases of explanatory remarks intended to dispel possible doubts of the reader about connections or references as meant by the author.

Pierangelo Garegnani has given an impressive contribution to economic analysis, extended on a wide range of themes, all concerning fundamental questions in economic theory. By publishing the starting point of his intellectual path, the Ph.D. dissertation, and placing side by side some of his most basic papers on either the critical front, the constructive front or the methodological front, this book allows the scholar to have an overall view of the theoretical framework he has contributed to elaborate in the perspective of an alternative approach to political economy.

Rome, Italy Roberto Ciccone

Introduction

I. Marginalist Theory and the Conception of Capital

1. The essays in this book turn on the alternative between the two broad approaches to a theory of distribution and relative prices which, at the cost of some simplification, can be said to have dominated economic thought in succession since its systematic inception in the 18th century. The first in order of time was founded on the notion of the surplus of which the community can dispose over the part of its product including the subsistence of workers, which must be used for continuing production on an unchanged scale. The incomes other than subsistence wages were traced to such a surplus. The early systematic formulation of this approach goes back to the Physiocrats, it was developed from Adam Smith to Ricardo, and Marx finally took it over when the main current of economic theory was already moving in a different direction. The second approach is the one which crystallized in the last quarter of the 19th century around the twin concepts of marginal utility and marginal productivity and has dominated since. It is founded on the conception of a substitutability between 'factors of production', and on the corresponding demand and supply functions for factors and commodities. It arose essentially out of an extension of the classical theory of rent to the division between wages and profits, thereby replacing the notion of surplus by which the classics had explained the same division.

One element can be said to have been of basic importance for the passage from the earlier to the later approach: it was the conception of capital as a single magnitude, a fluid susceptible of taking the form of any concrete capital good. As we shall presently see, in the absence of such a concept, the idea of a generalized substitutability between means of production and labour could hardly have occurred. The concept and the difficulties it raises for economic theory do accordingly play a central role in this book focussed as it is on the alternative between the two theories and a preliminary survey of the question, in the present section and the second of this Introduction, may help the reader to bring together elements he will find scattered in the following essays.

Elements concerning the classical alternative will enter the third section, and the fourth will provide an account of the essays contained in the book.

2. To understand the role of capital, the single magnitude, for the marginalist approach[1] it is necessary to start by recalling a basic feature of capital goods in a market economy which appears to have been largely forgotten in recent controversies. As Walras had lucidly pointed out nearly a century and half ago, in the eyes of their owners physically heterogeneous capital goods are in fact homogeneous in proportion to their values: they are elements of the single commodity 'perpetual net income'.[2] That is indeed the single commodity whose existence we imply when we assume competitive arbitrage to realize a uniform rate of riskless return on the price of such goods: the reciprocal of that rate is in effect the price of a unit of the Walrasian 'perpetual net income'. And nothing changes if, more in keeping with contemporary intertemporal general equilibrium, its finite horizon, and changing prices, we refer to 'income for next year', whose unit[3] has then a price given by the discount factor $(1+r_t)^{-1}$, r_t being the 'effectively' uniform rate of return for the year in question.[4]

Now, it is this single commodity yearly demanded by savers like other commodities, rooted in the experience and practice of wealth owners, and of the businesses in which they invest,[5] that has suggested in the first place the idea of a variability of the proportion in which the quantity of that commodity, 'capital', is employed with labour in production, analogous to the classical variability of the proportion of labour to land.[6] In fact the alternative production processes from

---

1 We prefer to call here 'marginal' or 'marginalist' rather than 'neoclassical' the dominant demand and supply theory. If the notion of 'margin' is less explicitly dominant in the present day reformulations of the theory, it clearly continues to be an essential ingredient of its general demand and supply framework. It is on the other hand difficult to trace today the continuity between that theory and the classical approach, that would justify the term 'neoclassical'.

2 Walras (1954), para. 242, pp. 274–76; also Garegnani, ([2003] 2011), para. 26. [*Editor's note:* the latter reference, which in the original draft was to para. 33 of the previous (2000) version of the essay, is here updated to the later version of the latter, rpt. in Part II of this volume].

3 It is a unit of *gross* income, because $\left(\frac{1}{1+r_{t+1}}\right)$ out of it will have to be set aside in $(t+1)$, if another similar unit of gross income is to be had in $(t+2)$.

4 The adverb 'effectively' is used above in order to remind the reader that this kind of uniformity of returns on capital is quite compatible with, and indeed requires, the 'nominal' diformity of the commodity own rates of interest, when changes in relative prices over the period of the loan are included in the system (below para. 8). In that case however the *numerical expression* of that uniform effective rate will differ according to the numeraire adopted, as it will coincide with the own interest rate of the latter.

5 Thus e.g. in (1975, p. 8), Bliss notes that capital "cries out to be aggregated". He does not however seem to notice the above simple reason for that.

6 Garegnani (1970), p. 407 [this volume, Part II, p. 147]. [*Editor's note*: in the original draft this footnote also contains the following incomplete reference: 'Wicksteed (see Kurz: 'Land')'. As suggested by professor Heinz Kurz, the reference presumably relates to an unpublished paper of him, titled 'Land' (which he kindly let us have), dealing with some Sraffa's manuscripts in which Wicksteed's *Coordination of the Laws of Distribution* (1894) is cited in connection with the same analogy Garegnani mentions in the text.

which that variability is made to descend, differ generally by the *kinds* of capital goods they employ other than by their *quantities* and the idea of a variability of their *proportion* to labour would hardly have occurred, unless those heterogeneous goods had been viewed as embodiments of different quantities of the same fluid—of the homogeneous commodity 'future income' or 'capital'.

3. Equally important from a strictly logical point of view, is the fact that only that single commodity or substance allowed expressing the capital endowment—a datum of each position as land and population were for classical rent—in a way which would be compatible with the above homogeneity of capital goods wealth owners. I am referring to the long period expression of that homogeneity, the tendency, under free competition, to a uniform 'effective' rate of return *on the supply prices* of the capital goods, for short from now on, the tendency to a "uniform return on capitals' supply prices" (or, if we prefer, to an equality of the latter with the respective demand prices).[7] That uniformity—the traditional competitive rate of profits—assumes in fact that the physical composition of the given capital endowment—defined as usual by sufficiently short lived produced means of production—be fully adjusted to the techniques adopted and the outputs produced,[8] and therefore implies an endogenous determination of that physical composition. This is in turn possible only if the capital endowment, a datum, as we said, is expressed as the single 'fluid' quantity, susceptible of taking any physical form.[9]

---

[7] For the distinction traced here between supply and demand prices of the capital goods cf., for example, Walras's own distinction between 'prix de revient' and 'cout de production' of such goods. Simple arbitrage will indeed always tend to impose a uniformity of the effective (riskless) rate on the prices of the capital goods, but that can always occur by lowering the demand price of the relatively abundant capital goods, which are therefore not currently produced, below their supply price.

[8] The uniformity of rate of return on capitals' supply prices of course excludes, as is generally done at this level of abstraction, the presence in the capital endowment of 'obsolete' capital goods—pertaining, that is, to methods of production dominated by other methods at all possible levels of the distributive variables. More embarrassingly for a theory in which the capital endowment is a datum is the fact that the same uniformity also excludes the presence in the endowment of kinds of capital goods which, though not obsolete, do pertain to methods of production other than those dominant in the current price situation. The latter question does not arise in Walras because of his assumption that all methods require the same kinds of capital goods though in different proportions, so that inappropriate *proportions* of them are the only cause of divergence of returns on the capitals' supply prices. The question is however highly important because it reflects the general case and re-enforces the marginalist need for capital as the single magnitude which can take the form of any concrete capital good.

[9] Cf. e.g. Hicks (1932a), pp. 20–21, on the need to refer to a marginal product of labour for which the 'quantity' but *not* the 'form' of the 'co-operating capital remains unchanged (see also n. 19 below).

Without this uniformity of effective returns on capitals' supply prices, on the other hand, the position of the economy referred to in the theory would be no more persistent[10] than a competitive position with, say, different wages for labour of the same quality, or with prices of products differing from their supply prices.[11] And persistency is instead the key feature of what we may indicate as the 'normal position' of the economy—the basis of economic theorizing since Adam Smith's 'natural price'. Such a normal position had in fact meant to be persistent enough for a repetition of transactions sufficient to allow compensation between the temporary, accidental deviations of observable from theoretical variables, and hence a correspondence of the latter to some average of the former.[12] The capital endowment, as a fluid susceptible of taking the form of any capital good, has thus characterized, with different degrees of explicitness, and with the single partial exception of Walras,[13] all mainstream expressions of marginal theory up to a few decades ago, and to the events to which we shall presently return.

4. This need for capital as a single magnitude raised however a problem, which, at the centre of controversy in recent decades, had in fact been simmering since the very origin of the theory. The 'quantity' of that special factor of production had to be measured independently of the distribution and the relative prices which it was brought to determine, just as the classical quantities of labour and land were. But the commodity demanded by wealth owners is not *directly* measurable in any such independent terms since its primary expression is in the *value* of the capital goods. The problem therefore was how to measure it in terms which would be both independent of prices, as the value of capital goods as such is not, and, at the same time, related appropriately to the value quantity on which wealth owners do take their decisions. The 'average period of production' over which the 'original' non-produced factors have to remain invested in order to produce a commodity was the road along which a conciliation of the two requirements was attempted. As is known, the attempt foundered on the compound rate of interest, on fixed capital, and on the plurality of the 'original' factors.[14]

---

10 'It is to the *persistence* of the influences considered, and the time allowed for them to work out their effects that we refer when contrasting Market and Normal price' (Marshall [1920] 1961, Bk V, Chap. 3, para 6, p. 348, our italics. The question is treated in Garegnani (1976) [this volume, Part II] and Garegnani (1989a). We use the word 'position', rather than 'equilibrium', when intended to cover also classical theory (where Smith and Ricardo's 'natural prices' cannot be properly described as the result of an 'equilibrium' between demand and supply forces).

11 The latter would in fact have to be the case for some capital goods when the uniformity of effective returns does not hold: see n. 7 above.

12 Garegnani (1976) [this volume, Part II].

13 The exception of Walras was 'partial' because at times, especially in his treatment of capital accumulation, he referred to 'increases' of capital seeming thereby to illegitimately suppose that increases in some components of the vector will occur with no fall in other components, so that capital could be conceived as a single magnitude in at least an ordinal sense.

14 Cf. in this volume Part I, *A Problem in the Theory of Distribution from Ricardo to Wicksell'*, Sect. I, Chap. 3, and Sect. II, Chap. 4 for, respectively, the notion of the average period of production and its shortcomings from the viewpoint of marginal theory.

The impossibility of consistently defining a concept as basic for the intended generalization of classical rent, as we claimed the single 'quantity of capital' was, might conceivably have led to the abandonment of the attempt in favour of some return to classical analysis, as had in fact happened when the 'wages fund' theories were abandoned around the middle of the 19th century. However, in the meantime the principles of factor substitution and the ensuing demand and supply explanation of distribution had apparently taken roots too deep for that outcome to be easily possible. Among the other circumstances Marshall's interpretation of Ricardo and the classical economists as primitive exponents of a demand and supply theory of prices simplified by an implicit assumption of constant returns, had succeeded in largely cancelling the traces of the classical alternative analysis. Thus, when it began to be recognized that capital could not be consistently treated as a single 'factor of production', the first reaction was to apply the theory and its principle of factor substitution to each kind of capital taken as a distinct 'factor', with little explicit consideration of the drastic difficulties such a change was bound to raise.

5. Hicks (1939) was probably the main influence for this way out of the difficulty adopted by mainstream theory. After basing his *Theory of Wages* (1932a) on normal positions and therefore on the usual notion of a 'quantity of capital' understood essentially as a value magnitude, he came to an early perception of the irretrievable inconsistency of that notion and,[15] in *Value and Capital* (1939), drawing on Swedish and other Continental precedents, he treated the capital endowment as a given in terms of a set of physically specified capital goods. It was the conception that since 1877 had been advanced by Walras, who had initially failed to realize its inconsistency with that uniformity of returns on the capitals' supply prices of the normal position—which he, had originally[16] intended to determine like all his predecessors and contemporaries.

The difficulties of this Hicksian way out were, on the other hand, the mirror image of the two reasons for which, we contended above, capital as the savers' single commodity had been at the origin of marginal theory—namely (*i*) the absence of substitutability between 'productive factors' when capital is conceived in the Walrasian way,[17] (*ii*) the inconsistency of that Walrasian conception with the endogenous treatment of the physical composition of the capital endowment necessitated by the persistency of the position and hence the possibility of correspondence between theory and observation. They were the difficulties which, perceived with varying degree of clarity, had apparently underlain the remarkable circumstance that—despite the fame of Walras and the known difficulties of the

---

[15] On the effect on Hicks of Shove's remarks on capital in his (1933) review of Hicks (1932a), cf. Garegnani (1976), p. 34, n. 13 [this volume, Part II, p. 216, n. 13].

[16] This volume, Part I, *A Problem in the Theory of Distribution from Ricardo to Wicksell*, Sect. II, Chaps. 2 and 3.

[17] Substitutability between the factors as conceived in Walras could of course be claimed to enter the system *over time* with gross investment as new more profitable capital goods replace the existing ones and therefore the savers' commodity (capital) enters in its direct form of the saving-investment flow. The fact however remains that substitution would be almost entirely absent in the initial equilibria and, in the logic of the theory, this is bound to affect all subsequent positions.

conception of capital as a single magnitude—Walras's own conception had failed to enter the mainstream during the six decades which elapsed between its 1877 formulation[18] and its Hicksian (1939) revival. Indeed Hicks himself in (1932b), not many years before *Value and Capital* (1939), had sceptically commented

> Walras and Pareto's theories of capital] are the last part of their work which one can consider as final or accept without the most careful consideration. (p. 297)

The about face of Hicks's on the Walrasian conception of capital, which seems to have passed surprisingly unnoticed in subsequent literature, may indeed by seen as an early signal of the crisis latent in marginal theory since the adoption of that conception[19] enforced by the inconsistency of the original one as a single magnitude.

Indeed, not unlike Walras's, Hicks's own treatment of capital in *Value and Capital* had initially little impact on mainstream theory. It drew little or no attention in what was then the centre of economic theorizing, the Cambridge of Pigou, Keynes, Robertson. It was in the America of Samuelson's *Foundations* (1947) that more notice of it was taken, but its influence might well have remained confined to groups of mathematical economists[20] out of the mainstream, were it not for the emergence of some striking results incidental to Piero Sraffa's work on the classical approach to prices and distribution in the same decades. The phenomena of the reswitching of techniques and of 'reverse capital' deepening, advanced in "preview" in the 1950s by the hands of Joan Robinson,[21] were indeed sufficient to soon render untenable the notion of capital as a single factor in pure theory. This opened the way to dominance for Hicks's reformulation—marking a deep 'Hicksian divide', as we may call it, in the evolution of marginal theory.

---

[18] Walras (1876–1877), 'Théorie Mathématique de la Richesse Sociale'. [*Editor's note*: the reference is to the Chapter 'Équations de la capitalisation', published in 1877. The third and fourth 'memoirs' of the 'Théorie Mathématique', concerning, respectively, the equations of production and the equations of capitalization, have entered into the second instalment of the 1st edition of Walras's *Eléments d'Économie Pure*, also published in 1877 (cf. Walras, 1954, p. 36, n. 2).]

[19] The two difficulties of the conception are not mentioned in *Value and Capital*. This is so, although the first of the two regarding substitutability had been prominent in a 1932 debate between Hicks and Robertson (cf. Hicks 1932b, Robertson 1931), in which the two authors agreed on the necessity of allowing capital to change 'form' to allow for marginal products and more generally decreasing demand functions for factors. The point returned with force in the *Theory of Wages* (1932a) where e.g. Hicks contrasts the 'full equilibrium' marginal product of labour with a 'short period' one, where the 'form', as well as the 'quantity', of the capital would *not* change: Hicks then dismisses the latter by stating 'it is very doubtful if this [short period marginal product of labour] can be given any precise meaning which is capable of useful application'. The contrast here between a "short period" and a "full equilibrium" marginal product of labour appears on the other hand to also imply awareness of the second deficiency of the vectorial conception of capital, i.e. the non-uniformity it entails of the effective returns on capitals' supply prices, an awareness present also in other passages of (1932a) e.g. where Hicks seems to imply that in Walras's system only *some* capital goods will be currently produced—owing, clearly, to the disparity of returns on their supply prices (or disparity between demand and supply prices).

[20] Indeed the Walrasian conception of capital had been used long before Hicks by mathematical economists with little notice of it being taken in mainstream literature. See e.g. Wald (1951).

[21] Cf. Robinson (1970), pp. 309–10, about her reliance on the Sraffa results.

II. Hicks's *Value and Capital* and the Later Capital Controversy: A 'Hicksian Divide' in Marginal Theory

6. With this we have reached the heart of the post-war capital controversy and also of what I see as its inconclusiveness so far. It is in fact a contention of this book that, contrary to what seems to be the view prevailing at present, the reformulations which emerged to dominance in the wake of the controversy, do not in fact avoid the dependence on the notion of capital as a single magnitude. The implications of the inconsistency of that notion remain therefore to be faced in marginal theory.

Indeed, as we saw, the point of the capital endowment given as a single quantity was to permit adjustment of its physical form to the production methods and outputs of the position of the economy under consideration—an adjustment which could of course only occur through the flows of gross savings and investment.[22] Now, these flows cannot but be present in the appropriate form in the reformulations based on the Hicksian-Walrasian notion of capital. It stands then to reason that such flows will reflect phenomena as objective as reswitching and reverse capital deepening which are the result of producers' behaviour in choosing both the outputs and the most profitable methods for producing them.[23] However, the way in which Hicks had introduced his reformulation of the theory in the relevant part of *Value and Capital* made it difficult for the controversy to focus on these basic terms of the question.

The essential question Hicks was dealing with in *Value and Capital* was the difficulties of the notion of capital for marginal theory, but the question is there almost totally overlaid by the declared need for a "dynamics" of dated prices and outputs, without making clear how that would solve the problems of capital or, indeed, what such problems exactly are. Hence the opacity of Hicks's account of the 'static' character of 'past theory' in which no less than three different kinds of equilibria appear to be mixed.

The first kind is (*i*) the confessedly 'rigid' (Hicks, 1939, pp. 115–16) representation of what 'static theory' should be if stated in what Hicks sees as the logically correct way. It consists of the equilibria analyzed in Parts I and II of *Value and Capital*, founded on Walras's given vectorial capital endowment. Hicks has however to admit that those equilibria cannot be taken to represent the thought of the "economists in the past" (*ibid.*, p. 115) as it actually was. Thus, a second kind of equilibrium was in effect implied in Hicks's notion of 'static theory', namely (*ii*) the 'normal position' actually used by those 'economists of the past'—indeed, by Hicks himself in (1932a)—the equilibrium which is in fact, if not in word, the real target of Hicks's 'static theory'.

---

[22] Garegnani ([2003] 2011) [this volume, Part II].

[23] For the idea that equilibrium in the markets for the future consumption made possible by today's savings alters the situation in this respect, cf. *ibid.*, para 24 and n. 51 [*editor's note*: our specification of paragraph and note].

However, the normal position with its twin basic features of the uniformity of the effective rate of return on capitals' supply prices and the resulting need of the given capital endowment as a single magnitude, nowhere explicitly emerges in *Value and Capital*. Hicks's tendency is instead to attribute to previous 'static theory', apart from the mentioned 'rigid' version (*i*), not the unmentioned normal position (*ii*), but rather a third, quite different notion, namely (*iii*) that of a stationary state.[24] However, the stationary state is radically different from the normal position. In the latter, the constancy of the capital endowment, treated as a *datum* of the equilibrium, is an abstraction from the changes it is admitted to undergo which is founded merely on the comparative slowness of those changes,[25] i.e. in the persistency of the normal position. In the stationary state instead the same constancy is the result of an equilibrium condition of zero net savings, and the capital endowment is accordingly an *unknown* of that equilibrium. Consequently the constancy of the equilibrium prices of the normal position is also an abstraction from the changes they are admitted to undergo in the real economy, contrary to the price constancy of a stationary state.[26]

Now, with their misleading representation under (*iii*) or under (*i*), the normal positions (*ii*) of 'the economists of the past' were suggested to have been respectively *either* eventual positions, distant in time, as stationary states inevitably are, *or* fleeting equilibria like those of Parts I and II of *Value and Capital*—in both cases equilibria hardly susceptible of being an effective realistic guide to observable phenomena. This was however the precise contrary of what the unmentioned normal position (*ii*) of those economists had always been meant to be, from Adam Smith's natural prices onwards—i.e. a centre around which the economy would oscillate long enough to be realized through an average of its actual positions over the period.

7. Thus the paradox of *Value and Capital* is that in its account of the "usual course of economists in the past", we do not find the normal position, the hallmark of economics down to Hicks's own *Theory of Wages* (1932a). That entails a second and even more striking paradox: that we do not find in *Value and Capital*

---

[24] In fact, Hicks passes from the equilibria (*i*) referred to in (1939, pp. 115–116) to directly attributing stationary states to previous economists (pp. 116–119).

[25] The slowness ought to be assessed relatively to the time required for broad compensation of accidental deviations of observed from equilibrium levels, letting the latter emerge as averages.

[26] Hicks's apparent confusion between normal and stationary position was of course made easier by the frequent use of the term 'stationary' to indicate also a normal position, because of its abstraction from changes in relative prices. However, Lionel Robbins (1930) had lucidly clarified already that ambiguity by his distinction between static and stationary positions of the economy. Hicks' misleading attribution of a proper stationary state, and not a normal position, to 'the economists of the past' is on the other hand made entirely clear when he writes that, in the stationary economy of those economists, the "quantity of intermediate products"—the quantity of capital—will be determined through "[t]he rate of interest ... fixed at a level which offers no incentive for net saving or dis-saving" (Hicks, 1939, p. 118).

any effective criticism of the normal position of such economists "in the past", the very position which Hicks wishes in fact to replace. The only criticism remains the generic one of the lack of realism of assuming the constancy of prices in the definition of an equilibrium—a criticism which would certainly be convincing if 'previous theory' had in fact rested, as it clearly did not, on Hicks's 'stationary states' (*iii*) or on his fleeting equilibria (*i*). But the dependence of current prices on expected prices was in fact all but overlooked with respect to normal prices—from Adam Smith's dichotomy of 'market' and 'natural' prices, down to Walras, Marshall, Pigou, Wicksell, and all others.[27] The question was simply that, to the extent in which the expected prices reflected merely 'accidental' circumstances, their effects could be ignored because they would be averaged out through the repetition of transactions, made possible by the persistency of the normal position. And to the extent in which the expected prices expressed instead changes in the data of the normal position, they would be dealt with by the comparison between the corresponding two normal positions.

The real point behind this alleged past oversight of price changes—point which however remains entirely implicit in *Value and Capital*—is that the *persistency* permitting the *abstraction* from them in the normal position of marginal theory, was made possible by the treatment of the capital endowment as a single magnitude, and that this is just what the Hicks of (1939), as distinct from the Hicks of (1932a), knew could *not* be done. Leaving aside the obviously unrealistic stationary state (*iii*), the marginalist normal positions (*ii*) had therefore to be replaced by equilibria of kind (*i*) whose fleeting character made the attempted remedy of a "dynamics of dated prices and quantities" all but inevitable. The need of a "dynamics" was, in other words, the *result* and not the *cause* of the change in the conception of capital, contrary to what is implied in Hicks's (1939) foreground argument.

8. That disappearance of the normal position from Hicks's (1939) argument was to weigh heavily on the controversies of twenty years later. It had there a series of effects which converged in what I see as almost completely blotting out the basic terms of the question of capital in marginal theory. These effects, I believe, can be summarized as follows.

(a) That disappearance did conceal the most glaring form of dependence of traditional marginal theory on capital as a single magnitude—its use as a datum in the factor endowment of the normal position. It thus made the reliance of previous theory on that magnitude difficult to understand and accordingly a confused

[27] In his (1939) Hicks probably counted for an easier acceptance of his methodological critique of "the usual course of economists in the past" (p. 115) because of the success in those years of Keynes's analysis with its reliance on expectations and its 'dynamics'. Cf. e.g. Hicks (1939), pp. 3–5; also Garegnani (1989).

bone of contention[28] rather than the simple historical fact it in fact is. Thus, when some authors on the critical side referred to the question as it emerges in the normal position, other authors, as in a Babel of languages, saw that endowment as either the unknown of the stationary position, or the given physical vector of the Hicksian 'temporary' or 'intertemporal' equilibria, or even, as we shall have to recall below, the single magnitude of an 'aggregate production function'.

(b) On the other hand, and more directly important, the misreading of normal position (*ii*) as equilibria (*i*) or stationary states (*iii*) led many participants in the controversies to take for granted the paradoxical charge that previous theory with its normal position was inapplicable to the 'real world'. This made it easier to overlook the impermanence of the new equilibria, which did *in effect* undermine the applicability of the theory. Hicks himself implicitly admits such an undermining when, in a little quoted passage of *Value and Capital*, he wrote that he assumed "the economic system to be always in equilibrium" (1939, p. 131),[29] an

---

28 The two roles which we saw above (paras. 2 and 3), of the 'quantity of capital' in previous marginal theory, have indeed been generally overlooked in the course of the capital controversy. Thus e.g. Hahn wrote

> it seems to me impossible (as a matter of intellectual history) to maintain that the possibility of perfect capital (or labour) aggregation is a neo-classical doctrine (Hahn 1982, p. 354)

where it is of course hard to see how e.g. Jevons, Clark, Böhm-Bawerk, Wicksell, Pigou etc. could use, as they did, the notion of a 'quantity of capital' without admitting the 'possibility' of that notion. (The passage also slips into the frequent confusion between the heterogeneity of capital goods, and that of labour. No equivalent of the uniform effective return on the heterogeneous capitals exists for heterogeneous labours, whose separate endowments can therefore be generally taken as given independently of each other (this volume, Part I, *A Problem in the Theory of Distribution from Ricardo to Wicksell*).

29 Cf. Garegnani (1976) [this volume, Part II]. Hicks' phrase above is immediately preceded by the following words: "so far as this limited sense of equilibrium is concerned, it is quite true that [....]". The "limited sense" evidently regards the 'week' to which Hicks's equilibrium is referred. However, the equilibrium of a 'week', unless tautologically defined to be what does actually happen (in which case its 'determination' is of course illusory), is no more likely to be fulfilled moment by moment than any other equilibrium, including that of a normal position. (Samuelson appears to underestimate the difficulty when, in the *Foundations*, he makes the analogy of a "cannonball as being at equilibrium ... at every point in its flight" (Samuelson, 1947, pp. 331–332). The dominant forces acting on the cannonball at each instant in time are comparatively few in number and their effects on the position of the cannonball are accordingly calculable with a degree of approximation sufficient to establish a correspondence between the theoretical and the observable position of the ball at each instant. Given instead the *numberless forces* of analogous strength which affect the economy *at each instant of time*, the observable instantaneous position cannot even in principle be determined with any approximation: only averages of observable positions reflecting the effects of the few most persistent among those forces can be determined; and the cumulation of the errors makes the path of the economy even less calculable than its instantaneous position. This, it seems, is what prompted Marshall to write

> dynamical solutions in the physical sense of economic problems are unattainable. And if we are to adhere to physical analogies at all, we must say that statical solutions afford starting points for *such rude and imperfect approaches to dynamical solutions* as we may be able to attain to (Marshall 1898, p. 39, emphasis added)

the 'approaches' in question being, essentially, the comparison of normal positions. But Marshall of course thought that capital as a single fluid could somehow be managed.

assumption which should have shocked the readers of *Value and Capital*. Nobody before had ever supposed the economy to actually be in an equilibrium except by a fluke: gravitation *around it* and not *achievement* of it, had in fact been what allowed for the significance of an equilibrium.[30] Thus Hicks's resort to the surprising assumption of an economy always in equilibrium was in effect an admission that his equilibria were too fleeting for the traditional form of correspondence through gravitation and that he could not or wished not to enter into the fundamental question of what form of correspondence, if any, would replace the traditional one.

(c) But as we saw (para. 5), the disappearance of the normal position in *Value and Capital* had been logically preceded by the disappearance of the key condition of that position under free competition, the traditional uniform rate of profits (i.e. the uniformity of the effective rate of return on the capitals' supply prices, or, if we prefer, the equality between the demand and supply prices of the capital goods), due to the impossibility to satisfy that condition on the basis of a Walrasian capital endowment.[31] As some critics attempted to break the silence on the matter, that condition, pertaining to the physical composition of the capital stock, came to be generally mistaken for an altogether different condition: the uniformity of the own commodity rates of interest, a mere synonym of a constancy of relative prices assumed in defining equilibrium, a second quite independent condition which is in fact incompatible with the first, whenever that constancy of prices is not assumed.[32] This misreading deepened of course the obscuration of the normal position, by hiding its basic rationale, that of *persistency* and not *constancy*.

(d) The confusion was made even worse when, in the fog created by the above multiple misunderstandings, the marginalist dependence on the notion of capital as a single magnitude came to be seen by some participants in the debate as pertaining to the empirical construct of an 'aggregate production function'; purporting, that is, to represent the output of the whole economy as a single homogeneous aggregate, produced by an equally homogeneous 'capital'. Thus, the question came to be confusingly taken as if the difficulties only pertained to an admittedly unrigorous approximation, and would presumably be absent when the several

---

[30] As Denis Robertson lucidly put itIt seems to me that anybody who rejects these two ideas, that a system can move towards equilibrium and that it may never get into it ... has made it extremely difficult for himself to interpret the course of events in the real world (1957, p. 96).

[31] For his Walrasian 'static equilibria' (*i*) of which above, Hicks does in fact drop Walras's equations of capital formation, where the uniformity of returns on capitals supply prices was expressly stated (Walras 1954, *e.g* para 238, pp. 271–272). [*Editor's note*: in the original draft the latter reference was blank. We have completed it by indicating a passage in the *Elements* which Garegnani shows elsewhere (Garegnani 1976, n. 15 [this volume, Part II, p. 217, n. 15]) to consider relevant to the matter at hand. But in fact there are many other points where Walras explicitly posits the condition of uniformity of the rates of return on the costs of production of capital goods: e.g. in para. 233, pp. 269-70 ('Under equilibrium conditions the … rate of net income, is the same for all capital goods').

[32] Garegnani ([2003] 2011) [this volume, Part II].

productive sectors are distinguished as in a general equilibrium system. The fact was thus overlooked that capital, the single magnitude, is required for the marginalist normal position, *whichever* the number of sectors into which we may wish to distinguish the economy.[33] In the marginal theories, capital, the single magnitude, has never been question of an aggregate production function *versus* general equilibrium, but, if anything, one of distinguishing between *two kinds of general equilibria*: the traditional one based on normal positions, exemplified by, say, Wicksell or even by Walras, as far as his original intentions went, *versus* the 'Hicksian' or 'neoWalrasian' ones that renounce such positions in the attempt to avoid that single magnitude.

9. Thus, in conclusion, it does not really seem excessive to look at the later phase of the capital controversies as having elements of a comedy of errors, which are still waiting to be cleared up. Thanks to the unambiguous phenomena of reswitching and reverse capital deepening, the controversy had been successful in its initial phase in discarding from pure theory the traditional version of the theory. Subsequently, however, when the implications of those phenomena inevitably became the main subject, the misapprehensions summarized above prevented decisive progress.

A certain unpreparedness on the critical side to extend the critique to the Hicksian reformulation of the theory aggressively advanced from the opposite side, was also relevant. Many of the critical authors had their roots in a Cambridge which, as we noticed, had essentially ignored the relevant part of *Value and Capital*, judging it unnecessarily complicated and unlikely to bear any serious fruit. In that opinion, it turned out, the Cambridge economists had underestimated the real potential of the Hicksian proposal, which was the defensive, not the constructive one. The inessentially heavy mathematical armour with which the proposal was increasingly equipped, did the rest in hampering the critical side at the time.

It is this complex of circumstances, we submit, which has left space for the credence that, whatever its methodological deficiencies, the equilibria of after the 'Hicksian divide' are immune from the inconsistencies on capital of previous marginal theory. That in turn has left space, I believe, for a second no less unwarranted consequence: a feeling that since the Hicksian reformulations confirm at the level of pure theory the substantial validity of the general demand and supply framework, they also provide some space for the admittedly imperfect previous concepts, above all that of a 'quantity of capital', as workable approximation in more applied work. I believe it can accordingly be said that the critique on capital, understood as the critique of marginal theory, has been only partly successful so

33 An example of that persisting confusion is present in Cohen and Harcourt (2005), where the aggregate production function seems to be viewed as essential for the neoclassical idea of scarcity—as if that idea had ever been made to rest on such a gross approximation, rather than on complex, subtle treatments like those of a Jevons, Walras, Marshall or Wicksell and indeed in their way the contemporary works subsequent to the "Hicksian divide".

far: it has ousted the traditional version of the theory from pure analysis, not the theory itself from economic analysis.

III. The Classical Alternative

10. But the critique of a theory can hardly be expected to advance to its full effects, unless a sufficiently developed and tested alternative is available. The lack of a known such alternative has certainly contributed to the half-way stop of the critical course. And here we return to the central theme of this book, namely the alternative between the two approaches which have dominated economic thought in succession.

The lack of an alternative theory may seem at first surprising, since results like the reswitching of techniques or reverse capital deepening which we saw played a central role in the capital controversy, had in fact resulted from an analysis of relative prices along the lines of the approach of Ricardo and the classical economists retraced by Piero Sraffa in the preceding years. That approach "submerged and forgotten",[34] in times clearly disturbed by the conflict between capital and labour that was to submerge Europe soon after the death of Ricardo, rather than abandoned after a well informed criticism,[35] could have provided a well tested alternative and the natural candidate for a reconstruction going hand in hand with the critique. However, the approach began to clearly emerge as the alternative to dominant theory it actually is, only in the 1960's and 1970's with Sraffa's *Production of Commodities* and related work, when, that is, the controversy had already run an important part of its course on the basis of a different reconstructive proposal.[36]

[34] The quotation is from Sraffa (1960, p. v).

[35] It may be relevant to recall here how soon after the death of Ricardo the conflict between capital and labour explode in Britain with the Chartist movement to submerge, then, continental Europe in the subsequent decades, and how the emergence of Socialism affected the attitude towards Ricardo's theory of value and distribution. Cf. e.g. Carey's reference to Ricardo's theory as a 'system of discords' (Carey 1856, p. 74) or the passage by Foxwell according to which "[Ricardo] did more than any intentionally socialist author to sap the foundations of that form of society which he was trying to explain" (1899, p. xli). On the influence on economics of the social and political climate in the England of the immediate post-Ricardian period, cf. Blaug (1958), Chap. 8.

[36] Elements of an alternative theory—partly influenced by the classical theory rediscovered by Sraffa—were in fact advanced in the initial stages of the controversy by Kaldor, Kahn, Robinson and other authors on the critical side of the controversy. The concern to rapidly fill the huge area of long-run problems which Keynes left "covered with fragments of broken glass" (Robinson 1956, p. v) may, however, have prevented deriving from the classical approach all it could offer, including, in my opinion, a consolidation and extension of Keynes's own achievements on aggregate demand (cf. para. 18 below).

And the process of comprehension of an analysis of distribution[37] and prices, as different from received theory, as classical analysis is, could only be difficult and slow.[38] Indeed, the situation was and still partly is one in which marginalist demand and supply are taken as almost synonyms of economic theory *tout court*—making scholars forget how the early systemization of the science by its founders from Quesnay to Adam Smith and Ricardo had run on basically different lines.

11. It was forgotten in particular how Ricardo had in effect arrived at establishing that, once the real wage is determined by its largely institutional circumstances (like the 'subsistence' accepted in the society under consideration) and the outputs are given with the corresponding technical conditions of production, the remaining distributive variables—in particular, the rate of profits—can be determined together with relative prices.[39] This determination of value and distribution constituted what we may call the 'core' of classical theory consisting essentially of the relations between prices and distributive variables which the competitive tendency to uniform levels of such variables necessarily entails. In it the real wage, outputs and technical conditions play the role so to speak of 'intermediate data', which determined by the theory, outside that 'core', allow determining the remaining distributive variables within it. This is true whether in that 'core' the determination of the distributive variables other than wages takes directly the form of a 'surplus' as happens in Quesnay, in Marx or in Ricardo's 'corn ratio' theory of profits, or the form of price equations like those we find in Sraffa's *Production of Commodities by Means of Commodities*.

But even more fundamental for defining the classical approach, was what underlies that determination—the way, that is in which that 'core' was set in a body of theory which ultimately appealed in effect, through its explanations of the 'intermediate data', to institutional and historical elements (of which the free competition shaping the 'core' is indeed one). This is exemplified in the just mentioned explanation of the division between wages and profits on the basis of a culturally determined subsistence wage. But it applies also to outputs which, free from the role later attributed to them, of providing a basis for demand functions of 'factors of production', were above all studied in connection with the theory of capital accumulation and growth with its dependence on the complex institutional and historical circumstances emerging when we read Adam Smith or Marx on the subject.[40]

---

37 An eminent example of that difficulty is provided by Samuelson when, in his frequent writings on Sraffa over the last 30 years, he insists on viewing the determination of prices in Sraffa (1960) as resting on an assumption of constant returns, following in this the lead of Marshall's old interpretation of Ricardo.

38 Demand and supply did indeed appear in the classical writers, but as single quantities, not functions, as sufficed for the role they had there of only ensuring the *tendency* of market prices to natural or normal prices, and not of determining the latter (Garegnani 2002a) [this volume, Part III].

39 We are of course simplifying here by ignoring questions like those of natural resources and joint production. However, the lines of their solution in way compatible with the essential classical elements indicated here ought to be well known by now.

40 Garegnani (1984) [this volume, Part III].

12. This composite nature of classical analysis is reflected in the composite nature of the methods it uses: mainly deductive in the 'core' and mainly inductive in the separate determination of the wages, outputs, and technical conditions taken provisionally as given in the deductive 'core'.[41] In this mixed inductive/deductive nature of classical theory we find, I believe, an important difference from marginal theory. Being simply a result of the competitive tendency to uniformity of the prices of each product and of the remuneration of each productive resource, the relations of the classical 'core' are also present in the marginal theories—at least up to the 'Hicksian divide' and the abandonment of the normal position in pure theory. However, the relations of the classical 'core' are there joined with the 'demand and supply' conditions for products and factors, which are deduced from consumer tastes and factor endowments, data which were unnecessary for, and absent from, classical distribution and relative prices. They can in fact be seen to have essentially the role of determining the division of the product between wages and profits thus replacing by the principle of factor substitution, the classical surplus principle and the institutionally determined real wage. In that way marginal theory unlike classical theory takes the shape of what is basically an entirely deductive system, with consumer 'tastes' and factor availability as ultimate data, together with the technical conditions of production.[42]

The paradox is that by its method classical theory satisfies much better than marginalism what Alfred Marshall, the author to whom the latter theory owes much of its success, argued to be the conditions of a satisfactory economic analysis. That analysis should, Marshall contended, avoid 'long chains of deductive reasoning' and leave room for 'specific experience' at key stages of the analysis.[43] Now, this is clearly just what classical theory does when, because of its explanation of wages and outputs largely separate from that of relative prices and the non-wage distributive variables, it avoids the marginalist long deductive chains, bringing from tastes and endowments down to prices and distribution. In that way classical theory provides indeed a more substantial break of those 'long chains' than the one Marshall himself was attempting by his method of partial equilibria,

---

[41] Contrary to a widespread opinion—founded essentially on a misapprehension of the analytical structure of classical theory with its 'intermediate data'—it can be held that Ricardo shared in that broader institutional and inductive general setting of the theory which came natural to the classical economists. In the *Principles* Ricardo was concerned essentially with correcting Smith on the central, but also highly specific point of the 'core' concerning the relation between the wage and the rate of profits, with all its manifold implications. He was therefore almost exclusively concerned with the deductive 'core' of classical theory. But he was clearly deferring to Adam Smith and his system for the rest of the theory. We may thus recognize both the highly deductive character of Ricardo's own specific work, and his participation in the institutional historical view of the economy which is so clear in Adam Smith or Marx. (A similar observation may indeed apply to Sraffa (1960), which is focussed on completing and elaborating the relations of the 'core' of the theory, for both constructive and critical purposes, but otherwise implicitly defers to the classical system as it developed from Adam Smith to Marx.)

[42] This volume, Part I, *A problem in the theory of distribution from Ricardo to Wicksell*, p. 51.

[43] Garegnani (2002a), p. 250 [this volume, Part III, p. 349].

which sends us ultimately back for its justification to general equilibrium and its 'long chains'. And that very same classical determination of wages and outputs broadly separate from prices, clearly leaves large space for Marshall's 'specific experience' in the treatment of those magnitudes.

Even more importantly, perhaps, by the methods they used for their analysis, the classical economists could stay largely clear of that postulate of reversibility of economic phenomena which is at the basis of demand and supply functions—and which, as Marshall again knew well, runs counter an essential character of most social phenomena, resulting from the fact that men's behaviour does change with experience.

It is interesting to note at this point how this change of content and method away from classical theory explains the often lamented absence in modern theory of the otherwise evident role of institutional and historical elements in economic phenomena. Indeed what marginalism has done has been nothing less than to replace the essentially social forces on which the classical economists ultimately relied for their explanation of a market economy, with forces which are as 'natural' as the human nature envisioned in marginal theory.[44] And 'natural' forces are independent of society for their *existence* (though of course not for their mode of operation) unlike 'social forces' which have in society their source as well as their outcome. This is a little noticed radical difference between the views of society underlying the two approaches.

IV. This Volume

13. The essays in this volume are expressions of the line of thought sketched above, taken in its three main aspects: the critique of marginal theories, the reconstruction and revival of the classical approach and, finally, problems pertaining to the doctrinal history relevant for the two previous aspects. The essays are grouped in Parts II, III, IV and V of the book, according to which of these three themes prevails in them.

All three aspects find however an initial treatment in the 1958 Cambridge Ph.D. dissertation *A Problem in the Theory of Distribution from Ricardo to Wicksell*, previously unpublished in English, and constituting Part I of the collection. The dissertation can supply, I believe, the kind of historical-analytical background,[45] against which, in my opinion, the question of capital in marginal theory has to

44 This may seem to run counter the frequent use of the word 'natural' by the early classics. It has however been often pointed out how 'natural' was used by them in a sense subtly different from the modern one counterposing, essentially, a natural world to a socially determined one, and referring instead to the *unimpeded* working out of forces which may well be social rather than natural in the modern sense.

45 A slightly revised version was published in Italian in Garegnani (1960). A commitment to publish the dissertation in English was also taken a few years later, but the intention to revise it in order to take into consideration Sraffa's *Production of Commodities* which had been published in the meantime, brought to procrastinations.

be viewed, but which has been largely missing in the controversies on the subject which erupted in those years: in that sense it provides a premise to the essays of the following four Parts. A primary element in that premise is the existence of the two broad approaches to value and distribution on the alternative between which we said the present book focuses. Thus, Sect. I of the dissertation, dealing with the problem of capital in Ricardo and the classical economists, begins with a presentation of their approach as I had then reconstructed under the influence of Piero Sraffa and Maurice Dobb's path breaking Introduction to Ricardo's *Principles* ([1821] 1951). And its Sect. II, devoted to capital in the marginal theories, starts by pointing to the differences between that approach and the classical one.

The focus of the dissertation is however on the specific problem of measuring capital independently of distribution, present in the classical no less than in the later approach. It is indeed contended there that the problem is what lies at the basis of the difficulties which Ricardo and Marx met in their theory of value and whose incomplete solution favoured the abandonment of the approach. A central difference is however argued there to exist on the question between the two approaches. While the demand and supply analysis of the neoclassical theories requires that the independent measurement be ultimately in terms of a single quantity, the same condition emerges as inessential within the classical approach.

The question of the consistent measurement of capital as a single magnitude arises, therefore, already in Sect. I of the dissertation, where it is shown how Ricardo and Marx's difficulties on value could be overcome if Böhm-Bawerk's average period of production could provide a satisfactory measurement of capital. The discussion of that measurement establishes however that its validity would require (*i*) the assumption of a simple rate of interest in the calculation of prices, in contradiction with the competitive uniform rate of return on capital at all stages of the production process; (*ii*) the absence of fixed capital.[46] An alternative measurement of capital in terms of the set of 'absolute periods of production'—the same developed later by Wicksell in a marginalist context—is then shown to allow for the classical determination of the rate of profits and relative prices without the unacceptable assumptions of the average period of production,[47] thus establishing the independence of the classical approach from the conception of capital as a single magnitude.

[46] This volume, Part I, *A Problem in the Theory of Distribution from Ricardo to Wicksell*, Sect. I, Chaps. 4 and 5.

[47] This method of 'absolute periods of production' had been applied to the Ricardian theory already in 1904 by the Russian economist Dmitrieff and then taken over from him by Bortkiewicz in an article of 1906–1907 in works of which I had no knowledge at the time (cf. this volume, Part I, *A Problem in the Theory of Distribution from Ricardo to Wicksell,* p. 41, n. 102). It was also only after completion of the thesis that I could get a view of Sraffa's alternative solution of the classical determination of profit rate and prices in terms of the vector of means of production—the possibility of which had emerged for me in the last stages of preparation of the dissertation under the stimulation of Seton (1957).

An interesting generalization of Ricardo's 'corn ratio' theory of profits comes to light in the course of the argument: it applies to the composite commodity or 'wage commodity' of which the classical given wage consists. Only the technical conditions of the goods entering directly or indirectly the wage goods are required, it emerges, for determining the general rate of profits of the economy. And in analogy with Ricardo's agriculture, this property is associated with the possibility of constructing a 'surplus equation' in which, that is, the profit rate can be directly determined in what we may call the 'integrated wage goods sector', on the basis of the difference between its product and the wages paid in it, both being physical quantities of the wage commodity. Capital in that sector can on the other hand also be measured in terms of the wage commodity as a simple function of the rate of profits by referring to the mentioned set of absolute time periods by which the wages are implied to be advanced with the methods of production in use.[48]

In more general terms allowing for some changes in the physical composition of the wage commodity, the 'surplus equation' with the profit rate as its sole unknown can also be formulated in terms of Adam Smith's old standard of value, 'labour commanded', i.e. with the wage as the unit in terms of which the output and wages of the integrated wage commodity sector will respectively equal the total labour force and the part of it employed in the direct and indirect production of aggregate wages.[49]

In either of these two forms the 'surplus equation' of the integrated wage good sector gives transparency to the circumstances determining the rate of profits, confirming and correcting as the case may be, the results Ricardo and Marx had achieved by their approximate 'surplus equation' based on labour values or on the 'corn ratio' of the early Ricardo.[50]

14. In Sect. II of the dissertation devoted to the problem of capital in marginal theory, the need for the measurement of capital by a single magnitude is made to emerge by means of the theories of capital of Walras and Wicksell. They are taken as representatives of the two broad alternative lines along which a solution of the problem of measuring capital can be attempted: time periods for which wages are advanced and physical quantities of the several capital goods, respectively.

With respect to Wicksell, his *Value, Capital and Rent* (1954) is considered with its failed attempt to measure capital in terms of the average period production. The measurement of capital to which Wicksell has to resort in his later *Lectures on Political Economy* (1934) is then examined. It consists of the same 'absolute periods of production' which were used in Sect. I of the dissertation to provide

[48] The function in question is what has become known in the meantime as the "reduction to labour" applied here to the wage commodity (cf. Sraffa 1960, Ch. VI).

[49] This volume, Part I, *A Problem in the Theory of Distribution from Ricardo to Wicksell*, Sect. I, Chaps. 4 and 5: it is there also shown how, under conditions of constant efficiency during its lifetime, fixed capital can be fitted into that scheme.

[50] *Ibid.*, Chap. 5.

a solution for the problem in the classical approach. It is there shown, however, that in the new demand and supply framework, with its conception of given factor endowments, Wicksell is forced to introduce capital as a single magnitude. The reason is that we already mentioned in Sect. I of this Introduction. Apart from the need to provide for a meaningful substitutability of factors, the capital endowment cannot be expressed as a vector of quantities (here a vector of periods of production) without contradicting the uniformity of effective returns on the capitals' supply prices—without contradicting, that is, the normal position, the basis of the analysis of Wicksell, as of all his contemporaries and predecessors. The inconsistency of the value measurement of capital to which Wicksell has then to resort is examined in detail by discussing his justifications for it in terms of Böhm-Bawerk's 'subsistence fund', and, later, in terms of what he indicates as 'real capital'.

The same need of capital as a single magnitude for the marginalist normal position is what had already emerged from Chaps. 2 and 3 of that Sect. II, dealing with Walras's theory of capital. It is there demonstrated that Walras' capital endowment, given as the physical vector of the capital goods, if it avoids Wicksell's inconsistent value measurement, prevents his complete system—including, that is, the equations of 'capital formation' for the uniformity of returns—from generally admitting a solution, for exactly the same reason which had forced Wicksell into his value measurement.

The marginalist need of capital as a single magnitude is there further confirmed, by pointing to the doubtful meaning of the 'equilibrium' we obtain when, in order to remove Walras's inconsistency, we renounce the reference to a normal position of the economy. It was the kind of 'short period' general equilibrium to which Walras himself ended by implicitly referring when, by the time of the fourth edition of the *Eléments*, he came to realize the inconsistency between his conception of capital and the normal position he had originally intended to determine.[51] That general equilibrium is of course the basis of those 'Hicksian' contemporary reformulation of the theory to which we referred above.

15. In the dissertation the measurement of capital in marginal theory is mainly discussed from, so to speak, the 'supply side'—the side, that is, of the given capital endowment of the normal position. After completing the dissertation I was however stimulated by the problems of comparative underdevelopment affecting then the Italian economy to attempt relating the critique in the dissertation to an analysis of the role of aggregate demand in a process of capital accumulation. The 'demand side' of 'capital' became then prominent through its expression in

[51] *Ibid.*, p. 63, n. 157 about a second error in Walras's argument in the first three editions of the *Eléments*, which clearly favoured his conviction at the time of being able to determine a normal position. On Pareto's apparent awareness of Walras's inconsistency in the *Cours* (1896–1897), followed by his abandonment of any formal treatment of capital in the 1909 *Manuel d'Économie Politique*, cf. this volume, Part I, *A Problem in the Theory of Distribution from Ricardo to Wicksell*, Appendix E.

investment demand. That attempt brought to light for me the phenomena which have since become known as 'reswitching of techniques' and 'reverse capital deepening',[52] i.e. how the variability of the relative value of the sets of capital goods pertaining to two production processes could overturn the inverse relation between interest rate and value of capital per worker traditionally assumed for the economy.

The question was then analyzed more systematically in the article 'Heterogeneous Capital, the Production Function and the Theory of Distribution' (1970) which finds place among the essays of Part II of the present book, devoted, as we said, to works in which the critique of marginal theory dominates. The simple model of Samuelson's 'Surrogate Production Function' (1962) permits there to show that no conceivable definition of capital allows its 'marginal product' to be equal to the interest rate—except when capital happened to consist of one and the same capital good in all alternative methods of production of the commodity produced and, moreover, the product is homogeneous with the capital good. The same model allowed then showing by a series of arithmetical examples how reswitching and reverse capital deepening allow for practically any relation between interest rate and value of capital per worker in terms of product that we might conceive, besides the inverse one postulated traditionally. The consequences of this for the uniqueness and stability of the marginalist normal positions were then analyzed. Also considered was the reason why the problem does not arise for normal positions as envisaged in the classical approach, where the division of the product between wages and profits is not determined by a 'substitutability' between corresponding factors of production, and the resulting demand and supply forces.

A first version of this paper was written in 1961, while a guest at the Massachusetts Institute of Technology, in the form of a criticism of an early draft of Samuelson's 1962 article which was circulating there at the time. During its long gestation up to 1970, the results of 'Heterogeneous Capital' were useful for a shorter work, also reprinted in Part II. It is the one I contributed to a Symposium in the *Quarterly Journal of Economics* (Garegnani, 1966). It was intended to exhibit the double mathematical error contained in a famous alleged theorem denying the possibility of 'reswitching' under sufficiently general conditions. The wider implications of the question raised in 'Heterogeneous Capital' were already sketched in the last pages of this earlier paper.

---

52 This was around 1959, when I started on what was later published as 'Notes on Consumption, Investment and Effective Demand' (Garegnani 1978–1979 [first published in Italian (Garegnani 1964–1965)]). Despite the fact that the possibility of reswitching had been already mentioned, although as a 'curiosum', by Joan Robinson (1956, pp. 109–10) in what she was later to describe as a "preview" of Sraffa (Robinson, 1970, p. 309) and which I had of course read at the time, and despite an actual preview of *Production of Commodities* I was given by Sraffa in his rooms after submitting my dissertation in December 1957, I had failed to recognize that what I had read then was the phenomenon I was striving for—a good example, I think, of the strong tendency to actually derive from reading only what one already broadly knows or expects.

16. The critique described above, whether from the side of the 'supply' of capital or from that of its 'demand', was conducted in terms of normal positions of the economy.[53] The remainder of the papers of Part II of the book are instead concerned with the 'neo-Walrasian' versions of the theory which came to dominance after the first stage of the capital controversy and with what we called the 'Hicksian divide' in marginal theory.

Those versions had in fact been already considered in their essential logic in Sect. II, Chap. 3 of the Ph.D. dissertation examining the alternative notion of equilibrium implied in the fourth edition of the *Eléments*, when Walras had come to realize the inconsistency which vitiated the three earlier editions.[54]

Thus, in the 1976 paper 'On a Change in the Notion of Equilibrium in Recent Work on Value and Distribution', after discussing the difficulties of capital underlying the striking about-face of Hicks on the Walrasian treatment of capital (para. 5 above), I drew from the material in the dissertation in order to point to the deficiencies of the way out attempted in *Value and Capital*. While noting the difficulty raised for factor substitution by the treatment of each kind of capital goods as a separate factor, the attention was focussed on the negative implications of the new notions of 'temporary' and 'intertemporal' general equilibrium for the possibility of a correspondence between theoretical and observable variables.

If this basic problem of method is at the centre of 'On a Change…', the article 'Savings, Investment and the Quantity of Capital in a System of General Intertemporal Equilibrium' (Garegnani [2003] 2011), turns to strict analysis and contends that the high methodological price paid by adopting the Walrasian conception of capital, may well have been paid in vain. We come there to the mentioned central argument in the present book, of how, though avoiding 'capital' as a single magnitude among the factor endowments, the new equilibria are, through investment demand and savings supply, as dependent on capital as a single magnitude, as the traditional normal equilibrium was. They are therefore subject, I contend there, to essentially the same difficulties discussed in terms of 'normal positions' of the economy in my 'Heterogeneous Capital…' (1970). In 'Savings, Investment and Capital …' it is shown, in particular, that contrary to what seems to be widely held at present, the equilibria in the market for future consumption which the intertemporal formulation allows connecting to today's savings, are of no avail for ensuring an equality between savings and investment decisions in the earlier periods. The latter equality continues to constitute an independent equilibrium condition no less than that between demand for, and supply of, labour in those earlier periods.

[53] Each point of the demand for 'capital' entering the determination of the 'normal position' of traditional marginal theory on which attention was focussed in my Garegnani (1970), pp. 423–24 [this volume, Part II, pp. 168-9] is in fact a potential normal position: the equilibrium that is, which would hold if the capital supplied happened to be that indicated by the schedule for that position.

[54] Cf. above, n. 51.

Appendix II to the essay just mentioned exemplifies, with reference to the Hahn (1982)'s and Bliss (1975)'s contributions, some of the misunderstandings which, I claimed in para. 8, have marred so far the controversy on capital.

17. Parts III and IV of the volume takes up as we said writings which mainly reflect the constructive line of argument founded on the classical approach. The essays are grouped under the self explanatory headings of, respectively, "Value and Distribution" and "Aggregate Demand".

As for the first group of essays, we may begin from the 1983 'The Classical Theory of Wages and the Role of Demand Schedules in the Determination of Relative Prices.' This short article focuses on what is for contemporary economists the most surprising feature of the classical approach: the absence of demand functions for the determination of commodity prices. The article shows how that feature is a direct consequence of the basic difference between that approach and marginal theory, namely the division between wages and profits explained by broader social and institutional circumstances, separately from prices.

A second article in the group, 'Value and Distribution in the Classical Economists and Marx' (1984) has then the more general aim of clarifying, by comparisons also with marginal theory, an analysis of the economic system, like that of the classical authors, which is independent of the idea of substitution between 'factors of production'.

The institutional and historical circumstances which Smith, Ricardo or Marx saw to affect economic phenomena are stressed in 'Misunderstanding Classical Economics? A Reply to Blaug' (2002a) also contained in Part III of the book. It was written as an answer to Mark Blaug's allegation that the revival of classical theory promoted by Sraffa overlooked the social and historical broadness of the classical authors, in favour of a narrow interpretation of their work through the lenses of linear production models. I point out in that article how, on the contrary, the interpretation of those authors in terms of the method of 'intermediate data' which Blaug criticizes, traces in the very analytical structure of classical theory the role played there by the broader social circumstances which Blaug rightly stresses.

Finally, the fourth article in the group of Part III, concerning Value and Distribution, namely 'On Some Supposed Obstacles to the Tendency of Market Prices Towards Natural Prices' (1997), deals with the problem which we would today indicate as the 'stability' of the classical normal position, i.e. the tendency of the actual, observable, variables towards their normal levels. The article had been stimulated by doubts advanced by several authors about Adam Smith's old conclusion on the general tendency of 'market prices' towards their 'natural' levels. The article focuses on the complexities due to the simultaneity and interactions between the deviations of 'market' from 'natural' prices. The upshot is there that the analysis of those interactions, absent in Adam Smith's pioneering analysis, does not appear to essentially alter Smith's conclusions, once the differences of classical theory from marginalist demand and supply are realized and taken into account with respect, in particular to the determination of the real wage, the key to the 'stability' of classical prices.

18. As we proceed to the group of essays of Part IV of the book—the group concerning 'Aggregate Demand' in the classical approach—some readers may feel puzzled as they recall Keynes' qualification of 'classical' for the position denying any role to such a demand. It should however have become clear by now that Keynes' qualification was in fact aimed at Pigou, rather than Ricardo and, more particularly, at the specific role which marginal theories attribute to the rate of interest for equilibrating decisions to invest with decisions to save, and which was totally absent in the old classical economists. Under the influence of Marshall's claim of continuity between his theory and that of Ricardo, Keynes had found it natural to attribute that theory of the rate of interest also to Ricardo on the strength simply of the latter's adherence to 'Say's law'.

The first of this group of articles, 'Notes on Consumption, Investment and Effective Demand' (1978–1979), in fact argues that Ricardo's adoption of Say's law, taken in its original form of supply creating its own demand—not to be confused with its marginalist form, that of a tendency to the full employment of labour[55]—was due to a direct identification between savings and investment, and not to any analysis of the corresponding decisions, and even less to any role of the rate of interest in equilibrating them. It is indeed contended in the article that such an equilibrating mechanism—the one which Keynes' analysis attempted to paralyze by resorting to expectations—is but the expression, from the standpoint of the rate of interest and of capital, of the marginalist explanation of distribution in terms of the demand and supply for 'productive factors', and that it accordingly falls when that explanation falls.

It is there argued that, on the contrary, Ricardo's analysis of value and distribution, with its independence of any equilibrium equality between demand for, and supply of, productive resources, and its determination of outputs separately from prices, is essentially open to a possible role of aggregate demand in determining the levels of economic activity. This is so, as soon as the distinction between decisions to save and decisions to invest is made clear. Indeed, when the division of the product between wages and profits is seen in terms of the classical broader forces regulating the size of the surplus of the product over wages, and not in those of an equilibrium between factor demands and supplies, the role of aggregate demand emerges as an altogether natural result. With aggregate output no longer determined by factor endowments, aggregate demand appears indeed to constitute an integral part of the separate determination of outputs. And this will be true with respect to the growth of the economy, and not only with regard to trade cycles.

The upshot of the 1978–1979 'Notes on Consumption' is therefore that the resumption of classical theory, and the critique of the marginalist theory of distribution associated with it, far from denying or weakening Keynes' conclusions on the role of aggregate demand, do indeed put those conclusions on a firmer basis

[55] One of the most important differences in the implications of the early classical versus neoclassical theory is of course the inexistence in the former of a competitive tendency to the full employment of an arbitrarily given labour endowment.

and above all make for their extension to long period analysis. The policy question that motivated the essay consisted indeed of the role which aggregate demand could play in the growth of a comparatively underdeveloped economy with a large reserve of unemployed labour, as was the Italian one of the time.

The same upshot, together with some further analysis of the implications of the classical approach for the role of aggregate demand in capital accumulation and growth, were taken up later in 'Two Routes to Effective Demand' (1985), also reprinted in Part IV. The long period implications stressed in that short essay were then explored more systematically in 'Some Notes for an Analysis of Accumulation' (1992), where their apparent contrast with the so called 'Cambridge equation', seemingly supporting a long period role of investment in determining the distribution between wages and profits, were also discussed. The same implications are concisely recalled in 'Accumulation of Capital', an article for *The Elgar Companion to Classical Economics* (1998), written in collaboration with Antonella Palumbo, where those results are compared with, and apparently confirmed by, the conclusions of economic historians.

19. With this we can come to the fifth and last Part of the book, devoted to questions of doctrinal history.

'Sraffa's Price Equations: Stationary Economy or Normal Position?' (2002b) is essentially a reply on the question of the 'stationarity' widely attributed to the prices of the equations in Sraffa's *Production of Commodities*. Those equations, I argue, refer instead to the 'normal prices' traditionally applied to a changing economy by the classical economists and also by marginalist authors before what we have called "Hicksian divide". The article was an occasion for attempting a less fragmentary treatment than I had given previously to the question of how changes of prices over time were dealt with, and can be dealt with, by means of the traditional normal positions, the question we touched upon already in para. 3 above.

Two articles deal then more generally with Sraffa's work, to whom we largely owe the revival of classical theory. In the first of the two, 'On Sraffa's Contribution to Economic Theory' (1989b), originally an interview on the occasion of his 80th birthday, I single out the three main contributions I see in his works, namely (*i*) the rediscovery of the approach to distribution and relative prices of Adam Smith and Ricardo; (*ii*) the development of that approach with respect to the problems of value that had remained partly open in Ricardo and Marx and, in strict connection with those first two contributions, (*iii*) the critique of marginal theory.

The last article, 'On a Turning Point in Sraffa's Theoretical and Interpretative Position in the Late 1920s', of 2005, exposes instead the route by which Sraffa appears to have come to his rediscovery of classical theory. It is a surprising route since, from a purely formal point of view, Sraffa might have arrived at his equations by simply applying to Marx's equations for prices-of-production, Marx's own suggestion (never carried out by him) of replacing the labour values on the input side of them with the unknown prices of production of the output side. Sraffa's route to his analysis started instead from a critique of the Marshallian subjective 'real cost' to which he counterposed the 'physical real cost' derived from the Physiocrats and, more broadly, from the old English classical economists.

This indirect route bears I believe a fascinating witness of the way in which the domination of marginal theory had succeeded in obscuring beyond recognition the basic, purely analytical, results which had been achieved, essentially, already by the time of Ricardo and Marx.

References

Blaug, M. (1958), *Ricardian economics*, New Haven and London: Yale University Press.

Bliss, C. J. (1975), *Capital theory and the distribution of income*, Amsterdam: North-Holland

Carey, C. H. (1856), *The past, the present and the future* (2nd ed), London: Trubner & Co.

Cohen, A. J. and Harcourt G. C. (2005), "Introduction. Capital theory controversy: Scarcity, production, equilibrium and time", in C. Bliss, A. J. Cohen and G. C. Harcourt (eds), "*Capital theory*", Vol. I, Cheltenham: Edward Elgar, pp. xxvii–lx

Foxwell, H. S. (1899), "Introduction to A. Menger", *The Right to the Whole Produce of Labour*, London: Macmillan, pp. v–cx

Garegnani, P. (1958), *A Problem in the Theory of Distribution from Ricardo to Wicksell*, Cambridge, Ph.D. Dissertation

Garegnani, P. (1964-65), Note su consumi, investimenti e domanda effettiva', *Economia Internazionale*, Parte I: 17(4), pp. 591-631; Parte II: 18(4), pp. 575–617

Garegnani, P. (1970), 'Heterogeneous capital, the Production Function and the Theory of Distribution', *Review of Economics Studies*, 37(3), pp. 407–436

Garegnani, P. (1976), 'On a Change in the Notion of Equilibrium in Recent Work on Value: a Comment on Samuelson', in M. Brown, K. Sato and P. Zarembka (eds), *Essays in Modern Capital Theory*. Amsterdam: North Holland, pp. 25–45

Garegnani, P. (1978-9), 'Notes on Consumption, Investment and Effective Demand', *Cambridge Journal of Economics*, Part I: 2(4), pp. 335-53; Part II: 3(1), pp. 63–82

Garegnani, P. (1983a), 'The Classical Theory of Wages and the Role of Demand Schedules in the Determination of Relative Prices', *American Economic Review*, 73(2), pp. 309–13

Garegnani, P. (1983b), 'Two Routes to Effective Demand', in J. A. Kregel (ed), *Distribution, Effective Demand and International Economic Relations*, London: Macmillan, pp. 69–80

Garegnani, P. (1984), 'Value and Distribution in the Classical Economists and Marx', *Oxford Economic Papers*, 36(2), pp. 291–325

Garegnani, P. (1989a), 'Some Notes on Capital, Expectations and the Analysis of Changes', in G. R. Feiwel (ed), *Joan Robinson and Modern Economic Theory*, London: Macmillan, pp. 344–367

Garegnani, P. (1989b) 'On Sraffa's Contribution to Economic Theory', in G. R. Feiwel (ed), *Joan Robinson and Modern Economic Theory*, London: Macmillan, pp. 368–74

Garegnani, P. (1992), 'Some Notes for an Analysis of Accumulation', in J. Halevi, D. Laibman and E. J. Nell (eds), *Beyond the Steady State*, London: Macmillan, 1992, pp. 47–71

Garegnani, P. (1997), 'On Some Supposed Obstacles to the Tendency of Market Prices towards Natural Prices', in G. Caravale (ed), *Equilibrium and Economic Theory*, London: Routledge, pp. 139–70

Garegnani, P. (in collaboraton with Antonella Palumbo) (1998), 'Accumulation of Capital', in H. D. Kurz and N. Salvadori (eds), *The Elgar Companion to Classical Political Economy*, Cheltenham: Edward Elgar, pp. 10–18

Garegnani, P. (2002a), 'Misunderstanding Classical Economics? A Reply to Blaug', *History of Political Economy*, 34(1), pp. 241–54

Garegnani, P. (2002b), 'Sraffa's Price Equations: Stationary Economy or Normal Positions?', in S. Boehm, C. Gehrke, H. D. Kurz, R. Sturn (eds), *Is There Progress in Economics?*, Cheltenham: Edward Elgar, pp. 389–401

Garegnani, P. (2002c), 'Sraffa: the theoretical world of the 'old classical economists'', in S. Nisticò and D. Tosato (eds), *Competing Economic Theories. Essays in Memory of Giovanni Caravale*, London: Routledge, pp. 67–79

Garegnani, P. ([2003] 2011) 'Savings, Investment and Capital in General Intertemporal Equilibrium'', in R. Ciccone, C. Gehrke and G. Mongiovi (eds), *Sraffa and Modern Economics*, Vol. I, Abingdon: Routledge, pp. 13–74

Garegnani, P. (2005) 'On a turning point in Sraffa's theoretical and interpretative position in the late 1920s', *European Journal of the History of Economic Thought*, 12(3), pp. 453–492

Hahn, F. H. (1982), 'The neo-Ricardians', *Cambridge Journal of Economics*, 6(4), pp. 353–74

Hicks, J. R. (1932a), *The Theory of Wages*, 2nd ed. London: Macmillan, 1963

Hicks, J. R. (1932b), 'Marginal Productivity and the Principle of Variation', *Economica*, No. 35, pp. 79-88

Hicks, J. R. (1939), *Value and Capital*, 2nd ed. Oxford: Clarendon Press, 1946

Kurz, H. D., 'Land', unpublished

Marshall, A. (1898), 'Distribution and Exchange', *Economic Journal*, 8(29), pp. 37–59

Marshall, A. ([1920] 1961), *Principles of Economics*, Ninth (Variorum) ed., London: Macmillan

Pareto, V. (1896–7), *Cours d'Économie Politique*, 2 Vols., Lausanne: Rouge

Pareto, V. (1909), *Manuel d'Économie Politique*, Paris: Giard & Brière [Eng. transl.: *Manual of Political Economy*, ed. by A. Montesano, A. Zanni, L. Bruni, J. S. Chipman, and M. McLure, Oxford: Oxford University Press, 2014]

Ricardo, D. ([1821] 1951), *On the Principles of Political Economy and Taxation*, In *The Works and Correspondence of David Ricardo*, edited by P. Sraffa with the collaboration of M. D. Dobb, Vol. I. Cambridge: University Press of Cambridge

Robbins, L. (1930), 'On a certain ambiguity on the notion of stationary state', *Economic Journal*, 40(158), pp. 194–211

Robertson, D. H. (1931), 'Wage-Grumbles', in *Economic Fragments*, London: P. S. King & Son, Ltd., pp. 42-57; rpt. in American Economic Association, *Readings in the Theory of Income Distribution*, Philadelphia/Toronto: The Blakiston Company, 1946, pp. 221–36

Robertson, D. H. (1957), *Lectures on Economic Principles*, Vol. I, Rochester: Staples Press

Robinson, J. (1956), *The Accumulation of Capital*, London: Macmillan

Robinson, J. (1970), 'Capital Theory up to Date', *Canadian Journal of Economics/Revue canadienne d'Économique*, 3(2), pp. 309–17

Samuelson, P. A. (1947), *Foundations of Economic Analysis*. Cambridge, Ma: Harvard University Press

Samuelson, P. A. (1962), 'Parable and Realism in Capital Theory: The Surrogate Production Function, *Review of Economic Studies*, 29(3), pp. 193–206

Seton, F. (1957), 'The "Transformation Problem", *Review of Economic Studies*, 24(3), pp. 149–60

Shove, G. F. (1933), Review of *The Theory of Wages* by J. R. Hicks, *Economic Journal*, 43(171), pp. 460–472

Sraffa, P. (1960), *Production of Commodities by Means of Commodities*, Cambridge: Cambridge University Press

Wald, A. (1951), 'On Some Systems of Equations of Mathematical Economics', *Econometrica*, 19(4), pp. 368–403

Walras, L. (1876-7), 'Théorie Mathématique de la Richesse Sociale', *Bulletin de la Société Vaudoise de Sciences naturelles*, 14(76), 1876, pp. 365-94 and 14(77), 1877, pp. 525–64

Walras, L. (1954), *Elements of Pure Economics or The Theory of Social Wealth*, 4th def. ed., Jaffé's Engl. ed., London: George Allen and Unwin

Wicksell, K. (1934), *Lectures on Political Economy*, Vol. I, New York: Kelley

Wicksell, K. (1954), *Value, Capital and Rent*, London: George Allen and Unwin

Contents

Part I
The Ph.D. Dissertation: A Problem in the Theory of Distribution from Ricardo to Wicksell

A Problem in the Theory of Distribution from Ricardo to Wicksell

Contents

The original version of the chapter has been revised: Incorrect details have been corrected. A correction to this chapter can be found at https://doi.org/10.1007/978-3-031-23643-3_18

P. Garegnani, *Capital Theory, the Surplus Approach, and Effective Demand*, Springer Studies in the History of Economic Thought, https://doi.org/10.1007/978-3-031-23643-3_1

Preface

A dissertation which has been the result of a few years' research and touches on so intricate a subject as the theory of capital cannot be written but with the awareness that the results expounded would undergo corrections and changes after a deeper analysis of some of the questions involved and after having gained a closer acquaintance with the concrete problems to the solution of which the theory must be applied. I am therefore conscious of the provisional nature of certain formulations and relative stresses, or of the possibility of mistakes at some points of the dissertation. These defects are also due in part to my having been unable to carry out an overall revision of the exposition, because detained by some problems which arose in the progress of the work.

I regard my contribution as consisting of: (a) bringing out how the difficulties Ricardo met in his theory of value and distribution can be reduced to a problem of consistently measuring capital similar to the one the marginal productivity theories also met and did not solve satisfactorily; (b) showing how a measurement of capital as a complex of quantities—obtained by generalizing Bortkiewicz's solution of Marx's 'transformation problem' may constitute a satisfactory basis for the solution of the problem in a theory of the Ricardian type; (c) showing how that same measurement of capital as a complex of quantities becomes unsatisfactory when applied to a marginal productivity theory.

Although in general statements it has often been admitted that unsolved difficulties lay behind the concepts of capital used in the marginal productivity theories, no attempt seems to have been made at a detailed discussion of the problem in the range of possible measurements and conceptions of capital (value in terms of some standard; average period of production, the complex of absolute periods of production of original factors; quantities of physically homogeneous capital goods). A first step in that direction is attempted in our examination of Walras's and Wicksell's theories of distribution in Section II of the dissertation, in connection with the argument directed to bring out point (c) above.

I wish here to thank Mr. Sraffa and Mr. Dobb who have successively supervised my work during the terms of research I have spent in Cambridge. My debt to them is double since it regards not only the guidance and encouragement they have given to me in the course of the preparation of the dissertation, but it refers also to the fact that the interpretation advanced here of the connection between Ricardo's theory of value and his theory of distribution, and, more generally, my interest in the subject, owe much to Sections IV and V of the Introduction to the *Principles* written by Mr. Sraffa with the collaboration of Mr. Dobb, and contained in Vol. I of their edition of Ricardo's *Works*.

Whenever I have been aware of being indebted to some particular authors for concepts or interpretations used in the following dissertation, the relevant works are mentioned in the footnotes.

Trinity College.

December 1958.

Introduction

At the cost of severe simplification, it seems that we can distinguish in the history of economic analysis, two broadly different approaches to a theory of the distribution of the social product among the members of the community.

The first one to appear had its centre in the concept of social surplus. It was first used in a systematic form by the Physiocrates; it became a part of what Smith has to say on distribution in the *Wealth of Nations*; it gave the basis to the analysis of Ricardo; finally Marx took it over and developed it at a time when the dominant trend of economic thought was already moving in another direction.

The other approach is the one which has been dominant in recent economic thought: it centres on the concept of a marginal productivity of homogeneous 'factors of production' and makes of the theory of distribution an application of a general theory of value, relating values to marginal increments in subjective satisfactions derived from commodities.

The aim is here to show how in the attempt to develop each of these approaches into a consistent theory of distribution the same theoretical difficulty has arisen and has not been satisfactorily solved. In the context of the first approach, the difficulty underlies Ricardo's search for an 'invariable' standard of value; it was inherited by Marx in the form of the determination of a link between 'values' and 'prices of production'. In the context of the second approach that difficulty arose in the attempts to give meaning to a 'marginal productivity of capital' on which to found the determination of the rate of interest.

The two approaches to distribution are basically different and the problem arose, in the two contexts, in a different form, in the form of different difficulties. But, it is submitted here, once these difficulties are stated in their simplest form, they can be reduced to the same problem which can be described as that of finding a way of measuring capital in terms which while bearing a definable relationship to the 'value' of capital are, at the same time, independent of changes in distribution.[1]

[1] What is meant by this, should become clear in what will be said below.

In Section I of the dissertation we shall examine the problem as it arises in the surplus theories of distribution and we shall consider the possibility of its solution within those theories. For that purpose we shall mainly refer to Ricardo's theory of distribution but, when discussing Bortkiewicz's 'transformation' of 'values' into 'prices of production', we shall also refer to the different way in which Marx faced the same problem.

In Section II we shall examine the problem as it arises in the marginal productivity theories of distribution. We shall there discuss and criticize the solutions Walras and Wicksell offered to the problem in that setting.

Section I, Chapter I: The Surplus Approach to Distribution and the Problem of Measuring Value Connected with It

Before examining the connection in which the problem of the measurement of capital arises in Ricardo's theory of distribution, it may be useful to indicate in this chapter some general features of the surplus approach he shares with the Physiocrats and Adam Smith.[2] This will allow us to indicate how a special problem of measuring value is connected with that approach.

Within the surplus approach the main problem in the theory of distribution is the determination of what regulates the size of the social surplus. The social product[3] is divided into two parts: the part which is given to the labourers and the remaining part, constituting the social surplus.

The determination of what governs the size of the social surplus can be schematically described in the following way: we start from the determination of the circumstances regulating the quantity of goods given to the labourers; then, if

[2] The use of the expression 'theory of distribution' to cover both the theories founded on the concept of surplus and those founded on marginal productivity, might be misleading to the extent in which it can hide a difference in the scope of the two types of theory. The surplus approach lends itself to applications in the field of accumulation and growth which are foreign to the theories of distribution as understood to-day. This remark seems particularly relevant in the case of Smith, where the surplus approach is used more for the analysis of reproduction and accumulation than for what he has to say on profits and rents. In this dissertation, when describing theories of distribution, we shall proceed in a very schematic way, trying only to bring out the elements which seem relevant for our purpose, and we shall often have to ignore such differences.

[3] If we had to use modern concepts we should here specify social product net of the replacement of capital since it is supposed to consist entirely of wages, profits and rents received during the period. But in the theories we are referring to, the conception of capital was different and not sufficiently consistent to allow the drawing of a distinction between gross and net social produce in the modern sense. As we shall have occasion to mention (below, p. 20), Smith often identifies capital with the wages paid during the period, usually assumed to be a year, so that the only replacement of capital, taking the community as a whole, appears to be the setting apart of the produce of a year to pay the wages of the next year (see, *e.g.*, the distinction between replacement of capital and revenue at p. 320 of *Wealth of Nations*, Vol. I, Cannan ed. [*editor's note*: the Cannan edition of the *Wealth of Nations* is the one that will be referred to in the remainder of the dissertation]).

we know what regulates the size of the produce, the size of the surplus in each given situation is determined by what remains of the produce over the wages of the labourers who produce it. In algebraic terms we could say that the size of the surplus is determined by an equation in three variables: the social produce, the portion of it which goes to the labourers and which, for brevity, we shall call 'necessary consumption',[4] and finally the social surplus; the first two variables are independent variables in the sense that, when determining the surplus, they can be taken as data in their size or variation; the social surplus, in its size or variation, is then the only unknown in the equation and can therefore be determined by it.

The basis on which this simple procedure rests is, it seems, the possibility of taking as given the wages (considered as an aggregate of commodities) per unit of labour, in the face of changes in the product obtained with the labour, and, when necessary, of taking as given the produce in the face of changes in wages. This feature, which explains and justifies the determination of the share of the product different from wages as a residual quantity, is related to the way in which the wages were determined. For the Physiocrats the quantity of goods retained by the 'productive' labourer could be assumed to be fixed at a customary subsistence level.[5] The same was true for Ricardo. The position of Smith was less clear-cut, but it seems safe to conclude that for him also the quantity of goods going to the labourers could be broadly assumed not to vary with variations of the produce.[6] Marx also did not hold a simple subsistence theory of wages, but he himself often stressed the importance of taking the wages as given in a theory of distribution as he understood it.[7]

We have up to now referred to the social produce and to the part of it given to the labourers, as the basic magnitudes on which the study of factors regulating the size of the social surplus operates. Social produce, necessary consumption, social surplus over a given period of time have an immediate meaning as aggregates of commodities. But, it is evident that the theories we have alluded to cannot stop at such a conception. We have seen that the theories conceive them as magnitudes which undergo definite quantitative variations in passing from one situation to another, and are homogeneous with each other so that the social surplus can

---

[4] Cf. 'The rate of profits must depend on the proportion of production to the consumption necessary to such production' (Ricardo, *Works*, Sraffa ed., Vol. VI, p. 108).

[5] *E.g.* see Turgot, *Reflections*, para VI.

[6] Smith relates the level of wages not to the actual greatness of the produce but rather to its 'progressive' or 'declining' state: a high rate of accumulation would tend to outrun the increase of population and to increase wages (*Wealth of Nations*, Vol. I, pp. 70–5). This kind of relationship would not prevent us from taking the wages as a datum in the sense relevant here. What would prevent us from doing that would be a functional relationship between the wages and the actual size of the produce like the one assumed in marginal productivity theories.

[7] In his *Theories of Surplus Value* (London, 1951), while commenting upon the Physiocratic doctrine he remarks: 'The conception of the value of labour power as something fixed, as a given magnitude, as indeed it is in practice in each definite case, is therefore one of the foundations of modern political economy, whose business is the analysis of capitalist production' (p. 45).

be obtained by subtracting necessary consumption from social produce. We need therefore a measurement of social produce and necessary consumption in terms of a common unit so that: (a) an unambiguous quantitative meaning can be given to the changes occurring in each of those aggregates of commodities, whatever the changes which may occur in the kind of commodities constituting them;[8] (b) the resulting magnitudes can be added to, and subtracted from one another.

In the case of the Physiocrats the problem hardly arose since the very limitations of their view of the economic process offered them an easy solution to it. For them a 'produit net' can arise only in agriculture so that the magnitudes determining the size of the surplus are the agricultural produce and the consumption of the farmer. In the type of agriculture the Physiocrats had in mind the consumption of the farmer consisted mostly of the staple agricultural commodities.[9] So that, at least for the broad problems the Physiocrats were interested in, the consumption of the farmers could be taken as physically homogeneoues with their produce,[10] and the aggregates determining the surplus could be conceived as physical quantities. If we then choose to measure them in value terms on the assumption of constant prices, the procedure would find a justification in that such value measurements would correspond to unambiguous physical quantities. The meaning of the value unit would be that of a physical unit of agricultural produce.[11] Variations in the 'produit net', or in the 'avances annuelles' will then always have an unambiguous meaning and we shall not, on this account, have any special difficulty.

The difficulty was, however, bound to arise as soon as, with Smith, a surplus was seen to originate in all branches of production and not only in agriculture and the surplus came to include both rent of land and profits on capital. The quantities relevant for the determination of the surplus then became the aggregate of the commodities produced in the economy, whether agricultural or not, and the part of them consumed by the labourers. In the more diversified economy which came

[8] *E.g.* we should be able to speak of a constancy of the social produce in the face of a rise of wages which will, in general, affect the relative demand for commodities and the physical components of the produce; or we should be able to define the size of the surplus in any given situation, independently of whether that surplus will be used for the consumption of its receivers or will instead be accumulated, which circumstance will affect the physical constituents of the surplus.

[9] Further, to the extent in which the consumption of the farmer (and the reintegration of the 'avances primitives') consisted of produce of the 'sterile' class, it could—from the Physiocrats' standpoint—be reduced to the given subsistence of the artisans and to the agricultural raw materials they used, that is to a given quantity of agricultural produce.

[10] Physical homogeneity in the meaning used here does not imply that produce and necessary consumption consist of one and the same commodity. It is sufficient if they consist of the same commodities in approximately the same proportions.

[11] This appears to be the procedure adopted by Quesnay in his *Tableau Economique*. In his 'Analyse du Tableau Economique' he says: 'Supposons donc un grand royaume, dont le territoire... rapporterait tous les ans une reproduction de la valeur de cinq milliards; et où l'état permanent de cette valeur serait établi sur les prix constants qui ont cours entre les nations commercantes...' (*Physiocrates*, ed. Daire, Vol. 1, p. 58).

into focus with this generalization of the Physiocratic scheme it becomes impossible to conceive social produce and necessary consumption as physically homogeneous. Also, the changes whose effect on the surplus the theory studies, are bound to affect the proportions of the physical components of the social produce. The basis for conceiving the magnitudes and their variations in physical terms falls and some other unit must be found consistent with the use of the measurements in the theory.

It is here that the problem of value arises within this type of theory of distribution, and the context in which it arises may help to explain some special features of the problem of value in the classical economists, in particular the concern for what they called a 'real' or 'invariable' standard of value.

The heterogeneous commodities constituting the social produce must be reduced to a satisfactory common standard. In economic reality they are exchanged for each other, and so they are in fact reduced to a common standard in terms of any of the commodities in circulation. If we take such ratios in exchange as the appropriate indication of the relative significance[12] of the several commodities within the magnitudes with which we have to deal, as the classical economists in general did, we shall have one of the requirements according to which the aggregates should be measured: in the resulting magnitudes the commodities must count according to their relative values in the situation to which the quantities refer. The quantities will have to be 'value' quantities and the standard a 'measure of value'.

That being so, a determination of what regulates relative values is an essential part of the search for an appropriate standard of value: we shall have to know how the values of the aggregates will behave, in the face of the changes to be examined, when measured in terms of the possible standards; this will offer the ground on which to discuss the further problem of which, if any, among those possible standards, gives measurements consistent with the use of the quantities in the theory. For, beside the requirement just mentioned, the use of such measurements in the theory imposes on the standard another special requirement. We shall examine that requirement in the following chapter in connection with Ricardo's theory. We can here notice, however, that to the extent in which the standard of value has to satisfy some special conditions, the classical economists had to face, as a result of their approach to the theory of distribution, a special problem of measuring value linked to, but distinct from, the one of what regulates relative values.[13]

---

[12] The way in which our exposition is conducted should not be taken to imply that the classical economists consciously faced this problem of the relative significance of the commodities. They rather took it for granted that the ratios in exchange are the measure of such relative significance.

[13] See also the appendix to this chapter regarding the problem of a 'real' measure of value in A. Smith.

Appendix to Section I, Chapter I: Smith's Distinction Between a Real and a 'Nominal' Price of Commodities

Smith had to face the question of valuation sketched in Chapter I when he introduced in the scheme of the *Wealth of Nations* the Physiocratic idea of surplus and, with it, the conception of social produce and the problem of its distribution among classes.[14] That seems to be the main context in which the discussion of Chapter VI in Book I, on the 'real' and 'nominal' price of commodities, should be seen.

The money unit must have immediately appeared to Smith as unsuitable for the purpose of measuring the value of the social produce, or its parts, in his analysis of the surplus: no relationship could be established between the variation of the social produce in the meaning Smith was groping for, and that of the money value of the corresponding aggregate of commodities. It was a fact recognized for some time that the price of commodities could and did vary with circumstances relating only to the monetary unit, like the debasement of coins or, as was brought into relief by the discussion on the cause of the rise in prices after the geographical discoveries, the change in the quantity of the precious metals available relatively to the need for them. The fact had been expressed as variability in the 'value' of money. For Smith changes in the value of the social produce arising from such circumstances were immaterial: *e.g.* a change in the money value of the social produce which left unaffected its physical constituents and their distribution among the members of the community, would have been no change of the produce in the meaning of it relevant for Smith's problem. So, the variations of the money value of the surplus had little or no significance for the questions with which Smith was mainly concerned: the prosperity of a community and its classes, and its power to accumulate. Accordingly Smith discarded money as a measure of value in his analysis, since 'gold and silver … like every other commodity vary in their value, are sometimes cheaper and sometimes dearer'.[15]

It could be argued that the difficulties connected with a money standard might be overcome through appropriate assumptions regarding the behaviour of the money unit; but it seems that the determination of the appropriate assumptions would correspond to what appeared to Smith as the search for an invariable measure of value. From Smith's point of view to make such assumptions would amount to assuming that the 'value' of money remains 'constant' in the face of the changes analysed: to do so we should first have to know what constancy in value means; in other words, we should already possess a 'standard' of value.

[14] Although, at times, Smith mentions the produce and its variations without referring to value, in most cases, and in particular where he must give a stricter quantitative meaning to the concept, he introduces value. *E.g.*, *Wealth of Nations*, Vol. I, pp. 56, 323, 325 etc..

[15] *Wealth of Nations*, Vol. I, p. 34.

Once having discarded money and the 'nominal price', Smith has to look for a 'real price' suitable for his analysis. For that he, following numerous precedents in English economic literature, and in particular that of his own Glasgow teacher Francis Hutcheson,[16] falls back on the quantity of labour a commodity can buy as the standard for measuring its 'real price': '[l]abour alone, ... never varying in its own value, is alone the ultimate and real standard by which the value of all commodities can at all times and places be estimated and compared'.[17]

The reasons he gives in Chapter V, Book I, for such a choice have often puzzled his critics, beginning with Ricardo.[18]

But, once the problem of the 'invariable measure of value' is also seen in the context of that need to measure and conceive in meaningful terms the social produce and its shares, which is connected with the approach inherited from the Physiocrats, then the choice does not appear to be so arbitrary as some interpreters have supposed.[19]

Labour commanded had some advantages for Smith over other possible standards of value from two points of view. On the one hand, it allowed a relationship to be established between the variations of the quantity of labour embodied in an aggregate of commodities and the variations of its value, stricter than would be possible with other standards of value.[20] On the other hand, the quantity of labour which an aggregate of commodities can command must have appeared to Smith as a particularly relevant magnitude by which to measure it in connection with the problems of accumulation. It may be worth while to see these two points in some more detail, starting with the latter.

The first advantage of labour commanded as a standard of value, is that the variations of the value of aggregates so measured are variations of a quantity of great importance from Smith's point of view: they are the variations in the number of people who can be employed with them. So, the constancy or variation at the 'real value' of what we have called necessary consumption, which is often identified

[16] F. Hutcheson, *System of Moral Philosophy*, Glasgow, 1755, Vol. II, pp. 58, 62, 63; quoted in Cannan's Introduction, *Wealth of Nations,* Vol. I, pp. XXXVII–XXXVIII.

[17] *Wealth of Nations*, Vol. I. p. 35.

[18] Ricardo, *Works*, Sraffa ed., Vol. I, pp. 13–20.

[19] 'The effect of this doctrine of real and nominal price was quite arbitrarily to select labour as the only thing which does not change in value ... Quite arbitrarily ... because there is no reason for saying the converse, namely, that commodities have not varied in value, but labour has become of greater value, inasmuch as more commodities will now have to be given in exchange for it' (E. Cannan, *A Review of Economic Theory*, London 1929, p. 166).

[20] It will be remembered that a direct measurement of value in terms of labour embodied was thought by Smith to be impossible once 'that early and rude state of society' in which neither 'stock has accumulated in the hands of particular persons', nor 'land has all become private property', has passed; since then profits and rents have become 'original sources of ... all exchangeable value' (*Wealth of Nations*, Vol. I, pp. 49–51 and p. 54).

by Smith with the capital which should always be at least replaced, determines whether the number of productive labourers is being maintained or varied. In other words the 'capital' which, according to Chapter III of Book II, should never be encroached upon, is measured in labour commanded: it is the constancy of that magnitude which, given the physical productivity of labour, guarantees constancy in the 'prosperity' of the country.[21] Also, the 'real value' of the surplus expresses for Smith the limit to the increase in the number of productive labourers which could be realised in the country at that time, and is therefore the best indication of its power to accumulate.[22]

The other advantage offered by labour commanded is connected with the theory of the 'natural price': according to Smith the 'natural price' of any commodity is determined by adding up three 'component parts', the wages of the labour, the profits of the 'stock', and the rent of the land employed for producing the commodity; all three components being calculated at their 'natural rate'.[23] If those component parts are measured in labour commanded, so as to obtain their 'real value', the first component, the wages, gives the quantity of labour embodied in the commodity. If we pass from the individual commodity to the social produce, we shall see that, to the extent in which the proportions of rent and profits in its value do not vary very much, the variations in its value so measured will tend to reflect proportional variations in the number of labourers productively employed; and we must remember that variations of the number of productive labourers are the main factor determining that 'progressive' or 'declining' state of the wealth of nations which is at the centre of Smith's concern. This relationship could not, in general, be established if the value were measured in terms of some other

[21] *E.g.*, referring to a situation where the 'value' of money has risen, Smith says: 'The capital of the country though it might nominally be the same, would really be augmented ... it would command a greater quantity of labour. The quantity of productive labour it could maintain and employ would be increased' (*Wealth of Nations*, Vol. I, p. 337; see also p. 320).

[22] '... the annual produce of its labour will always be sufficient to purchase or command a much greater quantity of labour than what was employed in raising, preparing, and bringing that produce to market. If the society were annually to employ all the labour which it can annually purchase, as the quantity of labour would increase greatly every year, so the produce of every succeeding year would be of vastly greater value than that of the foregoing'(*Wealth of Nations*, Vol. I., p. 56). In general the property of labour commanded of measuring the variation in the number of labourers which could be employed with a certain aggregate of commodities, is extensively used by Smith in Book II of the *Wealth of Nations*.

[23] *Wealth of Nations*, Vol. I, p. 57.

commodity, since then the value would be affected, in the first component, by the change in the wage rate in terms of that commodity.[24,25]

If labour commanded had for Smith those advantages as a measure of aggregates in connection with his theory of the surplus, its use within that same theory meets a very serious difficulty. The value of a commodity or aggregate of commodities, measured by it, varies as the proportion of profits and rent in the value varies. When, in a theory of distribution of the type examined in Section I of the dissertation, we are using the magnitudes social produce and necessary consumption in order to determine how certain circumstances affect distribution, it is clear that we cannot assume constancy in that proportion. Then in order to know how those circumstances affect the produce and the necessary consumption measured in labour commanded, we should first have to know how they will affect profits and rents, which is just what we have to determine on the basis of produce and necessary consumption; we seem to be moving in a circle.

In Smith the surplus approach to distribution was not yet developed enough to bring out the problem clearly. The main use of that approach in Smith was for the broad problems of accumulation where vaguer formulations could still give useful results. Where the difficulty would have arisen more acutely, in connection with the determination of the rate of profits and of rents, he fell back on other ideas whose inconsistency with the approach adopted in other parts of the work he did not seem to feel. However, the difficulty affecting Smith's standard of value was

[24] Labour commanded establishes a strict relationship between labour embodied and the first component of the natural price only. If the variation of the wage rate is associated with a variation of profits and rent as a rate to wages, another standard in terms of which the wage rate can vary may allow a stricter relationship between labour embodied and value than labour commanded, to the extent in which the variation of wages and that of rent and profits compensate each other. The commodities successively chosen as standard by Ricardo will be of that type. But if the change in the wage rate in terms of a commodity is due only to a change in the productivity of the labour employed in producing that commodity, the change of the wage rate need not be associated with a change in rents and profits, and value in labour commanded would tend to vary in step with variations of the labour necessary to produce the commodity.

[25] This property of labour commanded is often used by Smith, both in relation to individual commodities and in relation to aggregates. In the first connection, for instance, he says: 'As it costs less labour to bring those metals from the mine to the market, so when they were brought thither they could purchase and command less labour' (*Wealth of Nations*, Vol. I, p. 34); the same relationship between variations in 'value' and variations in the quantity of labour necessary to produce the commodity is at the basis of most of what is said in the digression, in Chapter XI, on the effects of 'the progress of improvement' upon the 'real price' of different sorts of 'rude produce' and of manufactures (*e.g.*, see p. 224); it is also often used to discriminate between changes in the value of money and changes in the value of commodities in the digression on the history of prices in that same chapter (*e.g.*, pp. 186–7). In the second connection, we have passages like: 'Every increase or diminution of capital, therefore, naturally tends to increase or diminish the real quantity of industry, the number of productive hands, and *consequently* the exchangeable value of the annual produce of the land and labour of the country, ...' (*Wealth of Nations*, Vol. I, p. 320, emphasis added); see also pp. 56, 321, 327, and in general the whole of Chapter III, Book II.

bound to become apparent to Ricardo as he attempted a general formulation of his theory of profits. He then, as we shall see in Chapter II of this section, had to face in a clearer form the requirements which the measurements of the relevant aggregates should satisfy to be consistent with their use in the theory of distribution. What has been said here and in Chapter I should bring out the conclusion that a special problem of 'measuring value' is connected with the type of theory of distribution which can be found in the classical economists. The recognition of this may help to understand the importance they set on the search for an 'invariable' measure of value. With regard to Ricardo that should now be universally recognized, after Mr. Sraffa and Mr. Dobb's introduction to the *Principles*,[26] but the question seems to be important also in explaining Smith's concern with the 'real' measure of value.[27]

---

[26] Ricardo, *Works*, Vol. I, pp. XXX–XLIX.

[27] According to a commoner view, Smith's problem was only the result of confusions connected with an attempt to find a measure of general purchasing power for purposes of historical and statistical description; a view which seems to have originated with S. Bailey's *Critical Dissertation* (see below, Appendix A). For example, in his *History of Economic Analysis* (New York, 1954) Schumpeter says: 'Smith replaces for purposes of interlocal and intertemporal comparison this monetary or 'nominal' price of each commodity by a real price in the same sense in which we speak, for example, of real wages as distinguished from money wages, that is, by price in terms of all other commodities. And these real prices he in turn replaces, in ignorance of the index-number method already invented in his time, by prices expressed in terms of labour .... But Smith flounders so badly in conveying the idea and, moreover, confuses it with philosophies concerning the nature of value ... that his fundamentally simple idea was misunderstood even by Ricardo' (p. 188). Undoubtedly some of the connections in which Smith uses his standard are those for which to-day a standard of general purchasing power would be used (see the discussion on the best way of preserving the 'value' of perpetual rents in Chapter IV of Book I, or the digression on the history of the variation of the value of silver in Chapter XI of the same Book). But it appears that the search for an invariable measure of value met in Smith an analytical need connected with his approach to distribution. Attempts to use those concepts to answer questions which now, in the light of later analysis on different lines, appear as distinct, are present. But to put the questions involved in his idea of the invariable measure of value in clear terms, would have required a more advanced stage of development of the theory than was achieved by Smith. A point may be mentioned here which might be of some significance in supporting the interpretation of Smith's problem we have advanced. In the early schemes of the *Wealth of Nations* (as recorded for us by the *Glasgow Lectures* (Oxford 1896), and by the draft found and published by Professor Scott, Part III of 'A. Smith as Student and Professor', Glasgow 1937, both dated at a time before Smith came into contact with the Physiocrats), where a theory of distribution appears, if at all, in a very rudimentary form, the distinction between 'real' and 'nominal' value does not yet appear. In those same works, an interest in the history of prices was already present, particularly in the draft where a full digression on the subject is planned (*Lectures*, p. 198; Scott, op. cit., p. 347).

Section I, Chapter II: Ricardo's Theory of Distribution, His Problem of Measuring Value Reducible to That of a Consistent Measurement of Capital

The surplus approach to distribution is woven by Ricardo into a theory of profits. We shall here sketch briefly the basic elements of that theory so as to be able to concentrate our attention on the form taken there by that problem of 'measuring' value which we have seen in the previous chapter to be connected with the surplus approach. That will offer the ground for indicating the general features of the problem of measuring capital which appears to lie behind Ricardo's difficulties in measuring value.

The theory of rent which Ricardo borrowed from Malthus,[28] allowed him to determine the corresponding share of the social product. In this way he could isolate that part of the product which is to be divided between wages and profits.[29] The part of it going to the labourers is determined once we know that, according to Ricardo, the wages are fixed at the subsistence level; the remainder is profits. Further: the ratio between the value (however measured) of that residual and the value of the aggregate of goods given to the labourers as wages will determine the rate of profit.[30]

How does Ricardo measure those quantities? In the *Essay on Profits* Ricardo measured them in physical terms, in terms of quantities of 'corn'. That procedure was valid to the extent to which it could be assumed that all the capital used in

[28] See editors' introduction to the *Essay on profits'*, Ricardo, *Works*, Sraffa ed., Vol. IV, pp. 6–8.

[29] We can note here a feature of the way in which total rent on land is eliminated from the social product in the *Principles*. The value of the social produce net of rent is related to the quantity of (homogeneous) labour employed in producing the entire social produce, rent included. This is correct because the value of the agricultural produce is related only to the quantity of labour necessary to produce it on the marginal land (or at the 'intensive' margin). It follows that the value of the social produce, including rent, will be higher than that corresponding to the labour actually embodied in it; the excess will be equal to the value of the goods constituting the share of the landowners, since the labour value of the rent on a piece of land is determined by the difference between the quantity of labour which should have been necessary if the corn grown on that land had been grown on marginal land, and the quantity of labour which was actually employed to produce it. In what follows of Section I of the dissertation we shall ignore the complications that the consideration of rent would introduce in the models: we shall assume that the social produce is divided only between wages and profits.

[30] The position of Ricardo about the identification of capital with the wages paid during the year is in no way as simple as the account given above would seem to imply, and we shall have to return to the question (below, pp. 19–20). But what is attempted here is to draw a very simplified scheme, ignoring for the moment the complications and contradictions contained in Ricardo's work.

agriculture consisted of agricultural products, of 'corn'. If we introduce elements of capital which are not corn, but are valued in corn, we have no longer that independence of the rate of profit on the capital employed in agriculture from the system of relative values which allowed him to study in agriculture the forces regulating the rate of profit in the whole economy.[31]

In the *Principles* that method, which Ricardo had clearly found unsatisfactory,[32] is abandoned and the determination of profits is studied in the economy as a whole. Ricardo is then faced by the problem of 'measuring value' referred to above. Here, in connection with his theory of profits, it is possible to be more precise about the terms of the problem.

The requirements which the reduction of commodities to a common standard should satisfy within Ricardo's theory of profits appear to be two.

Firstly, the commodities measured in the common standard will have to bear to each other the proportions in which they will, in equilibrium, be exchanged. This requirement is the one we have already mentioned in Chapter I.[33] There we explained it in relation to the relative significance of the commodities within the magnitudes with which the theory of distribution has to deal. As long as the question remains in those general terms there can be doubt as to whether a strict adherence to the proportionality with ratios in exchange in each of the situations considered is the only way to give the meaning required for the quantities measured by the standard. But in Ricardo the justification of this requirement is more specific. The problem for Ricardo is no longer only that of the circumstances regulating the *size* of the surplus; it is also that of what governs the profits as a *rate* on capital; it is the problem of what regulates the rate of profits ruling in the economy. In the economy the ruling rate of profits is calculated as a ratio between values (values of aggregates of commodities). Whether such values are money values or values in terms of any of the commodities has no importance, since the concern here is with a ratio and the ratio will be the same whatever the commodity chosen to measure profits and capital in economic reality. What has importance here is that, in these actual values, the commodities enter according to what their relative values are in the given situations. Now, if in the reduction of the commodities to the common standard used in this theory, their relative values are not respected, the theory will be unable to determine what variation in the actual rate of profits ruling in the economy will follow from certain hypothetical circumstances, for we

---

[31] On the point of the justification of the principle of the determining role of profits in agriculture, used in Ricardo's *Essay on profits*, see Mr. Sraffa and Mr. Dobb's introduction to Vol. I of their edition of Ricardo's *Works*, p. xxxi.

[32] See in this connection, for example, the discussion in the correspondence between Ricardo and Malthus of March–April 1815, on the case submitted by Malthus according to which the rise in the price of corn relatively to manufactures, could increase the profits of the farmers by diminishing the corn price of the manufactured elements of capital (Malthus's case is clearly stated in his letter to Horner of March the 19th, Ricardo, *Works*, Vol. VI, pp. 186–8).

[33] Above, p. 9.

shall be unable to say that the ratio between surplus and wages (capital) measured in terms of the standard used in the theory will be the same as the ratio between the values in the situation examined, however measured.[34]

Secondly, the common standard must be such that we should be able to postulate the effect of hypothetical circumstances on the aggregate of commodities measured by it, without knowing in advance the variations in the rate of profits, which will result from those circumstances. The reason for this requirement is clear: since we determine the rate of profits and its variation on the basis of magnitudes expressing the social product and the aggregate of goods given to the labourers as wages, we should be able to express those magnitudes in a way which does not require a previous knowledge of the rate of profits.[35,36]

Because of the first requirement, the starting point for Ricardo's problem of reducing heterogeneous commodities to a common standard must be a determination of what regulates the ratios in which commodities exchange.[37] For that purpose Ricardo inherits Smith's theory of the 'natural' price: the natural price is determined by adding up the wages of the labour which has produced the commodity, at their 'natural' rate, and the profits on the capital employed calculated at their 'ruling or 'natural' rate.[38]

---

[34] If, for example, labour embodied were used as the standard in the theory, an increase in the quantity of labour embodied in the goods given to the same number of labourers would be reflected, other things being equal, in a fall in the rate of profits calculated as a ratio between the labour embodied in the goods constituting profits and the labour embodied in the wages. But if we cannot say that commodities will exchange according to the quantity of labour embodied in them, we cannot say that the rate of profit in the economic reality will vary in the same way: the relative value of profit goods might vary in such a way as to keep constant or even increase the actual rate of profits. Also the possible question of the extent to which in certain problems that or another measurement of the aggregates may be taken as an allowable approximation, cannot be decided until we possess an exact measure in relation to which the degree of error involved can be ascertained.

[35] Cf. above p. 13. We shall see below (p. 21) that the simple fact of the variability of a given physical aggregate of commodities with changes in distribution, when measured in the standard, does not appear to disqualify the standard from being satisfactory for the purposes of Ricardo's theory of profits, provided that the resulting magnitudes can be fitted in the equation determining profits so that the only unknown in the equation will be the rate of profit. This should explain the wording chosen above for the second requirement.

[36] The idea underlying this second requirement was first suggested by the reading of Mr. Sraffa and Mr. Dobb's introduction to their edition of the *Principles*. See, in particular, the passage: 'Thus the problem of value which interested Ricardo was how to find a measure of value which would be invariant to changes in the division of the product' (Ricardo, *Works*, Vol. I, p. xlviii).

[37] Cf. above, p. 9.

[38] As we have seen above (p. 15), Ricardo eliminates rent of land by calculating the price of agricultural products according to their cost at the margin of cultivation. We can here remember that Smith and Ricardo's theory of price is founded on the assumption of constant returns to scale for manufactures, while the position of the margin in agriculture is given since it is treated as broadly determined by the level of accumulation and population.

If the proportion between wages and profits contained in the natural price were always the same for all commodities as it would be if, for instance, all commodities were produced by labour unassisted by fixed capital, applied uniformly over a year and paid at the beginning of the year—the quantity of labour embodied in the commodities could be the common standard we need. We could then use it either directly as labour embodied in the aggregates of commodities or indirectly by measuring the values of those aggregates in terms of a hypothetical commodity requiring always the same quantity of labour to produce it. The uniformity throughout the whole economy, in the level of wages and in the rate of profits in conditions of competitive equilibrium would guarantee that commodities exchange according to the quantity of labour embodied in them[39]; labour embodied would then satisfy the first requirement. The same standard would evidently satisfy also the second requirement since the quantity of labour embodied in given commodities is independent of changes in distribution and, in particular, of changes in the rate of profits.

Labour embodied is in fact the foundation on which Ricardo's theory of profits in the *Principles* rests. While being fully aware of the shortcomings of his own standard, Ricardo criticised the standard chosen by Smith and Malthus: labour commanded. In fact the latter standard, while obviously satisfactory from the point of view of the first requirement (the proportionality of the values of commodities as measured by it with ratios in exchange), was unsatisfactory from the point of view of the second requirement, since the value of commodities so measured changes simply as a result of changes in the rate of profits.[40]

But the proportions in which the natural prices of commodities are divided between wages and profits are not the same, and accordingly the ratios in which commodities exchange will change also with changes in the rate of profits. As a consequence labour embodied is no longer a satisfactory standard since it cannot satisfy the first requirement. Or, looking at the question in the way Ricardo tended to look at it, using as a standard of value a commodity produced always by the same quantity of labour,[41] it is the second requirement which appears to remain

[39] The quantities of labour embodied referred to here are quantities of homogeneous labour. We do not need to enter here into the difficulties connected with the reduction to homogeneity of labour of different 'quality'; we can here only remember that all that is needed by Ricardo, as later, it seems, by Marx, is the possibility of assuming the invariability, in the face of the changes examined, of the proportions between the wages for different types of labour (Ricardo, *Works*, Vol. I, pp. 20–22).

[40] Cf. above, p. 13, but see pp. 21–2.

[41] The other conditions of production of the standard commodity, which can be referred to as the 'capital' assisting the labour which has produced it, underwent changes in the successive writings of Ricardo on the subject (see a close analysis of those changes at pp. XII–XIV of the introduction to Vol. I of Mr. Sraffa and Mr. Dobb's edition of Ricardo). This point however need not detain us here.

unsatisfied: the value of a given physical aggregate of commodities measured by that standard will vary when nothing changes but the way in which the social product is distributed.[42]

On this problem Ricardo struggled without reaching a solution which could satisfy him. Before trying to see what underlies this problem, it may be useful to hint at another deficiency of Ricardo's determination of the rate of profits.

According to the scheme indicated above,[43] Ricardo tended to identify the capital to which the yearly profits should be referred in order to calculate their yearly rate, with the total wages paid to the labourers for the year. This procedure would be justified only if the process of production could be thought of as starting at the beginning of each year with the existing labour force unassisted by capital goods and reaching completion for all commodities at the end of the year. In that case the capital would consist entirely of the wage goods given to the labourers during the year, goods which must have been in the hands of the capitalists at the beginning of the year.

That scheme is a simplification of Ricardo's position. Ricardo recognised the existence of a fixed capital distinct from a 'circulating' capital, furthermore he reduced the distinction between the two types of capital to one of rapidity of circulation[44]: all the question of the modifications to the principle that commodities exchange according to the quantity of labour embodied in them, turns on the complications introduced by the different proportions or durabilities of capital. But it seems that where Ricardo comes to the circumstances affecting the rate of profits in the economy as a whole, he does not see that there is here a factor which can influence the rate of profits in a way completely independent of changes in the proportions in which the product is divided between labourers and capitalists[45]: if capital does not coincide with the wages paid during the year to which the product refers, and can therefore vary independently of them, the rate of profits can also vary independently of the proportions that wages bear to the produce.

[42] 'If the commodity chosen for Mr. Ricardo's measure, whose value confessedly consists of profit and labour, were divided in the proportion of 90 for labour and 10 for profit—it is manifest that with every rise of 1% in labour a commodity produced by labour alone would rise one per cent. If the measure was perfect it ought not to vary at all' (Ricardo, *Works*, Vol. IV, p. 373).

[43] P. 15. See in particular n. 30.

[44] 'According as capital is rapidly perishable, and requires to be frequently reproduced, or is of slow consumption, it is classed under the heads of circulating, or of fixed capital' and in a footnote 'A division not essential, and in which the line of demarcation cannot be accurately drawn (Ricardo, *Works*, Vol. I, p. 31). Further, in a letter to Mc Culloch, he said: 'All the exceptions to the general rule [that commodities exchange according to the quantity of labour embodied] come under one of time' (op. cit., Vol. VIII, p. 193).

[45] *E.g.* 'If the necessaries of the workman could be constantly increased with the same facility, there could be no permanent alteration in the rate of profits or wages, to whatever amount capital might be accumulated' (*Works*, Vol. I, p. 289).

On this point Ricardo inherits some of the contradictions and of the confusions which exist, on the subject, in the *Wealth of Nations*. In a well known passage Smith reaches the conclusion that whereas from the point of view of the individual producer the price of a commodity includes, besides the profits earned by him and the wages and rent paid by him, all that 'is necessary for replacing the stock', from the point of view of the community 'the whole price ... resolves itself either immediately or ultimately into the same three parts of rent, labour and profit'.[46] This may be a legitimate way of looking at the question if we take into consideration the whole period over which the commodity would have been produced by labour and land starting without any assistance of capital, the necessary capital goods being produced before they are used for the production of the commodity. This way of looking at capital is the one adopted in connection with attempts to reduce capital to periods of production. But the proposition that the entire price of a commodity and hence the entire value of the total produce of the community reduces itself into wages, rents and profits, cannot be true when the wages, rents, and profits, referred to, are those earned in the 'year' to which that produce refers. We do not need to enter into an examination of the contradictions in Smith's treatment of capital. All that is relevant here is to remark that Ricardo remained, in part, prisoner of these difficulties of the concept of capital and did not achieve a satisfactory treatment of the quantity to which the surplus must be referred in order to calculate the rate of profits: since he saw the value of the commodities as consisting entirely of wages and profits he thought that the variations of the proportions that wages bear to the produce was the only circumstance which could affect the rate of profits in the economy as a whole.[47]

We have hinted at this problem left unsolved by Ricardo, because it seems that a solution of the difficulties connected with the concept of capital becomes a condition for the solution of the question of 'measuring' value indicated above; it becomes such a condition when we recognise that in consequence of the difference in the proportions between wages and profits in the prices of the various commodities, the commodities do not exchange according to the quantities of labour necessary for their production.

If all commodities exchanged according to the quantity of labour embodied, the introduction of a capital not identical with the yearly wages would not give rise to any special difficulty with regard to the measurement of the magnitudes.

We could use labour embodied as the unit by which to measure the aggregate of the relevant capital goods existing at any moment in the economy and thus determine the rate of profits as:

$$\text{Rate of profits} = \frac{\text{yearly (net) social product} - \text{total yearly wages}}{\text{social capital}} \tag{I}$$

[46] *Wealth of Nations*, Vol. I, p. 52.

[47] K. Marx indicated this shortcoming of Ricardo's analysis as a mistaken identification between rate of profits and 'rate of surplus value' (*Theories of Surplus Value*, p. 329 and *passim*).

instead of the former:

$$\text{Rate of profits} = \frac{\text{yearly (net) social product} - \text{total yearly wages}}{\text{social capital}}$$

As we shall see, the latter are the terms in which Marx calculates the rate of profits when operating on 'values'. But when the proportions in which the 'natural' price is divided into wages and profits are different in different commodities, the problem of a satisfactory 'measurement' of capital emerges as a preliminary to the possibility of expressing in homogeneous terms all the relevant aggregates. Since profits and their variations will now have to be taken into account when measuring the value of commodities, any attempt to express those values without a previous knowledge of the ruling rate of profits will have to go a step back to try to measure the 'capital', to which those profits are functionally related, in a way independent of changes in distribution.

The difficulty for Ricardo was that, when a change in distribution occurred, the magnitude of an unchanged aggregate of commodities would appear to change when measured in terms of his standard.[48] For instance, a commodity which required 'more' capital per labourer to be produced than the standard would fall in its value measured by the standard when nothing but a change lowering the rate of profits occurred. The fact that such a value changes in this way would not be an obstacle if we could determine *how* it changes. It may seem that if we try to determine how the value of the commodity changes we should find ourselves in a vicious circle, because we should need to know at least the variation in the rate of profits, which is just what we want to determine through our measurements. But this is by itself a spurious vicious circle; the difficulty lies somewhere else: if the magnitudes of Eq. (I) above could all be expressed as known functions of an unknown rate of profits, the problem would have been solved; the only difference would be that, keeping the equations in that form, we should have the unknown rate of profits not only on the LHS but also on the RHS. As long as the rate of profits remains the only unknown in it, the equation is soluble as well as if all the magnitudes appearing on the RHS had been expressed independently of the rate of profits. But, and here we come to what appears to be the real difficulty, in order to determine the value of a given physical aggregate of commodities as a known function of the rate of profits, we need, besides the quantity of labour embodied in the aggregate, a quantity or set of quantities which we can take as a datum in the equation and which bears some known relationship to the value (measured in the same standard as the value of the aggregate) of the capital which has assisted the labourers in the production of the aggregate of commodities. In other words, it appears that the problem of the determination of profits on Ricardo's lines could be solved if it were possible to 'measure' capital in terms of a quantity or set of quantities given independently of the way in which the produce is divided between

[48] See above, pp. 18–9.

profits and wages, and which can be related in a known way to the value (in terms of some standard) of the capital they express.

Instruments for attempting such a measurement of capital have been developed in later economic analysis in the different context of the marginal productivity theories of distribution. In the second section of this dissertation we shall examine them in that context and attempt to evaluate how satisfactory they are in solving the similar problem of capital measurement existing in that type of theories of distribution. Here we shall use the period of production approach to the measurement of capital, within a theory of distribution on Ricardo's lines. In order to illustrate and clarify the conclusion we have reached about the problem lying behind the measurement of value in Ricardo, we shall indicate how the rate of profits could be determined if the average period of production, as elaborated by Böhm-Bawerk, were a satisfactory measure of capital. This will pave the way for a discussion in the successive chapters of the present section of the lines on which a solution of the problem can be attempted once the assumptions necessary for the use of the average period of production are dropped.

Section I, Chapter III: Ricardo's Problem Could Be Solved by Using the Average Period of Production

Were it not for the difficulties we shall presently indicate, the average period of production could be a magnitude satisfying the requirements mentioned at the end of Chapter II.

The aim of this chapter is to show how the average period of production could be employed in a Ricardian theory of distribution and to clarify some more general issues arising from the use of the period of production approach within a surplus theory of distribution.

The average period of production of a commodity used here is the one defined by Böhm-Bawerk: it is the arithmetical weighted average of the periods of time which must elapse between the moments in which the several quantities of labour necessary for the production of the commodity have been applied[49] and the moment in which the commodity is sold; the weight given to each of the periods of production entering the average, is the quantity of homogeneous labour[50] to which it refers.[51]

---

[49] The relevant moment from which the periods of time begin is not, strictly, the one at which the quantity of labour has been applied; it is the one at which the wages for that quantity of labour have been paid. Here we have assumed that those two moments coincide.

[50] On what is meant by homogeneous labour see above, n. 39.

[51] E. Böhm-Bawerk, *Positive Theory of Capital*, London, 1891, pp. 88–9. Meaning and implications of the average period of production will shortly be seen in some more detail.

For example, if a commodity or aggregate of commodities A, sold to final consumers at a moment 0, requires for its production a number of labour years L_a so distributed over time that a quantity l_{1a} has to be applied one year before moment 0, l_{2a} two years before, and so on,[52] its average period of production T_a will be:

$$T = \frac{l_{1a} + 2l_{2a} + 3l_{3a} + \ldots}{L_a} \tag{II}$$

In order to make the average period of production we have here defined, a measure of capital satisfactory for our purposes, we need two assumptions.

Firstly we must assume that profits are distributed among the capitalists according to the rules of the simple rate of interest; in other words, we must assume that profits cannot give rise to further profits. Only what is spent on wages receives profits over the time elapsing between the moment in which the payment of wages has occurred, and the moment in which the commodities produced with that labour are sold. It seems that we can describe the implications of this assumption by envisaging an economy where the profits included in the value at which the capital goods are sold, do not produce further profits and the aggregate of profits is so distributed among the owners of capital goods that they receive, in equilibrium, the same rate of profits on the wage costs of their capital goods.[53]

[52] It has often been pointed out why the fact that some fractions of the labour embodied in a commodity may have to be considered as having periods of investment tending to infinity, does not appear to constitute an insurmountable obstacle for the period of production conception of capital. Briefly, the reason is that the quantities of labour having a period of investment tending to infinity will be infinitely small quantities. So, with regard to the concept of average period, the periods of production tending to infinity weighted by quantities tending to zero, will give finite quantities and the average period will be a finite quantity. So, with regard to the more general use of the period of production approach here, the amounts of profits over periods of time tending to infinity being calculated upon infinitely small wage outlays, will have finite values.

[53] As to why it is necessary to use the simple rate, in order to be able to apply here the average period of production, see below, n. 56. As what has been said in the text may have already made apparent, the use of the simple rate involves us in contradictions with the principle that the rates of profits are the same in all branches of the economy, in conditions of equilibrium and free competition. To give an example: let us assume that two commodities A and B require the same quantity of labour to be produced and that all the labour has to be paid for at the same moment; let us also assume that whereas A is ready for sale one year after the moment in which the labour required has to be paid, B will take two years before it can be sold; if the price of the labour required is 100 and the ruling rate of profits 20%, the price of A will be 120, and that of B 140, but then the capitalists producing B would find it convenient to shift their capital to the production of A: by investing there 100 they would obtain after a year 120, which, reinvested entirely by buying more labour, would give after the second year a total profit of 44 instead of the 40 earned in producing B; equilibrium could be reached only when the price of B is to that of A as 144 is to 140. Or, more generally and looking at the same thing from another angle, if the relative prices were those corresponding to simple rate calculations, to the extent that the producers employ capital goods, they would receive a rate of profits smaller than the simple rate, since the profits received would bear that rate to the *wage costs* of the capital goods and not to the whole price for which they were bought, a price which always includes a profits element.

Secondly, we must assume that all capital is 'circulating' capital, meaning by this that each capital good in it will be entirely consumed in the production of commodities completed at a definite point in time, or over a period of time sufficiently short to allow us to consider it as a point of time.[54]

When those assumptions are made, the equilibrium value of any commodity or aggregate of commodities A, can be easily expressed as a function of the quantity of homogeneous labour necessary for its production, of the average period of production, and of the rate of profits. That can be done by using as a standard of value the wage unit, that is, using Smith's terminology: 'labour commanded'.[55] The total wage costs of A measured in yearly wage units will obviously be given by the number of labour years necessary to produce the commodity, that is L_a, and the amount of profits, in terms of the same unit, will be given by the ruling rate of profits over those wage costs for the appropriate set of periods of production. That same set of periods of production which, when using the simple rate of profits, can be replaced by the average period T_a. If V_a is the equilibrium value of A, and p the ruling rate of profits, we shall have:[56]

$$V_a = L_a(1 + pT_a) \tag{III}$$

Some remarks about the concept of capital involved in the relationship may be useful. We have seen that the term (pL_aT_a) expresses the value in wage units of the

[54] 'Circulating capital' as defined here coincides with what G. Åkerman calls variable capital' (see K. Wicksell, *Lectures on Political Economy*, London 1934, Vol. I, p. 258). We have chosen the expression 'circulating capital' to avoid confusion with Marx's terminology occurring below. The reason for which this assumption is necessary to our use of the average period of production, is analogous to that for which we need the assumption of the simple rate of interest (below, n. 56). Briefly, even when using simple rate, the discount on 1 for 2 years will not be the same as the discount on 2 for 1 year; it follows that the time elements in the relationship between values of inputs and values of outputs cannot be summarised in an average period of production independent of the interest rate (see also below, pp. 43–4).

[55] The value of any commodity A could of course be expressed while using as a standard of value any other commodity; but then we should know and introduce in the expression also the quantity of labour and the average period of production of the standard.

[56] If l_{1a}, l_{2a}, ... have the meaning defined above (pp. 22–3), we have:

$$V_a = l_{1a}(1 + p) + l_{2a}(1 + 2p) + l_{3a}(1 + 3p) + \ldots$$

$$= (l_{1a} + l_{2a} + l_{3a} + \ldots) + p(l_{1a} + 2l_{2a} + 3l_{3a} + \ldots) =$$

$$= L_a + pL_a \frac{l_{1a} + 2l_{2a} + 3l_{3a} + \ldots}{L_a} = L_a + pL_aT_a$$

It will be noticed how it is only the use of the simple rate which allows us to substitute in the equation (pL_aT_a) for $p(l_{1a} + 2l_{2a} + 3l_{3a} + \ldots)$. It is only when we use the simple rate that the profits on 1 for 2 years are the same as the profits on 2 for 1 year, under which condition only can the time periods appearing in the equation be expressed with T_a independent of the rate of interest.

profits contained in the value of *A*. That can be accounted for in two ways corresponding to two ways of looking at capital which lead to the same results.

According to the way of looking at capital adopted in constructing the equation, we consider the commodity or aggregate of commodities *A*, as if it had been produced by labour which began production without the assistance of any capital goods. We follow back in time the processes of production from which the capital goods employed in the last stages of the production of *A* arise, and, in this way, we reduce the cost-elements entering production, to quantities of labour and periods of production. We can look at the procedure as a device by which, in order to overcome the physical heterogeneity of the goods constituting capital, we project in time the several processes of production, processes which are carried on simultaneously in the equilibrium situation examined, and supply each other with their products. We have spoken of a device, because the relevant periods of production are not those which have actually elapsed in the course of the production of the commodities considered; the relevant periods are those which would have elapsed if the commodity had been produced at all the stages according to the techniques or, more generally, according to the forms of technical organisation of the processes of production which are in use in the equilibrium situation examined, and which are the ones relevant for the determination of the relative values. The periods of production needed for the theory will be identical with the ones which have actually elapsed in the production of the commodity only to the extent in which the equilibrium situation examined can be supposed to have existed unchanged in the past.[57]

If we take the view of the production process we have just described, the only 'capital' employed is the wages paying the quantity of labour L_a, whose value in the unit chosen here is L_a. The profits will then have to be calculated over the periods for which that capital has remained invested or, when using the simple rate, over the average period: they will then be (pL_aT_a).

But if all the stages of the production of *A* are carried out simultaneously and side by side, the process of producing *A* can be looked at in a second way. According to it, the application of a quantity of labour L_a, over however short a time, would *simultaneously* give rise to a *net* output of *A* embodying the same quantity of labour L_a. The wages paid for that quantity of labour would then appear to be paid out of the value of current production and not out of capital; but, at the same time, the simultaneity between the application of a continuous stream of labour and the continuous stream of net output embodying the corresponding quantity of labour, requires the existence at any moment of a definite aggregate of intermediate goods. We could say that such aggregate of intermediate goods

[57] What has been said here about periods of production is analogous with what was implied when speaking of that labour necessary to produce commodities which affects their relative values. The quantities of labour relevant for the purpose are not the ones which may have actually been employed in their production but are those which would be necessary in the conditions of the situation examined.

provides the suitable store of past labour from which the actual labour embodied in the outputs, which cannot be supplied by the current labour simultaneously applied, is drawn; at the same time, the place of such past labour is taken, in the store, by the labour currently employed: the store is being continuously depleted and simultaneously replenished so that, as long as the technical organisation of production does not change, it remains the same in the number and nature of its physical constituents. Now, if the number of labourers continuously engaged in the production of *A*, at all the stages of it,[58] is *n*, the number of labour years which must be embodied in that aggregate of intermediate goods, will be given by (nT_a): if it takes on the average 10 years before the labour applied now by a labourer gives rise to a finished commodity, in order to have the simultaneity of labour inputs and net outputs every labourer will have to be assisted on the average by a stock of intermediate goods embodying, in total, 10 labour years applied at the appropriate dates in the past; such past labour will continuously supply the labour necessary to bridge the 10 years average gap between the application of the labour of the workmen and the emergence of the final output.

An example will further clarify the point: we want to obtain from a forest a continuous stream of output of wood, such that the yearly rate of output will embody *L* labour years employed in the planting of the trees (we assume that no further labour is required after the tree is planted); we shall then have to keep a number *L* of labourers continually employed in planting trees; if to plant a tree requires a fraction $(1/x)$ of a labour year, and if the trees are cut after 20 years, we shall need a forest in which the number of trees, uniformly distributed over all the ages from 0 to 20, is $(x20L)$, and the quantity of labour embodied in the whole forest is $\frac{1}{x}(x20L)$, that is $(20L)$. This general relationship between periods over which labour has to remain invested (whether they are absolute periods or it is the average period used here) and quantities of labour embodied in the stock of capital goods necessary to make labour inputs and net outputs simultaneous, is self evident, when the two ways of looking at capital are seen clearly.[59] We could say that quantity of labour embodied in the stock of capital goods assisting a given number of labourers and average period of production are but two ways of visualising and describing one and the same magnitude measuring capital.

Returning to the aggregate of commodities *A*, if they have emerged from production as a uniform stream over a year, the number *n* of labourers continuously engaged in all stages of its production must be equal to (L_a); the quantity of labour embodied in the stock of capital goods which must have assisted those labourers in

[58] So that all but those engaged in the 'last stages' of the production of *A* are in fact engaged in producing the capital goods simultaneously consumed in the successive stages.

[59] See, for instance, a use of this relationship in Wicksell, *Lectures*, Vol. I, p. 204. The conception of capital as a stock of goods such as to make inputs and outputs simultaneous is stressed by J. B. Clark (e.g., *Quarterly Journal of Economics*, Vol. IX, pp. 267–8), but he sees it as exclusive of the period of production conception.

the production of A, will then be (L_aT_a); the value in yearly wage units of that capital will also, because of the assumption of simple rate of interest, be (L_aT_a)[60]; since A has continuously emerged from production over a year, the profits contained in its value will be the profits for one year over a capital worth (L_aT_a) in yearly wage units; their value will then be (pL_aT_a) as Eq. (III) above had shown.[61]

Concluding this digression, T_a, whether interpreted as average period of production or as quantity of labour embodied in the stock of capital goods assisting, on the average, one worker, would offer the basis for a magnitude measuring the capital employed in the production of A, a magnitude which is both independent of changes in distribution and related in a known way to the value in wage units of that capital. That being so, it is now easy to show how the rate of profits can be determined, within Ricardo's scheme, by using the average period of production.

If L is the number of labour years embodied in the yearly net social produce, that is, also, the number of labourers constituting the homogeneous labour force employed in the economy; if L_1 is the number of labour years embodied in the share of the produce given to the labourers as wages; if T is the average period of production of the yearly social produce, T_1 is the average period of the yearly aggregate of wage goods, and p is the unknown rate of profits, the value in yearly wage units of the net social product[62] will be given by: $L(1 + pT)$. The value of the aggregate of wages paid during the year will be: $L_1\,(1 + pT_1)$. The value measured in the same unit, of the aggregate capital used in production will be: LT. The unknown rate of profits which is the ratio between the value of the yearly surplus and the value of the capital, can then be determined by solving the following equation where all quantities but the rate of profits are data:

[60] This apparent contradiction for which, in contrast with all other commodities, the labour commanded by capital goods is equal to the labour embodied in them, is a contradiction inherent to the use of the simple rate of interest in the calculations (see above, p. 23, in particular n. 53).

[61] The result evidently does not depend on the assumption made in the text according to which A emerged from production over a year. If A had emerged as a uniform stream over any fraction $1/n$ of a year, the number of labourers continuously engaged in the production of A would have been (nL_a) since L_a, the quantity of labour embodied in A, is expressed in labour years; the labour years embodied in the stock of capital goods assisting them would have been (nL_aT_a); the value in yearly wage units of the profits on that capital for a fraction $1/n$ of a year would have been: $p\frac{1}{n}nL_aT_a = pL_aT_a$.

[62] The value indicated above must refer to the net social produce, that is, to the value of the gross produce minus the value of the capital goods consumed during the year and simultaneously replaced in the same physical form. We have seen above (p. 25) how, when we take the 'inputs simultaneous to outputs' view of capital, the value of the produce of a given quantity of labour is calculated on the assumption that the aggregate of physical capital goods existing at any moment is being kept intact; a part of the labour currently employed replaces the capital goods which are being consumed in the production of the stream of final output. If we take instead the period of production view of capital, that value will of course be that of the net product of the quantity of labour L, since there, by hypothesis, no question of capital replacement arises: the production started without the assistance of any capital goods.

$$p = \frac{L(1+pT) - L_1(1+pT_1)}{LT} \qquad \text{(IV)}$$

More simply, since the value in yearly wage units of the aggregate of wages paid to the labourers during the year, must obviously be equal to the number of labour years bought with it which is L, we shall have: $L = L_1(1 + pT_1)$. From which we obtain[63]:

$$p = \frac{L - L_1}{L_1 T_1} \qquad \text{(V)}$$

The simplification of Eq. (IV) into Eq. (V) is of some interest because it shows that the rate of profits in the economy is independent of the magnitude of the capital employed in the sector of the economy which is not engaged in the direct or indirect production of the goods bought by the labourers. We could express this by saying that the rate of profits depends only on magnitudes relating to the sector producing goods for the labourers: the proportion of the total homogeneous labour force which is employed in the production of wage goods (which is always equal to the proportion of the value of wages to the value of the net produce in that sector), and the capital per worker employed in the sector.[64] The economic explanation of this, at first sight, a somewhat surprising result, is, it seems, in that the prices of goods other than those produced in that sector can have no influence on the rate of profits of the sector, since they affect neither the revenue nor the wage or capital costs of the firms of the sector.[65] It follows that if in equilibrium there is to be one rate of profits in all branches of the economy, the prices of the non-wage goods will have to change relatively to those of the wage goods, so as to offer to their producers the rate of profits determined by the conditions existing

---

[63] Equation (V) can be obtained from Eq. (IV). In fact Eq. (IV) can be written:

$$pLT = L + pLT - L_1 - pL_1T_1$$

Eliminating the term (pLT) on the RHS and LHS and solving the equation for p, we obtain:

$$p = \frac{L - L_1}{L_1 T_1}.$$

[64] If we divide by L numerator and denominator of the term on the RHS of Eq. (V), the equation becomes:

$$p = \frac{1 - \frac{L_1}{L}}{\frac{L_1}{L} T_1}.$$

[65] The point made here about the independence of the rate of profits from the conditions existing outside the wage goods sector appears to be the same as the one which emerges from Bortkiewicz's solution of the 'transformation problem' and which we shall see below. We can note that the wage goods sector as understood here includes all the capital goods industries which, at one or more removes, supply the wage goods industries; therefore it includes both what Bortkiewicz calls the wage goods sector and a part of what he calls the capital goods sector. (See below, pp. 36–7).

in the wage goods sector. This is analogous to what has been said above[66] on the justification of the principle, used by Ricardo in the *Essay on Profits*, that the rate of profits in agriculture regulates the rate of profits in the whole economy: only here, evidently, the simplification of the procedure does not depend on any limiting assumption about the nature of the goods constituting capital.[67]

Another remark which can be made about Eqs. (IV) and (V) is that the quantities used there to determine the rate of profits, L and L_1, are given as quantities of labour embodied in aggregates of commodities, and T and T_1 can be taken either as time periods or as quantities of labour embodied in the stock of capital goods assisting, on the average, respectively, one worker in the economy as a whole and one worker in the wage goods sector (1).[68] This emergence of quantities of labour embodied as the determining magnitudes, might appear somewhat surprising since we have obtained those equations while using as a unit for the measurements labour commanded. But it appears that, in the problem, the distinction between labour embodied and labour commanded as measures of aggregates of commodities, can be reduced to a difference in the way of grouping and visualising the same quantities: for instance, we could read the RHS of Eq. (V) either as the ratio between the quantity of labour embodied in the social surplus and the quantity of labour embodied in the stock of capital goods used in the wage goods sector, or as the ratio between the quantity of labour commanded by the surplus and the quantity of labour commanded by the stock of capital goods, both magnitudes referring to the wage goods sector. The important feature is that, of the determining quantities, L and L_1 are here *given* to us as quantities of labour embodied, and T_1 either as an average of time periods or as a quantity of labour embodied.

If the proportionality between relative values and quantities of labour embodied could be assumed, the simplest way of conceiving and describing the determination of the rate of profits on the lines of Ricardo's approach, would have been by way of a ratio between the quantity of labour embodied in the social surplus and

---

[66] Pp. 15–6. See Mr. Sraffa and Mr. Dobb's introduction to Vol. I, Ricardo, *Works*, pp. xxxi–ii.

[67] Another difference between Eq. (V) and Ricardo's simplified procedure in the *Essay on Profits* is that in the equation, the determining magnitudes cannot be immediately measured in physical units of produce. But also in Eq. (V) L and L_1 could be substituted with physical magnitudes if we assumed, not unrealistically, that the workers employed outside the wage goods sector consume the same commodities in the same proportions as the workers employed in the sector. In that case produce and wages in the wage goods sector can be considered as physically homogeneous and can, accordingly, be measured with the same physical compound unit. The rate of profits could then, again, be visualised as a ratio between physical quantities, although the ratio would now have a more complicated form because of the introduction of T_1. What has been said about the possibility of simplifying the procedure of the determination of the rate of profits by limiting the analysis to the wage goods sector of the economy, is evidently independent of the use of the average period of production: we shall use it in the following chapter when operating with a set of absolute periods of production. (See below, pp. 39ff.).

[68] But see n. 67 above for the possibility of using physical quantities.

the quantity of labour embodied in the social capital.[69] In that case a commodity by which to measure value in a way independent of changes in distribution, could have been found: the commodity of 'invariable value' would have been one always produced by the same quantity of labour.

But when it is recognized that we cannot assume proportionality between labour embodied and relative values, Ricardo's way of approaching the problem, through the search for an 'invariable standard of value', was likely to lead him into a blind alley, since such a standard had to satisfy two contradictory requirements. On the one hand his use of a commodity as the standard involves proportionality of the measurements with the ratios in which commodities exchange; on the other hand, Ricardo expected those measurements to be independent of changes in distribution so as to constitute immediately the data for the determination of the rate of profits. Put in that way the problem was insoluble.

Concluding, we have tried to show in Chapter II how the difficulties Ricardo met in the problem of value in connection with his theory of profits, can be reduced to the problem of measuring capital in terms of a quantity or set of quantities which, while independent of changes in the distribution of the social produce, would at the same time bear some definable relationship to the value of that capital. This has been exemplified in the present chapter by showing that the determination of the rate of profits on Ricardo's lines, could take place if the average period of production were a satisfactory measure of capital. Why the average period of production does not appear to be satisfactory for the purpose has been touched on in connection with the two assumptions we had to make in order to be able to use that measurement: simple rate of profits and absence of fixed capital. In the following chapters of this section we shall examine and discuss the solution Bortkiewicz gave to the same problem in the form it took in Marx, that is the transformation of 'values' into 'prices of production'. We shall see in that connection how it appears that the deficiencies affecting the use of the average period of production can be overcome by expressing capital as set of quantities.

Section I, Chapter IV: The Difficulties Connected with the Use of the Compound Rate of Profits; An Assumption Implicit to Bortkievicz's Solution of Marx's 'Transformation Problem'

Marx took over from Ricardo the basic elements for his theory of distribution. From the point of view which is of concern in this dissertation, the important new element Marx introduced into Ricardo's theory of distribution was a conception

[69] Even under that assumption the rate of profits could have been determined while measuring the aggregate in terms of labour commanded. For instance, if we assumed that the production of all commodities starts at the beginning of the year with labour unassisted by capital goods, and reaches completion at the end of the year, the determining equation, using labour commanded as the standard, is $p = \frac{L(1+p)-L_1(1+p)}{L_1(1+p)}$; the equation can be immediately simplified into $p = \frac{L-L_1}{L_1}$.

of capital by which capital was no longer identified with the wages paid during the period to which the product is related.[70] Marx conceived capital as including, besides wages, a stock of capital goods, both aggregates being measured in terms of the labour embodied in them. Such a measurement of capital can be easily translated into that measurement in terms of the labour embodied in the stock of capital which coincides with Böhm-Bawerk's average period of production.[71] But if Marx put forward that conception of capital, he, in the manuscripts published after his death as Book III of *Capital*, did not elaborate a satisfactory set of relationships allowing us to determine the rate of profits with the quantities of labour embodied in the relevant aggregates, in the cases in which the commodities cannot be assumed to exchange according to the quantities of labour embodied. Attempts to undertake that task came later, after the publication of Books II and III of *Capital*, and gave rise to the discussion of what became known as the 'transformation problem', or problem of transforming, in Marx's terminology, 'values' into 'prices of production'. In more familiar terms the problem is that of finding a satisfactory set of relationships by which it is possible to determine the relative values of commodities, starting from quantities measured in labour embodied. As what has been said in the previous chapters may have already made clear, this problem is really one with that of the determination of the rate of profits: the relative values of commodities cannot be determined if we do not know the rate of profits; on the other hand, the rate of profits can be determined only simultaneously with the values, in some standard, of the relevant aggregates of commodities, determination which in turn implies the determination of the system of the 'prices' of commodities in terms of that standard.

The most important contribution to the discussion of the transformation problem came from L. von Bortkiewicz who advanced a solution.[72] We have seen in Chapter III how the rate of profits could be determined by means of the average period of production, if we could assume, besides the absence of fixed capital, a distribution of profits over capitals following the rules of the simple rate of interest. Bortkiewicz, on the contrary, appears to use Marx's data for a determination of the rate of profits according to the compound rate of profits.[73] This is done by implicitly introducing a special assumption with which it is possible to obtain from Marx's data, not only the relevant average periods of production, but also the relevant sets of absolute periods over which the labour embodied in the

---

[70] Cf. above, pp. 19ff.

[71] Above, pp. 25ff.

[72] References will be to the article published in July 1907 in *Jarbücher für Nationalökonomie*, translated by Sweezy under the title 'On the Correction of Marx's Fundamental Theoretical Construction in the Third Volume of *Capital*' and published as appendix to Sweezy's edition of Böhm-Bawerk's *Karl Marx and The Close of his System* (New York, 1949).

[73] In Bortkiewicz's equations the uniform rate of profits is calculated on the prices of production of the capital goods. Since the prices of production of the capital goods include the profits of their producers, such profits become a part of 'capital', that is, give rise to further profits.

commodities has remained invested. The aim of this chapter is to see the problems raised by the introduction of the compound rate into the type of theory of distribution examined here, and assess in that context the meaning of Bortkiewicz's solution. In Chapter V of this section we shall proceed to examine and discuss another assumption on which Bortkiewicz's solution rests: the absence of fixed capital.

It will be useful to see first a few points concerning Marx's conceptions and terminology with respect to capital. For Marx the capital employed in the production of commodities consists of two parts: 'variable' capital and 'constant' capital. The distinction is related to the classical economists' conception of a yearly process of production. For our purpose Marx's view of the overall organisation of the process of production can be described by means of the following simple scheme. The process of production for all commodities starts at the beginning of the year with a capital consisting: (a) of the goods which will be given to the labour force as wages, during the year, and this, measured in terms of the labour embodied in it, is the 'variable' capital; (b) of a stock of capital goods like machinery, raw materials, etc., and this, again expressed in labour embodied, is the 'constant' capital. At the end of the year the process of production reaches completion for all commodities and the entire gross produce of the year becomes available; that gross produce consists of three parts, all measured in labour embodied: one part, which we shall call c, consists of capital goods and goes to replace that part of the constant capital existing at the beginning of the year (here expressed by C), which has been consumed during the year; a second part, v, constitutes the wages of the labourers in the following year; that is, it replaces the variable capital used during the year; the remaining part, s, constitutes the income of the capitalists for the following year, and it is the source either of their consumption or of further accumulations; the ratio $r = \frac{s}{v}$ is what Marx calls 'rate of surplus value'. The ratio $\frac{C}{C+v}$ is called by Marx 'organic composition' of capital. Marx then, when calculating on 'values', determines the rate of profits as $p = \frac{s}{C+v}$.

Those definitions of capital are not immediately identical with the one we have seen to coincide with the average period of production measurement,[74] but the difference is due only to different suppositions about the organisation of the processes of production. There we established an equality between average period of production and quantity of labour embodied in the stock of capital goods assisting, on the average, one worker when the several successive processes connected with the production of a commodity are so co-ordinated as to give simultaneity between the stream of labour applied and a stream of the commodity containing that same quantity of labour; in that case Marx's variable capital disappears and wages are paid out of simultaneous production; its place in the capital is taken by an aggregate of goods in process composed of commodities in the last year of their period of production. If, for example, we assumed that Marx's scheme of the organization of production is so modified that the products come out as a continuous, uniform

[74] Above, pp. 25ff.

stream over a year instead of appearing as a batch at the end of the year, wages would no longer be a constituent of capital, and the stock of capital goods would embody a quantity of labour $(C + \frac{v+s}{2})$[75]; the average period of production of the net social produce would be $(\frac{C+\frac{v+s}{2}}{v+s})$.[76] But the average period of production of the net social produce can of course be obtained also for Marx's scheme: it will be given by: $T = \frac{C}{v+s} + 1$.[77] It is now evident that if we have in addition to the data considered up to now, the labour embodied in the stock of capital goods assisting the workers in the production of wages, we can easily pass from Marx's quantities to the ones appearing in Eq. (V)[78] and determine the rate of profits accordingly.[79] But that determination rests on the assumption of simple rate of profits. When the compound rate of interest is introduced the average period of production, or quantity of labour embodied in the capital stock, is no longer sufficient for measuring capital in the equation determining the rate of profits.

At this stage it may be useful to introduce some definitions and clarify some points connected with the modifications which the period of production measurement of capital seen in Chapter III must undergo when the compound rate of profits is used in the calculation. The essential modification is that, as we shall see, we must pass from the average period of production to the set of absolute periods of production.

We have seen above[80] that for any commodity or aggregate of commodities A, produced with a quantity of labour L_a, it is possible to envisage the process of its production as if A had been produced by labour starting production without any assistance of capital goods and applied at various dates up to the moment in which

[75] Such a change in the organization of production involves the addition to the previous constant capital assisting one worker, of a quantity of labour varying from 0 to 1 labour years and uniformly distributed, so that, for instance 1/10 of the labourers would be assisted by a capital containing an additional 1/10 of a labour year, another tenth by a capital containing an addition of 2/10 of a labour year, etc. With continuity in such distribution each labourer will be assisted by a capital increased, on the average, by ½ of a labour year. Since $(v+s)$ is the quantity of labour applied over one year, the aggregate of capital existing at any moment in the economy will embody $\frac{v+s}{2}$ labour units more than the previous constant capital used to embody (at the beginning of the year).

[76] Since $(v+s)$ is the quantity of labour applied by the total labour force over one year, and $(C + \frac{v+s}{2})$ is the labour embodied in the capital, the ratio between the latter and the former will be the number of labour years necessary to the total labour force to produce a similar capital stock: it will also therefore be the number of labour years embodied in the capital assisting, on the average, one worker; that is the average period of production in years (see above, pp. 25–6).

[77] If C were all the capital necessary to have simultaneity between the stream of labour inputs and that of outputs the average period would be $\frac{C}{v+s}$ (see the preceeding footnote); but in fact one more year is required before the labour passing through the capital stock can take the form of commodities ready for sale.

[78] Above, p. {52}.

[79] We should have: $L = v + s$; $L_1 = v$; T_1 would be determined from the constant capital employed in producing wages analogously to what we have seen above for T.

[80] Pp. 22–3.

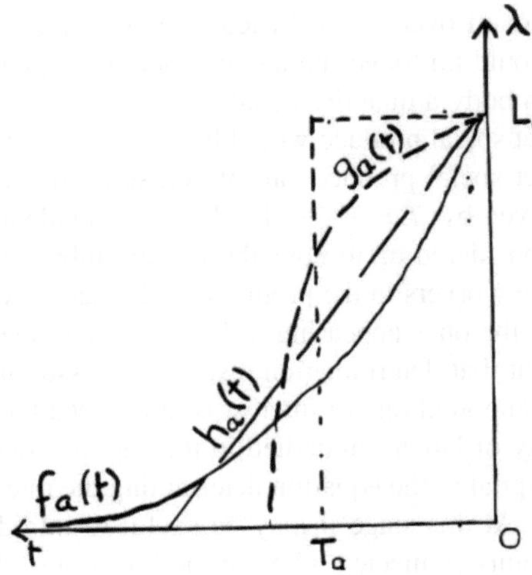

Fig. 1 Different investment functions having the same average period of production

A is sold.[81] We therefore referred, for the calculation of the average period of production, to quantities of labour l_{1a}, l_{2a}, l_{3a} ... applied, respectively, 1, 2, 3, ... years before the moment 0 at which *A* is sold. If we drop the assumption, convenient in Chapter III above, that labour is applied at moments in time at a distance of one year from each other, and we envisage instead labour as applied continuously over time, the quantities taking the place of l_{1a}, l_{2a}, l_{3a} etc. can be summarised in a function expressing the total quantity of labour λ_{-t} which had already been applied for the production of *A* at any moment $(-t)$, *t* years before moment 0. In such a function, which we shall call the investment function, *t* may have any values between 0 and $-\infty$, and λ will range from 0 to the value L_a at moment 0.

This concept of an investment function will be useful here mainly as a short way of referring to a set of quantities and expressing some relevant characteristics of that set. In fact, the function can be interpreted as giving us a complex of 'absolute periods of production': over any sufficiently small segment of time Δt_1, left or right of the point of time $(-t_1)$, a small quantity of labour $\Delta\lambda_{-t}$ is applied which will remain invested, in the form of intermediate products, for a period of time t_1. The relationship between the average period of production and the investment function can be seen from Fig. 1, where the average period of production T_a, corresponding to the investment function f_a (*t*), is the side of a rectangle whose other side is L_a (the quantity of labour embodied in *A*), and whose area is equal to the one enclosed below the f_a (*t*).[82] Evidently, the average period of production does not define uniquely the investment function: there can be an infinite number of investment functions having the same average period of production. In Fig. 1,

---

[81] This can be done on the condition that all capital is circulating capital. (See above, p. 24; in Chapter V below we shall see the problem introduced by fixed capital.)

[82] In algebraic terms: $T_a = \frac{\int_{-\infty}^{0} f_a(t)dt}{L_a}$.

for example, we have drawn with dotted lines the investment functions $g_a(t)$, $h_a(t)$, which have the same average period of production T_a as the $f_a(t)$; we can put these investment functions in an approximate order according to their increasing convexity to the t axis: $g_a(t)$, $h_a(t)$, $f_a(t)$.[83] In general, we have at one extreme the case in which all the labour embodied in the commodity has been applied at one and the same moment, so that we have only one period of production; towards the opposite extreme, on the contrary, we have cases where a large proportion of the labour has remained invested for relatively short periods of time, and, accordingly, a small proportion has remained invested for very long periods.

Now, when we used in our calculations the simple rate of interest, the shapes of the investment functions were irrelevant once we knew the average periods of production: the value in wage units of any commodity A, was always determinable as $V_a = L_a(1 + pT_a)$.[84] But when the compound rate of profits is introduced the value in the same unit can no longer be expressed as a function simply of L_a, p, and any single period of time which can satisfy that requirement of independence from changes in distribution which we saw (in Chapter II[85]) to be essential for a valid measurement of capital within a theory of distribution on Ricardian lines. It would of course be possible to force the relationship between V_a, L_a, p, into an analogous form $V_a = La(1 + p)^{T'_a}$; but then T'_a could no longer be one of the data for the determination of the rate of profits since, given the shape of the investment function, it would have to vary with the rate of profits (if L_a and V_a have to be the correct ones). T'_a should increase or diminish as p increases or diminishes.

Concluding, when the compound rate of profits is used in the calculation of the value of the commodities, the value in wage units of any commodity will vary not only with the quantity of labour embodied, the rate of profits and the average period of production; it will vary also with the shape of the investment function: given the rate of profits, the value will be the higher the more convex the investment function is. There seems to be no way of calculating the value of a commodity without taking into consideration the whole investment function.

If we apply this conclusion to the determination of the rate of profits it is evident that, once the compound rate of profits is introduced, p can no longer be determined by taking as data only the quantity of labour embodied in the yearly net social produce, the quantity of labour embodied in the yearly aggregate consumption of the workers, and the quantity of labour embodied in the aggregate of capital goods employed for the production of wage goods.[86] In fact, if the value V_a of any aggregate of commodities A, given L_a, T_a, and p, varies with the shape of the investment function, it follows that when V_a, L_a and T_a are given, it must be p that varies with the shape of the investment function. And the latter is the case

[83] Some quantity could probably be elaborated in order to measure the 'degree of convexity' of the investment function, if more precision should be needed for theoretical uses of this function.

[84] See above, n. 56.

[85] Above, pp. 21–2.

[86] We have used only those data in Eq. (V) of Chapter III (above, p. 28).

with the yearly aggregate of wage goods in the situation envisaged for the determination of the rate of profits: L_1 is a datum, so is T_1 (that is the quantity of labour embodied in the capital goods assisting on the average one worker of the wage goods sector) and so, finally, is L, the value in wage units of the yearly aggregate of wage goods which is always equal to the quantity of labour applied during the year; it follows that, as the shape of the investment function compatible with T_1 differs, p will have to be different. In approximate terms we could say that, given L_1, and L and T_1, p is the lower the more convex the investment function is. It is therefore clear that the rate of profits cannot be determined without taking into consideration also such 'convexity', that is the whole set of periods of production or investment function.

And this is what Bortkiewicz does once his solution is described in terms of the period of production view of capital. Briefly, his solution is correct only on the assumption that the key proportion between Marx's *aggregate* quantities of labour embodied, C and $(v + s)$,[87] referring to the capital goods section of the wage goods sector, holds not only between the aggregates for the section as a whole, but holds also between the C and the $(v + s)$ of the individual firms or industries constituting the section. We can now see this point in some more detail.

Marx, when, in Book II of *Capital,* he studied in detail the process of 'reproduction' of the social capital, divided the whole economy into two sectors: sector I producing capital goods and sector II producing consumption goods. His aim was there to examine the relationships which must exist between the outputs of these two key sectors if they were not either to fall short or exceed the markets they provide for each other at different levels of accumulation.[88] Bortkievicz, in his solution of the 'transformation' problem takes over from Marx that division of the economy and subdivides further sector II producing consumption goods into a sector II producing workers' consumption goods, and a sector III producing capitalists' consumption goods.[89] For the purpose of our discussion of Bortkiewicz's solution, we can here drop sector III and limit ourselves to Bortkiewicz's sector II and to that section of sector I which produces capital goods destined, at one or more removes, to the production of wage goods; the two sectors together constitute what we have defined as the wage goods sector in Chapter III above. We can limit the analysis to those two sectors since they are the only ones relevant for the

[87] Marx understands the organic composition as the ratio between C and v (see, for example, the second paragraph of Chapter XXV, Book I, of *Capital*). The proportion relevant for us here is instead that between C and $(v+s)$. It differs from Marx's organic composition because it can vary independently of the organic composition when r, that is, the rate of surplus value s/v, varies (see below the ratios Q_1 and Q_2, p. 39).

[88] See Chapters XX and XXI of Book II of *Capital.*

[89] See Bortkiewicz, op. cit., p. 200. We can here note that when dealing with the transformation of 'values' into 'prices of production' in Chapter IX of Book III of *Capital*, Marx did not divide the economy into a consumption goods sector and a capital goods sector.

determination of the rate of profits, and our only concern here is the way in which Bortkiewicz determines the rate of profits. Bortkiewicz assumes also that all the constant capital is consumed during the yearly process of production; that is C is equal to c.[90]

We have then as data for the determination of the rate of profits, the two sets of quantities of labour embodied c_1, v_1, s_1 and c_2, v_2, s_2, referring to the aggregate capitals and surpluses of, respectively, the sector producing capital goods to be used directly or indirectly for producing wage goods, and of Bortkiewicz's wage goods sector. Taking those quantities as aggregates, it is evident that there is no possibility of determining the investment function of wage goods. We can determine with them the average period of production of the wage goods,[91] but we cannot pass from it to the investment function because we do not know how c_1, on the one hand, and $(v_1 + s_1)$ on the other hand, are distributed among the firms or industries which serve sector II at one or two or three 'removes'.[92] According as the proportion between c and $(v + s)$ is higher than the average for sector I in the firms at the nearer 'removes', the same proportion will be lower than the average in the further 'removes', and the investment function of wage goods from the point on the left of the one having $t = -1$, would be less convex than if the opposite case as to the distribution of c and $(v + s)$ in the firms of sector I had been true. And accordingly, given L and L_1, the rate of profits would be higher. If we want to determine the rate of profits we shall have to distinguish the quantities c_1, v_1, s_1 according to the parts of them which enter the relevant individual processes; and take into consideration the several relationships established between the firms inside sector I which supply each other with their products. Looking at it from the period of production way of viewing capital, this will amount to constructing the investment function of the wage goods.

---

[90] Op. cit., pp. 199–200. This assumption amounts to the one that all capital is 'circulating' capital according to the definition of it given in Chapter III (above, p. 24). The significance of this assumption for Bortkiewicz's solution will be considered below, in Chapter V of the present section.

[91] With a procedure analogous to the one seen above, n. 76, we obtain

$$T_1 = \frac{c_1 + c_2}{(v_1 + s_1) + (v_2 + s_2)} + 1.$$

[92] The meaning of 'removes' here can be defined exactly in relation to the investment function (above, Fig. 1, p. 34). The firms or industries serving sector II at one remove are those where the labour applied is represented by $(\lambda_{-1} - \lambda_{-2})$ and in which the constant capital used is measured by λ_{-2}; the ones serving sector II at two removes are those whose $(v+s)$ is measured by $(\lambda_{-2} - \lambda_{-3})$ and whose c is represented by λ_{-3}, etc. It is of course possible that some firms or industries of sector I will serve sector II at more than one removes simultaneously (for instance a firm producing lathes used both for producing private cars and for producing machinery), in that case their $(v+s)$ and c will be divided in the proportion in which they have entered the two types of output, and will appear separately in the appropriate section of the investment function.

Bortkiewicz succeeds in determining the rate of profits because his solution assumes that the ratio between the aggregates for sector I, c_1 and $(v_1 + s_1)$, repeats itself unchanged in all the firms of sector I. In that case the 'price of production' per unit of labour embodied is the same for all kinds of capital goods,[93] and accordingly he can in his equations deal with sector I on the basis of the c_1, v_1, s_1 only.

In fact, Bortkiewicz's determination of the rate of profits can, for our purposes here, be summarized in the following two equations[94]:

$$\begin{aligned}(c_1x + v_1)(1 + p) &= (c_1 + v_1 + s_1)x \\ (c_2x + v_2)(1 + p) &= c_2 + v_2 + s_2\end{aligned} \tag{VI}$$

where x is the 'price of production' of a product of sector I measured by a produce of sector II embodying the same quantity of labour. It can now be seen from the first of the two equations of system (VI) that one price x is applied to the whole aggregate c_1 on the LHS and to the whole aggregate $(c_1 + v_1 + s_1)$ on the RHS; the implication is that either all the heterogeneous capital goods used and produced in sector I as a whole sell at one and the same price per unit of labour embodied, or the rate of profits can be determined on the basis of an 'average' price of capital goods.[95]

---

[93]Within sector I, then, exchanges would take place according to quantities of labour embodied.

[94]Cf. Eqs. (11) and (12) at p. 202, op. cit. The equations used there by Bortkiewicz include the sector III which we have found convenient to drop from our discussion of his solution (above, pp. 36–7). Those equations differ from Eq. (VI) also because Bortkiewicz makes an unnecessary use of Marx's equations of 'simple reproduction'. This question will be discussed in Appendix B below.

[95]A passage where, at a first reading, it may appear that the key assumption indicated in the text is stated by Bortkiewicz, is the following one: 'At the same time we shall assume that in the production of all three groups of means of production, that is, those which are used respectively in Departments I, II and III—the organic composition of capital is the same' (op. cit., p. 200). But the differences in organic composition ruled out in the passage are not the ones relevant for the assumption which concerns us, that is the differences between the organic compositions of the firms serving at two and more removes sector II. They refer rather to the differences between the organic composition of the *aggregate* capitals of three subsectors of Bortkiewicz's sector I; the one serving at one remove his sector III, the one serving at one remove sector II, and the one serving at two or more removes both sector II and sector III. This interpretation is borne out by the following passage: 'Suppose that the relation between the price and the value of the products of Department I is (*on the average*) as x to 1 ...' (op. cit., p. 201, our italics). The implication of that 'on the average' we have underlined is, clearly, that prices per unit of labour are different, and this in turn implies that the organic compositions of the capitals employed for their production are different. Bortkiewicz does not seem to realise that once the compound rate of profits is used, the rate of profits cannot be calculated on the basis of an average price of capital goods determined according to the average organic composition of his sector I. The sectors into which Bortkiewicz divides the economy in this article, and, in particular the distinction made between a wage goods sector and a capital goods sector serving also his sector III, may have helped to blur the distinctions which are relevant for the determination of the rate of profits and of the system of relative values: the ones between the firms or industries contributing to the production of wage goods at different removes.

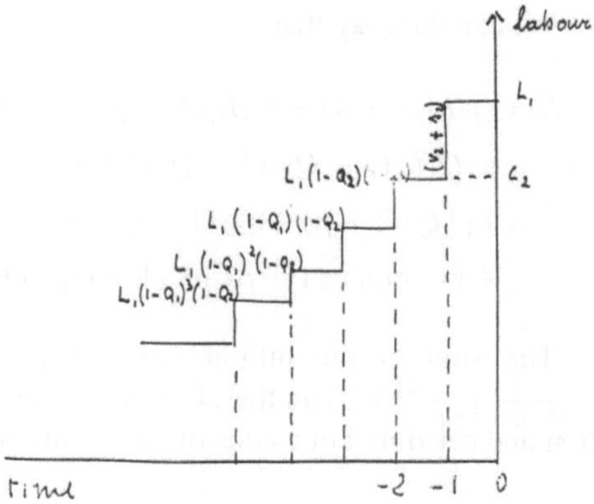

Fig. 2 Time distribution of the quantity of labour embodied in wage goods

If the assumption is made that all the firms within sector I have the same ratio between $(v + s)$ and $(c + v + s)$, it becomes easy to obtain from the quantities c_1, v_1, s_1, and c_2, v_2, s_2, the investment function of wage goods. We shall here do this briefly because it seems that a reconstruction of Bortkiewicz's procedure in terms of the period of production view of capital, may offer a useful basis both for bringing out more clearly the nature of the solution and for examining the possibility of its generalisation.

We shall assume with Bortkiewicz that $C = c$. The symbols p, c_1, v_1, s_1; c_2, v_2, s_2, L_1 (that is $[v_1 + s_1 + v_2 + s_2]$), L have the meanings already defined. To keep in step with Bortkiewicz's procedure we shall assume that the investment function is discontinuous so that the labour applied over any year is considered as if it had been all applied at the beginning of that year.

Of the quantity of labour embodied in the wage goods given to the labourers over the year between 0 and (+1), a fraction $Q_2 = \frac{v_2+s_2}{c_2+v_2+s_2}$ will have been applied at the moment (-1) within sector II, so that the value contributed by that quantity of labour, measured in wage units, will be given, at the moment 0 in which the wage goods are sold, by $Q_2L_1(1 + p)$; of the remaining portion of L_1, that is $L_1(1 - Q_2)$, a fraction $Q_1 = \frac{v_1+s_1}{c_1+v_1+s_1}$ will have been applied at the moment (-2) within sector I, and the value in wage units contributed by it will be given by $Q_1L_1(1 - Q_2)(1 + p)^2$; of the remaining portion of L_1, that is $L_1(1 - Q_1)(1 - Q_2)$, a fraction Q_1[96] will have been applied at the moment (-3) and the value contributed by it will therefore be: $Q_1L_1(1 - Q_1)(1 - Q_2)(1 + p)^3$, and so on (Fig. 2).

---

[96] It is here, of course, that the assumption of equality in the ratio between c and $(v+s)$ in the various firms of sector I becomes relevant: we are assuming that the capital goods entering production at the moments (-2), (-3), etc. will all have been produced with the same proportion Q_1.

We can then say that:

$$L = Q_2 L_1(1+p) + Q_1 L_1(1-Q_2)(1+p)^2 + Q_1 L_1(1-Q_2)(1-Q_1)(1+p)^3$$
$$+ Q_1 L_1(1-Q_2)(1-Q_1)^2(1+p)^4 + \cdots =$$
$$= L_1\{Q_2(1+p) + Q_1(1-Q_2)(1+p)^2[1+(1-Q_1)(1+p)$$
$$+ (1-Q_1)^2(1+p)^2 + (1-Q_1)^3(1+p)^3 + \ldots]\}$$

The sum of the infinite series $1, (1-Q_1)(1+p), (1-Q_1)^2(1+p)^2, \ldots$ is $\frac{1}{1-(1-Q_1)(1+p)}$.[97] We can therefore write, substituting that value in the previous equation and dividing both sides of the equation by L_1:

$$\frac{L}{L_1} = Q_2(1+p) + \frac{Q_1(1-Q_2)(1+p)^2}{1-(1-Q_1)(1+p)}$$

Noting that $\frac{L}{L_1}$ is equal to $(1 + r)$, where r is Marx's rate of surplus value defined above,[98] and solving the equation for the unknown $(1 + p)$, we obtain:

$$(1+p) = \frac{(1+r)(1-Q_1) + Q_2 \pm \sqrt{[(1+r)(1-Q_1)+Q_2]^2 - 4(1+r)(Q_2-Q_1)}}{2(Q_2-Q_1)} \qquad \text{(VII)}$$

The formula for the determination of the rate of profits offered by Eq. (VII) is the formula obtained by Bortkiewicz.[99]

---

97 The finite value of the sum of that infinite series, confirms here what we said above (n. 52) about the difficulty, sometimes raised against the period of production measurement of capital, that some of the periods of production will have to be considered as tending to infinity.

98 P. 32.

99 Bortkiewicz's formula is (cf. formula (24), op. cit., p. 203):

$$(1+p) = \frac{-(f_1 g_1 + g_2) \pm \sqrt{(f_1 g_1 + g_2)^2 + 4(f_1 - f_2) g_1 g_2}}{2(f_1 - f_2)}$$

where $f_1 = \frac{v_1}{c_1}; f_2 = \frac{v_2}{c_2}; g_1 = \frac{c_1+v_1+s_1}{c_1}; g_2 = \frac{c_2+v_2+s_2}{c_2}$

If we recall that in Eqs. (VI) above:

$$Q_1 = \frac{v_1+s_1}{c_1+v_1+s_1}; Q_2 = \frac{v_2+s_2}{c_2+v_2+s_2}; r = \frac{s_1}{v_1} = \frac{s_2}{v_2} \text{ so that}$$

$v_1(1+r) = v_1 + s_1$ and $v_2(1+r) = v_2 + s_2$; it can be easily shown that

$$f_1 = \frac{Q_1}{(1+r)(1-Q_1)}; f_2 = \frac{Q_2}{(1+r)(1-Q_2)}; g_1 = \frac{1}{1-Q_1}; g_2 = \frac{1}{1-Q_2};$$

if we now substitute these values for f_1, f_2, g_1, g_2 in Bortkiewicz's equation, and if we divide both numerator and denominator by $[(1+r)(1-Q_1)(1-Q_2)]$ we obtain Eq. (VII).

From Eq. (VII) it appears that the rate of profits, under the restrictions deriving from the assumptions we have seen above, depends only on three quantities: the rate of surplus value and the 'organic composition' of capital in sector II and of that section of sector I which supplies at one or more removes sector II.[100]

Bortkiewicz's actual results are founded on the assumption we have seen, but the important point in it appears to be that it implicitly overcomes the difficulty that the measurement of capital according to the average period of production, or quantity of labour embodied in the capital stock, meets in the compound rate of profits. In fact, once Bortkiewicz's limiting assumption is made explicit there is no difficulty in generalizing the determination of the rate of profits, so that it can be applied for any form whatever of the investment function of wage goods. If we use a continuously compound rate of interest, and if $f_1(t)$ is the investment function of the wage goods with a t ranging from any point $(-\tau)$ (which may be at $-\infty$) to 0, and if L is, as before, the quantity of labour applied by the labour force during the year, p could be determined from the equation:[101,102]

---

[100] Q_1 and Q_2 can in fact be obtained from the organic composition of capital, as defined by Marx (above, p. 32), and the rate of surplus value.

[101] It would be possible to achieve this generalization of Bortkiewicz's solution also on the lines of his own method consisting of a system of equations expressing the equality between costs and revenues obtained by applying the unknown prices of quantities of inputs and outputs measured in terms of labour embodied (see Eqs. (VI) above). Only now the number of sectors of the economy and, accordingly, the number of equations (and prices) should be increased so as to have a sector for any capital good or group of capital goods requiring different proportions of current to past labour, that is different ratios $\left(\frac{v+s}{c+v+s}\right)$. These equations, if kept in Bortkiewicz's form, would still imply an arbitrary assumption that the labour directly employed in each sector remains invested for one year before the product of the sector is sold; but that assumption could be dropped without much difficulty. We can notice that, to the extent in which we must insert in the system a special equation for each type of capital good entering the production of wage goods at any stage, and to the extent in which the wages of the labourers can be expressed as physical quantities of wage goods, it should be possible to measure the quantities to which the unknown prices are referred as physical quantities; since then the relevant quantities would be physically homogeneous, quantities of labour embodied and physical quantities would give equivalent measurements. (Cf., for instance, F. Seton, 'The Transformation Problem', *Review of Economic Studies*, June 1957, p. 151, n. 3, point (1)).

[102] At the time in which this chapter and the following one were first drafted, I was aware that, besides the article referred to in the text, Bortkiewicz had published another article on the transformation problem ('Wertrechnung und Preisrechnung im Marxschen System', in three instalments in *Archiv für Sozialwissenschaft und Sozialpolitik*, July 1906-September 1907; the second and third instalments are available in English in No. 2 of *International Economic Papers*). Since the article in the *Jarbücher* was published one year after the first instalment of the one in the *Archiv*, and since all recent discussions of the problem referred only to it, I assumed, at the time, that the former article contained Bortkiewicz's essential results and I postponed the reading of the latter one to some time before the intended re-drafting of the relevant part of the dissertation. Scarcity of time did not allow me to do such re-drafting. I have now studied the article from the *Archiv* and if I were to rewrite this chapter and the next I would modify them. For what regards this chapter, I would take into account that Bortkiewicz had there advanced equations involving a period of production view of capital, taken from the work of the Russian economist Dmitriev (whose work is not available in any of the languages at my disposal). A comparison however of

$$\int_{-\tau}^{0} \frac{d\lambda}{dt} e^{\rho t} dt. \tag{VIII}$$

Section I, Chapter V: The Difficulty Connected with Fixed Capital; Another Assumption Implicit to Bortkievicz's Solution; Possibility of Dropping That Assumption; Conclusions of Section I of the Dissertation

In Chapter III we saw that the average period of production measurement of capital meets a second main obstacle besides the one deriving from the calculation with the compound rate of interest. It is the obstacle connected with the existence of fixed capital.[103] Bortkiewicz's solution of the transformation problem, while it overcomes (though on the basis of a restrictive assumption) the compound rate of interest difficulty, does not, on the contrary, deal with the difficulty created by fixed capital. In fact such a solution rests on the absence of fixed capital.

Bortkiewicz's solution is obtained while assuming, in his own words, 'that the entire advanced capital (including the constant capital) turns over once a year and reappears again in the value or the price of the annual product'.[104]

The assumption that the capital existing at the beginning of the year is entirely consumed during the yearly process of production, or, in the symbols adopted in Chapter IV above, that $C = c$[105] implies that all capital is circulating capital, in the definition of it adopted above[106]: each capital good constituting the capital stock will be entirely consumed in the production of commodities completed at a definite point in time, namely at the end of the year. That assumption is then justified by Bortkiewicz by the need to simplify the presentation, and there is no indication of the fact that it is essential to that measurement of capital in terms of labour embodied which he uses throughout the article. In fact fixed capital brings in a

---

the two texts shows that Bortkiewicz was not aware that the solution in the later article was the one outlined in the *Archiv* limited by the assumption pointed out in this chapter. To this extent the criticisms made in this chapter maintain their validity. Bortkiewicz's failure to grasp fully the relationship between the period of production and the labour embodied views of capital may be explained by the fact that the two articles used equations first advanced by two different authors: Dmitriev in the one case and Tugan Baranowski in the other.

[103] See above, n. 54.

[104] Op. cit., pp. 199–200.

[105] Above, p. 37.

[106] Above, p. 24.

special theoretical difficulty. As has often been pointed out in various forms, it is impossible to define consistently the quantity of labour which is still embodied in a piece of fixed capital which has been in use for some time; and the Bortkiewicz determination of the rate of profits rests on data including the quantities of labour embodied in the fixed capital.

The fixed capital difficulty is independent of the type of rate of profits used in the calculation: it is there even when we use the simple rate of interest. It can be stated in either of two forms corresponding to the *equivalent* ways of looking at the quantity of capital. We can speak of the impossibility of determining in a way independent of the rate of profits, the period of time over which, on average, the labour embodied in a piece of fixed capital remains invested; it is, in other words, question of the impossibility of establishing a relationship of the form $V_a = L_k(1+p)^{T_k}$ between the simple sum[107] of the values contributed to the produce by a machine or piece of fixed capital K, and the quantity of labour L_K[108] necessary to produce the machine K. Or alternatively, we can speak of the impossibility of defining, in a way both independent of the rate of profits and consistent with the use of the resulting quantity in the theory, the quantity of labour which is embodied in a 'park' of machines of different ages.

The root of the difficulty is in that the relationship between the number of labour years L_K embodied in the machine K when new, and the simple sums of the values, in the yearly wage units, contributed by it to outputs of commodity A which we have called V_a, is given by the following equation:

$$L_k = \frac{V_a}{n_k}\frac{1}{(1+p)} + \frac{V_a}{n_k}\frac{1}{(1+p)^2} + \frac{V_a}{n_k} + \frac{1}{(1+p)^3} + \dots \frac{V_a}{n_k(1+p)^{n_k}} \quad \text{(IX)}$$

In the equation n_k is taken to be the years of the economic life of the machine and p, as usual, the rate of profits. We have there assumed, in order to isolate the fixed capital difficulty, that the machine K takes no time to be produced[109]; we have also assumed that the machine contributes the same value $\frac{V_a}{n_k}$ to the outputs during every year of its economic life and that the outputs come out of production at the end of each year.

[107] We speak of simple sum because the values of the outputs of the machine appearing at different dates are, in V_a, added without first bringing them to the same date by adding interest or subtracting discount. The usefulness of this approach will be seen later (below, pp. 45–6).

[108] In the formula above, we have assumed that all the labour embodied in K has been applied at one moment.

[109] If we take into consideration the periods of production of the labour producing the machine we must put on the LHS of Eq. (IX) the value in yearly wage units of a new machine calculated according to Eq. (VIII) of p. 42 above.

Equation (IX) can be written in the form[110]:

$$V_a = \frac{pL_k n_k (1+p)^{n_k}}{(1+p)^{n_k} - 1} \qquad \text{(X)}$$

Now, Eq. (X) cannot be reduced to the form $V_a = L_k(1+p)^{T_k}$, if T_k has to be independent of the rate of profits p. To be compatible with the correct values of V_a and L_k, T_k would have to increase as p diminishes, and vice-versa. Or, looking at the same thing from the side of the labour embodied view of capital, the quantity of labour which in our calculations should be considered to be embodied in a park of machines of uniform age distribution, should increase when the rate of profits diminishes, and vice-versa.[111] If that is so, the quantities of labour embodied in

---

[110]Equation (IX) can be written:

$$L_K = \frac{V_a}{n_K}\left[\frac{1}{(1+p)} + \frac{1}{(1+p)^2} + \cdots + \frac{1}{(1+p)^{n_K}}\right]$$

The n terms in the sum of the R.H.S. are in geometrical progression, and their sum will be given by $\frac{(1+p)^{n_k} - 1}{p(1+p)^{n_k}}$; substituting it into the equation and solving for V_a, we obtain:

$$V_a = \frac{pL_k n_k (1+p)^{n_k}}{(1+p)^{n_k} - 1}$$

[111]As we have repeatedly seen in the last three chapters, periods of production and quantity of labour embodied in the capital stock are but two ways of visualising and describing the same way of conceiving capital as a quantity. Hence, if as p decreases, the T_k of the equation $V_a = L_k(1+p)^{T_k}$, must increase if V_a is to be the correct one determined by Eq. (X), the quantity of labour embodied in the park of machines of uniform age distribution [necessary to render simultaneous the application (to the production of machines) of a quantity of labour L_k, and the coming out of an output of A in which the value contributed by the machines is V_a] will also increase, since such quantity of labour will be given by a number of' labour years ($L_k T_k$).

This can also be described in another way: since, when we use the period of production conception, the relationship we established between the labour embodied in a commodity A and the value in wage units contributed by it, is $L(1+p)^T = V$; since the value contributed each year by a machine K is, by hypothesis, $\frac{V_a}{n_k}$, it follows that the amortisation of the labour embodied in the machine in the first, second, etc., years of the life of K must, for the purposes of our calculations, follow the law:

$$l_{1k} = \frac{V_a}{n_k(1+p)};\ l_{2k} = \frac{V_a}{n_k(1+p)^2};\ \ldots l_{nk} = \frac{V_a}{n_k(1+p)^{n_k}};$$

where $l_{1k}, l_{2k}, l_{3k} \ldots l_{nk}$ are the parts of L_k amortised after the first, second, etc., year of the life of the machine, it will then follow that as p diminishes, the proportion of L_k amortised in the first year will diminish, and therefore the quantity of labour in a park of machines of type k, and of uniform age distribution, will increase. We can represent it geometrically in Fig. 3, where what we can call the disinvestment function becomes the less convex to the origin, the lower the rate of profits; if there were no profits the function would be represented by a straight line; the quantity of labour embodied in a park of machines of uniform age distribution requiring, to be kept intact, a yearly application of an L_k quantity of labour, will be represented by the area under the curve (that is $L_k T_k = \int_0^{n_k} F_k(t)\,dt$) and will evidently increase as p diminishes.

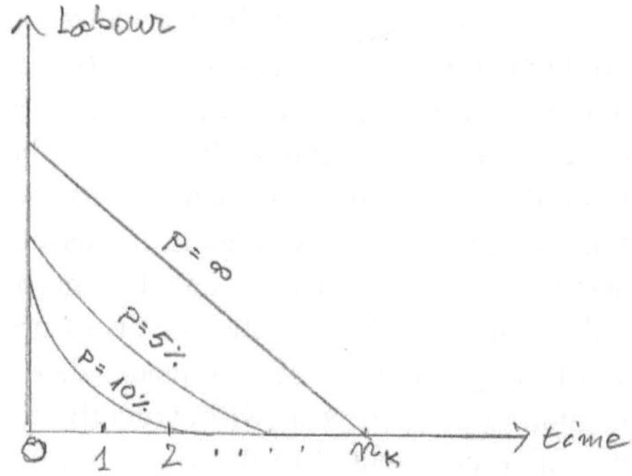

Fig. 3 The convexity of the disinvestment function is less, the lower the profit rate

the stock of 'constant' capital can no longer be taken as data when determining the rate of profits, and accordingly the basis of Bortkiewicz's solution falls.

But it appears that a way of dealing with fixed capital within the type of theory of distribution considered here could be evolved by dropping the concept of quantity of labour embodied in a stock of fixed capital, that is the concept of a period for which the labour embodied in a new piece of fixed capital remains invested. We should instead take as data the number of labourers continuously employed in replacing the fixed capitals of the several types, and the life of each type of fixed capital. The basis for that way of dealing with fixed capital would be the use of the relationship between L_k and V_a expressed in Eq. (X) above. That equation can in fact be interpreted as giving the relationship which must exist between the value, in yearly wage units, annually contributed by a park of machines of type K, of ages uniformly distributed between 0 and $n_{k,}$ and the number of labour years, or labourers, L_k, which are necessary in order to replace, at the end of each year, those machines which were in the last year of their lives.[112]

An example may be helpful to clarify the way in which Eq. (X) can be used to express the value of aggregates of commodities in the equation determining the rate of profits.

Let us assume, at first, that the wage goods are produced with a variable capital v, and that the constant capital consists entirely of a park of machines all of the

[112] Let us imagine that the park of machines of type K consists of a number of machines n_K, such that, at the beginning of the year, we have one machine for each age between 0 and $(n_k - 1)$. The value contributed by the n machines to the yearly output of A_1 will be $(\frac{V_a}{n_k} \cdot n_k)$; that is V_a. On the other hand at the end of each year the oldest machine, aged n_k, will have to be substituted by a new one and this requires that during the year a number of labour years L_k has been applied to the replacement of it, or that a number of labourers L_k has been continuously engaged in providing that replacement. The relationship has evidently general validity for any number of machines, provided that V_a is modified accordingly and that to L_k we give the more general meaning of quantity of labour years or number of labourers necessary in order to keep physically intact the park of machines.

same type K and uniformly distributed, at the beginning of the yearly process of production, among all ages between 0 and (n_k -1), where n_k is, as before, the life of that type of fixed capital. The number of machines constituting the park (assumed to be a multiple of n_k) is such that a number of labourers k is continuously engaged in producing the machines which must be replaced at the end of the year. To simplify the procedure, we shall at first assume that the k labourers do not require the assistance of any constant capital, either fixed or circulating; so that the only capital required for them, is the one necessary to pay their yearly wages. The value in yearly wage units of the new machines entering the wage goods production at the beginning of each year, will evidently be: $k(1 + p)$; hence, according to Eq. (X), the value contributed to the yearly produce of wage goods by the entire park of machines will be:

$$k(1+p)\frac{pn_k(1+p)^{n_k}}{(1+p)^{n_k}-1}$$

There is no difficulty now in constructing the equation determining profits on the basis of the equality between the value in yearly wage units of the yearly aggregate of wage goods and the total number of labourers employed in the economy, that is L. The equation is:

$$L=(v+s)(1+p)+k(1+p)\frac{pn_k(1+p)^{n_k}}{(1+p)^{n_k}-1} \qquad \text{(XI)}$$

Since L_1, the number of labour years embodied in the net produce of the wage goods sector of the economy (or number of labourers continuously engaged in producing wage goods, either directly, or indirectly by producing the machines K) is equal to ($k + v + s$), if we define $Q_1 = \frac{v+s}{k+v+s}$, Eq. (XI) can be written as[113]:

$$L=L_1[Q_1(1+p)+(1-Q_1)(1+p)\frac{pn_k(1+p)^{n_k}}{(1+p)^{n_k}-1}] \qquad \text{(XII)}$$

The only unknown in Eq. (XII) is the rate of profits p, which can therefore be determined.

If the types of fixed capital used in the final year of the production of the wage goods are more than one, we must consider all the k_1 k_2 … k_m and n_{k1} n_{k2} n_{k3} … n_{km}, for each of the m types of fixed capital. We must then add the respective expressions of the values yearly contributed by each of them, on the R.H.S. of Eq. (XI). If we drop the assumption that all the constant capital employed in the last year of the production of wage goods is fixed capital, it will be question of introducing in the equation beside the k_1 k_2 … k_m, an element c, whose value in wage units will be expressed, to the extent in which fixed capital has not entered its production at previous stages, according to the procedure which brought us to

[113] To the extent in which two or more types of fixed capital have the same life they can, for the purposes of Eqs. (XI) and (XII), be considered as one, and the respective k's can accordingly be added into one k.

Eq. (VIII) of Chapter IV[114]; and, to the extent in which fixed capital has entered its production at one or more removes, by introducing the appropriate k's. If we drop also the assumption that the fixed capital is produced without any constant capital, the value in wage units of the new fixed capital K_i entering the relevant stage of the production of wage goods, will cease to be expressed as: $k_i(1 + p)$; we shall have to express instead that value according to the same principles indicated for the value of the final product of wage goods. The equation and its solution would become very complicated, but it does not appear that we shall meet any difficulty of principle in constructing it. It would be mainly question of grouping the relevant quantities in the most manageable way by the help of appropriate concepts. As long as we can take as data the k's and the n_k's of the various types of fixed capital, the equation will always have only one unknown, the rate of profits.

The next question would be that of the extent to which, in the face of the changes the theory of distribution analyses, we can take as given (or determine in a non-circular way) the techniques of production adopted, that is the techniques of which the k's and n_k's are an expression.

The same problems underlie also the method used above in Chapter IV for overcoming the difficulty of the compound rate of profits. The investment function of which we spoke there is in fact an expression of the technique by which the wage goods are produced in so far as circulating capital is concerned.

The methods for dealing with the two difficulties of the compound rate and of the fixed capital, have in common the feature of abandoning the conception of capital as one quantity[115] in favour of the set of time periods over which labour has to remain invested in the process of producing the commodities: the set of absolute periods expressed by the investment function in the case of circulating capital, and the lives of the several kinds of capital goods in the case of fixed capital.

Summing up the results of our analysis of the problem of an adequate measurement of capital within a theory of distribution on Ricardian lines, it seems possible to conclude:

I. that for such a theory it is essential to 'measure' capital in terms of magnitudes which are both independent of changes in distribution and are related in a known way to the value, in some unit, of the capital they express;
II. that the average period of production appears to be unsatisfactory as a measurement of capital because, on the one hand, the assumption of a simple rate of profits leads us to contradictions with the principle of uniformity of the rate of profits under conditions of competitive equilibrium, and, on the other hand, it cannot deal with fixed capital;

---

[114] Above, p. 42.

[115] The importance of Böhm-Bawerk's average period of production is that it offers a consistent measurement of the capital assisting one labourer in terms of *one* quantity, so that we should then be able to refer unambiguously to a *proportion* between capital and labour. The relevance of this will be seen in detail in the second part of this dissertation, dealing with the marginal productivity theories of distribution.

III. that an attempt to overcome within such a theory of distribution the two difficulties besetting the use of the average period could be made by measuring capital as a set of magnitudes, in the forms appropriate to the circulating and fixed capitals.

The problem of the measurement of capital becomes then that of the extent to which the relevant set of periods of time and respective quantities of labour (that is, the set referring to the production of wage goods at all their stages), can be introduced as a datum in the equation determining the rate of profits. Such a set of quantities results from the technique adopted for producing, at all their stages, the relevant goods: to any technique there will correspond a definite set of periods of production and quantities of labour, so that any change in technique will involve a change in the set of quantities. The question can then be reformulated as one concerning the extent to which, in the face of the changes the theory of distribution must analyse, we can either take as given the techniques of production or determine in a non-circular way the changes that they will undergo. Such a question cannot be discussed without getting into the wider theoretical set up on which such theories of distribution rest. It is beyond the scope of this dissertation to attempt even a first examination of that question. But we can note here that the consideration of capital as a set of quantities may not meet, within a theory of distribution built on Ricardian lines, obstacles as serious as the ones we shall see in connection with the marginal productivity theories of distribution. The reason for that is that in the Ricardian theory the conception of capital as *one* quantity, given, in its size, *independently* of the changes occurring in the techniques of production and physical capital goods, does not seem to have the essential role it has in the marginal productivity theories which single out 'quantities of factors of production' existing in the economy as the main determinants of distribution. To the extent in which such a conception of capital is not essential, it should be possible to introduce in the relevant equation or equations of a Ricardian theory a measurement of capital on the lines of the set of quantities we have used in the last two chapters.[116]

[116] In the article 'Wertrechnung und Preischnung' already mentioned (n. 101), Bortkiewicz did introduce fixed capital in his equations, but the way in which he dealt with the question is unsatisfactory. He there resolves the contribution to the product of a piece of fixed capital into that of quantities of labour e_1, e_2, …, e_w, which remain invested (neglecting the construction period of capital good) for, respectively, 1, 2, …, w years, were w years is the life of the fixed capital. Such quantities of labour are obtained by discounting for 1, 2, …, w years, the contribution of the fixed capital to the value of the output of years 1, 2, …, w. In other words those quantities are the quantities l_{1k} l_{2k} … l_{nk} we have seen above (n. 111; Bortkiewicz does not measure value in wage units and introduces therefore in those relationships the unknown wage rate measured in his standard). He then inserts these quantities of labour and time periods in his equations, and uses them in the same way as the quantities of labour and times periods relating to circulating capital: he takes them as data for the determination of the rate of profits (*Int. Ec. Papers*, No. 2, pp. 18–21). This procedure is evidently incorrect: Bortkiewicz did not realise that since e_1 e_2 … e_w vary with the rate of profits (see above, n. 111), they cannot be taken as given when determining the rate of profits; they are unknowns for those equations, and, to that extent, Bortkwiecz's system of equations in that article cannot determine the rate of profits.

Section II, Chapter I: The Requirements for the Measurement of Capital in the Marginal Productivity Theories

In Section I we have examined in Ricardo the nature of the problem of measuring capital within a surplus theory of distribution. That has led us to consider on which lines a solution of that problem could be attempted, and to an examination of the solution advanced by Bortkiewicz for Marx's problem of transforming 'values' into 'prices of production'.

We have now to consider the similar problem of capital measurement as it arises in the marginal productivity theories of distribution. We shall do that by examining the attempts to solve the problem made by Walras and Wicksell in their theories of distribution. The object of this chapter is to offer the basis for the examination of those theories by first stating in their most general terms the elements of the problem.

The marginal productivity theories arose from a generalisation of the theory of rent used by Ricardo.[117] In Ricardo that theory was useful in so far as it allowed him to isolate the part of the social produce which must be distributed between capitalists and labourers. The surplus theory of distribution then entered to determine that distribution. The marginal productivity theories eliminate the need for a special theory of the distribution between capitalists and labourers by applying also to that distribution the principle Ricardo had used for the rent of land: as the proportion between land and labour (assisted by capital) governs the distribution between the two types of resources, so the distribution between capital and labour is thought to be governed in an analogous way by the proportion 'capital' bears to labour. Such a development had the attraction of leading to a unified and elegant theory of distribution and offered a way out of the confusion in which the theory of distribution had been thrown by the failure to follow up and develop the analysis underlying Ricardo's theory of profits. But it also implied difficulties which managed to remain hidden from the view of most and are only now beginning to be recognised as affecting the foundations of the elaborate structure built in the meantime.

As will become clear from what follows, a generalisation of the classical theory of rent to cover the distribution between capital and labour puts the main weight of that determination on a ratio between the capital and the labour existing in the economy, which implies a conception of capital as *one* magnitude given independently of the changes in distribution the theory examines, and independently of the connected changes in the techniques of production.[118]

[117] The belief that Ricardo invented the theory of rent, and that he was therefore the originator of the principle of the marginal productivity, has been convincingly shown to have no foundation by Mr. Sraffa and Mr. Dobb in their introduction to the *Essay on Profits* (*Works*, Vol. IV, pp. 6–8).

[118] The necessity of the measurement of capital by a single magnitude arises fundamentally from the fact that in competitive equilibrium there can be only one rate of interest. Such a necessity will become apparent in the course of the examination of Walras's and Wicksell's theories.

We have already indicated how this conception of capital as one magnitude does not appear to be essential for a Ricardian theory of distribution where, to that extent, a conception of capital as a set of magnitudes would appear to be satisfactory.[119] In fact the two problems of capital measurement arise in different connections in the two types of theories and the different connections explain the different characteristics of the two problems.

In the Ricardian theory the problem has its origin in the necessity of expressing in a way independent of distribution the value of the aggregates of commodities relevant for the determination of the rate at profits: produce, wages and capital. The necessity for such a measurement of the value of commodities, however, disappears in the marginal productivity theories. The analytical basis for Ricardo's determination of profits as a surplus was an assumption of independence between changes of the wage rate, conceived as a complex of wage goods, and changes in the physical quantity of produce obtained from a unit of labour.[120] For the marginal productivity theories on the contrary, the wage is functionally related to the produce and therefore any determination of profits as difference between produce and wages begs the question. Produce and wages are not taken as independent variables when determining profits; they can only be determined simultaneously with profits.[121] As profits can no longer be determined as surplus, so the need no longer arises of expressing the value of the relevant aggregates of commodities in terms independent of changes in distribution; together with this need disappears the problem of capital measurement in the form we discussed in Section I. The problem of value does enter the marginal productivity theories of distribution, but it enters it in a way which renders unnecessary any problem of measuring value not immediately identical with the problem of the determination of the system of relative values. In each enterprise or in each industry the share of the produce which goes to each unit of the several factors employed is determined, in competitive equilibrium, by the increment of the produce which results from an increase, by a sufficiently small unit, of the quantity employed of the factor in question, the quantity of the other factors remaining unchanged. Accordingly, in each enterprise or industry, distribution can be studied with the production function relating physical outputs to quantities of factors employed. The problem of value enters the theory of distribution when we study the whole economy and the distribution of the available quantities of factors among the industries: we have then to introduce the condition that the value of the marginal product of a factor must be the same in the whole economy; such value however can be measured in terms of any of the

---

[119] See above, p. 48.

[120] See above, p. 7.

[121] In this part of the dissertation we shall refer to the capitalists' share in the produce indifferently as profits or interests.

commodities and no special problem of measurement arises. More generally, we can say that in the marginal productivity theories the remuneration of each factor is determined simultaneously with the system of the relative values of commodities on the basis of three groups of data:

(a) consumers' preferences;
(b) techniques available in the given state of technical knowledge, as they are expressed by the production function of each industry;
(c) quantities of factors of production available in the economy in the situation examined.

It is here, in connection with the data of groups (b) and (c) and not in connection with a measurement of aggregates that the problem of capital measurement connected with this type of theory arises.

The quantities of factors of production constituting the data of group (c) and appearing as variables in the production functions constituting the data of group (b) should be measured (that is, conceived) in a way which makes those quantities independent of the way in which the produce is distributed among the factors. In other words we should need to conceive the quantities of factors which are employed for each of the techniques included in the production functions, or are available in the economy, in terms of units such that those quantities will remain unaffected by changes in distribution and can therefore be defined without knowing already the prices of the factors. Using Wicksell's expression we can say that the quantities of the factors must be measured in 'technical units'.[122] This requirement arises from the necessity of avoiding circular reasoning: if we cannot measure and therefore define the quantity of a factor before knowing the system of relative values, we shall be unable to use the theory, for the theory is so built that it allows us to determine the system of relative prices only if we have among our data both the quantities available of all the factors of production, and the production functions involving the quantities of factors as variables.[123] The point will be given some illustration presently when we shall discuss value as a possible measure of capital.

Such requirements for the measurement of the factors of production can be thought to be satisfied by the factors traditionally grouped as 'labour' and 'land'. Even for them there are difficulties connected with the heterogeneity of different kinds of labour and land. But for them it seems possible, within limits, to consider

[122] *Lectures*, Vol. I, p. 149. Wicksell however in that passage considers the measurement of capital as 'exchange va1ue' only as a 'theoretical anomaly which disturbs the correspondence which would otherwise exist between all the factors of production', and not as a basic deficiency involving the theory in circular reasoning.

[123] Cf. above, pp. 17 and 21–2 for analogous questions in the Ricardian theory of distribution.

each sufficiently homogeneous quality of labour or land as a factor of production of its own, and thereby avoid the difficulty.[124]

When we come to 'capital' the difficulty of satisfying the requirements appears. What we have under this heading is a collection of heterogeneous goods like stocks of raw materials or of finished goods in the hands of the producers, goods in process, buildings, machinery, etc. What they have in common, and has induced economic theory to consider them all as 'capital', can be reduced, it seems, to the following two basic characteristics: firstly, all these goods are produced in accordance with the principles valid for the production of other goods; secondly, these goods are consumed in the course of the production process and have to be replaced within a period of time sufficiently short to guarantee a tendency towards a definite relationship, controlled by the equilibrium rate of interest, between their costs of production and the value of the share of the produce they afford to their owners.[125]

The capital goods have then in common one quality economically relevant: value. It is in value that capital is usually reckoned in economic practice and it is from that commonsense idea of capital that the conception of capital as a factor of production has been borrowed by economic theory and has derived its appearance of reasonableness also in the new setting. But the value of the capital goods, whichever the unit in which that value is measured, does not satisfy the

[124] A limit to this possibility of overcoming the difficulty connected with the heterogeneity of labour or land is in the fact that the narrower the definition of a labour or land factor, the less realistic it becomes to assume the possibility of substituting the factors so defined for one another. Another limit arises from the difficulty of taking as data the quantities of the various kinds of labour available in the economy: the same labourer can offer labour of different qualities if he so wishes; the tendency is strengthened by the substitution in the labour force of young workers for old ones. This point has similarities with the one we shall see concerning changes in the relative quantities of capital goods of different types as disparities in the rates of net income earned on them arise. But the important difference is that while in the case of capital goods we appear to have no basis for determining the ratios by which those capital goods will 'transform' into one another, in the case of labourers one worker who can supply labour of different kinds as relative wages vary, will always remain one worker and the range of alternatives is definable as one between one labour-day or hour of qualities *A*, *B*, *C* etc. Accordingly, this variability of the relative quantities of labour of different qualities may be taken into account by way of appropriate supply functions (built on the basis of the existing population and of its preferences as to the qualities of labour it can supply) relating the quantities supplied of different kinds of labour to the system of relative wages. This difference between heterogeneity of labour and heterogeneity of capital seems to be ultimately reducible to the fact that labourers are not capital goods having a cost of production in the same sense as those goods, and are not therefore subject to anything like a tendency to uniformity in the rates of net income.

[125] These two characteristics are those which, as we shall see, make it necessary for the marginal productivity theories to consider all the capital goods as a single factor of production, the quantity of which existing in the economy is given for each situation examined, and therefore prevent a solution of the problem of heterogeneity along the lines indicated above for the heterogeneity of labour and land. This question will be at the centre of our examination of Walras's theory in the following chapters.

requirement of independence from changes in distribution: the same physical capital would appear to be different 'quantities of capital' when changes in distribution occur, since the value of any capital good in terms of any conceivable commodity will in general change even though nothing changes but the rates of profits and wages. The reason for which value cannot supply a conception of capital consistent with its use in the marginal productivity theories is therefore the circularity we have mentioned in explaining the necessity for a measurement of factors in technical units. We can now examine in some more detail that circularity as it applies to the value measurement of capital. It is useful for our purpose here to distinguish between the two connections in which the magnitude 'capital' appears in the system of equations determining distribution and prices: as a variable in the production function and as the datum 'quantity of capital existing in the economy'.

In the production functions of the several industries the relevant alternative techniques available with a 'given state of technical knowledge' are described by relating the quantities of physical outputs to the quantities of factors employed. In those functions therefore the measurement of 'capital' should be such that a given aggregate of capital goods physically defined should always be the same 'quantity' of capital, whatever the system of relative prices. In fact when the quantities of the other factors are given, a certain aggregate of capital goods defines the technique of production used, and with that the physical output obtainable; if that aggregate of capital goods is so measured as to be a 'quantity of capital' variable with changes in distribution, no unique relationship can evidently be established between 'quantity of capital' and physical produce. This would be the case if we measured capital as value: given the quantities of the other factors the same techniques and outputs would be compatible with different values of the capital, and the same value of capital could be made compatible with practically any of the techniques described by the production function by varying appropriately the wage and profit rates used in the calculation of its value. Let us, for instance, imagine a certain technique by which a given physical output of some specified commodity is obtained by applying given quantities of labour of various descriptions and a complex of capital goods physically defined. If we assume a variation in the rates of wages and profits the value of capital will vary, and in a different way according to the commodity chosen as measure: it might rise in terms of one commodity while falling in terms of another. That variation would contradict the pre-requisites of the marginal productivity theory: the quantities of other factors remaining constant, capital has varied and the physical produce has not changed. Should we say that the marginal productivity of capital in that combination of factors is zero? But we could equally well give to that same marginal productivity any large number of other values, provided we constructed suitable examples. The net of contradictions in which one is caught when one measures capital as value in the production function could be looked at in other aspects, but what has been said seems sufficient to conclude that no meaning can be given to the marginal product of capital and therefore to the marginal product of all other factors so long as capital is so measured. The marginal productivity of a capital measured by value, and with it the marginal productivity of other factors, can have a meaning for the individual producers who take as given the system of relative prices, but cannot have a meaning in the context in which the theories considered set it.

As regards the second role of capital quantity in the marginal productivity theories, the detailed criticism of the value measurement of the quantity of capital available in the economy, will be the subject of a successive chapter criticizing that procedure in Wicksell's theory of distribution and examining the arguments which have been advanced in defence of that measurement.[126]

The measurement of capital in the marginal productivity theories must satisfy a second requirement which is also analogous to the second requirement for capital measurement in Ricardo. That requirement was that the quantity or set of quantities measuring capital should bear a definable relationship to the value (in terms of some standard) of the capital so expressed.[127] In the marginal productivity theories the corresponding requirement is that the single magnitude measuring capital independently of distribution, should bear a definable relationship to the value (in terms of some standard) of the capital it expresses.[128]

It is not difficult to show why this requirement must be satisfied; if there were no such requirement the problem could be easily solved by measuring capital goods according to some of their common physical properties: the weight or volume of capital goods is obviously independent of changes in the distribution of the social produce. It should be sufficient in order to justify the requirement to remember that the marginal product of capital must be related to the value of the marginal unit of capital in order to determine the rate of interest. If no relationship can be postulated between the magnitude measuring capital and its value, no rate of interest can be determined. But the necessity of the requirement can be traced further back into the theory. Without the possibility of postulating a relationship between the magnitude measuring capital and the value of the corresponding capital goods, it would not be possible to have a production function. We could define the production function as the function giving us the *minimum* quantity of a factor compatible with a given physical output and with given quantities of all the other factors.[129] Now it could be asked: why does the production function include only

---

[126] What is needed at this stage of the argument is to state the two general requirements which the measurement of capital in the marginal productivity theories must satisfy and, at the same time, to rule out those formulations in which a conception of the production function with capital measured as value—a conception which can have a meaning only for the individual producer or a small industry—is used as the basis of a general theory of distribution.

[127] Above, pp. 21–2.

[128] The difference in the formulation of the requirement in the two types of theories reflects what we said at the beginning of the chapter on the necessity for the marginal theories of conceiving capital as a single magnitude.

[129] In this proposition, the output referred to must be understood not to be beyond the point at which, given the quantities of all other factors, any increase of the variable factor cannot increase the output. Otherwise there would be no quantity of the variable factor compatible with that output.

these among all the technically possible combinations of factors? The answer is clear: the same quantity of a commodity can certainly be produced with different quantities of factor *A*, the quantities of the other factors remaining the same, but no entrepreneur will employ three units of *A* if he can obtain the same output with two units. That answer, however, holds only in so far as we can assume that three units of *A* will always be more costly to the entrepreneurs than two units, whatever the system of relative prices. Now, that could not be said if for instance we measured capital by weight: if an entrepreneur can obtain the same results with two alternative and completely different sets of capital goods weighing respectively two and three tons, we have no reason to postulate that he will always use the first rather than the second; the choice will depend on the relative value of the two sets which need not bear any relationship to their relative weight. We cannot therefore have a production function if we cannot postulate some definable relationship between the magnitude measuring capital and the value of the same capital.

Summing up the results of this preliminary analysis of the marginal productivity theories, we can say that the validity of those theories appears to depend on the possibility of measuring capital by a single magnitude satisfying two requirements:

(a) that the 'quantity of capital' constituted by a given physical aggregate of capital goods should not vary simply as a result of changes in distribution; (b) that a definable relationship should exist between the quantity of capital so expressed and the value (in some standard) of the aggregate of capital goods it expresses. These points will be clarified in the following chapters since we shall have to return to them again and again in the course of our examination of Walras's and Wicksell's theories of distribution.

It seems possible to say that the more serious attempts to solve the problem of capital measurement in the marginal productivity theories have been made in two distinct directions characterised by the way in which capital is measured in the production functions: we have, on the one hand, a conception of capital as a set of quantities of capital goods physically defined, and, on the other hand, we have a conception of capital as average period of production or as a set of periods of production. It has seemed to us that the most comprehensive[130] and cogent examples of these attempts are to be found respectively in Walras and in Wicksell. Their theories of distribution have therefore been chosen for examination.

[130] Walras and Wicksell had in common the awareness that the theories of distribution they were expounding were general theories of distribution and had therefore to be formulated in terms of the general equilibrium of the economic system; for only in that setting can all their implications be examined.

Section II, Chapter II: Walras's Theory of the Rate of Interest; Impossibility of Satisfying Simultaneously His Equations of Capitalisation[131]

In Part III of the *Elements of Pure Economics*[132] Walras solves the problem of the pricing of consumers' goods on the assumption that the quantities of them available in the economy are given. He then proceeds, in Part IV, to the analysis of production. There he takes as given the quantities of the various kinds of land, labour and 'capital goods proper' which are the source of corresponding streams of productive services. In Part IV he sets forth the system of equations which determines simultaneously both the prices of consumers' goods and the prices of the productive services of the various physical specifications; that is the wages of different kinds of labour, the gross rents of different kinds of land and the prices of the services of the several types of capital goods.

Part V is the one we have to examine here: it is there that we have Walras's theory of the rate of interest. It takes the form of the determination of the prices of the 'things' whose services (measured as time rates) are the productive services. They are the 'things' which fall within Walras's broader definition of 'capital' which includes, besides capital goods proper, personal and land capitals.

Evidently the determination of the prices of 'capitals', once the prices of their services are determined, is the same thing as the determination of their rate of interest: the rate of interest is governed by the ratios between the two sets of prices.

Walras determines the interest rate exclusively in relation to the 'capital goods proper', since they only, being products, are subject to that law of equality between costs of production and prices which is the centrepiece of Walras's theory of interest. The prices of land and personal capitals are obtained by capitalising the prices of their services at the rate of interest determined for the 'capital goods proper'.[133] It is therefore to 'capital goods proper' that we shall refer in what follows.

Walras first distinguishes between the 'gross' price of a productive service—the one determined in Part IV of the *Elements*—and its 'net' price, obtained by deducting from the 'gross' price given fractions of it μ and ν for, respectively, depreciation and insurance. For our purpose here we can express the two coefficients μ and ν by one coefficient c_k, which is given for each type of capital good (k). The rate of interest or 'rate of net income' is then defined as the ratio between

---

[131] Walras for most of his arguments assumes fixed coefficients of production. On the extent to which it is justified for our purpose to consider his theory as a marginal productivity theory, see Appendix C below.

[132] References will be to W. Jaffé's English edition (London, 1954).

[133] Op. cit., pp. 270–71.

the net price of the annual service of the capital good and the price of the capital good, that is

$$i = \frac{p_k - c_k P_k}{P_k} \tag{I}$$

where i is the rate of interest, p_k is the gross price of the annual service of the capital good, P_k is price of the capital good itself, and c_k has the meaning just defined.[134]

After that, there comes, in the *Elements*, a rather perplexing passage where Walras asserts that if there is neither accumulation nor decumulation of capital in the economy, there can be no rate of interest and no prices of capital goods, because 'these goods could only be exchanged for one another in ratios proportional to their *net* incomes; and such transactions being theoretically without rational motive, could not give rise to any prices of capital goods in terms of *numéraire*'.[135] If there is no price of capital goods how can the capital goods exchange according to their *net* incomes since, as Walras himself has just said, the net incomes are obtained by deducting from the gross incomes the given fractions of the *prices of the capital goods* constituting amortisation and insurance?[136] In fact there appears to be no reason why even in a stationary economy a rate of interest and prices for capital goods should not arise.[137] The origin of this assertion, however, is to be found in the method Walras uses for determining the rate of interest. As we shall presently see the existence of savings is essential to Walras's determination of a single rate of interest. The incorrectness of the above quoted statement appears to be a corollary of his incorrect theory of interest.[138]

---

[134] Op. cit., pp. 268–69.

[135] Op. cit. p. 269 (emphasis in the original).

[136] This contradiction is likely to have survived from the first edition of the *Elements* where it was not evident since the amortisation and insurance, to be deducted from the gross price to obtain the net price, were assumed to be given amounts and not given fractions of the value of capital goods. (Cf., for the change, Jaffé's collation note (b), op. cit., p. 586). It is clear, on the other hand, that the amortisation quota cannot be taken to be a fixed amount in equations which determine, among others, the prices of capital goods.

[137] The only situation in which it would be possible to envisage absence of prices of capital goods would be that of an economy where all capital goods lasted *forever* and where a set of social conventions existed for which they could not be bought and sold for money. What is difficult to see is how such an economy would enable us to apply Walras's other general equilibrium equations. Even if it were possible to imagine a modern economy which is stationary and where capital goods last forever, capital goods would have a price because of individual savings and dissavings cancelling each other out in the economy taken as a whole.

[138] See below, pp. 68–9.

After that passage Walras goes on to show how the interest rate is determined in the case of a progressive economy. As he first announces it, the argument is:

> New capital goods are exchanged against the excess of income over consumption; and the conditions of equality between the value of the new capital goods and the value of the excess, gives us the equation required for the determination of the rate of net income and consequently for the determination of the prices of capital goods. Moreover, new capital goods are products; and the condition of equality between their selling prices and their costs of production gives us the equations required for the determination of the quantities manufactured.[139]

The argument so summarised is developed in the remaining paragraphs of lesson 23 and we shall expound it here briefly. If we have l types of capital goods: K, K', K'', ..., whose selling prices are respectively $P_k, P_{k'}, P_{k''}$, ..., their selling prices will be given by the capitalisation of the net prices of their annual services. We shall therefore have the following equations[140]:

$$\begin{cases} P_k = \frac{p_k}{i+c_k} \\ P_{k'} = \frac{p_{k'}}{i+c_{k'}} \\ \dots\dots \\ \dots\dots \\ \dots\dots \end{cases} \qquad \text{(II)}$$

On the other hand, in competitive equilibrium, the selling prices will have to be equal to the costs of production of the new capital goods. If $k_p, k_{p'}, \dots, k_t, k_{t'}, \dots, k_k, k_{k'}, \dots$, are the n invariable coefficients of production for capital goods of type K[141]; if $k'_p, k'_{p'}, \dots, k'_k, k'_{k'} \dots$, are similarly the coefficients of production for a capital good of type K' etc., and if $p_p, p_{p'}, \dots, p_t, p_{t'}, \dots, p_k, p_{k'}, \dots$, are the n gross prices for the yearly services of the productive services of types $P, P', \dots, T, T', \dots, K, K', \dots$, we shall have the following other l equations[142]:

$$\begin{cases} P_k = k_p p_p + k_{p'} p_{p'} + \cdots + k_t p_t + k_{t'} p_{t'} + \cdots + k_k p_k + k_{k'} p_{k'} + \cdots \\ P_{k'} = k'_p p_p + k'_{p'} p_{p'} + \cdots + k'_t p_t + k'_{t'} p_{t'} + \cdots + k'_k p_k + k'_{k'} p_{k'} + \cdots \\ \dots\dots \\ \dots\dots \\ \dots\dots \end{cases} \qquad \text{(III)}$$

139 Op. cit., pp. 269–70. See also a similar statement in the preface to the fourth edition (op. cit., p. 46).

140 Op. cit., p. 272. From Eq. (I) above we have $iP_k + c_k P_k = p_k$; hence $P_k = \frac{p_k}{i+c_k}$.

141 Coefficients of production are the quantities of productive services of types $P, P', \dots, T, T', \dots, K, K', \dots$, entering the production of a unit of the good in question, in this case one capital good of type K.

142 Op. cit., p. 271.

Walras then introduces the condition of the equality between gross savings[143] and total value of the new capital goods currently produced, both magnitudes being measured as all other value quantities, in terms of the commodity 'numeraire' A. For that purpose he defines a commodity (E) as 'perpetual net income', the price of which—that is the price to be paid for a perpetual net income of 1 numeraire unit—is evidently the reciprocal of the interest rate: $p_e = \frac{1}{i}$. The aggregate demand D_e for such a commodity in the whole economy is given as a function of the entire system of prices and of the rate of interest: in fact both the incomes of the potential savers and their choices as to the allocation of their incomes between savings and consumption depend on those prices. So that we shall have:

$$D_e = F'_e(p_b p_c \ldots p_m, p_p \ldots p_t \ldots p_k \ldots i)$$

The total amount of savings E will be given in any situation by the quantity of commodity E demanded, that is D_e, times its price p_e: $E = D_e p_e$. Since p_e is the reciprocal of the rate of interest, we can write the equation:

$$E = F_e(p_b p_c \ldots p_m, p_p \ldots p_t \ldots p_k \ldots i) \qquad \text{(IV)}$$

On the other hand total savings E must also be equal in equilibrium to the value of all the new capital goods produced during the period. If the quantities produced of new capital goods of types K, K', K'' …, are respectively D_k, $D_{k'}$, $D_{k''}$, …, we shall have one more equation[144]:

$$E = D_k P_k + D_{k'} P_{k'} + D_{k''} P_{k''} + \cdots \qquad \text{(V)}$$

In systems (II) and (III), and in Eqs. (IV) and (V), we have in total $(2l + 2)$ equations which, Walras concludes, will together determine the $(2l + 2)$ unknowns that the problem of capital formation ('capitalisation') has introduced in the equations of general equilibrium, namely the l prices of capital goods proper: P_k, $P_{k'}$, $P_{k''}$, …; the l quantities of them newly produced in the period: D_k, $D_{k'}$, $D_{k''}$, …; the amount of gross savings E, and the rate of interest i.[145]

For convenience of reference in the remainder of our argument, we can eliminate the unknowns P_k, $P_{k'}$, $P_{k''}$, …. by substituting the values for them given by system (II) into system (III), obtaining the following system:

$$\begin{cases} \dfrac{p_k}{i + c_k} = k_p p_p + \cdots + k_t p_t + \cdots + k_k p_k + \cdots \\ \dfrac{p_{k'}}{i + c_{k'}} = k'_p p_p + \cdots + k'_t p_t + \cdots + k'_k p_k + \cdots \\ \ldots\ldots \\ \ldots\ldots \end{cases} \qquad \text{(A)}$$

---

[143] Gross savings are intended, because they include all excess of gross income over consumption.

[144] Op. cit., pp. 275–76.

[145] Op. cit., Sect. 243, p. 276.

Similarly, we can eliminate E in Eq. (V) by using the value of it given by Eq. (IV):

$$F_e(p_b \ldots p_m, p_p \ldots, p_t \ldots p_k \ldots, i) = D_k P_k + D_{k'} P_{k'} + \ldots \tag{B}$$

We are then left with $(l + 1)$ equations to determine the $(l + 1)$ unknowns[146]: the rate of interest and the quantities of capital goods newly produced. But the fact that the number of independent equations is equal to the number of the unknowns to be determined is not, of course, by itself a guarantee that those equations can determine those unknowns. Our criticism of the theory we have expounded will in fact aim at two conclusions.

First, we shall attempt to show that since Walras takes as data the quantities of each type of capital good available for use in production in the economy, it will be impossible, in general, to satisfy simultaneously the two equilibrium conditions:

(a) that the selling prices of all the capital goods should be equal to their costs of production;
(b) that the rates of net income (rates of interest) on all the capital goods should be the same.

Secondly, we shall try to show that the attempt Walras makes to bring about equality between the rates of net income on the capital goods involves him in a mis-conception of the way in which the quantities of newly produced capital goods are determined in an equilibrium situation.

We have said that in system (A) and in Eq. (B) the unknowns are the quantities of new capital goods D_k $D_{k'}$ ..., and the rate of interest i. Let us have a closer look at the other variables appearing in the equations.

We have first of all a number (ln) of production coefficients: k_p ... k_t ... k_k ...; $k'_p \ldots k'_t \ldots k'_k \ldots; k''_p \ldots k''_t \ldots k''_p \ldots$. These coefficients are taken by Walras as given at this stage of the argument. The l constants c_k $c_{k'}$ $c_{k''}$ ..., are also taken by Walras as given.

We are then left with the $(m + n - 1)$ prices of both consumers' goods and productive services: p_b... p_p... p_t ... p_k .... These prices cannot be immediately taken as a given in the determination of the rate of interest and of the quantities of new capital goods produced. The reason is the following one. In Walras the achievement of equilibrium in the capital market will require two kinds of adjustments: (a) changes in the total value of new capital goods so as to equalise it to gross savings (see Eq. (B)); (b) changes in the relative outputs of the various types of capital goods. These adjustments will involve shifting productive services between the different branches of the economy, and such shifts may bring about changes in the prices of the productive services (and hence, in the prices of consumers' goods) if the overall proportions in which the services are employed in the sectors are different.

If that is so, the question to be answered before deciding whether or not we can take as given the prices of services and goods appearing in Eqs. (A) and (B)

---

[146] Instead of P_k $P_{k'}$ we could have put on the RHS of Eq. (B) either the LHS or the RHS of the appropriate equation of system (A).

is: is there any reason to assume that the differences in the proportions of productive services employed in the sectors affected by the adjustments are such as to make of the resulting changes in the prices of the services and goods an element of appreciable importance in the process by which equilibrium is achieved in the capital market? If the answer is negative we can, as a first approximation, neglect the variations of the prices of goods and services when dealing with the problems of equilibrium in the capital market. And this appears to be the case in point here. It seems that those variations will in general be of the type which is usually ignored in economic analysis.[147]

It appears therefore that we can here assume the $(m + n - 1)$ prices appearing in Eqs. (A) and (B) to be given. It is now easy to show what we wanted.

In the l equations of system (A), all variables can be taken as given but for one: the rate of interest i. We have a case of overdetermination: we have l independent equations and one unknown. Except by a chance depending on the data determining the equilibrium system, system (A) will not determine one interest rate; it will determine as many rates of net income as there are capital goods. The reason for this can be easily seen in intuitive terms. Among the data Walras takes to determine the whole equilibrium system of prices we have the quantities available of each kind of capital good: the $q_k\ q_{k'}\ q_{k''}$ .... owned by individuals in the community.[148] Given those quantities, the prices of the productive services of the capital goods will be determined simultaneously with the prices of other productive services (and of consumers' goods) on the basis of the system of preferences of the consumers, and there is no reason why they should bear a uniform ratio to the costs of production of the capital goods.

Passing now to Eq. (B) we meet there two difficulties. First, what will be the rate of interest to be put on the RHS of the equation? Since there will not be a unique ratio between the cost of production of the capital good and the net price of its service, we shall not have, until some other assumption is introduced, a unique rate of interest.[149] Secondly, even if one rate of interest can be put on the RHS of Eq. (B), we should not be able to determine the l quantities $D_k\ D_{k'}\ D_{k''}$ ... since we have l unknowns in one equation. This is only to be expected since, in each equilibrium situation, the distribution of net savings between the different types of capital goods newly produced, will presumably depend, if an equilibrium must be maintained, on the shape of the marginal productivity curves of the capital goods on the right

---

[147] We shall deal further with this point in the following chapter, where we shall examine also the hypothesis of highly specialised factors of production.

[148] Op. cit., pp. 238–9.

[149] Any rate of interest we might choose would call forth the corresponding amount of savings, so that the equation would always be satisfied. In fact we could say, using approximate terms, and ignoring effects of secondary importance, that Eq. (B), when correctly interpreted, would determine the *amount* of savings called forth at the rate of interest (and system of prices) determined by the marginal productivity of capital goods. This would be strictly true if variations in the amount of savings and in the relative outputs of the capital goods in course of production did not affect the prices of the productive services.

of the present point of equilibrium; relatively more units will be produced of the capital goods whose marginal productivity function is more elastic.[150,151] Walras does not introduce in Eqs. (A) and (B) data referring to such elasticities; it is therefore not surprising to find that the relative outputs of new capital goods cannot be determined. The idea that those equations can determine the relative outputs of new capital goods seems to be founded on a misconception of the forces which, in equilibrium, regulate the amounts of new capital goods produced. This misconception is related to Walras's attempts to show that one ratio between costs of capital goods and net prices of their productive services can be determined in his system. We shall have therefore occasion to return on this point in the following chapter where we shall examine in detail how far Walras appears to have been aware of the difficulty of determining one rate of interest, and how he thought it could be shown that one rate of interest is determined within his system of equations.

Section II, Chapter III: Criticism of Walras's Detailed Analysis of How Equilibrium in the Capital Markets Is Reached; Conclusions on Walras's Theory of Capital and Distribution

Walras was aware that all was not well with his equations for the equilibrium of the capital market.

In Lesson 23, he does not go further than the statement already quoted:

> [N]ew capital goods are products; and the condition of equality between their selling price and their cost of production gives us the equations required for the determination of the quantities manufactured.[152]

The statement is further elucidated only by the following passage referring to the selling prices of the capital goods:

> If their selling price is greater than their cost of production, the quantity produced will increase and their selling price will fall; if their selling price is lower than their cost of production the quantity produced will diminish and their selling price will rise.[153]

---

[150] This evidently refers to the allocation of *net* savings. The allocation of the amounts devoted to replacement will be predetermined, in an equilibrium situation, by the need to replace the capital goods of different types which have come to the end of their productive life during the period.

[151] It might be objected that the existence of net savings in itself would contradict the conditions of equilibrium: if the relevant economic quantities are expected to change, the relationship between them cannot be formulated only in terms of their values at a given moment; expected values should also be taken into account. But, of course, this would reduce to very little, if anything, the possibilities of useful static economic analysis; a less restrictive concept of equilibrium where the possibility of net savings is allowed for must be referred to.

[152] Op. cit., pp. 269–70.

[153] Op. cit., p. 271.

Walras does not explain, there or after, why the *selling price* should fall or rise as the quantity of the capital good which is being produced rises or falls. In fact the idea expressed in the passage is incorrect, and he himself will contradict it in Lesson 25.[154] By the selling price of capital goods which can be above or below the respective costs of production, Walras means the prices of the capital goods determined by the equations he gives (at p. 272) and corresponding to our system above: they are determined by the price of the annual services and by the rate of interest. Now there is no reason why these prices should be significantly affected by changes in the relative outputs of new capital goods: the price of the annual service depends on the quantity of the capital good which is *already in existence* and not on the quantity of it which is being currently produced and has not therefore yet been employed in production[155]; the rate of interest, on the other hand, is not affected by changes in the relative outputs of capital goods which leave unchanged the total amount currently saved. There is in particular no reason why the selling price of a capital good should fall or rise as the quantity of it currently produced rises or falls.[156,157]

---

[154] In Lesson 25, Walras tries to show how the equations are in fact solved by the 'groping' in the relevant markets. There he refers to the effect on the selling price of a new capital good of changes in the relative outputs of new capital goods: thus 'all these substitutions can hardly affect the rate of net income and consequently can hardly affect the selling price in any significant degree' (p. 293). For an explanation of this contradiction see n. 156 below.

[155] As Walras himself clearly states, 'Although the economy is becoming *progressive*, it remains (for the time being) *static* because of the fact that the new capital goods play no part in the economy until later in a period subsequent to the one under consideration' (op. cit., p. 283, emphasis in the original).

[156] Expectations are evidently ruled out by the hypothesis of static equilibrium on which the equations are based.

[157] The passage we have commented upon is interesting because it may provide a clue to the root of Walras's error in the theory of interest. One may advance the hypothesis that Walras at first thought of the equalisation between selling prices and costs of production of the new capital goods, on the basis of an incorrect analogy with the case of consumption goods. There changes in the relative outputs of the goods do affect relative selling prices (see op. cit., pp. 244–7). It was probably only in the later development of his thought on the subject, that Walras became fully aware of the difference between the two cases: prices of consumption goods depend on the relative time rates of output or relative outputs of the goods, whereas prices of productive services depend on the relative quantities of the capital goods already in existence. When he became aware of the difference he had, in order to defend the theory, to shift the entire weight of the equalisation between selling prices and costs for capital goods on a rise or fall of the *costs* as the relative output of a capital good rises or falls. A weight which, when Walras's argument is cleared of some misunderstandings, the cost cannot bear. The hypothesis we have advanced, while it makes it easier to understand how Walras could resort to the unsatisfactory arguments we shall be examining in the text, can be supported by some evidence which should, however, be integrated, before reaching conclusions on the point, by a closer comparison of successive editions than I have had the possibility of doing. The evidence can be summarised in the following points:

(A) The striking contradiction between the passage we have criticised, and which appears to have been at that point of the argument since the first edition of that part of the *Elements*

The difficulties hidden behind those propositions appear in Lesson 25, where Walras attempts to describe how through successive adjustments in prices and quantities the market will move towards an equilibrium where all the Eqs. (A) and (B) are simultaneously satisfied. As Walras himself says: 'it is not immediately apparent, as it was in the case of the inequality between selling prices and the costs of production of consumers' goods, how changes [in the quantities of new capital goods manufactured] can bring [selling prices and costs of production] into

---

(cf. also the earliest version of the theory of interest in *Théorie Mathématique de la Richesse Sociale*, Lausanne 1883, pp. 87–88), and the passage of Lesson 25 quoted above (n. 154) which is part of a drastically changed argument first introduced in the fourth edition (cf. Jaffé's collation note (n) at p. 594, op. cit.). The first passage speaks only of selling prices rising or falling with changes in the outputs of capital goods, so that one is led to believe that the equalisation between selling prices and costs will be achieved mainly by the variation of selling prices; the second passage, and the argument of which it is a part, supposes the equalisation to be brought about entirely by the variation of costs of production.

(B) The passage in question may well have remained in the fourth edition by mistake. In fact a striking change occurred in the fourth edition of the *Elements* as regards the mechanism by which selling prices and costs of production of new capital goods are brought into equality. Before the fourth edition the equalisation had been thought to result from selling prices falling and costs of production rising as the quantity newly produced of a capital good increased. As expressed in the earliest version of the theory—a paper delivered in the winter 1875-6, at Lausanne—the argument was: 'si on augmente ou diminue la quantité D_k on augmente ou diminue légèrement, d'une part, les prix de tous les services producteurs qui entrent dans la confection du capital (*K*), c'est-à-dire qu'on augmente ou diminue sensiblement le prix de revient de ce capital exprimé par le premier membre de la … inégalité, tandis qu'on diminue ou augmente sensiblement, d'autre part, le prix du revenue producteur (*K*), c'est-à-dire qu'on augmente ou diminue sensiblement le prix de vente du même capital exprimé par le second membre de cette même inégalité' (*Théorie Mathématique de la Richesse Sociale*, pp. 102–3). Walras does not say *why* the price of the productive service of (*K*) should decrease as the quantity of it in course of production increases: he probably took that for granted, on the basis of the analogy with consumption goods. That argument seems to have remained fundamentally the same in the first three editions of the *Elements*. It was only before the fourth edition that Walras must have realised that there is no reason why the price of the productive service should decrease (or increase) as the quantity of the capital good in course of production in the situation considered increases (or decreases). Accordingly the whole weight is then thrown on the costs, and the argument becomes the one we shall criticise in the text (see for a summary of this change from the third to fourth edition, Jaffé's collation note already mentioned).

(C) The significant Sect. 267 (p. 308), to which we shall refer in the text and where reservations are made about the possibility of satisfying simultaneously all the equations of system (A), appeared for the first time in the fourth edition. It is also in the fourth edition that, in Section 258, the possibility is admitted that the quantities of some types of capital goods produced will be zero, an admission which implies the impossibility of equalising their prices to their costs.

(D) More generally, the extensive changes that the whole of this part of the *Elements* underwent between the third and fourth edition and, earlier, between the first and second edition, seem to point to a dissatisfaction of Walras with this part of his theory.

equality with each other', since 'it is not obvious at first glance that these selling prices and costs of production are functions of the quantities manufactured of new capital goods'.[158]

In order however to demonstrate that selling prices and costs of production are in fact functions of the quantities manufactured Walras enters into a chain of substitutions in the equations of general equilibrium the aim of which, stated in economic terms, is to bring out that the prices of productive services are functions of the relative quantities produced of all the goods and so, among the others, of the quantities of new capital goods manufactured.[159] Using this relationship Walras transforms the equations of system (A) into equations where $D_k\ D_{k'}\ D_{k''}$ ... appear, and he proceeds to attempt to demonstrate that the l equations so obtained can be used to determine the l quantities of new capital goods produced.[160] What is there in Walras's argument? It appears that the only thing that there can be is what we had occasion to mention above (pp. 60–1) when we said that the prices of productive services (and consumers' goods) could not strictly be taken as given when relative outputs of new capital goods change: to the extent in which the proportions of the productive services employed in the sectors involved in the adjustments necessary to fulfil Eqs. (A) and (B) differ, the prices of the productive services will undergo some change as a result of the adjustments. We decided there that we could, at that stage in the argument, take those prices as given since there appears to be no reason why the differences between the proportions of factors employed in the relevant sectors should be such as to make the resulting variations in the costs of production of the new capital goods an element of appreciable importance for the equilibrium in the capital markets.

The variation of the costs of production of new capital goods due to that cause are, however, all that remains of Walras's arguments that changes in the relative outputs of the new capital goods will equalize the rates of net income on all types

---

158 Op. cit., pp. 290–1.

159 In fact the substitutions indicated by Walras (op. cit., p. 291) amount to the following procedure. The basic system is the one of the (n) equations stating the equality between quantities of productive services employed and quantities offered (system (4) in Walras). Now, the quantities offered for productive use expressed on the RHS depend on the prices both of the productive services and of the consumption goods; but since the prices of consumption goods must in equilibrium be equal to their costs (Walras's system (5)) they can be expressed in terms of the prices of productive services, so that on the RHS of the basic system the only prices appearing are those for productive services. On the LHS, the quantities of productive services employed depend on the quantities produced both of consumption goods and of new capital goods; the consumption goods produced depend both on their prices and on the prices of productive services (on the latter prices consumers' incomes depend) and since the former category of prices can be expressed in terms of the latter by using the costs of production equations, it follows that the quantities of productive services employed in production can be expressed as functions only of the quantities of new capital goods and of the prices of productive services. Taking now LHS and RHS of the equations of the basic system so transformed we can express the price of each productive service as a function of the quantities of new capital goods.

160 Op. cit., pp. 291ff.

of capital goods, once Walras's arguments have been freed from the errors we shall mention presently.

After the chain of substitutions mentioned above Walras proceeds to argue his case in some more detail. He begins by saying:

> if we increase indefinitely the prices of all productive services which are used in the manufacture of a capital good, and consequently raise its cost of production, we cause the offer of these services, and therefore the quantity manufactured of this capital good, first to increase from zero and then to fall to zero again (at infinity). In other words, the quantity manufactured of a capital good is a function which first increases from zero and then decreases to zero (at infinity) as the cost of production ... increases. It is precisely this law of variation of the quantity manufactured as a function of the cost of production which enables us to bring the cost of production and the selling prices of new capital goods into equality with each other.[161]

We can stop and examine the first sentence of the passage. Why should the increase here considered in the quantity manufactured of a capital good, imply an increase in the total quantities available for productive purposes of 'all' the services employed in the manufacture of the capital good?[162]

Walras himself assumes in the remainder of Section 257 and in Section 258 that the groping he is studying involves only changes in the *relative* outputs of the l new capital goods[163]: in that case the quantities of productive services required for increasing the output of a type of capital good, would be freed by a corresponding reduction in the output of one or more other types of capital goods. It is true that if the proportions of factors employed in the sectors involved are different, some factors will become scarcer and some more abundant. The prices of productive services would then change in opposite directions, and, with the elastic supply of productive services assumed by Walras, the supply of them available for productive use might also change in opposite directions. But even then we shall not have that increase in prices and quantities available of '*all* productive services' of which Walras speaks. The introduction of supply functions of the productive services only helps to obscure the issue which is one of *relative* changes in outputs.

The only other passage in which Walras tries to explain how Eq. (A) can be simultaneously satisfied in equilibrium is the following one:

> Let Δ_k be the quantity of capital good (K) to be manufactured which, when substituted for D'_k in the process of groping will render the two sides of the first inequality ... equal [see

[161] Op. cit., p. 292.

[162] It is evidently this total quantity of a productive service which, due to the assumed possibility of direct use of the service by his owner, rises from zero as the price of the productive service increases.

[163] He does so by assuming that profits and losses due to disparity between prices and costs compensate each other in the production of new capital goods (op. cit., p. 292). Even if the process of groping to fulfil equations (A) involves increases in the quantities of all or most of the new capital goods produced the output of consumers goods would have to be simultaneously decreased and the additional quantities of productive services required for the capital goods would come from the consumers' goods sectors.

system (A)†]; let $\Delta_{k'} = 0$ for the moment, on the assumption that the cost of production of the capital good (K') is greater than its selling price; and let $\Delta_{k''}$ be the quantity of the capital good (K'') to be manufactured which, when substituted by groping for $D'_{k''}$ renders the two sides of the third inequality equal ... It is immediately seen that for any capital good, let us say (K): (1) the substitution of Δ_k for D'_k of (K) must raise its cost of production appreciably, (2) the substitution of zero for $D'_{k'}$ of (K') and for all the other quantities of capital goods which are discontinued cannot lower the cost of production of (K) at all significantly, (3) the substitution of $\Delta_{k''}$ for $D'_{k''}$ of (K'') and similar substitutions of quantities of capital goods which will continue to be manufactured cannot increase the cost of production of (K) very much, and (4) all these substitutions can hardly change the rate of net income and consequently can hardly affect the selling price in any significant degree. Under these circumstances, it is possible that the effect of changes in the output of any new capital good making for equality between the cost of production of that capital good and its selling price will be stronger than the contrary effect of interrelated changes in the output of other capital goods, tending towards the undoing of that equality.[164]

Let us have a closer look at the second sentence of the passage, to see what follows that rather misleading 'it is immediately seen'. For convenience of exposition let us group the l types of new capital goods into two divisions: those like (K) and (K") whose output will be increased in the process of adjustment, and those like (K') whose output will be diminished or reduced to zero. Now, the cases are two: either the proportions in which the n productive services enter these two groups of capital goods, considered as a whole, are the same, or they are not.

In the first case the consequences indicated by Walras under (l) (2) (3) will not take place, the costs of production of each capital good will not vary as its output changes. Changes in the relative outputs will therefore fail to equalise the rates of net income on the l types of capital goods.

We must then fall back on the second case even if Walras has not specified that his argument relates only to it, nor has given us any reason why the relevant proportions of production coefficients should of necessity be different. In that case the price of some productive services will rise while that of others will fall [165]; the costs of production of each type of capital good will increase with its output since the effect on it of the fall in the price of some services will be more than compensated by the rise in the price of the other factors. It appears then that in this case there will be some variations of the costs of production of capital goods in the directions indicated in Walras's points (l) (2) and (3). But was Walras justified in concluding

† [*Editor's note*: the addition of the superscript '" for the quantities and prices Walras refers to in this context, as distinctive from his system (A), reflects the premise that the magnitudes he is here dealing with are supposed to be 'determined at random' (cf. *Elements*, para. 252).]

[164] Op. cit., p. 293.

[165] These propositions about the behaviour of the prices of factors are founded on the assumption that the 'numeraire' is produced with proportions of the productive services intermediate between those of the two groups of capital goods. But the assumptions about the 'numeraire' are here of importance only for the exposition: what is important for the argument is the change in the relative values of the two groups of capital goods.

that those variations could be such as to guarantee the simultaneous equalisation of prices and costs for all capital goods? It seems that the only hypothesis under which the variations of costs of production could approach the magnitude required by Walras's argument, would be that the services required for each kind of capital good are so highly specialised that all or most of them can be employed only in the production of that capital good. But in that case we should meet immediately other difficulties as basic as the one we are trying to avoid: if the productive services are highly specialised we shall no longer have that substitutability between services which is the essential postulate of any marginal productivity theory. So, in all likelihood, we shall have indeterminacy of the prices of services arising from the number of factors being higher than the number of commodities in which they enter[166]; this cause of indeterminacy refers to the case of fixed production coefficients, but in so far as the highly specialised services envisaged here are concerned, the production coefficients can hardly be thought to be anything but fixed.[167]

It appears then that that hypothesis should be discarded since it seems to fill one gap in the theory only at the cost of opening another one not less wide.

We are then left with a conception of the productive services sufficiently wide to allow each one of them to be employed in all or most industries. But that is also the case in which the variations of the costs of production as the outputs of new capital goods change, are likely to be very small. It becomes then evidently impossible to assume that the process envisaged by Walras can bring about the equalization of costs of production and selling prices.

But the main criticism to be levelled against Walras's theory is not so much the impossibility of bringing about the equalization of the rates of interest on different capital goods. It is rather that his methods for bringing about such equalization is founded on a misconception of what determines in an equilibrium situation the distribution of savings between the different capital goods producible. In fact even if we assumed that through sufficiently large changes in the relative outputs of new capital goods the rates of net income can be equalized, the possibility of actually bringing about such equalization would depend on the size of the current amount

[166] See below, Appendix C.

[167] Or even if that cause of indeterminacy could be somehow avoided, changes in the relative demands for capital goods could hardly affect the quantities produced since, for Walras, the quantities of productive services available are given; the only effect of such changes in demand would be drastic variations in the prices of the specialised services, including those for capital goods. The implausibility of such results in a theory of distribution which should, as a general theory, be a 'long run' analysis, is evident. Further, in the situation envisaged here, also the prices of the productive services of the capital goods newly produced, far from being 'hardly affected' as Walras says in point (4) of the above quoted passage, would be considerably affected, one way or the other, to the extent in which that type of capital good is employed for producing capital goods. The effect on the selling price of the capital goods of these variations in the price of the services wlll be magnified by the capitalization, and it is therefore conceivable that the selling prices of some capital goods would, as the outputs of them change, move in the same direction as the costs, but more rapidly, thereby widening and not narrowing the gap between costs and prices.

of savings: the greater the time rate of savings, the more likely that the equality will be achieved since the possible changes of the relative outputs can be larger. This brings us to the surprising conclusion that the very existence of one rate of interest (and of the equality between costs and prices of capital goods) and hence the very existence of equilibrium at the moment considered, depends on whether or not the savings which are being simultaneously made are above a certain minimum level. There is evidently something wrong with the procedure which forces us to this conclusion.

The flaw is in the idea that the allocation of savings between different types of capital goods is determined, in a situation of equilibrium, by a necessity of equalizing the rates of net income through changes in their costs of production. If there is equilibrium the rates of net income on all producible capital goods must be equal whether net savings are being simultaneously made or not: the net savings will be allocated between the capital goods according to the relative elasticities of the respective marginal productivity functions if equilibrium is to be maintained as the new capital goods enter production.[168]

On the other hand the mechanism by which the rates of net income on capital goods are equalized, while satisfying at the same time the condition of equality between the prices of capital goods and their costs of production, will have to be looked for in another direction. The relative quantities of capital goods available in the economy in the equilibrium situations ought to be considered as unknowns in the general equilibrium equations and not to be taken as data as Walras does. It will then be the variability of the relative quantities of capital goods in existence which will bring the marginal productivities of their services and therefore the net prices of those services, into a uniform ratio with the costs of production of the capital goods: a ratio which will also be the equilibrium rate of interest. In other words, in order to obtain a single equilibrium rate of interest, it is necessary to allow the physical capital goods to be transformed into each other in the process of achieving equilibrium, and accordingly the quantities of them existing in the equilibrium situation can be determined, if at all, only simultaneously with the rate of interest and the general system of prices. This in turn requires a conception of that total 'quantity' of capital available in the economy, which for the marginal productivity theories is one of the main determinants of distribution (and prices), as a single magnitude which can freely assume the form of any physical capital good like a fluid which can be freely poured from one container into another.[169]

[168] For the allocation, in that situation, of the part of gross savings constituting the replacement of capital see above, n. 150.

[169] It is not difficult to indicate schematically how the determination of the rate of interest would take place within the theory so reformulated. The unknowns introduced would be $(l+1)$: the quantities of each type of capital good in existence in equilibrium and the rate of interest. The determining equations would be the l of system (A) above, establishing *equality in the rates of net income*, and one equation stating the equality between the 'quantity' of capital constituted by the quantities of capital goods of different types in existence in equilibrium, and the given 'quantity' of capital available in the economy.

Walras in the fourth edition of the *Elements*, seems to have come close to realising the deficiency affecting his theory of capital and interest.[170] In a significant passage of Section 267, a section first introduced in that edition,[171] he says: "In an economy like the one we have imagined, which establishes equilibrium *ab ovo*, it is probable that there would be no equality of rates of net income". This amounts to saying that the situation examined will not be an equilibrium one. But then, we can ask, what will be the usefulness of the system of prices so determined, if it is recognised not to be the equilibrium system of prices? We should be referring to a hybrid situation where all is supposed to conform to equilibrium, but for the relative quantities of capital goods of different types. It seems that if we allow time for all quantities to conform to equilibrium, and that implies for instance allowing the time necessary for the capital goods of the same type to be allocated between industries so as to receive the same prices for their services, then also the relative quantities of capital goods will have tended to change so as to conform to the condition of a uniform rate of net income, and the resulting system of prices will be different from the one we have determined. On the other hand, if we do not allow sufficient time for the relative quantities of the various kinds of capital goods to change, it appears that there will be no possibility of the other quantities conforming to the equilibrium conditions either; in that case the system of prices in the economy to which the data refer could be anything. It seems therefore hardly possible to interpret the results of such a theory of prices and distribution even as referring only to a usefully defined situation of temporary equilibrium: there does not seem to be much reason why the time necessary to shift physical resources of all kinds between all industries should be appreciably shorter than the time required for the changes in the relative quantities of the physical capital goods. And, in any case, it seems that such a definition of equilibrium, even if possible, could not be accepted as the setting for a general theory of distribution. After the sentence we have just commented upon, Walras continues:

> On the other hand, in an economy in normal operation, which has only to maintain itself in equilibrium, we may suppose the last l equations [corresponding to system (A) in our exposition] to be satisfied.

This statement does not seem to go beyond the tautology: in equilibrium there will be equilibrium. If the economy *is* in equilibrium, then, by the definition itself of equilibrium on which the general equilibrium equations are built, there is equality in the rates of net income on the capital goods, that is the equations of system (A) are all simultaneously satisfied. But then in order to determine a single rate of interest (in order, that is, to satisfy simultaneously all the equations of system (A)) some of the data, the quantities of capital goods available, must be known to be the ones compatible with the equilibrium situation.

[170] Cf. above, n. 157, for a hypothesis on the origin of Walras's inconsistencies in the theory of capital and interest.

[171] See Jaffé's collation note (a), *Elements*, p. 599.

If the data from which we start depend on the equilibrium quantities we aim to determine, if, in other words, in choosing the data we must know already that they refer to an established equilibrium position, we shall be moving in a vicious circle. Our theory, it seems, will enable us only to determine an equilibrium system of prices, if we have already an economy in equilibrium from which to take the data; but then we shall be determining what we know already: the system of prices ruling in the economy from which we have taken the data. Instead of taking the data we could have taken directly the system of prices. For instance, if we had to examine the problem of how the raising of certain general tariffs, or the introduction of a certain general tax, is likely to affect wages and interest rates, we should be able to say very little, since we could not determine what the situation of equilibrium will be *after* the change has occurred: to determine such a situation we should need to know already what the allocation of the existing 'quantity of capital', or any other 'quantity of capital', will be between the various types of capital goods in the new equilibrium situation; an allocation which we shall not know and have no way of finding out until the new equilibrium situation has actually come about. To solve this problem we should need to take among the data not the quantities of capital goods in existence; we should need instead to take as datum a 'quantity of capital' measured in such a way that it can freely assume the form of different capital goods.

We are now in a condition to draw some conclusions from our examination of Walras's theory. In the first place, if our argument is right, it can be said that Walras's theory gives us no satisfactory determination of the rate of interest and, with it, of the prices of all productive services.[172] This is so because one of the assumptions on which the theory is built—that the quantities of the several kinds of existing capital goods are among the data—is incompatible with the determination of the equilibrium price system: either we determine distribution and, more in general, the price system, for a situation which cannot be one of equilibrium, or we shall have to take some of the determining quantities from a situation of equilibrium already established in economic reality, in which case, it appears, the theory, considered as a general theory of distribution, moves in a circle.

In the second place, it appears that this deficiency of Walras's theory can be overcome only to the extent in which the quantities of physically homogeneous capital goods in existence in the economy can be taken as unknowns in the system of equations of general equilibrium; and the extent to which this can be done depends on the possibility of measuring the datum 'quantity of capital available in the economy' in terms of one magnitude which can take the form of any of the capital goods. We are therefore faced again with the problem of measuring capital indicated in Chapter I of this section. Walras's theory solves it, in so far as that measurement is required in the production functions,[173] by referring to physical

[172] As a consequence also the determination of the system of relative prices of commodities is not satisfactory to the extent in which it depends on data (like the quantities of capital goods available in the economy) inconsistent with an equilibrium situation.

[173] In so far, that is, as we need quantities of capital for the production coefficients, whether those coefficients are taken to be fixed or variable.

quantities of capital goods of different kinds. But the problem arises again in connection with the measurement of the given quantity of capital in existence, since there the measurement in terms of a set of quantities contrasts with the existence, in competitive equilibrium, of a single rate of interest on all types of capital goods. The question outlined here is strictly analogous to the one we shall meet again in discussing the theory of distribution that Wicksell put forward in the *Lectures*. Here as there the problem of the measurement of capital is solved, in so far as that measurement is required in the production functions, by a measurement in terms of a set of quantities: in Walras's case physical quantities of capital goods, in Wicksell's case absolute periods of production of labour and land. But in both cases this measurement fails when applied to the quantity of capital existing in the economy and the problem of adequate measurement reappears. Wicksell thought it could be solved by referring to a value measurement of capital. The deficiency of Walras's theory could also be easily overcome if we could measure the capital existing in the economy in value terms. But such a measurement would meet the same difficulties we shall examine below when discussing Wicksell's solution.[174]

[174] It seems rather surprising that, as far as I have been able to see, the inconsistency of Walras's theory discussed here, has not been pointed out in the critical literature on that work. G. J. Stigler, in his *Production and Distribution Theories*, summarizes Walras's argument without comment (pp. 248–50), and his criticisms of the theory of capital and interest (pp. 254–55) do not touch upon the issue we have examined. Schumpeter also, in his *History of Economic Analysis* (New York, 1954) seems to have taken for granted the internal consistency of Walras's arguments. He affirms that in the theory of capital formation Walras arrived, 'as regards determinateness and stability, to results analogous to those arrived at in the cases of multi-commodity exchange and of production' (p. 1018). Among the earlier critics, Wicksell might perhaps be seen not to be very far from the point raised here when, in *Value, Capital and Rent* (London, 1954) he says: 'If only durable goods are regarded as capital then a certain *rent* is fixed for each group of these by the above-mentioned equations, but *not* the *capital value* of the goods itself, nor, consequently, the *rate* of interest either...' (p. 167, emphases in the original). But the point so formulated does not seem to hold since, as we have seen, there is no difficulty in calculating the costs of production and values of capital goods in Walras's theory. The suspicion that Wicksell's criticism may be founded on a misunderstanding of Walras is strengthened by the reason he adduces for that criticism: 'Walras calls capital and treats as 'capital' *only* durable goods, but not raw materials and half finished products and not the means of subsistence of workers. What the owner of the circulating capital advances to the workers, landowners, etc., is therefore not treated by Walras as capital at all. It is therefore implicitly assumed by Walras that workers and other producers maintain themselves during production and receive remuneration for their productive services from the proceeds of the products in question only after completion of the production. This is obviously incorrect. In this interpretation the true role of capital is completely overlooked' (*ibid.*, emphasis in the original). This criticism of Walras's approach to capital does not appear to be justified. Wicksell does not seem to see that periods of production and quantities of concrete capital goods assisting the 'original factors' in order to render simultaneous the inputs of those factors and the corresponding outputs of produce are but two ways of measuring capital which are, a priori, equally legitimate. And if we choose the second, there is no question of capital being 'advances' for the payment of original factors, since the application of the productive services and the produce obtained are simultaneous and so the factors can be paid out of current production. The important problem in comparing the two approaches to the measurement of capital is elsewhere: which of these approaches, if any, is better able to solve the difficulties inherent to a measurement of capital in terms consistent with its use in the theories of distribution.

Section II, Chapter IV: Wicksell's Use of the Average Period of Production, Deficiencies of That Measure of Capital; Wicksell's Theory of Distribution in the *Lectures*; His Treatment of Fixed Capital

Wicksell's theory of capital is built on the basis laid by previous attempts to relate the role of capital in production to the time elapsing between the moments at which wages are paid and the moment or moments at which the commodities become ready for sale and consumption. The idea can be traced as far back as the classical economists, mainly Ricardo; but the first to use time as a measure of capital in a marginal productivity theory of the rate of interest was Jevons; Böhm-Bawerk in his 'third ground', and by introducing the concept of average period of production, attempted to overcome some of the obvious difficulties which stood in the way of a development of the idea thrown out by Jevons. Böhm-Bawerk's work offered to Wicksell his starting point. Wicksell modestly saw his task as no more than 'to present Böhm-Bawerk's principal ideas in an abridged and, if possible, clearer and more comprehensible form'.[175] But in reality Wicksell did much more than that, for giving a clearer and more comprehensible form to Böhm-Bawerk's principal ideas and setting them in the frame of the general equilibrium, implied to become aware of the difficulties involved and to attempt their solution. We shall for instance see how Wicksell relied at first on Böhm-Bawerk's average period of production as a measure of capital in the production functions, and how later, in the *Lectures*, that concept disappears; we shall also see how Wicksell became increasingly conscious of some of the inconsistencies involved in the use of Böhm-Bawerk's subsistence fund conception of capital.

The concept of average period of production, or 'investment period of capital',[176] as Wicksell prefers to call it, is the basis on which a theory of distribution on marginal productivity lines is advanced in *Value, Capital and Rent*, first published in 1893.[177] We shall give a brief summary of the theory and we shall then

---

[175] *Lectures*, Vol. I, London 1934, p. 147.

[176] *Value, Capital and Rent*, London, 1954, p. 125, last paragraph. References will be to that edition.

[177] Wicksell at first assumes that labour is uniformly distributed over an absolute period of production t; in this case the average period of production is $t/2$ which is also the variable appearing in the equations he sets forth on the basis of that first assumption. That assumption is evidently a device apt to make it easier for the reader to grasp the conception of capital he is advancing. The assumption is accordingly dropped later in the argument and what is in fact the average period is introduced. But even there Wicksell seems unwilling to part company with the absolute period t; he substitutes for $t/2$ the expression εt, where ε is an 'appropriate fraction' of the absolute period t; but at the same time he says that 'the distribution of labour over the period of production can itself be altered and ε is therefore in reality a variable quantity', so that εt have to be considered in his equations as 'a single variable' (op. cit., pp. 125–126). That variable is evidently Böhm-Bawerk's average period of production. In the *Finanztheorische Untersuchungen*, published three

examine the deficiencies which appear to prevent the use of the average period of production as a satisfactory measure of capital in the marginal productivity theories.

In our summary we shall assume (as Wicksell does at first) that land is free,[178] and that only one commodity is produced in the economy.[179] Further, all capital is assumed to be circulating capital according to the definition of it given in Section I.[180]

If all capital is circulating capital it will always be possible to determine for how long each fraction of the labour necessary to produce the commodity will have to remain invested in a given technique of production of the commodity: we can therefore calculate Böhm-Bawerk's average period of production for each of the techniques available in a given state of technical knowledge. We can then obtain a production function expressing the physical quantity p of the commodity obtainable from a given quantity of labour, *a labour year*, as a function of the average period T expressed in years: $p = f(T)$.

Using the simple rate of interest, as Wicksell does and as we must do in order to use the average period, we can write the following equation asserting

---

years after *Value, Capital and Rent*, Wicksell did in fact introduce the average period as defined by Böhm-Bawerk. We shall not examine here the theory of capital and distribution of that work since, for our purpose here, it appears to be fundamentally the same as the one of the earlier work. A difference, the introduction of an average period of production for land distinct from the one for labour, will be mentioned below.

[178] Op. cit., p. 146 [*editor's note*: actually, here Wicksell announces that he is about to integrate Böhm-Bawerk's theory, up to that point exposed (cf. earlier in Wicksell's book, e.g. p. 119) in the free land hypothesis proper to it, by allowing for a positive rent of land].

[179] The corresponding assumption in Wicksell is that the proportional increase in the physical productivity of labour as the average period is lengthened is the same in all branches of business (op. cit., pp. 126–7). From that assumption it follows that in equilibrium the average period of productlon will be the same in all business. Further, that implies that the relative values of the commodities will not change as the period of production varies (as the proportion of profits and wages in the costs of production will be the same for all commodities, the commodities will in each equilibrium situation exchange according to the quantities of labour embodied; and since as the average period varies the quantities of labour embodied in the physical units of the commodities change in a uniform proportion, their relative values will remain constant). We can therefore measure outputs, wages and capital in the theory in unambiguous terms by using value in terms of any of the commodities. This, from the point of view of the exposition, is the same as if we assume a one commodity economy and then proceed to measure wages and output in physical terms, and to measure capital as value, in terms of the commodity. Wicksell's assumptions are the same as the ones Böhm-Bawerk makes in the *Positive Theory of Capital*. As a 'curiosum' one can remark that this assumption amounts to that assumption of equality in the 'organic composition' which Böhm-Bawerk reproached Marx for using: when that assumption is made, commodities always exchange according to the quantities of labour embodied.

[180] Above, p. 24. For the same assumption in *Value, Capital and Rent* see p. 120, where Wicksell says that 'the tools are assumed to be worn out and valueless' when production is completed.

the equilibrium equality between the produce of *a labour year* and the wage w paid for it plus the interest at the equilibrium rate i over the average period of production:[181]

$$p = w(1 + iT) \tag{I}$$

Another equation is obtained by Wicksell by the following reasoning: assuming that the entrepreneurs are capitalists, they will evidently choose, for any given rate of wages w, that average period T which will maximise the rate of interest i; the corresponding mathematical condition (obtained by differentiating with respect to T both the LHS, where p is given as a function of T, and the RHS of Eq. (I)) is[182]:

$$\frac{dp(T)}{dT} = wt \tag{II}$$

The unknowns the theory of distribution must determine are three: the wage rate w, the interest rate i, the average period T; we need therefore a third equation. The missing equation is supplied, as in all the marginal productivity theories, by the condition regarding the given quantity of capital existing in the economy. Wicksell measures that datum as a sum of values in terms of the product. The reasoning by which the equation is constructed is the following: since in the economy a large number of similar processes of production are simultaneously carried out, each one at a 'different stage of progress', if continuity is assumed in the gradation of such processes (that is, if we assume that the number of such simultaneous processes tends to infinity),[183] the total, at any moment, of the wages paid to each worker and not yet re-paid by the sale of the corresponding product, is, on the average, given by (wT); further, since we are calculating with simple interest, the interest not yet paid through the sale of the product does not bear further interest; and therefore (wT) is all the capital invested in each worker. If the number of workers in the economy is A, the 'total capital' is given by (wAT). If K is the value

[181] Cf. Eq. (13) at p. 121, op. cit. On the usual assumption of linearity and homogeneity of the production function, implicit to Wicksell's equations, see below, n. 187.

[182] Cf. Eq. (14), p. 122, op. cit. The same equation could be obtained by assuming that the entrepreneurs are workers and, for any given rate of interest, choose the T which maximizes the wage rate w.

[183] The view of the organisation of production taken here is the same we described in Chapter III of Section I, when we spoke of the view of capital associated with simultaneity between labour inputs and outputs of finished product embodying the corresponding quantity of labour (above, pp. 25ff).

of the capital available in the economy, a value measured in terms of the product, we have the following equation[184,185]:

$$K = wAT \tag{III}$$

We have then three independent equations for determining the three unknowns. The problem of distribution—within the limits set by the initial assumptions—appears to be solved.

Before passing to an examination of what happens once we drop the assumptions which allow Wicksell to use the average period of production, we can stop for a moment and make some remarks on the value measurement of the quantity of existing capital appearing in Eq. (III). The inconsistency of such a value measurement in theories which, like the one we have outlined, take the quantity of capital as a datum will be examined in detail in the next chapter where we shall also consider the subsistence fund conception of capital, the one adopted by Wicksell in *Value, Capital and Rent*. All we need do at the moment is to point out that, as long as capital can be measured in the production function as the average period of production, the value measurement of the given quantity of existing capital is not essential. That flaw in the theory could be eliminated by applying to the measurement of existing capital the same measurement as is used in the production function. The quantity of capital is expressed in the production function purely by T. Now if we take the view of capital as the stock of capital goods necessary to render simultaneous the inputs of labour and the corresponding (net) outputs of produce, T can be identified with the quantity of labour embodied in the capital stock

[184] Cf. Eq. (15) at p. 126, op. cit. Our account of the way in which Eq. (III) is constructed differs from Wicksell to the extent to which we refer directly to the average period T, instead of Wicksell's half of the absolute period t. A simple and less ambiguous way of describing the equation is perhaps the one adopted in Sect. I of the dissertation (above, pp. 26–7): since the equilibrium capital stock will embody (AT) labour years its value (which, when calculating with simple interest, is equal to its wage costs) will be (wAT).

[185] As one would expect from a supporter of the subsistence fund conception of capital, the description Wicksell gives of the datum K is ambiguous. In the immediate context we have expressions like 'total existing capital' or 'capital invested'. But it we take a wider context the meaning becomes clear: what Wicksell has in mind (and identifies with the total subsistence fund) is the value, in terms of the product, of the physical capital in existence in the economy. So, when describing what he means by constancy of the 'productive factor' capital in the definition of a 'stationary community', he says: 'Though in this case the forms (of capital) change, its total value remains unchanged, since in place of the consumed capital goods new ones of equivalent value enter successively' (op. cit., p. 103; see also p. 119 where, while referring to physical capital goods, he says: 'all existing capital goods are united in one sum' for 'the theoretical determination of the level of interest and of wages', and discusses whether 'the capital *value* of all railways, buildings etc.' (emphasis added) should be included in that 'sum', or those physical capitals should not rather be considered as rent goods; also p. 106, where he speaks of the necessity for the theory of uniting all 'capital-goods' in one 'sum'; etc.). We shall see below the same ambiguity in Böhm-Bawerk. In the *Lectures*, when the value measurement of capital is used, Wicksell is, in general, clearer and speaks of the 'value of capital'.

assisting, on the average, one worker.[186] In the units we have defined for the above equations, T will be the number of labour years embodied in such a stock. The labour years embodied in the aggregate capital stock will then be (AT). If we take as given the capital K' existing in the economy in terms of labour years, we shall have the following equation:

$$K' = AT \tag{IIIa}$$

If now we substitute Eq. (IIIa) for Eq. (III), the three unknowns w, i, T, can be determined without resorting to Wicksell's value measurement. The theory so modified would be immune from the criticism that the value of capital cannot be a determinant of distribution since the value of capital goods varies simply as a result of changes in the division of the product.[187] The quantity of labour

---

[186] See above, pp. 25ff.

[187] The *internal* consistency which the introduction of Eq. (IIIa) would bring to the theory considered as a marginal productivity theory, can be seen, for example, from the fact that only then can w and i be shown to be determined in the three equations by the marginal products of labour and 'capital' respectively. In fact the LHS of Eq. (II) (above, p. 75) read in discrete terms, is the increment in physical produce obtainable by increasing by one year the average period of production of labour, that is by increasing by one labour year 'capital' per worker; such increment of produce will determine the equilibrium price of the service of a unit of 'capital', and the equilibrium rate of interest will be the ratio between that price and the equilibrium value of a unit of 'capital' given by w. The same principle does not hold if 'capital' is the value magnitude of Eq. (III); the equilibrium i is higher than $\frac{dp}{dk}$(k is here the value of the capital assisting on the average one worker). Similarly it can be shown that the wage rate, as jointly determined by Eqs. (I), (II), (IIIa), is the marginal product of labour (if the production function is homogeneous and linear, as is implied by the equations, since product per worker is there assumed to depend only on T, and not also on the total number of workers employed). In fact if we increased the number of labourers in the economy from A to ($A+1$), the aggregate yearly produce would increase by p but for the reduction in capital per worker from $\frac{K'}{A}=T$ to $\frac{K'}{A+1}=T\frac{A}{A+1}$, which, since A is assumed to be very large, will reduce product per worker by $\frac{dp}{dt}(T - T\frac{A}{A+1}) = \frac{dp}{dT}\frac{T}{A+1}$, and aggregate produce by $\frac{dp}{dT}\frac{T}{A+1}(A+1) = \frac{dp}{dT}T$. So that the net increment in aggregate produce obtained by the unit increase in labour is $w'=p-\frac{dp}{dT}T$; but from Eq. (I), when we substitute on the RHS i with the value $\frac{\frac{dp}{dT}}{w}$ determined by Eq. (II), we have: $p=w(1+\frac{\frac{dp}{dT}}{w}T)=w+\frac{dp}{dT}T$; if we put this value of p in the expression giving the value of w', the marginal product of labour, we obtain $w'=(w+\frac{dp}{dT}T)-\frac{dp}{dT}T=w$; the wage is equal to the marginal product of labour. The same proposition would not hold if we repeated the reasoning using the K of Eq. (III) instead of the K' of Eq. (IIIa), obtaining a marginal product of labour w''; w'' would be larger than w; this is not surprising since the marginal product of 'capital' as defined by Eq. (III) is, as we have seen, smaller than i. We shall discuss in Chapter VI below Wicksell's interpretation of such a divergence of i from the marginal product of the 'capital' he has defined. But we can here notice how it arises from measuring K in units which are not the same as the ones to which the marginal product of 'capital' (as determined by the production function) is referred: in Eq. (II) we have the average period of labour embodied; in Eq. (III) we have a value magnitude.

embodied in the capital goods on the contrary is invariant as the division of the product changes.[188]

The previous summary has shown how the average period of production could be used as a consistent measurement of capital in a marginal productivity theory. But the assumptions we have to make in order to be able to use the average period are so drastic as to prevent its use in any general theory of distribution. The three relevant assumptions are: (a) that interest on capital is distributed according to the rules of the simple rate of interest; (b) that all capital is circulating capital; (c) that there is only one factor of production besides capital.

The reasons why the first two assumptions are essential to the use of the average period have already been discussed in Section I of this dissertation.[189] What we specifically saw there was why, when compound rate and fixed capital are introduced, it is no longer possible to establish a relationship between the value of a commodity and its wage costs based on a single period of time independent of the rate of interest. And this is the same as saying that the value of the physical capital assisting the workers in the production of a commodity cannot be related to a single period of time (or quantity of labour embodied).[190] Now this contradicts one of the two requirements which must be satisfied by the magnitude measuring capital in the marginal productivity theories: that it should be possible to relate it in a known way to the value of the corresponding capital stock.[191] It is for instance possible that in a technique requiring circulating capital measured by a shorter average period of production, the capital is more costly than the one for a technique involving a longer average period; to obtain that result it is sufficient that the investment function in the first technique should have a higher 'convexity', and that the rate of interest should be above a certain level; this shows that a production function could not even be constructed on the basis of the average period.[192]

---

[188] The problem of the extent to which, in the face of changes in the techniques of production, we could postulate the constancy (or the size of the variation) of the existing capital stock conceived as a quantity of embodied labour cannot be entered since we have no experience of an actual economy where the three assumptions necessary for the validity of the average period measure are verified. But it would appear that if we could imagine such an economy, an actual tendency to 'keep intact' capital as a quantity of stored up labour would not be unlikely: the constancy or variation of capital so conceived could, for instance, be ascertained by using the wage unit as an approximate practical standard (as we have seen, when using simple rate of interest the value of capital goods is equal to their wage costs).

[189] See above, pp. 23–4 and passim.

[190] Strictly the above statement is true if the value of capital is measured in wage units. If a different standard is used then of course the relationship between average period and value of capital involves also the average period of the standard and the quantity of labour embodied in it (unless the standard is itself a capital good in which case its average period is irrelevant because of the simple rate assumption).

[191] Above, pp. 54–5.

[192] See the example of the weight measure, above pp. 54–5. The impossibility of using a single time period when introducing compound interest and fixed capital can also be seen by looking at Eq. (I), where we need on the RHS a term measuring the share of profits in the produce, measured there by (iwT); or by looking at Eq. (II), where on the RHS we need the value of the addition to 'capital' measured there by w; if we cannot postulate a relationship between the time period measuring capital and the value of the capital stock we cannot evidently have equations like (I) and (II).

Besides the difficulties connected with the compound rate and with fixed capital, the use of the average period in a marginal productivity theory runs into a third difficulty which we did not meet when discussing the use of that measure in a surplus theory of distribution. As soon as the assumption that only one factor—homogeneous labour—exists besides capital is dropped, it will in general be impossible to measure capital by a single average period, even when using simple interest and assuming away fixed capital. If, for example, we introduced the factor 'homogeneous land', the application to production of the services of such a factor will be no more simultaneous to the emerging of the finished product than the application of labour: there will be a set of periods of time over which the services of land will remain invested. Of course, so long as compound interest and fixed capital do not interfere, we can calculate an average period of production of land, corresponding to each possible technique for producing the commodity, in the same way as we calculated the average period of production of labour, and the use of both average periods does not appear to introduce a special difficulty in so far as we are looking at the problem of capital measurement only from the angle of the possibility of constructing a production function. But as regards the measurement of the existing quantity of capital we shall, in general, have only two possibilities. The first is to take as data two distinct quantities, one for labour capital (or number of embodied labour years) and one for land capital (number of embodied acre-years); but then we shall have one equation in excess in the system so long as in equilibrium there must be a single interest rate[193]; we are meeting another instance of the principle that the existence in equilibrium of a single rate of interest prevents the marginal productivity theories from measuring the 'existing capital' as a set of quantities. The second possibility is to allow land capital to be transformed into labour

[193] The system of equations referred to could be schematically set out in the following way, where the new symbols introduced are: K_1 the existing labour capital, K_2 the existing land capital, B the number of acres of land available in the economy, b the land assisting one worker; r the rent per acre of land measured in terms of the product; T_1 and T_2 the average periods of production for labour and land respectively:

$$\begin{cases} p = w(1+iT_1) + rb(1+iT_2) \\ \dfrac{\delta p}{\delta T_1} = iw \\ \dfrac{\delta p}{\delta T_2} = irb \\ \dfrac{\delta p}{\delta b} = r(1+iT_2) \\ b = \dfrac{B}{A} \\ K_1 = AT_1 \\ K_2 = BT_2 \end{cases}$$

We have seven independent equations brought to determine six unknowns: i, w, r, b, T_1, T_2. For the system to be soluble we should allow two equilibrium rates of interest; one for labour capital, one for land capital.

capital (or vice-versa), in the process of achieving equilibrium; in this case we should have to find a 'par' according to which the two capitals can be transformed into one another; or, in other words, we should take the two capital quantities as unknowns and we should be back at the problem of measuring the existing capital by a magnitude in terms of which the two capitals can be reduced to homogeneity; the value magnitude would, again, open the theory to the criticisms we shall consider in the following chapter.

In *Value Capital and Rent* there is little if any analysis of these limitations on the measure of capital used there in the production function.

As regards the compound rate difficulty, when Wicksell drops the initial assumption of a uniform distribution of labour over an absolute period of production and introduces what is in effect the average period,[194] he says that the equations will undergo 'no essential alterations, at least when calculating simple interest'.[195] But he does not explain what kind of 'essential' alteration might become necessary when not calculating with a simple rate.[196]

With regard to fixed capital, Wicksell notices the difficulty but avoids it in part by considering highly durable capital goods as rent-goods, in part by referring to an 'average life' of the capital good as 'an indication of the average length of the period of production'.[197]

With regard to the multiplicity of factors other than capital, he does in fact introduce land as a scarce factor at a later stage of the argument, but the special assumption made there that labour and land are, at all stages of the production

[194] Cf. above, n. 177.

[195] Op. cit., p. 126.

[196] In n. 1 of p. 123, Wicksell shows what form the equations corresponding to our Eqs. (I) and (II) would take when using the compound interest. But at that stage he was still assuming uniform distribution of labour over an absolute period. This assumption obviously implies that a change in the 'proportion' of capital to labour can be achieved only by altering the absolute period of production and this rules out all the difficulties connected with the changes in the 'convexity' of the investment functions (see above, pp. 34–5). We can notice that neither in that footnote nor elsewhere in *Value, Capital and Rent* Wicksell considers the modifications that the equation corresponding to Eq. (III) here would undergo with compound interest, even while assuming uniform distribution of labour over the production period. Interest would have appeared in the value of capital and he would have found it difficult to conciliate the resulting equation with the principle that 'capital', as it turns over during the period of production, 'will be paid out in wages up to the last penny' (op. cit., p. 146). The apparent consistency between Eq. (III) and that view of capital is the result only of the use of the simple rate.

[197] Op. cit., p. 118.

process, applied in one and the same proportion, allows him to keep a single time period in the equations.[198,199]

The scanty concern shown by Wicksell with the limiting assumptions on which the use of a single time period in *Value, Capital and Rent* is founded, may partly be ascribed to the fact that Wicksell tended to regard the average period only as a simplifying device which could be dropped without meeting difficulties of principle. He was right in so far as we can rely on the value measurement of existing social capital as a determinant of distribution. But once, as is contended here, it is realised that such a measurement brings us back to the circularity avoided by introducing time periods in the production function, then the use of a single average period of production becomes not a simplifying device which, if not allowable, can be dropped at the cost only of more complex calculations; it becomes instead a condition *sine qua non* for the validity of the type of theory used.

This brings us to the conclusion which, it seems, can be drawn from this examination of Wicksell's theory in *Value, Capital and Rent*. The average period of production there used could afford a basis for a measurement of capital consistent with its use in a marginal productivity theory. But the assumptions necessary to the use of such a concept appear to be so drastic as to rule it out as a basic concept in a general theory of distribution. We shall presently see how Wicksell in the *Lectures* and in a later article drops all the three limiting assumptions but at the cost of dropping the measurement of capital in the production function by a single time period. Consequently the value measurement of the 'given' quantity of capital becomes essential to the later formulations.

In the first volume of the *Lectures* the average period of production is abandoned. In its stead we have two alternative treatments of capital in the theory of distribution, neither of which require the restrictive assumptions of the simple rate of interest calculation.

One of them is the famous wine case,[200] where the proportion of capital to other factors in the production function is measured by one absolute period of

[198] Op. cit., p. 147. In that case it would be possible to have also an equation similar to Eq. (IIIa) since the proportions of labour to land capital would remain the same as the period of production varies. But even that assumption would not allow to measure social capital according to an equation of the type of (IIIa) if the change examined with the theory involves a change in the proportions of original factors available (or, when more than one commodity is produced, if the proportions in which labour and land are applied in the two commodities are different, and their relative outputs vary). In these cases to satisfy all the equations of equilibrium, land capital must be transformable in labour capital and vice-versa.

[199] In the later work *Finanztheorische Untersuchungen* Wicksell uses in the determining equations two distinct average periods, one for labour and one for land, related to one another by a value measurement of the existing social capital.

[200] *Lectures*, pp. 172–184.

production. That analysis need not detain us. It is founded on the assumption that labour and land are all applied at one and the same point in time, after which the produce increases in value without any further application of original factors. In that case we have on the one hand a single period of time, so that, given the available quantities of labour and land, existing capital could be measured in terms independent of distribution[201]; and, on the other hand, the period is an absolute one, so that compound rate calculation can be used.

The other way of dealing with capital is much more general in scope and of the three assumptions we saw to be necessary for the validity of the theory based on the average period of production, only the exclusion of fixed capital remains.

The procedure by which this is achieved is analogous to the one we saw in analysing the solution Borkiewicz proposed for the problem of value and distribution in a surplus theory. It consists essentially in abandoning the attempt to reduce capital in the production function to one time period, and in considering instead the distribution over time of the labour and of the other original factors.

The way in which Wicksell fits this into a production function is by making that function depend on the quantities of a complex of factors of production, each consisting of the labour or land applied at a given distance in time from the moment in which the finished product emerges. So that what we can loosely define as an increase in the proportion of capital to original factors will be reflected in an increase of the quantities of the factors at a longer time distance from the moment in which the produce arises, relatively to the quantities of the factors at a shorter time distance. These changes are controlled by the condition that the marginal productivities will bear to each other the proportions dictated by the new equilibrium levels of wages, rents, and interest rates.[202]

In order to simplify the exposition, we assume that only one commodity is produced in the country: then

$K =$ value in the one commodity of the quantity of capital available in the economy.

$A =$ number of labourers.

$B =$ acres of land.

$A_0\ A_1\ A_2 \dots A_{(n-1)}$ quantities of labour (labour-years) applied 0, 1, 2 … $(n-1)$ years before the emerging of the produce and $B_0\ B_1\ B_2 \dots B_{(n-1)}$ are the corresponding quantities of land.

$w =$ yearly wage of one labourer measured as a physical quantity of the commodity.

$r =$ yearly rent of an acre of land measured as a physical quantity of the commodity.

$i =$ interest rate.

---

[201] Wicksell seems reluctant to take existing capital as a definitive value sum. The argument is conducted more in terms of existing capital being just sufficient or more or less than sufficient for a certain storage period (pp. 173–6, 179) rather than in terms of the neat scheme of equations we saw in *Value, Capital and Rent*.

[202] *Lectures*, Vol. I, pp. 203–206. Wicksell's determination supposes two commodities.

The quantities Wicksell takes as given in the determination of the equilibrium are A, B, K. If labour and land are distributed over any number (n-1) of years,[203] the number of unknowns will be ($2n$ + 3): ($2n$) for $A_0\ A_1 \ldots A_{n-1}$; $B_o\ B_1 \ldots B_{n-1}$; the rate of interest; the wage and the rent rates.

We are given a production function $P = f(A_0\ A_1\ A_2 \ldots A_{n-1}, B_0\ B_1\ B_{n-1})$. From it we can obtain ($2n$) independent equations establishing the relationships which must hold, in equilibrium, between the marginal productivities of the ($2n$) factors appearing in the production function[204]:

$$\begin{cases} \frac{\delta P}{\delta A_0} = w \\ \frac{\delta P}{\delta A_1} = w(1+i) \\ \ldots \\ \ldots \\ \frac{\delta P}{\delta A_{n-1}} = w(1+i)^{n-1} \end{cases} \qquad \begin{cases} \frac{\delta P}{\delta B_0} = r \\ \frac{\delta P}{\delta B_1} = r(1+i) \\ \ldots \\ \ldots \\ \frac{\delta P}{\delta B_{n-1}} = r(1+i)^{n-1} \end{cases} \tag{IV}$$

Two more equations are given by the conditions that the quantities of labour and land applied to all the various stages of production simultaneously carried out in the economy, must be equal to the total quantity of labour and land available in the economy[205]:

$$\begin{cases} A_0 + A_1 + \cdots + A_{n-1} = A \\ B_0 + B_1 + \cdots + B_{n-1} = B \end{cases} \tag{V}$$

Finally, we have the condition that the value of the capital made necessary by that time distribution of labour and land should be equal to the given capital value

---

[203] The fact that nowhere labour works unassisted by capital, may make n tend to infinity. The A_{n-1} and B_{n-1} will be infinitesimal quantities so that they can be left out of account. But, in principle, it should be possible to take into account also the variations in the relative quantities of these infinitesimal quantities of labour and land: as n increases, number of equations and number of unknowns increase in step.

[204] Wicksell uses the equations corresponding to system (IV) to express the quantities $A_2\ A_3 \ldots$ $B_1\ B_2 \ldots$ as functions only of $A_0\ A_1\ B_0$ (op. cit., p. 203. [*Editor's note*: for B_0 the subscript 0 has been inserted here in place of the subscript 1, present in the original, for consistency with the order that is natural to use, and that in fact Garegnani himself adopts a few lines below in this same note. Curiously, the incongruence seems to be inherited from Wicksell's exposition on the page Garegnani refers to, where, for the two production processes that are considered there, Wicksell reduces the unknowns to A_0, A_1 and B_1 (rather than the obvious option B_0) for the first process, and to A_0^1, A_1^1 and B_0^1 for the second one.]) This corresponds, in terms of the equilibrium equations used here, to using the $2n$ equations of system (IV) in order to eliminate $2n$ unknowns: namely the ($2n - 3$) quantities $A_2\ A_3 \ldots A_{n-1}$; $B_1\ B_2 \ldots B_{n-1}$; and the wage rate w, the rent per acre r, the rate of interest i. We should then have only three unknowns in the equilibrium equations, namely $A_0\ A_1\ B_0$, which would be determined by the three Eqs. (V) and (VI) we shall see in the text.

[205] Cf. Wicksell's first two equations at p. 204, op. cit..

available. The expression for it is obtained by remembering that for each A_j there will be j elements of capital each embodying a quantity A_j of labour applied at the beginning of each of the years which have elapsed between the moment 0 and the moment $-j$. We have then the following equation:[206]

$$K = wA_1(1+i) + wA_2[(1+i) + (1+i)^2] + \cdots$$
$$+ wA_{n-1}[(1+i) + (1+i)^2 + (1+i)^{(n-1)}] + rB_1(1+i) + rB_2[(1+i) + (1+i)^2] + \cdots$$
$$+ rB_{n-1}[(1+i) + (1+i)^2 + \cdots + (1+i)^{(n-1)}] \tag{VI}$$

We shall then have $(2n + 3)$ independent equations with which to determine the $(2n + 3)$ unknowns of the system.[†]

This solution, we have said, is subject to the limitation that all capital is circulating capital or, as Wicksell prefers to call it, is 'variable capital'. But once we are prepared to measure capital as a set of quantities and therefore to refer to the quantity of capital existing in the economy as a value sum, there is no basic difficulty in introducing fixed capital. One could introduce it along Walras's lines, by considering each capital good a factor of production of its own and considering the quantities of such capital goods as unknowns determined by the condition that the net rates of returns on the value of each type of capital good should be equal to the rate of interest, and by the condition that the value of the whole stock of them available should be, together with that of the circulating capital, equal to a given capital value.

Wicksell dealt with the problem of fixed capital in an article published, in 1923, reviewing Åkerman's *Realkapital und Kapitalzins*.[207] In it Wicksell reformulated in algebraic terms the theory put forward by Åkerman and conducted an analysis of the relationships between the variables involved. The fundamentals of the theory of distribution applicable to the case of fixed capital can be summarized in a few equations. To simplify—and it is here purely a question of simplification because multiplicity of types of fixed capital, multiplicity of commodities, presence of circulating capital complicate the problem but do not introduce conceptual difficulties—we can assume one commodity produced by 'free' labour assisted only by one kind of fixed capital; the machines in question are supposed to require only unassisted labour to be produced; the length of their life is supposed to vary according to the quantity of labour employed in producing them.

If we have a production function $P = g(x, y)$ where the yearly physical produce P is given as a function of the number of labourers y employed, and of the

---

[206] Cf. op. cit., p. 204, the last two paragraphs.

[†] [*Editor's note*: the number of independent equations and unknowns is actually one more, $(2n+4)$, for it should also include, respectively, the production function and the quantity of produce P.]

[207] The article is published, in an English translation, as Appendix (2) to Vol. I of the English edition of the *Lectures* already quoted.

numbers of machines x assisting those labourers, and if b is the yearly rent (measured in terms of the product) paid for the service of a machine and w is the yearly wage, the marginal productivity principle requires that in conditions of free competition the following equations should be satisfied in equilibrium:

$$\begin{cases} \dfrac{\delta P}{\delta x} = b \\ \dfrac{\delta P}{\delta y} = w \end{cases} \tag{VII}$$

We are given the length n (in years) of the life of a machine as a function of the quantity of labour a (in labour-years) employed in its production:

$$a = f(n) \tag{VIII}$$

The maximization of profits of the part of the producer of the finished product, together with the equilibrium condition of the equality between the value of a new machine and its costs of production, guarantee that in equilibrium the cost of lengthening by one year the life of a machine will be equal to the value of a yearly service of the machine discounted at the ruling rate for the appropriate period of time. That is, using interest at a continuously compound rate ρ:[208]

$$w\frac{da}{dn} = be^{-\rho n} \tag{IX}$$

On the other hand the competitive equilibrium of the machines producing industry guarantees the equality between the value of a new machine and its cost of production[209]:

$$wa = b\int_0^n e^{-\rho t}dt \tag{X}$$

If the total labour force is A, of which M labourers are continuously engaged in replacing (or maintaining) the machines we shall have:[210]

$$y = A - M \tag{XI}$$

$$x = \frac{M}{a}n \tag{XII}$$

[208] Cf. Eq. (6), op. cit., p. 277, where Wicksell calculates on the basis of the defined form he gives to the equation corresponding to our Eq. (VIII).

[209] Cf. Eq.(4), op. cit., p. 276.

[210] Cf. op. cit., p. 287, last paragraph.

Finally, the value of the stock of machines of uniform age distribution, for (t) varying between 0 and n, will have to be equal to the given capital value existing in the economy[211]:

$$K = \frac{M}{a}\int_0^n (n-t)be^{\rho t}dt \qquad \text{(XIII)}$$

We have then eight unknowns: x, y, b, w, ρ, a, n, M; and eight independent equations.† The problem can be solved.[212]

In conclusion. the three difficulties which prevent the average period of production used in *Value, Capital and Rent* from being a valid measure of capital are solved by Wicksell in the later formulations of the theory of distribution, by measuring capital in the production function as a set of factors of production. But this implies the *necessity* of a value measurement of the existing social capital if the conditions of equilibrium, in particular the existence of a single rate of interest, are to be satisfied. It appears therefore that the whole structure of Wicksell's theory of distribution rests on the value measurement of capital as one of the determinants of distribution. In the following chapter we shall discuss that measurement in connection with the possible justifications of it.

[211] Wicksell does not commit himself clearly to this equation in the article we have been referring to; and this is not surprising since, as we shall see in Chapter VI below, Wicksell had by that time become doubtful about the consistency of taking the value-capital as a datum. In the article in question, the first section (pp. 274–84, op. cit.) is concerned with the determination of the life of the machines and of the rate of interest, when the wage rate and the yearly rent of a machine are given. When Wicksell later considers w and b as unknowns, he obtains five equations with six unknowns: he then chooses the life (n) of a machine as the datum and takes K as an unknown (op. cit., p. 289, last paragraph); but he can do so only because of the assumption that no capital exists besides machines of a single type. If, for example, a second type of machine is introduced, their lives could not be taken as data without contradicting the equilibrium condition of uniformity in the interest rate; to satisfy that condition capital-value would have to be taken as given as in the *Lectures*. Wicksell approaches the problem of the general relationships between quantity of 'capital' on the one hand, and, on the other hand, amount of produce and prices of factors, in the last pages of the essay. Also there he avoids taking clearly as a datum value-capital and prefers to refer to its variation: he aims at showing 'the validity of the principle that an increase in capital (*measured* in units of the product, or the value of the product remaining unaltered) must, *as a general rule*, always produce an increase in the volume of production' (op. cit., pp. 293–4; emphases in the original); but he seems to me to fail to demonstrate his point: his argument starts by assuming that 'real capital' has increased (p. 297, third paragraph), without showing that such a larger 'real capital' will necessarily be associated in the new equilibrium situation with that larger 'capital, measured in units of the product' of which he had set out to treat.

† [*Editor's note*: the author slips here into the same omission about the number of equations and unknowns mentioned above (p. 84, editor's note †).]

[212] If we dropped Åkerman's assumption of variability in the life of each kind of capital good we should no longer have Eqs. (VIII) and (IX), but n and a would now cease to be unknowns and become data. The solution, but for the simplifying assumptions used here, would not differ from one given on Walras's lines. Åkerman's assumption however of variability in the life of fixed capital, allows for a greater substitutability between factors.

Section II, Chapter V: Criticism of the Value Measurement of the Datum 'Capital Existing in the Economy': The Subsistence Fund Conception of Capital, the 'Real Capital' Conception

In the preceding chapter we have seen how Wicksell at first relied on the average period of production as the measure, in the production function, of the proportions 'capital' bears to labour and how he later in the *Lectures* and in his analysis of Åkerman's problem abandoned it and introduced instead in the production functions the absolute periods of production of 'original' factors with regard to circulating capital, and the lengths of the lives of the different types of capital goods with regards to fixed capital.

Through these changes Wicksell's theory of distribution retains two important characteristics.

Firstly, the capital element in the production functions is expressed by quantities other than value quantities: average or absolute periods of production, dated or undated quantities of 'original' factors of production (labour and land), number of machine services simultaneously available. Thus Wicksell avoids the more obvious form of circular reasoning involved in constructing a production function on quantities which are themselves part of the system of relative prices to be determined.

Secondly, the 'quantity of capital' existing in the economy in each situation analysed is taken as a datum measured by the value of the stock of capital in terms of the consumption good produced or of one of the consumption goods produced.

The second characteristic is the one which we shall now have to examine. Our contention is that by it Wicksell has fallen back into that same circularity he has avoided in the production function by expressing the capital element as periods of production.

We shall discuss the value measurement of the datum 'quantity of capital' in relation to two distinguishable meanings which can be attributed to the 'quantity of capital in existence in the economy' in each situation. They are: Böhm-Bawerk's 'Subsistence Fund' and what we can express as 'Real Capital'.

After having attempted in this way a clarification of the fundamentals of the problem we shall pass to examine in Chapter VI below how far Wicksell appears to have been or to have become conscious of the unsolved difficulty which remains at the very basis of the structure of his theory of distribution.

The notion of capital as an aggregate of wage goods which can be taken as given in the face of changes in distribution, goes back to the wage fund theories of wages. That same conception seems to have passed into some of the later more sophisticated theories of distribution founded on the marginal productivity principle. On it Jevons's theory of the rate of interest is built[213]; it appears again in Böhm-Bawerk's theory of distribution; from Böhm-Bawerk it passed into Wicksell's versions of the theory of distribution.

---

[213] See for example the following passage: 'Capital as I regard it, consists merely in the *aggregate of those commodities which are required for sustaining labourers of any kinds or class engaged in work*'. *Theory of Political Economy*, London, 1911, p. 223 (emphasis in the original).

Since the conception of capital as a subsistence fund in a context similar to Wicksell's has been most fully stated by Böhm-Bawerk, it appears convenient to see and discuss it in the form it takes in the *Positive Theory*.

There Böhm-Bawerk asserts as a proposition of fundamental importance to his entire theory of distribution: 'In any economical community the supply of subsistence, available for advances of subsistence is ... represented by the total sum of its wealth.'[214]

A few pages later he enlarges the statement thus:

> The entire wealth of the economical community serves as subsistence fund, ... and, from this, society draws its subsistence during the period of production customary in the community. All goods which appear to-day as the stock or parent wealth of society, so far as they are not already consumption goods, will, in the more or less near future, after a certain addition of finishing labour, ripen into consumption goods, and will consequently cover, for a more or less lengthy time to come, the people's demand for consumption.[215]

The proposition is fundamental to his theory because it is used for what amounts, in algebraic terms, to Eq. (III) of our account of Wicksell's theory in *Value, Capital and Rent*.[216]

He does so in Book VII of the *Positive Theory*, where he establishes the quantative relations determining wages and interest rate. The simplifying assumptions underlying the treatment there are the same as we have already seen in Wicksell's first work. Land is free, simple interest rate is used in the calculations, labour is uniformly distributed over the period of production, and the same proportional increase in the physical productivity of labour, as the period of production lengthens, is assumed for all branches of production; the last assumption, as we saw,[217] allows us to measure unambiguously produce and wages as value in terms of any of the consumption goods.

With the help of arithmetical tables Böhm-Bawerk then determines the period of production adopted, wages and the rate of interest. He first shows how for each possible rate of wages there will be one production period which offers to the capitalists the highest rate of profit on capital. He then shows that there will be one rate of wages (and, accordingly, one period of production and rate of profit) at which the 'existing stock of wealth', given as a value sum measured in terms of the same standard as produce and wages, will just employ all the labourers available by supplying them with the subsistence corresponding to that rate of wages over that period of production.[218] These rates of wages, of produce, and of interest will be the equilibrium ones.

---

214 *Positive Theory of Capital*, London, 1891, p. 319.

215 *P. Th.*, p. 322.

216 Above, p. 76.

217 Above, n. 179.

218 *P. Th.*, pp. 381–94.

Now such a theory is meaningful only if we have in each situation of the economy for which we want to determine wages and the rate of interest a 'National Subsistence Fund' of an amount definable *before* wages, rate of interest, period of production have been determined: Böhm-Bawerk must take the subsistence fund to be 1500 m. in order to conclude that in equilibrium with that labour force, the yearly wage is 50 and the rate of interest is 10%.[219] Otherwise wages and rate of interest will be completely indeterminate.

Such a 'National Subsistence Fund' is for Böhm-Bawerk 'the total sum of wealth in possession of the community'. Since the 'wealth' of the community will at any given moment consist only to a very small extent of subsistence goods, the size Böhm-Bawerk puts on the subsistence fund cannot be anything else than the value in the subsistence goods unit of the wealth of the community. And the 'wealth' that is relevant here can be taken as consisting mostly of those 'intermediate' products whose aggregate Böhm-Bawerk had previously defined as Social Capital.

If that is so, then Böhm-Bawerk's theory rests on the possibility of identifying the value, in a subsistence goods unit, of the existing stock of capital with a stock of subsistence goods which, so to speak, will always be there at the disposal of the community whatever the technique (period of production) chosen and whatever the levels of wages and rate of interest. If, that is, the intermediate goods constituting capital will in any relevant case (and at the right time) 'ripen' into an amount of subsistence goods determinable independently of the unknowns that the theory of distribution must determine. But that is not so.

The value of a capital good in terms of a subsistence goods unit will tend, it is true, to bear some definite relationship to the output of subsistence goods for obtaining which it is employed, but the relationship is such that the value of the capital good, far from being independent of the technique in which it will be employed and of the ruling level of wages and rate of interest, will instead be, in most of the relevant situations, entirely the outcome of just these factors.

For example, let us take the case of an intermediate product: the amount of consumption goods which will be finally obtained from it and the moment in the future at which they will be obtained will of course depend on the technique adopted for the remaining stages of the production process; the value of the intermediate product in terms of consumption goods will at any moment tend to be equal to that amount of consumption goods minus the wages of the further labour required together with the interest on them for the period for which they remain invested, minus the interest on the value of the capital good itself for the time between now and the moment in which the final produce is expected.

This shows that in no way can we attribute to the value in a subsistence good unit of the capital stock the meaning of a definite quantity of subsistence which will in any case be added to the amount otherwise at the disposal of the

---

[219] *P. Th.*, p. 391.

community. In fact the value so measured of a given physical stock of capital is in no way definable independently of the techniques of production according to which it is used, and of the levels of wages and interest which will rule in the future; accordingly, since that value is dependent on just the quantities Böhm-Bawerk aims to determine, we cannot take it as the measure of a potential subsistence fund in the sense Böhm-Bawerk needs for his theory.

All that we have is the fact that the existing capital goods will be employed together with current and future resources in the production of consumption goods and that their value in terms of the produce will tend to be equal to what is left over from the produce after interest, wages and rent over the period before the produce arises have been paid. As such it will be entirely dependent on what we expect to determine by taking it as datum. By making various hypothesis about the levels of wages and interest, the value of capital can be made anything we want down to zero. To take an extreme example: let us imagine that we had a stock of physical capital corresponding to a certain equilibrium situation; a change in technical knowledge occurs for which current 'free capital' will be invested in a form which offers a much higher output per man employed (at all stages of the production process) so that there is room either for a big increase in the rate of profits or of the wage rate (or for a fall in the relative price of the commodity, if we are considering a particular industry), or of both: the effect of this will be that soon the rate of profits or of wages or of both will rise (or the relative price of the commodity will fall); the existing stock of capital goods which can be used only according to the previous method of production will diminish in value; that value might even fall to nothing: it is common experience that capital goods are scrapped before the end of their physical life because at the levels of remuneration made possible by new techniques, their value has become negative.

It could be argued that the argument by which we rejected the conception of capital as a potential subsistence fund has been conducted while ignoring the relationship between the value of capital goods and their costs of production.

If the value of a capital good is equal to its costs of production[220] then—one could argue—there is a sense in which the value in subsistence of a capital stock is equal to an amount of subsistence which will be available in the future *because* of the existence of that aggregate of capital goods. Since—the argument would run—wages and in general the remuneration of all the resources appearing in the production function express, in equilibrium, their respective marginal productivities, it would follow that the costs of the capital goods in the subsistence unit will be equal to the 'contribution' which the resources embodied in it will ultimately make to the output of consumers' goods, that is to the 'contribution' which, at the margin, the capital good in question will make to the output; were it not so the

[220] To simplify the question, the argument is referred to circulating capital: in the case of a piece of fixed capital which has already been in use for some time, the relationship between its value and its costs of production will of course not be one of equality. But what will be said is evidently equally applicable to fixed capital.

resources employed in producing the capital good would have been misemployed and we could not be in equilibrium if the value of the capital good is equal to its costs of production. The equality between value of the capital good and its 'contribution' to output at the margin would mean that if we wished to dis-invest it, we could obtain an increase in subsistence equal to the value of the capital good, by devoting the resources, otherwise necessary to replace it, to the direct production of subsistence goods where also their produce will be equal to their remuneration.

This argument does not seem to answer the question: the costs of production vary with changes in distribution and cannot be taken as given when determining distribution. Further, the equality between costs and values of existing capital goods implies that the physical stock of capital is the *equilibrium* one: the one consistent with the techniques most profitable at the levels of wages and interest rate ruling in the economy in that situation, which is then bound to be an equilibrium situation. But then the subsistence fund conception of capital, since it would depend on such an equality, would make sense only so long as we remained in the same equilibrium situation. It would then be of no use to us since its function should be that of supplying us with a conception of capital as a fluid which can freely and without changing its magnitude pass from one concrete capital good into another as we pass from one equilibrium situation into another: if the subsistence fund embodied in a capital stock ceases to be a meaningful definite quantity out of one given equilibrium situation it fails just when we need it. In fact no sooner does the need for a change in the physical form of the 'capital' arise than the previous equality between values and costs is broken: on the one hand, values and costs of existing capital goods will vary because these are now calculated on the basis of the relevant new rate of profits obtainable by introducing the new techniques (and the new wage rate, if, as is likely, the ruling rate has also been affected): on the other hand, a divergence is bound to arise between the values and the costs of production of the previous capital goods: otherwise the kinds of capital goods will not be changed and the existing capital goods will be replaced in the same form.

It appears therefore that the idea according to which a capital stock can be considered as a subsistence fund in the sense that it will contribute a definite amount of subsistence goods to the future outputs of society is untenable. It is useless to attempt to establish what is the contribution that the whole capital stock will make to the future output of society and to expect to find a definite quantity.

The most general meaning—i.e. a meaning valid both for the case in which the equality with costs of production holds and for the case in which it doesn't—we can attribute to the value in subsistence of a capital good is that of measuring claims on the future output of society associated with the ownership of the capital good and, as such, it cannot but be an outcome of the way in which the social produce is distributed. If that is so any attempt to use the value of the 'existing capital' as a determinant of distribution can only result in circular reasoning, whether, as in Böhm-Bawerk, it is founded on a subsistence fund conception of capital or whether it is justified in relation to a somewhat different conception of capital like the one we shall consider in the next section.

Concluding, I think that the criticism of Böhm-Bawerk's subsistence fund attempted here can be very well summarized by applying to it Böhm-Bawerk's own conclusions on the wage fund theory of wages:

> In explaining then, the rate of wages by an amount which is itself conditioned by the rate of wages the … theory describes a circle.

We may also judge how justified Böhm-Bawerk appears to have been in maintaining:

> My subsistence fund, on the other hand, starts with a *fixed given* amount—the stock of wealth accumulated in the community.[221,222]

If the subsistence fund conception offers no solution to the marginal productivity theorists' problem of what is to be understood by the datum 'quantity of capital' to which they have to refer, and if accordingly we cannot use this conception to justify Wicksell's value measurement of that datum, we have now to consider attempts at a conception of capital which appears distinguishable from the subsistence fund one and evaluate in relation to it Wicksell's value measurement of the datum capital. The reason for which the value measurement of capital appears to be unsatisfactory also in relation to this second conception of capital is the same as we saw in the case of the subsistence fund conception: the variability of the value of a given physical aggregate of capital goods with changes in distribution.

According to the approach which concerns us here, the 'quantity of capital' should be conceived not as a store of potential subsistence, but rather as an aggregate of capital goods. So that if we had two situations in which the inventory of capital goods was exactly the same, we should without hesitation say that the two quantities of capital are the same even if the remuneration of the factors and, accordingly, the value of that capital stock in a subsistence goods unit is different in the two situations. The difficulty of course is that the capital goods are physically heterogeneous, so that we have no obvious unit by which to measure and compare such 'real' capitals. This is the way of approaching the problem that we have indicated in the introduction to the present section of the dissertation, where we referred to the necessity of conceiving the stock of physical capital in terms of a magnitude invariant in the face of changes in distribution.

---

[221] *P. Th.*, p. 420 (emphasis added).

[222] The reasoning in this section has been conducted on the assumption that a unique meaning can be given to the variations of the value of physical capital measured in 'subsistence goods'; that, in other words, we have an unambiguous subsistence goods unit. That was a corollary of the assumptions indicated at p. 88 above. When those assumptions are dropped changes in distribution will also change the relative values of different subsistence goods; accordingly, constancy of the 'subsistence fund 'when measured in terms of one consumption good is compatible with decreases or increases which that identical 'subsistence fund' will show when measured in terms of another consumption good. This brings out another manifestation of the inconsistency of using the value of capital as a determinant of distribution.

We have now to examine more closely what we mean by measuring the stock of physical capital in terms of a magnitude invariant in the face of changes in distribution.

Let us imagine an economy where all capital consists of machines of a given type: we should then have no difficulty in determining the equilibrium distribution in the economy, because we should have in the number of machines in existence at any moment, the datum quantity of capital[223] and the same magnitude could be used to express capital in the production functions.[224]

It might appear that even then there would exist doubts about the extent to which this conception of capital is satisfactory in so far as the amount or proportion of resources (labour and machines) necessary to the production of a machine varies, due to changes in technical knowledge or in other data. If a machine could be produced in situation B with half the amount of both labour and machine services necessary before in situation A, it could be argued that it is misleading to say that capital has remained constant if we have in B the same number of machines of the same age distribution as we had in A: in some sense the 'amount of resources embodied in the capital stock' has halved. But where we can give a definite meaning to the idea of a quantity of embodied resources, and where it appears to be relevant, we can always take it into account while measuring capital as a number of machines: if we had, for instance, reason to suppose that in passing from situation A to situation B the community tends to modify the number of machines so as to keep constant the 'quantity of resources' embodied in them, then we could determine the effect of that change in technical knowledge by calculating equilibrium distribution in the situation B on the assumption that the number of machines is double the one of machines in situation A. What is important is, it seems, that since the machines in existence at any moment will be of the type which are required in any of the possible equilibrium situations, a change somewhere in the data defining an equilibrium will not necessitate the substitution of those capital goods with others of a different type and we can therefore use a machine as the physical standard for the measurement of the datum we need for the theory of distribution. Here then we should have that 'magnitude invariant to changes in distribution' satisfying the requirements of a 'real' capital conception. But the difficulty is solvable here simply because we have assumed away its source: the heterogeneity of the capital goods.

---

[223] Complications might arise in connection with a non uniform age distribution of the stock of machines, but we do not need to enter into them; what we need here is only an illustration.

[224] The problem of capital measurement in the marginal productivity theories is really one in the sense that a satisfactory measure of' the datum 'quantity of capital' would also at the same time be satisfactory for the measurement of capital in the production function; on the other hand a solution of the problem in the production function which is not at the same time a solution of the problem of measurement of the datum does not seem to get us any nearer to a valid solution of the problem.

What, if any, justification can be found for Wicksell's value measurement of that datum quantity of capital in connection with a 'real capital' conception?

It is obvious that the value of the capital stock in terms of a consumption good does not satisfy that condition for a 'real' measurement of capital which the average period of production did satisfy: the value in these terms of a given aggregate of capital goods does change when nothing but the distribution of the social produce changes. This immediately prevents us from maintaining that such a value measurement can offer a valid basis for a 'real' capital conception. In fact where the expression 'real' capital crops up in Wicksell, it is almost always in order to differentiate or contrast it with his own value measurement of the 'amount' of capital.

But sometimes in the *Lectures*, when as we shall see, Wicksell had partly come to recognize the circularity of' his own measurement of a given quantity of capital, there seems to be the feeling that the value measurement of capital, if it cannot be a strictly valid measurement, can at least be taken as a workable approximation to a something defined as 'real' capital.[225]

What such a justification seems to ignore is that in order to be able to speak of a magnitude as a workable approximation to another magnitude, we should first be able to define the second magnitude. Only in that case shall we be able to ascertain what the degree of approximation is likely to be in the problems we have to deal with, and accordingly whether the approximation is a workable one or not. Now the real capital magnitude is just what, in most relevant cases, we do not have.

All that we can know is that in those special cases where we have such a generally acceptable capital magnitude—as where we are comparing two situations in which the physical capital stock is the same although distribution has varied, or where we make the hypothesis that all capital consists of machines of the same type—the value magnitude of capital can vary to any degree whatever, while real capital remains constant, and while the levels of wages and interest are varied. Moreover it is possible to have value capital changing in opposite directions with given changes in wages and interest (real capital remaining constant), according to which commodity is chosen as standard.

Summing up, if we compare the problem of the measurement of the datum 'quantity of capital' examined here with the one of having satisfactory quantities by which to express capital in the production functions, it appears that what has been gained by the introduction of the periods of production has been only the possibility of conceiving and constructing in consistent terms a production function. But the theory of distribution based on the marginal productivity principle will not have gained by it so long as we are unable to relate the quantities appearing in the production function to quantities of factors of production which can be taken as data for the determination of the equilibrium distribution; more

[225] See for instance, in its context: 'it may be difficult—if not impossible—to define this concept of social capital with *absolute precision* as a definite quantity. In reality, it is rather a *complex* of quantities' (*Lectures*, vol I, p. 165, first emphasis added).

specifically to quantities which can be supposed to remain unaffected by changes in the system of prices involved in the process of achieving equilibrium.That condition may be supposed to be satisfied for the factors traditionally grouped as labour and land but it does not appear to be possible to satisfy it for the factor capital.

Section II, Chapter VI: The Subsistence Fund Conception in Wicksell, Particular Applications of It; Wicksell's Groping for a 'Real Capital' Conception in the *Lectures*; Conclusions of Section II of the Dissertation

In the last chapter we have examined the question of the value measurement of the datum 'quantity of capital existing in the economy' in general terms. We propose now to see how Wicksell justified the use of that measurement in the successive versions of his theory, and to consider how far he became aware of the essential deficiency of his procedure. We should specify that what is attempted here is in no way an exhaustive examination of the development of Wicksell's capital theory or of his attitude to the results he obtained. Such an exhaustive examination could not be done without a careful study and comparison of the numerous successive articles and essays which Wicksell devoted to the problems of distribution over more than thirty years. Our concern will only be to refer to some passages from *Value, Capital and Rent* and from the third edition of the *Lectures* which appear relevant for bringing out clearly the conceptions of capital underlying the two works.

In *Value, Capital and Rent* there seems to be little sign of an awareness of the difficulties involved in the value measurement of a given quantity of capital.

On the one hand Wicksell was probably still inclined to take it for granted that constancy in the quantity of capital in face of the changes examined by the theory, could with reasonable approximation be taken to mean constancy in the value of capital in terms of the commodities or of one of the commodities produced. So he did not feel that any special justification was needed for the following statement referring to capital in the static state assumed in his analysis[226]: 'Though in this case the forms of [capital] change, its total value remains unchanged, since in place of the consumed capital goods new ones of equivalent value enter successively.'[227]

[226]Wicksell expresses it as 'stationary state'. We have preferred the expression 'static state' for Wicksell's *assumption* of constancy in the quantities of factors, in order to avoid possible confusion with 'a stationary state where the constancy in the quantity of factors is not assumed but is instead one of the resultants of the equilibrating process (cf. L. Robbins, 'On a Certain Ambiguity in the Conception of Stationary Equilibrium', *Economic Journal*, 1930).

[227]*Value, Capital and Rent*, London, 1954, p. 103.

On the other hand, in that early work, Wicksell saw his theory of distribution as being mainly an algebraic formulation and generalization of Böhm-Bawerk's theory and tended therefore to follow Böhm-Bawerk's procedure.

In fact the conception of capital underlying and justifying the value measurement in *Value, Capital and Rent* appears to be that of a 'subsistence fund' similar to the one Böhm-Bawerk had used. The view Wicksell takes of concrete capital appears there to be that of an aggregate of capital goods whose value in terms of product measures an amount of potential subsistence which will be realised and re-invested, in the same or in different capital goods, as the capital goods turn over during the period of production. When, for instance, he contrasts his theory with the wage fund theories, he says: 'The whole capital, at least in so far as it is 'turned over' during the period of production,[228] will subsequently appear in the form of money and means of subsistence, and, when no account is taken of ground rent and the like, will be paid out in wages up to the last penny, but ..., not *in one year*, but during a period of time...'.[229] So the difference between the wage fund theories and his own is seen to be only in the introduction of the average period of production; the underlying conception of capital as a subsistence fund is understood to be the same.

It is not difficult to find in *Value, Capital and Rent* specific instances which bring clearly into light that conception of capital and some of the inconsistencies connected with its application to the theory of distribution. We may single out two of them, the first of which may help to bring into sharp relief the distinction between the 'subsistence fund' and the 'real capital' conceptions of capital, and the second of which is of some special interest in itself.

The first application of the subsistence fund conception occurs when Wicksell notices an 'ambiguity' in the problem of the most profitable period of production compatible with a given capital. If—he says—the capitalists combined and, without altering the existing quantity of capital, adopted periods of production longer than the ones most profitable in conditions of free competition, they would achieve the result of lowering the wage and raising the rate of interest. The reasoning is simple. Since the number of workers A and the quantity of capital K (measured as value according to Eq. (III) above)[230] are given, if the capitalists lengthened the average period of production T, the 'wage-capital available each year' would fall since it is given by $\frac{K}{T}$. Accordingly, the wage rate which is given by the 'wage capital available each year' divided by the number of labourers, or $\frac{K}{AT}$, would have also to fall. The lengthening of the average period would increase, or at least not diminish, the produce, and the fall in wages would therefore be accompanied by a rise of the amount of interest in terms of product. Since, finally, by hypothesis, the

228 The limitation of the statement appears to refer to those capital durable goods which are considered by Wicksell as rent goods (see above, p. 80).

229 Op. cit., p. 146 (emphasis in the original).

230 Above, p. 76.

value, in terms of the product, of the aggregate capital has not changed, the rate of interest must have increased in proportion to the amount of interest.[231]

We said before that this case brings into relief the distinction between the 'subsistence fund' and the 'real capital' conceptions. In fact here constancy of capital according to the latter conception would have meant constancy in the average period of production in the face of the fall of wages (the same physical capital assisting the same number of workers is measured by the same average period of production). Wicksell instead understands as constancy in the quantity of capital, constancy in the value of capital in terms of the product. It is the 'subsistence fund' conception.

We can now consider some of the implications of the use of that conception of capital in this particular argument. The way in which Wicksell envisages the process is: since capital is a (potential) subsistence fund of given size a fall in the wage rate can be maintained (or obtained) only by lengthening the average period and thereby reducing the 'wage capital available for each year'.[232] If for example the capitalists combined in order to raise their share of the produce by halving the wage rate, Wicksell's argument implies that unless they simultaneously agree to double the average period, there will be a special problem of disposing of half of the 'capital' available, which will otherwise become 'superfluous'[233] and tend to force wages up to their previous level.[234] What Wicksell does not seem to see in his argument is that the superfluous capital subsistence fund is nothing but the increase in the amount of interest consequent upon the fall of wages and that there is no problem of absorbing it by a longer average period; in fact no sooner have the wages been halved that the value in terms of product of the same physical capital owned by the same capitalists (which is for Wicksell the measure of the 'potential' subsistence fund available) has also halved[235] without anyone doing anything to it, and has therefore freed the capitalists of the troublesome half of their capital.

The nature of this false problem in which the subsistence fund conception of capital involves Wicksell may become clearer with an example. Let us imagine an economy where each worker engaged in the direct of indirect production of corn is assisted, on the average, by a stock of physical capital measured by an average period of production of 5 years (that is, the stock of capital assisting one worker

[231] Wicksell, op. cit., pp. 128–30.

[232] 'But then each lengthening of the average period of production will prove in the end to be remunerative, provided it is undertaken simultaneously in all businesses; since the wage-capital available for each year is diminished and wages must consequently fall' (op. cit., p. 129).

[233] Cf., for instance, p. 127, op. cit., for a use of the expression 'superfluous capital' in a similar connection.

[234] The assumption of a combination of capitalists evidently frees Wicksell, and us, from satisfying in the situation where wages are lower, the equality between rate of interest and wages and the marginal productivity of, respectively, the average period and labour.

[235] Following Wicksells's argument we are assuming simple interest.

embodies on the average 5 labour years); the yearly produce per worker, after providing for the yearly physical replacement of capital,[236] is 1000 tons of corn.

Of those 1000 tons, 600 are given to him as yearly wage, and 400 constitute interest on the capital (which will have, on the assumption of simple rate, the value of 5 times 600 tons of corn, 3000 tons of corn). If now the capitalists combine and agree to lower to 300 tons the yearly wage, that implies that out of the unchanged product of 1000 tons they will give to the worker 300 tons, and that therefore the yearly interest can rise to 700 tons of corn without infringing on the physical capital. Wicksell on the contrary would argue that unless the average period is doubled to 10 years, the yearly wage-capital available for a worker will still be $\frac{3000}{5} = 600$ tons of corn and that it will therefore be impossible to carry out the intended reduction of wages. But that could only mean that the capitalists are refusing to accept increases of interest which, according to Wicksell, were the aim of the whole operation; that they continue for a time to accept as interest no more than the previous 400 tons and obstruct the change in the division of the product they had decided upon.[237]

---

[236] In other words the product per worker is calculated by dividing the aggregate corn produce by the number of workers engaged in a completely vertically integrated process of production of corn. In still other words, the number of labourers includes not only the labourers producing corn on the land but also those producing the iron ore, coal, iron tools, etc. necessary to keep intact the list of capital goods existing at any moment in the vertically integrated 'corn factory'.

[237] Our criticism of the argument of Wicksell discussed here can be viewed as an attempt to show how the subsistence fund conception of capital involves us into contradicting any acceptable conception of capital, net income, and net savings. Our standpoint is that in the case discussed, to 'keep capital intact' means (after as well as before the change in wages has occurred) to replace each *capital good* consumed with an identical one, so that (after as before the change in wages) 'net' produce per worker is 1000 tons of corn and if the wages are 300, the interest, the remaining share of the net product, must be 700. Wicksell's reasoning, on the contrary, implies that as the wage falls to 300, the capitalist will for a time continue to retain as yearly income (interest) only 400 tons of corn, and will attempt to re-invest in *additional* capital goods the corresponding of 300 tons of corn, considered as part of 'capital replacement'; it would then be true that they will succeed in keeping wages at 300 to the extent in which they lengthen the average period: that is, to the extent in which they can reduce the production of corn per worker to a total of 700 and employ instead the labour which used to produce (at all stages) 300 tons, for the production of the *additional* capital goods which will later enter corn production and lengthen the average period of production there. But why should the capitalists continue to consider as yearly interest only 400 tons of corn once the wages have fallen? Was not their aim to increase interests and is it not apparent that exactly the same capital goods and exactly the same scale of production can be maintained while retaining (and consuming) as yearly interest the corresponding of 700 tons of corn? Such a behaviour would not even achieve, in any conventional period of account, the aim of bringing back the value of the physical capital to the level it had before the wages fell. If for example the accounts are closed one year after the fall in wages, and even if we assume that all the corresponding of 300 tons of corn has been successfully invested in *additional* capital goods of that value, the value of capital per worker will be 1500+300=1800 and not 3000. To get back to that value in a year, interest would have not to remain at 400; it should became 700-1500=-800: in other words even if no interest is paid over a year, and the corresponding of 700 tons of corn is reinvested as capital replacement, the capital account will still show a loss of 800. What these results show, are the oddities to which the subsistence fund conception of capital could bring us.

Wicksell' s argument follows from thinking of the value of capital as a given subsistence fund: since that value was 3000, as long as the average period is only 5 years, there will be 600 tons of corn becoming 'free capital' each year and looking for employment; but in fact no sooner have the wages fallen to 300 tons a year than the value of the same physical capital has halved itself to $300 \times 5 = 1500$ tons of corn; so that now the yearly wage capital will be $\frac{1500}{5}$, that is 300, just what is needed for the yearly wage.[238] And this is not surprising once it is understood that the value of a piece of fixed capital is determined by the way in which the produce is divided between capitalists and labourers: using with Wicksell simple interest, the value of the existing capital can vary, in our example, between 0 and 5000 as the wage rate varies between 0 and the entire net produce of 1000.

We can now pass to the second instance of the use of the subsistence fund conception chosen here. Böhm-Bawerk had summarized his determination of the rate of interest in the following way: 'the level of the rate of interest is to be deduced from the relation of the last surplus return to the sum of subsistence which allows the last extension of production'.† To it Wicksell objects that the statement is 'misleading' unless the qualification 'at an unchanged rate of wage' is added to it.[239] What Wicksell means is that 'the sum of subsistence which allows the last extension of production' is in fact larger than the one in relation to which the rate of interest is determined. Wicksell proves his point by a mathematical treatment of the ratio between the increase of the produce and the increase of the value of capital (in terms of product) consequent upon the marginal lengthening of the average period, which leads to the conclusion that this ratio will always be smaller than

[238] It might be argued: as the existing physical capital wears out and is replaced, the same capital goods will have a lower value and a part of the amortization quotas becomes excessive and can be consumed; there would therefore be a sense in which dissaving occurs. But this would be the same argument we have criticized in the text, stated in different words. The excess amortization quotas are Wicksell's 'excess wage capital' looked at from the point of view of firms vertically disintegrated and not, as Wicksell looked at it, from the point of view of an entirely vertically integrated firm. The point may become clearer with an example. Let us imagine a completely vertically integrated firm producing, for instance, cars: there would be no amortization in the firm as a whole; the rise of interest in the firm would be entirely due to the fall of the share of wages in the total revenue (which is also the 'net' revenue) of the firm. If now we fragment the integrated firm into a number of firms carrying out different processes for the production of the cars (the further the fragmentation is carried, the larger, given the final output of cars, the volume of transactions between the firms and the larger the value of the aggregate 'gross' product of the firms (using as a value standard a car). The rise of interest in each firm will only in part result from the fall of the wages paid to the workers in the firm; the further the fragmentation is carried, the more, it seems, the rise in interest in the firm will be due to the fall in the wages of the workers engaged in the firms serving (directly or indirectly) the firm in question, fall reflected in the fall of the amortization necessary to keep the capital physically intact in the firm. It appears therefore that the excess amortization quotas, as Wicksell's 'excess wage capital', are, in each firm, but a part of the increment in interest resulting from the fall of wages, a part the larger the higher the degree of vertical disintegration among the firms.

† [*Editor's note*: as quoted by Wicksell, op. cit., p. 136.]

[239] Op. cit., p. 136.

the rate of interest determined by his equations.[240] In fact the increase in the value of capital per worker can, in the situation Wicksell envisages, be divided into two value quantities which can be described as: (a) the value of capital goods embodying the unit of labour which must be added to the quantity of labour embodied in the previous capital stock in consequence of the unit lengthening of the average period[241]; (b) the increase in the value of the capital goods embodying the same quantity of labour as was embodied in the previous capital. The equilibrium rate of interest is determined by the ratio between the increment of produce and only the first of the two quantities; it will therefore be larger than the ratio between increase of the produce and increase in the value of capital.[242]

Wicksell's interpretation of this result is that the increase in the value of capital due to the rise in the wage rate (quantity (b) in our exposition) is to be considered an increase in the 'sum of subsistence' constituting the 'national capital', which fails to have any effect on the produce since the increase in wages 'swallows it up'.[243] It is therefore implied that *that* increase in the value of capital can be considered as implying an increase in the subsistence fund of the same kind as is implied by the increase due to quantity (a)[‡]: an increase in the capital-subsistence fund involving an act of savings. Also here the interpretation of the value of capital as a subsistence fund seems to involve Wicksell in a fallacy strictly analogous to the one we have examined above: as there Wicksell thought that a reduction of the wage rate required a lengthening of the period of production in order to absorb all the 'existing capital', so here he thinks that a rise in wages, by itself, 'swallows up' and requires an increase in the existing capital. Here as there Wicksell does not see that such a change in the 'wage capital available for the year' does not require new capital in any acceptable sense since as the share of wages in the produce changes, the share of interest changes by the same amount and in the opposite direction. The increase in the value of capital due to quantity (b), on the contrary, implies, to the extent in which the problem can at all be discussed in this framework, that the community as a whole should reduce its aggregate consumption by some amount (produce a capital good embodying a labour year instead of producing and consuming commodities embodying a labour year).

To attempt to see clearly into this rather entangled question let us try to isolate the change in the value of capital connected purely with the rise of wages by assuming, for a moment, that the rise of wages occurs while the technique of production and therefore both the average period and the physical capital have

---

240 Op. cit., pp. 137–8.

241 Cf. above, n. 187.

242 If i is the interest rate and p the yearly produce per worker, w the wage, k the value of capital per worker, and Δw, Δk the increments associated with the lengthening of T by ΔT, we have that:
$i = \frac{\Delta p}{(w+\Delta w)\Delta T}$ is larger than $\frac{\Delta p}{\Delta k} = \frac{\Delta p}{(w+\Delta w)\Delta T + \Delta w T}$.

243 Op. cit., p. 137.

‡ [*Editor's note*: erroneously (b) in the original.]

not changed. We shall later drop this assumption. The case then evidently is the same as the one discussed with the corn example above. Let us imagine that the wage rate has risen from 600 to 700 tons of corn. The 'increase' of 100 tons in the yearly wage capital necessary to 'advance' the wage of the workers will come from the reduction of yearly interest per worker, from 400 to 300 tons. Worker and capitalist taken together will consume, if they wish, as much as before, 1000 tons, while the physical capital is being maintained as before. It seems difficult to speak in any meaningful sense of anyone having saved anything. To say that savings for 100 have been made, would not be very different from saying that if out of 1000, *A* gets 600 and *B* gets 400 in a year, and *A* 700 and *B* 300 the next, the community constituted by *A* and *B* has saved 100 in passing from that year to the next. We could equally well say that the community has dissaved 100 since A now consumes that much more. In fact if we calculated the value of capital with compound interest, as we should do, it is quite conceivable that the value of the same physical capital should have fallen as a result of the rise in wages: for that it is enough that the product should have, speaking in approximate terms, a shorter period of production than the capital goods, a case of very likely occurrence once fixed capital is introduced.[244]

Should we then say that since capital is now a 'subsistence fund' destined to the payment of both wages and interest, the community has dissaved since the wage fund part of it has increased by less than the interests fund has decreased? And that, when we know that the community as a whole can continue to consume as much as before forever (that is while keeping its physical capital intact)? It seems clear that such a change in the value of capital is a question of change in the relative values of commodities with changes in distribution; it has to do with the standard of measurement and not with the community increasing or decreasing its consumption. It is only a manifestation of the unsatisfactory nature of the subsistence fund conception of capital discussed in Chapter V of this section.

We can now drop the assumption that the period of production has not changed and consider in its entirety Wicksell's case: wages have risen in connection with the extension of the average period of production. Taking up again the corn example let us imagine that the average period has been lengthened from 5 to 6 years, the corn produce per worker, calculated net of what is necessary to keep physical capital intact, has risen from 1000 to 1060, the yearly wage has risen from 600 to 700,[245] the value of the capital per worker has increased from $600 \times 5 = 3000$ to $700 \times 6 = 4200$. The additional difficulty here arises from the fact that the new 6 years average period technique will in general imply substituting the capital goods of the 5 years average period technique with different ones. If we could imagine that the more 'roundabout' technique implies the same physical capital per worker as the previous one, but for the addition of a capital good embodying

---

244 See below, n. 247.

245 We have respected in these figures the equality between wage and marginal productivity of labour calculated as above (n. 187).

a labour year, all that we said before would apply as to the meaning of the rise of the value of the unchanged capital goods from 3000 to 3500. The only part of the increase in the total value of capital from 3000 to 4200 to which the meaning of 'new saving' may be given is the 700 tons of corn necessary to pay the 5 labour years which produced the additional capital good. The other 500 required for a yearly wage capital of 700 over an average of years would come from the fact that the interest instead of taking 400 out of a yearly produce of 1000, would take 360 out of a yearly produce of 1060.[246] If all the capital goods connected with the new technique are different there seems to be little if any general possibility of determining the amount of new savings required to move from the former to the new equilibrium position: it will all depend on the way in which the substitution of the old capital goods for the new ones comes about (on the series of disequilibrium situations preceding the new equilibrium). The conclusions of this lengthy attempt to criticize the meaning Wicksell gives to the variations of the value of capital connected with the change of the wage rate can be put in a few words: Wicksell was induced by the subsistence fund conception of capital into seeing a phenomenon of capital formation (new saving) where—to the extent at least in which we can at all get hold of a consistent measurement of capital—there is only an instance of changes in the relative values of commodities due to changes in distribution, which is independent of any change in the amount of product the community can consume while maintaining intact its physical capital.

If in *Value, Capital and Rent* the subsistence fund conception dominates Wicksell's treatment of the given quantity of capital existing in the economy, in the *Lectures* there are clear signs of dissatisfaction with it and of a groping towards what we have defined as a 'real capital' conception. The value measurement of a given quantity of capital remains since Wicksell cannot dispense with it without leaving his theory of distribution indeterminate, but that measurement is no longer defended as the conceptually exact measurement of a capital-subsistence fund. In fact, in a passage we shall discuss, Wicksell comes very near to a recognition of the circularity involved in its use.

The change in Wicksell's position is not to be understood as the substitution of a clear-cut conception for another, lucidly distinguished by Wicksell. The subsistence fund conception lingers on in the *Lectures*. So the divergence between the rate of interest and the ratio between the increases of produce and capital is still explained, as in *Value, Capital and Rent*, by the fact that the increase in wages

---

[246] A clear example for bringing out our point may be offered by Wicksell's wine case in the *Lectures*. There the community in order to lengthen the period of production from 4 to 5 years must give up one yearly output of 4 years old wine consisting of one million hectolitres, whose value is 100 million shillings. But the value of capital has increased by 108 million shillings since the value of the same wine 0, 1, 2 and 3 years old has increased by 6 million shillings as a result of the change in distribution (op. cit., pp. 176–7). It seems clear that it would be difficult to attribute such 8 million shillings increase of the capital to the saving of a corresponding amount of subsistence, amount 'swallowed up' by the combined effect of the rise in wages and rents and fall in the interest rate.

and rents 'absorbs' a part of the new capital formation, although the statement is now more captious and ambiguous[247]; and in the following paragraph he speaks of the divergence as due to the value measurement and defines that measurement as 'a theoretical anomaly which disturbs the correspondence which would otherwise exist between all the factors of production.'[248] The subsistence fund conception makes its appearance also in other passages; for instance where Wicksell, although more cautiously, repeats the arguments we have cited from *Value, Capital and Rent* about the difference between his theory of capital and the wage fund theories.[249]

But, in the *Lectures*, the stress tends to fall not on capital as a subsistence fund but on capital as an embodiment of past services of labour and land in an attempt to get hold of some concept of 'real capital'. In the largely illustrative and less rigorous introductory treatment of capital and interest, we have, for instance, the following definition: 'Capital is saved-up labour and saved-up land. Interest is the difference between the marginal productivity of saved-up labour and land and of current labour and land'[250] and this idea of capital is adhered to as much as possible in the section. Or, in another connection where he has to define a case of constancy in the quantities of factors employed in producing a commodity: 'If we suppose ... that a given proportion of the available labour, land, and capital—i.e., in the last resort, given quantities of original factors of different years ...'.[251]

An indication of the direction in which Wicksell is groping can be gathered from the following criticism of Böhm-Bawerk which appears to be of particular interest since it is it seems to be the nearest Wicksell gets to a direct criticism of the subsistence fund conception:

> Böhm-Bawerk was not entirely consistent, for in his account of the quantative factors determining interest he reverts, probably for reasons of exposition, to the earlier Jevonian conception of capital as a *subsistence fund*, a sum of (potential) wages; so that capital

[247] *Lectures*, Vol. 1, pp. 148–9. This explanation of the divergence in question can be found also in the 1923 article 'Real Capital and Interest' (p. 292) and the context is of particular interest. The mathematical treatment of fixed capital brings out there the possibility that the rate of interest might be larger than the ratio between increases of produce and capital (that is, the value of the same physical capital might fall as a result of the increase in wages). This result clearly contradicts Wicksell's explanations of the phenomenon in terms of the subsistence fund (he, even in the *Lectures,* does not consider interests as part of the subsistence fund, see p. 188, n. 1) and he defines the result as 'strange' or 'puzzling'. Wicksell appears to be worried by that result not only because it contradicts his explanation of the divergence, but also because it may prevent the statement that an increase in the value of capital is always associated with a fall of the interest rate and a rise of wages (see the doubt expressed at p. 183, 2nd para.).

[248] Op. cit., p. 149. A few lines below the divergence is considered a 'defect' of the theory. The whole passage has many half-statements.

[249] Op. cit., pp. 194–195.

[250] Op. cit., p. 154 (sentence entirely in italics in the original).

[251] Op. cit., p. 201: 'given quantities of original factors of different years' amount to the same as current labour assisted by the capital consisting of given quantities of 'saved-up labour and saved-up land' of the previous definition (cf. above, p. 82).

again becomes the primary, and the capitalistic process of production the derivative, concept.[252]

What is clear from this passage is that Wicksell is dissatisfied with the subsistence fund concept of capital, although that concept still underlies much of what is said in the *Lectures*. What is at first sight less clear is what Wicksell proposes to substitute for it, what is that 'capitalistic process of production' which should be considered as the 'primary' and no longer as the 'secondary' concept. But once those expressions are seen in the context of passages where capital is described as 'the total of a number of years accumulation of labour and land' or more explicitly as a 'complex of quantities', Wicksell's meaning becomes clearer: capital ought to be conceived as the absolute periods of time for which original factors have to remain invested in the capitalistic process of production; it is to these time periods that we should refer primarily and regard 'capital' as the complex of intermediate products which must exist at any moment in order to render simultaneous the application of the original factors (labour and land) and the emergence of the corresponding outputs of finished goods. But how can we apply such a conception of capital to the measurement of the quantity of capital existing in the economy, a datum for the determination of the equilibrium distribution in the marginal productivity theory?

The condition that a single rate of interest should exist in the economy and govern the ratios between the marginal productivities of original resources having different periods of investment necessarily implies that the relative quantities of such dated original resources change in the process of achieving equilibrium. Labour capital or periods of investment of labour must be allowed to transform themselves into periods of investment of land and vice-versa; longer periods must be transformed into shorter periods and vice-versa. In mathematical terms, if the quantities $A_0\, A_1\, A_2 \ldots, B_0\, B_1 \ldots$ had to be taken as data, the $(2n)$ equations of system (IV)[253] could not be solved, we should have $(2n)$ equations and only one unknown, the rate of interest. The equations would determine not a single rate of interest, but $(2n)$ rates of interest: one for each dated quantity of labour and land.[254] To obtain a single rate of interest, the dated quantities of original factors must be allowed to transform themselves into each other. But then, if distribution (and more generally, the system of prices) are not to remain indeterminate, we shall need another relation which, in the marginal productivity theories, ought to be supplied by the existing 'quantity' of capital conceived as a fluid which can indifferently take the form corresponding to any of those dated quantities. It does not seem therefore that consideration of that 'capitalistic process of production' can offer a substitute for the concept of capital quantity, so long as the basic approach of the marginal

[252] Op. cit., p. 168.

[253] Above, p. 83.

[254] And the same is the case when fixed capital, not considered in the *Lectures*, is brought into the equations: one type of machine must be allowed to transform itself into another, machines with a shorter life into machines with a longer life and vice-versa.

productivity theories is retained. The choice, characteristic of those theories, of the determining quantities in the distribution equations, that is the idea that the main determinants of distribution are the existing quantities of factors of production, prevents us from making of the 'quantity of capital' a 'derivative' concept, an unknown of the equilibrium system rather than a determinant of it.[255]

In fact also in the *Lectures* Wicksell, although with evident reluctance,[256] has to introduce the value of social capital as a datum when he has to bring determinacy into the equations of general equilibrium. So, when he comes to the conclusion of his treatment of the general equilibrium in an economy where two commodities are produced, he says:

'We have thus obtained five independent relations, but we still require a sixth. This can be obtained from an assumption concerning the amount of capital', and after having shown how the value of the physical capital can be obtained from the quantities $A_0 A_1 \ldots B_0 B_1$ he says:

> If these values are summed and are put equal to a certain given quantity—the total exchange value of the capital employed in *the two industries together*, expressed in terms of the first commodity, we shall then obtain the necessary *sixth relation*, and the problem will at last be completely determinate.[257]

But if Wicksell has ultimately to measure the datum quantity of capital in value terms in the same way as he did in '*Value, Capital and Rent*, now that he no longer feels secure about the subsistence fund conception of capital, he cannot repress his doubts about the meaning of his value measurement of the given total capital. He asks himself what 'importance' can be given to the claim that in the static state (the one supposed by the theory where consumers' tastes, technical knowledge, quantities of factors are given)[258] the value of capital is given. His answer is a double one. The first part is:

> In equilibrium, the capital employed in production has already assumed a certain technical dimension and composition, as well as a certain exchange value (expressed in terms of one of the commodities). It can now be asserted that, so long as capital of this magnitude and composition, or even of this exchange value, is maintained and utilized from year to year, equilibrium cannot be disturbed if, from the beginning, the other conditions of stability are fulfilled.[259]

This does not seem to go further than the statement: in equilibrium there is equilibrium. If the value of capital is that of an already established equilibrium situation, of a situation, that is, where all conditions of stability are fulfilled, then, by the definition itself of stability, there will be stability so long as, all the other quantities remaining the same, capital also remains the same in composition and value.

---

[255] Accordingly, Böhm-Bawerk's subsistence fund is what brings determinacy into his theory, and cannot be there only for reasons of exposition.

[256] See, e.g. above, n. 211.

[257] Op. cit., pp. 204–5 (emphases in the original).

[258] Cf. above, n. 226.

[259] Op. cit., p. 202.

That this is so can be of little interest when it is question of taking as a datum a value of capital which is not the one taken from the equilibrium situation we have to determine.

The second part of the answer is more interesting:

> But it would clearly be meaningless—if not altogether inconceivable—to maintain that the amount of capital is already fixed before equilibrium between production and consumption has been achieved.[260]

If it is true that—as Wicksell says here—it is 'meaningless'—if not 'inconceivable', to maintain that we can know the amount of capital before equilibrium has been achieved, we may ask what such a theory would enable us to know. To be able to determine the equilibrium distribution and system of prices we need, among the other data, the quantities of the factors of production. If for what refers to one of the factors, capital, we cannot know its quantity before equilibrium has been achieved, we shall be able to determine only what we can know without the theory: the distribution and prices of that already achieved equilibrium situation from which we should take the value of capital.[261] In any other case, the value of capital cannot be taken from the already established equilibrium situation, for the reason that we do not know what the equilibrium situation will be like before we have determined prices and distribution in it. We are evidently in a vicious circle: we cannot know the equilibrium situation unless we have the quantity of capital and we cannot know the quantity of capital before we have the equilibrium situation. The possibility of forecast is ruled out: if we asked what is likely to be the influence on distribution of a certain tariff or change in technical knowledge, we cannot answer because we cannot say what the value of capital will be in the equilibrium which will result after the change. This is so unless some other meaningful relationship is brought in to replace the missing one. But it is just the characteristic of the marginal productivity theories that the relationship is supplied by the given 'quantity of capital'.

A few lines after the passage quoted above, Wicksell continues:

> This indeterminateness … is of course primarily due to the fact that capital, unlike labour and land, is not an original factor of production which can exist (even hypothetically) independently of, or antecedently to, production.

This statement, it seems, can be interpreted as a criticism of a theory of distribution which depends for its validity upon the concept of capital as a factor of production whose existence as a definite magnitude can be assumed independently of the economic variables we have to determine. Wicksell continues:

> But [this indeterminateness] has another more deep-seated cause. In reality, the amount of capital is not determined by physical conditions but by the equilibrium between psychical forces which, on the one hand, drive us to save and accumulate capital and, on the other,

---

[260] *Ibid.*.

[261] For the similarity with the implications of the passage of Walras's discussed in Chapter III of this section, see above, pp. 70–1.

> to consume already existing capital. In other words *the accumulation of' capital* is itself, even under stationary conditions, a necessary element in the problem of production and exchange.[262]

It appears that in this passage Wicksell confuses two questions which ought to be kept separate: (a) the question of measurement of capital in units consistent with the use of capital quantity in his theory of distribution, that is the question of what we can mean by capital quantity in a marginal productivity theory; (b) the question of the extent to which, once capital has been consistently defined and is therefore measurable, we can apply to it the concept of a 'static state', that is we can assume that the quantity of capital so conceived will not vary during the time necessary for equilibrium to be achieved; a question of the same nature as the one regarding the extent to which the quantity of labour available, or technical knowledge or consumers' preferences, may be assumed not to change during the time that equilibrium takes to be achieved. The 'indeterminateness' of which Wicksell had begun to speak arises from question (a),[263] and he brings in, to explain it, question (b) which may also be a cause of indeterminateness but in another sense.

The distinction between the two questions is brought out by considering that if we do not know what the existing quantity of capital is, we have no basis for taking into account those psychical forces on which the accumulation of new capital or the consumption of already existing capital is supposed to depend: the action of those forces cannot but be related to levels of income, and the levels of income cannot, in Wicksell's theory, be determined if we do not know what the existing quantity of capital is.[264]

We may now pull together the threads of Section II of the dissertation and summarize the conclusions in the following points.

I. The choice of the capital existing in the economy as one of the determinants of distribution imposes on the marginal productivity theories the condition that physical capital should be measured as a single magnitude invariant to changes in distribution and related in a known way to the value, in some standard, of the stock of capital it expresses. In fact capital could be measured in the production function also as a set of magnitudes satisfying those requirements, but such a set of quantities could not be taken as given when determining distribution without contradicting the condition of the existence of a single equilibrium rate of interest on the value of all capital goods.

II. Walras measures the quantity of capital existing in the economy as a set of quantities of capital goods of different kinds. This leads to the result that if his procedure is accepted it will in general be impossible to satisfy simultaneously all the equations of general equilibrium. Walras's attempt to show that such equations can be simultaneously satisfied appears to be unsuccessful,

[262] Op. cit., pp. 202–3.

[263] Cf. the paragraph preceding the one of the passage last quoted (op. cit., pp. 201–2).

[264] See the Appendix to this chapter.

and to involve him in a misconception of what determines the equilibrium allocation of savings among the different kinds of capital goods.

III. Wicksell, in the earlier versions of his theory, measured capital in the production functions as the average period of production of labour. But the assumptions necessary for a valid use of that measure (simple rate of interest, absence of fixed capital, one homogeneous factor of production besides capital) prevent its use in the production functions and therefore prevent it from being a possible basis for a consistent measurement of the quantity of capital existing in the economy as a single magnitude.

IV. Wicksell in the later versions of his theory abandons the average period of production and introduces in the production function circulating capital as a set of absolute periods of production of original factors, and fixed capital as the number of machines of given types. But, such magnitudes being more than one, we cannot use them as the data measuring the capital existing in the economy. Wicksell measures the existing capital as a given value sum. But this contradicts the condition that the magnitude measuring capital should be invariant to changes in distribution: the value of any physical stock of capital varies with changes in distribution and cannot therefore be taken as a determinant of distribution.

Appendix to Section II, Chapter VI: Capital and Distribution in a Stationary Economy

We may here indicate a way in which the physical forces mentioned by Wicksell in the above quoted passage,[265] might be thought to lead to a solution of the problem of distribution. That could be done by eliminating the datum 'quantity of capital existing in the economy', and substituting for the missing equation one expressing the condition that at the equilibrium levels of income and system of prices, the amount of net savings currently made should be zero. In other words instead of analysing and comparing situations in which the 'quantity of capital' is given, we should limit ourselves to analysing and comparing stationary situations, that is situations where the tendency to accumulation has spent its force.[266] In that case the value of capital could be taken as an unknown; the other data would be the same as before: the system of consumers' preferences, the state of technical knowledge expressed by Wicksell's production functions, the existing quantities

---

[265] Above, pp. 106–7.

[266] Difficulties may exist as to the possibility of defining zero net accumulation. But it seems that, since the hypothetical situation corresponding to any arbitrary value of capital would be an equilibrium situation, if the whole of the incomes determined for such a situation were consumed, capital would remain the same in its physical components. We should then have the ground for defining unambiguously zero net accumulation as the one we have where, on the basis of the existing propensities to save, those incomes are consumed in their entirety.

of the factors of production other than capital.[267] The process of determination of such an equilibrium situation could be described in these terms. For each arbitrary value in terms of any of the commodities produced, we shall have, according to the procedure indicated in Wicksell's scheme of general equilibrium, a system of prices and distribution; on the basis of that system of prices and distribution it will be possible to determine whether a tendency will exist to have accumulation of new capital or consumption of already existing capital, using for the purpose the functions relating the savings of each member of the community to the level of his income and to the other relevant economic variables. The value of capital for which net accumulation in the community as a whole is zero, would define the situation of equilibrium we are looking for.

But the assumptions on the basis of which we could determine the system of relative values would be extremely restrictive. We should have a theory which determines the system of distribution only for special 'stationary states' defined by the condition that accumulation should be zero. It may be doubted whether such theory would be useful for any problem but that of what self-consistent systems of prices would yield no net accumulation.

If we had to study the effect of a certain event affecting some of the data (for instance a change in the techniques available in order to produce the same commodities), all that we could do would be to compare two price situations A and B, in which A is the system of prices and distribution which would have existed before the event, if, the data remaining what they were before the 'event', there had been enough time to reach a stationary situation as to the accumulation of capital, and, on the other hand, B is the system of prices and distribution which would come into existence if, after the event has taken place, no further changes in data should occur before a new stationary situation is reached as to the accumulation of capital.

The possibility of taking as given the quantity of capital would have allowed us to compare the systems of relative values for situations of equilibrium in which tendencies to accumulation or decumulation may exist and so, presumably, we could have obtained results which could have been more relevant for forecasting the effects of the 'event' in an economic reality where constancy in the data, but for the event considered, can the less be assumed, the longer the period of time the effects of the event take to work themselves out. For it seems safe to assume that the economy is at any moment nearer in time and, hence, in its system of relative values, to a hypothetical equilibrium situation founded on a complete adjustment between production and consumption based on the existing quantity of the factors

[267] I have found an indication of what appears to be a similar way of dealing with the problem of capital in professor Hicks's *Value and Capital* (Oxford, 1939) where it is said 'if entrepreneurs do not desire to increase or diminish their stock, their net borrowing must be nil. If the demand and supply for loans are to be in equilibrium, net saving must therefore be nil. … We therefore have … equations to determine the size of the stock of capital goods and the rate of interest; consequently both are determined' (p. 118).

of production, than to a hypothetical stationary situation where, all the relevant data remaining the same, the tendency to accumulate has spent its forces; and, if we have to take into consideration the effects of an accumulation of capital proceeding up to the point where net accumulation becomes zero, the assumption 'other things remaining equal' referred to data such as consumers' preferences, population, technical knowledge, can hardly be held.[268]

Appendix A: Points on Bailey's Attack on the Classics' Theories of Value

What has been said in Chapters I and II of Section I about the surplus approach to the theory of distribution to be found in the classical economists, should have brought into light how the necessity of dealing with aggregates of commodities as homogeneous quantities whose variations can be postulated independently of changes in distribution (rates of profits and wages), raises a problem of value which has two aspects: determination of the circumstances governing relative values and search for a way of expressing the values of commodities in terms of magnitudes given independently of the way in which the social produce is distributed. It was this second aspect of the value problem which was tackled by Ricardo (and, to some degree and amid confusions, by other classical writers), in the form of the search for an 'invariable' measure of value and for a 'real' or 'absolute' value underlying the relative values. This connection between the theories of distribution of the classical economists and their search for an 'invariable' measure of value and for 'real' values, was not seen by most post-Ricardian economists. In 1825, that is two years after the death of Ricardo, Samuel Bailey published his essay *A Critical Dissertation on the Nature, Measure and Causes of Value*.[269]

This pamphlet seems to have had a considerable influence in inducing subsequent economists, with the exception of Marx, to abandon Ricardo's concepts of an 'absolute' or 'real' value and of an 'invariable' measure of value, abandoning with them both the search for a clarification and a solution of the very real

[268] It might be thought that a similar 'stationary' state is necessary for equilibrium analysis, independently of the problem connected with the concept of a given quantity of capital: if savings are currently made the equilibrium will be disturbed in the future and expectations of changes in the price system will influence decisions together with the present price system. But, as we have mentioned above (n. 151), if there must be any useful static analysis, it appears that a less restrictive concept of equilibrium must be referred to.

[269] The essay has been reprinted by the London School of Economics in 1931.

theoretical problems which lay behind those concepts and the possibilities for a development of the analytical structure of Ricardo's theory of distribution.[270]

In that essay Samuel Bailey, starting from Smith's definition of the exchangeable value of a commodity as 'the power of purchasing other goods which that object conveys', reaches the conclusion that the meaning of exchangeable value is that of the ratio in which the two commodities exchange for each other. So that it is meaningless to speak of the value of a commodity if one does no immediately specify another commodity supplying the other term of the ratio. Bailey believes therefore that he has a solid ground for rejecting as self contradictory and therefore meaningless the idea that there can be a commodity which is in itself invariable in value while its ratio to another commodity varies. Accordingly, he regards the concepts of an 'invariable' measure of value and of 'real' or 'absolute' value in Smith, Ricardo and other economists as purely the result of conceptual confusions.

In assessing the importance of Bailey's indictment of the classical economists two points should be made.

On the one hand in the classical economists there were, chiefly before Ricardo, many unconscious identifications of distinct problems which prevented a clear statement of the aim or aims of those concepts. To that extent Bailey's criticism, although conducted purely on the level of verbal consistency, might have helped to stimulate a clarification of the issues involved.

On the other hand the fact that Bailey did not see that behind the verbal inconsistencies there were real problems, and, together with it, the inadequacy of the answers from the Ricardians, had the effect of stopping the work on those problems until they arose again in a very different context.

Appendix B: On Some Points Recently Discussed with Regard to the 'Transformation Problem'

What has been said in Chapters III and IV of Section I on the determination of the rate of profits in Ricardo's and Marx's theories of distribution may be helpful for a clarification of some issues raised in recent discussions of the 'transformation problem'.

A first point is whether and in what sense, if any, the rate of profits correctly determined within the Marxian model depends on Marx's 'conditions of reproduction', that is whether the rate of profits is influenced by the level of the accumulation which the economy is simultaneously carrying out.

---

[270] Schumpeter in his *History of Economic Analysis* considers Bailey's work the 'peak performance' among those of the critics of Ricardo's theory of value, and he notices that 'it became clear in time that he had in fact turned the tide and dealt a fatal blow' to Ricardo's analytic structure (p. 599).

Bortkiewicz, in the article we have repeatedly referred to, had employed for his solution Marx's equations of 'simple reproduction' expressing conditions in which no net accumulation takes place.[271] P. Sweezy in his *The Theory of Capitalist Development* follows closely that procedure.[272] J. Winternitz, in a note 'Value and Prices' on the *Economic Journal* of 1948, obtained the same solution Bortkiewicz had obtained, but without using the equations of simple reproduction.[273] He therefore pointed out that the rate of profits in the Marxian model is independent of the level of accumulation, in contrast to what would have appeared from the Bortkiewicz solution. But that argument did not apparently convince K. May who argued that since the quantities $c_1\ v_1\ s_1$ and $c_2\ v_2\ s_2$ determining the rate of profit and the prices of production in the Winternitz solution are dependent on the 'equations of reproduction', those equations are relevant to the solution even if they are not explicitly introduced.[274] It would therefore follow, although May does not explicitly draw this conclusion, that the rate of profits varies simply as a result of the rate of accumulation. The point is of some importance and is worth clearing up.

In fact May's argument is based on a misreading of the equation determining profits due to the unsatisfactory way in which the solutions of the transformation problem have been put forward. Although the *absolute* quantities $c_1\ v_1\ s_1$ and c_2

[271] See Eqs. (11), (12) and (13) at p. 202, Appendix to Böhm-Bawerk's *Karl Marx and the Close of His System*, New York, 1949.

[272] P. Sweezy, *Theory of Capitalistic Development*, New York, 1942, p. 117.

[273] *Economic Journal*, 1948, p. 278. It is not difficult to point out within Bortkiewicz's own equations why the introduction of the equations of simple reproduction was quite unnecessary. At p. 202 of op. cit., Bortkiewicz formulates three of the four determining equations of his solution in the following way:

$$(1+p)(c_1x+v_1y) = (c_1+c_2+c_3)x$$
$$(1+p)(c_2x+v_2y) = (v_1+v_2+v_3)y$$
$$(1+p)(c_3x+v_3y) = (s_1+s_2+s_3)z$$

where $c_1c_2c_3$, $v_1v_2v_3$, $s_1s_2s_3$ have the meaning seen in Chapter IV above (p. 38) and where x, y, z, are the prices of production of commodities of sectors I, I, III embodying a labour unit, while p is the rate of profits. But those three equations could be substituted by the following three ones:

$$(1+p)(c_1x+v_1y) = x(c_1+v_1+s_1)$$
$$(1+p)(c_2x+v_2y) = y(c_2+v_2+s_2)$$
$$(1+p)(c_3x+v_3y) = z(c_3+v_3+s_3)$$

These latter equations, which express the equilibrium equality between the costs of production (LHS) and the revenues (RHS) in each of the sectors, do not bring in the equations of simple reproduction, and give the results obtained by Bortkiewicz.

[274] *Economic Journal*, 1948, p. 599. M. H. Dobb seems to take the same view in his 'A Note on the Transformation Problem' in *On Economic Theory and Socialism*, London, 1955, p. 276, last paragraph.

v_2 s_2 appear in Winternitz's equation for the rate of profit, the only magnitudes relevant for the determination of the profit rate are certain *ratios*, namely the rate of surplus value, the organic composition of sector II and the organic composition of that section of sector I which produces capital goods directly or indirectly necessary for the production of wage goods.[275] Or, both more concretely and more generally,[276] the rate of profits depends only on the quantities of wage goods constituting the wage rate and on the technique by which those goods are produced. If that is so the question of whether or not the rate of profits depends on the level of accumulation *simultaneously* carried out, answers itself: it does to the extent only in which it affects either the real wage rate or the technique by which the wage goods are produced; these are questions which are evidently beyond the scope of the transformation problem and which are connected with the wider theoretical context in which the type of theory of value and distribution examined here is used.

What has just been said in connection with the first point, can be used to clarify another question of some importance recently discussed: it refers to the independence of the rate of profits from the data concerning the production of goods other than the wage goods. As we have already mentioned,[277] Bortkiewicz pointed out that his equation determining the profit rate was independent of the data for his sector III. K. May, on the basis of the argument just examined dissents: since, he argues, the quantities c_1 v_1 s_1 and c_2 v_2 s_2 determining profits are linked by the equations of reproduction to the quantities c_3 v_3 s_3, it follows 'that the rate of profits is not independent of division three'.[278]

In other words, what May appears to think is that since Bortkiewicz's sector I supplies capital goods to sector III, the data c_1 v_1 s_1 will depend on the output and organic composition of the sector producing goods consumed by capitalists, and therefore also the rate of profits will depend on the data for sector III.

This argument appears to be founded on a confusion created by the way in which Bortkiewicz divided the economy into sectors. As we have already seen, the only datum for sector I relevant for determining the rate of profits is the organic composition of that section of the sector which directly or indirectly supplies sector II. Therefore those variations of the whole sector I (either in the aggregate capitals c_1 and v_1 or in the organic composition) which are due to variations in its section serving directly or indirectly sector III (and these are the variations of the data of sector I associated with variations of the data for sector III) cannot affect the rate of profits.

[275] See above Eq. (VII) at p. 40, where the rate of profits is determined exclusively by the quantities Q_1, Q_2 and r.

[276] More generally because this formulation is valid also when we drop the special assumption about the shape of the investment function underlying Bortkiewicz solution and justifying the distinction between the two sectors.

[277] Above, n. 65.

[278] Op. cit., p. 599.

We may finally comment on the view expressed by Mrs. Robinson that the whole point at issue in the transformation problem is 'purely formal and of no importance'.[279] The reason for such a view appears to be 'that the whole argument is condemned to circularity from birth, because the '*values* which have to be 'transformed into prices' are arrived at in the first instance by transforming prices into *values*'.[280]

What the argument quoted above seems to ignore is that while the quantity of labour embodied in a commodity is independent of the rate of profits and can therefore be used by Marx as a datum for determining the rate of profits, the price depends on the rate of profits and therefore Marx cannot start from it when he has to determine that rate. In fact what has become known as the 'transformation problem' deals with the basic relationships of Marx's and Ricardo's theories of distribution and value.

Appendix C: Walras's Assumption of Fixed Coefficients of Production; Some Points on the Use of Fixed Coefficients in the Theory of Distribution

In Chapters II and III of Section II we have considered Walras's theory of distribution as a version of the theories of distribution based on the marginal productivity principle. This note is intended to answer possible doubts about the extent to which we were justified in doing so, and to indicate a few points about the nature of a theory of distribution founded on fixed coefficients of production.

The doubts referred to might arise because, whereas in the more common versions of the marginal productivity theory the main weight of the determination of the prices of the factors of production is put on the variability of the coefficients of production, Walras, on the contrary, expounds the main points of his theory while assuming that the proportions of the productive services required for producing a unit of a commodity are given and cannot be varied in the process of achieving equilibrium. A first answer to such doubts is that for Walras that was only a simplifying assumption, and that, from the very first published version of his theory, he explained how the coefficients were really unknowns of the equilibrium system which could be determined by the condition of minimising the costs of production. The fact however remains that his theory is expounded as if it did not essentially depend on the variability of production coefficients.

We can immediately remark that for what concerns us here the problem is not important, since an appropriate measurement of the 'quantity of capital' is essential for this type of theory of distribution independently of whether the production

[279] *Collected Economic Papers*, Vol. 1, London, 1951, p. 149.

[280] Op. cit., p. 150 (emphases in the original).

coefficients are taken to be fixed or variable. But it may still be useful to look at some points connected with such a version of the marginal productivity theory.

It may be misleading to draw a sharp distinction between theories based on fixed coefficients and the more commonly accepted theories.

For both types of theory the determination of the prices of the factors of production rests on the possibility of substituting one factor for the others. The difference is in that, whereas the latter theory can rely both on a technical substitutability (due to the possibility of varying the proportions of factors required to obtain a given physical output of a specified commodity), and on a substitutability for the consumers between commodities requiring different proportions of the factors, the former theory can rely only on a substitutability between factors arising from the second cause.

From this difference some consequences follow.

Firstly, we can mention that when the coefficients of production are taken as fixed, we cannot measure the marginal product of a factor in homogeneous physical terms: the marginal product of a factor, if it can at all be determined, can only be thought of as the algebraic sum of quantities of different commodities.[281] We must then bring in the system of relative values, but that does not introduce any additional difficulty since also when the production coefficients are variable the physical marginal product of a factor in a firm or industry can be determined only when the quantities of all the factors there employed are determined, and such quantities can be determined only simultaneously with the system of relative prices.

[281] A simple example will illustrate this. Let us have an economy in which only two commodities *A* and *B* are produced using two factors of production, *X* and *Y*, in proportions defined by the production coefficients a_x a_y for *A*, and b_x b_y for *B*; we shall also assume that the proportion of *X* required is higher for *A* than for *B*: ($\frac{a_x}{a_y} > \frac{b_x}{b_y}$). Then a marginal increase of the quantity of *X* available (the quantity of *Y* remaining constant) would allow us to increase the output of *A* while giving up some output of *B*: the marginal product of *X* will then be defined by the difference between the value of the increase of *A* and the value of the decrease of *B*, and, in competitive equilibrium, the price of the marginal increase of *X* will be equal to that difference. In mathematical terms: if we forego one unit of *B*, b_x units of *X* and b_y units of *Y* will be freed; with them we can produce $\frac{b_y}{a_y}$ units of *A*, if we can dispose of ($\frac{b_y}{a_y}a_x - b_x$) more units of *X*. Hence, in the equilibrium situation, if p_a p_b p_x are the prices respectively of *A*, *B*, *X*, we must have:

$$p_x = \frac{\frac{b_y}{a_y}p_a - p_b}{\frac{b_y}{a_y}a_x - b_x}$$

With analogous procedure we can determine p_y from the equation:

$$p_y = \frac{\frac{a_x}{b_x}p_b - p_a}{\frac{a_x}{b_x}b_y - a_y}$$

The second and more important consequence is that when we have fixed coefficients of production some special conditions must be satisfied if the prices of the factors of production are to be determinable, once the quantity of them available for productive purposes is rigidly fixed.[282] The prices of the factors of production are determinable only when the proportions in which the factors enter into the commodities are different[283]; otherwise the possibility open to the consumers to substitute one commodity for another, as their relative prices change, will no longer give rise to a substitutability between factors of production.

Another condition for the determinacy of the prices of the factors, which is perhaps less obvious than the one just mentioned, is that taking any possible group of commodities, characterized by the fact that they are the *only* commodities in the economy for which two or more specified factors of production are required, the number of commodities should always be equal or greater than the number of factors which are only employed in their production. A special case of this condition is when all factors enter all commodities; then the condition becomes that the total number of commodities in the economy should be equal to or greater than the total number of factors; in Walras's notation $n \leq m$. But when not all the factors enter all the commodities, that condition is insufficient, since more than one group of commodities of the type mentioned above can be found.[284]

---

[282] We shall presently see how the introduction of a price elasticity of the supply of factors for productive purposes modifies the conclusions reached on the assumption that the quantities of factors available for production are fixed.

[283] Referring to the example given in note 281 above, the indeterminacy of p_x and p_y when $\frac{a_x}{a_y} = \frac{b_x}{b_y}$ is apparent. If $\frac{a_x}{a_y} = \frac{b_x}{b_y}$, it follows that $\frac{b_y}{a_y} = \frac{b_x}{a_x}$. Substituting $\frac{b_x}{a_x}$ for $\frac{b_y}{a_y}$ in the RHS of the equation determining p_x we have:

$$p_x = \frac{\frac{b_x}{a_x}p_a - p_b}{\frac{b_x}{a_x}a_x - b_x} = \frac{\frac{b_x}{a_x}p_a - p_b}{0}$$

The value of p_x is indeterminate; with analogous procedure it is easy to show that the same is true for p_y.

[284] I am not sure that the formulation of the condition given above is the best one. But a simple mathematical demonstration of it can be given. One of the systems of equations of general equilibrium is the one expressing the equality between total quantities of productive services available in the economy and the quantities of them used in order to produce the equilibrium outputs of commodities $A\ B\ C$ .... Using Walras's notation, the variables involved are:

$D_a D_b \ldots$	the quantities of the m commodities A, B ... produced and consumed in equilibrium
$O_t \ldots O_p \ldots O_k \ldots$	the quantities of the n productive services available in the economy
$\begin{Bmatrix} a_t \ldots a_p \ldots a_k \ldots \\ b_t \ldots b_p \ldots b_k \ldots \end{Bmatrix}$	the $(m \cdot n)$ fixed production coefficients of commodities A, B, ...

The system is

$$\left\{\begin{matrix} a_t D_a + b_t D_b + c_t D_c + \cdots = O_t \\ \cdots \\ a_p D_a + b_p D_b + c_p D_c + \cdots = O_p \\ \cdots \\ a_k D_a + b_k D_b + c_k D_c + \cdots = O_k \end{matrix}\right\} \quad n \text{ equations} \qquad (1)$$

This general condition of determinacy is the less likely to be fulfilled the more the factors are highly specialized.

Comparing the two conditions of determinacy just mentioned we can see that the fixed coefficients determination of the prices of productive services is beset by two causes of indeterminacy of which the one is the more likely to be present the less the other is, and vice-versa. In fact the more the factors employed in the production of a commodity tend to be specialised, the less the first cause of indeterminacy will make itself felt and the more the second cause of indeterminacy is likely to be present; and vice-versa.[285,286]

In the general equilibrium equations the n quantities of factors available and the $(m \cdot n)$ production coefficients are given. The only unknowns appearing in system (1) are the m quantities of commodities produced: $D_a D_b$ …; the equations of system (1) on the other hand are n in number; the condition $m \geq n$ follows immediately; if it is not satisfied, and if the equations are independent, we shall have over-determination.

More generally, if the general condition mentioned in the text is not satisfied we shall be able to single out in that system at least one group of r equations in which only a number s of quantities of commodities appear on the LHS, where $s < r$; they will be the equations corresponding to the r productive services (or factors) which enter the production only of those s commodities. In that group of equations we shall have s unknowns and r equations: the equations are insoluble.

In fact if $s < r$, and if all the equations are independent, we have overdetermination: all the conditions those equations impose on D_i, $D_{i'}$ … cannot be simultaneously satisfied. In economic terms, there cannot always be a set of s outputs D_i, $D_{i'}$ … such as to employ the given quantities of the r factors. There remains then the case in which the quantities available of at least $(r - s)$ among those productive services are given so as to be compatible with the D_i … determined by the equations referring to the remaining s productive services. But then $(r - s)$ among the r equations will not be independent equations. Accordingly, taking now all the equations of general equilibrium together, they will consist of a number of independent equations diminished of $(r - s)$ and the unknowns will therefore outnumber the independent equations.

The conditions of determinacy demonstrated here, as well as the first one mentioned in the text, could be derived from the fact that, on the assumption of fixed production coefficients, the price of a factor of production is determinable to the extent in which it is possible, through marginal alterations in the relative outputs of the commodities, to absorb an increase in the quantity of that factor by one unit while keeping constant the quantities of the others. When $r > s$, that will not be possible because, as we have seen, there will not be outputs of the s commodities which can absorb any set of quantities of the r factors.

[285] The point can be seen clearly if we imagine what appear to be the two limiting cases as to the divergence in the proportions of the coefficients of production: on the one hand we have all commodities produced with the same factors in the same proportions; on the other hand we have each commodity produced with factors which do not enter into any of the others.

[286] It appears that the first cause of indeterminacy can be brought under a more precise statement than the second one if the relevant number of commodities to be compared with the number of productive services is taken to be not the one empirically given, but the one of commodities with differences in the proportions between production coefficients: the first cause of indeterminacy would then be simply a special case where $m = 1$ and $n > 1$.

Thirdly, even when the conditions of determinacy are satisfied, the validity of a marginal productivity theory appears to be weakened by the assumption of a fixity in the coefficients of production. Other things being equal, fixity of production coefficients diminishes the price elasticity of the demand for each productive service: very small changes in the quantity of a productive service available are more likely to bring about relatively large changes in its price (and in that of the others); so that the prices of the factors would tend to be left practically indeterminate. And this, it seems, would be a reason for thinking that the forces chosen for determining distribution in such a theory, are unlikely to be the most important ones.

The points indicated above have been reached on the assumption that the quantities of productive services available for productive use in each situation are given independently of their price, so that all the weight of the determination of their price rests on the demand for them, on their marginal productivity.

Walras instead assumed that the owners of productive services have the alternative of using them for direct consumption in quantities determined by the usual conditions of the equilibrium of the consumers. As a result the quantities of productive services available for production will depend on their price.

From the formal point of view this assumption is very useful: if the shape of such supply functions is appropriate, we may be able to determine the prices of the productive services even when the conditions of determinacy indicated above do not hold. The weight of the determination would be borne by the satisfactions to be derived by directly using the productive services.

But the economic validity of a theory of distribution which would determine the level of the rate of interest, of rents and of wages, on the basis of the satisfaction of the owners of given capital goods (or the owners of given natural resources, or the labourers) can derive from employing respectively their capital goods, natural resources, labour for direct use seems very doubtful. Concluding, it appears that when production coefficients are taken as fixed, the resulting theory of distribution is thereby impaired in its validity for the following reasons:

(a) unless the number of factors of production is less than the number of commodities with differences in the proportions between coefficients of production, the distribution of the social produce among the owners of the existing quantities of the factors of production will remain indeterminate;
(b) even when that condition is satisfied, the elasticity of the marginal productivity functions, other things being equal, will be smaller;
(c) the introduction of a price elasticity of the supply of productive services available for productive use makes determinacy of distribution more likely, but is of doubtful validity when compared with economic reality.

On the other hand the difficulties connected with an adequate measurement of the given 'quantities of capital' are always present whether the coefficients of production are considered to be fixed or variable.

Appendix D: Professor Knight's Theory of the Rate of Interest

In the thirties a controversy on the theory of capital took place, mainly on British and American scientific periodicals. The controversy, which had apparently been stimulated by concern with theories of the trade cycle accounting for the economic instability of the period, came to touch on the problem which interests us here: the connection between theory of distribution and theory of capital.

A prominent part in the controversy was taken by Professor F. H. Knight who, in a series of essays and articles,[287] criticised the theories of capital based on the concept of period of production on which Professor Hayek's work was based, and attempted to show how a satisfactory theory of the rate of interest on marginal productivity lines could be obtained without resorting to a measurement of capital by periods of production.

We have thought that Professor Knight's theory of the rate of interest may be usefully considered here as one of the most recent attempts to deal with the problem of capital in a marginal productivity context.

We should make clear that we are not attempting an exhaustive examination of Professor Knight's arguments: we shall refer only to the points which seem to us to be more relevant for the problem discussed in Section II of the dissertation. We shall also accept in most of our argument more of the setting in which Professor Knight determines the rate of interest, than appears to be generally acceptable. It will be our purpose to show how, even in that setting, the solution advanced does not appear to be satisfactory.

The basic contentions on which Knight attempts to build a theory of the rate of interest can be reduced, it seems, to the following two. Firstly we have the contention that for the determination of the rate of interest we do not need to refer to the concept of a 'quantity of capital'; the rate of return can be determined by referring

[287] 'Capitalistic Production, Time and the Rate of Return' in *Economic Essays in Honour of Gustav Cassel*, London, 1933; 'Capital, Time and the Interest Rate', *Economica*, August 1934; 'Professor Hayek and the Theory of Investment', *Economic Journal*, March 1935; 'The Ricardian Theory of Production and Distribution', *Canadian Journal of Economics and Political Science*, February 1935; 'The Theory of Investment Once More: Mr. Boulding and the Austrians', *Quarterly Journal of Economics*, November 1935; 'The Quantity of Capital and the Rate of Interest', *Journal of Political Economy*, August and October 1936; 'On the Theory of Capital: in Reply to Mr. Kaldor', *Econometrica*, 1938; see also the article 'Interest' in the *Encyclopaedia of Social Sciences*, Vol. 8, edited by E. R. A. Seligman, New York, Macmillan, 1932.

only to a marginal investment, without any need to bring in the existing quantity of capital.[288]

Secondly, in the case of the marginal investment the rate of interest can be determined by comparing the 'perpetual income', which will be the result of that investment, with the *cost* of the investment as determined by the prices of the productive services entering the capital good or goods of which the investment consists. In other words Knight contends that the value of the marginal increment of capital can, for the problem of the rate of interest, be non-circularly determined by referring to the costs of production of the concrete capital goods of which the marginal increment consists.[289]

These two contentions granted, there is no difficulty in writing an equation from which the rate of interest can be determined. In Knight we have an equation where the costs of production of the capital good appear on the LHS[290] and, on the RHS, we have the value of the capital good calculated as the discounted value of all future 'income' which can be derived from the investment: in competitive equilibrium the costs of production must be equal to the price of the capital good. Since, according to Knight, the rate of interest will be the only unknown in that equation, the equation will determine the rate of interest.

Let us take as an example the equation put forward by Knight in his article in *Economica*: the capital good or capital goods which constitute the marginal

[288] In the equations we shall mention later, Knight always refers to a single new investment: the rate of interest is there determined by the condition that the cost of that investment should be equal to the value of the discounted flow of the increase in the produce obtained by adding that investment to an existing combination of productive agencies. The following passage from the article in the *Journal of Political Economy* shows what difficulty Knight was trying to avoid by referring only to the marginal investment: 'The ultimate meaning of the interest rate does not involve a quantity of capital at all, but only a relation between an instantaneous rate of investment and a resulting instantaneous rate of growth in potential income … And at an instant the magnitudes involved are not of the nature of capital quantity and income yield but of rates of change in these … It remains true that a (finite) quantity of capital must be defined in terms of a rate of interest; but because the rate is definable without reference to capital quantity, the vicious circle disappers' (*Journal of Political Economy*, 1936, pp. 434–5).

[289] 'The rate of interest is essentially "determined" by "cost of production" … The resources which would yield a certain consumption income are used instead, for a certain interval, to yield wealth, which in turn will yield and represent a certain perpetual income' (*Economic Essays in Honour of Gustav Cassel*, p. 335). 'The immediate way out of the difficulty of circularity raised by the view that capital quantity is arrived at by capitalization … is the notion that the quantity [of capital] is determined independently of the yield by the cost of production of capital goods' (*Journal of Political Economy*, 1936, p. 434).

[290] To give an unambiguous meaning to the costs of production appearing on the LHS of the equation we need the assumption that costs of production of capital goods are independent of the scale of output. Knight recognizes this need (see *Economic Essays*, p. 336; *Economica*, 1934, p. 281).

investment require the yearly expenditure of S on 'resources' over a period of construction of C years; after the moment in which the capital good has been completed, it will yield an income of R per year for a period of use of L years. The equation expressing the equality of costs of production and values of future incomes (both quantities being referred to the moment in which the capital good is ready to enter production) will then be

$$\frac{S\left[(1+i)^C - 1\right]}{i} = \frac{R\left[(1+i)^L - 1\right]}{i(1+i)^L} \tag{A}$$

where i is the rate of interest we are aiming to determine.[291] Equation (A) will determine the rate of interest i if all the other variables appearing in it can be taken as given when determining the rate of interests; in other words, we should be able to consider S and R in Eq. (A) as *known* quantities. Knight seems to take it for granted that such quantities can be taken as known while determining the rate of interest.[292] We can now pass to an examination of the validity of the theory of interest summarized here and for that purpose we shall have to see to what extent Knight was justified in taking as given the S and R quantities of Eq. (A).

One of the difficulties in criticizing Professor Knight's theory of the rate of interest as put forward in the articles indicated above, is the vagueness of the formulation at key points, so that one is left in doubt about what is meant and different interpretations appear as equally plausible. Because of this we shall have to examine one by one the possible interpretations and see where each of them leads.

The simplest way of pointing out the basic deficiency of Knight's procedure is perhaps by looking more carefully at the S on the LHS of Eq. (A). S, we have seen, are the annual costs borne during the construction of the capital good, that is the remuneration of the productive agents employed in producing the capital item. Now, with respect to these productive agents the cases may be two: either they do or they do not include capital goods.

In the second case, we may grant, for the purpose of our argument here, that the S quantities can be taken as given in Eq. (A); but then the resulting theory of capital and interest would be nothing but an application, from a very limited angle, of just that theory of capital reducing it to periods of time over which 'original

[291] *Economica*, 1934, p. 265.

[292] In the article on the *Journal of Political Economy*, after an equation similar in meaning to the one given above, Professor Knight says: 'The known magnitudes depend on the conditions under which investment actually takes place, which conditions are assumed to remain unchanged during the course of the investing operation' (*Journal of Political Economy*, 1936, p. 442).

factors' have to remain invested.[293] In fact Eq. (A) would then determine the rate of interest on the basis of the marginal productivity of original factors remaining invested over the time distribution of inputs and outputs defined by the periods of time C and L. Such an interpretation of Eq. (A) must be excluded: one of the main criticisms Knight advances against the period of production theories is just that the capital goods are never produced by 'labour' and 'land' only: they always require for their production the co-operation of other capital goods.[294]

We are then left with the case in which the quantities S do include the renumeration for the services of capital goods. But then how can we take as given, when determining the rate of interest, that portion of S which is the remuneration of the productive services of other capital goods?

On this fundamental point Professor Knight is ambiguous:

> On the cost side ... the direct outlays incurred [for producing the capital good] will practically always include a proportion, which may be small or large, of payments to pre-existing "capital items". These, of course, may take the form of "rent" in the ordinary business sense, a payment to the owner of a concrete instrument for its use, or of "interest", paid for the use of "capital", a sum of abstract value.[295]

There Knight stops. How and why can we take as given the 'rents', or the capital, 'a sum of abstract value', when calculating the rate of interest in Eq. (A), he does not say. That is what we must see now.

The possibilities about the nature of the payments for capital services put forward in the passage quoted above are two: rents for physically defined capital goods services, or the rate of interest on capital considered as a sum of (abstract) value. It is convenient for our purpose to distinguish between these two possibilities and examine them in turn, beginning with the second one.

---

[293] In this case the quantities S would be constituted entirely of wages or rents paid for productive services other than those of capital goods. But how far is it allowable to assume, as Professor Knight does, that the prices of those services remain unchanged during the course of the investing operation (see n. 292)? We may interpret it as meaning that since the marginal investment considered in Eq. (A) cannot appreciably affect those prices, we can take them from the situation in the economy for which we want to determine the rate of interest. But then it is difficult to see what we gain by Eq. (A). The possibility of forecast is in general ruled out: if we have to determine what effect a certain event (like a change in technical knowledge, or a change in consumers' tastes, etc.) will have on the rate of interest, we shall not in general be able to take as given the wages or rents any more than we can take as given the rate of interest. We could interpret Professor Knight as meaning that those prices can be taken as given in Eq. (A) since they can be determined simultaneously with the rate of interest by the conditions of general equilibrium. But then we should introduce in those equilibrium equations just that 'capital quantity' we are trying to avoid by way of Eq. (A). We must therefore return to the first interpretation and conclude that even if in the calculation of the costs of the marginal investment we could avoid the difficulties of capital costs, the theory of interest of Eq. (A) would seem to be of little use.

[294] See, for instance, *Economica*, 1934, pp. 279–80.

[295] *Economica*, 1934, pp. 261–2.

If we have to evaluate the capital costs of the capital good as the rate of interest on the value of the capital goods employed, we shall be moving in a vicious circle: it is true that we can freely introduce on the LHS of Eq. (A) the unknown rate of interest; but that is not sufficient: in order to evaluate capital costs in that way we need the *value* of the capital goods used in producing the first capital good and we have no way of knowing such a value; in fact we introduced the *S* series just in order to determine in a non-circular way the value of the capital good which constitutes the marginal investment; now it appears, we have only been begging the question, since in order to know the *S* quantities we must know the value of the capital goods employed in producing the first capital good: we are back at where we started.[296] If we interpret Professor Knight as saying that the capital costs in the *S* quantities appearing on the LHS of Eq. (A) are to be calculated as 'interest paid for the use of 'capital', 'a sum of abstract value', then his determination of the rate of interest is illusory: we do not have the basis on which it is supposed to rest the cost of production of the capital good constituting the marginal investment. Unless we want to think that the costs of production of the capital good can be ultimately reduced to the rate of interest and to the prices of the services of factors of production other than capital: the value of capital goods entering the production of the first capital good can then be determined as their costs of production and so on and so on, until going sufficiently far back in time, all the costs of production appear to be made up of the prices of 'original' factors plus the unknown rate of interest on them over the period for which they have remained invested. But again, this would be a version of that period of production theory of capital and interest, which Professor Knight considers erroneous, with all the additional limitations of the initial set of assumptions.

We have up to now considered only the LHS of Eq. (A). Difficulties would appear also on the RHS. What sort of production function will give us the physical quantities for the *R* series, that is the increase in 'income' to be obtained by adding the new capital good to an existing combination of factors of production?[297] Who tells us that the most profitable addition to an existing combination of factors of production is always the addition of a certain capital good without any change in

[296] Since the value of a capital good must be equal to the discounted value of future (net) incomes, to take as given the value of capital goods amounts to taking as given the interest rate to be determined.

[297] An intepretation of the *R* series would be that the increase in physical produce obtainable by the addition of the capital good (or goods), constituting the investment expressed by Eq. (A), to the existing combination of factors is known by experience in the situation considered and can be taken as given in the equation. Then the same remarks made above (n. 293) would be to the point here. The same remarks would again apply in connection with the additional difficulty of the prices to be applied to the product in order to obtain the *R* series, if we interpret Professor Knight as taking those prices from the situation considered (cf. the passage quoted above, n. 292).

the previously existing capital stock?[298] The mention of these questions should be sufficient to indicate what sort of other difficulties we should run into. We are then left with the other possible interpretation of Professor Knight's equation: the capital costs on the LHS of Eq. (A) appear as rents for physically specified types of capital goods services.

With such an interpretation the theory of interest expounded by Knight would avoid the deficiencies we have just seen. We could think that on the LHS of Eq. (A) the prices of the productive services obtained from physically specified types of capital goods can be taken as given in the sense that they are quantities which can be determined simultaneously with the rate of interest by the conditions of general equilibrium, once the quantities of capital goods of the different types available in the economy are given. For the RHS of Eq. (A) the R connected with the marginal investment will be determinable for each type of capital good since we can have a production function in which the produce is related to the quantities of productive services of a physically specified type employed in production, while the prices of products can be determined simultaneously with the prices of the productive services.

According to this interpretation behind Eq. (A) there would really be a theory of capital and of the rate of interest analogous to the one we have seen in connection with Walras: there is no such thing as capital or one factor of production; there are instead capital goods of many different types, the remuneration for whose services is a rent determined according to the marginal productivity principle once the quantity of them, together with that of the other sources of productive services and all the other data, are given.[299]

But then the same criticisms we advanced against Walras's theory of the interest rate could also be advanced against Knight's way of determining the rate of interest.

---

[298] If this condition does not hold it will evidently be impossible to identify the marginal investment with a definite capital good, and with that the basis for Knight's procedure is lacking: we are back at the problem of capital quantity.

[299] This may be what Knight had in mind. In a book recently published (*The Economic Organization*, New York, 1951) we have, for instance, the following passage 'When durable goods are bought and sold, their value is determined by the operation called capitalization. That is, their value is simply the capital sum which, put at interest at the *current* rate will yield an income equal to the annual net product of the property sold. The product itself … approximates the addition which a small unit of such property is capable of adding to the total product of a large combination of such property and the auxiliary productive factors effectively organized and coordinated in production'(p. 111).

Appendix E: The Theory of Capital in Pareto[†]

Summary: I. Introduction.—II. The theory of distribution in the *Cours*.—III. Its criticism: the impossibility of satisfying the equilibrium condition relative to the uniformity of net rates of return.—IV. The disappearance of capitalisation from the general equilibrium equations in the *Manuel*; the resulting deficiencies for this version of general equilibrium theory.—V. Criticism of some statements in the *Manuel* on the possibility of avoiding the notion of capital.—VI. Conclusion.

I

Chapters II and III of the second section tried to show how the measurement of available capital adopted by Walras—the existing physical quantities of each type of capital good—necessarily leads to a contradiction of the equilibrium condition of a uniform net rates of return and cannot therefore be accepted. But the analysis in these two chapters would be incomplete without examining what happened to Walras's theory of capital in the work of Pareto, the main continuer of general equilibrium theory. One question in particular springs to mind: up to what point was Pareto aware of the inconsistency implicit in Walras's theory of capitalisation and, if he was aware of it, how did he try to overcome it?

To find an answer, it seems a distinction must be made between the Pareto of the *Cours* and the Pareto of the *Manuel*. While the theory of capitalisation in the *Cours* remains Walras's, apart from some ambiguities to be discussed below, in the *Manuel* Walras's theory of capitalization disappears from the general equilibrium equations and, as we shall see, nothing replaces it. It is this disappearance of the

[†] [*Editor's note*: English translation from the author's *Il capitale nelle teorie della distribuzione* (1960). In the text as published in the latter book, the references to Pareto's two volumes of the *Cours d'Economie Politique* (Paris, 1896-7) and to his *Manuale d'economia politica* (Milan, 1906) were, respectively, to the Italian edition of the *Cours* (Turin, 1953) and to the 1909 French edition of the *Manuale* (*Manuél d'economie politique*, Paris, 1909); for the present edition of the Appendix, however, it seemed appropriate to convert the references to the Italian edition of the *Cours* into references to the original French edition. In the English draft of this Appendix the quotations had been translated by the author, as no English editions were extant for either of Pareto's mentioned works at the time, and this is still the case for the *Cours*. For the *Manuel*, however, we have been able to make use of the relatively recent English edition (*Manual of political economy*, Oxford, 2014, derived from the 1909 French edition), and references to the latter will integrate those to the French edition. Garegnani's quotations from the *Manuel* are, however, left in the English translation edited by him: although the differences from the now extant English edition appear to be limited to options between equivalent terms, it seemed that for excerpts Garegnani considered particularly significant the 'form' in which he recognized them should be privileged, and even more so in the case of added emphases.]

theory of capitalisation between two works separated by an interval of about ten years[300] which is most striking[301] and requires an explanation.

In the following section, we will give a brief exposition of the theory of capitalisation in the *Cours*, examining it and criticising it in Section III. Sections IV and V will discuss what Pareto says, or doesn't say, on the subject in the *Manuel.*

II

It is in Part One of the *Cours d'Économie Politique*, the 'Principes d'économie pure', that we find the general equilibrium equations and, with them, the essential structure of the theory of capital and distribution. There we find, first and foremost, the definition of capital: 'we call capital whatever economic good which serves production more than once'.[302] This is followed by a classification of capital into three categories, similar to those of Walras: personal capitals, capital goods proper and land capitals.[303] The capitalisation equations are included in a mathematical note in which they are formulated together with the other equations of general equilibrium theory.[304] We set out here briefly all those equations.[305]

The symbols used by Pareto are:

m number of types of the consumable products $A, B, C, \ldots$
n number of types of the capitals $S, T, \ldots$
θ number of the individuals community;

[300]The two volumes of the *Cours d'Économie Politique* were published in 1896–97, and the Manuale d'economia politica in 1906; in 1909 the French version of the *Manuale* appeared, revised and corrected by Pareto himself (but, as far as the issues of capital are concerned, the French version does not appear to present major changes compared to the Italian edition of 1906). The English translations of both works have been checked by the present author.

[301]This was noted by Hicks. Thus, replying to an article by H. Schultz: 'Marginal Productivity and the Lausanne School' (*Economica*, 1932), he writes: 'their theories of capital, suggestive as they are, are the last part of their work which one can consider as final, or accept without the most careful consideration. And I am not sure that Pareto would not have agreed with me. For it is surely significant that Walras' elaborate theory of capitalisation does not reappear in the later work of Pareto, while there is nothing very substantial to take its place' (*Economica*, 1932, p. 297).

[302]*Cours*, Vol. I, para. 90, p. 40.

[303]Pareto introduces in that same para. 90 the concept of 'savings-capital' ('épargne-capital'). For a discussion of this concept and its validity, see further on, n. 339.

[304]Vol. I, para. 135, n. 1, pp. 59–61.

[305]Unlike Walras, Pareto does not treat the group of equations and unknowns introduced with capitalisation separately from the others.

$q_{1s}, q_{1t}, \ldots$ $q_{2s}, q_{2t}, \ldots$	the quantities of the capitals *S*, *T* .... owned respectively by the individuals 1, 2, ..., quantities also defined as the quantities of services (measured as rates per unit of time to which the quantities produced and consumed refer, for example a year) at the disposal of the individuals 1, 2, ...,
$r_{1s}, r_{1t}, \ldots$ $r_{2s}, r_{2t}, \ldots$	the quantities of services of the capitals *S*, *T*, ... sold by the individuals 1, 2, ... [306];
$r_{1a}, r_{1b}, \ldots$ $r_{2a}, r_{2b}, \ldots$	the quantities of the products *A*, *B*, ... bought and consumed by the individuals 1, 2, ... during the year;
$R_s, R_t, \ldots$	the total quantities of services of the capitals *S*, *T*, ... sold by the individuals to the entrepreneurs;
$R_a, R_b, \ldots$	the total quantities of the products *A*, *B*, ... bought and consumed by the individuals during the year;
$r_{1\varepsilon}, r_{2\varepsilon}, \ldots$	the net annual saving of the individuals 1, 2, ... expressed in units of the numeraire *A*;
R_ε	the total net annual saving of the community;
$p_b, p_c, \ldots$	the prices of the products *B*, *C*, ... in terms of the numeraire *A*;
$p_s, p_t, \ldots$	the *net* prices of the productive services of the capitals *S*, *T*, ...;
$p'_s, p'_t, \ldots$	the *gross* prices of these productive services;
$\pi_s, \pi_t, \ldots$	the prices of the capitals *S*, *T*, ...;
$y_s, y_t, \ldots$	the given fractions of the existing amounts of the capitals *S*, *T*,... which must be reproduced annually in order to maintain the existing physical capital intact[307];
$a_s, a_t, \ldots$ $b_s, b_t, \ldots$ ...... $s_s, s_t, \ldots$ $t_s, t_t, \ldots$	the coefficients of production of the products *A*, *B* ... and the capitals *S*, *T*, ...;

[306] As Walras had done before him, Pareto supposes that the services of *S*, *T*, ... may represent a direct utility for individuals, such that, for instance, r_{1s} may be different from q_{1s}.

[307] Cf. *Cours*, Vol. I, para. 133, p. 58. Since Pareto includes 'personal capitals' (and 'land capitals') among the capitals *S*, *T*, ..., the significance to attribute to the respective *y* and the respective 'coefficients of production' is not clear (compare equations [VII] later). Presumably they must be considered as equal to zero.

The equations of general equilibrium formulated by Pareto are the following: θ budget equations for the individuals[308]:

$$p_s r_{1s} + p_t r_{1t} + \cdots = p_a r_{1a} + p_b r_b + \cdots + r_\varepsilon; \tag{I}$$

$\theta \cdot (m + n)$ equations which express, for each individual, the equality between the weighted 'elementary ophelimities'[309]:

$$\begin{array}{l} \phi_{1a}(r_{1a}) = \frac{1}{p_b}\psi_{1b}(r_{1b}) = \cdots = \frac{1}{p_s}\psi_{1s}(q_{1s} - r_{1s}) = \cdots = \psi_{1\varepsilon}(r_{1\varepsilon}) \\ \phi_{2a}(r_{2a}) = \frac{1}{p_b}\psi_{2b}(r_{2b}) = \cdots = \frac{1}{p_s}\psi_{2s}(q_{2s} - r_{2s}) = \cdots = \psi_{2\varepsilon}(r_{2\varepsilon}) \\ \ldots\ldots\ldots\ldots\ldots\ldots\ldots\ldots\ldots\ldots\ldots\ldots \\ \ldots\ldots\ldots\ldots\ldots\ldots\ldots\ldots\ldots\ldots\ldots\ldots; \end{array} \tag{II}$$

$(m + n + 1)$ equations which express the total quantities of products A, B, ... consumed as sums of the quantities consumed by the individuals, and the total quantities of the services of each capital, as well as the quantities of savings, lent to the entrepreneurs as (algebraic) sums of the quantities lent by the individuals[310]:

$$\begin{array}{l} R_a = r_{1a} + r_{2a} + \ldots \\ R_b = r_{1b} + r_{2b} + \ldots \\ \ldots\ldots\ldots \\ \ldots\ldots\ldots \\ R_s = r_{1s} + r_{2s} + \ldots \\ \ldots\ldots\ldots \\ \ldots\ldots\ldots \\ R_\varepsilon = r_{1\varepsilon} + r_{2\varepsilon} + \ldots \end{array} \tag{III}$$

308 Cf. Eq. [1], *ibid.*, para. 135, p. 59, n. 1.

309 Cf. Eq. [2], *ibid.* The $\phi_{1\varepsilon}(r_{1\varepsilon}), \ldots$ represent the 'elementary ophelimities' for the individuals 1, 2 ..., of a unit of saved income. It may seem surprising that Pareto expresses these ophelimities as functions only of the sums saved and not also of the rate of interest, that is of the permanent future income they would give rise to: in para. 106, p. 50, under (β), he stated that one of the two reasons for which an individual saves is 'the advantage which he will gain from such saving by lending it to entrepreneurs...'.

310 Cf. Eqs. [3], *ibid.*, p. 60.

We shall then have an equation which expresses the equality between total net annual savings and the value of the capital goods produced during the year. In this, Pareto supposes that ν types of 'old' capitals S, T, ... are produced, and ν' types of 'new' capital goods[311] H, K, ..., in quantities to be determined R'_s, R'_t, ... and R_h, R_k,:[312]

$$R_\varepsilon = \pi_s R'_s + \cdots + \pi_h R_h + \cdots ; \qquad \text{(IV)}$$

$(\nu + \nu' - 1)$ equations that express the equality between the net rates of return of the capital produced[313]:

$$\frac{p_s}{\pi_s} = \cdots = \frac{p_h}{\pi_h} = \cdots ; \qquad \text{(V)}$$

$(m + \nu + \nu')$ equations which express the equality between the prices of all the products and their production costs[314]:

$$\begin{cases} 1 = a_s(p_s + y_s\pi_s) + a_t(p_t + y_t\pi_t) + \ldots \\ \ldots\ldots \\ \ldots\ldots \\ \pi_s = s_s(p_s + y_s\pi_s) + s_t(p_t + y_t\pi_t) + \cdots \\ \ldots\ldots \\ \ldots\ldots \\ \pi_h = h_s(p_s + y_s\pi_s) + h_t(p_t + y_t\pi_t) + \cdots \end{cases} \qquad \text{(VI)}$$

Lastly, we obtain the n equations which establish the equality between the total quantities of productive services sold by the individuals and the quantities of services used in production[315]:

$$\begin{aligned} R_s &= a_s R_a + \cdots + s_s y_s R_s + s_s R'_s + \cdots + h_s R'_h + \cdots \\ R_t &= a_t R_a + \cdots + s_t y_s R_s + s_t R'_s + \cdots + h_t R'_h + \cdots \\ &\ldots\ldots\ldots\ldots\ldots\ldots\ldots\ldots\ldots\ldots \\ &\ldots\ldots\ldots\ldots\ldots\ldots\ldots\ldots\ldots\ldots \end{aligned} \qquad \text{(VII)}$$

[311] The significance attributable to these $(\nu + \nu')$'old' and 'new' types of capital goods will be discussed later.

[312] Cf. Eqs. [4], *ibid.*

[313] Cf. Eqs. [4], *ibid.*; we may note that Pareto, unlike Walras, does not explicitly introduce the interest rate, equal to the uniform net rate of return of the capital.

[314] Cf. Eqs. [5], *ibid.* The expressions $(p_s + y_s\pi_s)$, $(p_t + y_t\pi_t)$, ... constitute the gross prices of the productive services of capitals S, T, ... As is well-known, Pareto expounds equilibrium equations even for monopoly cases, equations which we shall leave aside since the deficiencies of the theory of capital which we are interested in discussing are independent of the market hypotheses on which the equations are based.

[315] Cf. Eqs. [6], *ibid.*.

The Eqs. (I), (II), (III), (IV), (V), (VI), (VII) are in all:

$$\theta + \theta(m+n) + (m+n+1) + 1 +$$
$$+ (\nu + \nu' - 1) + (m + \nu + \nu') + n$$

But, as is well-known, any one of the Eqs. (VII) may be obtained by the Eqs. (I), (IV), (VI), and by the remaining Eqs. (VII).[316] The independent equations are therefore:

$$\theta(m+n+1) + 2(m+n) + 2(\nu+\nu')$$

The unknowns, according to Pareto, are:

$r_{1a}, r_{2a}, \ldots r_{1s}, r_{2s}, \ldots r_{1\varepsilon}, r_{2e}, \ldots$	in number	$\theta(m+n+1)$
$R_a, R_b, \ldots R_s, \ldots R_\varepsilon$	in number	$(m+n+1)$
$p_b, p_c, \ldots p_s, \ldots$	in number	$(m+n-1)$
$R_s{}', \ldots R_h' \ldots$	in number	$(\nu+\nu')$
$\pi_s, \ldots \pi_h, \ldots$	in number	$(\nu+\nu')$

The unknowns would thus be in total $\theta(m+n+1) + 2(m+n) + 2(\nu+\nu')$, equal therefore, Pareto concludes, to the number of independent equations.[317]

III

Before coming to the point which interests us the most—the possibility of simultaneously satisfying the Eqs. (V) and (VI) in so far as the latter refer to capital goods proper—it is necessary to examine a novelty introduced by Pareto into Walras's capitalisation equations. It concerns the current production of ν' types *H*, *K* ... of 'new' capitals that, apparently, are capitals of types different from existing ones. On the introduction of these capitals, no explanation is supplied by Pareto, either in the mathematical note where the equations appear or in the text of the *Cours*. Some explanation might have been required, however, given that the types of the capitals *H*, *K*, ... bring into Eqs. (V) the prices of their services, namely $p_h, p_k, \ldots$. Are these prices unknown variables or data? Pareto does not include them among the unknowns of the system, nor could he have done so without the number of unknowns exceeding the number of independent equations by ν': in other words, since capitals of that type are not used for any of the productions that take place in

[316] Cf. *ibid.*, p. 61.

[317] Cf. *ibid.* The total number of the equations is different in Pareto because he does not count among the equations our (III) and therefore does not count among the unknowns the $(m+n+1)$ quantities $R_a, R_b, \ldots, R_s, \ldots, R_\varepsilon$.

the economy, the general equilibrium equations do not permit a determination of the prices of their services. It is on the other hand clear that such prices cannot be considered as data of the general equilibrium system.[318]

In fact, the supposition of a current production of ν' types of capital different from existing ones appears irreconcilable with the hypotheses on which Pareto's equations are constructed and cannot therefore be accepted. The production of capital goods of types different from existing ones in fact implies the existence of an *incentive* to adopt techniques of production which require capital goods different from those available; in such conditions equilibrium cannot be reached on the basis of the givens chosen by Pareto, which include the existing technical capital. There is, therefore, a contradiction between the supposition that an equilibrium has been reached on the basis of those givens and the supposition that there is a current production of capital goods of types different from existing ones.[319] In the rest of our argument we shall therefore suppose that system (V) consists only of the $(\nu - 1)$ first equations; we shall also regard as eliminated the last ν' equations of system (VI), as well as the last ν' terms of the sums to the right of Eq. (IV).

We have just overcome this first obstacle to an understanding of the theory of capitalisation in the *Cours* when we are immediately faced with another one. Which of the n types of existing capitals constitute the ν types of 'old' capital goods, among which Pareto supposes net savings are distributed in the situation of equilibrium? Walras distinguished clearly among the n types of existing capital (which included persons and land), the l types of capital goods 'proper', producible like any other good, and referred his capitalization equations *to all* of the latter.[320] Pareto, too, as has already been recalled, distinguishes the n types of capital existing in personal, land and capital goods proper[321]; but when he introduces the capitalisation equations, he does not explicitly say that ν is the number of *all* the types of producible capital goods in existence.[322] The importance of this will become clear later, when we consider the consequences of a possible

[318] This would be equivalent to supposing that the prices (in numeraire) of the services of those capital goods may be known independently of the other prices, and therefore independently of the 'ophelimities' which the direct uses of those capitals or the indirect ones (consisting in the production of consumer goods) will have for consumers.

[319] Pareto seems to have fallen into this inconsistency in order to insert into his equations the commonly observed fact that at any one time in the economy one may have a production of capital goods which are different from existing ones; he does not seem to have asked himself to what extent this element of reality was compatible with the hypotheses on which his system of general equilibrium rests.

[320] Cf. system (A) in Section II, Chapter II, p. 59 of this dissertation.

[321] *Cours*, Vol. I, para. 90, p. 40. We may note here how in that paragraph the distinction is left vague and there is a tendency to present it as non-essential.

[322] He simply states: 'We shall suppose that ν old capitals are produced.' (*ibid.*, para. 135, p. 60, n. 1).

different interpretation of ν.[323] Furthermore, were ν not to include all the producible capitals, something should be said about the way of determining in which of them savings are invested and since Pareto says nothing clear about this, we shall first examine the theory of the *Cours* as if ν included all the existing producible capitals.

In this case, and once the inconsistency regarding the 'new' capital goods is eliminated, the theory set out above is the same as that of Walras. It is therefore subject to the same criticism laid out in Chapter II of the second section, which we shall briefly recall here, adapting it to the particular way in which Pareto expounds the equations.

If we remember that $p_s, p_t,...$ are the net prices of the services of the capitals of the type S, T .... and that they are obtained from the corresponding gross prices $p'_s, p'_t, \ldots$ by subtracting, respectively, the amounts $y_s\pi_s, y_t\pi_t,...$ for amortisation and insurance, the Eqs. (VI) may be written in the following way:

$$\frac{p'_s - y_s\pi_s}{\pi_s} = \frac{p'_t - y_t\pi_t}{\pi_t} = \ldots$$

or rather

$$\frac{p'_s}{\pi_s} - y_s = \frac{p'_t}{\pi_t} - y_t = \ldots \tag{VIII}$$

Replacing, in (VIII), $\pi_s, \pi_t, \ldots$, with the corresponding values given by (VI), we obtain[324]:

$$\frac{p'_s}{s_s p'_s + s_t p'_t + \cdots} - y_s = \frac{p'_t}{t_s p'_s + t_t p'_t + \cdots} - y_t = \ldots \tag{IX}$$

Equations (IX) are wholly analogous to equations (A) of Walras.[325] We may therefore apply to them the argument which led us to the conclusion that they could not be satisfied simultaneously.

Let us consider the variables which appear in the Eqs. (IX), for instance. We have the coefficients $y_s, y_t, \ldots$ for amortisation and insurance; they are givens. Then there are the coefficients of production $s_s, s_t, \ldots, t_s, t_t, \ldots$; at this stage of the argument, they too are assumed to be given by Pareto.[326]

[323] It may suffice to note here that the exclusion from current production of some types of producible capital goods would imply the existence of a divergence, in equilibrium, between the ratios (net price of the service)/(cost of production), for the various types of capital goods.

[324] To the right of (VI), the expressions $(p_s + y_s\pi_s), (p_t + y_t\pi_t)$, ... are simply the gross prices of the services of S, T, ..., namely p'_s, p'_t.

[325] Cf. above, Section II, Chapter II, p. 59.

[326] The variability of the coefficients of production is examined by Pareto in the second volume of the *Cours,* paras. 717ff. It is useful to recall here that the hypothesis of variability of the coefficients of production would not weaken, but rather reinforce the conclusion at which we are aiming: the impossibility of obtaining a uniform net rate of return on the capitals in Pareto's system.

All that remains in (IX) are the gross prices $p'_s, p'_t, \ldots$ of the productive services. These prices will be affected by variations in the quantities of capitals produced $R'_s, R'_t, \ldots$ (these are the additional unknowns which the problem of capitalisation introduces into Pareto's system of general equilibrium) only to the extent in which such productive services are used in different proportions in the production of $S, T, \ldots$.

Now, for the reasons set out in Chapters II and III of this section,[327] it seems possible to conclude that the influence of the variations of $R'_s, R'_t, \ldots$ on the prices of the productive services will be generally so weak as to allow us to assume the prices of the productive services as given when the equations of capitalisation are considered.[328]

We therefore find ourselves in (IX) with a number $(\nu - 1)$ of independent equations in which no unknown appears. It will not be possible to satisfy them in general; it will not be possible, that is, to satisfy, at the same time as the other conditions of equilibrium, the ones relating to the uniform net rate of return on producible capital. In Pareto, as in Walras, the reason for this lies in the choice of the quantities of producible capitals existing among the givens of the system. This may also be explained in intuitive terms: given the available physical quantities of the different types of producible capital goods, the equations of production and consumption will broadly determine the gross prices of their services and, by determining at the same time the prices of all the other productive services, they will also determine the costs of production of the producible capitals; the ratio (net price of service)/(cost of production) will therefore already be determined, for each type of capital good, by the conditions of equilibrium of production and consumption; if we now add the extra condition of the equality of this ratio for all capital goods, this condition cannot, in general, be satisfied.[329]

What does Pareto say about the way and possibility of reaching an equality between the net rates of return postulated by the Eqs. (IX)? One thing which is striking in the theory of capitalisation in the *Cours* is the very lack of an unambiguous explanation of this. Walras had tried to show how the equations of capitalisation could be satisfied,[330] only to come very close to admitting the deficiency of

[327] Cf. above, pp. 60–1 and 66–8.

[328] For the different case of highly specialised productive services, cf. above, pp. 67–8.

[329] Cf. above, pp. 65–6. One consequence of the impossibility of satisfying all the Eqs. (XI) will be the impossibility, until some other condition is introduced, of determining the quantities of capitals currently produced $R'_s, R'_t, \ldots$. The reasons are the same as those which we saw for the analogous quantities of $D_k, D_k, \ldots$ in Walras (cf. above, pp. 61–2).

[330] Cf. the passages already quoted above, pp. 66 and 66–7.

his theory in a paragraph inserted into the IV edition of the *Eléments*.[331] Pareto, on the other hand, in the mathematical note cited, does not go further than setting out the equations, nor is there any reference to what Walras stated about the matter.[332]

In the rest of the text, the most significant passage on the topic is probably the following:

> How will savings be distributed among the various capitals? We are lacking a condition to solve this problem. What makes it indeterminate is the circumstance that costs of production are not equal to selling prices.[333]

Pareto goes on to introduce, with the concept of free competition,[334] the condition of equality between the selling prices and the costs of production of the capitals produced, and he continues:

> If free competition exists among entrepreneurs, they will turn to the most lucrative destination of investments. Their efforts will thus end up by leveling out all the differences which the transformation of saving into new capitals presents as far as profit is concerned.[335]

The ambiguity of these passages calls for them to be carefully examined. It is not clear, in fact, whether Pareto is referring to one or the other of two ways in which it is conceivable that the tendency for entrepreneurs to invest savings in the most lucrative way may lead to a leveling of the net rates of return on producible capitals; ways which must be kept separate since their consequences are different for the validity of Pareto's theory.

The first of these two ways is the only one which does not entail changes in the givens which determine the system of equilibrium, and it is the one which we considered above when we discussed Pareto's equations: changes in the current relative productions of the various types of producible capital should modify the respective *costs of production* so as to render uniform the ratio (net price of service)/(cost of production) for all types of capital. We have already seen the reasons for which uniformity of the net rates of return cannot be achieved in this way.

The second process to which Pareto may be referring in the passages cited is completely different. It recognizes that, *given the existing quantities* of producible capitals, the ratios (net price of service)/(cost of production) of the various types of producible capital cannot be equalized. But it adds: current savings, being

---

[331] Cf. above, p. 70.

[332] 'We shall suppose that ν old capitals are produced from which the quantities $R'_s, R'_t, \ldots$ will be obtained, and ν' new capitals, from which the quantities $R_h, R_k, \ldots$ will be obtained. The equations $(\nu + \nu')$ will result...': there follow the Eqs. (IV) and (V) in our text above (*Cours*, Vol. I, para. 135, n. 1, p. 60).

[333] *Ibid.*, para. 130, p. 56.

[334] *Ibid.*, para. 131, pp. 56–7, Pareto states that he will consider the case of monopolies in the production of capital goods later, a case with which we are not concerned here (cf. n. 314 above).

[335] *Ibid.*, para. 132, p. 57.

wholly invested in the type with the highest net rate of return, will increase its *existing* quantity compared to those of the other types of capital goods; therefore the price of that service will gradually fall along with its respective net rate of return, until it becomes the same as that of the type of capital with a net rate of return immediately below it, and so on, until the uniformity of the ratio (net price of service)/(cost of production) is reached, for all types of capital. Now, this way of reaching the uniformity of the net rates of return is incompatible with the equations of general equilibrium. The situation in which the condition of uniformity of net rate of return (and the equality between the prices and costs of capital goods) will be satisfied cannot be the one determined by Pareto's equations, because it would require a variation of the existing quantities of capital goods. Besides, the situation to which Pareto's equations refer cannot be one of equilibrium because the proportions of the existing capital goods are not those of equilibrium. Since there is no equilibrium, there is no reason to suppose that equations different from (IX) could be satisfied: the system of prices may be anything and we would not have the means to determine it.[336]

Could this second process be what Pareto is referring to in the second of the cited passages? The expressions used there would permit this interpretation, which would draw support from the fact that, as we shall see, this will be the version given by Pareto in the *Manuel*, of the way in which one attains an equality of net rates of return. This interpretation might also explain the ambiguity, which we have already noted, in which Pareto leaves the definition of the number ν of the types of capitals currently produced. In fact, by not defining ν as the number of all the types of existing producible capitals, one is led to suppose that current savings are invested only in some of the producible capitals; those for which the net rate of return is the highest.[337,338]

---

[336] Cf. above, pp. 70–1 [*editor*: for the analogous problem in Walras]. We reached a negative conclusion there also on the possibility of attributing to the situation determined by the general equilibrium equations the significance of a temporary equilibrium.

[337] Strictly speaking, the savings should be invested in capital of a single type, that which presents the highest value of the ratio (net price of service)/(cost of production). There would then no longer be any difficulty in satisfying the Eq. (IX): they would be replaced by inequalities.

[338] But we may note here how this interpretation of the cited passages would lead to a contradiction of the supposition, made by Pareto in his equations, that existing capital goods are replaced by others of the same type, as they are consumed (compare the terms $s_s y_s R_s, s_t y_t R_t$, ... appearing to the right of equations [VII], and expressing the quantities of the services S, T, ... used to replace the capitals S, T, ... consumed in the period considered). Now, if the net saving is invested only in one (or some) of the producible capitals, those for which the ratio (net price of service/cost of production) is the highest, the interest rate will have to adjust to that ratio, and the price of the other types of capital goods (obtained by capitalizing the price of their respective services by that rate of interest) will have to be lower than the respective prices of production. If these capital goods are nonetheless produced in such a way as to replace the existing quantity of them, one should suppose that the entrepreneurs who produce those capital goods are producing them at a loss, losses which do not appear at any point in Pareto's system; or that the owners of those capital goods behave irrationally, investing the amortisation in capital goods which will yield a lower net rate of return than that obtainable by investing in other capital goods.

Whether one wishes to interpret the theory of the *Cours* in this way, or whether one wishes to interpret it as if ν included all the types of producible capitals, the conclusion remains valid that, in that theory, there is a contradiction between the condition of equilibrium relating to the uniformity of net rates of return and the choice of the existing quantities of capital among the givens of the system.[339]

IV

If what we have said about the theory of capitalisation in the *Cours* is correct, it should come as no surprise that the theory disappears in the *Manuel*. The

[339] Before ending our discussion of the theory of capital in the *Cours*, it may be useful to discuss the concept of 'savings-capital' which Pareto uses in both the *Cours* and the *Manuel*. In the *Cours* Pareto defines savings-capital in this way: 'Savings used to make advance payments for production is a capital. We shall call it savings-capital' (*Cours*, Vol. I, para. 90, p. 40; cf. also para. 87, p. 39). Thus, in the mathematical note where the equations of production are set out, he states that 'among the capitals *S*, *T*, ... there is savings-capital, destined to transform future goods in present goods' (*ibid.*, para. 100, n. 1, p. 46).

Pareto does not explain further what this 'savings-capital' consists of, which is owned by the individuals in the community and is lent by them to the entrepreneurs in the same way that other capitals are lent. The fact that this capital is expressed directly in terms of numeraire, so that the price of its service is immediately the interest rate, as well as the lack of further explanations on the subject, might lead one to think that Pareto was thinking of monetary funds. This, however, would in no way resolve the problem raised by the lack of simultaneity between the productive inputs and the corresponding products. The possession of a monetary fund enables an individual entrepreneur to begin production by purchasing the necessary productive services before he has been able to sell the corresponding output; but even here, after the initial period, the productive services will be paid with the earnings which are simultaneously obtained and the initial monetary fund will be permanently invested in the range of intermediate goods (stock, goods being produced) whose existence is what permits one to obtain simultaneity between expenses and earnings. Thus, looking at the community as a whole it is clear that the possession of a monetary fund, no matter how large, for 'advance payments' will not allow it to start productions which require time: the return on productive services paid in cash will be spent on goods ... which do not exist, because they have not yet been produced. For production to take place, either there will have to be in the economy an aggregate of consumer goods, or else an aggregate of intermediate goods (circulating capital) such that production and consumption can take place simultaneously. The second solution, which is the only one compatible with the hypothesis of continuous and uniform production flows made in the equilibrium equations, is the one adopted by Walras when, in the IV edition of the *Eléments*, he considered circulating capital. It is therefore clear that 'savings-capital' understood as a monetary fund does not permit a solution of the problem of the 'transformation of time' which Pareto believes he can resolve with it. If, then, one wished to view Pareto's 'savings-capital' not as a monetary fund but as the value, in numerals, of intermediate goods (circulating capital), we would be faced with another difficulty. Pareto takes the amount of 'capital-savings' existing in the hands of the various individuals as a given: how would it be possible to take as given the value of the intermediate goods owned by the various individuals in equations which must determine the system of prices itself?

In the *Manuel* the concept of 'savings-capital' reappears (op. cit., pp. 437–8 [*Manual of political economy*, p. 221]) but from what Pareto says, it does not appear to be easy to understand what he means by it: it seems to concern consumer goods necessary for advance payments to the owners of productive services. The impossibility would in any case remain of measuring the value of the reserves of consumer goods which constitute the given quantities of 'savings-capital' owned by each individual.

ambiguity about the types of capital produced perhaps indicates that, already at the time of the *Cours*, Pareto was aware of the weakness of that part of the theory of general equilibrium. The absence, in the *Manuel*, of any theory of capitalisation appears to suggest that, in the years between the publication of the two works, Pareto had become convinced that the weakness of the theory of capital presented in the *Cours* could not be easily overcome, and it was therefore necessary to eliminate capitalisation equations from the equations of general equilibrium—even at the cost of opening up a large gap in the foundations of his theory.

Thus, in the mathematical appendix to the *Manuel*, where the equations of general equilibrium are formulated and discussed, we only find the equations of equilibrium of consumption and production. It is in paragraphs 80–3 of this appendix that the system of general equilibrium is set out for the hypothesis of free competition. Here a distinction is made between the 'goods' or 'capital services' *A*, *B*, ... available in given quantities $a_{10}, b_{10} \ldots a_{20}, b_{20}$, for the individuals 1, 2, ... and the goods *X*, *Y*, *Z*, ... which are produced by using *A*, *B*, ... According to a now familiar process, given the technical conditions of production, given the tastes of consumers, and given the quantities $a_{10}, b_{10}, \ldots, a_{20}, b_{20}, \ldots$ the conditions of equilibrium of consumption and production allow one to determine the system of relative prices for *A*, *B*, *C*, ... *X*, *Y*, *Z*, ... along with the other unknowns. In the mathematical appendix there is no mention of savings nor prices of producible capital, nor therefore of net rates of return, uniform or not, nor interest rates. As for capital, all that the equations of the *Manuel* permit one to determine are the gross prices of the productive services of each of the various types of capital in existence. The deficiency of a theory of distribution which does not enable us to determine the rate of return on capital is obvious in itself and such as to call into question the usefulness of the theory. But deeper deficiencies lurk behind this failure to determine the rate of interest in the *Manuel*.

If all the goods used in production were like land and labour, which cannot be produced according to the laws that regulate the production of goods, the theory of the *Manuel* would not give rise to objections: in a world like that, there would be no capital, in the sense commonly attributed to the term, and the task of economic theory would be much easier than it is. But clearly the most important characteristic of the economy in which we live is the fact that production requires the use of goods producible like any other good, and the majority of these goods are consumed during a relatively short period of time.[340] At least two important consequences stem from this, in whose light we must consider the theory of the *Manuel*.

In the first place, if production must continue it has to replace capital goods as they are consumed. The lack of a theory of capital forces Pareto to ignore this phenomenon in the *Manuel*, and therefore to alter the significance which the equations of general equilibrium had in Walras. We have in fact seen that in the equations of the *Manuel* it is supposed that *X*, *Y*, *Z*, ... are produced by *A*, *B*, *C*, ... Among

[340] Cf. above, p. 52.

A, *B*, *C*, ..., Pareto says, are to be found 'commodities'; one must also find there producible capital services of a sufficiently short life span; now, both the former and the latter are consumed (the former totally, the latter in part) in the processes of production which take place during the period of time to which the equations refer. These goods and capitals do not, however, appear among the products of the period, which consist solely of the commodities *X*, *Y*, *Z*, ... Should we then conclude that in the period considered the individuals consume their entire gross income, therefore making it impossible to produce in the subsequent period, since the available quantity of 'commodities' included among *A*, *B*, *C*, ... will be zero? That the replacement of *A*, *B*, *C*, ... is not implicitly included by Pareto among the products *X*, *Y*, *Z*, ... appears to be demonstrated by the fact he attributes to individuals distinct functions of 'ophelimity' for each of the goods (or services) *A*, *B*, ... *X*, *Y*, ..., so that they will sell a part of $a_{10}, b_{10}, \ldots$ owned, so as to procure the quantities $x'_1, y'_1, x'_2, y'_2 \ldots$ consumed.[341] Furthermore, if one wished to include among the products also *A*, *B*, ..., we would have to determine the respective quantities produced. But this could not take place without taking into account the net rates of return and therefore introducing the very equations of capitalisation which are missing from the general equilibrium scheme of the *Manuel*; and with them the problems that one had sought to avoid would be introduced. That is what we might have expected: the problems of capital are inseparable from the problems of production and consumption; and a theory of consumption and production which seeks to do without them cannot fail to present gaps such as those which we have just considered.

In the second place, the fact that producible goods are used in production and consumed in a relatively short period of time leads, in conditions of free competition, to a tendency towards the uniformity of their net rates of return. It does not therefore appear possible to postulate a situation of equilibrium without introducing a condition relating to this uniformity. Therefore, if in the equations of the *Manuel* one attempted to insert a theory of capitalisation, one would meet with the same difficulties encountered in the *Cours*. In the *Manuel*, too, the available quantities of the various types of capital are taken as given; the uniformity of the net rates of return cannot therefore be obtained. This means that the situation to which the equations of the *Manuel* refer cannot be a situation of equilibrium and therefore the system of prices which will be obtained in that situation cannot be determined.

Pareto recognizes, in the text of the *Manuel*, the existence of this tendency towards the uniformity of the net rates of return. Moreover, in at least one passage he sheds the ambiguity in which the subject was left in the *Cours* and states that this uniformity is attained by *modifying the proportions of the existing capital goods*:

341 Cf. Eqs. (A) and (B) on p. 610, *Manuel* [*Manual of political economy*, p. 297]. Let us recall that in the *Manuel*, as in the *Cours*, it is supposed that *A*, *B*, ... also have a direct ophelimity for individuals, who will consume quantities $a'_1, b'_1, \ldots, a'_2, b'_2, \ldots$ of them.

free competition tends to equalize the net return of the capital goods which can be produced via savings: in fact, savings are evidently transformed into those capitals which yield the most returns, up to when the *abundance of these capitals makes their net return fall to the common level*'.[342]

This implicitly recognizes the impossibility of reaching the equilibrium of capitalisation on the basis of the givens in the system of general equilibrium. But there is no indication of the consequences which this brings for the validity of the theory, nor is there any attempt to treat the ideas expressed here and in other passages in terms of equations and unknowns.

V

In the *Manuel* there are however certain statements regarding capital which, because of the way in which they are formulated may have aroused in readers the impression that the concept of capital and the problems linked to it are not essential to the theory of general equilibrium. They may therefore have appeared to be an indirect justification for the absence of equations of capitalisation in the mathematical appendix to the *Manuel*. Before ending our discussion of the *Manuel* it will be useful to examine these statements.

A series of paragraphs in Chapter V of the *Manuel* is entitled: 'The theory of economic equilibrium with and without the notion of capital'.[343] The idea announced by Pareto here is summed up in the following passage, referring to production in general:

> In order to produce these things, one may consider exclusively consumption, and in this case one moves away from the concept of capital; or one may consider the consumption of certain commodities and the use of certain capital goods. One will achieve substantially the same result. In both cases it is necessary to take account of transformations over time. These two ways of considering the phenomenon are borne out in real life, more or less. Before one can get bread and feed oneself there is an obstacle, namely one must have an oven to bake this bread in. The oven appears as a capital here; by way of certain expenditure, it will last indefinitely and will always produce bread. Or the obstacle consists in getting the things (bricks, mortar, etc.) which, when consumed and transformed, will make the oven. In this form there is no longer any capital; there are only consumptions which are shared out over a greater or lesser quantity of bread produced. On top of this, there will be the cost of transformations over time, which we shall not deal with at this point.[344]

---

[342] *Manuel*, p. 361; our italics [*Manual of political economy*, p. 183].

[343] *Manuel*, p. 296 [*Manual of political economy*, p. 150; differently from the author's translation reported in the text, in the *Manual* the French 'notion' is translated as 'concept'].

[344] *Id.* The cited passage continues: 'Dans les pays civilisés, le four, et toutes les choses nécessaires pour construire le four, sont considérés comme équivalents à leur prix en numéraire; c'est-à-dire que les capitaux comme les consommations peuvent être remplacés par leur prix en numéraire. L'obstacle nous apparaît ici sous une troisième forme, à savoir qu'il nous faut faire une certaine dépense' (*Manuel*, pp. 296–7 [*Manual of political economy*, p. 150]). This third way of considering capital is not distinguishable from the first two from the standpoint of the equations of general equilibrium: in both cases the 'expenditure' will always be considered in the equations when unknown prices are applied to the physical quantities of the consumption or use of capital.

Pareto thus states that the production of any good may be considered in two alternative and equally legitimate ways: either as the exclusive result of 'consumptions', or as the result of the consumption of 'certain commodities' and the use of 'certain capital goods'. In the first case, in which Pareto is perhaps implicitly referring to the theories of the period of production, he professes to believe that 'there is no longer any capital'.

Now the meaning of this assertion clearly depends on what Pareto means by that capital which 'is no longer there'. But if, as the context of the passage may lead some to think, he means to say that, when production is seen as a series of consumptions distributed over the period preceding the emergence of the finished product, the problems of capital and its measurement disappear, the assertion is untenable. In a theory, such as that of Pareto, in which the prices of the productive services come to depend—once the tastes of the consumers and the techniques of production have been given—on the quantities of such productive services existing in the economy, the temporal structure of production and therefore the system of prices cannot be determined without reference also to conditions set, in the final analysis, by the available capital.

Let us take a closer look at the way of viewing production for which—Pareto says—'there is no capital'. Let us even admit that the difficulties which one encounters when one wishes to consider production as the sole result of consumption—difficulties of which Pareto does not speak—may be overcome.[345] In the equations of general equilibrium we could then express the quantity produced of every good as a function of 'consumptions' (of other products, of labour and of services of scarce natural resources) and of the set of periods of time ranging between these consumptions and the moment in which the good in question is ready for sale. But in order that production conceived in this way can take place it will be necessary that the products to be used in production are already available, as well as those which will make up the remunerations for work and the natural resources used. Or if one adopts the viewpoint of uniform and continuous flows of all products (usually adopted in general equilibrium theories), and if therefore one supposes that the goods consumed for a productive process are simultaneously reproduced by other productive processes, production as a certain temporal structural of 'consumptions' will require the existence in the economy of a certain set of 'intermediate goods'. Whatever the hypothesis made about the continuous or discontinuous way in which production is organized, one therefore rediscovers 'capital' in the form of the set of commodities which must exist in the economy

[345] The difficulty is the one represented by fixed capital, which we have had repeated occasion to deal with in the dissertation. To use the example provided by Pareto himself in the passage quoted: if a certain number of workers produces a ton of bread in one day by using an oven, what part of the bricks, mortar, etc. used in the construction of the oven should we consider as used in the production of that ton of bread; or rather, what are the coefficients of production of the bread relating to bricks, mortar, etc.? A solution can be looked for along the lines indicated above in Section I, Chapter V.

at any given moment, if the production of certain commodities according to certain techniques is to take place. The 'capital' has not disappeared because of the fact that one has chosen to express the techniques of production in terms of 'consumptions' and periods of time, instead of 'uses of capital goods'. In particular, in a theory of the kind used by Pareto, one would be faced once again with the problem of the measurement of existing capital. Without such data it would not in fact be possible, in that type of theory, to determine what will be the structure of production (understood as structure of 'consumptions' and associated periods of time) in equilibrium: that is, what will be the relative outputs of the various goods and (in the case of variable coefficients of production) what will be the technique adopted for the production of each good. And together with the indeterminacy of the equilibrium outputs one would also have the impossibility of determining the other unknowns in the system: in particular the system of relative prices.

Now, if the necessary data relating to existing capital were given the expression adopted by Walras and Pareto, i.e. the physical quantities of the capital of various types, the impossibility of determining a uniform net rate of return on the various types of capital would re-emerge in the form of the impossibility of applying the same rate of interest (over the respective periods of time) to the values of the sets of 'consumptions' corresponding to the uses of the various types of capital. If, on the other hand, the existing capital were conceived as 'subsistence', or were however measured in terms of its value, the theory would be involved in the circular reasoning examined in connection with the theories of Wicksell and Böhm-Bawerk.[346]

VI

In conclusion, what has been said above seems to allow us to state that in Pareto the deficiency of Walras's theory of capitalization—the impossibility of satisfying the conditions of equilibrium relating to the equality of the net rates of return on various types of capital goods—has not been in any way overcome, not could it have been since the cause of that deficiency in Walras—the measurement of existing capital in terms of the set of physical quantities of the various types of capital goods—is also present in Pareto's theory. In the *Cours* the deficiency manifests itself in the mutual contradictions of the equations of capitalisation. In the *Manuel*, on the other hand, since there is no theory of capitalisation, the deficiency remains implicit. However, in the *Manuel* the elimination of the equations of capitalisation causes further deficiencies in the theory, in so far as the replacement of capital goods consumed in the course of production is not taken into account.

[346] Cf. in particular above, Section II, Chapter VI. For the reference in Pareto's passage here to 'trasformations over time' of which one should take account whether he adopts the standpoint of the 'consumptions' or the view of the 'consumption of certain goods and the use of certain capitals', cf. n. 339 above on the concept of 'savings-capital'.

Bibliography

Åkerman, J. G. (1923–24). *Realkapital und Kapitalzins*. Centraltrycketeriet (Part I 1923, Part II 1924).

Bailey, S. (1825). *A critical dissertation on the nature, measure and causes of value*. R. Hunter.

Böhm-Bawerk, E. (1888). *Positive theory of capital*. Macmillan, 1891.

Bortkiewicz, L. (1906–7). Wertrechnung und Preisrechnung im Marxschen System. In *Archiv für Sozialwissenschaft und Sozialpolitik*, Part 1, Vol. 23, 1906; Part 2 and Part 3, Vol. 25, 1907; Parts 2 and 3 published as 'Value and Price in the Marxian System', *International Economic Papers*, No. 2, 1952.

Bortkiewicz, L. (1907). Appendix. On the correction of Marx's fundamental theoretical construction in the third volume of capital. In P. M. Sweezy (ed. and intro) (1949), *Karl Marx and the close of his system* by Eugene von Böhm-Bawerk & *Böhm-Bawerk's Criticism of Marx* by Rudolf Hilferding. Augustus M. Kelley, 1949, pp. 197–221 (first published as 'Zur Berichtigung der grundlegenden theoretischen Konstruktion von Marx im dritten Band des "Kapital"', *Jahrbücher für Nationalökonomie und Statistik*, Vol. 34, 1907).

Cannan, E. (1904). Introduction to Smith (1776), pp. xiii–xiviii

Cannan, E. (1929). *Review of economic theory*. A. M. Kelley.

Clark, J. B. (1895). The origin of interest. *Quaterly Journal of Economics*, 9(3), 257–278.

Dobb, M. (1955). A note on the transformation problem. In M. Dobb (ed.), *On economic theory and socialism. Collected Papers*. Routledge & Kegan Paul.

Hicks, J. R. (1932). A reply. *Economica*, 37, 297–300.

Hicks, J. R. (1939). *Value and capital*. Oxford University Press.

Hutcheson, F. (1755). *A system of moral philosophy*, 3 Bks. Foulis, Glasgow University.

Jevons, W. S. (1911). *The theory of political economy* (4th ed.). Macmillan.

Knight, F. H. (1932). Interest. In E. R. A. Seligman (Ed.), *Encyclopaedia of the social sciences* (Vol. 8, pp. 131–144). Macmillan.

Knight, F. H. (1933). Capitalistic production, time and the rate of return. In *Economic essays in honour of Gustav Cassel* (pp. 327–342). George Allen and Unwin.

Knight, F. H. (1934). Capital, time and the interest rate. *Economica*, 1(3), 257–286.

Knight, F. H. (1935). Professor Hayek and the theory of investment. *Economic Journal*, 45(177), 77–94.

Knight, F. H. (1935). The Ricardian theory of production and distribution. *Canadian Journal of Economics and Political Science*, 1(2), 171–196.

Knight, F. H. (1935). The theory of investment once more: Mr. Boulding and the Austrians. *Quarterly Journal of Economics*, 50(1), 36–67.

Knight, F. H. (1936). The quantity of capital and the rate of interest. *Journal of Political Economy*, Part I, 4(4), 433–463; Part II, 4(5), 612–642.

Knight, F. H. (1938). On the theory of capital. In reply to Mr. Kaldor. *Econometrica*, 6(1), 63–82.

Knight, F. H. (1951). *The economic organization*. Augustus M. Kelley.

Malthus, R. T. (1815). Letter to F. Horner (March 14th). In (edited by P. Sraffa with the collaboration of M. Dobb). *The works and correspondence of David Ricardo* (Vol. VI, pp. 186–188). Cambridge University Press, 1951.

Marx, K. (1951). *Theories of surplus value*. Lawrence & Wishart.

May, K. (1948). Value and price of production: A note on Winternitz's solution. *Economic Journal*, 58(232), 596–599.

Pareto, V. (1896). *Cours d'Économie Politique*, Tome Premier. F. Rouge.

Pareto, V. (1896–7). *Corso di Economia Politica*. UTET, 1971.

Pareto, V. (1897). *Cours d'Économie Politique*, Tome Second. F. Rouge.

Pareto, V. (1906). *Manuale di Economia Politica*. Milano. Società Editrice Libraria.

Pareto, V. (1909a). *Manuel d'Économie Politique*. Paris. V. Giard & E. Brière.

[Pareto, V. (1909b). *Manual of political economy. A critical and variorum edition*, ed. by A. Montesano, A. Zanni, L. Bruni, J. S. Chipman, & M. McLure. Oxford University Press, 2014.]
Quesnay, F. (1766). Analyse de la formule arithmétique du *Tableau Économique* de la distribution des dépenses annuelles d'une natione agricole. *Journal de l'agricolture, du commerce et des finances*, juin. Republished in M. E. Daire (ed.), *Physiocrates*, Première Partie (pp. 57–78). Librairie de Guillamin, 1846.
Ricardo, D. (1815). *An essay on the influence of a low price of corn on the profits of stock*. In (edited by P. Sraffa with the collaboration of M. Dobb) *The works and correspondence of David Ricardo* (Vol. IV, pp. 9–41). Cambridge University Press, 1951.
Ricardo, D. (1820), Letter to J. R. McCulloch (June 13th). In (edited by P. Sraffa with the collaboration of M. Dobb) *The works and correspondence of David Ricardo* (Vol. VIII, pp. 191–197). Cambridge University Press, 1951.
Ricardo, D. (1821). *On the principles of political economy and taxation*. In (edited by P. Sraffa with the collaboration of M. Dobb) *The works and correspondence of David Ricardo* (Vol. I, pp. 5–443). Cambridge University Press, 1951.
Robbins, F. L. (1930). On a certain ambiguity in the conception of stationary equilibrium. *Economic Journal*, 40(158), 194–214.
Robinson, J. V. (1951). The labour theory of value. In *Collected economic papers* (Vol. One, pp. 146–151). Basil Blackwell (first published as review of Sweezy (ed.), 1949 [see above, reference to Bortkiewicz (1907)], *Economic Journal*, June, 1950).
Schultz, H. (1932). Marginal productivity and the Lausanne School. *Economica*, 37, 285–289.
Schumpeter, J. A. (1954). *History of economic analysis*. Oxford University Press.
Scott, W. R. (1937). *Adam Smth as Student and Professor*. Jackson Son & Co.
Seton, F. (1957). The transformation problem. *Review of Economic Studies*, 23(3), 149–160.
Smith, A. (1896). *Lectures on justice, police, revenue and arms* (edited by E. Cannan). Clarendon Press.
Smith, A. (1776). *An inquiry into the nature and causes of the wealth of nations*, Cannan ed. (Vol. I). Methuen & Co., 1904.
Stigler, J. (1941). *Production and distribution theories*. Macmillan.
Sweezy, P. M. (1942). *Theory of capitalistic development*. Dennis Dobson.
Turgot, A .R. J. (1766). *Reflections on the formation and distribution of wealth*. E. Spragg, 1793.
Walras, L. (1926). *Elements of pure economics*. George Allen and Unwin, 1954.
Walras, L. (1883). *Théorie Mathématique de la Richesse Sociale*. Corbaz.
Wicksell, K. (1893). *Value, capital and rent*. George Allen and Unwin,1954.
Wicksell, K. (1896). *Finanztheoretische Untersuchungen nebst Darstellung und Kritik des Steuerwesens Schwedens*. Gustav Fischer.
Wicksell, K. ([1901]). *Lectures on political economy* (Vol. I). George Routledge & Sons, 1934.
Wicksell, K. (1923). Real capital and interest (English transl.). In Wicksell ([1901] 1934) (pp. 258–259).
Winternitz, J. (1948). Value and prices: A solution of the so-called transformation problem. *Economic Journal*, 58(230), 276–280.

Part II
Critique of Marginal Productivity Theories

Heterogeneous Capital, the Production Function and the Theory of Distribution†[1,2]

The notion of capital as a "factor of production", on which the theories of production and distribution dominant since the latter part of the last century ultimately rely, has been the object of considerable discussion in recent years. As is well known, these theories had their origin in a reformulation in terms of homogeneous land and "intensive" margins, of the Malthusian theory of rent. It was shown that the rent of land—which had appeared as the residuum left after deducting the share of wages and profits calculated at the rate given by the marginal product of a dose of "labour with capital"—could also be viewed as the marginal product of land, with the sum of wages and profits as the residuum. The two factors, land and "labour with capital", could then be put on the same footing and the theory extended to any number of factors.

The way was thus open, it was thought, to explaining in terms of marginal productivity the division of the product between labour and capital, which the Classical economists had analyzed by altogether different principles. But in order

The original version of the chapter has been revised: Incorrect details have been corrected. A correction to this chapter can be found at https://doi.org/10.1007/978-3-031-23643-3_18

†Previously published in *The Review of Economic Studies*, 37(3), 1970. All necessary permissions acquired.

In addition to the previously published text, the present edition of the article is supplemented by the Mathematical Note which was available in the Marshall Library of the University of Cambridge (UK), and which is published here for the first time. Thanks are due to Dr. Daria Pignalosa and Dr. Paolo Trabucchi for their help with editing.

[1]A paper containing the material before included in Sections I–III of the present paper was submitted for publication in April 1963 and accepted for publication subject to revision shortly afterwards. The present paper is a revised version of the extended paper, including three new sections, which reached the Editors in October 1968.

[2]I wish to thank Mr. Sraffa for his comments and criticisms. I am also grateful for the help derived from discussion of this paper in seminars at the Faculty of Economics in Cambridge, and at the Consiglio Nazionale delle Ricerche in Rome. Professor Gandolfo of the University of Siena has been of considerable help with the mathematics underlying some propositions of Section IV.

P. Garegnani, *Capital Theory, the Surplus Approach, and Effective Demand*, Springer Studies in the History of Economic Thought,
https://doi.org/10.1007/978-3-031-23643-3_2

to explain the rate of profit along these new lines, capital had to be conceived, ultimately, as a single magnitude: and had accordingly to be measured as a value quantity, unlike labour or land which were physical quantities. The extension of the "law of rent" to distribution between labour and capital therefore raised the danger of circular reasoning: the value of a capital good, like that of any product, changes with those very rates of wages and interest which are to be explained by means of "quantities" of capital. Some of the originators of these theories were conscious of the difficulty, but their attempts to deal with it were limited to very special hypotheses. It is therefore not surprising that in recent literature instances should have cropped up showing that the basic propositions of the theory are in fact controvertible. Up to now, however, little or no attempt seems to have been made to see the implications of the failure of these propositions for the problem of value and distribution. An attempt to do this is the main aim of the present article.

We shall begin by discussing a defence of traditional theory put forward by Samuelson [1] and claiming that in some cases heterogeneous capital goods can be reduced to quantities of a homogeneous "capital", the marginal product of which equals the rate of interest: this, Samuelson thought, would display the corresponding version of traditional theory as a useful "parable" giving "insights into the fundamentals of interest theory".[3]

Sections I and II of this paper will therefore examine the relations between the wage, the rate of interest and the product per worker in the two-commodity economy—with only a consumption good and a capital good—which Samuelson used for his argument.

Section III will then show that a production function giving the interest rate as the marginal product of capital is compatible with these relations *if, and only if*, the conditions of production of the capital good are always identical with those of the consumption good: an hypothesis which turns the original "heterogeneous capital model" into one where capital, besides being homogeneous and hence measurable in physical terms, is also homogeneous with the consumption good.

In Section IV, the results reached that far will be generalized from Samuelson's two-commodity economy to one where any number of commodities are produced.

In that more general setting, Sections V and VI will consider how the discussion in the earlier sections bears on various formulations of traditional theory. Attention will be focussed on the idea that in a competitive economy wages and interest are governed by the demand and supply for "capital" and labour, the core of traditional theory in all its versions. The fact that "capital intensity" in the economy need not increase as the rate of interest falls (the wage rises), undermines, it will be argued, the explanation of distribution in those terms. In the Appendix, these negative conclusions will be illustrated by numerical examples showing how far the relations between the rate of interest, the wage, the value of capital and the physical product per worker may differ from what received theory claims.

---

[3] Cf. Samuelson [1], p. 193. [For editorial reasons, footnotes are numbered here in sequence over the entire article instead of per single page as in the original.]

The final pages of Section VI will then consider some of the problems which arise when that explanation of value and distribution is abandoned. In this connection, we shall refer to the different approach used by the Classical economists up to Ricardo.

I. Production with a Single "System"

The economy Samuelson assumes in his article is one where production takes place in yearly cycles and where a single consumption good A exists, obtainable by a number of alternative "systems of production", α, β, γ, etc. Each "system", e.g. α, consists of two "*methods of production*": a method for the direct production of A by means of fixed quantities $l_a^{(\alpha)}$ of labour, and $c_a^{(\alpha)}$ of a capital good $C^{(\alpha)}$ specific to the method; and the method for producing $C^{(\alpha)}$ by $l_c^{(\alpha)}$ of labour and $c_c^{(\alpha)}$ of itself. The capital good $C^{(\alpha)}$ is assumed to decay according to a yearly "rate of mortality" $d^{(\alpha)}$, independent of age.[4] Constant returns to scale are assumed in both industries and, hence, for the "system of production" as a whole.

Further, the system is such that: (i) a surplus can be obtained over the pure replacement of machines (i.e. , $1 - d^{(\alpha)}c_c^{(\alpha)} > 0$); (ii) the capital good enters the production of both commodities (i.e., both $c_c^{(\alpha)}$and $c_a^{(\alpha)}$ differ from zero); (iii) some labour is required directly or indirectly to produce each of the two commodities (i.e., $l_c^{(\alpha)}$ differs from zero, as do either $l_a^{(\alpha)}$, or $d^{(\alpha)}$, or both).

To begin with, suppose that only one system is known. The hypotheses of a uniform rate of interest or of profits r, and of a uniform wage w, enable us to write the two price equations.

$$\begin{aligned} 1 &= l_a w + c_a p_c (r + d), \\ p_c &= l_c w + c_c p_c (r + d), \end{aligned} \tag{1}$$

where we assume w to be paid at the *end* of the production cycle, and where p_c is the price of the capital good C, expressed, like w, in terms of A. In system (1), l_a, c_a, d, l_c, c_c are all known quantities, while r, w, and p_c are the three unknowns. The two equations are then sufficient to define the relation between r and w in the economy, given by

$$w = \frac{1 - c_c(r + d)}{l_a + (l_c c_a - l_a c_c)(r + d)} \tag{2}$$

Assumptions (i), (ii) and (iii) we made about the system of production ensure that for $r=0$ there is a positive "maximum wage" which we shall indicate by W. On the same assumptions, as r rises from zero, w falls as a continuous differentiable function of r, reaching zero for a finite "maximum rate of interest" R. It can also

[4] Samuelson [1], p. 197. This way of dealing with the life of capital goods evades the problems of joint production, specific to *fixed* capital (cf. below, p. 160). In Sects. 2–4, however, we shall retain the assumption of a "rate of mortality" d, with $d=1$ for the case of circulating capital, as in Sect. 5 and the Appendix [*editor's note*: for better clarity, footnote text slightly amended from the original].

be shown that for $0 \leq r \leq R$ the price p_c of the capital good is positive.[5] The curve representing function (2) in the relevant interval $0 \leq r \leq R$ (Fig. 1) is Samuelson's "Factor-price Frontier": we shall call it the *wage-curve* of the given system of production.

It is now convenient to introduce the notion of "integrated consumption-good industry". By that we shall mean the composite industry where the proportion I of the C industry to the A industry is the one which just ensures the replacement of the capital goods consumed in the composite industry. The proportion I can be easily calculated. To a unit of the A industry, there must correspond a size of the C industry sufficient to replace the quantity $c_a d$ of C consumed in the A industry *plus* the quantity $c_a Id$ of it consumed in the C industry at its size I. The proportion I is therefore given by $I = c_a d + c_c Id$, i.e.

$$I = c_a d/(1 - c_c d)$$

(In what follows we shall, for short, refer to the "integrated consumption-good industry" as the *integrated industry*).

Recourse to the integrated industry is necessary if the *net* product—the product to be divided between wages and interest—is to consist of a *physical quantity* of the consumption good. An economy with zero net accumulation merely consists of the integrated industry.

A few important quantities and relations can now be read from the wage-curve *WR* of Fig. 1.

---

[5] For $r=0$, function (2) gives $W = \frac{1-dc_c}{l_a(1-dc_c)+dl_c c_a}$ where W must be positive by assumption (i) above, and finite by assumption (ii). Similarly for $w=0$ we have $R=(1-dc_c)/c_c$, with R as the net "rate of reproduction" of the capital good, positive by assumption (i) and finite by assumptions (ii) and (iii). We now note that function (2) defines a straight line in the special case $l_c c_a - l_a c_c = 0$, and a rectangular hyperbola with asymptotes parallel to the r and w axes in the general case where $l_c c_a - l_a c_c \neq 0$. In the first case we have the *decreasing* straight line:

$$w = \frac{1 - dc_c}{l_a} - \frac{c_c}{l_a} r.$$

In the case of the hyperbola, the product of the distances of each point of the curve from the asymptotes is the *positive* quantity $\frac{l_c c_a}{(l_c c_a - l_a c_c)^2}$, and consequently we have a *decreasing* hyperbola. The positive intercepts, W and R, then imply that the segment of the curve for $0 \leq r \leq R$ lies on a single portion of the hyperbola, and is therefore continuous and differentiable.

Turning now to the positivity of p_c, we note that system (1) in the text gives p_c as the following function of r:

$$p_c = \frac{l_c}{l_a + (l_c c_a - l_a c_c)(r + d)}$$

It follows that if $l_c c_a - l_a c_c \geq 0$, then p_c is positive for any non-negative value of r. In the remaining case, where $l_c c_a - l_a c_c < 0$, we have $p_c > 0$ for $r < \frac{l_a}{l_a c_c - l_c c_a} - d$; but $\frac{l_a}{l_a c_c - l_c c_a} - d > R$ because $R = \frac{1}{c_c} - d$, and we can conclude $p_c > 0$ for $0 \leq r \leq R$.

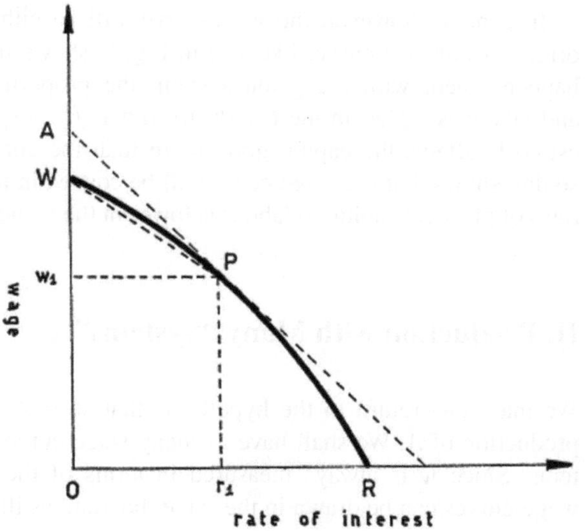

Fig. 1 The "wage-curve": *OW* is the net physical product per worker; tan w_1PW is the value of capital per worker when the wage is Ow_1

(i) the segment *OW*—measuring the wage when interest is zero—also measures the net *physical* product per labourer obtainable from the "integrated industry" with the given system of production;

(ii) as a result, given a wage Ow_1, the segment w_1W measures the amount of the consumption good received as interest for each worker employed in the integrated industry;

(iii) the tangent of the angle w_1PW measures the value, relative to the consumption good, of physical capital per worker in the integrated industry at the wage Ow_1. This is so because:

$$\tan w_1PW = w_1W/w_1P = w_1W/Or_1 = \frac{\text{interest per worker}}{\text{rate of interest}} = \text{value of capital per worker.}$$

(For brevity we shall refer to the tangent of the angle w_1PW as the *slope* of *WP*);

(iv) Since physical capital per worker in the integrated industry is a fixed physical quantity of capital good *C*, the change in the slope of *WP*, as we move along the wage-curve *WR*, indicates how p_c changes with changes in the division of the product between wages and interest.

It follows from (iv) that p_c is constant only when the wage-curve is a straight line. This will be the case if the proportion between physical capital and labour is the same in the two industries (i.e. $c_c/l_c = c_a/l_a$). Then, as r varies, the change in interest-costs relative to wage-costs must affect the two products equally, leaving their relative value p_c unchanged.

In general, however, the wage-curve will be either concave or convex to the origin. A concave curve, like *WR* in Fig. 1, shows that p_c rises with r. That will happen when, with the given system, the proportion between physical capital and labour is higher in the *C* industry (i.e. $c_c/l_c > c_a/l_a$), so that the rise in interest-costs affects the capital good more than the consumption good. Similar reasoning shows that the wage-curve will be convex in the remaining case, where the ratio of physical capital to labour is lower in the *C* industry.

II. Production with Many "Systems"

We may now return to the hypothesis that several systems are available for the production of *A*. We shall have as many wage-curves as there are alternative systems. Since w is always measured in terms of the same commodity *A*, all the wage-curves can be drawn in the same diagram, as illustrated in Fig. 2 for the case of two systems.

At any level of the rate of interest, producers will choose the cheaper way of producing *A*. But, clearly, the costs of *A* produced with different systems will depend on the system which happens to be in use. We may take the example of Fig. 2. If α is in use at r_2, the wage is $w_2^{(\alpha)}$ and the prices of $C^{(\alpha)}$ and $C^{(\beta)}$ are calculated for r_2 and $w_2^{(\alpha)}$. If however β, and not α is in use at r_2, the wage is $w_2^{(\beta)}$: the prices of $C^{(\alpha)}$ and $C^{(\beta)}$ are different and thus the costs of *A* produced with the two alternative systems will also differ from what they are when α is in use. The question is then whether the order of the two systems as to cheapness might not itself change according as system α or β is in use. If the order should so change we

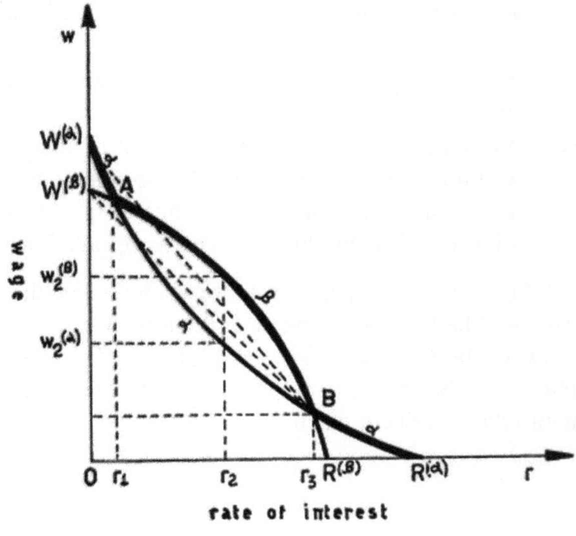

Fig. 2 Production with two systems and the "wage-frontier"

would have endless switching back and forth between α and β, or, alternatively, no tendency to change whichever system happens to be in use.

These possibilities, however, can be ruled out: the cheaper system will be the same at both wage rates and price systems. Moreover, the tendency of producers to switch to whichever system is cheaper in the existing price situation, will bring them to the system giving the highest w; while systems giving the same w for the same r will be indifferent and can co-exist.[6] It follows that the relation between r and w will be represented by the "outside" broken line generated by the intersecting wage-curves: the line which Samuelson named "north-east frontier" and which we shall call *wage-frontier*. Where the "wage-frontier" has a "corner" a switch of systems occurs, while at the "corner" itself the two systems, which we may call "adjacent", can co-exist. Thus, in the example of Fig. 2, the "wage-frontier" is $W^{(\alpha)}ABR^{(\alpha)}$, with switches from α to β, and back from β to α occurring as r rises from zero to its maximum $R^{(\alpha)}$.

---

[6] Let us suppose that, at a given level r^* of r, *a system α is in use*, and a second system β is considered in order to know the price $p_{c\beta}^{(\alpha)}$ of $C^{(\beta)}$ and have the price (cost) $p_{a\beta}^{(\alpha)}$ of A produced with β. We shall assume that r^* is smaller than $R^{(\alpha)}$ and $R^{(\beta)}$ so that neither $w^{(\alpha)}$ nor $w^{(\beta)}$ is zero. To determine $p_{c\beta}^{(\alpha)}$ and $p_{a\beta}^{(\alpha)}$, we must add to the price-equations of $C^{(\alpha)}$ and A produced with α, those of $C^{(\beta)}$ and A produced with β:

$$\begin{aligned} 1 &= l_a^{(\alpha)}w^{(\alpha)} + c_a^{(\alpha)}p_c^{(\alpha)}\left(r^* + d^{(\alpha)}\right), & p_c^{(\alpha)} &= l_c^{(\alpha)}w^{(\alpha)} + c_c^{(\alpha)}p_c^{(\alpha)}\left(r^* + d^{(\alpha)}\right), \\ p_{a\beta}^{(\alpha)} &= l_a^{(\beta)}w^{(\alpha)} + c_a^{(\beta)}p_{c\beta}^{(\alpha)}\left(r^* + d^{(\beta)}\right), & p_{c\beta}^{(\alpha)} &= l_c^{(\beta)}w^{(\alpha)} + c_c^{(\beta)}p_{c\beta}^{(\alpha)}\left(r^* + d^{(\beta)}\right). \end{aligned} \tag{i}$$

Using the value of $w^{(\alpha)}$ resulting from the first two equations, we can determine $p_{c\beta}^{(\alpha)}$ and hence $p_{a\beta}^{(\alpha)}$; system β will be cheaper or dearer than α (in the price situation corresponding to α) according as $p_{a\beta}^{(\alpha)}$ is less or more than 1. If β, and not α, had been in use we would have had:

$$\begin{aligned} p_{a\alpha}^{(\beta)} &= l_c^{(\alpha)}w^{\beta} + c_a^{(\alpha)}p_{c\alpha}^{(\beta)}\left(r^* + d^{(\alpha)}\right), & p_{c\alpha}^{(\beta)} &= l_c^{(\alpha)}w^{(\beta)} + c_c^{(\alpha)}p_{c\alpha}^{(\beta)}\left(r^* + d^{(\alpha)}\right), \\ 1 &= l_a^{(\beta)}w^{\beta} + c_c^{(\beta)}p_c^{(\beta)}\left(r^* + d^{(\beta)}\right), & p_c^{(\beta)} &= l_c^{(\beta)}w^{(\beta)} + c_c^{(\beta)}p_c^{(\beta)}\left(r^* + d^{(\beta)}\right). \end{aligned} \tag{ii}$$

Now, w and the prices of the four commodities (A produced with α appearing as different from A produced with β) which result from equations (ii) will generally differ from those obtained from equations (i). But the difference can be seen to arise here purely from a change of the value-unit, which was A produced with α in (i), and is A produced with β in (ii). (It should be noted that this result is due purely to the fact that the two systems have no common commodity-input, and does not hold for more complex systems of production). The ratios between the prices and the wage are therefore the same in both systems of equations, and we have $\frac{w^{(\beta)}}{w^{(\alpha)}} = \frac{1}{p_{a\beta}^{(\alpha)}} = p_{a\alpha}^{(\beta)}$. Since when $p_{a\beta}^{(\alpha)} \lesseqgtr 1$, then $p_{a\alpha}^{(\beta)} \gtreqless 1$ the order of the two systems as to cheapness is the same at both systems of prices. Moreover, $p_{a\beta}^{(\alpha)} < 1$ if, and only if, $w^{(\beta)} > w^{(\alpha)}$: thus the systems giving a w higher than $w^{(a)}$ are cheaper than α at the prices corresponding to α. Accordingly, whichever the system initially in use, the switch to cheaper methods will finally bring us to the system giving the highest wage. On the other hand, when $w^{(\alpha)} = w^{(\beta)}$, $p_{a\beta}^{(\alpha)} = 1$: systems giving the same w are therefore equally profitable at the given level of r, and can co-exist.

We could now examine how net physical product and value of capital per worker in the integrated industry change as r varies and producers switch from system to system. So, for example, Fig. 2 shows that, at r_3—with r rising—producers switch to system α, having a *higher* product per labourer (measured by $OW^{(\alpha)}$, larger than $OW^{(\beta)}$) and having, at r_3, a *higher* value of capital per worker (measured by the slope of $W^{(\alpha)}B$, steeper than that of $W^{(\beta)}B$). These results are both in striking contrast with received theory, as is the fact that in the highest range of r producers "switch back" to a system which had already been in use for low levels of r. It is convenient however to postpone these matters, and make some further assumptions which—while necessary for a discussion of Samuelson's surrogate production function—will allow us to meet traditional theory on the more familiar ground where systems of production "change continuously" with r.

We shall assume, accordingly, that the four coefficients l_a, d, c_c and $(l_c c_a)$[7] can change as given continuous functions of a parameter u: i.e. to each value of u included in a certain range, there will correspond a unique set of values of the coefficients and, hence, a system for the production of A. (As an example, we might imagine "wine" being produced with a continuously variable quantity of direct labour, where the "wine" produced with a given quantity of labour requires a specific *quality* of grapes, in turn produced by themselves and labour in fixed quantities.).[8]

We shall also suppose that the "family" of systems thereby defined is such that: (i) the wage-curve of each system cannot contribute segments, but only points, to the "wage-frontier"; (ii) that the "wage-frontier" no longer shows any "corner". The "wage-frontier" then becomes a smooth "envelope" which is tangent at each point to one wage-curve, and encloses the whole family of them from above. An illustration is given in Fig. 3, where we have drawn some members of one such family of wage-curves having E as their "envelope".[9]

---

[7] Function (2) depends on $l_c c_a$, and not on l_c and c_a taken separately. This is as we should expect, since the arbitrary choice of the physical unit of C (which affects l_c and c_a, but not $l_c c_a$) cannot alter the relation between r and w.

[8] The assumption of continuity in the text is made only in order to show that the criticisms of traditional theory raised in this paper are independent of whether or not we assume systems of production which change by indefinitely small steps. In fact this assumption would be justified if the qualitative differences in the means of production used in different systems could be reduced to quantitative differences of the single input "capital". But when differences in the kinds of input have to be taken into account, the only acceptable hypothesis is that of a finite number of alternative systems.

[9] In mathematical terms the position is as follows. The four coefficients are given by the functions $l_a = v_1(u)$, $l_c c_a = v_2(u)$, $c_c = v_3(u)$ and $d = v_4(u)$, defined for an interval of u in which all four functions are positive. Substituting these functions in function (2) (see p. 149 above), we obtain.

$$w = \frac{1 - v_3(u)\{r + v_4(u)\}}{v_1(u) + \{v_2(u) - v_1(u)v_3(u)\}\{r + v_4(u)\}}, \tag{2.1}$$

where (2.1) is the "parametric equation" of the family of wage-curves. When the functions giving the four coefficients are appropriate, the family of curves defined by (2.1) admits a "smooth" envelope enclosing them from above. The equation of the envelope, or its points, can then be found by well-known procedures (cf. e.g. Courant [2], pp. 171–174).

Fig. 3 *E* is the "envelope" of the wage-curves

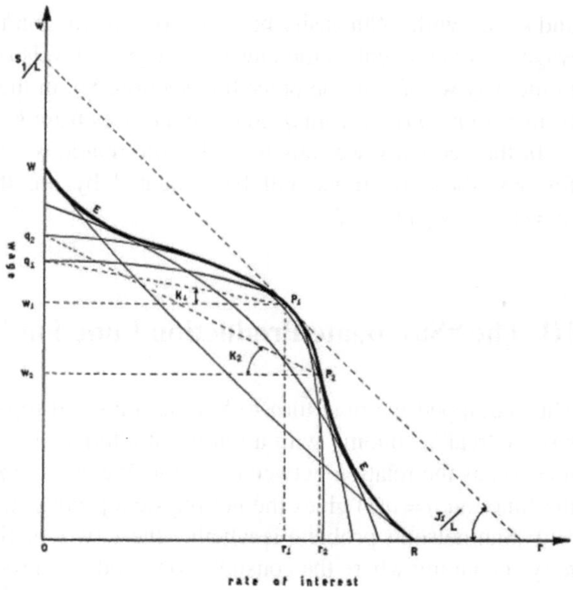

On these assumptions, the system of production—i.e., the level of *u* defining the system in use— "changes continuously" with *r*. By this expression we mean that: (i) any change of *r*, however small, brings about a change of system; (ii) one system only is in use at each possible level of *r*.

Let us now consider the properties of an economy meeting these hypotheses. As the rate of interest rises, the wage must fall because the "envelope" is tangent to a decreasing curve at each point. Little however can be said about its curvature. Where the envelope is tangent to wage-curves which are either convex to the origin or straight lines, the envelope must be convex: but where the wage-curves are concave, the envelope may well be concave or a straight line. The envelope may therefore have any curvature, with convex and concave segments alternating.

As we have just seen, at any possible level of *r*, a single system is in use in the economy.[10]

We shall therefore find in the "integrated industry" (p. 150) a determinate physical product and a definite physical capital per worker. We shall indicate this net product by *q*, using *k* for the value of the physical capital per worker, expressed in terms of *A* and calculated at the given level of *r*. The way in which *q*

[10]The hypothesis of a "smooth" envelope has ruled out the co-existence of "adjacent" systems, shown by "corners" of the wage-frontier. A second kind of co-existence is however conceivable: that in which two or more wage-curves are *tangent* to each other. Indeed, we might conceive families of wage-curves where two or more of them are tangent to each point of the "envelope". These possibilities have been ignored in the text. (Cf., however, note 43 below in the Appendix.)

and k vary with r can easily be seen from the diagram of the envelope. We take the wage-curves tangent to the envelope at given levels of r: q and k can then be read in the way we saw in the preceding section. So, in the example of Fig. 3, as r rises from r_1 to r_2, q rises from q_1 to q_2, and k rises from k_1 to k_2.

In the economy we thus have definite relations between w, q, k and r. In what follows, these relations will be indicated by the three single-valued functions $w=e(r)$, $q=q(r)$, $k=k(r)$.

III. The "Surrogate Production Function"

Thus equipped we may turn to Samuelson's "surrogate production function". We have a "real" economy with a family of alternative systems giving the "envelope" $w=e(r)$ as the relation between r and w. We assume zero net accumulation so that the function $q=q(r)$ gives the net physical product per worker in the "real" economy. Samuelson's problem is whether these two relations might hold in an "imaginary" economy where the consumption good A is produced by labour and a capital homogeneous with A, and w and r are therefore determined by the marginal products of the two factors.

The problem can be restated as follows. We are asked to define a function $S=S(J, L)$ homogeneous of the first degree—with S as the quantity of (net) product, J that of capital, and L that of labour—satisfying the following two conditions:

(i) $\partial S/\partial L=e(\partial S/\partial J)$, where $w=e(r)$ is the relation between w and r in the "real" economy;

(ii) $S/L=q(\partial S/\partial J)$, where $q=q(r)$ is the relation between net product per worker and r in the same "real" economy.

The function $S(J, L)$, if it existed, would be a "surrogate production function" for the "real" economy in the sense that it would determine the relations between r, w and q once J—the quantity of "surrogate capital"—has been appropriately defined. This would in fact show that heterogeneous capital goods can be expressed as quantities of an appropriately defined homogeneous capital, in accordance with what Samuelson calls the "Clark-Ramsey parable".

To see whether the "surrogate function" can be defined, we begin by using Euler's theorem to write $S(J, L)$ in the form

$$S/L = (\partial S/\partial L) + (\partial S/\partial J)(J/L). \tag{3}$$

In the "imaginary" economy, the equilibrium rate of interest would always be equal to $\partial S/\partial J$. Condition (i) then permits us to write function (3) in the form.

$$S/L = e(r) + r(J/L). \tag{3.1}$$

Differentiation of function (3) with respect to $\partial S/\partial J$ gives[11]

$$J/L = -\frac{d(\partial S/\partial L)}{d(\partial S/\partial J)} \tag{4}$$

and, using condition (i) again,

$$J/L = -e'(r), \tag{4.1}$$

where $e'(r)$ is the derivative of the envelope-equation for the "real" economy.

Result (4.1) is of some interest and, by itself, sufficient to rule out the "surrogate function" in a first class of cases. It shows that, *if* $S(J, L)$ is to give the relation between r and w in the "real" economy, *then* to each level of $\partial S/\partial J$ there must correspond a ratio J/L equal to the "slope" of the envelope at the point where $r = \partial S/\partial J$. We saw, however, that the "real" economy may give an "envelope" which—in parts or throughout—is *concave* to the origin. Then J/L would *rise* with $\partial S/\partial J$, and the function $S(J, L)$ could not be a production function: equilibrium in the "imaginary" economy of the "Clark-Ramsey parable", requires that the marginal product of "capital" should *not* rise when the ratio of "capital" to labour J/L rises. A straight-line envelope, which we saw was also conceivable, would be in even more striking contrast with the "parable": we should then have to admit that the "marginal products" change, when the ratio of capital to labour does not.[12] But even the convexity of the relation between r and w does not ensure the existence of the "surrogate function": the conditions for that are stricter.

To find them, let us return to function (3.1) and, using result (4.1), re-write it in the form

$$S/L = e(r) + r\{-e'(r)\} \tag{3.2}$$

It is now clear that condition (i) above is *sufficient* to define the function $S(J, L)$. No freedom is left for adapting $S(J, L)$ so as to satisfy condition (ii): we can only ascertain whether S/L as defined by (3.2) is identical with $q = q(r)$. That this is in general *not* so can be easily seen from the graph of the envelope (cp. Fig. 3). Function (3.2) gives S/L as the intercept on the w axis of the *straight-line* tangent to the "envelope" at the corresponding level of r. On the other hand, q is the intercept on the w axis of the *wage-curve* touching the envelope at the same point.

---

[11] We first obtain:

$$\frac{d(S/L)}{d(J/L)}\frac{d(J/L)}{d(\partial S/\partial J)} = \frac{d(\partial S/\partial L)}{d(\partial S/\partial J)} + \frac{J}{L} + \frac{\partial S}{\partial J}\frac{d(J/L)}{d(\partial S/\partial L)},$$

and then, since $d(S/L)/d(J/L) = \partial S/\partial J$, we have.

$$\frac{J}{L} = -\frac{d(\partial S/\partial L)}{d(\partial S/\partial J)}$$

[12] In fact, in the case of a straight-line envelope, no differentiable homogeneous function can satisfy condition (i) above.

Fig. 4 The "envelope" when the consumption good is homogeneous with the capital good

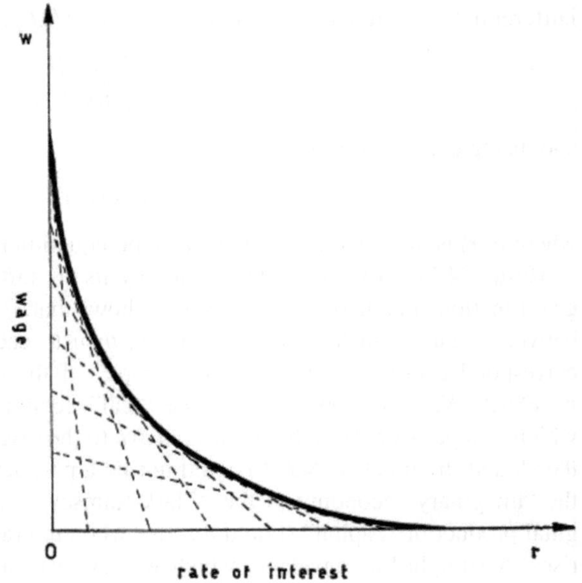

Function (3.2) therefore over-estimates q at all levels of r where the system in use gives a wage-curve concave to the origin (see Fig. 3 at the point where $r=r_1$). It underestimates q when the wage-curve is convex. It only gives the correct q when the wage-curve is a straight line. Consequently, function (3.2) satisfies condition (ii) as well as condition (i) and a "surrogate production function" exists, *if and only if* all wage-curves are straight lines (see Fig. 4).

The implications of this condition must now be traced. We know from Section I that the wage-curve is a straight line when, in a given system, the proportion of capital goods to labour is the same in the A and C industries, so that the relative value of the two commodities is constant as the division of the product between wages and interest changes. We may now go further and note that, but for the arbitrary choice of the capital-good unit, the input-coefficients of the two industries are identical. The system is therefore *indistinguishable* from one where A is produced by itself and labour.[13] Indeed, since "heterogeneity" of commodities can here be properly defined only as a difference in their conditions of production, a straight-line wage-curve *means* that A is produced by itself and labour.

[13] Samuelson writes: "under our postulations, one can rigorously estimate (surrogate capital) by

$$J = V = P_\alpha K_\alpha + P_\beta K_\beta + \ldots$$

where the equilibrium market (numeraire) prices of the heterogeneous physical capitals are weights which *most definitely do change* as the real wage and interest rate are higher along the factor price frontier" ([1], p. 201, our italics). But in fact, under Samuelson's hypothesis of "equal proportions of inputs", the prices of the "heterogeneous" physical capitals are "weights" which do *not* change as r and w change.

When this is true for the whole family of systems, we have that A is produced with varying proportions of itself to labour: the proportions indicated by the "slopes" of the wage-curves. It is then no surprise that the relations between r, w and q are compatible with the "Clark-Ramsey parable". The assumption of equal proportions of inputs has turned the "real" economy with "heterogeneous capital-goods" into the "imaginary" economy of the "Clark-Ramsey parable", where, in Samuelson's own words,

"Labor and a homogeneous capital ... produce a flow of *homogeneous net national product* which can consist of consumption goods or of net capital ... formation, *the two being infinitely substitutable* (in the long run, or, possibly even in the short run) *on a one-for-one basis*".[14]

In fact "surrogate capital" and "capital" are one and the same thing: at any given level of r, J/L, the "slope" of the envelope, is also the "slope" of the wage-curve tangent to the envelope at that rate of interest, and measures the proportion of A to labour required to produce A with the system in use at that level of r. Samuelson's "surrogate production function" is thus nothing more than the production function, whose existence in such an economy no critic has ever doubted.[15]

---

[14] Samuelson [1], p. 200; our italics. It should be noted how Samuelson himself emphasizes that when the price of "consumption" is constant relative to "net capital formation" (i.e. in his words: "the two [are] infinitely substitutable ... on a one-for-one basis"), the two commodities are homogeneous (i.e., they constitute "a flow of homogeneous net national product").

[15] We have supposed a stationary economy (above, p. 156). This is in fact the assumption we must make in order to discuss the "surrogate function" in the case where A and C are heterogeneous (if A and C are homogeneous, the level of accumulation is irrelevant). For, with some net accumulation, the net product would consist of A and of capital goods different at different levels of r. Then, as r changes, the net product per worker (a product measurable only in value terms) reflects also the changes in the composition of output—a circumstance quite distinct from the changes in the system of production, which alone the production function is meant to express. So, for example, should the economy grow in scale year by year, at a proportional rate equal to the rate of interest, the value relative to A of net product per worker would be equal to the S/L of Eq. (3.2) (cf. Bhaduri [3], p. 288 and, for a more general discussion of the ratio of capital to labour in conditions of accumulation, Spaventa [4]): but it would be incorrect to describe this case as one where the traditional production function is valid. By doing so we would have to admit, whenever the envelope is concave, equilibrium with rising "marginal products": or even, should the envelope be a straight line, "marginal products" changing without any change in the proportions of the factors (p. 157 above).

The problem of the "surrogate function" has been associated by Samuelson with the measurement of relative shares of labour and capital by means of the elasticity of the wage-curve (cf. [1], pp. 199–200). Now, if in Fig. 1 (p. 151) we draw the tangent AP to the "wage-curve at the point P, the elasticity of the curve at that point is Ow_1/w_1A. On the other hand, relative shares in the stationary economy are Ow_1/w_1W at P (cf. proposition (ii) on p. 151). Consequently, the elasticity of the wage-curve does not measure relative shares in the stationary economy unless the wage-curve is a straight line. (In the latter case, A and C being homogeneous, the elasticity of the wage-curve measures relative shares, whatever the level of accumulation.) When A and C are heterogeneous, the elasticity measures relative shares only when the proportional rate of accumulation equals r.

IV. A Generalization

Suppose now, for a moment, that a second consumption good was produced in the economy besides A, and let it be a "luxury good", a good not consumed by workers. The introduction of this good would not have affected the relation between r and w. Each "system" for the production of A—i.e. a "method of production" of A, and the "method of production" of the corresponding capital good—would still give the two Eqs. (1); and these would determine the relation between r and w *independently* of the new price-equations for the "luxury good" and any means of production specific to it. The part these additional equations would play is only that of determining the prices of the "luxury good" and its means of production (once r, w and p_c are known).

What we have here is the application of a principle which Ricardo first perceived[16]: in any economy, the relation between the wage and the rate of interest depends exclusively on the methods of production of the commodities that are either wage-goods *or* means for their direct or indirect production. The way is now open for extending the inquiry of the preceding sections to an economy with any number of commodities.

Let us consider an economy where commodities A_1, A_2, ..., are produced in yearly cycles, each in a distinct industry. By assuming an industry for each commodity we rule out joint production, and thus the possibility of a satisfactory treatment of fixed capital. We shall therefore complete the step and assume that the means of production are entirely consumed in each yearly cycle of production. As before, we suppose that no scarce natural resources exist, and that each industry has constant returns to scale. To begin with, we shall also assume that only one "method of production" is known for each industry. Thus, the production of a unit of commodity A_1 requires fixed quantities l_1 of labour and a_{11}, a_{21}, ..., of commodities A_1 A_2, etc.: these quantities define the "method of production" of A_1. Similarly the "methods of production" of A_2 A_3, etc., are defined, respectively, by the sets of input-coefficients l_2, a_{12}, a_{22}, ...; l_3, a_{13}, a_{23}, ...; etc.

The wage w is paid at the end of the yearly production cycle, and is a quantity of the *wage-commodity G* consisting of the *h wage-goods* A_1, A_2, ..., A_h taken

[16] Both in letters of 1814 and in his *Essay on the effect of the low price of corn on the profits of stock* (1815), Ricardo maintained that "it is the profits of the farmer that regulate the profits of all other trades" ([5], Vol. VI, p. 104; cf. also Vol. IV, p. 23). As Mr Sraffa pointed out, that principle is founded on the assumption that "corn" is the only constituent of the wage, and requires only labour and itself to be produced ([5], Vol. I, p. XXXI): "corn" is then the only commodity "entering the wage", and the conditions of its production determine the rate of profits in the economy, once the wage is given. The principle was then taken up in a more general form by L. von Bortkiewicz ([6], English tr. p. 209; [7], English tr., p. 21; cf. also Pasinetti [8], p. 85. For the principle and comments on its formulation in Bortkiewicz, see, by the author, [9], pp. 31–33, 54n, 202 [*editor's note:* corresponding points can be found in Part I of this volume, respectively Sect. 1, Ch. III, pp. 27–30; Sect. I, Ch. IV, p. 38, n. 95; Appendix B, p. 113].

in the quantities $\lambda_1, \lambda_2, ..., \lambda_h$, respectively.[17] We can now sort out from among all the commodities those which are means of production for the h wage-goods, or means of production for those means of production, etc. We shall indicate by $m(m \geq h)$, the number of commodities which either are wage-goods or enter (directly or indirectly) the production of the wage-goods. For short, we shall call these m commodities, "commodities entering directly or indirectly the wage", or simply *commodities entering the wage.* We shall indicate them by $A_1, A_2, ..., A_m$. The methods of the m "commodities entering the wage" constitute the *system of production* of the "wage commodity" G.

The assumption of a uniform wage and rate of interest allows us to write the following $m+1$ equations, the last of which defines G as the value unit:

$$\begin{aligned}
p_1 &= l_1 w + (a_{11}p_1 + a_{21}p_2 + \ldots a_{m1}p_m)(1+r)\\
p_2 &= l_2 w + (a_{12}p_1 + a_{22}p_2 + \ldots a_{m2}p_m)(1+r)\\
&\ldots\ldots\ldots\ldots\ldots\ldots\ldots\ldots\ldots\ldots\ldots\ldots\ldots\ldots\\
&\ldots\ldots\ldots\ldots\ldots\ldots\ldots\ldots\ldots\ldots\ldots\ldots\ldots\ldots\\
p_m &= l_m w + (a_{1m}p + a_{2m}p_m + \ldots + a_{mm}p_m)(1+r)\\
1 &= \lambda_1 p_1 + \lambda_2 p_2 + \ldots \lambda_h p_h
\end{aligned} \qquad (5)$$

where $l_1, a_{11}, ..., a_{m1}; l_2, a_{12}, ..., a_{m2}; ..., l_m, a_{1m}, ..., a_{mm}$ are all known quantities, as are $\lambda_1, \lambda_2, ..., \lambda_h$. There are $m+2$ unknowns: r, w and the prices $p_1, p_2, ..., p_m$.

Having $m+1$ independent equations for $m+2$ unknowns, system (5) has one degree of freedom, which we may use to obtain w and the prices as functions of r.

To analyse the relation between r and w, it is first necessary to distinguish those commodities, if any, which are used either directly or indirectly as means of production of *all* the m commodities. These commodities we shall call commodities (or products) *basic to the system.*[18] (E.g., in the systems discussed in the preceding sections, C, the capital good, was "basic" while A, the consumption good, was not.) We shall now make the following assumptions about the "system" for producing the wage-commodity G:

[17] Changes in the wage level are generally associated with changes in the kinds and proportions of the commodities consumed by workers. It may then appear that a changing wage, measured in terms of an unchanging set of "wage-goods", becomes an abstract value-quantity on the same footing as the wage in terms of any other commodity. However, certain commodities always play a primary role in workers' consumption and therefore provide a more significant measure of the wage. In addition, when, as in most concrete problems, the concern is for non-drastic changes in distribution around a given situation, the goods consumed by workers in that situation can be legitimately singled out as "wage-goods".

[18] Cf. Sraffa [10], pp. 7–8. Mr Sraffa defines as basic commodities those which enter directly or indirectly the production of all commodities in the economy. This stricter definition seems inconvenient here since the relation between r and w depends only on the conditions of production of the commodities "entering the wage".

(i) the system is viable, i.e. is capable of yielding a surplus over the pure replacement of the means of production;
(ii) at least one of the m commodities is basic to the system;
(iii) the direct production of at least one of its basic products requires some labour (so that labour enters directly or indirectly into the production of all m commodities);
(iv) where a group of non-basics exists such that each of them enters directly or indirectly the production of all commodities in the group, the group's "own net rate of reproduction" is greater than the "net rate of reproduction" of the basic products.[19]

Assumptions (i), (ii) and (iii) are the generalization of the parallel assumptions (on p. 149) for our earlier two-commodity systems. (There, assumption (iv) was unnecessary because consumption good A, the non-basic product, did not enter its own production.)

We can now return to the relation between r and w as determined by system (5). Assumptions (i), (ii), (iii) and (iv) ensure that, for $r=0$, we shall have a positive "maximum" wage W, and that, as r rises from zero, w falls as a continuous differentiable function of r, reaching zero for a finite "maximum" rate of interest R. The same assumptions imply that, for $0 \leq r \leq R$, the prices of the m commodities are positive and finite.[20] The system for the production of G therefore defines a "wage-curve" (Fig. 5) as with Samuelson's two-commodity systems, except that, under the present more general assumptions, concave and convex segments may alternate along the wage-curve.[21]

Let us now take the m industries in the unique set of proportions which ensures a net physical product consisting entirely of G,[22] and call the resulting composite industry the "integrated wage-commodity industry" or, for short, the *integrated industry*. Then, for the reasons we saw in Section I (p. 151), the vertical intercept OW of the wage-curve (Fig. 5) measures the net physical product per worker in the "integrated industry"; while the "slope" of the straight line WP measures the value—relative to the wage-commodity—of physical capital per worker in the same industry, at point P.

[19] The "net rate of reproduction" of the basic products is Mr Sraffa's "Standard ratio" ([10], p. 21). The "own net rate of reproduction" of a group of connected non-basics is the analogous concept obtained by considering those non-basics as if their production did not require as means of production any commodity outside the group.

[20] It should be noted that assumptions (i), (ii), (iii) and (iv) do not ensure, for $0 \leq r \leq R$, positive prices for the "luxury goods" or their specific means of production: zero or negative prices for some of these goods would mean that they cannot be produced at the given rate of interest.

[21] The wage-curve is a ratio between a polynomial of the mth degree and one of the $(m-1)$th degree in r. By a known property such rational functions admit up to $(3\,m-6)$ points of inflexion (cf., e.g. Enriques [11]). Further inquiry would be needed to find whether that maximum number can be reached in the relevant interval $0 < r < R$.

[22] Cf. the notion of a "sub-system" in Sraffa [10], p. 89.

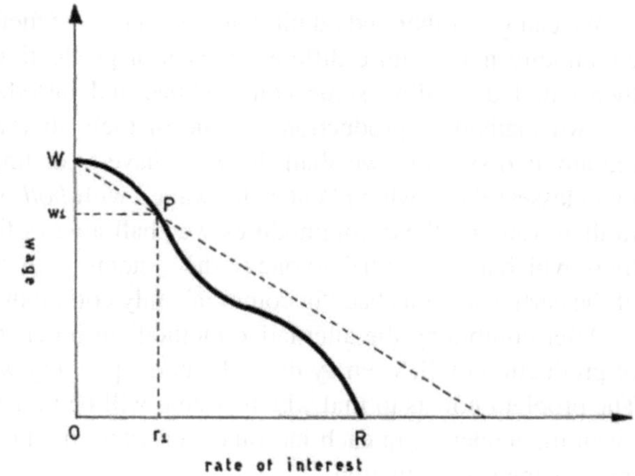

Fig. 5 The wage-curve for systems with many commodities

A straight-line wage-curve therefore indicates that the value of the physical capital used in the integrated industry does not change relative to the wage-commodity G as the division of the product between wages and interest changes. In that case, the equations of system (5) can be reduced to the following single price-equation for the wage-commodity:

$$1 = lw + a(1 + r)$$

where l (given by $l_1\lambda_1 + l_2\lambda_2 + \ldots l_h\lambda_h$) is the quantity of labour necessary for the direct production of a unit of G, and a, a constant, results from the commodity-input coefficients of the m industries. This single price-equation shows that the conditions of production of G are identical to those of its means of production: G and its means of production are therefore homogeneous (pp. 158–9 above).

In all other cases, the value (in terms of G) of the capital employed in the integrated industry changes with r, and—as is shown by the alternation of convex and concave segments along the curve—the direction of change will itself change as r rises from zero to R.

So far, we have assumed that only one method is known for producing each of the commodities "entering the wage". Let us now assume alternative methods for some or all the m commodities. Each *combination of* m *methods, one for each commodity*, constitutes a system for the production of the wage-commodity G. (If i_1 i_2, ..., i_m are the number of alternative methods of production of A_1 A_2, ..., A_m respectively, we have $i_1 \times i_2 \times \ldots\ i_m$ alternative systems).[23]

[23] It should be noted that a change in the method of production of a commodity may entail a change in the list of basic products. It is also conceivable that certain sets of available methods may give rise to systems having no basic products. This last possibility will be ignored here, in accordance with assumption (ii) of p. 162 above.

We can go further and admit that the alternative methods of production of some commodity may require different means of production. Changing a method may then entail discarding some commodities and introducing new ones, each with its own method of production (or one of their alternative methods). In comparing any two systems, we shall therefore have to distinguish the commodities into two classes: those which "enter the wage" with *both* systems and are "common" to them (among these commodities we shall always find the h wage-goods), and those which are "specific" to one of the systems. (E.g. the two-commodity systems of the earlier sections had "in common" only commodity A, the wage-good.).

After combining the alternative methods in order to form all possible systems of production of G, we may draw the corresponding wage-curves in one diagram. The problem now is to find which system will be in use at any specified level of r, given the tendency, in each industry, to switch to whichever method is cheaper in the existing price situation.

Here, as in Section II (pp. 152–3), the question is complicated by the fact that the price situation, on the basis of which the methods are chosen, itself depends on the system which happens to be in use. It can be proved however that, whichever the system initially in use, the switch to cheaper methods will eventually bring into use the system giving the highest w. When two (or more) systems give the same w for the given r, and that w is higher than those of all other possible systems, the two (or more) systems give the same prices for all commodities they have in common, and can therefore co-exist.

The more general hypotheses of this section do not therefore affect the main conclusion in Section II about the relation between r and w in an economy with many systems for producing the wage-commodity. That relation is represented by the "wage-frontier" generated by the intersecting "wage-curves": methods, and hence systems of production, change at the "corners" of the frontier, at which points two "adjacent" systems (p. 153) can co-exist. The same wage-curve however may now contribute more than two separate segments to the wage-frontier since any two wage-curves may intersect more than twice.

If we were prepared to make the necessary assumptions,[24] we could imagine the "wage-frontier" becoming a "smooth" envelope enclosing the family of wage-curves from above. The problem of a "surrogate production function" could then be approached in the same way as in Section III.

Let $w = e(r)$ be the equation of the envelope, and $q = q(r)$ be the relation between r and the net product per worker in the integrated wage-commodity industry. The problem is whether there is a function $S = S(J, L)$, homogeneous of the first degree, such that $\partial S/\partial L = e(\partial S/\partial J)$ and $S/L = q(\partial S/\partial J)$. For the reasons given above (p. 157), the function exists if, and only if, all the wage-curves are straight lines. We have already noted that a system giving a straight-line

[24] The number of commodities "entering the wage" should not change from system to system, and the $m(m+1)$ input coefficients should be appropriate functions of a single parameter u (cf. above, n. 9).

wage-curve implies that G is produced by itself and labour. It follows that $S(J, L)$ exists only when G is produced by variable proportions of itself and labour. Then J is the capital used *in the production of* G, and $S(J, L)$ is the production function of G.

But, in contrast to what we saw in Section III, the condition that all wage-curves are straight lines is now insufficient to ensure the existence of a "surrogate production function", i.e. a function giving not only the relation between r and w, but also the relation between r and the net product *in the economy as a whole.* This is so because "luxury goods" can be produced in addition to G. The value relative to G of the net product per worker in the economy will then depend on the relative size of the various industries and will differ from $S/L = q$.[25] This, however, only confirms the conclusion we reached in Section III: a "surrogate production function" exists only for an economy where a single commodity is produced by itself and labour.

V. Heterogeneous Capital and the Premises of the Traditional Theory of Distribution

Our inquiry into the properties of economies with heterogeneous capital goods now offers a convenient basis for examining the validity of traditional theory from an angle less special than that of Samuelson's "surrogate production function". This we shall do by discussing three questions which, as we shall see, correspond to three different versions of the theory. The discussion will be conducted on the basis of the economy considered in the last section, with constant returns to scale, no joint production and no scarcity of natural resources.

The first question is whether there exists an *aggregate* production function in which quantities of labour and "capital" explain both the level of the national product and, by means of the "marginal products" of the two factors, its distribution.[26] A second question is whether a similar production function can be conceived for any *single* commodity. The third and most important question concerns the basic premise of the traditional theory of distribution in all its formulations: the notion that a fall of r will cheapen the more capital-intensive processes of production.

[25] A similar difference between S/L and the value of the net product per worker in the economy could arise if the wage-goods were produced in proportions other than those in G. However, the assumption of a multiplicity of wage-goods can hardly be maintained where all wage-curves are straight lines: it would indeed be a fluke if G, consisting of different commodities in given proportions, required as means of production *those* commodities in *those* proportions in *all* alternative systems.

[26] Cf. Samuelson [1], pp. 193–4.

Our discussion of Samuelson's "surrogate function" makes it easy to dismiss the first question. Either a single commodity is produced in the economy, and no problem of aggregation arises, or different commodities are produced, and no "aggregate production function" exists. But, despite the fashion for "aggregate production functions" in recent economic literature, they are only of secondary interest. In traditional theory, distinct production functions were generally attributed to each consumption good, and consumer demand was brought in to determine the proportions in which these goods are produced.

We therefore get nearer to the core of traditional theory when we turn to the notion that the technical conditions of production for any commodity A_i can be represented by a production function with "capital" and labour as the factors. In these versions of traditional theory it is claimed that, in any equilibrium situation, the ratio of "capital" to labour in the production of A_i would be that for which the marginal product of "capital" is equal to the ruling rate of interest. To that ratio, there would correspond a "marginal product" of labour, giving the wage in terms of A_i, and a determinate physical product to be divided between wages and interest.

To discuss this view of production we must refer to the notions of "system of production" and "integrated industry", applying them to the commodity A_i.[27] In parallel with the assumptions of continuity inherent in the notion of "marginal products", we must assume that the system for the production of A_i "changes continuously" with r. What we saw about the relations between r, w, and q, and their representation by means of the "envelope" of wage-curves, can then be applied to the relations between r, the wage in terms of A_i, and the net physical product per worker in the production of A_i. The question we must now ask is whether these relations could result from a production function, with labour and an appropriately defined "capital" as the two factors.

This is simply Samuelson's problem of the existence of a "surrogate production function", re-stated for the production of a single commodity A_i, and not for aggregate production. And, for exactly the reasons we saw above (pp. 158–9), the function exists if, and only if, A_i is produced with varying proportions of itself and labour.[28]

[27] So far, we have used these notions only for the wage-commodity G, but they can be applied to any commodity A_i. A "system of production" for A_i is a set of methods of production; one method for A_i and one for each of the commodities which enter directly or indirectly the production of A_i. Appropriate proportions of these industries will give the "integrated industry" of A_i.

[28] The hypothesis that each commodity in the economy is produced by itself and labour would involve logical difficulties, unless we supposed that G, the wage-commodity, consisted of a single wage-good. This is so because each wage-good would have a distinct net "rate of reproduction". Consequently, as r reaches the minimum of those "rates", say that for A_1, the price of all wage-goods other than A_1 would be zero in terms of A_1. Thus, at that level of r, where the wage is zero in terms of G (but still positive in terms of wage-goods other than A_1), the economic system would become unworkable. (This difficulty is due to the fact that the systems of production of G would have no "basic" product.)

But expressing the conditions of production of a commodity in terms of a production function with "capital" as a factor is a feature of only *some* versions of the traditional theory of distribution. They are the versions stemming from authors like Marshall or J. B. Clark, who thought that the principle of substitution, drawn from the reformulation of the Malthusian theory of rent in terms of homogeneous land and "intensive" margins, could be applied *without modification* to labour and "capital". In production with unassisted labour and land, variable proportions of the factors can be shown to imply equality between the marginal products of the two factors and the rates of wages and rents in terms of the product. It was therefore thought that, in production with "capital" and labour, a similar equality would hold between the rates of interest and wages and the marginal products of these factors.

But this analogy between "capital" and labour or land was misleading. To give a marginal product equal to the *rate of interest*, "capital" must be conceived as a magnitude homogeneous with the product and must therefore be measured as the *value* of the means of production and not in physical units as is the case with labour or land. This value, however, like that of the other products, changes as r and w change. Consequently, the "quantities" of capital per worker corresponding to each system—and with it, the "production function" where those quantities appear—cannot be known independently of distribution. Every conclusion reached by postulating the contrary cannot be defended on *that* ground. And we have just seen that *one* of those conclusions is invalid: no definition of "capital" allows us to say that its marginal product is equal to the rate of interest.

The trap of drawing such a close analogy between capital and labour or land has been avoided in other versions of traditional theory. As we shall see, traditional theory—reduced to its core as the explanation of distribution in terms of demand and supply—rests in fact on a single premise. This premise is that any change of system brought about by a fall of r must increase the ratio of "capital" to labour in the production of the commodity: "capital" being the value of physical capital in terms of some unit of consumption goods, a value which is thought to measure the consumption given up or postponed in order to bring that physical capital into existence. Now, this proposition about "capital-intensity" was one of the conclusions reached by postulating a production function in which "capital" is included as a factor: the principle of decreasing marginal products would ensure that, as r falls, the ratio of capital to labour rises, causing the marginal product of capital to fall in step with r. Some authors however thought that the proposition could be defended on other, more consistent grounds.

This was the position assumed by Böhm-Bawerk and Wicksell in what are, perhaps, the most careful formulations of the traditional theory. In their production functions, the capital goods appear in the form of a magnitude or set of magnitudes (Böhm-Bawerk's "average period of production" or Wicksell's "dated quantities of labour") which are independent of distribution: it is to these magnitudes that the marginal productivity conditions are applied. "Capital", the value magnitude, comes in at a second stage; when, to lay the basis for explaining interest and wages in terms of supply and demand, it is argued that a fall of r will result in a relative cheapening of the systems of production requiring capital goods of a smaller value per worker.[29]

We must therefore turn our attention to the proposition that systems with a higher "capital-intensity" become profitable at lower levels of r, and thus to the third of the questions outlined above (p. 165). That proposition is strictly associated with a second one, which claims that a fall of r lowers the relative price of the consumption goods whose production requires a higher proportion of capital to labour. Both propositions are in fact expressions of a single principle, according to which a fall of r cheapens the more capital-intensive processes of production. Granted this principle, the way is open for explaining distribution in terms of demand and supply. As r fell, both the change in the system of production for each consumption good, and consumer substitution in favour of the more capital-intensive goods, would raise the ratio of "capital" to labour in the economy. If we then assume that the quantity of labour employed remains equal to its supply (and the supply rises or, in any case, shows no drastic fall as w rises with the fall of r), it will follow that the amount of capital employed in the economy *increases* as r falls. This relation between r and the amount of capital employed could then be viewed as a demand function for capital; and competition in the capital market could be thought of as ensuring the absorption of "net saving" through appropriate falls of r.

On the other hand, the assumption of a persisting equality between the employment of labour and its supply would be justified by a parallel mechanism at work in the labour market. A regular demand function for labour would exist for any given amount of capital employed in production, and competition could be thought of as bringing the wage to the level where all labour finds employment.

(After Keynes, this alluring picture of a tidy interplay between demand and supply in the labour and capital-markets would of course be qualified as applying "in the absence of risk and uncertainty",[30] or where monetary authorities offer a visible beneficent hand should the invisible one fail.)

This elaborate theory of distribution therefore rests on the principle that a fall of r cheapens the more capital-intensive processes of production relative to the others. But this principle is no more valid than that of the equality between the rate of interest and the marginal product of capital: in just the same way, it is invalidated by the dependence of the value of capital goods on distribution.[31]

[29] On the theories of Böhm-Bawerk and Wicksell, and the reasons for the failure of their arguments supporting the principle about "capital-intensity", cf. the author's [12], pp. 563–4 [this volume, Part II, pp. 204–5], and the references given there.

[30] Cf., e.g., R. Solow, [13], p. 81.

[31] If the relative value of the two sets of capital goods required by any two systems of production remained constant as r changes, a fall of r could not fail to cheapen the more "capital-intensive" of the two systems. But the fall of r can *reduce* the relative value of the set of capital-goods used in the *less* capital-intensive system: and this reduction may well make that system cheaper than the more capital-intensive one.

Fig. 6 The relation between rate of interest and value of capital per worker with the family of systems of Fig. 3 (p. 155)

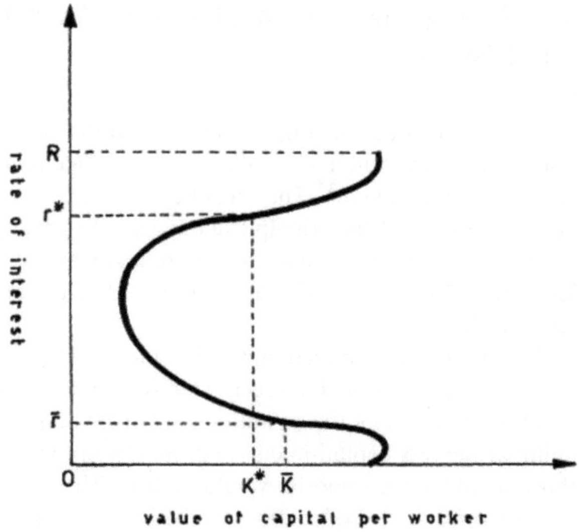

That a fall of r may cheapen the *less* capital intensive systems of a commodity A_i can be seen from the examples given for the consumption good in Samuelson's two-commodity systems. So, at point B of Fig. 2 (pp. 152–3), the switch with falling r is in favour of system β, whose capital goods have, at switch-point prices, the lower value per worker. And the position would not be altered if we assumed that the system of production of the commodity "changes continuously" with r. So, in the family of systems of Fig. 3 above, a fall of r can lower, as well as raise, the value of physical capital per worker in terms of the product (a value which we shall here indicate by k_i). Fig. 6 shows the relation between r and k for that family of systems. Other examples of that relation are shown in Fig. 9 of the Appendix, relating to families of systems which we shall examine there: as some of these examples show, k_i and r may fall together even in the lowest range of r.[32]

We have seen that a fall of r may cheapen the less "capital intensive" of two systems for the production of a commodity. The same applies if the two systems relate to distinct commodities. Then by the traditional analysis of consumer choice we should conclude that, as r falls, substitution among consumption goods may lower, as well as raise, the ratio of capital to labour in the economy.

[32] In the examples referred to in the text, k_i is measured in terms of the commodity whose production we are considering. But the conclusion that k_i and r may fall together over any range of r is not affected if any other commodity is chosen as value unit. It should be noted however that the direction in which k_i changes with r may be different with different value-units since the relative value of such units will itself change with r.

VI. Heterogeneous Capital and the Theory of Value and Distribution

Particular theoretical examples have forced the admission, in recent economic literature, that the switch of systems might operate in a direction contrary to the one traditionally assumed.[33] The tendency however has been to label those cases as "exceptions": as if the principle about capital-intensity had resulted from observed regularities, always liable to exception, and was not a pure deduction from postulates (like Böhm-Bawerk's "average period of production") now generally admitted to be invalid.

Instead, it must be recognized that the traditional principle, drawn from incorrect premises, is itself incorrect. Moreover, the examples of the Appendix do not seem to indicate that the conditions in which a fall of r results in a relative cheapening of the less capital-intensive productive processes are any less plausible than those in which the opposite would be true. This appears to undermine the ground on which rests the explanation of distribution in terms of demand and supply for capital and labour.

To see why that is so, we may begin from the relation between r and the value, in the chosen unit, of the physical capital employed in the economy. This value we shall indicate by K. The relation between r and K—the traditional "demand function" for capital (saving)—was based on two assumptions: (*a*) that in the situation defined by each level of r, the labour employed is equal to the supply of it at the corresponding level of w; (*b*) that the composition of consumption output is that dictated by consumer demand at the prices and incomes[34] defined by the level of r. We shall now grant these assumptions, but we shall restrict the choice of the consumers by supposing, at first, zero net savings (i.e., in each situation, the capital goods are consumed and reproduced in unchanging quantities year by year). From these assumptions, and from what we saw about changes in the systems of production and the relative prices of consumption goods, it follows that K may fall or rise, as r falls.

To clear the ground, we must now grant traditional theory two further assumptions in addition to (*a*) and (*b*): namely that (*c*) a tendency to net saving (i.e. a fall in consumption) appearing in the situation defined by a given level of r, brings about a fall of r; (*d*) as r and w change, with systems of production and relative

[33] Cf. Robinson [14], p. 106; also [15], pp. 109–10, 418; Champernowne [16], pp. 118–19, 128–9; M. Morishima [17], p. 126; Hicks [18], p. 154. Cf. also D. Levhari [19], and the ensuing Symposium [20].

[34] In order to determine, simultaneously with the wage and prices, the incomes of consumers and hence the quantities of goods demanded and produced, some hypothesis is necessary regarding the distribution of the ownership of the capital-goods in the situation defined by each level of r.

outputs changing accordingly, net savings realized in the economy can still be meaningfully defined, and can be measured—however broadly—by the difference between the K of the final and that of the initial situation.[35]

Let us now imagine that the economy is initially in the situation defined by the level r^* of the rate of interest, with K^* as the amount of capital.[36] Then a tendency to positive net savings appears (i.e. consumption is reduced). We assume that, after a time, the tendency to net saving disappears so that, if a new equilibrium is ever reached, the level of consumption will become that of the situation which corresponds to the new lower equilibrium value of r.

We must now ask whether—as r falls from r^* to some level $\overline{r}$ because of the initial tendency to net saving—a new situation can always be found with an additional quantity of capital ΔK representing the net savings which the community intended to make during the period. The form of the relation between r and K implies that such a new situation cannot always be found: however high r^* is, and however small ΔK, there may well not exist any lower rate of interest $\overline{r}$ at which $\overline{K} = K^* + \Delta K$. Or, to find a situation with an amount $\overline{K}$ of capital just larger than

[35] These assumptions are themselves highly questionable. It is beyond the scope of this article to discuss fully assumption (*d*). It should however be noted that, in order to justify this traditional assumption, we should once more refer to the economy of Samuelson's "parable", where a single commodity is produced by itself and labour. In that economy, physical capital and K would be one and the same thing. No change of relative outputs could arise there, and changes in the systems of production would not require any qualitative change of the existing physical capital. Then, once we admit, with traditional theory, a tendency to the full utilization of resources, any change of K could be seen as resulting from an equal opposite change in consumption. But in an economy with heterogeneous capital goods, none of the conditions listed above is verified. The changes in systems of production or in relative outputs will affect the capital stock by changing the *kind* of capital goods, or by increasing the quantity of some capital goods and decreasing that of others. The possibility of referring to *physical increments* of the capital stock will fail, and with that will fail the possibility of any meaningful notion of "net saving", not to mention "net saving" in terms of K. Then, even if we could grant traditional theory the existence of a tendency to the full utilization of resources, we would have to admit that the changes in total consumption imposed by given changes in the physical capital stock would depend on the *kind* of changes in the stock, and on the speed with which they have been accomplished—more than upon the difference between the K of the final and that of the initial situation.

As for assumption (*c*), we may note that Keynes's negative conclusions about the flexibility of r can only be strengthened if, as we shall argue in the text, changes in r provide no mechanism for equalizing "demand" and "supply" of capital (saving).

[36] Unless we suppose that the system for the production of each commodity changes "continuously" with r, K can assume, at any level of r where two systems co-exist, any value between the extremes set by the two systems.

K^*, we may need a fall of r so drastic (cf. Fig. 6 above) as to make it clear that, in this case too, it is impossible to determine r by the supply and demand of "capital" (saving).[37]

This is not all. We saw (p. 168) that, in traditional theory, our assumption (*a*)—of a persisting equality between the quantity of labour employed and the supply of it—found its justification in the idea of a demand function for labour. But the fact that, given the quantity of labour employed, K may rise as r rises, implies that the labour employed with a constant K must *fall* with the corresponding fall of w. Thus—even if, by assumption (*d*), we grant that, in the face of changes in systems of production and relative outputs, we can speak of a constancy of capital and take that to mean constancy of K—there is no reason to suppose a tendency to equality between the demand and supply for labour. Assumption (*a*) is then unwarranted: the failure of a demand and supply analysis, which we first saw from the viewpoint of the capital market, has its mirror-image in the labour market.

Analogous results would have been reached had we imagined an initial rise in consumption (i.e. a tendency to negative net saving); or an initial change in the "demand" conditions for capital and labour (i.e. a change in the relation between r and K due to changes in consumer tastes or in the methods of production available).

Thus, after following in the footsteps of traditional theory and attempting an analysis of distribution in terms of "demand" and "supply", we are forced to the conclusion that a change, however small, in the "supply" or "demand" conditions of labour or capital (saving) may result in drastic changes of r and w. That analysis would even force us to admit that r may fall to zero or rise to its maximum, and hence w rise to its maximum or to fall to zero, without bringing to equality the quantities supplied and demanded of the two factors.

Now, no such instability of an economy's wage- and interest-rates has ever been observed. The natural conclusion is that, in order to explain distribution, we must rely on forces other than "supply" and "demand". The traditional theory of distribution was built, and accepted, in the belief that a fall of r—an increase in

[37] This conclusion would not be affected if we chose to measure capital in the economy by means of the chain-index method proposed by Champernowne [16] and supported by Swan ([21] pp. 348ff). It is beyond our scope to discuss this measure of capital or the claim that it permits us to consider as the increase of capital brought about by net saving "not the change in the value of the stock [in terms of consumption goods], but rather the value of the change" ([21] pp. 349 and 356) (cf. however n. 35 above on "physical increments" of the capital stock). It is sufficient to remark here that when measured in these terms the amount of capital per worker may fall together with r (though it cannot do so in the immediate proximity of $r=0$). In similar cases, Champernowne asserts "the only way that investment could remain positive ... would be for food-wages to leap up and the rate of interest to leap down to levels where capital equipment ... [giving a higher ratio of capital to labour] became competitive" ([16] p. 118).

w—would always raise the proportion of "capital" to labour in the economy: the theory becomes implausible once it is admitted that this principle is not always valid.[38]

The idea that demand and supply for factors of production determine distribution has become so deeply ingrained in economic thought that it is almost viewed as an immediate reflection of facts, and not as the result of an elaborate theory. For the same reason, it is easily forgotten how comparatively recent that theory is. In the first systematic analysis of value and distribution by the English classical economists up to Ricardo, we would look in vain for the conception that demand and supply for labour and "capital" achieve "equilibrium" as the proportions in which those "factors" are employed in the economy change with the wage and rate of profits. Thus, Ricardo saw no inconsistency between free competition and unemployment of labour. In his view lower wages could eliminate unemployment only by decreasing the growth of population or by favouring accumulation.[39]

What we find in the Classical economists is the idea that the wage is ruled by the "necessaries of the labourer and his family". Since they regarded these "necessaries" as determined by social as much as physiological conditions, we may see them as recognizing that distribution is governed by social forces, the investigation of which falls largely outside the domain of the pure theory of value. The proper object of value theory was seen to be the study of the *relations* between the wage, the rate of profits and the system of relative prices. These relations would then

[38] According to Professor Hicks, the failure of the principle about capital intensity leaves us in a position which, though not satisfactory, "has parallels in other parts of economic theory" ([18], p. 154). He thus seems to suggest that the possible fall, as r falls, in the value of capital per worker does not affect traditional theory any more than do the well known anomalies of the demand for inferior goods. This seems to ignore that the case of inferior goods did not call into question the general supply-and-demand analysis of prices only because it could be plausibly argued that: (*a*) should those anomalies give rise to a multiplicity of equilibria, the equilibrium position with the highest price would be stable, while that with the lowest price would, in all likelihood, be stable too; and (*b*) if the latter equilibrium were unstable, the rest of the economic system would not be affected since all we would have is that once the price has fallen below the level of that equilibrium the commodity would not be produced due to a lack of demand willing to pay the supply price. No analogous arguments have been advanced by Professor Hicks with respect to the fall of capital-intensity as r falls.

[39] E.g., in his Chapter "On Machinery" in the *Principles* Ricardo wrote: "the discovery and use of machinery may be attended with a diminution of gross produce; and whenever that is the case, it will be injurious to the labouring class, as some of their number will be thrown out of employment, and population will become redundant, compared with the funds which are to employ it" ([5], Vol. I, p. 390).

An interesting expression of the contrast between Ricardo and later theorists can be found in Wicksell's criticism of this position of Ricardo. Wicksell holds that the decrease of "gross produce" of which Ricardo speaks, is not possible because "as soon as a number of labourers have been made superfluous by these changes, and wages have accordingly fallen, then, as Ricardo failed to see [other] methods of production … will become more profitable … and absorb the surplus of idle labourers" ([22], p. 137).

provide the basis for studying the circumstances on which depends the distribution of the product between classes.

The distinction thus made by the Classical economists between the study of value and the study of the forces governing distribution goes together with a separation between the study of value and that of levels of output. Since the inception of the marginal method this separation has been thought no more tenable than that between value and distribution. But the weakness of the marginalist position should now be apparent.

The outputs of commodities and, hence, consumer choice, can influence relative prices, *either* by modifying the technical conditions of production (i.e., the set of methods available for producing each commodity), *or* by affecting the rates of wages and profits.

The first possibility arises because increases in the output of a commodity may, on the one hand, bring about an increase of the division of labour in any of its possible forms and, on the other hand, where scarce natural resources are used, may force the adoption of methods which increase the output obtained from those resources. But with regard to the changes in the division of labour due to increases in output, the traditional analysis of the firm has in fact restricted the theory of a competitive economy to those technical improvements that are "external" to the firm. At the same time, the approach in terms of outputs of single commodities has ruled out the technical improvements deriving from the economy's general growth. Consequently, the only "economies of scale" considered were those "external to the firm", but "internal to the industry"—the class which, it has been noted, "is most seldom to be met with."[40] There remains the case of scarce natural resources. This—as Ricardo showed—can be conveniently treated by first assuming the outputs of the commodities to be given, *then* moving on to inquire about the technical changes associated with changes in outputs, and the consequent changes in the relations between r, w, and the prices (including the prices for the use of natural resources). This method would also allow a less restricted treatment of the "economies of scale".[41]

The second way in which consumer choice and, hence, outputs can influence relative prices is by affecting the relative scarcity of labour and capital, and thus the wage and rate of interest, given the supply of the two factors and the state of technical knowledge. This link between prices and outputs is one and the same thing as the explanation of distribution by demand and supply of factors of production: and it becomes untenable once that explanation is abandoned.

---

[40] Sraffa [23], p. 540 [rpt. 1952, p. 186].

[41] This method is apparently the one Mr. Sraffa points to, when in the Preface to *Production of Commodities by Means of Commodities* he writes "No changes in output ... are considered, so that no question arises as to the variation or constancy of returns" and adds: "This standpoint, which is that of the old classical economists from Adam Smith to Ricardo, has been submerged and forgotten since the advent of the marginal method" ([10], p. v).

Thus, the separation of the pure theory of value from the study of the circumstances governing changes in the outputs of commodities, does not seem to meet any essential difficulty. On the contrary, it may open the way for a more satisfactory treatment of the relations between outputs and the technical conditions of production. Moreover, by freeing the theory of value from the assumption of consumers' tastes given from outside the economic system, this separation may favour a better understanding of consumption, and its dependence on the rest of the system.

With this, the theory of value will lose the all-embracing quality it assumed with the marginal method. But what will be lost in scope will certainly be gained in consistency and, we may hope, in fruitfulness.

Postcript

A mathematical note has been omitted for reasons of space [*editor's note*: the reader will find the mathematical note, published here for the first time, next to the Appendix]. In paras. 1–6 of that note a demonstration is given of the propositions set out at p. 162 of the text on the positivity of prices and the properties of the relation between r and w. Then in paras 7 and 8 a proof is given of the statements on p. 164 on the relative profitability of alternative systems of production. A copy of the note is available to students in the Marshall Library at Cambridge.

Appendix

The purpose of this Appendix is to show by a selection of numerical examples how far the relation between the rate of interest and the value of capital per worker in the production of a commodity can differ from what traditional theory postulates. For simplicity of calculation, we shall refer to the two-commodity systems of production discussed in Sections I and II of the paper. We shall indicate by k_i the value, expressed in terms of the product, of capital per worker in the integrated production of a commodity A_i (cf. p. 150 in the text); by w_i, the wage expressed in the same terms; and by q_i, the level of the net physical product per worker.

We shall begin by considering the family of systems giving the wage-curves and "envelope" of Fig. 3 (p. 155). To give a more complete idea of the freedom with which k_i may vary as r changes, we shall then show how families of systems may be found giving *any* relation between r and k_i within an area defined purely by the shape of the envelope (cf. the area *STQO* in Fig. 9).

I

We assume circulating capital, i.e. $d=1$; and choose as the unit of any capital-good C the quantity of it requiring a labour-year for its direct production, so that $l_c=1$ in each system. Let the remaining three coefficients be defined by the following functions

$$
\begin{aligned}
l_a &= \frac{30 + 11u^{\frac{11}{10}} + u^{\frac{11}{5}} - 27e^{-2u}}{6 + u^{\frac{11}{10}}} \\
c_a &= \frac{27e^{-2u}}{\left(6 + u^{\frac{11}{10}}\right)^2} \\
c_c &= \frac{5 + u^{\frac{11}{10}}}{6 + u^{\frac{11}{10}}}
\end{aligned}
\qquad \text{(i)}
$$

where $u \geq 0$ is the variable parameter, and e is the base of natural logarithms. The family of systems defined by the functions (i) is such that, as l_a increases (i.e. u increases), c_a decreases and c_c increases (cf. Table 1).

Substituting the expressions for the five coefficients in function (2) of the text (p. 149), we obtain the equation of the family of wage-curves,

$$
w = \frac{1 - \left(5 + u^{\frac{11}{10}}\right) r}{\left(5 + u^{\frac{11}{10}}\right) + \left\{27e^{-2u} - \left(5 + u^{\frac{11}{10}}\right)^2\right\} r}.
$$

The system defined by $u=0$ gives a wage-curve convex to the origin and having $W=R=0{\cdot}20$, shown in Fig. 7a. As u increases, both W and R, given by $1/\left(5 + u^{\frac{11}{10}}\right)$, decrease. At the same time, the ratio of C to labour decreases in the A industry and increases in the C industry; as a result the wage-curves become progressively less convex to the origin. Thus, the system for $u \cong 0{\cdot}034$ gives a straight line wage-curve, while the wage-curves corresponding to still higher values of u are concave.

Table 1 Family of systems as functions of the variable u

Parameter u	Production of a unit of the consumer good		Production of a unit of the capital good	
	Labour l_a	Physical capital c_a	Labour l_c	Physical capital c_c
0·000	0·500	0·750	1	0·833
0·250	2·584	0·424	1	0·839
0·500	3·930	0·237	1	0·845
0·750	4·834	0·133	1	0·851
1·000	5·478	0·075	1	0·857
1·250	5·974	0·042	1	0·863
1·505	6·391	0·023	1	0·868

Table 2 Series of systems in use at increasing levels of the interest rate

Rate of interest % r	System in use u	Wage w_i	Net phys. prod, per worker q_i	Value of capital per worker k_i
00·0	0·000	0·200	0·200	1·080
2·6	0·250	0·175	0·192	0·635
4·1	0·500	0·169	0·183	0·393
6·1	0·750	0·159	0·175	0·257
8·3	1·000	0·151	0·167	0·184
10·5	1·250	0·144	0·159	0·148
12·9	1·505	0·129	0·152	0·179
14·4	1·250	0·105	0·159	0·379
15·1	1·000	0·083	0·167	0·552
15·9	0·750	0·061	0·175	0·715
16·9	0·500	0·041	0·183	0·850
17·5	0·250	0·026	0·192	0·947
20·0	0·000	0·000	0·200	1·000

The fall of W and R on the one hand, and the increasingly concave shape of the wage-curves on the other, are such that each cuts the wage-curves corresponding to any lower u twice, and shows a middle section above all of them (see Fig. 7a). This is so up to the point where $u = 1{\cdot}505$. As u rises further, the wage-curves recede towards the origin and the corresponding systems are less profitable than others at *all* possible levels of r.

As is clear from Fig. 7a, the family of wage-curves for $0 \leq u \leq 1{\cdot}505$ admits an envelope E. Each wage-curve touches E twice (with the exception of that for $u = 1{\cdot}505$ which touches E only once), and each system will be in use at *two* levels of r. Thus, as r rises from zero to the maximum of 20 per cent admissible in the economy, we shall run through the whole series of systems twice: first (up to $r = 13$ per cent) in the order of increasing u, and then in the opposite order (Table 2). Accordingly q_i, the net physical product per worker in the integrated industry will first fall as r rises, and then rise, as shown by Fig. 7b (cf. also Table 2). The same is true for k_i (see Fig. 7c).

The relation between k_i and q_i is shown by the curve of Fig. 7d, whose loop-like shape requires some explanation. As r rises from zero, we enter the diagram from the right and move in the direction of the arrows: q_i and k_i decrease together. But, as we reach $r \cong 12$ per cent, while q_i continues to decrease, k_i starts rising and we move down and to the right. Then, as r increases beyond 13 per cent, q_i also begins to rise and we move along the lower part of the loop. Thus, for the same q_i—indicating that the same system is in use—we have two levels of k_i due to the *two* levels of r at which the same physical capital is evaluated. So long as the systems are those in use for the middle range of r (i.e. the systems having a proportion of C to labour higher in the C than in the A industry), k_i is higher at the second (higher) rate of interest. The contrary is true for the systems in use in the

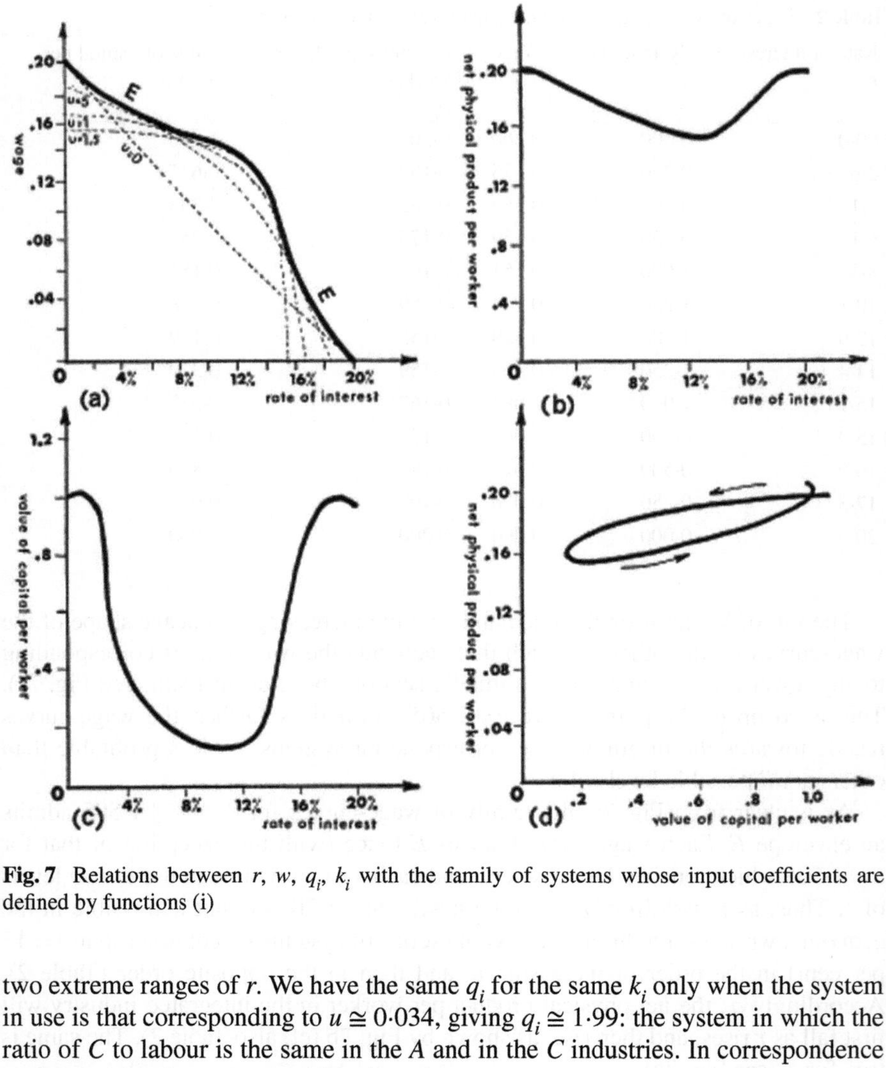

Fig. 7 Relations between r, w, q_i, k_i with the family of systems whose input coefficients are defined by functions (i)

two extreme ranges of r. We have the same q_i for the same k_i only when the system in use is that corresponding to $u \cong 0{\cdot}034$, giving $q_i \cong 1{\cdot}99$: the system in which the ratio of C to labour is the same in the A and in the C industries. In correspondence to that system the two parts of the loop intersect.

II

Suppose a decreasing rectangular hyperbola with asymptotes parallel to the r and w axes, which intersects both positive semi-axes: for short, we shall call *segment* the part of this hyperbola included between the two intersections. It can be shown that when the "segment" is *concave* to the origin, it can always be interpreted as the wage-curve for a two commodity system of the kind used for our numerical examples: i.e., the equation of the curve is always compatible with positive values of all the four coefficients l_a, $(c_a l_c)$, c_c, d.[42]

Let us now take the parabola defined by the equation

$$w = -20r^2 - r + 1$$

and call E the part of that curve included between the points of intersection (0, 1) and (0·2, 0) with the positive semi-axes (Fig. 8).

Consider the possible families of "segments" having E as the envelope enclosing the family from above: an infinite number of such families can be conceived. Since E is concave to the origin, any family must include only concave "segments", and is therefore a possible family of wage-curves. Accordingly, E can be conceived as the relation between r and w for any among an infinite number of possible families of systems of production.

We may now define each family j of such systems in terms of the function $k_i^{(j)} = k_i^{(j)}(r)$, relating the rate of interest and the value of capital per worker in the family. To see the conditions which $k_i^{(j)}$ must satisfy, let us consider in Fig. 8 the wage-curve QPS of the family j, tangent to E at the point P for $r = r^*$, where $0 < r^* \leq 0 \cdot 2$: the "slope" of the straight line QP measures $k_i^{(j)}(r^*)$ (see proposition (iii) of p. 162 in the text). If E is to enclose all wage-curves of the family j from above, that "slope" must be lower than the "slope" of the straight line drawn to P from T, a slope given by $(1 - w^*)/r^* = 1 + 20r^*$. Further, $k_i^{(j)}(0)$— the slope for $r = 0$ of the wage-curve tangent to E at point T—must equal the "slope" of E at T, which is 1. Thus, the function $k_i^{(j)}(r)$, defining a possible family of systems having E as the envelope, must satisfy the conditions:

$$k_i^{(j)}(0) = 1; \text{ and } k_i^{(j)}(r) < 1 + 20r, \text{ for } 0 < r \leq 0.2 \qquad \text{(ii)}$$

[42] The equation of the hyperbola assumed in the text is

$$w = \frac{1 - xr}{y - zr}$$

where x, y, z are positive and such that $(xy - z) > 0$. On the other hand, the equation of a wage-curve (see function (2), p. 149 above) can be written as.

$$w = \frac{1 - \frac{c_c}{1-dc_c} r}{\frac{l_a + (l_c c_a - l_a c_c)}{1-dc_c} + \frac{l_c c_a - l_a c_c}{1-dc_c} r}.$$

Equating one by one the coefficients of the two functions we obtain the following three equations

$$\frac{c_c}{1 - dc_c} = x; \ \frac{l_a + (c_a - l_a c_c)}{1 - dc_c} = y; \ \frac{c_a - l_a c_c}{1 - dc_c} = z;$$

which give

$$l_a = \frac{y + dz}{1 + dx}; \ c_c = \frac{x}{1 + dx}; \ l_c c_a = \frac{xy - z}{1 + dx};$$

where l_a, c_c and $(l_c c_a)$ are positive because x, y, z, $(xy - z)$ and d are positive.

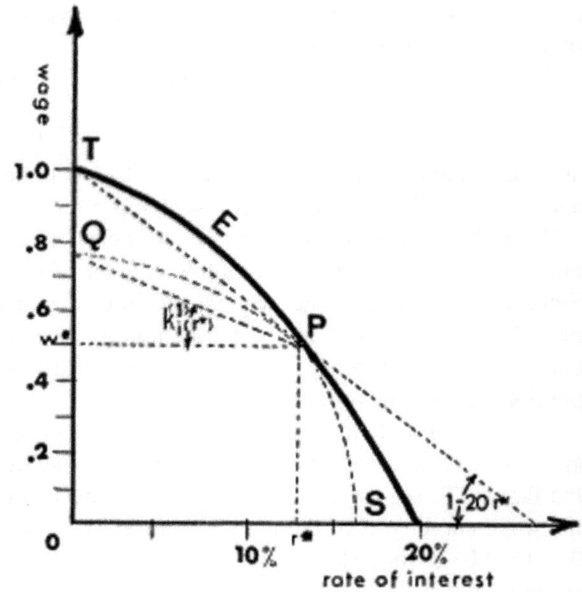

Fig. 8 E is the envelope of the family of systems j defined by the function $k_i^{(j)}(r)$

To any function $k_i(r)$ satisfying these conditions there corresponds a family of wage-curves having E as its envelope.[43] It follows that families of systems can be conceived giving as the relation between r and k_i any curve which, in Fig. 9, has Q as its point for $r=0$, and then keeps within the area $STQO$—an area depending upon the curve E of our example.[44]

---

[43] Conditions (ii) above are sufficient to exclude that a wage-curve tangent to E would also intersect it. By equating the function of the hyperbola giving the wage-curve with that of the parabola giving E, we obtain an equation of the third degree in r. Of its three possible roots, two are accounted for by the point of tangency, while the third root can be shown to be negative.

[44] If we considered the possibility that *two* systems be in use at the same level of r (cf. n. 6 above) the relation between r and k_i would be given by an area. An example is provided by the shaded area in Fig. *a*: as r falls from its maximum of 20 per cent down to zero, the possible values of k_i narrow down to a single intermediate value *OB*.

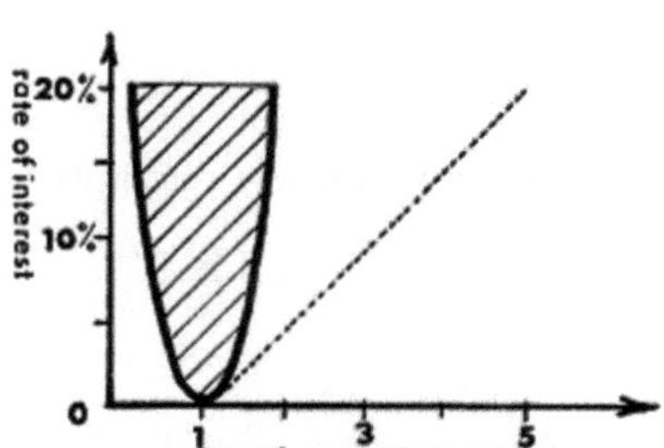

Fig. *a* The shaded area is a possible relation between k and r

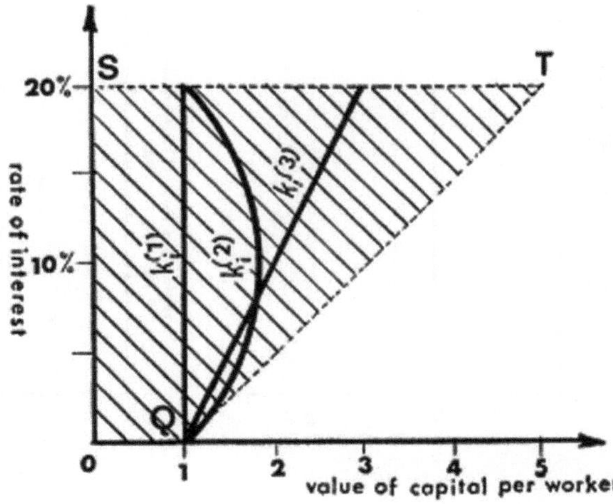

Fig. 9 Any curve $k_i^{(j)}$ which starts from Q and stays within the area *STQO* is a possible relation between the value of capital per worker k_i and the rate of interest

We have chosen to illustrate this freedom of the relation between r and k_i by considering the families of systems defined by the following three functions, represented in Fig. 9:

$$k_i^{(1)} = 1$$
$$k_i^{(2)} = 1 + 10r$$
$$k_i^{(3)} = 1 + 18r - 90r^3$$

As in the preceding example we suppose $d=1$ and $l_c=1$. The coefficients l_a, c_a, c_c are functions of the parameter u, chosen so that the system defined by any value u^* of u is adopted at the level $r=u^*$ of r.

In what follows, we give for the three families of systems: (*a*) tables with the numerical values of the coefficients for some of the systems; and with the values of r, w, q_i and k_i in the situation where those systems are in use; (*b*) diagrams of the relation between net production and value of capital per worker (it should be noted how the curves differ from those rising and concave from below, generally assumed) (Fig. 10 and Tables 3, 4 and 5).

Mathematical Note[45]

Rates of reproduction

1. Let **B** be the matrix of the commodity-input coefficients a_{ij} of the m commodities 'entering the wage', with a column j for each industry and a row i for each

[45] I am grateful to Dr. Giancarlo Gandolfo of Rome University and to Professor Antonio Andreatta of Pavia University for their mathematical assistance in the preparation of this Note.

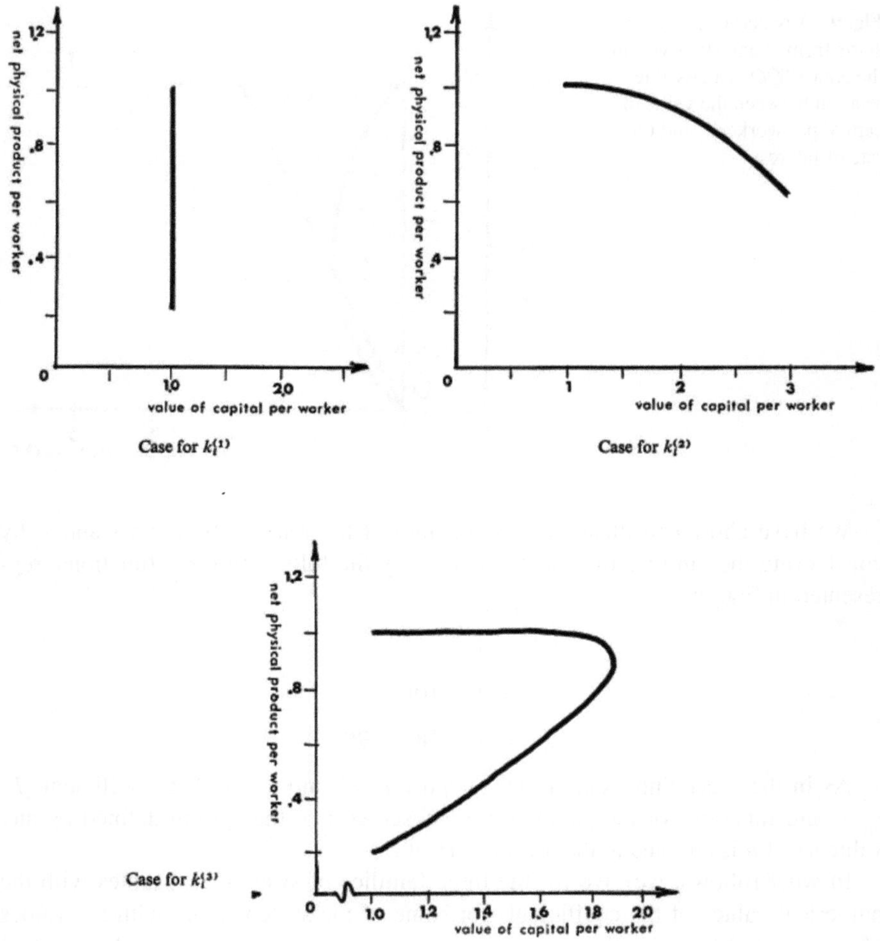

Fig. 10 Relations between q_i and k_i for the three families of systems of the example

Table 3 The case $k_i^{(1)} = 1$

Systems of production						In use at		Value of capital per worker k_i
Param u	Input-coefficients (*)				Net phys. prod, per worker q_i	r	w	
	l_a	c_a	l_c	c_c				
0	0·976	0·0006	1	0·976	1	0	1	1
0·05	1·027	0·0017	1	0·932	0·95	0·05	0·9	1
0·10	1·216	0·0037	1	0·892	0·80	0·10	0·7	1
0·15	1·750	0·0097	1	0·857	0·55	0·15	0·4	1
0·20	4·537	0·0772	1	0·833	0·20	0·20	0	1

Table 4 The case $k_i^{(2)} = 1 + 10r$

Systems of production						In use at		Value of capital per worker
Param u	Input-coefficients (*)				Net phys. prod, per worker q_i	r	w	k_i
	l_a	c_a	l_c	c_c				
0	0·968	0·0010	1	0·969	1	0	1	1
0·05	0·959	0·0006	1	0·915	0·975	0·05	0·9	1·5
0·10	0·986	0·0159	1	0·873	0·9	0·10	0·7	2
0·15	2·978	0·0359	1	0·845	0·775	0·15	0·4	2.5
0·20	1·204	0·0772	1	0·834	0·6	0·20	0	3

kind of input. Assumption (ii) in the text (see Section IV of the paper) about the existence of at least one 'basic' product ensures that appropriate changes of the order in which the commodities are listed in the matrix (i.e. appropriate permutation of the rows and corresponding columns) will give **B** in the 'normal form':

$$\begin{bmatrix} \mathbf{B}_1 & \mathbf{B}_{12} & \mathbf{B}_{13} & \cdots & \mathbf{B}_{1g} \\ \mathbf{0} & \mathbf{B}_2 & \mathbf{B}_{23} & \cdots & \mathbf{B}_{2g} \\ \mathbf{0} & \mathbf{0} & \mathbf{B}_3 & \cdots & \mathbf{B}_{3g} \\ \cdots & \cdots & \cdots & \cdots & \cdots \\ \mathbf{0} & \mathbf{0} & \mathbf{0} & \cdots & \mathbf{B}_g \end{bmatrix} \tag{I}$$

where: (a) the sub-matrix $\mathbf{B}_1$ is irreducible, and the other sub-matrices $\mathbf{B}_2$, $\mathbf{B}_3$, …, $\mathbf{B}_g$ *on the diagonal* are either zero or irreducible; (b) all matrices below the diagonal are zero; (c) in *each* column 2, 3, …, g of (I), at least one of the sub-matrices *above* the diagonal has a non-zero element.

In **B** reduced to its form (I), the first column represents the industries of the basic products, and $\mathbf{B}_1$ is accordingly the matrix of their commodity-input coefficients. Columns 2, 3, …, g, on the other hand, result from the industries of the non-basic products. Two cases are possible for these commodities. In the first case, the non-basic commodity does not enter either directly or indirectly *its own production*: its industry will then by itself form one of the columns in (I), and the element on the diagonal of that column will be zero (all zero matrices on the diagonal are of order one). In the second case, the non-basic enters directly or indirectly its own production: it must then be part of a group of one or more non-basics such that each enters directly or indirectly the production of all in the group. The industries of the group will give one of the columns (among 2, 3, …, g) in (I), whose element on the diagonal is an irreducible matrix.

It can now be seen that condition (c) above is necessary to ensure that the commodities of row 1 of **B** in its form (I) are basic, i.e., that they also enter directly or indirectly the production of the commodities of the other rows. In fact, the

Table 5 The case $k_i^{(3)} = 1 + 18r - 90r^2$

Systems of production						In use at		Value of capital per worker k_i
Param u	Input-coefficients (*)				Net phys. prod, per worker q_i	r	w	
	l_a	c_a	l_c	c_c				
0	0·958	0·0017	1	0·958	1	0	1	1
0·05	0·928	0·0083	1	0·907	0·984	0·05	0·9	1·675
0·10	1·010	0·0142	1	0·875	0·890	0·10	0·7	1·900
0·15	1·394	0·0211	1	0·850	0·651	0·15	0·4	1·675
0·20	4·537	0·0772	1	0·833	0·200	0·20	0	1

commodities of row 1 enter directly or indirectly into this commodity, or group of commodities, of row 2, *if and only if* $\mathbf{B}_{12}$ has a non-zero element; this condition being satisfied, the commodities of row 1 will enter those of row 3 if and only if *either* $\mathbf{B}_{13}$ *or* $\mathbf{B}_{23}$ has a non-zero element: and so on — where, as we move to columns further to the right, a *single* non-zero matrix above the diagonal is *sufficient* to ensure that the commodities of row 1 enter directly or indirectly the commodities whose column we are considering, provided that the same condition is satisfied in all columns to the left.

2. Let us now ask whether a vector $\mathbf{x}_1$ of productions for the basic industries exists such that the product and its means of production are homogeneous, i.e. they consist of the same commodities taken in the same proportions. The vector $\mathbf{x}_1$ must satisfy the following equations (whose number is that of the basic commodities):

$$\mathbf{B}_1\mathbf{x}_1 = z_1\mathbf{x}_1 \tag{II}$$

where z_1 is the unknown ratio between the means of production and the product. We know that the sub-matrix $\mathbf{B}_1$ has no negative elements and is irreducible. A well known theorem (cf. Gantmacher, *Applications of the Theory of Matrices*, New York, 1959, pp. 65–75) then ensures that among the values of z_1 satisfying equations (II) there is *one and only one* value z_1^* with which a vector $\mathbf{x}_1$ is associated — unique but for a factor of proportionality — each of whose elements is non-zero and of the same sign. The same theorem states that z_1^* is positive, and is the 'dominant characteristic root' of $\mathbf{B}_1$ (i.e. is no less in absolute value than any other characteristic root): since z_1^* is also simple, it follows that it must be larger than any other solution of (II). On the other hand, our assumption that the system is capable of giving a surplus over replacement (see assumption (i), p. 162 above) ensures that z_1^* is smaller than one. Thus, (positive) *proportions* of the basic industries giving a product homogeneous with its means of production exist and are unique. We can therefore refer to a unique 'net rate of reproduction' of the basic commodities, given by $(1 - z_1^*)/z_1^*$, positive and finite because $0 < z_1^* < 1$.[46]

Let us turn to possible groups of non-basics where each non-basic enters directly or indirectly the production of all commodities in the group: as we saw (para. 1), to any such group there corresponds an irreducible matrix, say $\mathbf{B}_2$, on the diagonal of $\mathbf{B}$ in form (I). Let us then consider the production of the non-basics of group $\mathbf{B}_2$ *as if they did not require any means of production outside the group*: the sub-matrix $\mathbf{B}_2$ defines these restricted conditions of production. Our reasoning above for the basic commodities can then be repeated for these non-basics. It will lead to the conclusion that (positive) proportions of such non-basic industries, giving a product homogeneous with the commodities of the group used to produce it, both exist and are unique. We can then refer to the 'net own rate of reproduction' $(1 - z_2^*)/z_2^*$ of the group, where z_2^*, the ratio between means of production and product, is the 'dominant root' of sub-matrix $\mathbf{B}_2$. Assumption (iv) in Section IV of the paper — about the 'own rate of reproduction' of any such group of non-basic exceeding the 'rate of reproduction' of the basic products — can therefore be expressed by

$$z_1^* > z_i^* \qquad \text{(III)}$$

where z_1^* is the dominant root of sub-matrix $\mathbf{B}_1$, and z_i^* for $i = 2, 3, \ldots, g$, is the dominant root of any non-zero sub-matrix on the diagonal of $\mathbf{B}$ in its form (I). (Condition (III) will also be satisfied by zero matrices on the diagonal since their dominant roots are zero.)

Rate of Interest and Prices with a Zero Wage

3. For $w = 0$, the price equations (cf. Equations (5) in Section IV of the Paper) become

$$\begin{aligned}
p_1 &= (a_{11}p_1 + a_{21}p_2 + \ldots + a_{m1}p_m)(1 + r) \\
p_2 &= (a_{12}p_1 + a_{22}p_2 + \ldots + a_{m2}p_m)(1 + r) \\
&\ldots\ldots\ldots\ldots\ldots\ldots\ldots\ldots\ldots \\
p_m &= (a_{1m}p_1 + a_{2m}p_2 + \ldots + a_{mm}p_m)(1 + r) \\
1 &= \lambda_1 p_1 + \lambda_2 p_2 + \ldots + \lambda_h p_h
\end{aligned}$$

i.e.

$$\mathbf{pB} = s\mathbf{p} \qquad \text{(IVi)}$$

$$1 = \lambda_1 p_1 + \lambda_2 p_2 + \cdots + \lambda_h p_h \qquad \text{(IVii)}$$

[46] Cf. the notions of 'Standard system' and 'Standard ratio' in Sraffa, *Production of Commodities by Means of Commodities*, Cambridge, 1960, Ch. IV.

where **B** has the meaning already given, **p** is the price-vector ($p_1, p_2, \ldots, p_m$), and $s = 1/(1+r)$ is the reciprocal of the interest factor $(1+r)$. A theorem (cp. Gantmacher *op. cit.*, pp. 92–94) about matrices reducible to form (I) ensures that, when condition (III) above is satisfied, among the values of s satisfying equations (IVi) there is one and only one value s^* of s associated with a vector **p** whose elements are all non-zero and of the same sign. Since s^* is the 'dominant root' of **B** and hence the highest of the 'dominant roots' of the sub-matrices $\mathbf{B_1}, \mathbf{B_2}, \ldots, \mathbf{B_g}$, condition (III) above ensures that s^* is equal to z_1^*. Further, by excluding that any z_i^* (for $i = 2, 3, \ldots, g$) is equal to z_1^*, , condition (III) also ensures that s^* is a *simple* characteristic root of **B**: the associated vector **p** is therefore unique, but for a proportionality factor. Thus, once we introduce equation (IVii), the vector **p** (whose elements are all non-zero and of the same sign) will give a unique set of positive values for $p_1, p_2, \ldots, p_m$.

We can therefore conclude that for $w = 0$, the price equations will determine a unique series of positive prices; and that with these prices is associated a 'maximum rate of interest' $R = (1 - s^*)/s^*$, given by the 'rate of reproduction' of the basic products $\left(1 - z_1^*\right)/z_1^*$, and hence positive and finite (para. 2).

Rate of Interest and Prices with a Positive Wage

4. Let us assume for a moment a wage w' which, unlike the wage w, is paid at the *beginning* of the yearly production cycle; the only change required in the price equations given in Section IV of the paper will be to replace w with $w'(1+r)$ in the first m equations. This device of an 'anticipated' wage enables us to replace the wages paid in each industry with the quantities of wage-goods constituting them, and then to add these quantities to the means of production. In fact, using equation (IVii), we can write

$$w' = w'(\lambda_1 p_1 + \lambda_2 p_2 + \cdots + \lambda_h p_h)$$

and, substituting this into the price equations,

$$\begin{aligned}
p_1 &= l_1 w + (a_{11}p_1 + a_{21}p_2 + \cdots a_{m1}p_m)(1+r) \\
p_2 &= l_2 w + (a_{12}p_1 + a_{22}p_2 + \cdots a_{m2}p_m)(1+r) \\
&\ldots\ldots\ldots\ldots\ldots\ldots\ldots\ldots \\
&\ldots\ldots\ldots\ldots\ldots\ldots\ldots\ldots \\
p_m &= l_m w + (a_{1m}p + a_{2m}p_m + \cdots + a_{mm}p_m)(1+r) \\
1 &= \lambda_1 p_1 + \lambda_2 p_2 + \cdots \lambda_h p_h
\end{aligned}$$

Writing these price equations in matrix notation we have

$$\mathbf{pB^+} = s\mathbf{p} \qquad \text{(V)}$$

where s and $\mathbf{p}$ have the meaning already given, and $\mathbf{B}^+$ is the family of matrices

$$\mathbf{B}^+ = \begin{bmatrix} a_{11}+l_1w'\lambda_1 & a_{12}+l_2w'\lambda_1 & \cdots & a_{1m}+l_mw'\lambda_1 \\ a_{21}+l_1w'\lambda_2 & a_{22}+l_2w'\lambda_2 & \cdots & a_{2m}+l_mw'\lambda_2 \\ \cdots & \cdots & \cdots & \cdots \\ a_{h1}+l_1w'\lambda_h & a_{h2}+l_2w'\lambda_h & \cdots & a_{hm}+l_mw'\lambda_h \\ a_{h+1,1} & a_{h+1,2} & \cdots & a_{h+1,m} \\ \cdots & \cdots & \cdots & \cdots \\ a_{m1} & a_{m2} & \cdots & a_{mm} \end{bmatrix}$$

having w' as the variable parameter.

By assumption (iii) in Section IV of the paper, labour enters directly or indirectly into the production of all the m commodities. It follows that, when the positive wage is resolved into the h wage-goods, each of them, and hence each of the m commodities 'entering the wage', enters directly or indirectly into the production of all. All the m commodities are then on the same footing as the basic products, and matrices $\mathbf{B}^+$, unlike matrix $\mathbf{B}$, are irreducible.

Equations (V) are then of the same form as equations (II) in para. 2 above, and the theorem we used there to ascertain the existence of positive solutions for z_1 and $\mathbf{x}_1$ can be applied here to s and $\mathbf{p}$. We can therefore conclude that, among the values of s satisfying equations (V), one and only one value s^* (the largest of them) is associated with a vector $\mathbf{p}$—unique, but for a proportionality factor—whose elements are all non-zero and of the same sign. Equation (IVii) defining the value-unit will then give a unique series of *positive* prices.[47]

5. If we now choose r, and not w (or w'), as the independent variable, the price equations become linear homogeneous equations. It follows that when they admit a non-zero solution for the wage and prices, the solution is unique but for a proportionality factor-a factor which is then determined by the equation defining the value-unit. The results of the preceding two paragraphs can then be stated by saying that for $r = R$ (when $w = 0$) the prices of all m commodities are positive and finite and that the same is true for any r giving $w' > 0$.

Mr. Sraffa has shown, on the other hand, that as r decreases from R to zero the posticipated wage w must rise and must therefore be positive for $0 < r < R$.[48] Consequently, in that interval, also the anticipated wage $w' = w/(1+r)$ must be positive, and the m prices are accordingly positive and finite.

Consider then the point for $r = 0$. The wages must there be equal to the value in terms of the 'wage-commodity' of what remains of the physical product after

[47] Mr. Sraffa (*op. cit.* Ch. V, in particular p. 28 n. 1) has given a demonstration of the positivity of prices limited to the hypothesis that all commodities are basic goods. Cf. also Newman, "Production of Commodities by Means of Commodities", *Schweizerische Zeitschrift Fuer Volkswirtschaft und Statistik*, March 1962.

[48] Sraffa , *op. cit.*, pp. 38–40.

deducting the means of production (we can always re-dimension the industries so that the production of each commodity is no less than the quantity of it used as means of production). All prices being positive and finite, the wages must be positive and finite and we have accordingly for $r = 0$ a positive and finite level W of wage rate w.

We can therefore conclude that as r falls from R to zero, w rises from zero to a finite level; the prices of the m commodities being always positive and finite.

6. There remains now to show that the decreasing relation between r and w is continuous and differentiable. From the price equations, we obtain

$$w = \frac{\begin{vmatrix} a_{11}(1+r)-1 & a_{21}(1+r) & \cdots & a_{h1}(1+r) & a_{h+1,1}(1+r) & \cdots & a_{m1}(1+r) & 0 \\ a_{12}(1+r) & a_{22}(1+r)-1 & \cdots & a_{h2}(1+r) & a_{h+1,2}(1+r) & \cdots & a_{m2}(1+r) & 0 \\ \cdots & \cdots & \cdots & \cdots & \cdots & \cdots & \cdots & \cdots \\ a_{1m}(1+r) & a_{2m}(1+r) & \cdots & a_{hm}(1+r) & a_{h+1,m}(1+r) & \cdots & a_{mm}(1+r)-1 & 0 \\ \lambda_1 & \lambda_2 & \cdots & \lambda_h & 0 & \cdots & 0 & 1 \end{vmatrix}}{\begin{vmatrix} a_{11}(1+r)-1 & a_{21}(1+r) & \cdots & a_{h1}(1+r) & a_{h+1,1}(1+r) & \cdots & a_{m1}(1+r) & l_1 \\ a_{12}(1+r) & a_{22}(1+r)-1 & \cdots & a_{h2}(1+r) & a_{h+1,2}(1+r) & \cdots & a_{m2}(1+r) & l_2 \\ \cdots & \cdots & \cdots & \cdots & \cdots & \cdots & \cdots & \cdots \\ a_{1m}(1+r) & a_{2m}(1+r) & \cdots & a_{hm}(1+r) & a_{h+1,m}(1+r) & \cdots & a_{mm}(1+r)-1 & l_m \\ \lambda_1 & \lambda_2 & \cdots & \lambda_h & 0 & \cdots & 0 & 0 \end{vmatrix}} \tag{VII}$$

The determinant at the numerator is a polynomial of the mth degree in r — and that at the denominator a polynomial of the $(m-1)$ th degree in the same variable. Being thus a ratio of two polynomials in r, function (VII) is continuous and differentiable over any interval of r where the polynomial at the denominator does not become zero.

Now let us take any value r^* of r such that $0 < r^* < R$. If the determinant at the denominator were zero, then by a well known property of linear and homogeneous equations, the following system

$$\begin{aligned} &[a_{11}(1+r^*)-1]p_1 + a_{21}(1+r^*)p_2 + \cdots + l_1 w = 0 \\ &a_{12}(1+r^*)p_1 + [a_{22}(1+r^*)-1]p_2 + \cdots + l_2 w = 0 \\ &\cdots\cdots\cdots\cdots\cdots\cdots\cdots\cdots\cdots\cdots \\ &a_{1m}(1+r^*)p_1 + a_{2m}(1+r^*)p_2 + \cdots + l_m w = 0 \\ &\lambda_1 p_1 + \lambda_2 p_2 + \cdots + \lambda_h p_h = 0 \end{aligned} \tag{VIII}$$

would admit non-zero solutions in the $(m+1)$ unknowns $w, p_1, p_2, \ldots, p_m$. The first m equations in (VIII) are our price equations and, as we have seen (cp. para. 4 for the case $r = R$ and para. 5 for $0 \leq r^* < R$), they determine prices which are *all of the same sign*. But then the last of equations (VIII) cannot be satisfied. Thus system (VIII) does not admit any non-zero solution, which shows that the determinant at the denominator cannot be zero for $0 \leq r^* \leq R$. It follows that function (VII) is continuous and differentiable in that interval.

The Switch to Cheaper Methods and the 'Wage-Frontier'

7. In what follows, wages and prices will refer to a given level r^* of the rate of interest, zero or positive and smaller than the lower R of the systems compared (so that the wage given by any of the systems is not zero). We shall indicate by $w^{(\alpha)}$ and $p_i^{(\alpha)}$ respectively the wage and price of any commodity A_i at $r = r^*$ when system α is in use for the production of G: and by $w^{(\beta)}$ and $p_i^{(\beta)}$ the same variables with system β. (It should be noted that, if A_i is a commodity specific to α, and not therefore one of the m_β commodities entering the wage in system β, $p_i^{(\beta)}$ will be obtained from the α price equation with $w^{(\beta)}$ as the wage and for β prices of its means of production.) Finally, by $p_{i\alpha}^{(\beta)}$ we shall indicate the β price of the commodity A_i produced with the α method, and not with the β method.

To prove what is stated in the text (p. 164) about the system which producers will adopt for producing G, we need to establish three propositions.

I. Suppose that G is being produced with a system β, and a method cheaper than that in use exists for producing the commodity A_j: *then, system α, resulting from β when the cheaper method is adopted for the production of A_j, must give a higher wage.*

To see why this is so let us consider how the prices change as producers switch from β to α. If A_j were a wage-good not used in the production of any of the other commodities, its price p_j/w *expressed in terms of the wage* would fall in the proportion.

$$\frac{p_{j\alpha}^{(\beta)}}{p_j^{(\beta)}},$$

while the prices of the other commodities would remain unchanged when measured in terms of the wage-unit. These latter prices can thus be affected only to the extent in which A_j enters directly or indirectly into their production, in which case they must fall. Since A_j, a commodity 'entering the wage' (p. 161 above), either is a wage-good, or enters (directly or indirectly) into the production of at least one wage-good, the price in wage-units of G must also fall: i.e. its reciprocal, the wage, must rise.

II. *Given two systems α and β for the production of G, differing by any number of methods and such that $w^{(\alpha)} > w^{(\beta)}$, then for at least one commodity the method of production of system α is cheaper than the method of system β, at the wage and prices of system β.*

We assume at first that systems α and β have every commodity in common (cf. p. 164 above). Let us introduce $P_1, P_2, \ldots, P_m$ such that:

$$P_1 = \frac{p_1^{(\alpha)}}{p_1^{(\beta)}} \quad P_2 = \frac{p_2^{(\alpha)}}{p_2^{(\beta)}} \ldots P_m = \frac{p_m^{(\alpha)}}{p_m^{(\beta)}}$$

where the ratios P_1, P_2, …, P_m are all finite and positive (para. 4 above); and let P_j indicate a P such that no P is lower.

To begin with, we must show that, letting P_0 indicate the ratio $w^{(\alpha)}/w^{(\beta)}$, we must have $P_0 > P_j$. In effect since the composite wage-commodity G is the value-unit in both systems, we have that *either* the price of each wage-good is the same in the two systems, or the price of at least one wage-good is lower in the α system. So P_j cannot be larger than one; and since $P_0 > 1$, we must have $P_0 > P_j$.

We can now prove the main proposition: that some commodity A_j exists for which $p_{j\alpha}^{(\beta)} < p_j^{(\beta)}$. Indicating by V the ratio $p_j^{(\alpha)}/p_{j\alpha}^{(\beta)}$, we can write

$$V = \frac{p_j^{(\alpha)}}{p_{j\alpha}^{(\beta)}} = \frac{l_j^{(\alpha)}w^{(\alpha)} + a_{1j}^{(\alpha)}p_1^{(\alpha)}(1+r^*) + a_{2j}^{(\alpha)}p_2^{(\alpha)}(1+r^*) + \ldots + a_{mj}^{(\alpha)}p_m^{(\alpha)}(1+r^*)}{l_j^{(\alpha)}w^{(\beta)} + a_{1j}^{(\alpha)}p_1^{(\beta)}(1+r^*) + a_{2j}^{(\alpha)}p_2^{(\beta)}(1+r^*) + \ldots + a_{mj}^{(\alpha)}p_m^{(\beta)}(1+r^*)}$$

After multiplying the terms at the numerator by $w^{(\beta)}/w^{(\beta)}$, $p_1^{(\beta)}/p_1^{(\beta)}$, …, $p_m^{(\beta)}/p_m^{(\beta)}$, respectively, we obtain:

$$V = \frac{P_0y_0 + P_1y_1 + P_2y_2 + \cdots + P_my_m}{y_0 + y_1 + y_2 + \cdots + y_m}$$

where $y_0 = l_j^{(\alpha)}w^{(\beta)}$, $y_1 = a_{1j}^{(\alpha)}p_1^{(\beta)}(1+r^*)$, …, $y_m = a_{mj}^{(\alpha)}p_m^{(\beta)}(1+r^*)$. In relation (IX), V appears as the weighted average of P_0, P_1, …, P_m for non-negative weights y_0, y_1, …, y_m; V is therefore intermediate between the highest and the lowest of the P's with a non-zero weight (if such two P's are different).

We must now distinguish two cases. In the first case, the production of commodity A_j with the α method requires some direct labour or a means of production with a P larger than P_j — that is either y_0 is non-zero, or at least one of the other weights y applied to a P larger than P_j is non-zero. Then we must have $V > P_j$, i.e.

$$\frac{p_j^{(\alpha)}}{p_{j\alpha}^{(\beta)}} > \frac{p_j^{(\alpha)}}{p_j^{(\beta)}};$$

and we can conclude that $p_{j\alpha}^{(\beta)} < p_j^{(\beta)}$. There remains the case where A_j is produced with no direct labour and all its means of production have a P equal to P_j. We must then consider one by one those means of production, and, if necessary, their *own* means of production, until we find a commodity A_k to which the reasoning of the first case can be applied. (That we shall eventually find one such commodity follows from assumption (iii) in Section IV of the paper, according to which labour enters directly or indirectly into the production of all commodities).

We can now drop the initial assumption that systems α and β have all commodities in common, and compare the ratios P of the commodities 'entering the wage' *with system* α, whether or not they 'enter the wage' with system β as well. We must then begin by showing that the P of any commodity specific to α cannot be lower than the lowest of the P's for commodities common to the two systems. Let us consider the case of the commodities specific to α, whose production does not require, either directly or indirectly, any commodity common to the two systems: their P's would all be equal to P_0, and larger than P_j. The P of any commodity specific to α can therefore be different from P_0 only to the extent that some commodity common to α and β enters directly or indirectly its production. It cannot therefore be lower than the lowest P of these commodities: it can equal the lowest P only if the commodity requires no direct labour, and its means of production have that P.

As a result, when we choose a P_j no greater than any other P_i, for $i = 1, 2, \ldots, m$, *either* A_j will already be a commodity common to the two systems, *or* the analysis will have to proceed to A_j's means of production until we find a commodity which, while having the lowest P, requires for its own production some direct labour or some means of production with a higher P, — and this commodity must be common to the two systems. In either case we shall reach a commodity to which the previous demonstration applies.

III. *Given two systems α and β such that $w^{(\alpha)} = w^{(\beta)}$ where this common level of the two wages is the highest obtainable with the available systems, the price of each commodity must be the same in the two systems.*

Suppose this not to be true, so that the price of at least one of the commodities is lower in one of the systems, say α. If, as before, we indicate by P_j the lowest of the ratios between the prices of systems α and β for the commodities entering the wage with system α, we would have $P_j < 1$. Since the ratio P_0 between the two wages is here 1, we would have $P_j < P_0$. Then, for the reasons we saw in the previous demonstration, at least one of the α methods would be cheaper than the β method at the β prices. But system γ obtained from β by introducing the cheaper method would then, by proposition above, give $w^{(\gamma)} > w^{(\beta)}$—contrary to the initial hypothesis that no system existed giving a wage higher than that of α and β. Thus, the price of each commodity must be the same in the two systems.

8. From proposition (II) it follows that when, at r^*, the system of production in use is not the one giving the highest w, producers will have an incentive to change the method of production for one or more of the commodities. Proposition (I) then ensures that, as a result of such a switch or switches, w will rise. This process will continue until the 'wage-frontier' is reached. There, by proposition (I), no incentive to change any of the methods in use can any longer exist.[49]

The problem then arises of what is the nature of the situation indicated in 'corners' on the wage-frontier: i.e. *whether* either of the two adjacent systems can be in use, but *not* the two of them simultaneously; *or whether* the two systems can

[49] A proof that the tendency to minimise costs will eventually bring into use the system giving the highest wage for the given rate of interest has been given by D. Levhari in "A Nonsubstitution Theorem and Switching of Techniques", *Quarterly Journal of Economics*, LXXIX (February 1965). His demonstration refers to systems where all commodities are 'basic' and which have in common all the commodities.

co-exist. Proposition (III) ensures that the second is the case. (The same proposition would ensure the co-existence of systems whose wage-curves were the one tangent to the other at a point on the wage-frontier: cf. n. 6 in the text of the paper.)

We can therefore conclude that, whichever system is in use initially, the switch to cheaper methods will eventually bring into use the system giving the highest wage for the given r. We can also conclude that where, at the given rate of interest, more than one system gives the same *highest* wage, such systems can co-exist.

Systems for the production of any commodity

9. The discussion in this Note has been carried out for systems of production of wage-commodity G. But the fact of G being the wage-commodity has affected the discussion only in so far as w and the prices were measured in terms of it. It follows that all the results of this discussion are applicable to systems of production of any (simple or composite) commodity provided that commodity is used as the value-unit.

References

1. Samuelson, P. A. (1962). Parable and realism in capital theory: the surrogate production function. *Review of Economic Studies, 29*, 193–206.
2. Courant, R. ([1936]1962). *Differential and integral calculus* (Vol. II). London.
3. Bhaduri, A. (1966). The concept of the marginal productivity of capital and the Wicksell Effect. *Oxford Economic Papers, 18*, 284–288.
4. Spaventa, L. (1968). Realism without parables in capital theory, in *Recherches récentes sur la fonction de production* (Namur), pp. 13–45.
5. Ricardo, D. (1951–73). *Works and correspondence* (Sraffa edition, 11 Vols). Cambridge.
6. von Bortkiewicz, L. (1949). Zur Berichtigung der Grundlegenden Theoretischen Konstruktion von Marx im Dritten Bande des 'Kapitals', *Jahrbuecher fuer Nationaloekonomie* (July 1907): English translation in the Appendix to Paul Sweezy's edition of E. Böhm-Bawerk, *Karl Marx and the Close of his System*, pp. 199–221. New York.
7. von Bortkiewicz, L. (1952). Wertrechnung und Preisrechnung im Marxschen System, in three parts, *Archiv fuer Sozialwissenschaft und Sozialpolitik* (July 1906–Sept. 1907): English translation of parts 2 and 3 in *International Economic Papers, 2*.
8. Pasinetti, L. L. (1960). A mathematical formulation of the Ricardian system. *Review of Economic Studies, 27*, 78–98.
9. Garegnani, P. (1960). *Il capitale nelle teorie della distribuzione*. Milano.
10. Sraffa, P. (1960). *Production of commodities by means of commodities*. Cambridge.
11. Enriques, F. (1915). *Lezioni sulla teoria geometrica delle equazioni e delle funzioni algebriche*, Vol. I. Bologna.
12. Garegnani, P. (1966). Switching of techniques. *Quarterly Journal of Economics, 80*, 554–567.
13. Solow, R. (1956). A contribution to the theory of economic growth. *Quarterly Journal of Economics, 70*, 65–94.
14. Robinson, J. V. (1953–54). The production function and the theory of capital. *Review of Economic Studies, 21*, 81–106.
15. Robinson, J. V. (1956). *The accumulation of capital*. London.

16. Champernowne, D. G. (1953–54). The production function and the theory of capital: a comment. *Review of Economic Studies*, 21, 112–35.
17. Morishima, M. (1964). *Equilibrium, stability and growth*. Oxford.
18. Hicks, J. R. (1965). *Capital and growth*. Oxford.
19. Levhari, D. (1965). A non-substitution theorem and switching of techniques. *Quarterly Journal of Economics*, 79, 98–105.
20. Pasinetti, L. L., Levhari, D., Samuelson, P. A., Bruno, M., Burmeister, E., Sheshinski, E., & Garegnani, P. (1966). Symposium, paradoxes in capital theory. *Quarterly Journal of Economics* 80.
21. Swan, T. W. (1956). Economic growth and capital accumulation. *Economic Record*, 32, 334–361.
22. Wicksell, K. (1935). *Lectures on political economy* (Vol. I). London.
23. Sraffa, P. (1926). The laws of returns under competitive conditions. *Economic Journal* 36, 535–50; rpt. in G. J. Stigler & K. E. Boulding (eds), *Readings in price theory*. Chicago, 1952, 180–97.

Switching of Techniques†*

I. Introduction

In the second part of an article recently published in this *Journal*[1] Dr. Levhari—following, he says, a conjecture of Professor Samuelson—attempts to demonstrate that, given an economy where n commodities can be produced by a number of alternative methods, it is impossible that a "system of production" (i.e., a set of n methods, one for each commodity), which has ceased to be profitable because of a change of the rate of interest, or of profits r, should again become profitable as r changes further in the same direction.

In what follows, we intend, first to point out where Levhari's argument fails and then to show—by means of the numerical example appended to this paper—that such a "return" of a system of production (or "switch-back") is possible on Levhari's own assumptions.[2] The last section of the paper will comment on the origin and implications of the error which the "return" of a system reveals in traditional theory.

†Previously published in *Quaterly Journal of Economics*, 80(4), 1966. All necessary permissions acquired.

*In the present version the numbering of the notes is progressive, and in this it differs from the original version in which, without obvious justification, twice in the course of the paper the sequence is interrupted and starts again from number 1.

[1] D. Levhari, "A Nonsubstitution Theorem and Switching of Techniques", *Quaterly Journal of Economics*, 79(1), 1965, pp. 98–105.

[2] Levhari's conclusions were first challenged by Dr. Pasinetti in a paper delivered at the Congress of the Econometric Society, September 1965.
The possibility of the "return" of a system had been stated—with a view to its implications for a critique of the traditional theory of distribution—by Mr. Sraffa in his *Production of Commodities by Means of Commodities* (Cambridge: Cambridge University Press, 1960), §§ 92 and 94. That possibility had earlier been noticed by Mrs. Robinson ("The Production Function and the Theory of Capital", *Review of Economic Studies*, 21(2), 1953–54, 106; also, *The Accumulation*

P. Garegnani, *Capital Theory, the Surplus Approach, and Effective Demand*, Springer Studies in the History of Economic Thought,
https://doi.org/10.1007/978-3-031-23643-3_3

II. Levhari's Argument

To show Levhari's errors we must first restate his argument. He considers an economy where commodities 1, 2, ... n are produced in yearly cycles, in n industries (one for each commodity), using labor and a circulating capital made up of the commodities themselves. There are k_j alternative methods for the production of each commodity j, so that we have $k_1 \times k_2 \times ... \times k_n$ "systems of production", each formed by taking n methods (of which one at least differs from system to system), one method for each commodity. We indicate these systems by A, B, ... Each system A is therefore described by a vector $a_0=(a_{01}, a_{02}, ...a_{0n})$ of labor-input coefficients and a square matrix $a=(a_{ji})$, for $i, j=1, 2, ... n$, of the commodity-input coefficients a_{ji}, relating to the quantity of commodity j entering the production of a unit of commodity i. Levhari assumes that the matrices a, b ... of systems A, B ... are all "indecomposable".[3]

It is known that given one such system A, the hypothesis of a uniform rate of interest r and a uniform wage w is sufficient to determine single-valued functions $w^{(A)} = w^{(A)}(r)$, $p_j^{(A)} = p_j^{(A)}(r)$, where $w^{(A)}$ is the wage in system A, and $p_j^{(A)}$ is the price in system A of any commodity j, both $w^{(A)}$ and the $p_j^{(A)}$'s being measured in terms of any given commodity. It has also been shown that the function $w^{(A)} = w^{(A)}(r)$ is a continuous decreasing function which, in a "viable" system, gives a positive value $w_{max}^{(A)}$ for $r=0$, while $w^{(A)}=0$ for a finite positive value of r; $r=r_{max}^{(A)}$. Further, for $0 \leq r \leq r_{max}^{(A)}$ all the prices $p_j^{(A)}$ are positive.[4] Levhari chooses as a measure of value the wage unit; this unit has the peculiarity that all the $p_j^{(A)}$'s become monotonic increasing functions of r, for $0 \leq r \leq r_{max}^{(A)}$.[5]

Suppose now that system A is in use at $r=r'$, $(0 < r' < r_{max}^{(A)})$, and let p_1', p_2', ... p_n', indicate the prices in wage units corresponding to r' in system A.[6] Call B any other system. The assumption that A is in use means that, in each industry, production with the method of system A is *at least as cheap* as production with

of Capital, London: Macmillan, 1956, pp. 417–18) and by Mr. Champernowne ("The Production Function and the Theory of Capital: A Comment", *Review of Economic Studies*, 21(2), 1953–54, 119, 130). The contention in Levhari's article was apparently that, while the "return" of a method is possible, the same is not true for a system (*op. cit.*, p. 103).

[3] In Mr. Sraffa's terms, the n commodities are all "basic products" i.e., each enters directly or indirectly the production of all commodities (Sraffa, *op. cit.*, § 6).

[4] Cf. Sraffa, *op. cit.*, Chaps. IV-VI.

[5] Levhari, *op. cit.*, p. 100.

[6] Since in the relevant part of Levhari's article only the prices relating to system A appear, we may drop the indication of the system of production from the price notation. A question is raised by the fact that the prices corresponding to a given level of r will differ according to which system of production is in use. Might not the conclusion as to which system is more profitable at the given r, change according to the system for which the prices are calculated? It has been shown that this cannot be so (cf. Sraffa, *op. cit.*, §§ 93–94).

the method of system B (the methods of A and those of B must differ in at least one industry, B and A being different systems). We have therefore the following n relations:

(1)

$$\begin{aligned}&(1+r')(a_{0i}+a_{1i}p'_1+\cdots+a_{ni}p'_n)\\ &\leq (1+r')(b_{0i}+b_{1i}p'_1+\cdots+b_{ni}p'_n) \quad (i=1,\ldots,n)\end{aligned}$$

(It should be noted that the sign = applies in *all* relations (1) only if A and B can both be in use at $r=r'$). Since $(1+r')>0$, we may divide each of the (1) by $(1+r')$, and obtain[7]

(1.1)

$$(a_{1i}-b_{1i})p'_1+\cdots+(a_{ni}-b_{ni})p'_n \leq b_{0i}-a_{0i} \quad (i=1,\ldots,n)$$

At this point of his argument Levhari attempts to demonstrate that a semipositive vector $x^*=(x^*_1,\ldots,x^*_n)$ of levels of production of the various industries always exists, such that, at those levels of activity *either* system A requires more of all kinds of commodity-inputs than B, or the contrary is true, or, finally, A and B require the same quantities of all those inputs. The vector x^* should therefore satisfy the following two conditions[8]:

(2)

$$x^*_i \geq 0 \ \text{ and} \sum_{i=1}^{n} x^*_i > 0 \quad (i=1,\ldots,n)$$

and, for all $j=1,\ldots,n$

(3) $$\textit{either} \sum_{i=1}^{n}(a_{ji}-b_{ji})x^*_i > 0 \quad \textit{or} \sum_{i=1}^{n}(a_{ji}-b_{ji})x^*_i < 0$$

$$\textit{or} \sum_{i=1}^{n}(a_{ji}-b_{ji})x^*_i = 0$$

We shall discuss later whether in fact such a vector x^* always exists. But first we shall see where Levhari's argument leads. Multiplying each of the (1.1) by the corresponding x^*_i we obtain:

---

[7] Relationships (1.1) are written by Levhari in matrix notation as $a_0(\lambda I-a)^{-1}(a-b) \leq b_0-a_0$ (*op. cit.*, p. 104); where a_0, b_0, a, b, are the input vectors and matrixes we have defined in the text; I is the unit matrix of the nth order, and $a_0(\lambda I-a)^{-1}=p$ (cf. Levhari, *op. cit.*, p. 100) is the price vector $(p_1,\ldots,p_n)$ corresponding to the system of production A, at a level of $\lambda=\frac{1}{1+r}$ for which A is in use.

[8] *Ibid.*, pp. 104–5.

(4)

$$\{(a_{1i}-b_{1i})p_1'+\cdots+(a_{ni}-b_{ni})p_n'\}x_i^*\leq(b_{0i}-a_{0i})x_i^*\quad(i=1,\ldots,n)$$

and adding these n relations we have[9]
(4.1)

$$p_1'\sum_{i=1}^{n}(a_{1i}-b_{1i})x_i^*+\cdots+p_n'\sum_{i=1}^{n}(a_{ni}-b_{ni})x_i^*\leq\sum_{i=1}^{n}(b_{0i}-a_{0i})x_i^*$$

The expression appearing on the left-hand side of (4.1) is the value for $r=r'$ of the function of r (the prices $p_1,\ldots,p_n$ are functions of r) which Levhari calls $\psi(r)$, i.e.,

(5)

$$\psi(r)=p_1\sum_{i=1}^{n}(a_{1i}-b_{1i})x_i^*+\ldots+p_n\sum_{i=1}^{n}(a_{ni}-b_{ni})x_i^*$$

Function (5) must be a monotonic function of r for $0\leq r\leq r_{max}^{(A)}$. This is so because for $0\leq r\leq r_{max}^{(A)}, p_1,\ldots,p_n$ are positive and are monotonic increasing functions of r, while condition (3) ensures that the constants in (5) are all of the same sign, or all zero. In particular $\psi(r)$ is a monotonic increasing function if $\sum_{i=1}^{n}(a_{ji}-b_{ji})x^*>0$, $(j=1,\ldots,n)$; $\psi(r)$ is a monotonic decreasing function if, for each j, $\sum_{i=1}^{n}(a_{ji}-b_{ji})<0$, and, finally, $\psi(r)$ is the constant $\psi(r)=0$ if, for each j, $\sum_{i=1}^{n}(a_{ji}-b_{ji})x_i^*=0$.[10]

We now come to the last step of Levhari's argument. Supposing that, at r', system A is in fact *more* profitable than B (and not, *at least as* profitable as B, as we assumed initially), and supposing that as r rises from r' to r'' ($(0<r'<r''<r_{max}^{(A)})$ producers switch to system B; then according to Levhari we must have $\psi(r'')>\psi(r')$.[11] His reason for believing this is evidently that, at r', where A is *more* profitable than B, the stricter condition $\psi(r')<\sum_{i=1}^{n}(b_{0i}-a_{0i})x_i^*$ should hold, thus excluding the possibility $\psi(r')=\sum_{i=1}^{n}(b_{0i}-a_{0i})x_i^*$, admitted in (4.1). Similarly, at

[9] Cf. Levhari's relation $a_0(\lambda I-a)^{-1}(a-b)x^*\leq(b_0-a_0)x^*$, i. e., $p(a-b)x^*\leq(b_0-a_0)x^*$(*ibid.*, p. 105).

[10] *Ibid.*, p. 105.

[11] Levhari considers the case where producers switch from A to B as λ rises (i.e., r falls). He writes: "In a case in which a has been used and we switch with higher λ to another matrix b, [the derivative] $\psi'(\lambda)$ must be negative at the switch point" (*ibid.*, p. 105; surely we should read the passage as saying "$\psi'(\lambda)$ must be *positive* at the switch point").

r'', where B is more profitable, we should have $\psi\left(r''\right) > \sum_{i=1}^{n}(b_{0i} - a_{0i})x_i^*$. A switch from A to B when r rises from r' to r'' could then occur only if $\psi(r'') > \psi(r')$.

This would in turn imply that the monotonic function $\psi(r)$ is a monotonic *increasing* function. We could then conclude that as r rises further above r'' no switch back to A can occur; because at any r such that $r_{max}^{(A)} \geq r > r''$, we would have $\psi(r) > \psi\left(r''\right) > \sum_{i=1}^{n}(b_{0i} - a_{0i})x_i^*$, showing that B is more profitable than A. We could also conclude that if r fell from the initial level r' to any level r such that $r' > r \geq 0$, A would remain more profitable th B since $\psi(r) < \psi\left(r'\right) < \sum_{i=1}^{n}(b_{0i} - a_{0i})x_i^{*\cdot}$

Since A and B are any systems, we could assert that as r moves in one direction within the range between zero and the maximum r admissible in the economy, producers cannot switch back to a system which, in the course of that movement, has been superseded by another.

III. A First Flaw in Levhari's Argument

Up to this point we have just stated Levhari's argument. We must now see where it fails. To do so, it is convenient to begin by noticing and correcting a first flaw in Levhari's reasoning. We shall then be able to proceed to the main error occurring where Levhari argues there always is a vector x^* satisfying conditions (2) and (3).

The flaw we are now concerned with, occurs when Levhari asserts that a switch from A to B as r rises from r' to r'' requires $\psi(r'') > \psi(r')$. That is not necessarily so. It is true that at r', where A is more profitable than B, the sign $<$ must apply to at least one of the relationships (1.1). Since however, by condition (2), some of the levels of production may be zero, we may, in (4), have multiplied by zero the one or more relations (1.1) to which $<$ applied, thus obtaining $0 = 0$ in their place. Then the sign $=$ would apply to all the relations in (4), and hence to their sum in (4.1), so that $\psi\left(r'\right) = \sum_{i=1}^{n}(b_{0i} - a_{0i})x_i^*$. Similarly at r'', where B is more profitable than A, we might have reduced to zero the industries where the advantage of B appears, and have $\psi\left(r''\right) = \sum_{i=1}^{n}(b_{0i} - a_{0i})x_i^*$. But then $\psi(r'') = \psi(r')$, and the fact that $\psi(r)$ is a monotonic function (in this case, a zero constant)[12] does not exclude that producers may switch back to A as r rises beyond r''.

[12] The possibility $\psi(r) = \text{Const.}$ is in fact considered by Levhari (although he does not seem to realize that in this case $\psi(r) = 0$). He there asserts that if Const. $= \sum_{i=1}^{n}(b_{0i} - a_{0i})x_i^*$, then A and B are indifferent at any r (*ibid.*, p. 105). This is incorrect.

The validity of Levhari's conclusions requires therefore, in this respect, that the semipositive vector x^* be such that a nonzero level of production x^* is applied to *at least one* of those industries for which, at r' or r'', the methods of systems A and B are *not* indifferent: i.e., condition (2) should be replaced[13] with the following stricter condition (where $p_1'', \ldots, p_n''$ are the prices for $r = r''$):

(2.1)

$$\begin{aligned}
&x_i^* \geq 0 \quad \text{and} \\
&x_i^* > 0 \quad \text{for at least one } i\ (i = 1, \ldots, n); \ \text{such that} \\
&p_1'(a_{1i} - b_{1i}) + \ldots + p_1'(a_{ni} - b_{ni}) < b_{0i} - a_{0i} \\
&\text{and/or} \\
&p_1''(a_{1i} - b_{1i}) + \ldots + p_1''(a_{ni} - b_{ni}) > b_{0i} - a_{0i}.
\end{aligned}$$

However, *if* Levhari's argument about the existence of a vector x^* satisfying (2) and (3) were valid, that same argument could be used, with a slight modification, to show the existence of an x^* satisfying (2.1) and (3).[14] The discussion of Levhari's demonstration can therefore be narrowed down to the part of his argument which claims there is always a vector x^* satisfying conditions (2) and (3): if that part were valid, the whole argument could be made to stand.

IV. The Main Error

Levhari's argument about the existence of the vector x^* is so concise, that we can quote it in full[15]:

> we can observe that [the commodity-input matrices] a and b can be looked upon as the output and input matrices of a von Neumann model. As we know, there exists a maximum rate of expansion α and an activity level $x^* \left[= \left(x_1^*, \ldots, x_n^*\right)\right]$ such that $\sum_{i=1}^{n} a_{ji} x_i^* = \alpha \sum_{i=1} b_{ji} x_i^* > 0$, for $j = 1, \ldots, n$, where $x^* \geqq 0$; if $\alpha > 1$, then

[13] Indeed, when the two systems considered do not differ in all their methods of production, an infinity of vectors x^* satisfying conditions (2) and (3) can be found simply by assuming zero production of the industries whose methods differ in the two systems, and letting the production of the remaining industries assume any positive level whatever. These vectors would be of no avail to Levhari's argument.

[14] Cf. below, fn. 15.

[15] [*Editor's note*: the quotation which follows in the text differs from Levhari's original in that the mathematical relations are presented in non-matrix form.]

$\sum_{i=1}^{n} a_{ji}x_i^* - \sum_{i=1}^{n} b_{ji}x_i^* > 0$; if $\alpha < 1$, $\sum_{i=1}^{n} b_{ji}x_i^* = \frac{1}{a}\sum_{i=1}^{n} a_{ji}x_i^*$ and $\sum_{i=1}^{n} b_{ji}x_i^* - \sum_{i=1}^{n} a_{ji}x_i^* > 0$; if $\alpha = 1$, then $\sum_{i=1}^{n} a_{ji}x_i^* - \sum_{i=1}^{n} b_{ji}x_i^* = 0$.[16]

Levhari does not say from whom "we know" the proposition which forms the premise of his argument in that passage. If his source is von Neumann's well-known article, there we find a demonstration of a quite different proposition: i.e., that there always exists a semipositive vector x^* of activity levels which maximizes in $\sum_{i=1}^{n} a_{ji}x_i^* \geq \alpha \sum_{i=1}^{n} b_{ji}x_i^*$, for $j=1, \ldots, n$, where the possibility indicated by the sign $>$, ignored by Levhari, is introduced to take care of the "free goods".[17] And if the doubt should arise that the sign $>$, rather than $=$, makes no difference to Levhari's argument that doubt is easily dispelled by observing that for $\alpha<1$, and for any commodity i such that we obtain $\sum_{i=1}^{n} a_{ji}x_i^* > \alpha \sum_{i=1}^{n} b_{ij}x_i^*$, we may have all three possibilities $\sum_{i=1}^{n} a_{ji}x_i^* - \sum_{i=1}^{n} b_{ji}x_i^* \gtreqless 0$. For $\alpha<1$, von Neumann's x^* may, therefore, give rise to quantities $\sum_{i=1} \left(a_{ji} - b_{ji}\right)x_i^*$ positive for some commodities j and negative for some other j's, in contrast with condition (3).[18]

---

[16] Levhari, *op. cit.*, p. 105. It can now be seen that if the proposition Levhari attributes to von Neumann were true, we could easily show that there always exists a vector x^* of levels of activity, satisfying the stricter conditions (2.1) and (3), and not just (2) and (3). This is so because von Neumann does not assume that the number m of his (joint production) processes is the same as the number n of the commodities (cf. von Neumann, "A Model of General Equilibrium", *Review of Economic Studies*, 1945–46, pp. 1–2). We could therefore single out the m industries ($m \leq n$) of A and B in which, at r' or r'', costs of production with the method of system A differ from those with the method of system B, and then write $\sum_{i=1}^{m} a_{ji}x_i^* = \alpha \sum_{i=1}^{m} b_{ji}x_i^* > 0$. Discussion of the cases $\alpha \gtreqless 1$ would then show that the vector x^*—which, being semipositive, must now satisfy (2.1)—satisfies (3).

The fact that von Neumann puts no restriction on the number m of processes can be used also for a *reductio ad absurdum* of the proposition Levhari attributes to that writer. For if $m=1$, then clearly we have no reason to expect $a_{j1}x_1^* = \alpha b_{j1}x_1^*$ for any $x_1^* \neq 0$, and $j=1, \ldots, n$.

[17] Cf. relations (7) and (7') in von Neumann, *op. cit.*, p. 3. We may note here, incidentally, that Levhari's assumption that matrixes a and b are "indecomposable" does not coincide with von Neumann's condition $a_{ji}+b_{ji}>0$ (cf. relations (9) in von Neumann, *op. cit.*, p. 3).

[18] For $\alpha>1$ Levhari's reasoning holds. For $\alpha=1$, we can conclude only that $\sum_{i=1}^{n} a_{ji}x_i^* - \sum_{i=1}^{n} b_{ji}x_i^* \geq 0$ for $j=1, 2 \ldots n$: the possibility indicated by the sign $>$ would not, however, affect Levhari's argument, because when for one or more j's the sign $>$ applies, $\psi(r)$ must be a monotonic increasing function *even if*, for the remaining j's, the sign $=$ applies. Condition (2)—or condition (2.1)—has therefore been stated in an unnecessarily strong form: semipositive or seminegative (instead of strictly positive or negative) vectors $\sum_{i=1}^{n} \left(a_{ji} - b_{ji}\right)x_i^*$ for $j=1, \ldots, n$, would have been sufficient for Levhari's argument.

Thus von Neumann gives no support to Levhari's assertion that an x^* satisfying (2) and (3) always exists. Nor can that proposition be proved in any other way since it is false:[19] conditions (2) and (3) may well be incompatible.

As a result, when we return to the whole of Levhari's argument, we are forced to choose between, on the one hand, a semipositive vector of levels of production not satisfying condition (3), and a vector satisfying (3) but including some negative components. In the first case Levhari's argument fails because $\psi(r)$ need no longer be monotonic: the inequality $\psi(r')<\psi(r'')$ becomes then compatible with $\psi(r''')<\psi(r'')$ (for $0 \leq r' < r'' < r''' \leq r^{(A)}_{max}$), and the sequence of systems of production, *A—B—A* cannot be excluded on this ground. In the second case Levhari's argument fails because, in passing from (1.1) to (4), some of the inequality signs may be reversed: then all three possibilities $\psi\left(r'\right) \gtreqless \sum_{i=1}^{n}(b_{0i} - a_{0i})x_i^*$ are compatible with *A* being more profitable than *B*, and the fact that $\psi(r)$ is monotonic does not exclude the sequence *A — B—A* as *r* rises (falls).

So far we have seen that Levhari's demonstration of the impossibility of a sequence *A—B—A* is invalid: this need not imply that such sequence is in fact possible. The numerical example in the appendix shows however that the sequence *A—B—A* is possible on Levhari's own assumptions. Thus the proposition Levhari set out to demonstrate is itself false.

V. The "Return" of a System and the Theory of Distribution

The possibility, just stated, of the "return" of a system contradicts a basic proposition of the theory of production and distribution dominant in the last seven or eight decades. That theory supposes that, given a number of alternative "techniques"

[19] Consider, e.g., the following two matrixes a and b and their difference $(a-b)$:

$$a = \begin{pmatrix} 0.5 & 0.6 \\ 0.4 & 0.5 \end{pmatrix}, \quad b = \begin{pmatrix} 0.4 & 0.5 \\ 0.5 & 0.6 \end{pmatrix}, \quad a - b = \begin{pmatrix} 0.1 & 0.1 \\ -0.1 & -0.1 \end{pmatrix}$$

Given any semipositive vector $x = (x_1, x_2)$, we have

$$(a_{11} - b_{11})x_1 + (a_{12} - b_{12})x_2 = 0.1x_1 + 0.1x_2 > 0$$

and

$$(a_{21} - b_{21})x_1 + (a_{22} - b_{22})x_2 = -0.1x_1 - 0.1x_2 < 0$$

for the "integrated" production[20] of a commodity by means of labor and capital goods, the techniques can be ordered according to their "capital intensity"; the theory then asserts that any change of technique as the rate of interest falls will be in favor of the more capital-intensive one. Clearly, if this were true, the "return" of a system—implying as it does the return of techniques for the production of one or more commodities,[21] would be impossible: it would force us to the contradictory statement that a technique is both less and more capital-intensive than others.

Before concluding this paper, it is natural to ask ourselves how that fallacy came to be accepted into the body of economic theory, and what its exposure entails for the validity of the traditional explanation of distribution.

The above proposition about changes in capital intensity has resulted from the attempt to apply to "capital" and labor (or, more generally, "capital" and other factors), a principle which was first formulated for factors like labor and land, measurable independently of the distribution of the product. But capital, to be the factor the price of whose service is the rate of interest, must be conceived ultimately as the value, in some unit, of capital goods: and the value of any capital good, like the value of any other product, changes with distribution. Then, to apply the principle of changes in factor proportions to production with capital goods, it would

[20] By "integrated" production of a commodity, we mean production taking place in a composite industry, which consists of the industry producing the commodity and the industries producing directly or indirectly the means of production for that commodity: the industries being taken in the proportions which just ensure the replacement of the means of production used in the whole composite industry. (Cf. Sraffa's concept of "sub-system" in *op. cit.*, Appendix A). Recourse to "integrated production" is necessary if the product to be divided between wages and interest (i.e., the *net* product) is to consist of a physical quantity of the commodity, as supposed in the traditional theory of production.

It should be noted that the word "technique" is employed in the text to denote technical conditions for the "integrated" production of a given commodity, so as to distinguish them from the conditions indicated by "method" or by "system" of production.

Difficulties which cannot be dealt with here arise with the notion of "integrated production"—and in some other respects, when we admit fixed capital and hence joint production. The statements in the text should therefore be taken as relating to systems of the kind discussed by Levhari, where only circulating capital exists.

[21] Change in a method changes not only the "technique" of the commodity to which the method refers, but also the "techniques" of all commodities in whose production the first enters directly or indirectly. Thus, e.g., in Levhari's "indecomposable" systems, change in a method entails change in all n techniques. More generally, change in the method of production of a "basic" product changes the techniques for all products in the economy; whereas change in the method of a "nonbasic" product affects only the technique of that product, and of such "nonbasics" in whose production it might enter. (For the notion of "basic" product cf. above, n. 3.)

first have been necessary to face this peculiarity of capital, showing the meaning and validity of the principle when capital is included as one of the factors.[22]

For the only general attempt to deal with these problems, we must turn to Böhm-Bawerk and Wicksell, and to their "average period of production," measured independently of distribution. As is well known, they conceived capital as the "subsistence fund" necessary for the "roundabout" use of labor. Its size relative to labor would depend on the "average period of production" (which would supply the criterion independent of distribution for ordering the techniques according to their capital intensity), and on the wage rate. Böhm-Bawerk and Wicksell could then show that, as the rate of interest falls (the wage rate rises), the techniques brought into use would be those with a longer average period of production, requiring a "subsistence fund" larger relative to the quantity of labor employed.

This notion of "average period of production"—which Wicksell himself abandoned in his later work—depended however on the unacceptable assumptions of a simple rate of interest, absence of fixed capital, and the existence of only one factor other than capital.[23] And, apart from this attempt, the principle of the increase

---

[22] To illustrate the difficulties arising when capital is included as a factor, let us consider two techniques *A* and *B*, by which a commodity *G* can be produced, and suppose, to start with, that land and labor, but no capital, are required. Let a_x, a_y be, respectively, the quantities of land and labor necessary to produce, in a yearly cycle, a unit of *G* with technique *A*; b_x, b_y the analogous quantities for *B*; and let p_x, p_y be the rates of rent and wages (in terms of any specified commodity) expressing the division of the social product between the two factors. Then the ratio between p_a, the unit cost of *G* when *A* is used, and p_b, the analogous cost with *B*, is.

$$\frac{p_a}{p_b} = \frac{a_x p_x + a_y p_y}{b_x p_x + b_y p_y} = \frac{\frac{a_x}{a_y}\frac{p_x}{p_y} + 1}{\frac{b_x}{b_y}\frac{p_x}{p_y} + 1}\frac{a_y}{b_y}.$$

The expression after the second sign of equality makes it clear that any fall of rent relative to the wage, results in a relative cheapening of the more land-intensive technique: e.g., if $a_x/a_y > b_x/b_y$, p_a/p_b falls when p_x/p_y falls.

But suppose that *x* is now "capital" (i.e., value of physical capital in terms of the chosen commodity), and not land. Then, in the first place, knowledge of the two techniques is no longer sufficient to give a_x and b_x. To know these two quantities we must also know the system of production in use in the economy (cf. above, n. 6), and the distribution of the product expressed by p_x/p_y (the ratio between rate of interest and wages). Secondly, when the system of production is given, and—with p_x/p_y known—the prices of the capital goods are known, the reasoning used for the labor-land case breaks down because a_x and b_x *vary* with p_x/p_y. Thus, supposing, e.g., that *both* before and after a given fall of p_x/p_y we have $a_x/b_y > b_x/b_y$, that fall might still result in a *rise* of p_a/p_b if a_x rises sufficiently relative to b_x. As will be mentioned later in the text, this is in fact possible.

[23] For a discussion of the hypotheses on which Böhm-Bawerk's "average period of production" rests cf., by the author, *Il capitale nelle teorie della distribuzione* (Milano, 1960), pp. 35–39, 61–65, 131–135 [*editor's note*: for arguments broadly corresponding to the parts of the Italian book referred to, see this volume, Part I, *A Problem in the Theory of Distribution from Ricardo to Wicksell*, Sect. I, Chs. III and IV, and Sect. II, Ch. IV].

Of the above three assumptions, two—i.e., absence of fixed capital and production with only labor and capital—underlie the present discussion as well. It should be clear, however, that the negative conclusions reached here would apply all the more when these two assumptions are abandoned.

in the proportion of capital to labor as the rate of interest decreases, seems to have rested exclusively on the illegitimate extension of conclusions reached for special cases (like wine or wood produced with labor and land applied at a single point of time), or simply on the apparent plausibility of treating capital as a factor like the others.[24]

In reality, once we correctly recognize how the value of capital goods depends on distribution, the very possibility of ordering the techniques according to the proportions of capital to labor slips from our hands; that order may change as prices and distribution change.

And no way out of this difficulty can be found by relating capital per man to some magnitude independent of distribution (like Böhm-Bawerk's "average period of production"), which would then be taken as the measure of capital intensity: the "return" of a technique shows that any such measure, even if it could be found, would lead to contradicting the principle of an inverse relationship between rate of interest and capital intensity.

But, renouncing all attempts to express the capital intensity of a technique independently of distribution, we could limit our attention to a switch point between two techniques. It might then be claimed that the technique we switch to, as interest falls, is always the one which—when the capital goods of both techniques are evaluated at the prices of the switch point—shows the higher value of capital per man. This claim would be groundless. As the rate of interest falls, the switch can be in favor of the technique requiring capital goods of a smaller, and not a larger value per man.

Further, if we then wished to compare two situations in the production of a commodity—each with a given rate of interest defining the technique in use and the prices ruling in the situations, we might well find the smaller value of capital per man at the lower rate of interest.[25]

---

[24] Wicksell, after abandoning the notion of average period of production used in his early *Value, Capital and Rent* (1893), showed some uneasiness about the validity of that principle. Thus, e.g., in the *Lectures on Political Economy*, he wrote: "it appears inconceivable a priori that an increase of capital could, *ceteris paribus,* coincide with a decrease of both wages and rent—*though the question should be further investigated* (*op. cit.*, Vol. I; 2nd. ed., 1911; English ed., London, 1934, p. 183; italics added to last sentence). It is interesting to note how these doubts seem to have been forgotten in subsequent decades.

[25] In fact, in most traditional literature, the principle of increasing capital intensity as interest falls is ultimately taken to mean that, at a lower rate of interest, we shall find a higher value (in some unit) of capital per man. An example of this is offered by Wicksell's position in the *Lectures*. He there reduced physical (circulating) capital to labor- and land-services "saved up" for different periods of time. But, as the rate of interest changes, and we pass from technique to technique, some of these dated quantities of labor- and land-services will rise and some fall, without any determinate pattern. Wicksell had therefore to fall back on the value of these quantities (i.e., of the capital goods), and express the result of changes in technique with falling interest as a rise of the proportion that value bears to the quantities of "current" labor and land (cf., e.g., the passage quoted in the preceding footnote).

The last two possibilities have been admitted sporadically in recent economic literature when particular theoretical examples have forced their recognition.[26] Up to now, however, the tendency has been to dismiss such instances as "exceptions": as if the traditional principle they contradict resulted from observed empirical regularities liable to exception, and was not purely a deduction from postulates generally recognized as invalid. What these instances really show, is that the traditional principle—drawn from incorrect premises—is itself incorrect.

The consequences of admitting this, however, are far-reaching, because on that principle has been erected the dominant theory of distribution. From the rise of the proportion of capital to labor in the economy as interest falls,[27] there have been deduced "demand functions" for "capital" (i.e., "saving") and for labor; and, with them, the idea of distribution as governed by a tendency to the equality between demand and supply for these "factors of production." Hence, in particular, the explanation of interest (profits) by the scarcity of "capital" and as the reward for "waiting." It is hard to see how this elaborate structure can stand, when its premise is found wanting.[28]

Let us consider two systems of production, A and B, in an economy where two commodities, 1 and 2, are produced by means of labor and of commodities 1 and 2. The systems can be described by the vectors $a_0=(a_{01}, a_{02})$ and $b_0=(b_{01}, b_{02})$ of the labor-input coefficients in industries 1 and 2, and by the matrixes a and b of the commodity-input coefficients. (In the matrixes we refer each row to inputs

---

[26] Cf. J. Robinson, "The Production Function", *op. cit.*, p. 106; *The Accumulation of Capital, op. cit.*, pp. 109–10, 418; Champernowne, "The Production Function" *op. cit.*, pp. 118–19, 128–89; M. Morishima, *Equilibrium, Stability and Growth* (Oxford: Clarendon Press, 1964), p. 126. Cf. also J. R. Hicks, *Capital and Growth* (Oxford: Clarendon Press, 1965), p. 154.

[27] That rise should result, according to traditional theory, both from changes in the technique used for producing each commodity, and from the rise in the relative output of the consumption goods produced with a larger proportion of capital to labor. The reason advanced for the second effect is that the relative price of these goods falls with the rate of interest, leading to a rise in the relative quantity of them demanded by the consumers. This argument meets the same difficulties as the first. To see why that is so, it is sufficient to refer to the illustration given in n. 22 above, and envisage the techniques A and B not as alternative techniques for producing commodity G, but as techniques for producing two distinct goods. Then, in particular, the possible rise of p_d/p_b as p_x/p_y falls, shows that, as the rate of interest falls, the relative price of the consumption good produced with capital goods having a higher value per man may *rise*, as well as fall.

[28] As is known, "demand functions" for labor and "capital" deduced from changes in the proportions of those "factors of production," were foreign to the thought of the classical economists up to Ricardo. (The failure of the traditional principle on proportions of capital to labor, and the implications of that for distribution theory, have been more fully discussed by the author in "Note su consumi investimenti e domanda effettiva (Parte Prima)", *Economia Internazionale*, XVII(4), 1964, pp. 620–31 [Engl. vers. 'Notes on consumption, investment and effective demand: I', this volume, Part IV]).

consisting of the same commodity, and each column to inputs of the same industry). Let the systems be as follows:

$$A\begin{cases} a_0 = \begin{pmatrix} \frac{89}{10} & \frac{9}{50} \end{pmatrix} \\ a = \begin{pmatrix} 0 & 1/2 \\ 379/423 & 1/10 \end{pmatrix} \end{cases} \quad B\begin{cases} b_0 = \begin{pmatrix} \frac{89}{10} & \frac{3}{2} \end{pmatrix} \\ b = \begin{pmatrix} 0 & 1/4 \\ 379/423 & 5/12 \end{pmatrix} \end{cases}$$

As the equality of the first columns of $\begin{pmatrix} a_0 \\ a \end{pmatrix}$ and $\begin{pmatrix} b_0 \\ b \end{pmatrix}$ shows, the two systems have in common the method for producing commodity 1. Further, the matrixes a and b are both "indecomposable" (i.e., the two commodities are "basic" in both systems).

To see how producers switch from A to B as r changes between zero and its maximum, we shall consider the functions, one for each system, relating the wage w, in terms of the same commodity (e.g., commodity 1), to the rate of interest r. At any given r, if $w^{(A)} > w^{(B)}$, then A will be preferred to B; if $w^{(A)} < w^{(B)}$, B will be preferred to A; and if, finally, $w^{(A)} = w^{(B)}$, A and B will be indifferent and can coexist.[29]

To find the functions $w^{(A)}(r)$ and $w^{(B)}(r)$ we first write the price equations of the two systems, using commodity 1 as the measure of value.

(i)

$$\left.\begin{aligned} 1 &= (1+r)\left(\tfrac{89}{10}w^{(A)} + \tfrac{379}{423}p_2^{(A)}\right) \\ p_2^{(A)} &= (1+r)\left(\tfrac{9}{50}w^{(A)} + \tfrac{1}{2} + \tfrac{1}{10}p_2^{(A)}\right) \end{aligned}\right\}$$

(ii)

$$\left.\begin{aligned} 1 &= (1+r)\left(\tfrac{89}{10}w^{(B)} + \tfrac{379}{423}p_2^{(B)}\right) \\ p_2^{(B)} &= (1+r)\left(\tfrac{3}{2}w^{(B)} + \tfrac{1}{4} + \tfrac{5}{12}p_2^{(B)}\right) \end{aligned}\right\}$$

From equations (i) we obtain

(iii)

$$w^{(A)} = \frac{2\{4230 - 423(1+r) - 1895(1+r)^2\}}{9\{8366(1+r) - 685(1+r)^2\}}$$

[29] It can be demonstrated that at any level of r for which $w^{(A)} = w^{(B)}$, we must have $p_2^{(A)} = p_2^{(B)}$; that at any level of r for which $w^{(A)} > w^{(B)}$, costs of producing commodity (2) with the method of system B will exceed costs with the method of A, both within system A (i.e., for $w = w^{(A)}, p_2 = p_2^{(A)}$) and within system B (i.e., for $w = w^{(B)}$, $p_2 = p_2^{(B)}$); and finally, that the contrary is true at levels of r for which $w^{(A)} < w^{(B)}$. For brevity the demonstration is not given here.

(iv) giving, for $r=0$, $w^{(A)}_{max} \cong 0.0553$

and $w=0$ for $r=r^{(A)}_{max} \cong 38.7\%$

and from equations (ii)

(v)

$$w^{(B)} = \frac{10\{1692 - 705(1+r) - 379(1+r)^2\}}{3\{50.196(1+r) - 13.335(1+r)^2\}}$$

(vi) giving, for $r = 0$, $w^{(B)}_{max} \cong 0.0550$

and $w=0$ for $r = r^{(B)}_{max} \cong 37.8\%$.

Lastly we find the levels of r, if any, at which the two systems are equally profitable, i.e., where $w^{(A)}=w^{(B)}$. To do so we first equalize functions (iii) and (v), and obtain the equation:

$$(1+r)^2 - \frac{23}{10}(1+r) + \frac{66}{50} = 0$$

The roots of this equation, i.e., $(1+r) = \frac{11}{10}$ and $(1+r) = \frac{6}{5}$, give the two values of r at which systems A and B are equally profitable, i.e.,

(vii)

$$r^* = 10\%$$
$$r^{**} = 20\%$$

Results (iv), (vi) and (vii) show how the curves representing $w^{(A)}$ and $w^{(B)}$ would behave, the one in relation to the other, when drawn in a diagram with r and w, on the horizontal and vertical axes, respectively. We know that the two curves are continuous in the ranges $0 \leq r \leq r^{(A)}_{max}$ and $0 \leq r \leq r^{(B)}_{max}$, respectively. Then, since $w^{(A)}_{max} > w^{(B)}_{max}$, the curve $w^{(A)}$ must, as r increases from zero, be above the curve $w^{(B)}$ until we reach their first intersection[30] for $r=10\%$. The curve $w^{(A)}$ then passes below $w^{(B)}$ and stays there until the two intersect again at $r=20\%$. Then $w^{(A)}$ finally passes above $w^{(B)}$ to reach the r axis for $r^{(A)}_{max} \cong 38.7\%$. This means that A would be in use for $0 \leq r \leq 10\%$; B for $10\% \leq r \leq 20\%$; then A would again be in use for $20\% \leq r \leq r^{(A)}_{max} \cong 38.7\%$.

[30] The possibility that, at r^* and r^{**}, the two curves touch without intersecting is excluded because r^* and r^{**} are the roots of a quadratic equation (calculation shows, e.g., that, at $r=15\%$, $w^{(B)}=0,03,155 < w^{(A)}=0,03,160$.).

On a Change in the Notion of Equilibrium in Recent Work on Value and Distribution: A Comment on Samuelson †

1. Introduction

Some days ago I found myself wondering how to discuss today Professor Samuelson's paper which, by then, I knew I would be unable to read before the event. I was however given a clue: his paper would overlap with an earlier note of his (Samuelson, 1975). And since that note prompted me to some reflections, I decided to come and talk about them, knowing that I would be peripheral to what Professor Samuelson would have said today (though not, I now realize, to the historical vein in which he said it).

In that earlier note Samuelson (1975) answers a charge from Robinson (1975b) that he had used relations valid across different 'long-period equilibria' (i.e. equilibria where the prices of products yield a uniform rate of profits on the supply prices of the capital goods)[1] in order to determine the effects of a process of capital accumulation. My concern today will be with the issue on which Robinson and Samuelson seem to agree: the illegitimacy of studying the *permanent* effects of changes in conditions of the economy by means of the comparison between the two 'long-period equilibria' corresponding to conditions before and after the change.

This agreement, which reflects a position increasingly held in theoretical work, constitutes a drastic departure from what had long been the accepted method in the

† Previously published with the North-Holland Publishing Company in *Essays in Modern Capital Theory*, ed. by M. Brown. K. Sato and P. Zarembka, 1976. All necessary permissions acquired.

[1] Samuelson (1975) and Robinson (1975b) refer to the long-period equilibria of economies in 'steady-state growth'.

P. Garegnani, *Capital Theory, the Surplus Approach, and Effective Demand*,
Springer Studies in the History of Economic Thought,
https://doi.org/10.1007/978-3-031-23643-3_4

theory of value and distribution. The study of the permanent effects of changes by means of comparisons between positions of the economic system characterized by a uniform rate of profits was in fact the method used by Ricardo and the English classical economists, when they explained profits in terms of the surplus product left after paying wages at the rate determined by independent economic or social circumstances (see Garegnani, 1970, pp. 426–427 [this volume, Part II, pp. 172–3]). But fundamentally the same method was preserved after Ricardo, across the deep change which the theory underwent in favour of a symmetric explanation of profits and wages in terms of the equilibrium between the forces of demand and supply for labour and capital.

It was only in the last few decades that this method, which was centred on 'long-period positions' of the system—as we may call them in order to cover both the long-period equilibria of the later theories and the analogous notion of the classical theories[2]—was increasingly challenged: be it in favour of short-period equilibria, which do not imply a uniform rate of profits on the supply price of the capital goods, or be it in favour of Robinson's 'analysis of processes'.

What I shall try to suggest today is that this departure from tradition has not been due to weaknesses of the method as such, but rather to weaknesses of the dominant theory of distribution and, in particular, of the conception of capital it relies on. The attempt to overcome the deficiencies of the received notion of capital while retaining the basic supply and demand approach, provides, I shall argue, the main explanation of the move towards short-period equilibria and their sequence in time as the new basis for the theory of value and distribution.

Our concern will here be with this move towards short-period equilibria, but in Sect. 6, after considering the role which Keynes may have had in favouring the move, we shall also advance some remarks about the different ground for Professor Robinson's rejection of the traditional method.

2. The Traditional Method and the 'Long-Period Positions' of the System

We have been speaking of 'long-period equilibria' or, to cover the similar Classical notion, of 'long-period positions' of the system. But the expression most frequently used today in describing situations with a uniform rate of profits on the supply price of the capital goods, are 'stationary' or 'steady states'. This change in terminology reflects the change in method we are discussing. The abandonment of the method of long-period positions seems indeed to have been generally justified

---

[2] Since, as just mentioned, the classical economists did not resort to the 'opposite forces of supply and demand' in their explanation of distribution and relative prices, the word 'equilibrium' does not seem appropriate to describe the position of the economic system characterized by 'natural' prices, wages and profits.

by arguing that, in an economy where the conditions determining the long-period prices are changing through time, the decisions of individuals will be affected by future price changes (whether correctly foreseen, or simply expected); and this will prevent the long-period prices and position from being a guidance to the actual prices (and position) of the economy.[3]

This, however, was not the view which the older theorists took of the applicability of their method. Even if we leave aside Ricardo, who did not intend his theory of profits for a 'stationary' or 'steady state' England, it was not for such an economy that Marshall wrote: 'an increase of material capital... will much increase the national dividend ... and since ... it will have forced down the rate of interest, ... the joint product of a dose of capital and labour will now be divided more in favour of labour' (Marshall, [1920] 1949, VI, xi, 4, p. 553); or Walras stated: 'In a progressive economy the rate of net income will fall appreciably' (Walras, 1954, lecture 36, para. 333, p. 391). Nor did the older theorists ignore that actual prices change day by day and are expected so to do, whether because of changes in long-period conditions or for other reasons.

As we all know, they understood the long-period position as the 'centre' towards which the competitive economy would gravitate in the given long-period conditions. The basis of the argument had been laid down by Adam Smith with his distinction between the 'market price' and 'natural price' of a commodity. The actual or market price could, at any given moment, be above or below the natural price, i.e. the price just sufficient to cover at their 'natural rates' the wages, profits and rents to be paid in order to produce the commodity. The market price would exceed the natural price when the quantity of the commodity 'brought to market' falls short of the 'effectual demand', i.e. the quantity demanded by those willing to pay the natural price. But just this excess of the market price would cause the quantity supplied to increase towards the effectual demand and thus undo itself. The converse would be true when the market price is below the natural price. As a result, Smith could conclude that: 'the natural price ... is ... the central price to which the prices of all commodities are continually gravitating' (Smith, [1776] 1910, Vol. I, Bk. I, Chap. 7, pp. 48–51).

It was because of this 'gravitation' that the 'long-period values' of the variables (i.e. their values in the 'long-period positions' of the system) were thought to be those relevant for an analysis of lasting changes in the system. In the words of Ricardo ([1821] 1951, Chap. 4, pp. 91–92):

> Having fully acknowledged the temporary effects which, in particular employments of capital, may be produced on the prices of commodities, as well as on the wages of labour, and the profits of stock, by accidental causes, without influencing the general price of commodities, wages or profits, since these effects are equally operative in all stages of society, we will leave them entirely out of our consideration, whilst we are treating of the laws which regulate natural prices, natural wages, and natural profits...

---

[3] Cf., for example, the passage in Hicks (1946, pp. 116–117), on which we shall comment below, pp. 213–4.

where the argument for 'leaving entirely out of consideration' the deviations of market from natural values of the variables rests intimately on the 'temporary' nature of these deviations in contrast with Ricardo's concern with lasting changes.

And a similar argument about 'long-period normal' values was still used by Marshall ([1920] 1949, V, iii, 7, p. 291) a century later:

> The actual value at any time, the market value as it is often called, is often more influenced by passing events, and by causes whose action is fitful and short lived, than by those which work persistently. But in long periods these fitful and irregular causes in large measure efface one another's influence; so that in the long run persistent causes dominate completely.

The persistent, or non-temporary nature of the causes of long-period values, which was thus stressed by both Ricardo and Marshall, explains why the relevance of these values was not thought to be confined to the analysis of economies which are stationary[4] or in steady growth. That persistence was thought to ensure that changes in the causes, if continuous, would be sufficiently slow as not to endanger the gravitation towards the (slowly moving) long-period values. That same persistence would ensure that, should the changes be rapid, they would be once-for-all changes, and that, after a period of transition, gravitation to the new long-period values would again assert itself.

The forces which Marshall and post-Ricardian theory introduced to determine the normal rates of wages and profits were fundamentally different from those envisaged by Ricardo for his natural rates. Consequently, the gravitation towards such rates (and the corresponding long-period prices) raised very different problems in the two theories. Ricardo and the other classical economists—who considered the real wage as determined *before* profits and relative prices, and not *simultaneously* with them by the 'forces of demand and supply'—were able to separate the determination of outputs from the determination of prices and profits (see Garegnani, 1970, pp. 426–428 [this volume, Part II, pp. 172–5]). When thus separately determining the outputs, they could deal with the interactions between outputs and the effectual demands, both with respect to the system as a whole[5] and with respect to each industry. Accordingly, the adjustment of individual outputs involved in the gravitation towards natural prices could be conceived of as an *adaptation to quantities already fixed*, i.e. *determined in another part of the theory.* Hence, for example, the notion by Smith referred to above, and so striking to the modern reader, of 'effectual demand' as a single definite point and not as the definite schedule of later theory.

Marshall and the post-Ricardian theorists, on the other hand, who brought demand and supply to determine the division of the product between wages and profits, could only determine outputs simultaneously with relative prices and

[4] 'Cf. below, n. 11, about a contrary opinion of Hicks on Marshall.

[5] As we shall mention later (below, n. 33), this separation between determination of relative prices and determination of outputs leaves the Ricardian theory of value 'open' with respect to the possibility of deficiencies of effective demand.

the rate of profits. Accordingly, the interactions between quantities supplied and demanded became an essential part of the gravitation to the normal rates of wages and profits and the corresponding normal prices. And the difficulties involved in the process of gravitation as conceived in these later theories started to become apparent with Keynes' *General Theory* (1936).

But whatever the differences between the two kinds of theory, and however basic the difficulties raised by gravitation for the later theories, what concerns us here is only to point out that the notion of 'long-period positions' as 'centres' of gravitation was fundamentally the same in the two cases and did not depend for its application on the hypothesis of a stationary (or steady-state) economy.

3. The Criticism Based on 'Price Expectations'

What then are the deficiencies of the method based on 'long-period positions' which caused its abandonment in favour of an analysis founded on short-period equilibria of demand and supply?

If we turn to Hicks' *Value and Capital* (1946), the first influential work in which the long-period method was thus abandoned in a general treatment of value and distribution, we find, we shall argue, two distinct lines of criticism against what is there comprehensively named 'static theory', but which the context specifies as being essentially the traditional long-period theory.[6]

'Static theory', Hicks argues in his first line of criticism, would be applicable to the 'real world' only 'if we could say that the system of prices existing *at any moment* depends upon the preferences and resources existing at that moment and upon nothing else.' This, Hicks continues, is not the case because 'the current supply of a commodity depends not so much upon what the current price is as upon what entrepreneurs have expected it to be in the past', and, correspondingly, 'the current position in the factor markets' depends on what the prices of the products are expected to be in the future. In order to have an applicable theory, we must then allow for the fact that 'supplies (and ultimately demands too) are governed by expected prices quite as much as by current prices', and abandon 'static theory' (Hicks, [1939] 1946, pp. 116–117, our italics).

[6] 'Static theory' is there defined simply as that in which the quantities do not have to be 'dated' (Hicks, 1946, p. 115). This definition, however, covers both the long-period theory we have been discussing (which was also that of Hicks, [[1932] 1963]) and the short-period theory where, as in the general equilibrium system of the 'static' part of *Value and Capital*, profits appear as rentals of the capital goods, and will not generally bear a uniform rate to the supply price of such capital goods: Hicks' criticism of static theory on the ground that it ignores the effects of future price changes has evidently very different force in the two cases (cf. below, pp. 219–20). The generality of the criticism of previous theory, and the passages where such theory is charged with 'often' introducing 'a "factor of production" capital and its "price" interest' (Hicks, 1946, p. 116n.) make it clear, however, that the real target of criticism is long-period theory.

Taken literally, this criticism would seem to accuse previous theory of having ignored the fact that since production takes time, the supply of commodities cannot adapt instantaneously to price. This non-instantaneous adaptation was however so little ignored by, for example, Adam Smith that, in discussing the 'market price', he treated the quantity of the commodity 'brought to market' at any given time as fixed independently of the price it would fetch. Incorrect price expectations entertained in the past might indeed be a way of describing some of the factors that make the market prices deviate from the natural prices. But the real point of the method criticized was that there were to be forces capable of eliminating the deviations. It was these forces which gave to the long-period prices their true status: that of 'centres' of gravitation, and not that of 'prices existing at any moment', to which Hicks refers at the beginning of his passage.

Hicks' criticism of previous theory would have been more pointed if he had disputed the gravitation of the market prices towards such centres.[7] This, however, might have raised doubts about the forces of demand and supply which traditional theory had introduced to explain such 'centres': i.e. might have raised doubts about the *theory* and not only about its static *method.* The argument concerning price expectations used here by Hicks has in fact to be read remembering that the *General Theory* had been published not many years before:[8] but Keynes had in fact disputed the gravitation to a demand-and-supply equilibrium in the factor markets and had thus raised, we shall suggest below, as many questions about the theory as he had about its static method. And, as we shall now attempt to show, it is to the theory rather than to its method that Hicks' own second line of criticism in fact points.

4. The Criticism Relating to the 'Quantity of Capital'

This second line of criticism appears when it is asserted that 'static theory' is 'quite incompetent to deal properly with capital', a problem, as Hicks continues, where 'the dating of economic quantities is of the first importance'.[9] And

[7] A few pages after the passages we have quoted Hicks does mention 'stationary-state theorists' who 'regarded reality as "tending" towards stationarity', and adds that 'the existence of such tendency is more than questionable' (Hicks, 1946, p. 119). But, as we shall see below, n. 11, the 'stationary state' there referred to is not 'the long-period equilibrium' of traditional theory and, therefore, the 'tendency' to the former is a different question from a tendency to the latter. In the later (1965) book, Hicks' doubts extend to equilibrium proper and the validity of static theory is there questioned on the two grounds that 'it is by no means inevitable that an equilibrium should exist' and that '[e]ven if the equilibrium exists, it has still to be shown that there is a tendency to it' (Hicks, 1965, pp. 17–8). These drastic statements, however, are only followed by passing references to imperfect competition and the 'cobweb theorem'.

[8] Cf. below, n. 21.

[9] The full passage refers to 'static theory' as 'quite incompetent to deal properly with capital, or interest, or trade fluctuations, or even money—problems where the dating, etc.' (Hicks, 1946, p. 116). In an earlier article referred to below, n. 21, the abandonment of static theory in favour of dynamic theory was motivated only with the need to deal with capital (Hicks, 1935, pp. 268–270).

for the reader wondering how previous theory, incompetent to deal with capital, could still have dealt with the rates of wages and profits (interest), Hicks adds in a footnote:

> people … would often introduce into their static theory a 'factor of production' capital and its 'price', interest, supposing that capital could be treated like the static factors. … That some error was involved in the procedure would not have been denied; but the absence of a general dynamic theory, in which all quantities were properly dated, made it easy to underestimate how great the error was (Hicks, [1939] 1946, pp. 116, n. 1).

We are not told exactly what the error was. The fact that this passage is immediately followed by those concerning the dependence of current on future prices, and by a recognition of the legitimacy of static theory in the case of the stationary state may lead the reader to think that the error is due to capital accumulation which, while causing changes in the long-period prices, at the same time causes, through investment, a dependence of current prices and outputs on price expectations. And to the older theorists argument that the changes brought about by accumulation would generally be slow enough to be ignored,[10] the reader will answer by thinking of the difficulties deriving from expectations which Keynes had pointed out not many years before, and which Hicks himself discusses in later parts of *Value and Capital*.

But when, two pages later, Hicks comes back to capital he in fact points in a different direction. After arguing that 'static theory' would only come into its own in the case of a 'stationary state' in which 'it would not be necessary to distinguish between price expectations and current prices', he unexpectedly moves on to quite a different question:

> One thing, however, is evident when we look at this stationary economy. … This is the dependence of the input–output relations (the production functions) on the quantity of intermediate products carried by the system. How will the quantity of intermediate products—the quantity of capital—be determined?

Hicks' answer is that in a stationary economy the 'quantity of capital' will be determined by the condition of a zero (net) propensity to save (Hicks, 1939 [1946], pp. 118–119).

This fortunate coincidence, for which the same stationary state that makes it unnecessary to distinguish between price expectations and current prices also takes care of the separate difficulty about the 'quantity of capital', does not, however, really answer the question which Hicks had asked. As we saw above, previous marginal theorists had not generally assumed the stationary state Hicks refers

[10] See above, p. 212.

to.[11] The condition of zero net savings was accordingly not available to them: how, then, did they 'determine' the quantity of capital?

The answer is: in the same way which Hicks himself had adopted in his *Theory of Wages* ([1932] 1963) not many years before *Value and Capital*, namely by taking it as a magnitude given in some value unit and slowly affected over time by net saving.[12] This procedure, the deficiencies of which Hicks may have become more aware of after Shove's review of his earlier book,[13] was indeed the generally

---

[11]Above, pp. 210–1, Hicks writes (1946, p. 117) that the 'hallmark' of the Austrian economists (Böhm-Bawerk and Wicksell are mentioned) is 'concentration on the Stationary State', the stationary state being then defined in the way we saw. This seems misleading: both Böhm-Bawerk and Wicksell assumed the amount of capital in the economy to be a given (value) magnitude and not an unknown determined by the condition of zero net saving (cf. Böhm-Bawerk, 1891, pp. 391 and 420; Wicksell, 1954, p. 126; 1934, p. 207). As Robbins (1930), pointed out, two distinct conceptions of the stationary state were present in the literature: in one, the constancy over time of the quantities of factors is *assumed,* while in the other this constancy is one of the results of the equilibrating process. Böhm-Bawerk and Wicksell generally used the expression 'stationary state' for the former conception (e.g. Wicksell, 1954, p. 153; 1934, p. 152) whereas Hicks' description of it unambiguously refers to the latter. On the same subject, Hicks (1965, p. 47) writes about Marshall 'seeing' that 'when it came to capital theory ... all that could be done [by the static method] was the analysis of a stationary state'. This also seems misleading. Hicks quotes the passage where Marshall ([1920] 1949, V, v, 8, p. 315n) says that a 'theoretically perfect' long period would involve 'the supposition of a stationary state of industry'. But in the text to which the passage is appended as part of a footnote, Marshall had written that 'the remainder of the present volume is chiefly concerned... with the normal relations of wages, profits, prices etc. for rather long periods', as distinct from the 'very gradual or *Secular* movements of normal price, caused by the gradual growth of knowledge, of population *and of capital*' [latter emphasis added]: the normal long-period relations are thus held to be compatible with 'the very gradual growth of ... capital'. The passage quoted by Hicks has to be read—it seems—while remembering other passages, where Marshall writes that only in a stationary state would the 'normal price' *coincide* with an average of the actual prices, and where this 'coincidence' is clearly held to be non-essential for the relevance of 'normal price' (Marshall, [1920] 1949, e.g. V, v, 5, p. 309; V, iii, 6, p. 289).

[12]For equilibria where the amount of capital is treated as a given (or independently variable) magnitude see Hicks ([1932] 1963, pp. 114–115, 127, 187–188, 205–207). For the value measurement of such magnitude cf., for example, the passage in Hicks ([1932] 1963, p. 20n.) where the anticipated scrapping of a machine A to replace it by a machine B having the same original cost, is said to require 'the use of new capital ... to an amount equal to [the] deficiency of the replacement fund'.

[13]Shove pointed out that, contrary to what Hicks had argued ([1932] 1963, p. 188), a rise of wages not accompanied by a fall in the interest rate cannot render relatively more profitable the more capitalistic methods of production, since the long-period prices of capital goods would then rise in the same proportion as wages have risen (Shove, 1933, pp. 470-1; rpt. in Hicks [1932] 1963, pp. 264–265). Shove's argument relies on a peculiarity of interest as the price of a factor measured in value terms: if, for example, the two factors had been labour and land a rise of (money) wages with constant (money) rent, would in fact have rendered relatively more profitable the more land-intensive methods of production, in analogy with Hicks' original contention.

accepted one, having been used with various degrees of explicitness and circumspection by such diverse writers as J. B. Clark, Böhm-Bawerk, Wicksell and Marshall in their determination of long-period equilibria.[14]

The only outstanding exception had been Walras who, in his *Elements* (1954), had conceived the capital endowment of the economy as a set of given quantities: as many as there are kinds of 'capital goods proper'.[15] But since Walras, no less than the authors just mentioned, attempted to determine a long-period equilibrium, he was simply incorrect in believing this to be compatible with treating each kind of 'capital good proper' as a separate factor in given supply. With a capital endowment conceived in these terms, the forces of demand and supply can only reach a *short-period equilibrium*, i.e. an equilibrium where the prices of the services of the capital goods will not generally be compatible with a uniform rate of profit on the (actual or potential) supply prices of the respective capital goods.[16]

It thus emerges that marginal theorists not only generally conceived the capital endowment of the economy as a value magnitude, but also had no alternative to doing so if they were to be consistent with the conditions of long-period equilibrium:[17] that very 'full equilibrium' in which, to paraphrase Hicks ([1932] 1963), the marginal product of labour is the one resulting when the 'quantity', but not the 'form', of the 'co-operating capital' remains unchanged.[18]

---

[14] With respect to Böhm-Bawerk and Wicksell, see the references given in n. 11 above. As regards Marshall, see ([1920] 1949, VI, ii, 4, p. 443), and the conception of the 'general fund of capital' used there.

[15] Cf. the equations in Walras (1954, para. 238, pp. 271–272) expressing, as Walras writes, the condition that in equilibrium [the] selling prices [of capital goods proper] and their costs of production are equal'. (For Walras' error see Garegnani, 1960, Parte II, Cap. III [closely corresponding to Sect. 2, Chap. 3 of *A Problem in the Theory of Distribution from Ricardo to Wicksell*, in Part I of this volume]. In his paper for this conference Dr. Nuti mentions the latter book, without giving page reference, as containing the accusation that an implicit assumption of malleable capital exists in the multi-commodity multi period model' (Nuti, 1976, p. 55). No such multiperiod model is however considered there.)

[16] This short period equilibrium was contemplated by Professor Hicks in his *The Theory of Wages* when he contrasted the "full" equilibrium' marginal product of labour with a "short"-period' one. He had then dismissed the latter by saying: it is very doubtful if this [short period marginal product of labour] can be given any precise meaning which is capable of useful application' (Hicks, [1932] 1963, pp. 20–1).

[17] Cf. below, n. 22 for the case of steady growth.

[18] Hicks ([1932] 1963, p. 20). In *Capital and Growth* (1965, pp. 40–48) Hicks conjectures that the conception of a 'homogeneous capital substance' was introduced in economic theory in order to avoid the problem of the allocation of saving among diverse capital goods and the consequent need to introduce future prices. This conception of 'capital substance' is then traced back to Ricardo's 'corn-capital' in the *Essay on Profits*, and to the labour-embodied measurements of the *Principles*. Hicks accordingly writes of Ricardo's 'herculean effort' to retain by these means the 'self-contentedness of the single period' (1965, p. 47). Here we cannot deal fully with the many perplexing aspects of this interpretation of Ricardo. It may be sufficient to remark that while Hicks' account of the *Essay on Profits* provides evidence of the role played there by the

(What we have just said may help to clear up a frequent misapprehension—there seem to be examples of it in Nuti (1976)—according to which the measurement of the capital endowment as a value magnitude is required only for the versions of marginal theory explaining distribution in the community by means of a single aggregate production function. In fact, however, the capital endowment of the economy can be a datum compatible with long-period equilibrium only if it is expressed as a value magnitude. Wicksell's *Lectures* (1934) and most of Hicks' *Theory of Wages* ([1932] 1963) are about many commodities and general equilibrium just as much as is Hicks' *Value and Capital* (1939 [1946]).)

There is no need to say here what difficulties beset this conception of capital. As the emergence of the phenomena of 're-switching' and 'reverse capital deepening' have begun to show, Hicks' question about the 'determination' of the 'quantity of capital' in 'static' (long-period) marginal theory was pointing only, it seems, to the most visible among these difficulties, i.e. that of determining the relative prices of commodities, capital goods included, while taking as a given or independently variable magnitude, the value of the capital endowment of the economy.[19]

What concerns us here is to point out that this difficulty over the determination of the quantity of capital is independent of the divergence between current and expected prices. The same need to measure the quantity of capital would arise if we wanted to determine long-period equilibrium while assuming that tastes, techniques and resources are not going to change in the future[20]: a situation in which, as Hicks says, 'actual prices do not need to be distinguished from expected prices'.

It is therefore apparent that this difficulty, unlike that concerning the influence of future prices,[21] regards the *theory,* i.e. the way in which the centres of

---

assumption of homogeneity *between capital and output* in one sector of the economy (and not of homogeneity among capital goods in the whole economy, as required in order to support Hicks' interpretation), no evidence is given by Hicks of Ricardo's concern for the allocation of savings, or for 'the self-containedness of the single period'. It would be a surprising coincidence if Ricardo's efforts, quite clearly directed to measuring capital and output independently of the rate of profits (in order to achieve a non-circular determination of the rate of profits as the ratio between surplus product and capital) should result to be also directed to the preservation of the 'static method'. The passage from the *Principles* quoted on p. 212 above suggests that Ricardo's 'static' concern for long-period positions of the economy had a different, and better-known, basis than the homogeneity of capital indicated by Hicks.

[19] Thus, the relation between interest and capital stock was there described as follows: 'A fall in the rate of interest would encourage the adoption of longer processes, requiring the use (at any moment) of larger quantities of intermediate products.' We now know that the 'length of processes' or 'quantities of intermediate products' need not increase as the rate of interest falls.

[20] I.e. taking the economy to be stationary according to the first of the two conceptions of a stationary state referred to above, n. 11.

[21] In an article which Hicks published after *The Theory of Wages*, but before Keynes' *General Theory* and in which the dynamic theory of *Value and Capital* was first introduced, Hicks' criticism of previous theories was directed only at their notions of capital, held to be inapplicable outside the stationary state (Hicks, 1935, pp. 268–269). Though price expectations played a key role in that article, no criticism was there raised on the ground of a failure of previous theories to distinguish between price expectations and current prices (cf. also above, n. 8).

gravitation of the system are determined, and not the static *method* of analysis based on such 'centres'. Thus, no similar difficulty arises for the classical economists who used the same method but did not determine the centres of gravitation as equilibria between supply and demand, and had accordingly no need to conceive of capital as a single 'quantity' measurable independently of distribution.

5. The 'Short-Period' General Equilibrium

If Hicks' line of criticism concerning the quantity of capital regards theory rather than method, it is none the less true that an abandonment of the method based on long-period positions of the system was entailed in the attempt to overcome the deficiencies of the traditional notion of capital while preserving the basic demand and supply approach.

The way had already been shown by Walras to those willing to take it.[22] All that was needed was to renounce Walras' own inconsistent attempt at determining a long-period equilibrium and accept instead as a basis the short-period general equilibrium of demand and supply compatible with given quantities of the several capital goods.[23]

It is evident, however, that this short-period general equilibrium cannot be determined independently of the changes it will undergo over time (as was done by Walras who was thinking of a long-period general equilibrium). The competitive tendency to a uniform rate of profits will be powerful and quick in bringing about changes in the composition of the capital stock and, hence, given the almost complete absence of substitutability in such a system, appreciable changes in the prices of productive services and commodities. The 'persistence' of the governing forces which justified the determination of a long-period equilibrium

[22] We may here leave aside the 'dynamic' analysis based on the hypothesis of steady proportionate growth which would not be defended as a basis for the general theory of value and distribution. We may. however, note that some of the attraction of this kind of demand and supply analysis lies in the fact that the 'quantity' of capital per labourer having a physical composition compatible with a uniform rate of profits, can here be left to be determined by the propensities to save: thus avoiding (as in Hicks' stationary state') the dilemma between short-period equilibrium and reliance on a capital endowment given in value terms.

[23] As Hicks prefers to describe it, 'heterogeneity of capital stock can be dealt with by using our formal theory of many factors ... and ... this now makes it unnecessary to insist that the economy is to be taken to be in a state of full equilibrium, in the sense that there is perfect equalization of yields on every sort of capital goods' (Hicks, 1963, p. 346). Accuracy would however require replacing the phrase 'unnecessary to insist that the economy is to be taken to be', by the phrase 'impossible to suppose that the economy is'.

independently of the changes the latter may be (slowly) undergoing, is clearly absent here.[24]

This analysis had therefore to shed the static method and consider the effect of future conditions on the markets for current commodities and productive services.[25] This it did in either of two ways: by introducing price expectations in the short-period equilibria, as was done by Hicks for his 'temporary equilibria' in *Value and Capital*, or, alternatively, by expanding the analysis into a theory of general intertemporal equilibrium based on the hypothesis of complete futures markets.[26]

We must here leave aside the question of whether these two kinds of analysis have in fact overcome the deficiencies of demand-and-supply theory with respect to capital. We may instead mention two shortcomings which are the direct consequence of the withdrawal from the long-period basis of previous marginal theories. The first regards the meaning we should attach to the short-period equilibrium which forms the basic element of the analysis in both its versions. Even if this equilibrium could be formally shown to be stable,[27] that same impermanence of causes which, as just seen, imposed consideration of its changes over time, would seem to prevent it from being conceived as a centre of gravitation of the economic system: the forces governing it would lack the persistence necessary to distinguish them from those other accidental forces which, at any given time, are likely to keep the economy out of this short-period equilibrium.[28] Thus, before the recurrence of demand and supply flows has been sufficient to correct, or compensate,

[24] It may also be noted that the above-mentioned competitive tendency considerably narrows the possibility of studying changes by means of comparisons of equilibria. In fact, over any appreciable period of time, the proportions between the several capital stocks will be governed by the tendency to a uniform rate of profits, and consequently the stocks cannot be treated as independent variables as could be done for the quantity of capital in the long-period equilibria. The changes occurring in the economic system must then be studied through sequences and not through comparisons of equilibria, and a second reason emerges why the analysis has to become 'dynamic'.

[25] This need to consider future conditions does not seem to arise, or to arise to the same extent, in the case of Marshall's short-period partial equilibrium. Behind the short-period supply price of the individual industry are the forces which govern the factor prices, or the range in which these vary with the output of the industry. These forces, which are included in the *ceteris paribus* assumption, are, it seems, ultimately long-period forces, so that Marshall's short-period equilibrium appears to be a complement to the long-period equilibrium of the system and not an alternative to it.

[26] Cf. e.g. Debreu (1959).

[27] I.e. stable under the assumption of constancy in the forces determining the equilibrium position.

[28] Marshall's short-period analysis, it seems, does not incur this difficulty because of its ultimate reliance on long-period forces (cf. n. 25 above). This seems to have partly remained the case in Keynes' extension of Marshall's short-period analysis to the system as a whole: the wage unit provides the base on which is erected a system of relative prices (implicit in the aggregate supply function), which can only reflect a system of long-period prices with degrees of distortion depending on the relative elasticities of the short-period supply curves of the individual industries, and on the level of the aggregate output.

previous accidental deviations, the equilibrium position itself will have changed considerably, and the equilibrium can then provide little if any guidance to the behaviour of the economy.[29,30]

The other shortcoming which should be mentioned appears when, in order to avoid the hypothesis of complete futures markets (and its evident lack of basis in reality), price expectations are introduced in their stead and 'temporary' equilibria are preferred to the 'intertemporal' equilibrium. In traditional theory, not only the long-period position, but also the gravitation towards it were generally explained without introducing price expectations. It may be objected that a particular treatment of price expectations was in fact always implied: that, for example, Smith's argument about the tendency of the market price to fall when it exceeds the natural price implies that producers should expect the high market price to last long enough for them to reap an extra profit by acting now in order to produce more of the commodity later. But the important point of Smith's procedure is precisely that this effect upon the minds of people of a market price exceeding the natural price appeared to be so inescapable as to permit proceeding directly to its objective consequence, increased production. This would seem to be the procedure to be aimed at with respect to 'expectations' in the theory of value: to relate them uniquely to objective phenomena, so as to bypass them and relate the facts explaining the expectations directly to the actions of the individuals. The procedure which Hicks (1939 [1946]) adopted, by which unobservable quantities, the expected prices, are introduced as independent variables, runs the risk of depriving the theory of any definite results, as Hicks himself had earlier come close to admitting.[31] The values which the unknowns assume in a situation which is fully defined in its objective data can be made to vary almost indefinitely by varying the hypotheses about expected prices.

These considerations regarding the new notion of equilibrium and the treatment of price expectations may help to explain why the long-period positions remained for so long the undisputed basis of the theory of value and distribution.

---

[29] This difficulty seems to be close to the one which Hicks admits to have been inherent in the temporary equilibrium method he used in *Value and Capital*: namely, the doubtful legitimacy of assuming that prices remain unchanged throughout the single period; and that these prices are equilibrium prices' (Hicks, 1965, p. 73).

[30] Moreover, where a sequence of such short-period equilibria is taken into consideration (as is the case, e.g. in the general 'intertemporal' equilibrium) the danger arises of a cumulation of errors due to the uncompensated deviations from equilibrium in preceding periods.

[31] In his review of Keynes' *General Theory*, Hicks had written that the method [of expectations] is thus an admirable one for analyzing the impact effects of disturbing causes, but it is less reliable for studying the further effects', since, 'it is probable that the change in actual production during the first period will influence the expectations ruling at the end of that period, and there is no means of telling what the influences will be. The more we go into the future, the greater this source of error, so that there is the danger, when it is applied to long periods, of the whole method petering out' (Hicks, 1936, p. 241).

6. Keynes' 'Short Period'

We noticed in Sect. 3 the influence of Keynes in the criticism which Professor Hicks raised against previous theory on the ground that it ignored price expectation. A further indirect role of Keynes in favouring the abandonment of the long-period method may be traced to the fact that the *General Theory* caused attention to be moved on to problems concerning the equilibrium of the system as a whole, away from the partial equilibrium analysis that had long kept the notion of capital and its deficiencies in a dimly perceived background.

In considering now whether the modern withdrawal of value theory from its previous long-period basis might not be traced to some more direct, or more deep-rooted, influence of Keynes' book (rather than, as we have argued so far, chiefly to the problem of capital) it seems necessary to start from one fact. Keynes' primary concern was not a re-examination of the orthodox theory of value from the angle of the short period: it was to establish a single basic proposition, namely that it is the level of incomes which ensures equality between saving and investment.

This basic proposition was, in itself, independent of the 'method of expectations' and was not necessarily confined to the short period. It was, however, in direct conflict with the dominant theory of distribution on its two main fronts—the doctrine that competitive wages gravitate towards a level where the demand for labour is equal to its supply, and the symmetrical notion that the interest rate equilibrates the demand and supply of savings, i.e. the demand and supply of capital in its free form.[32] Owing to his notion of the 'propensity to consume', Keynes succeeded in narrowing the ground of this conflict down to the rate of interest: and it was there, in the critique of the orthodox theory of interest, that 'expectations' played an essential role in the *General Theory*, through liquidity preference and the instability of the 'marginal efficiency of capital'.

This distinction between the constructive core in the ideas of the *General Theory*, free from the method of expectations, and the mainly negative, critical

---

[32] The doctrine symmetrical with that of wages equalizing demand and supply of labour is more strictly what we find, when, for example, Marshall writes: 'interest, being the price paid for the use of capital in any market, tends towards an equilibrium level such that the *aggregate demand for capital* in that market, at that rate of interest, is equal to the *aggregate stock forthcoming* there at that rate' (Marshall, [1920] 1949, VI, ii, 4, p. 443, our italics). Keynes (1936, pp. 175–6, 186–7) quotes this passage and interprets it as *in fact* saying that 'the rate of interest necessarily comes to rest under the play of market forces at the point where the *amount of investment* at that rate of interest is equal to the *amount of saving* at that rate' (p. 175). In effect, what form can an 'aggregate demand for capital' and a 'stock [of it] forthcoming' ever take for the interplay of these two factors to determine the rate of interest—if not that of a sequence over time of demands and supplies of saving in which capital assumes its free form? It was in fact through this sequence over time that the rate of interest was understood to gravitate about the equilibrium level Marshall writes of while, at the same time, the wage gravitated towards its long-period (full-employment) level. Cf., e.g. Marshall ([1920] 1949, VI, vi, 6, p. 492).

part centred on the rate of interest, is thrown into relief in these passages written by Keynes (1937, pp. 250–2, our italics) one year after his book:

> the initial novelty [of the ideas in the *General Theory*] lies in my maintaining that it is not the rate of interest, but the level of incomes which ensures equality between saving and investment. The arguments which lead up to this initial conclusion are *independent* of my subsequent theory of the rate of interest, and in fact I reached it before I had reached the latter theory. But the result of it was to leave the rate of interest in the air.

And, after mentioning an initial approach in terms of a rate of interest 'determined in some sense by productivity', he continues:

> It was only when this line of approach [failed] that I hit on what I now think to be the true explanation. … It would be true to say that [the liquidity-preference theory] does not carry us very far. But it gives us firm and intelligible ground from which to proceed.

Or again, two pages later:

> To speak of the 'Liquidity-preference Theory' of the Rate of Interest is, indeed, to dignify it too much. … I am simply stating what it is, the *significant theories on the subject being subsequent* (our italics).

These passages are interesting in more than one respect. They stress the independence of the 'initial novelty' in the *General Theory* from the theory of interest advanced there. They also imply that the main role of the latter was to provide an alternative to the orthodox doctrine of interest as the equilibrator of saving and investment. And, above all, they indicate that Keynes tended to regard his 'liquidity preference', with its reliance on expectations, as something 'which does not carry us very far', a provisional basis 'from which to proceed'.

It might then appear that expectations, and even the confinement to the short period of an analysis which Keynes thought had implications going far beyond it, had the main role of providing him with a provisional way out of the conflict between his 'initial novelty' and the dominant theory of distribution. The task of fully facing the conflict—i.e. of pursuing the critique of that theory further, and developing 'the significant theories on the subject'—was to be 'subsequent'.

Looking at Keynes' work in this perspective, it may also be appreciated how the deficiencies of the idea of a substitutability between capital and labour which have since emerged with reswitching and reverse capital deepening, may be relevant to accomplishing the negative part of that task. On the substitutability between labour and capital must in fact rest ultimately—with the demand and supply theory of distribution of which it is a part[33]—any long-run role of the interest rate in adjusting investment to the capacity to save.

---

[33] Cf. above, n. 31. We may here consider Keynes' (1933) interpretation of the controversy between Ricardo and Malthus about the possibility of a 'general glut of commodities', and the consequent assimilation of Ricardo to later theorists with respect to the theory of the rate of interest (Keynes, 1936, p. 32 and *passim*). Keynes' interpretation—while correct in pointing out the similarity between the *question* raised by Malthus against Ricardo and the one Keynes' was raising against his contemporaries—becomes misleading when it also proceeds to suggest a similarity in the *analysis* of such a question. As has been frequently pointed out in the meantime

If this is so, the *General Theory* does not seem to offer real ground for the contemporary attempt to rework traditional theory in terms of short-period equilibria: though the use of expectations and the short period made in that book may have favoured a climate of professional opinion more ready to accept, or overlook, the peculiar difficulties entailed by a shift of the theory of value to a short-period basis.

This brings us to a few brief comments on Professor Robinson's position on method which we mentioned in Sect. 1. The upshot of her analysis of accumulation lies in the rejection of any general tendency of the economic system to the full employment of labour, in the long run no less than in the Keynesian short period.[34] Her analysis thus clearly implies the impossibility of studying long-run changes by comparing *equilibria of demand and supply*, characterized, as such, by the full employment of labour. It does not however necessarily imply the impossibility of studying changes by comparing *long-period positions* of the economic system. 'Long-period' positions, as we can see in Ricardo,[35] do not as such imply full employment of labour. And Professor Robinson herself seems in fact often to rely on the method of long-period positions in her analysis of changes,[36] as is shown by the presence there of the method's central feature: the general rate of profits.

(Meek, 1950–1951, p. 156n.; Schumpeter, 1954, p. 641; Robbins, 1958, p. 248; Corry, 1959), both Malthus and Ricardo always took it *as a fact* that any saving would be invested, i.e. used to employ 'productive labourers' (see Malthus, 1836, pp. 322–30); no question could therefore arise between Malthus and Ricardo about interest being the factor which adjusts investment to saving. Ricardo's opinion on the impossibility of general gluts seems thus to have been due to a failure to distinguish between decisions to save and decisions to invest, and not to a theory of the rate of interest similar to that of Keynes' contemporaries.

It may indeed be suggested that Ricardo's theory of distribution and value was 'open' with respect to the possibility of deficiencies of aggregate effective demand. Because of the absence of the idea of a 'substitutability' between labour and capital, his theory did not provide premises for a tendency of investment to adapt to the full-capacity saving. At the same time the theory did not rely on such a tendency for its validity: Ricardo's determination of the wage was compatible with unemployment of labour and this had already been allowed for in his long-period positions of the economy (cf. Garegnani, 1970, p. 427 [this volume, Part II, p. 173]). Finally, the separation between determination of value and determination of outputs, characteristic of this theory, provided a setting in which the effect of aggregate effective demand on output and employment could be most conveniently studied. (For a fuller discussion of both Ricardo's position with respect to 'general gluts', and Keynes's interpretation of it, cf. Garegnani, 1964, pp. 599–605 [Engl. ver. 'Notes on Consumption, Investment and Effective Demand: I', this volume, Part IV, pp. 390–4]).

[34] Cf. her distinction between 'unemployment' and 'non-employment' of labour (Robinson, 1962, p. 54).

[35] Cf. above n. 33.

[36] See, for example, her comparison between the value in terms of consumption goods of a given piece of capital equipment as it is before, and after, a rise in the real wage due to accumulation (1956, p. 143-4).

What restricts Professor Robinson's use of this method and at the same time prevents it from emerging clearly has to be traced back to the arguments leading to her denial of a tendency to the full employment of labour. These arguments seem to be ultimately reducible to those same factors of 'uncertainty' and 'expectations' which Keynes had used for his critique of the orthodox theory of interest.[37] Given the specificity of physical capital to certain industries and methods of production (i.e. its 'non-malleability'), uncertainty and incorrect expectations would prevent investment from gravitating around the level, and the physical composition, compatible with equilibrium and its preservation over time. Accordingly, the relevance of the notion of equilibrium to the study of the actual behaviour of the economy and, in particular, to the study of capital accumulation is drastically denied. But it is a peculiarity of this line of argument that while the gravitation to equilibrium is denied, the traditional notion of demand and supply forces is not openly disputed. Consequently, equilibrium as a potential centre of gravitation is, so to speak, still there to be reached: in Professor Robinson's view it *would* be reached if uncertainty and incorrect expectations were absent, or made innocuous by a sufficient 'malleability' of capital.[38]

The persistence, in this particular sense, of the traditional notion of a demand-and-supply equilibrium[39] provides, we submit, the main explanation of Professor Robinson's position regarding the impossibility to study changes by means of comparisons. The positions to be compared (which can only be conceived of as 'centres' of gravitation of the economy) are implicitly identified with the traditional equilibria still seen as *the* (potential) centres of gravitation, and thus

[37] Cf. for example the passage: 'what mechanism … keeps accumulation going at the right rate? The argument of the *General Theory*, which shows that there is no such mechanism in a private-enterprise economy, cannot be true at each moment of time and yet untrue in the long run' (Robinson, 1962, p. 14; cf. also 1956, p. 180). As for the key role attributed to expectations and lack of foresight, cf. Robinson (1962, p. 133).

[38] Cf. for example Robinson (1975a, p. vii), where it is stated that if capital is assumed to be malleable 'putty', then 'there is no role for expectations, because equilibrium is instantly restored after any change. … Say's law is restored and household saving governs industrial investment. Full employment of the available labour force is always provided.' Cf. also the following passage, in Robinson (1974, p. 4): 'In the context of accumulation, "putty" is a way of getting rid of differences between the future and the past'.

[39] Until recently Professor Robinson (1962, pp. 31, 132–4) did not dispute the main basis of the traditional theory of distribution: the notion of a technical substitutability between capital and labour. She has, however, since abandoned her former view that 'at any moment there is a range of possible techniques, co-existing in time in the form of blueprints, among which choices are made …' (Robinson, 1975a, pp. ix–x). The notion of a potential equilibrium which lack of foresight (or the 'non-malleability' of capital) prevents the economy from achieving seems, however, to persist (e.g. 1975b, p. 36; 1974, p. 3), although, once technical substitution is denied, it is difficult to see which are the forces acting on the demand side of the 'equilibrium' in the market for factors (the indirect substitution between factors deriving from substitution between consumer goods plays no prominent role in Professor Robinson's analysis). When, in recent works, equilibrium is exemplified by constructs such as 'putty-capital', alternative techniques are in fact admitted (Robinson, 1974, p. 9).

rejected. This leads to ignoring at this methodological level the possibility of 'long-period positions', which, as exemplified in the classical economists, may be determined by forces altogether different from the demand and supply of marginal theory.

References

Böhm-Bawerk, E. (1891). *Positive theory of capital.* Macmillan.

Corry, B. A. (1959). Malthus and Keynes. *Economic Journal,* 69(276), 717–724.

Debreu, G. (1959). *Theory of value.* Yale University Press.

Garegnani, P. (1960), *Il capitale nelle teorie della distribuzione,* Milano: Giuffrè.

Garegnani, P. (1964–1965), 'Note su consumi, investimenti e domanda effettiva' , Pts. I and II, *Economia Internazionale*, XVII(4), pp. 591–631 and XVIII(4), pp. 575–617 [Engl. ver. 'Notes on consumption, investment and effective demand', I and II, this volume, Part IV].

Garegnani, P. (1970). Heterogeneous capital, the production function and the theory of distribution. *Review of Economic Studies,* 37(3), 407–436.

Hicks, J. R. ([1932] 1963]). *The theory of wages* (2nd ed.), London: Macmillan.

Hicks, J. R. (1935). Wages and interest: The dynamic problem. *Economic Journal*, 45(179), as rpt. in Hicks (1932), pp. 268–85.

Hicks, J. R. (1936). Mr. Keynes' theory of employment. *Economic Journal,* 46(182), 238–253.

Hicks, J. R. ([1939] 1946). *Value and capital* (2nd ed.). Clarendon Press.

Hicks, J. R. (1963). Commentary, in Hicks ([1932] 1963), Sect. III, 305–84.

Hicks, J. R. (1965). *Capital and growth.* Clarendon Press.

Keynes, J. M. (1933). Thomas Robert Malthus: the first of the Cambridge economists. In *Essays in biography*, 2nd ed.. Hart-Davis, 1951, pp. 81–124.

Keynes, J. M. (1936). *The general theory of employment, interest and money*. Macmillan.

Keynes, J. M. (1937). Alternative theories of the rate of interest. *Economic Journal,* 47(186), 241–252.

Malthus, T. R. (1836). *Principles of political economy* (2nd ed.). Pickering.

Marshall, A. ([1920] 1949). *Principles of economics* (8th ed.), Macmillan: London (reprinted and reset 1949).

Meek, R. L. (1950–1951). Thomas Joplin and the theory of interest. *Review of Economic Studies,* 18(3), pp. 154–63.

Nuti, D. M. (1976). On the rates of return on investment. In M. Brown, K. Sato, & P. Zarembka (eds), *Essays in Modern Capital Theory*. North-Holland, pp. 47–69 (rpt. from *Kyklos*, 27(2), 1974, pp. 346–69).

Ricardo, D. ([1821] 1951). *On the principles of political economy and taxation.* In *The works and correspondence of David Ricardo*, Sraffa ed., Vol. I. Cambridge University Press.

Robbins, L. (1930). On a certain ambiguity in the conception of stationary equilibrium. *Economic Journal,* 40(158), 194–214.

Robbins, L. (1958). *Robert Torrens and the evolution of classical economics*. Macmillan.

Robinson, J. V. (1956). *The accumulation of capital.* Macmillan.

Robinson, J. V. (1962). *Essays in the theory of economic growth.* St. Martin's Press.

Robinson, J. V. (1974). *History versus equilibrium.* Thames Polytechnic.

Robinson, J. V. (1975a). Introduction. In *Collected economic papers*, Vol. II, 2nd ed. Basil Blackwell.

Robinson, J. V. (1975). The unimportance of reswitching. *Quarterly Journal of Economics,* 89(1), 32–39.

Samuelson, P. A. (1975). Steady state and transient relations: a reply on reswitching. *Quarterly Journal of Economics,* 89(1), 40–47.
Schumpeter, J. A. (1954). *History of economic analysis*. Oxford University Press.
Shove, G. F. (1933). Review of *The theory of wages* by J. R. Hicks, *Economic Journal,* 43(71), as rpt. in Hicks (1932), pp. 249–67.
Smith, A. ([1776] 1910). *The wealth of nations*, Vol. I. Dent & Sons.
Walras, L. (1954). *Elements of pure economics*, 4th def. ed., Jaffé's Engl. ed.. George Allen and Unwin.
Wicksell, K. (1934). *Lectures on political economy*, Vol. I. Routledge & Kegan Paul.
Wicksell, K. (1954). *Value, capital and rent*. George Allen & Unwin.

Savings, Investment and Capital in a System of General Intertemporal Equilibrium*†

1. Introduction

1. The criticism of the neoclassical theory based on the inconsistency of the concept of a 'quantity of capital' has been met from the orthodox side essentially with the claim that contemporary reformulations of the theory do not rely on any such

---

* Previously published with Routledge in *Sraffa and Modern Economics*, ed. by R. Ciccone, C. Gehrke and G. Mongiovi, Vol. I, 2011. All necessary permissions acquired.
[*Editor's note*: Pierangelo Garegnani did not have the time to see the publication of the 2011 book just mentioned, nor did he have the opportunity to follow its preparation, and in the plan of the present collection he included this essay as published in 2003 (Garegnani, 2003). Although the 2011 book took up the essay as it was in the 2003 edition, in that republication it was possible to correct various material errors (largely due to the extensive occurrence of symbols and algebraic relations). For the present publication we have therefore chosen to use the 2011 edition of the essay, which on the occasion has also been cleared of residual misprints still present in the latter. Thanks are due to Dr. Daria Pignalosa for her precious assistance in the editing of the essay.]

† The present chapter reproduces Garegnani (2003), which in turn was a revised version of Garegnani (2000). The revision has entailed the addition of an Appendix II and the shift to an Appendix I of the material previously in Section 4. I thank for useful comments the participants at several seminars held in Italy and elsewhere, where the ideas contained in this chapter have been discussed since 1992. Thanks are due in particular to Profs. R. Ciccone, J. L. Eatwell, J. Geanakoplos, G. Impicciatore, H. D. Kurz, F. Petri, B. Schefold, F. Serrano, D. Tosato and Dr. F. Ravagnani. Special thanks are owed to Dr. M. Tucci and Prof. M. Angrisani for help on the mathematical parts of the chapter (see Dr. Tucci's Mathematical Note at the end of the chapter). I am grateful to Luisa Milanese for her assistance through the numerous versions of this chapter.

P. Garegnani, *Capital Theory, the Surplus Approach, and Effective Demand*,
Springer Studies in the History of Economic Thought,
https://doi.org/10.1007/978-3-031-23643-3_5

concept.[1] The present chapter is intended to show that the claim is unfounded and that the deficiencies of the concept undermine the reformulations no less than they do the traditional versions.[2]

In Sect. 2 we shall introduce for this purpose the very simple model of intertemporal equilibrium which Hahn put forward in 1982 to counter what he took to be the 'neo-Ricardian' critique. This model will allow us to bring out the decisions to save and to invest of any 'year' which are implied in an intertemporal general equilibrium (GE).[3] In Sect. 3 we shall then define what can be described

---

[1] For example, that is the basic contention in Prof. Hahn's (1982) article on the 'neo-Ricardians' (see Appendix II at the end of the chapter). See also 'equilibrium theory (say of an intertemporal equilibrium) […] does not need aggregate notions like 'capital'' (Bliss, 1975: 117n). Similarly, Prof. Samuelson had written earlier:

> Repeatedly in writings and lectures I have insisted that capital theory can be rigorously developed without using any Clark-like concept of aggregate "capital", instead relying upon a complete analysis of a great variety of heterogeneous physical capital goods and processes through time.
>
> (Samuelson, 1962: 193)

The claim seems to have been widely accepted also from the critically inclined side of the controversy (see e.g. Currie and Steedman, 1990).

[2] The 'traditional' version of neoclassical theory is here understood to be that which has dominated neoclassical pure theory until comparatively recent decades, and is characterised by equilibria with the adjusted physical composition of the capital endowment imposed by the condition of a uniform *effective* rate of return on the supply prices of the capital goods (but see n. 8 below on today's frequent confusion between this concept of equilibrium and the quite different notion of a stationary or steady state). That equilibrium was however inconsistent with expressing as a vector of capital goods its given capital endowment (cf. Appendix II, para. (iv) below), and was in fact accompanied by a treatment of it as a single 'quantity of capital', which could change its 'form', so as to allow for the rentals of the several capital goods to come into line with the above uniform rate (e.g. Hicks, 1932: 20). Walras had been the outstanding exception in relying on a vector of capital goods but, sharing as he did that traditional notion of equilibrium, his treatment of capital was simply inconsistent. A return to Walras's conception of the capital endowment as a physical vector, accompanied however by the abandonment of the traditional notion of equilibrium, occurred when, with Hicks (1939), the impossibility of consistently conceiving capital as a single magnitude began to be in fact admitted. That return characterises what we indicated above as the 'contemporary' versions of neoclassical theory.

The italicised word 'effective' by which we qualified the uniform rate of return was meant, on the other hand, to take care of the fact that the definition of that uniform rate will entail a non-uniformity of the own commodity rates of interest as soon as changes in relative prices over time are considered, as happens in the 'contemporary' versions of the theory. In the capital controversies, that inequality of own rates of interest, due to price changes, has indeed been often confused with the inequality of effective rates on the supply prices of the capital goods, due instead to the unadjusted physical composition of the capital endowment pertaining to Walrasian theory. The confusion, which has contributed considerably to the opacity of the capital controversies, is discussed in Appendix II below, with particular respect to the form it took in Hahn (1982).

[3] We shall here be exclusively concerned with intertemporal equilibria based on complete 'futures' markets and leave aside 'temporary equilibria'. It should, however, be evident that if the 'quantity of capital' underlies the savings-investment decisions of intertemporal equilibria, that quantity will not be any less entailed in those of a 'temporary equilibrium'.

as the 'general-equilibrium saving-supply schedule' and the 'general-equilibrium investment-demand schedule' for such a 'year'. The detailed determination of those schedules—which may be left aside at a first reading—has been postponed to Appendix I and to the Mathematical Note attached to the chapter. Sect. 4 will examine the general information which the schedules provide about the behaviour of the system, while Sect. 5 will deal with the effects on investment demand of changes in techniques and in consumption outputs as intertemporal prices change.

The above will enable us to approach in the final section the question of how a 'quantity of capital' enters intertemporal equilibrium. That will involve pointing out first how misleading can the idea be that the adjustments in intertemporal consumptions (i.e. in decisions to save and invest) raise no more problems than adjustments in contemporary consumption do.[4] Whereas the latter imply a shift of resources between the respective *contemporary* productions and can be activated *directly* by the disequilibrium prices, the analogous disequilibrium in intertemporal prices (own rates of interest), due, for example, to excess savings, can only adjust the respective intertemporal productions *indirectly*, through the intermediate link of an incentive given to entrepreneurs to change methods of production and/or relative consumption outputs, so as to increase the 'amount of means of production' relative to labour and other primary factors employed in the economy in that year. The corresponding additional investment is indeed what should, on the one hand, absorb in the production of the capital goods, the resources of time $(t-1)$ set free by the additional savings of t and, on the other, increase the productivity of primary factors in $(t+1)$, $(t+2)$, etc. to provide for the future increased consumption which the savers have planned. It will then be seen how the impossibility of measuring that 'amount of means of production' independently of distribution entails that no such 'increase' in means of production needs to follow from the competitive fall of the prices of commodities of early, relative to those of later dates (fall of the respective own rates of interest) caused by excess savings. The conclusion will thus be that treating under the same heading intertemporal and contemporary consumptions can obscure, but not do away with the differences between the two cases—the "quantity of capital" re-emerging essentially unchanged in its relevance, and in its deficiencies, for the determination of the equilibria. Indeed, in proportion to their value, heterogeneous capital goods are for savers perfectly substitutable means of transferring purchasing power over time, so that savers' decisions about capital goods will refer to that 'quantity',[5] which will accordingly have to be implicitly or explicitly present in the system like that

[4] Cf. e.g. the view that when it is recognised that in any discussion of savings and investment ('intertemporal allocation'), the proper variables are 'today's prices for future goods' there is 'a perfectly consistent story that does not look any different from the story about choosing commodities today' (Arrow, 1989: 155).

[5] Bliss has rightly claimed that 'capital cries out to be aggregated' (1975: 8). He does not however seem to have uncovered the reason of that 'cry': the perfect substitutability of capital goods for savers.

of any other good on which individuals exert their demand and supply decisions. Appendix II completes the chapter by examining some flaws in the mathematical argument Professor Hahn has conducted in his 1982 article. Those flaws will allow bringing out some misunderstandings which appear to have seriously hindered communication between the two sides in the course of the capital controversies.

Our analysis of general equilibrium will be conducted by analytical instruments, other than excess demands generated by treating *all* prices as independent variables and used since Hicks (1939). As indicated, we shall use 'general-equilibrium demands and supplies' of particular commodities or factors, assuming that all markets other than the specific ones on which we focus our attention are in equilibrium.[6] An equilibrium in the particular market considered will then imply an equilibrium of the whole system. The advantage of these instruments is the possibility they offer to trace the effects of peculiarities of that market on the general equilibrium and its properties. Thus we shall here centre on those commodity markets which constitute the savings-investment market, and study the effects of the phenomenon of 'reverse capital deepening' which directly affects such markets. The reader is thus asked for some effort in entering a less familiar method of analysis, which however, we hope, may turn out to allow for some novel results and for a better economic grasp of key phenomena affecting a general intertemporal equilibrium. In particular, the reader should try to take these unfamiliar instruments on their logic, and resist the temptation to translate them too quickly into the language with which he is more familiar.

2. Decisions to Save and Invest in a System of Intertemporal General Equilibrium

2. To have a first, bird's eye view of the ground we shall travel, it might be useful briefly to focus our attention back on the traditional versions of the theory.

We need to consider the seeming contradiction between the varying physical capital underlying the demand function and that underlying the supply function for capital,[7] the single 'factor' characterising those versions.[8] For the sake of a definite

[6] Cf. para. 9 for consistency with the aggregate of budget equations ('Walras's law').

[7] For these general-equilibrium demand and supply functions of 'capital' in traditional neoclassical theory, cf. Garegnani (1970: 425 [this volume, Part II, pp. 170–1]). To develop analogous concepts applicable to intertemporal equilibria will, as we said, be a main aim of the present chapter.

[8] Cf. above, n. 2. In the course of the capital controversies, the 'traditional' concept of equilibrium, in which the capital endowment is a *given*, has often been identified with the altogether different concept of a 'stationary' or 'steady state' of the economy where it is instead an *unknown*. The confusion has been favoured by the fact that a price constancy is today generally explained in terms of 'steady states'. However, the traditional price constancy was a *direct assumption*, founded only on the *persistence* attributable to those equilibria—a result largely of the

example we may refer to Wicksell's *Lectures* (1934: 204–205) where a 'quantity of capital' demanded, expressed as a value in terms of consumption goods, is equalised to the economy's endowment of it.

The seeming contradiction lies in the fact that, whereas in the demand schedule the physical capital which the quantity *K demanded* at each interest rate should express is that corresponding to the techniques and outputs most profitable at such a rate and changes with it, the physical capital making up the *supply*, or endowment of *K* is the stock in existence in the economy and will of course generally differ physically from the unknown one of the equilibrium to be determined. Thus, while in equilibrium 'quantity' demanded and supplied of 'capital' are equal, the two apparently refer to altogether different aggregates of capital goods.

However, clearly, this contradiction is only apparent: what is in fact meant in the supply schedule of 'capital' is that the physical form of the stock appropriate to the equilibrium position will be assumed by the existing stock *over a period of time* as, each 'year', a part of the capital goods in existence has to be replaced and a corresponding proportion of the labour force is set free to be re-equipped by investing the gross savings of the year.[9]

The implications of this for us here are important. The demand and supply schedules for 'capital' (the fund) envisaged in Wicksell and the other traditional writers for their equilibria, were in fact intended to analyse forces supposed to operate *through* the demand for gross investment, and the supply for gross savings (the flows). The attention was concentrated on the *fund* (capital) rather than the *flow* (savings-investment) concepts, in order to analyse that key case of substitution of factors in a purer form, undisturbed by the monetary and other phenomena which would have interfered when dealing with a savings-investment market. Now, once that is made clear, it should also be clear that all the phenomena traditionally treated by means of the 'quantity of capital', and therefore the 'quantity of capital' itself, cannot be absent in the new intertemporal versions of the theory, where each 'year' will of course entail investment and savings.[10]

---

assumption of an adjusted physical composition of the capital endowment. That assumption and the persistence it attributed to the equilibrium had the advantage of cutting through the difficulties which the dating of equilibrium variables entails: from the arbitrariness of the initial instant, to that of the final horizon, or to the meaning of a stability for such dated equilibria.

The assumption had however the decisive disadvantage that, in neoclassical theory, adjusted physical composition of capital and uniform effective rate of return on the supply prices of capital goods entailed conceiving the capital endowment as a single magnitude (n. 2 above).

[9] Cf. the frequent use among those authors of expressions like 'free' or 'fluid' or 'floating' capital, as opposed to 'invested' or 'fixed' or 'sunk' capital e.g. Jevons ([1871] 1957: 242–244), Marshall (1920: 62, 341), Wicksell (1954: 156; 1934: 145, 234; 1935: 192).

[10] Indeed, under our present assumptions of circulating capital only, and of yearly production cycles, the demand for gross investment and the supply of gross savings for the year would coincide with the demand for, and supply of, 'capital' of the traditional theories (for a more detailed examination of the connection between the two notions, see Garegnani, (1978): 352 [this volume, Part IV, pp. 407–8]). We may take this occasion to note how the relationship between demand for

Our task now will therefore be, first of all, to render explicit the savings supply and investment demand which pertain to each 'year' in the equations of general intertemporal equilibrium: this will be done in this section, leaving for the next the presentation of the method we shall use for analysing their changes as prices vary in the intertemporal system.

3. A very simple model will suffice for that purpose. Assume an economy with two goods only, a and b, each being both a consumption and a (circulating) capital good. The economy lasts two 'years' in all, $t = 0$ and $t = 1$, indicated by their initial moments 0 and 1. Production therefore occurs in a single cycle for $t = 0$, with all outputs becoming available at the end of that 'year' (a second production cycle in $t = 1$ would make no sense, because it is completed when the economy ceases to exist). As usual, all markets occur at 'moment' zero, so that the prices P_{a1} and P_{b1} of commodities a_1 and b_1 available for the year $t = 1$ are discounted to moment zero, when they are quoted together with the prices P_{a0} and P_{b0} of the spot commodities a_0 and b_0, and with the wage W.

We may at first suppose that one method only is known for producing each of the two commodities (this assumption will be abandoned in Sect. 5); l_a, a_a, b_a and l_b, a_b, b_b are the corresponding production coefficients, which for simplicity we shall assume to be all strictly positive. The methods are of course assumed to be 'viable', i.e. capable of producing a surplus over the mere replacement of the means of production.

We shall then have the following equilibrium relations:

$$\begin{cases} P_{a1} = l_a W + a_a P_{a0} + b_a P_{b0} \\ P_{b1} = l_b W + a_b P_{a0} + b_b P_{b0} \end{cases} \quad (1e)$$

$$P_{b1} = 1 \quad (2e)$$

$$\begin{cases} A_0 \geq D_{a0} + (a_a A_1 + a_b B_1), \text{ if sign} > \text{applies, } P_{a0} = 0 \\ B_0 \geq D_{b0} + (b_a A_1 + b_b B_1), \text{if sign } > \text{applies, } P_{b0} = 0 \\ L \geq L_a A_1 + L_b B_1, \text{if sign} > \text{applies, } W = 0 \quad (3e) \\ A_1 = D_{a1} \\ B_1 = D_{b1} \end{cases} \quad (E)$$

investment and demand for 'capital' has often been obtained by referring to the demand for capital at a lower rate of interest, and by then spreading the 'net investment' required in order to bring the capital stock to that level, over some given time period of adjustment. However, such a procedure either reflects a turnover period of aggregate capital, in which case our argument provides a foundation for it, or is arbitrary, as it overlooks the fact that even under constant technical conditions, capital accumulation generally entails changing most kinds of capital goods and not adding new capital goods to those in existence. Capital accumulation can only be generally conceived as one process with the replacement of the existing physical capital.

In system (E), Eqs. (1e) are the usual competitive price relations for the products a_1 and b_1,[11] while Eq. (2e) chooses b_1 as the numéraire. The first two relations (3e), on the other hand, regard the supply of commodities a_0 and b_0, provided by endowments A_0 and B_0, and the demand for them, given by consumptions D_{a0} and D_{b0}, plus investment $(a_aA_1 + a_bB_1)$ and $(b_aA_1 + b_bB_1)$, respectively; the third relation regards the demand and supply of labour, while the remaining two express the utilisation of the two outputs A_1 and B_1 for (only) the consumptions D_{a1}, D_{b1}.

System (E) thus has eight relations, only seven of which are independent, with seven unknowns: i.e. the four prices, the wage and the two outputs A_1 and B_1. Beyond the first test of consistency given by these numbers, the enquiry into the existence and character of the solutions of (E) will be part of the analysis we intend to conduct by means of the above-mentioned general-equilibrium savings-supply and investment-demand schedules (see system (F) para. 7).

It may now be important to observe first that we have here simplified the system by ignoring the possibility of storing the two goods between $t = 0$ and $t = 1$, thus 'transforming' a_0 into a_1, and b_0 into b_1—a simplification which does not affect the limited conclusions aimed at here, but the implications of which will be recalled below when necessary.[12] It is this simplification which justifies the

---

[11] It may be interesting to notice here the form which these price relations assume with undiscounted prices (indicated by the small letters)

$$p_{a1} = l_a w + (a_a p_{a0} + b_a p_{b0})(1 + r_b)$$
$$p_{b1} = l_b w + (a_b p_{a0} + b_b p_{b0})(1 + r_b),$$

similar to that of the traditional price equations, except of course for the different prices applied to the same good according as it appears as input or as output; for the connected dependence of the level of the uniform effective rate of profit upon the chosen numéraire cf. n. 2 above and passim (for the relation between these undiscounted prices and the discounted ones cf. below, para. 21, n. 47).

[12] It may thus be interesting to note that, had we considered the possibility of storage, system (E) would have needed to be modified by replacing the last two equations in (3e) with the following relations:

$$\begin{cases} D_{a1} = A_1 + T_i(1 - \alpha_a) \\ D_{b1} = B_1 + T_i(1 - \alpha_b) \end{cases} \tag{3e'}$$

where T_i is the quantity of commodity i stored ($i = a_0, b_0$).

Further, Eqs. (1e) in (E) would have to be modified by introducing an inequality sign

$$P_{i1} \leq l_i W + a_i P_{i0} + b_i P_{i0}, \tag{1e'}$$

and the following relations would also have to be added

$$P_{i0} \leq P_{i1}(1 - \alpha_i) \tag{1e''}$$

indicating the price P_{i0} low enough to make it convenient to provide the commodity of period $t = 1$ by the storage of that of period $t = 0$, at a cost of storage here assumed to consist of a *physical* wastage $\alpha_i < 1$. Now, the cases will be three, depending on T_i relative to D_{i1}.

assumption that both commodities are produced, and that, therefore, relations (1e) hold with a strict equality sign (cf. also below, Appendix II, para. [iv]).

A second observation may be in order about system (E). The choice of b_1 as numéraire in Eq. (2e) entails that the variables P_{a0} and P_{b0} emerge from (E) as the relative prices P_{a0}/P_{b1} and P_{b0}/P_{b1} which involve commodities of the two different dates, and which we shall accordingly call 'intertemporal relative prices'. We shall distinguish them from 'contemporary relative prices', e.g. P_{a0}/P_{b0}, since we shall find that the properties of the two sets differ in important respects.[13]

4. We can now come to the decisions to save and to invest implied in system (E) for each of the two years' life of the economy. Indeed, some readers might have been surprised by our reference in para. 3 to savings distinguished by year in a context of intertemporal equilibrium—where all contracts are made in an initial 'moment', and therefore all income is received and disposed of in that single 'moment'; and furthermore it will be disposed in consumption only (if 'final' capital is zero). However, reflection shows that *outputs*, including of course capital goods, have to flow out year by year, and accordingly the *incomes* making up the prices of those outputs must also be distinguishable by year, together with their savings component.

The fact that, given the two years' life of the economy, production only makes sense in $t = 0$, entails investment and savings will also only make sense for year $t = 0$. The aggregate decisions to invest I_{a0} of that period are the value of two physical components I_{a0} and I_{b0}, consisting of the parts of the two initial stocks A_0 and B_0 which are used as the means for the production of a_1 and b_1, and have already appeared in the first two relations (3e). We thus have

$$\begin{aligned} I_0 &= (a_a A_1 + a_b B_1) P_{a0} + (b_a A_1 + b_b B_1) P_{b0} \\ &= I_{a0} P_{a0} + I_{b0} P_{b0}. \end{aligned} \tag{4}$$

If $T_i = 0$, the relation (1e′) for commodity i will hold with an equality, and (1e″) generally with an inequality.

If $0 < T_i < D_{i1}$, i.e. the demand for i in $t = 1$ is satisfied by storage only in part and therefore the needs of i in $t = 1$ will be partly satisfied by storage and partly by production, both the respective relations in (1e′) and (1e″) will hold with an equality sign.

If, finally, $T_i = D_{i1}$ relation (1e″) will be satisfied with an equality sign, (1e′) being generally satisfied with an inequality.

Conditions (1e″) will on the other hand allow determining the two new unknowns T_a and T_b.

[13] An example is provided already by relations (1e″) in n. 12 above,which establish a constraint on 'intertemporal' prices which has no substantive correspondent for 'contemporary' prices. We shall also see (point IV in para. 14, and paras. [7] and [12] in Appendix I) that the principle for which the zero price of one commodity in terms of one scarce commodity, entails a zero price in terms of *any other* scarce commodity does not appear to apply to intertemporal prices.

Similarly, gross savings S_0 will be part of the social gross income Y_0[14] of $t = 0$—which, unlike the income Y_1 of $t = 1$, will not be the counterpart of a social gross product, and will consist instead of the initial stocks, A_0 and B_0. Thus S_0 will be expressed as the following difference between the gross income Y_0 and the aggregate consumption G_0 in year $t = 0$:

$$\begin{aligned} S_0 &= Y_0 - G_0 \\ &= (A_0 P_{a0} + B_0 P_{b0}) - (D_{a0} P_{a0} + D_{b0} P_{b0}) \\ &= (A_0 - D_{a0}) P_{a0} + (B_0 - D_{b0}) P_{b0} \\ &= S_{a0} P_{a0} + S_{b0} P_{b0}, \end{aligned} \tag{5}$$

where the physical components of the aggregate saving decisions S_0 are distinguished by S_{a0} and S_{b0} and where the equilibrium magnitudes of system (E) imply $S_{a0} = I_{a0}$, $S_{b0} = I_{b0}$ and therefore $S_0 = I_0$.[15]

As for the year $t = 1$, we shall have

$$\begin{aligned} S_1 &= Y_1 - G_1 \\ &= (LW + S_0) - (D_{a1} P_{a1} + D_{b1} P_{b1}). \end{aligned}$$

where $(LW + S_0)$ is the value of the gross social product from the income side, and where, however, the last two Eqs. (3e) stating that the entire output of $t = 1$ is consumed, entail $I_1 = 0$[16] and $S_1 = 0$.[17]

5. It may now be of interest to note how, in the individual 'wealth equations', relating to the entire lifetime of the economy, the savings of each year disappear (contributing perhaps to the misleading view that the problems raised by savings

---

[14] It should be noted that, contrary to general usage, we need to include in the gross investment, and hence in both 'gross' social product and 'gross' savings, the replacement of circulating means of production (the only means of production of our model).

[15] From the first two Eqs. (3e) we obtain $I_{a0} = A_0 - D_{a0}$, and $I_{b0} = B_0 - D_{b0}$; and since in relations (5) we have $S_{a0} = A_0 - D_{a0}$; $S_{b0} = B_0 - D_{b0}$, we obtain $I_{a0} = S_{a0}$; $I_{b0} = S_{b0}$ and, finally, $I_0 = S_0$. We have here assumed the relevant relations (3e) to be equations. Should the inequality sign apply in any of the two, the corresponding price would be zero and the 'excess savings' in that commodity would not affect the value equality, $I_0 = S_0$.

[16] It may be asked why the income LW is being excluded from Y_0 in Eq. (5) and is included instead in Y_1. However, 'yearly' production cycles, as distinct from continuous production, force us to distinguish between the period in which the participation of resources to production has occurred (in the present case $t = 0$) and the period in which the corresponding income must be supposed to accrue, *if* the equality between the *social income* and value of the *social product* is to be maintained. This does not preclude wages being 'advanced' in $t = 0$, but that would be out of the savings of capitalists in $t = 0$, unlike what we have assumed here in Eq. (5).

[17] The relations we are describing are in the nature of accounting identities and would hold whether the economy is in equilibrium or out of it—whether, more generally, they refer to *realised* savings and investment or, instead, to *decisions* to save and invest under some a priori specified, hypothetical circumstances. The latter is the case in Eqs. (4) and (5), where we have applied those relations to the equilibrium quantities of system (E), just as it will be the case when we shall apply them to the partly different hypothetical circumstances of system (F) of the next paragraph, implying equilibrium in some markets and not in others.

and investments disappear leaving place to a question 'not any different from [...] choosing commodities today').[18]

The equation in question is in fact simply the sum of the *yearly* individual budget equations of the kind just seen, and in that sum the savings on the 'expenditure side' of the budget equation for any year t, reappear on the 'income side' for $(t+1)$, and must therefore cancel out with the latter (the exception being any savings of the final year of the economy which will of course be zero, if terminal capital is to be zero).

Thus, for example, the yearly budget equations of an individual in our two-year economy can be written as follows, where the small letters y, g, s stand for the individual's income, consumption and gross savings for the respective year, and l, a_0, b_0 stand for initial endowments:

$$\begin{cases} (y_0) = a_0 P_{a0} + b_0 P_{b0} = g_0 + s_0 \\ (y_1) = lW + s_0 = g_1 \end{cases} \tag{5a}$$

In summing Eq. (5a), the s_0's cancel out and we are left with

$$(y_0 + y_1) = a_0 P_{a0} + b_0 P_{b0} + lW = g_0 + g_1,$$

where the terms after the first equality sign constitute the 'wealth equation'.[†]

Non-zero gross savings and investments being possible in our model only for $t = 0$, we shall henceforth simplify our notation by dropping the zero deponent from the savings and investment variables.

3. The General-Equilibrium Schedules of Savings-Supply and Investment-Demand

6. Our task is now to bring out how the savings and investment decisions of Eqs. (4) and (5) vary with prices and can accordingly affect the equilibria of the system. This is what will be done here by means of the two constructs mentioned already: 'the general-equilibrium investment-demand schedule' and 'the general-equilibrium savings-supply schedule'.

The two schedules will be obtained from the relations of system (E) by (i) treating one of the two own rates of interest of period $t = 0$, say r_b, as the

---

[18] See the quotation in n. 4 above.

[†] [*Editor's note*: the material error of not subtracting s_0 also from the left-hand side of this equation is in fact irrelevant to the author's conclusion about the equality between the second and third members and its meaning.

independent variable[19]; (ii) waiving the equality between I and S implied in (E).[20] This requires, first of all, the introduction of the definitory equation

$$r_b = \left(\frac{P_{b0}}{P_{b1}}\right) - 1 \tag{6}$$

The release of condition $I = S$ on the other hand, allows for either $S_a \neq I_a$, or $S_b \neq I_b$, or both, and therefore a difference between what we may now call the total demand for a_0 given by $A_0^D = D_{a0} + I_a$ (cf. the R.H.S. of the first of the relations (3e) in para. 3) and its total supply $A_0^S = A_0$, which can also be expressed as $A_0^S = D_{a0} + S_a$ (cf. Equation (5), para. 4)—and similarly for the total demand for, and supply of, b_0.

7. The result is seen in system (F) below where,

1. the two unknowns A_0^D, B_0^D replace the data A_0 and B_0 in the relations (3e) which now, in their form (3f), with an equality sign only define the two total demands;
2. the data A_0, B_0, re-labelled as A_0^S, B_0^S, appear instead in the relation (5f) defining savings;

---

[19]We have referred to two own rates of interest for period $t = 0$. As is well known, when the relative price of the two goods changes from $t = 0$ to $t = 1$, arbitrage will impose a lower nominal interest rate for loans in terms of the good, say a, whose relative value rises from $t = 0$ to $t = 1$, in order to compensate the advantage its lender would otherwise have relative to lenders of b, and so as to realise what is *in effect* a uniform rate of interest. This rate takes then a numerical expression dependent on the numéraire, not unlike what happens for commodity prices (cf. n. 2 above and Appendix I, par [9]).

[20]Cf. ns. 8 and 15 above. The nature of these two constructs can perhaps be more easily grasped when we realise that they follow the simple logical procedure which underlies, in an elementary textbook, the representation of, say, the demand for labour, when the quantity demanded L^D is directly derived from the marginal product of the labour employed with the given supply λ of land, the only other productive factor. At any point along that demand schedule, the following equations will therefore hold:

$$Q = f\left(L^D, \lambda\right);\ w = f_L^D\left(L^D, \lambda\right);\ \rho = f_\lambda\left(L^D, \lambda\right);\ L^S = L$$

The wage w is the independent variable, leaving four unknowns in the four equations, i.e. the corn output Q, the rent rate ρ and the quantities demanded and supplied L^D and L^S of labour, where for simplicity we have supposed the factor supplies L^S and λ to be rigid. At any relevant level of w, equilibrium will hold in the remaining two markets: for corn, where Q is equal to the corn expenditure ($L^D w + \lambda\rho$) from the owners of the two factors, and for land, where the supply λ is fully employed. The two schedules $L^D(w)$ and $L^S = L$ resulting as w varies, will therefore be 'general-equilibrium schedules' in the sense meant in the text: general equilibrium will hold in the labour market, i.e. when either $L^D = L^S$, or $L^D < L^S$ with $w = 0$, or $L^D > L^S$ and the wage is at its maximum for which $\rho = 0$. We may note for future reference how that disequilibrium in a single market—that of labour—is here compatible with the sum of budget equations (Walras's law) because the labour income in the economy is taken to be $L^D w$, i.e. that corresponding to the quantity L^D of labour *demanded*, and not to the endowment L: cf. para. 9 below in the text for the similar problem in the savings-investment market.

and where the unknowns I and S constitute the points of the two schedules corresponding to the given level of the independent variable r_b:

$$
\begin{array}{lr}
\begin{cases} P_{a1} = l_a W + a_a P_{a0} + b_a P_{b0} \\ P_{b1} = l_b W + a_b P_{a0} + b_b P_{b0} \end{cases} & (1f) \\
P_{b1} = 1 & (2f) \\
\begin{cases} A_0^D = D_{a0} + (a_a A_1 + a_b B_1) \\ B_0^D = D_{b0} + (b_a A_1 + b_b B_1) \\ L \geq l_a A_1 + l_b B_1 \text{ if inequality, then } W = 0 \\ D_{a1} = A_1 \\ D_{b1} = B_1 \end{cases} & (3f) \\
I = (a_a A_1 + a_b B_1) P_{a0} + (b_a A_1 + b_b B_1) P_{b0} & (4f) \\
S = \left(A_0^S - D_{a0}\right) P_{a0} + \left(B_0^S - D_{b0}\right) P_{b0} & (5f) \\
r_b = \left(\frac{P_{b0}}{P_{b1}}\right) - 1 & (6f) \\
\frac{A_0^D}{B_0^D} = \frac{A_0^S}{B_0^S} & (7f)
\end{array}
\qquad (F)
$$

All markets are here assumed to be in equilibrium except those of savings and investments, i.e. as we saw, the markets where saved and investible quantities of a_0 and b_0 are traded.[21] System (F) in fact implies equilibrium:

1. in the market for labour (see the respective relation in (3f));
2. in the markets for commodities a_1 and b_1 (see the last two equations in (3f));
3. in the markets of a_0 and b_0 for consumption (see the inclusion of D_{a0} and D_{b0} in Eq. (5f)).

However, if we exclude Eq. (7f) to be presently discussed, system (F) has eleven relations, ten of which are independent, containing eleven unknowns (the five prices, the two outputs A_1, B_1, the two aggregate quantities demanded A_0^D, B_0^D, and, finally, I and S).[22] Were it not for Eq. (7f), system (F) would therefore possess the

---

We may also note how the schedules may clarify the economic rationale of the necessary existence of an equilibrium, once excess supplies of factors are admitted for a zero price of their services. Not only an *excess supply* $L^S > L^D$ permits an equilibrium for $w = 0$, but also an *excess demand* $L^D > L^S$ does so for w at its maximum, since that situation is, in fact, just the same case with land in the place of labour: i.e. excess supply of land with zero rent, when land used can be scaled down to employ no more than the labour supply so any relative position of the schedules entails equilibria. Once excess supply and zero prices are admitted, the existence of solutions can be seen as a rather clear implication of the aggregate of budget equations (and, of course, of the continuity of the functions). Uniqueness, stability and more generally plausibility of the "equilibria" are what the neoclassical demand and supply rested on and the principle of substitution was for.

[21] See below, para. 9 (and n. 20 above), for the 'adjustment in expenditures' which allows the disequilibrium to be confined to the single market of savings and investment.

[22] The changes in methods of production which we might expect to occur along the schedules as r_b varies will be introduced in Sect. 5. It should however be noted that the schedules determined by (F) would already allow for the 'substitutability' between factors arising from consumer choice in $t = 1$.

one degree of freedom which we could expect since, essentially, we replaced with the two new unknowns A_0^D and B_0^D, the single unknown P_{b0} of (E) which becomes a given in (F) in the shape of the given $r_b = P_{b0} - 1$ of Eq. (6f).

Before discussing that degree of freedom, and its closure by means of (7f), we may, however, re-write the Eqs. (3f), (4f) and (5f) in the more transparent form which we shall frequently use in what follows.

$$\begin{cases} A_0^S = D_{a0} + S_a \\ B_0^S = D_{b0} + S_b \\ A_0^D = D_{a0} + I_a \\ B_0^D = D_{b0} + I_b \end{cases} \tag{3f'}$$

$$I = I_a P_{a0} + I_b P_{b0} \tag{4f'}$$

$$S = S_a P_{a0} + S_b P_{b0} \tag{5f'}$$

8. In fact, the economic meaning of the degree of freedom we would have in (F) but for Eq. (7f) is quite simple. We have aggregated all decisions to invest into the single magnitude I, but nothing has been specified about the *physical composition* of the investment flows of schedule I: this is what is done by means of Eq. (7f) which in fact fixes I_a/I_b jointly with D_{a0}/D_{b0} since A_0^D/B_0^D is a weighted average of those two ratios.

That physical composition cannot, however, be specified arbitrarily. Our use of the I and S schedules in order to analyse the properties of system (E) imposes two requirements. The first and stricter requirement is that when $S = I$, the aggregate demands for a_0 and b_0 should also be equal to the respective supplies. And the same correspondence should hold for possible 'extreme' equilibria at the level $r_{b\,min}$ with $S > I$ or with $W = 0$, for $S < I$ (see para. 14 below, points I and IV respectively, and Appendix I). This will in fact be the case when the proportion A_0^D/B_0^D in which the two commodities are there 'demanded' is the same as the proportion A_0^S/B_0^S in which they are supplied, as is imposed by Eq. (7f) (cf. paras. 15–16). The second, less strict, requirement is that the proportion A_0^D/B_0^D should reflect a non-implausible out-of-equilibrium behaviour of the economy. And Eq. (7f) seems to provide a description of an out-of-equilibrium behaviour as plausible, it seems, as any equally general condition (cf. below, paras. 17–18).

9. There remains a rather technical point we need to consider in order to complete our account of system (F). It concerns the consistency of the system with the sum of the individual budget equations underlying it (Walras's identity) and the often supposed impossibility of a disequilibrium confined to a single market, such as we have assumed in (F).[23] However, that impossibility would follow only if the

[23] The fact that the single market for I and S involves in effect the two markets, for a_0 and b_0, is irrelevant here.

individuals could spend for the commodities available in $t = 1$ according to the total income which they would derive from selling exactly the quantities of a_0 and b_0 they wish to sell at the going prices (i.e. A_0^S, B_0^S in the aggregate, if we include in the demand the consumption by owners) and realise the corresponding savings for $t = 0$, but that is just what cannot happen when $S \neq I$. When, on the other hand, the purchasing power for $t = 1$ originating from the savings S_0 is appropriately 'adjusted' to what the going level I would allow them to sell of a_0 and b_0—and this is what we have assumed in (F)—the contradiction disappears and system (F) is consistent.[24]

[24] The question is essentially the same as the one concerning the adjustment in the power to purchase 'corn' in the simple example of general-equilibrium demand for labour in n. 20 above. We implied that adjustment when we attributed an income only to the workers employed L^D. In the present model, let us indicate by D'_{a1}, D'_{b1} the consumption demands in $t = 1$ resulting from the equations of consumer equilibrium on the usual hypothesis that they dispose of the income resulting at the given prices from all the resources they own. Summing the budget equations through consumers and the two 'years', we get, after some simple transformations,

$$(A_0^S - D_{a0})P_{a0} + (B_0^S - D_{b0})P_{b0} + LW = D'_{a1}P_{a1} + D'_{b1}P_{b1} \tag{8a}$$

Clearly the L.H.S. of Eq. (8a) gives both the social income Y'_1, and the value of the purchases the individuals would carry out at $t = 1$, under the stated assumptions of complete sales of A_0^S, B_0^S, besides L. Then using relation (5) of para. 4, we have.

$$Y'_1 = D'_{a1}P_{a1} + D'_{b1}P_{b1} = S + LW \tag{8b}$$

On the other hand, the value Q_1 of the gross social product for $t = 1$, as it results from the system (F) by substituting for prices in accordance with Eqs. (1f), is given by.

$$\begin{aligned} Q_1 & \\ &= A_1P_{a1} + B_1P_{b1} \\ &= A_1(l_aW + a_aP_{a0} + b_aP_{b0}) + B_1(l_bW + a_bP_{a0} + b_bP_{b0}) \\ &= (l_aA_1 + l_bB_1)W + (a_aA_1 + a_bB_1)P_{a0} + (b_aA_1 + b_bB_1)P_{b0} \end{aligned}$$

and using Eq. (4f),

$$Q_1 = (I + LW) \tag{8c}$$

Thus the purchasing power $(S + LW)$ in Eq. (8b) would face commodities of the value $(I + LW)$ in Eq. (8c), and if we had used D'_{a1}, D'_{b1} in the system (F), the system would have been inconsistent. The 'adjustment' of purchases mentioned in the text can, on the other hand, be represented by the following equations, in which we indicate by D_{i1}, as distinct from D'_{i1}, the 'adjusted' purchases in $t = 1$ appearing in our system (F):

$$D_{i1} = D'_{i1}\frac{LW + I}{LW + S} \qquad (i = a, b).$$

It follows that the 'adjusted' aggregate expenditure and income Y_1 in $t = 1$ is now given by.

The 'adjustment' in expenditure we assume here, when compared with the more usual procedure of admitting disequilibrium in at least one further market, has the advantage of being compatible with a constancy in the employment of labour as r_b varies, thus providing a more transparent basis for deducing the shapes of the S and I schedules. It also allows for a simpler and perhaps better than any equally general representation of the out-of-equilibrium behaviour of the system, in the sense just mentioned that households failing to sell part of their A_0^S and B_0^S resources because of excess savings can hardly exert excess demand on the commodities of $t = 1$.[25]

10. Some preliminary observations concerning our method of analysis may in fact be useful at this point. The general-equilibrium nature of the two schedules and condition (7f) entail that any equilibrium in the market they represent is also an equilibrium of the system and that the converse is true (paras. 15–16). The properties of the general equilibrium relevant for its uniqueness and stability, and their dependence in particular on the circumstances of the savings and investment market then become visible in a form not unlike that of a partial equilibrium problem. It is in this way that in Sects. 4–6 the two schedules will render visible a cause of multiple and unstable equilibria which does not appear to have yet been sufficiently analysed in the literature. That cause is the way in which investment changes as intertemporal prices change (see Fig. 1).

Possibilities of non-uniqueness and instability of the equilibria have in fact been in the foreground of current general equilibrium literature. However, those possibilities seem to have been investigated in what we may describe as a mainly

---

$$\begin{aligned} Y_1 &= \sum_i D_{i1} P_{i1} \\ &= \frac{LW + I}{LW + S} \sum_i D_{i1} P_{i1} \\ &= \frac{LW + I}{LW + S} (LW + S) \\ &= LW + I = Q_1 \end{aligned}$$

and consistency has been brought back into the system (F). We may note that, by definition, consumption purchases for $t = 0$ remain unchanged, i.e. $D_{a0} = D'_{a0}$, $D_{b0} = D'_{b0}$, and so does therefore S, the amount of the decisions to save in $t = 0$.

[25] Apparently less plausible is the behaviour assumed in the opposite case of $I > S$, where the purchases for $t = 1$ would have to exceed what is possible with the purchasing power obtained from the full sale of the A_0^S and B_0^S endowments. However, the extra purchasing power implied in our adjustment of expenditures may be taken to express the tendential relative rise of purchasing power available in $t = 1$ because of the excess demand in $t = 0$ and a resulting tendential rise in the prices of commodities a_0 and b_0 (in terms of which savings are effected) *relative* to those of a_1 and b_1.

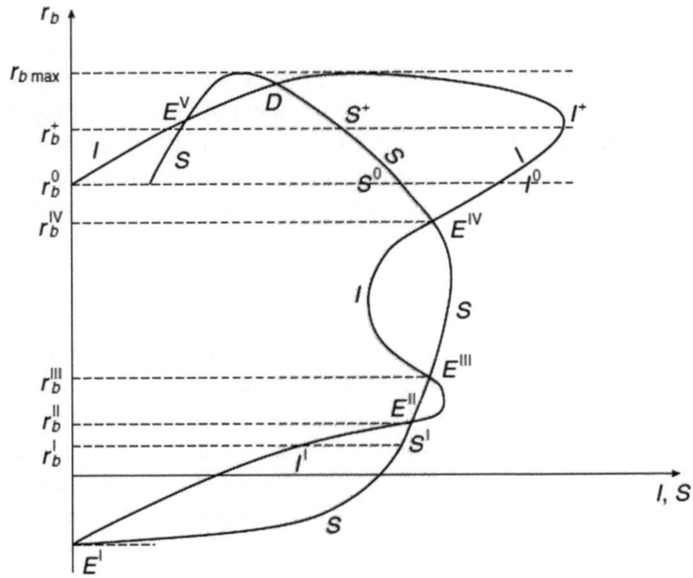

Fig. 1 Possible shape of investment demand *I* and savings supply *S*: points *E* indicate intertemporal general equilibria in the model

negative and economically unspecific way. The attention has been focused, that is, either on the impossibility of establishing uniqueness and stability under the more general premises of the theory, or on some sufficient, rather than necessary conditions for such properties.[26] Similarly, the efforts seem to have been concentrated on systems of pure exchange, or of production without capital—this, despite the fact that the implications of reverse capital deepening and reswitching which had been pointed out for the traditional versions of neoclassical general equilibrium should have alerted scholars to the possible implications of those phenomena for intertemporal theory (cf. para. 2).

Thus, with regard to the *causes* of multiplicity and instability of the equilibria, recent literature does not seem to have added substantially to what, owing to a more simplified, but also better focussed analysis, had been known, since Walras, Marshall or Wicksell,[27] about income effects and their causes. The paradox seems then to be that general conclusions about those properties that are at times presented as drastically negative for neoclassical theory[28] have in effect favoured the

[26] Cf.: 'Unfortunately, necessary conditions are unlikely to be available' (Arrow and Hahn, 1971: 242).

[27] See e.g. Marshall (1920: III, vi, 4: 109–110; V, xiii, 5: 391n; APP. H, 2: 665); Walras (1954: 112–3); Wicksell (1934: 56–63).

[28] See e.g. Kirman (1989).

comparatively comfortable, but unwarranted belief that the difficulties in question all have their origin in income effects—with which the theory has, after all, long managed to co-exist—and thus have had little dissuasive effect on the actual practice of the profession.[29]

11. Our general-equilibrium demand and supply schedules may be seen as part of an attempt to remedy this situation by tackling again such central properties of the equilibria in the way Marshall, Walras or Wicksell approached them, that is by starting from specified economic conditions susceptible of causing the difficulties in order to arrive at their consequences for the equilibrium. This has led to an analysis of production with capital, and to focussing on the savings- investment market—on which reverse capital deepening impinges directly—in order to ascertain how those phenomena can affect the properties of a general intertemporal equilibrium (Fig. 1).

A word of caution must now be added concerning our application of the method of general-equilibrium demand and supply schedules. Just because of its greater specificity, these tools of analysis bring to light questions which, apparently buried in the mathematical formalism previously used, require now[30] definite answers. Where possible, those answers have been attempted here, however provisionally. At other times the questions have been treated by referring to specific, more manageable sub-cases which do not however alter the generality of the *negative results* the paper is concerned with, since the sub-case is part of the general case.[31] It may incidentally be stressed that when sub-cases have been resorted to, they have been specified so as to grant more favourable conditions to the theory. In particular, care has been taken to avoid mixing the cases of non-uniqueness, instability or zero factor prices emerging here, with the altogether different cases which might be due to income effects.

12. Passing now from the method to the content of our argument, the reader may ask why we have introduced the *aggregate* savings and *aggregate* investment of system (F) in order to discuss a system (E) which was in fact formulated independently of any such aggregates. The answer will of course have to come from

---

[29] Thus Hicks could conclude in 1939 about the stability of equilibrium in exchange, and with reference to income effects:

> It cannot indeed be proved a priori that a system of multiple exchange will be necessarily stable. But the conditions of stability are quite easy conditions, so that it is quite reasonable to assume that they will be satisfied in almost any system with which we are likely to be concerned.
>
> (Hicks, 1939: 72)

and he even thought that such a conclusion could be strengthened when introducing production (1939: 104).

[30] See e.g. the distinction between 'intertemporal' and 'contemporary' relative prices in para. 3 above. (For its implications, cf. point V in para. 14 and para. 8 in Appendix I.)

[31] Essentially, the resort to a sub-case has occurred once, namely for the monotonic rising change of P_{a0} as r_b rises (cf. point II in para. 14 below).

what follows in this chapter. However, we have indicated already how the total demands for a_0 and b_0 which we find on the right-hand side of the first two relations in systems (3e), or (3f), are in fact made up of two quite heterogeneous elements each: the consumption demands D_{a0}, D_{b0} (which we assumed to be always satisfied along the I and S schedules) and the investment demands I_a and I_b. Now, the investment demands are ruled by principles that are totally different from those which govern consumption demands: hunger can be satisfied by corn, and not by coal; but desire for future income, the motive of the demand for capital goods from savers, can surely be satisfied by tractors, as well as by looms or any of the thousands of other capital goods, whichever of them offers a higher rate of return. It can here be indifferently satisfied by a_0 or b_0 lent for production. In fact, as we shall see in para. 26, different capital goods are perfect substitutes for the savers.[32]

Now, in view of the different principles thus regulating investment demands as distinct from consumption demands, and in view above all of the perfect substitutability of heterogeneous capital goods for the saver, but of course not of consumption goods for the consumer—it does *prima facie* stand to reason that the separation of the two kinds of demand and, then, the aggregation of the capital goods demanded for investment, might lend transparency to the workings of the system.

13. In para. 8 we mentioned 'stability' among the properties of the equilibrium which might be inquired into by means of our two schedules. That implies that the schedules should be applied to discuss adjustments to the equilibrium. Although only hints of that analysis will be contained in the present chapter (paras. 17–18), we should perhaps clarify what can be meant by 'adjustments' and 'stability' here, in a context of dated equilibria.

In fact, as I have argued elsewhere (1976: 38 [this volume, Part II, pp. 220–1]), an analysis of stability, capable of fulfilling its traditional role of ensuring 'correspondence' between theoretical and observable magnitudes, has to be founded on the possibility of a sufficient repetition of transactions on the basis of approximately unchanged data. If a tendency to equilibrium could be established on that basis, it could also be generally supposed that disequilibrium deviations would tend to compensate each other, letting the equilibrium levels emerge as some average of observable levels, and be capable, therefore, of providing some guidance to reality. Essentially, the question in this respect would be to allow for a time setting in which

> fitful and irregular causes in large measure efface one another's influence; so that ... persistent causes dominate value completely.
>
> (Marshall, 1920: V, iii, 7, 291)

That meaning of the positions of the economy to which theory refers its variables, and the corresponding notion of its stability, appear in fact to have been the

[32] They are not of course perfect substitutes in production.

unanimously accepted basis of economic analysis from Adam Smith, and before, until comparatively recent decades. At those earlier times, however, such a necessary repetition of markets on approximately unchanged data could be grounded in the conception of a normal position of the economy, a sufficient persistency of which was ensured by the uniform rate of return on the supply prices of the capital goods and by the corresponding adjusted composition of the capital endowment—which in neoclassical theory depends on the conception of the capital endowment as a single magnitude.[33] If the abandonment of the corresponding notion of equilibrium (fundamentally different, recall, from that of 'stationary' or 'steady states') was by itself sufficient to undercut *in fact* the previous meaning of an analysis of stability, by imposing data too impermanent to allow for a sufficient repetition of markets, the 'dating' of the equilibria has jettisoned it even in principle by excluding repetition as such.[34] This appears to leave in some obscurity the precise significance of present-day analyses of stability, quite independently of their negative results.

Our present critical purpose seems, however, to exempt us from entering further into the question and allows us to adopt the formal way out generally taken when the concern are still variables determinable by the equations of general equilibrium, and not the essentially indeterminable variables of a path-dependent

---

[33] See above, n. 2.

[34] Thus in *Value and Capital*, 1939, where the new notions of equilibrium and the associated 'dating' of equilibrium variables were used for perhaps the first time in influential Anglo-American work, Hicks felt forced to assume that transactions carried out at non-equilibrium prices would have very little effect on the amounts transacted, so that equilibrium prices could be realised on his 'Mondays' (1939: 127–128: the stability of those equilibria was evidently taken for granted). However, both in that book and in much subsequent work in pure theory, it is not mentioned that the question in the preceding literature was that of a compensation of deviations through repetition, and not that of the price actually hitting its equilibrium level. Thus Bliss (1975) refers to the 'Herculean programme' of constructing 'the complete theory of the behaviour of the economy out-of-equilibrium' necessary, in his view, in order to validate equilibrium 'as something that would be expected to be realised' apparently overlooking that repetition of transactions on unchanged data and not the truly Herculean 'complete theory etc.' had been the question—so long as one could rely on the traditional notion of equilibrium. We get however closer to the basic difficulty, when Bliss continues

> Furthermore, even if equilibrium were to be stable there might not be enough time within the space of a "week" for the prices to adjust to an equilibrium
>
> (Bliss, 1975: 28)

where Bliss sees the importance for the significance of the equilibrium of a sufficient lapse of time under approximately unchanged data. But, then, why not an equilibrium like the traditional one which would last more than a week, without falling in the limited relevance of the "steady state"? Here again (cf. n. 5 above) Bliss does not seem to ask himself the question, clearly relevant for the theory of capital to which he devotes his book (we shall indeed see in the Appendix II, para. viii, the very particular way in which he reconstructs the traditional equilibrium of Wicksell).

equilibrium. This formal way out is, of course, that of 'recontracting', or of 'tâtonnement', as it has come to be named with a misleading reference to Walras.[35] In the modern fictitious theoretical world into which we shall enter by means of that assumption, the repetition of transactions—thus in fact admitted to be essential for an analysis of stability—is supposed to take place in some initial 'moment', or period, before the actual time, measured out by 'dated' equilibria, has rendered such repetition impossible.

14. Though the model is simple, the discussion of system [F] and the determination of the schedules become complex as soon as we wish to go beyond the mere formal demonstration of the existence of solutions of system (F)—for which see the Mathematical Note at the end of the chapter—and we attempt to gain an understanding of their properties and economic meaning. We have accordingly placed that discussion in Appendix I and shall here confine ourselves to listing the conclusions we shall use in the rest of the chapter; references being given to that Appendix for the supporting argument.

I. When we suppose, as is done above, that neither commodity can be stored, the economically meaningful interval of r_b extends from $r_{b\,min} = -1$, for $P_{b0}/P_{b1} = 0$ (Appendix I para. [1]) to a level $r_{b\,max}$, the highest among those for which $W = 0$ (see point IV below).

II. Changes in the intertemporal relative price $r_b = [(P_{b0}/P_{b1}) - 1]$ need not affect in one direction rather than the other total relative demands for the two contemporary commodities a_0 and b_0, i.e. the ratio $(D_{a0} + I_a)/(D_{b0} + I_b)$, and therefore the relative contemporary price P_{a0}/P_{b0} necessary to satisfy Eq. (7f). Making then the further reasonable supposition that such a contemporary relative price will not be much affected by changes in r_b, we assume

[35] Walras introduced re-contracting only in the 4th edition of the *Elements* (1900). In the previous editions, the word *tâtonnement* had covered only the process of repetition of actual transactions, which in his view (confirmed up to the posthumous 5th 'definitive' edition of 1926):

> is perpetually tending towards equilibrium without ever actually attaining it [...] like a lake agitated by the wind, where the water is incessantly seeking its level without ever reaching it.
>
> (Walras, 1954: 380)

Re-contracting with 'bons' (tickets) was introduced in the 4th edition of 1900 and exclusively in order to avoid considering the changes occurring in the capital stocks during the process of gravitation around the equilibrium (1954: 242 and Jaffé's collation note [h] pp. 582–583; Garegnani, 1960). [*Editor's note*: in Garegnani (1960) the place where the analysis comes close, albeit in more general terms, to the issue discussed here is on pp. 116–8. In the author's Ph. D. dissertation *A Problem in the Theory of Distribution from Ricardo to Wicksell*, published in Part I of this volume, which the Italian book was derived from, the corresponding argument is on pp. 70–2.] Thus, it seems, re-contracting was adopted in order to rigorously analyse a *real* repetition of transactions (in which, he thus implied, changes in the capital stocks over the relevant period would not make appreciable difference) and not in order to have a *notional* repetition of transactions when a real one was prevented even in principle by the dating of the equilibria.

that the intertemporal price P_{a0}/P_{b1} moves in the same direction as P_{b0}/P_{b1} and hence r_b in the interval $r_{b\,min} < r_b < r_b^+$ in which $W > 0$. This suffices to ensure a unique solution in an interval $r_{b\,min} < r_b < r_b^0$ where $r_b^0 \leq r_b^+$ is, as we shall see under point IV below, the minimum level for which we find $W = 0$ (Appendix I, paras. [5]-[7]).

III. Two other important consequences follow from that assumption. The first is that the monotonic relation between P_{a0}/P_{b1} and P_{b0}/P_{b1} entails a decreasing relation between W and the intertemporal price P_{b0}/P_{b1} and hence r_b over the whole interval $r_{b\,min} < r_b < r_b^+$, along what we shall call 'the main branch' of the relation between r_b and the unknowns in (F), in particular between r_b and I and S. That 'branch' is of course where, as we saw under point II, we have unique solutions, but only up to r_b^0 and not for $r_b^0 \leq r_b \leq r_b^+$ where a continuum of positions for $W = 0$ will exist (see point IV below). The second important consequence of the monotonic direct relation between the intertemporal prices P_{a0}/P_{b1} and P_{b0}/P_{b1} is that r_a will move in the same direction as r_b allowing us to refer unambiguously to a rise or fall of the own interest rates (Appendix I paras. [8]-[9]).

IV. Should labour continue to be supplied at $W = 0$—as would generally be necessary for ensuring the continuity of the functions and the existence of solutions of system (E) (ibid. para. [10])—then at that zero level of W we shall find a continuum of solutions of (F) for levels L^D of labour demanded in the interval $0 \leq L^D \leq L$, and for the corresponding levels of r_b in the interval $r_b^0 \leq r_b^+ \leq r_{b\,max}$ where, with r_b^0 as the minimum such level, $r_{b\,max} \geq r_b^0$ is the maximum one (ibid. para. [6]: see also Fig. 2).

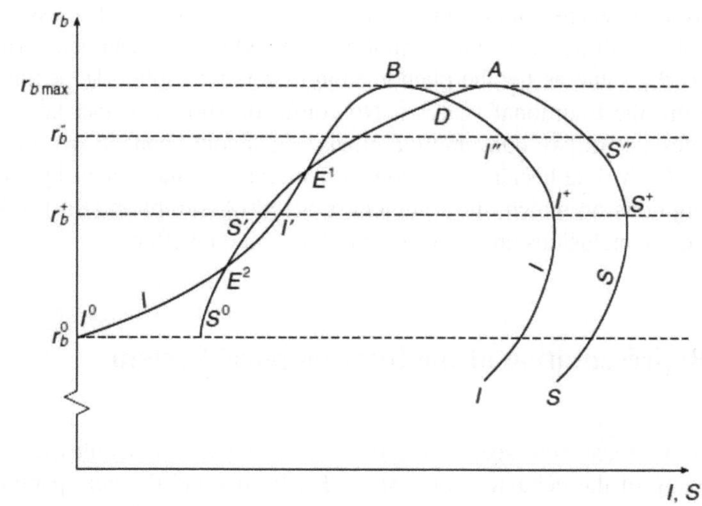

Fig. 2 The upper reaches I^+I^0 and S^+S^0 of the I and S schedules represent positions (F) for $W = 0$ characterised by different levels of labour employment and therefore of the investment required to equip them

V. The minimum level $r_{b\,min} = -1$ corresponding to the *intertemporal* price $P_{b0}/P_{b1} = 0$ does not entail, as one would perhaps expect, that b_0 is a free commodity so that, for example, also $P_{b0}/P_{a0} = 0$. On the contrary, there are reasons which force us to admit that, as $P_{b0}/P_{b1} \to 0$, the *contemporary* relative price P_{b0}/P_{a0} will generally tend to a positive and finite level, with all commodities available in $t = 0$ having zero price in terms of all commodities available in $t = 1$ (ibid., paras. [7] and [12]).

VI. As for the shape of the two schedules (see Fig. 1) what we can say generally is that: (i) the choice of b_1 as our numéraire entails, as just said, that for $r_b = r_{b\,min} = -1$ both P_{a0} and P_{b0} are zero, so that both the S and I schedules intersect the vertical axes at $r_b = -1$; (ii) as we saw under point III a 'main branch' of the S and I schedules will exist in the interval $r_{b\,min} \leq r_b \leq r_b^+$: along it W will decrease from W_{max} for $r = r_{b\,min}$ down to zero for r_b^+; (iii) the two schedules will then continue beyond r_b^+ in order to represent the continuum of positions indicated under point IV above, with the I schedule finally reaching the vertical axis with $L^D = 0$ (ibid. para. [14]); (iv) it does not seem however that anything general can be said about the overall shape of the schedules in the intermediate interval $0 \leq r_b \leq r_b^0$ except for the single-valued character of the schedules seen under point II and the bias towards rising S and I schedules due to our choice of b_1 as numéraire, and therefore of P_{a0} and P_{b0} rising as r_b rises (a bias which is of course innocuous as far as the properties of the equilibria are concerned, which only depend on the ratio S/I at each level of r_b); (v) in particular, the impossibility of supposing a necessarily falling I schedule is not however due to that bias. Nor is it due to the fact that alternative techniques have not yet been considered: possibilities of substitution between labour and means of production are already present in the system because of consumer choice between a_1 and b_1. The essential reason why a falling I schedule cannot be assumed will be seen below (para. 19) and is the same as for the phenomenon of reverse capital deepening, familiar from the traditional analysis. No confusion should in fact be caused by the presence of two consumption goods which could conceivably engender a rising I schedule because of income effects: as we make clear by one of the assumptions on which our argument is based (Assumption (IIIa), ibid. para. [5]), our conclusions are independent of any income effects.

4. The Representation of the Intertemporal System

15. What we must now see, therefore, is how the two schedules can aid our understanding of the behaviour of system (E). In this and the next paragraph we shall see how the schedules can represent the equilibria of the system and then, in the following two, we shall consider the information they can provide on out-of-equilibrium behaviour.

A 'position' (F) of the system (i.e. the solution of (F) for a particular value of r_b) will also be an equilibrium (i.e. a solution of E) when the first two relations in (3e) of para. 3, concerning the aggregate demand for, and supplies of, a_0 and b_0 happen to be satisfied: all other relations of (E) are in fact already present in (F). Leaving aside at first the case of 'extreme' equilibria occurring, that is, for $r_{b\,min}$ or for $W = 0$, it can be asserted that when the system is in equilibrium the two schedules S and I intersect, and that the converse is also true.

As for the first proposition, when r_b is in that intermediate interval, or also in the upper interval $r_b^+ \geq r_b \geq r_b^0$ along the 'main branch' of the S and I functions (point III in para. 14), and P_{a0}, P_{b0} are accordingly strictly positive, any solution of (E) entails that the first two relations in (3e) of para. 3 above are satisfied with an equality sign,[36] i.e.

$$A^S = A^D \text{ and } B^S = B^D \tag{3a}$$

and hence (see relations (3f′) in para. 7)

$$I_a = S_a, \quad I_b = S_b \tag{3a}$$

and

$$I_a P_{a0} + I_b P_{b0} = S_a P_{a0} + S_b P_{b0}, \text{ i.e. } S = I. \tag{3b}$$

The general equilibrium of the system thus entails an intersection of the two schedules.

As for the converse proposition, when we have an intersection of the schedules in that same interval (see Fig. 1, para. 10), Eq. (3b) is satisfied and therefore, after adding $D_{a0}P_{a0} + D_{b0}P_{b0}$ to both sides, we obtain

$$A_0^D P_{a0} + B_0^D P_{b0} = A_0^S P_{a0} + B_0^S P_{b0} \tag{3c}$$

Indicating then, by the constant γ, the common value of the ratios appearing on the two sides of Eq. (7f), we may write Eq. (3c) above as follows:

$$\gamma B_0^S P_{a0} + B_0^S P_{b0} = \gamma B_0^D P_{a0} + B_0^D P_{b0}, \text{ i.e. } B_0^S(\gamma P_{a0} + P_{b0}) = B_0^D(\gamma P_{a0} + P_{b0}) \tag{3d}$$

from which $B_0^S = B_0^D$ and hence, from Eq. (3c), $A_0^S = A_0^D$, thus fulfilling all relations (3e) in system (E), and ensuring that we are in a general-equilibrium position.

16. Turning now to the representation of possible 'extreme' equilibria of the system, we may note that equilibria in the upper interval $r_b^0 \leq r_b \leq r_{b\,max}$ will also be shown by intersections of the two schedules, but the converse proposition will not be true. Since different (F) positions may correspond to the same level of r_b, an intersection between I and S may occur in that interval at a point representing an (F) position on the I schedule, and a different one on the S schedule. The

[36]The level $r_b > r_{b\,min}$ entails $P_{b0} > 0$ and hence, by assumption (iii) para. [5], Appendix I, $P_{a0} > 0$.

intersections representing equilibria have then to be traced by checking whether the I and S points of the intersection pertain to the same (F) position. This will be possible in the diagram because, starting, for example, from points like I^+ and S^+ (see Fig. 2), the two schedules will go through exactly the same values of r_b in exactly the same sequence: 'couples' of I and S points corresponding to the same (F) position can therefore easily be singled out.[37] The reasoning conducted in the preceding paragraph will then apply to those points of intersections which represent the same (F) position on both schedules.

As we proceed to $r_{b\,min}$, at the opposite extreme, although the zero intertemporal prices P_{a0}, P_{b0} yield $S = I = 0$, we shall generally have definite non-zero physical quantities I_a, I_b, S_a, S_b (para. [13] in Appendix I). We need first of all to note here that the assumption about both goods being scarce for consumption in $t = 0$ as well as in $t = 1$ (see Assumption (ii) in para. [3] of Appendix I) entails that the position (F) for $r_b = -1$ is the one characterised by the 'collective' zero intertemporal price of all commodities available in $t = 0$ relative to those of $t = 1$, which we mentioned under point VI of para. 14 and discussed in paras. [7] and [12] of Appendix I.

Now, that (F) position is an equilibrium when, as $r_b \to r_{b\,min}$, $S_b > I_b$. At that position savings would generally exceed investment when expressed in contemporary prices by means of either a_0 or b_0. Then, by a reasoning analogous to the one conducted in para. 15 for Eqs. (3c) and (3d) we could in fact conclude $S > I$; $S_b > I_b$ and therefore we have an 'extreme equilibrium' with $A_0^S > A_0^D$; $B_0^S > B_0^D$. When however $S < I$ as $r_b \to r_{b\,max}$ no equilibrium will generally exist at $r_{b\,min}$.[38]

17. While thus representing the equilibria of the system, the two schedules can, as we said, provide elements for a discussion of its out-of-equilibrium behaviour. Suppose first an (F) position for $r_b = r_b'$ in the interval as $r_{b\,min} < r_b' < r^0$ such that $S' > I'$ (see Fig. 1, para. 10). As we just saw, the inequality $S > I$ entails $A^s > A^D$ and $B^s > B^D$. It would then seem natural to suppose an 'initial' reaction in the markets for a_0 and b_0, more directly affected by the disequilibrium, which would occur *before* adjustments can take place in connected markets: in our case under the reasonable assumption of excess supply for both commodities, that 'initial' competitive reaction could only be a fall of intertemporal prices P_{a0}/P_{b1} and P_{b0}/P_{b1}. However, the connected markets will then tend to adjust, so that we may envisage an out-of-equilibrium behaviour in the recontracting dominated by movements centring on the two general-equilibrium schedules. In this respect Eq. (7f), assuming a proportionate change of the algebraic excess demands for a_0 and b_0, seems to be as reasonable an assumption as can be made at a general level: it may indeed be taken to represent a condition of 'even flexibility' of the price system, in

[37] Thus, should the schedules be representable as in Fig. 2, intersection D would not indicate an equilibrium because, of the two successive (F) positions, (F') and (F''), that we meet in sequence at r_b as L^D falls from the full employment level of I^+ and S^+, point D corresponds to (F') on the I schedule, but to (F'') on the S schedule. Intersections E^1 and E^2 however are equilibria since each corresponds to the same (F) position on both schedules.

[38] Except for the fluke case of $S_a = I_a$, and therefore, $S_b = I_b$ exactly achieved for $r_b = -1$, which would of course be compatible with both $S > I$ and $S < I$ in the proximity of $r_{b\,min}$.

the sense of allowing for the excess demands for a_0 and b_0 to change in the same proportion. Our critical aim strengthens on the other hand the legitimacy of assuming that the dominant out-of-equilibrium movement will be along the schedules: if deficiencies of the demand and supply apparatus result under that assumption, they would seem to be all the more plausible when obstacles to the adjustments to equilibrium are also considered in the connected markets, which the schedules assume instead to be broadly kept in equilibrium.

Then, as we start moving along the schedules, the 'initial' fall of both P_{a0}/P_{b1} and P_{b0}/P_{b1} in response to the assumed excess savings will result in a movement downward along the schedules with a fall of both own rates r_a and r_b (see point III in para. 14). This result can indeed be taken to be general—largely independent, that is, of our assumption about the monotonic rise of P_{a0}/P_{b1} with P_{b0}/P_{b1} (cf. point II in para. 14, and para. [8] in Appendix I).[39]

[39] It would be correct to say that the cause of the possible rise of one own rate, call it r_a, as the other falls because of excess savings, is quite different from the excess savings, which cause the other to fall and would generally make for a fall of *both* rates. A fall of all consumption goods prices for $t = 0$, relative to those for $t = 1$ is in fact what we would expect from excess savings, i.e. excess supply of consumption goods *in general* in $t = 0$, and excess demand for them *in general* in $t = 1$. A rise of r_a as we move along the schedules because of excess savings can only result from a strong dislocation of contemporary relative prices for which the relative price of a to b were to rise for more between $t = 0$ and $t = 1$ than it did at a higher level of r_b (cf. Appendix I para. [9]).

A seeming puzzle connected with opposite movement of the own rates should perhaps be sorted out at this point. Should r_a rise in the proximity of an equilibrium as r_b falls because of excess savings, would not a representation of the same (F) position with r_a in place of r_b on the vertical axis (see Figure A) lead to opposite conclusions about the stability of the equilibrium? The answer is of course negative since the *adjusted* spontaneous competitive change consequent to excess savings would, with an apparent paradox, be a rise and not a fall of the interest rate—owing to the change in the relative-prices factor of Eq. (6a) in loc. cit. Appendix I. Figure A illustrates the 'upside-down' representation of an equilibrium E and of the neighbouring positions (F′) and (F″) when r_a is put on the vertical axis.

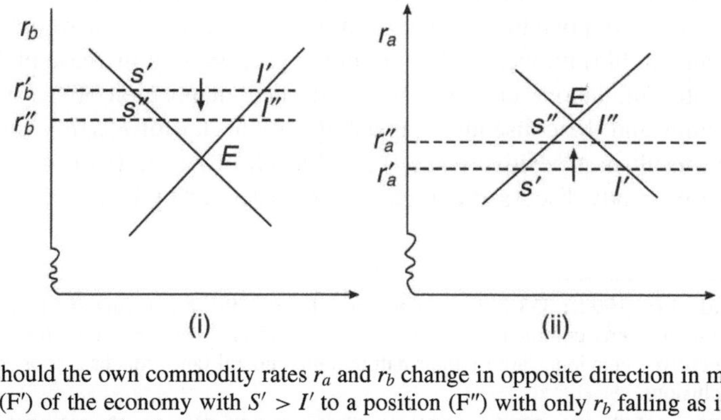

Figure A Should the own commodity rates r_a and r_b change in opposite direction in moving from a position (F′) of the economy with $S' > I'$ to a position (F″) with only r_b falling as indicated by the arrow in diagram (i)—then the spontaneous competitive movement in diagram (ii), with r_a on the vertical axis, would be upwards. [*Editor's note*: In both graphs, the designation of the functions *S* and *I* appears to have been interchanged.]

Similarly to what could be argued in any partial equilibrium use of the schedules—we have then elements for arguing a tendency e.g. toward equilibrium E^{III} in Fig. 1 of para. 10, where the I schedule cuts the S schedule from above and where therefore for any given initial position in the interval $r_b^{\text{III}} < r_b < r_b^{IV}$, r_b can be expected to fall, and to rise for any r_b in $r_b^{\text{II}} < r_b < r_b^{\text{III}}$. A tendency away from equilibrium can instead be argued when, as we move from left to right, I cuts S from below (see E^{II} and E^{IV} in Fig. 1).[40]

18. As we turn to 'extreme' values of r_b, we may note that if we happened to have $S > I$ in the proximity of $r_{b\,min} = -1$, the fall of r_b, which we can assume in the presence of $S > I$, would imply competitive recontracting to tend to the equilibrium with the zero intertemporal (but not contemporary) prices of both a_0 and b_0 we saw in para. 16.[41]

As we could expect, some novel problems are met when we shift our attention to the upper extreme for r^0 of the S and I schedules (where with $L = L^D$ and $W > 0$ we have all the conditions for the out-of-equilibrium behaviour considered in para. 17). In all other (F) positions of that interval, we shall have excess supply of labour with $L > L^D$ and a zero wage. The I schedule will tend to finally extend leftward so as to reach the vertical axis for the (F) position corresponding to $L^D = 0$ (cf. para. [14] in Appendix I) and, as we just saw in para. 16, any equilibrium will be shown by the two schedules intersecting, and intersecting for the same (F) position.

Outside any such equilibria, if in the given position (F) we have $I < S$ (see e.g. points I'' and S'' in Fig. 2) it would be natural to suppose that the excess savings, i.e. the excess supply of a_0 and b_0, will cause the 'initial' fall of both P_{a0}/P_{b1} and P_{b0}/P_{b1} we admitted for intermediate levels of r_b.

However, with $W = 0$ and the available excess supply of labour making it possible to expand outputs, that temporary 'initial' fall of the prices of a_0 and b_0, relative to those of their outputs a_1 and b_1 would make it profitable for entrepreneurs to raise outputs, and as adjustments occur we would tend to move along the I schedule towards the right in the direction of an increase of the labour employment L^D and therefore of the investment required to equip that labour. Prices P_{a0} and P_{b0} will have to move in the opposite direction and so may therefore do r_a and r_b. Unless an equilibrium were to be met in the process, that increase of L^D would continue until full labour employment is reached in position (F^+) for $r_b = r_b^+$. Excess savings and the consequent persisting 'initial' fall of P_{a0}/P_{b1} and P_{b0}/P_{b1} would then result in a positive wage W, and a fall of r_b: the (F) positions would become those already discussed in para. 17, characterised by $W > 0$.

[40] As I remarked in (1990c: 358 [this volume, Part III, p. 379]), arguments about stability conducted like the one here, confined essentially to signs of changes, while finding ready confirmation in competitive behaviour, 'are by their nature quite general [and] render ... possible equally general conclusions'.

[41] No tendency would be there to the 'fluke' equilibrium mentioned in n. 38 above, when $S_a = I_a$, $S_b = I_b$ at $r_{b\,min}$ but $S < I$ as $r_b \rightarrow r_{b\,min}$.

In the case in which, in that same upper interval of r_b and for $W = 0$, we instead had $I > S$ in the (F) position—as exemplified by points I' and S' in Fig. 2, for the same level of r_b of the just discussed position (F) with excess savings—then, an opposite process of decreases of employment L^D and investment would have to be expected. It would lead leftwards along the I schedule to an equilibrium which would then have to exist. As we just recalled, investment I has in fact to change continuously down to zero, while S also changes continuously, though generally without reaching zero. Then, with I starting to the right of S and having to pass finally to its left while going through exactly the same levels of r_b, it is inevitable that the two schedules will cross—as exemplified by E^2 to the left of the points I' and S' in Fig. 2.

5. Alternative Techniques and the Investment Demand

19. System (F), like system (E) which generates it, still rests on the assumption that only one method of production is available for each commodity. It is time to drop that assumption and consider the existence of several alternative methods for each commodity, all sharing the properties we mentioned in para. 3. We may call a set of 'methods of production', one for the commodity in question and one for each of its (direct and indirect) means of production, 'the system of production' or 'technique of production' of the commodity. Here, the 'technique' or 'system' of production of the commodity will accordingly include two 'methods of production', one for the commodity and one for the other commodity as means of production of the former. Thus one 'technique' for producing a, will also be a 'technique' for producing b, and we may therefore refer to techniques $i = 1, \ldots, n$ without mentioning the commodity they refer to.

Despite our assumption that all alternative methods of production require the same three factors, there is no assurance that marginal products, even of the discontinuous kind, will exist.[42] For the determination of the method that would be the cheapest at current prices and would therefore be chosen by competitive entrepreneurs, we must therefore resort to the more general approach we find in Sraffa's *Production of Commodities*: namely, comparing the expenses for producing the commodity by the alternative methods. However, at each level of r_b the comparison can only be done in terms of prices P^i_{a0}/P^i_{b0} and the wage W^i holding for the particular technique i 'in use'—meaning here by 'in use' that the technique is the one whose adoption we assume to be generally planned at the stage reached

[42] Marginal products, whether of the discontinuous or continuous variety, require that the available techniques be susceptible of being ordered so that they can be made to differ by the quantity of only one factor at a time. That, it seems, cannot generally be done when the factors are more than two: weighted averages of the different methods available which could give the above result will not make general economic sense, since it would be an exception when the methods entering such averages could co-exist.

by the recontracting.[43] Maximisation of entrepreneurial profits will then entail that the re-contracting proceeds to any method for each commodity which happens to be cheaper at those prices.

A question which is well known from the 'traditional', non-intertemporal assumptions then arises, about whether the *order* of the alternative methods of production of the commodity as to cheapness, might not itself change with the technique 'in use': with the possibility of either endless switching between techniques, or of the technique finally adopted depending on the one initially 'in use'. Our critical intent, however, will again allow us to grant the assumptions most favourable to the theory criticised and therefore to assume what has been demonstrated to be true under the traditional assumptions: that the order of cheapness of an alternative method is the same, whichever the technique in (planned) use at the given level of r_b.[44] We can thus suppose that entrepreneurs' choice will always arrive at one and the same method(s) for each of the two commodities, so that at any given r_b the cheapest technique(s) or 'system(s) of production' can be uniquely determined, together with the corresponding series of the prices, the outputs, and the I and S quantities, where the plurals above take care of the possible co-existence at some r_b of two (or more) methods for the same commodity and hence of the technique(s) differing from i by the method of that single commodity which will then entail the same wage and prices for the given level of r_b.

20. We can therefore proceed to reporting below the family (Fi) of systems of equations defining the two schedules under the assumption of a multiplicity of techniques of production $j = 1, 2, 3, \ldots$. Each member of that family is a system of equations like (F) defined in para. 6, but applied now to the technique i which happens to be the one no dearer than any other at the given level of r_b. Thus, to any level r_b in its relevant interval there will correspond a system (Fi) containing, as well as the relations (F) pertaining to the technique i adopted, as many quadruplets of relations, (8fi) and (9fi), as there are alternative 'techniques' or 'systems of production' $j \neq i$. The first two equations (i.e. 8fi) reckon the production expenses of a_1 and b_1 with the respective methods j. The second couple of relations, namely (9fi), states that no method j for producing each of the two commodities is cheaper than the method pertaining to the technique i 'in use'.[45]

---

[43] A sufficient unanimity concerning the technique to be adopted has evidently to be assumed in order to let the corresponding prices emerge from the re-contracting. That unanimity has then to be replaced by a similar one concerning a second technique which had been found to be cheaper at those earlier prices, and so on and so forth. The way out of this conundrum is of course the further fiction of the auctioneer.

[44] For the question in its traditional context, cf. Sraffa (1960, Chap. XII) and the subsequent literature referred to in Kurz and Salvadori (1995: 151).

[45] Comparisons regard in fact methods of production of each commodity rather than techniques: and changes in technique, in particular those leading to the cheapest technique i, are best envisaged as resulting from changes of methods for one commodity at a time. However, referring to techniques, as above, rather than to methods, has no drawback here when one remembers that there will then be no one-to-one correspondence between method and technique, the same method appearing in several techniques differing from each other by the method of the remaining commodity.

$$
\left.\begin{array}{ll}
\left\{\begin{array}{l} P^i_{a1} = l_{ai}W^i + a_{ai}P^i_{a0} + b_{ai}P^i_{b0} \\ P^i_{b1} = l_{bi}W^i + a_{bi}P^i_{a0} + b_{bi}P^i_{b0} \end{array}\right. & (1\text{fi}) \\
P^i_{b1} = 1 & (2\text{fi}) \\
\left\{\begin{array}{l} A^{Di}_0 = D^i_{a0} + \left(a_{ai}A^i_1 + a_{bi}B^i_1\right) \\ B^{Di}_0 = D^i_{b0} + \left(b_{ai}A^i_1 + b_{bi}B^i_1\right) \\ L \geq l_{ai}A^i_1 + l_{bi}B^i_1 \\ A^i_1 = D^i_{a1} \\ B^i_1 = D^i_{b1} \end{array}\right. & (3\text{fi}) \\
I^i = \left(a_{ai}A^i_1 + a_{bi}B^i_1\right)P^i_{a0} + \left(b_{ai}A^i_1 + b_{bi}B^i_1\right)P^i_{b0} & (4\text{fi}) \\
S^i = \left(A^S_0 - D^i_{a0}\right)P^i_{a0} + \left(B^S_0 - D^i_{b0}\right)P^i_{b0} & (5\text{fi}) \\
r_b = \left(\frac{P^i_{b0}}{P^i_{b1}}\right) - 1 & (6\text{fi}) \\
\frac{A^{Di}_0}{B^{Di}_0} = \frac{A^S_0}{B^S_0} & (7\text{fi}) \\
\left\{\begin{array}{l} P^i_{aj1} = l_{aj}W^i + a_{aj}P^i_{a0} + b_{aj}P^i_{b0} \\ P^i_{bj1} = l_{bj}W^i + a_{bj}P^i_{a0} + b_{bj}P^i_{b0} \end{array}\right. \quad \text{any } j \neq i & (8\text{fi}) \\
P^i_{a1} \leq P^i_{aj1}, P^i_{b1} \leq P^i_{bj1} \qquad \text{any } j \neq i & (9\text{fi})
\end{array}\right\} \quad (\text{Fi})
$$

where i at the exponent indicates that the variable in question is calculated under the assumption that technique i is being planned for use at the given r_b, whereas j at the deponent indicates the alternative technique to which there pertains the variable in question, coefficient of production or price based on such coefficients (no deponent has been given to the same variables pertaining to technique i). The equality signs in (9fi) take care of the possible co-existence between technique $j \neq i$ and other techniques for same levels of r_b, when the equality sign will apply to both the relations (9fi).

Correspondingly, also system (E), determining the equilibrium of the system, should now be written in the form of the following family of systems (Ei) allowing for alternative techniques:

$$
\left.\begin{array}{ll}
\left\{\begin{array}{l} P^i_{a1} = l_{ai}W^i + a_{ai}P^i_{a0} + b_{ai}P^i_{b0} \\ P^i_{b1} = l_{bi}W^i + a_{bi}P^i_{a0} + b_{bi}P^i_{b0} \end{array}\right. & (1\text{ei}) \\
P^i_{b1} = 1 & (2\text{ei}) \\
\left\{\begin{array}{l} A^S_0 \geq D^i_{a0} + \left(a_{ai}A^i_1 + a_{bi}B^i_1\right) \text{ with } P^i_{a0} = 0 \text{ if sign} > \text{applies} \\ B^S_0 \geq D^i_{b0} + \left(b_{ai}A^i_1 + b_{bi}B^i_1\right) \text{ with } P^i_{b0} = 0 \text{ if sign} > \text{applies} \\ L \geq l_{ai}A^i_1 + l_{bi}B^i_1 \text{ with } W^i = 0 \text{ if sign} > \text{applies} \\ A^i_1 = D^i_{a1} \\ B^i_1 = D^i_{b1} \end{array}\right. & \\
\left\{\begin{array}{l} P^i_{aj1} = l_{aj}W^i + a_{aj}P^i_{a0} + b_{aj}P^i_{b0} \\ P^i_{bj1} = l_{bj}W^i + a_{bj}P^i_{a0} + b_{bj}P^i_{b0} \end{array}\right. \quad \text{any } j \neq i & (8\text{ei}) \\
P^i_{a1} \leq P^i_{aj1}, P^i_{b1} \leq P^i_{bj1} \qquad \text{any } j \neq i & (9\text{ei})
\end{array}\right\} \quad (\text{Ei})
$$

where, as for (E) in para. 3, the relations corresponding to Eqs. (4fi), (5fi), (6fi) and (7fi) do not need to appear, $S = I$ being implied in (Ei).

21. The main question which the existence of alternative methods of production raises for us here is the changes in the investment requirements I due to changes in the cheapest technique as r_b varies. We might perhaps expect that owing to those changes (as well as to those of the relative outputs A_1/B_1 already determined in system F) the schedule I would generally show a negative slope. However, such an expectation has no better foundation for the present investment-demand schedule than it had for the capital-demand schedule in the 'traditional' setting.

A simple line of reasoning seems sufficient to show this. As has been pointed out,[46] the roots of reverse capital deepening, as well as those of the re-switching of techniques, lie in the effect of changes in distribution (rate of profits) upon the *relative value* of the alternative sets of capital goods required by the processes of production which are being compared—whether such processes are alternative methods of production for the *same* consumption good, or the methods for two different consumption goods. In the traditional, non-intertemporal setting, it is the changing relative value of such two sets of capital goods that can make a more 'capital-intensive' technique become more profitable, or a more capital-intensive consumption good fall in price, as the interest rate rises. And it is that same change in the relative value of the alternative sets of capital goods that can bring about 're-switching' among alternative techniques. Now, the same variability of the relative value of alternative sets of capital goods is clearly present in an intertemporal setting.

To see the thing in more definite terms, let us consider first the case of alternative techniques as distinct from that of competing consumption goods. From Eqs. (8fi) and (9fi) we may see how, at the given level of r_b, the choice between the cheapest technique i and any other alternative technique j differing, say, by the method of production of a alone, hinges on the following relative costs of the two methods:

$$\frac{P^i_{ai1}}{P^i_{aj1}} = \frac{l_{ai}W^i + a_{ai}P^i_{a0} + b_{ai}P^i_{b0}}{l_{aj}W^i + a_{aj}P^i_{a0} + b_{aj}P^i_{b0}}, \tag{10}$$

the method of technique i for a_1 being more profitable than the j one at the given r_b when $P^i_{ai1}/P^i_{aj1} < 1$. Defining now

$$C^i_{ai} = a_{ai}P^i_{a0} + b_{ai}P^i_{b0},$$
$$C^i_{aj} = a_{aj}P^i_{a0} + b_{aj}P^i_{b0},$$

where the C^i_a's are the respective capital expenses estimated at the given level of r_b and for i prices, we may then write the relative production expenses (10) of the two methods as follows:

$$\frac{P^i_{ai1}}{P^i_{aj1}} = \frac{l_{ai}W^i + C^i_{ai}}{l_{aj}W^i + C^i_{aj}}, \tag{10a}$$

[46] Cf. Garegnani (1978: 349–52 [this volume, Part IV, pp. 404–7]).

with (C^i_{ai}/l_{ai}) and (C^i_{aj}/l_{aj}) as the respective ratios of capital to labour in the (direct) production of a_1. We then have

$$\frac{P^i_{ai1}}{P^i_{aj1}} = \frac{W^i + C^i_{ai}/l_{ai}}{W^i + C^i_{aj}/l_{aj}} \cdot \frac{l_{ai}}{l_{aj}}. \tag{10b}$$

Assume now, without loss of generality, that $C^i_{ai}/l_{ai} > C^i_{aj}/l_{aj}$. Should the C^{i}_a's be measured so that they are independent of changes in W, clearly P^i_{ai1}/P^i_{aj1} could only fall as W rises (and r_b falls: point III, para. 14). Any changes of method could only be in favour of the more "capital intensive" one (from j to i in our case). Since however the C^i_a's and therefore the key ratio C^i_{ai}/C^i_{aj} are not so independent, the rise of W (fall of r_b) need not entail the fall of P^i_{ai1}/P^i_{aj1} we might have expected: a sufficient rise of C^i_{ai}/C^i_{aj} may well make P^i_{ai1}/P^i_{aj1} rise, and not fall as W rises. This means that the rise of W may well result in the less capital-intensive method j becoming the more profitable one of the two, and therefore being adopted.

The same change of C^i_{ai}/C^i_{aj} in the relative value of the sets of capital goods of the two alternative processes of production may entail, as can be shown by replacing P^i_{aj1} with P^i_{bi1}, that the less 'capital-intensive' consumption good b_1 may become cheaper relative to a_1 as W rises (r_b falls), so that regular substitution in consumption has "perverse" effects on factor demands. Hence the freedom with which we were able to draw the shape of the I schedule in our Figs. 1, 2 or 3.[47]

[47] To make r_b appear explicitly in Eq. (10b) we should turn to the undiscounted prices, here indicated by the small letter p (cf. n. 11 above). By itself, this change in the equations does not, of course, entail any change in the assumptions of the model (in particular in the assumption of complete future markets or of an 'initial' contracting period): it only requires that each price be notionally referred to the date of delivery of the good by taking as numéraire for it the good b of the same date. Then the wage W and the undiscounted prices of a_1 and b_1 are numerically equal to the discounted ones because already expressed in terms of b of $t = 1$:

$$p_{b1} = P_{b1} = 1; p_{a1} = P_{a1}; w = W.$$

As for the undiscounted prices of a_0 and b_0, using Eq. (6f) we have:

$$p_{b0} = 1 = P_{b1} = \frac{P_{b0}}{(1 + r_b)}$$

and since $P_{b0} = 1 + r_b$, we also have.

$$p_{a0} = \frac{P_{a0}}{P_{b0}} = \frac{P_{a0}}{(1 + r_b)}.$$

The two relations (1f) can then be written as follows:

$$\begin{aligned} p^i_{a1} &= l_{ai}W^i + \left(a_{ai}p^i_{a0} + b_{ai}p^i_{b0}\right)(1 + r_b) \\ p^i_{b1} &= l_{bi}W^i + \left(a_{bi}p^i_{a0} + b_{bi}p^i_{b0}\right)(1 + r_b) \end{aligned} \tag{3fi'}$$

6. Some Conclusions

22. We can now use the schedules to see some properties of a general intertemporal equilibrium and thereby how 'capital' as a single 'quantity' enters intertemporal equilibrium. The question may usefully be approached by showing how misleading is the widespread idea that savings and investment in an intertemporal equilibrium raise no more problems than do relative demands for contemporary commodities and can therefore be subsumed under a single theory of consumer choice.[48] It is of course true that if we assume no capital to be left at the final date, the (gross) savings at t must consist of demand for consumer goods at future dates $(t+\tau)$, at the expense of demand for the same or other consumer goods at t. It is then equally true that any excess of saving decisions over investment decisions at t must necessarily take the form of an excess supply of consumer goods at t, and an excess demand for them at future dates. Thus, imagine that initial recontracting had brought the economy to the position $(\hat{F})$ of quantities and prices which the system (Fi) associates with the interest rate $\hat{r}_b$ (see Fig. 3), and suppose that $(\hat{F})$ would coincide with an equilibrium $(\hat{E})$ except for a positive excess of savings $\Delta\left(\hat{S}\right)=\left(\hat{S}-\hat{I}\right)$, $\left(\hat{S}\right)$ and $\left(\hat{I}\right)$ being estimated at the prices of $(\hat{F})$.

From the households budget equations in (Fi) for $\hat{r}_b$ we obtain

$$\begin{aligned}\Delta\hat{S}_a &= -\left(\hat{P}_{a0}\Delta D_{a0}+\hat{P}_{b0}\Delta D_{b0}\right)\\ &= \hat{P}_{a1}\Delta D_{a1}+\hat{P}_{b1}\Delta D_{b1},\end{aligned} \tag{5b}$$

---

and the first equation of each couple of (8fi) is.

$$p^i_{aj1}=l_{aj}W^i+\left(a_{aj}p^i_{a0}+b_{aj}p^i_{b0}\right)(1+r_b) \tag{9fi'}$$

Expressing now the undiscounted capital expenses as

$$\begin{aligned}c^i_{ai} &= a_{ai}p^i_{a0}+b_{ai}p^i_{b0}\\ c^i_{aj} &= a_{aj}p^i_{a0}+b_{aj}p^i_{b0}\end{aligned} \tag{10'}$$

by transformations analogous to those operated in passing from Eqs. (10) to (10b) in the text, we obtain.

$$\frac{p_{ai1}}{p_{aj1}}=\frac{1+\frac{c^i_{ai}}{l_{ai}}\cdot\frac{1+r_b}{W^i}}{1+\frac{c^i_{aj}}{l_{aj}}\cdot\frac{1+r_b}{W^i}}\cdot\frac{l_{ai}}{l_{aj}} \tag{10b'}$$

where the change in p_{ai1}/p_{aj1} can now be seen to depend on the ratio $(1+r_b)/W$.

[48] For an example cf. the quotation in para. 1, n. 4.

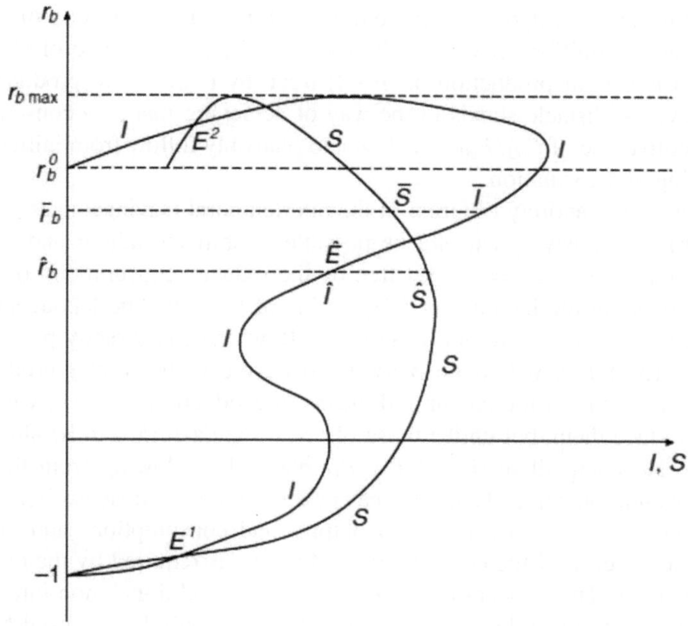

Fig. 3 Starting from $\hat{r}_b$ equilibrium would only be found at E^1, with a negative rate of interest, just as starting from $\overline{r}_b$ the equilibrium would be reached at E^2, with $W = 0$ and labour unemployment

where the ΔD's indicate the differences in the respective quantities demanded between positions $\widehat{F}$ and $\widehat{E}$ (where savings would have been equal to $\widehat{I}$); which, for simplicity, we have supposed to be *both* negative in $t = 0$ and positive in $t = 1$.[49] Undoubtedly, Eq. (5b) *looks* similar to that holding in the case of contemporary commodities, should $(\hat{F})$ have failed to be an equilibrium simply because of an excess demand for b_0 relative to a_0, giving

$$-\hat{P}_{a0}\Delta D_{a0} = \hat{P}_{b0}\Delta D_{b0}. \tag{5c}$$

23. However, the analogy between Eqs. (5b) and (5c) remains at the surface of the two phenomena and hides a basic difference between them which emerges as soon as we consider the adjustments which should lead to a new equilibrium and therefore the forces warranting it in the two cases. That basic difference can be best brought out if, for a moment, we extend our two-year model to the three years (−1), (0), (1), with the commodities a_0 and b_0 accordingly coming from production in $t = -1$ by means of L_{-1} labour and A^S_{-1}, B^S_{-1} initial stocks.

[49] Equation (5b) holds before the adjustments of purchasing power mentioned in para. 9.

Now, for the contemporary commodities of Eq. (5c) the question of achieving a neighbouring equilibrium will be the comparatively simple one of shifting the labour and means of production of $(t-1)$ freed by $(-\Delta D_{a0})$ to producing ΔD_{b0} and no obvious obstacle stands in the way of achieving that as a consequence of the competitive rise of P_{b0}/P_{a0}, which would plausibly follow from initial competitive bidding in the situation.

The position is entirely different in the intertemporal (savings/investment) case of Eq. (5b). Obviously, it will *not* be possible to shift the labour and the means of production of period $t = -1$, set free by the reduced consumption of $t = 0$, to *directly* producing the increments ΔD_{a1}, ΔD_{b1} of Eq. (5b): the labour and means of production of $t = -1$ are not those of $t = 0$, which *can* directly produce ΔD_{a1} and ΔD_{b1}. Even less will it be possible to devote to the direct production of ΔD_{a1} and ΔD_{b1} any of the labour and means of production of $t = 0$, which *could* directly produce them, but unlike those of $t = -1$ are assumed to be already fully employed. No competitive rise of P_{b1}/P_{b0} plausibly following from the relative rise of consumption demands in $t = 1$ can achieve either of those two feats.

How, then, can we raise the $t = 1$ outputs and consumptions and, moreover, do so at the expense of the consumptions of $t = 0$, as required by the excess savings of Eq. (5b)? The answer clearly remains that of traditional, non-intertemporal theory. This change of relative outputs over time can only be achieved by raising the gross productivity of the already fully employed labour L_0, by means of an increase, in some sense, of the quantity of means of production cooperating with it. It is a question, that is, of producing in $t = -1$ quantities ΔI_a and ΔI_b while decreasing production by quantities ΔD_{a0} and ΔD_{b0}, and then using the increments of investment with the constant quantity of labour L_0 to produce increments ΔD_{a1} and ΔD_{b1} of consumption. But, and here comes the essential point, those increments of investment can only be motivated by the rise of the intertemporal prices of a_1 and b_1, relative to b_0 and a_0, i.e. by the fall of the interest rates: no question of the increments of investment being caused *directly* by the additional consumptions ΔD_{a1}, ΔD_{b1} entailed in the savings of Eq. (5b)—contrary to the case for the contemporary consumptions of Eq. (5c).

The idea that savings and investment in intertemporal equilibrium cause no more problems than relative demands for (contemporary) commodities should rather be turned upside down into the one that intertemporal equilibrium raises the problem of savings and investment in basically the same terms as traditional equilibrium does.

24. The problem then is of course that what the capital controversies taught about 'capital reversing' and 're-switching' in traditional equilibrium—and has been confirmed for the present context in para. 19—entails that the rise of the intertemporal prices $P_{i,t+1}/P_{i,t}$ $(i = a, b)$, i.e. a fall of the own rates of interest $r_{i,t}$ might fail to provide the entrepreneurs with a motive for that increase 'in some sense' of I_i which is required for the *intertemporal* adjustments in consumption. The result might then be the striking one that, however small the initial excess savings, the theory could force us to admit movement to an equilibrium with drastic changes

in wages and prices (cf. in Fig. 3 above, the equilibrium E^1 to which there would be a tendency starting from the position $\hat{F}$ for $\hat{r}_b$ in our original two-year model). Further, if the position $\hat{F}$ with excess savings happened to be that for $\hat{r}_b < r''_b$ in Fig. 1 (para. 10) the theory would force us to admit a tendency to negative interest rates if not to the zero intertemporal prices P_{a0} and P_{b0} for our economy with non-storable goods.[50] And as indicated in para. [12] of Appendix I such zero intertemporal prices far from being a result of satiety, would mean that the attempt of some individuals to take care of even more acute scarcities in $t = 1$ runs counter to the inability of the market forces, as envisaged in the theory, to transfer consumption from $t = 0$ to $t = 1$.[51]

Alternatively we might find an equilibrium in which it is W which has to become zero,[52] with the attending labour unemployment, when the initial contracting had brought to a level r_b for which $\overline{I} > \overline{S}$ (see Fig. 3), the equilibrium E^2 to which there would be a tendency when the economy happened to start from $r_b = \overline{r_b}$.[53]

25. The above difference between the cases of contemporary and intertemporal consumptions allows us to begin seeing how the concept of a quantity of capital enters intertemporal general equilibrium. What we have analysed in paras. 23–24 is no less and no more than the process of substitution between labour and "capital", the single factor, which underlies the determination of distribution between wages and profits in the traditional versions of the theory, exemplified by

---

[50] Thus it seems incorrect to hold, with evident reference to reverse capital deepening and the reswitching of techniques, that.

> it is only because we want to have some kind of geometric average, called the rate of interest, that we get some of these paradoxes.
>
> (Arrow, 1989: 155).

The paradoxes are present, whether we refer to the intertemporal prices which, as Arrow states there, are 'what we are really interested in', or to the single rate of interest in the case of the traditional equilibrium. Only the language for describing them changes (cf. n. 39 above).

[51] It is perhaps ironical that Keynes should have been incorrect when he wrote: 'If savings consisted not merely in abstaining from present consumption but in placing simultaneously a specific order for future consumption, the effect *might* indeed be different. For in that case … the resources released from preparing for present consumption could be turned over to preparing for the future consumption' (Keynes, 1936: 210–211, out italics). In fact, the order for future consumption could remain unfulfilled if the reaction of the interest rates failed to incentivize entrepreneurs to 'deepen' capital in the economy. However, the 'might' we have italicised indicates, perhaps, Keynes' doubt that his 'struggle of escape from habitual modes of thought' (1936: p. viii) could have gone further.

[52] Cf. e.g. 'Certainly … we should not be much interested in an equilibrium with a zero real wage' (Arrow and Hahn, 1971: 354–355).

[53] It may seem paradoxical that it should be excess investment that accompanies here labour unemployment. However, in the model, excess investment is excess demand for the *given* stocks of a_0 and b_0, with whose owners labour competes in sharing the product available in $t = 1$ (see Eq. (1a) in Appendix I, para. [2]): zero wages due to deficient investment need at least three periods in order to emerge.

our reference to Wicksell's *Lectures* in para. 2. The process was there viewed as involving the entire capital and labour endowments, whereas here it has been dealt with from the viewpoint of flows and not funds. But if 'capital' was what Wicksell and traditional theorists dealt with for their determination of wages, interest and prices, then—as indeed we foresaw in para. 2—'capital' is also what we have dealt with when studying the forces that should correct a surplus or deficit of savings over investment, thus determining the prices, in particular the own interest rates, of our simple intertemporal equilibrium and their properties.

Thus we duly found there the central relevance of an inverse relation between the own interest rates and the 'amount' of means of production, i.e. of capital per worker in the economy: as we saw, only if that inverse relation holds, can entrepreneurs operate adjustments towards plausible equilibria in intertemporal consumptions. And that inverse relation is of course the same which was required to ensure adjustments to plausible equilibria in the market for 'capital' and the other factors in the traditional version of the theory. Also the consequences of the impossibility of measuring that 'amount', i.e. 'capital', in terms independent of distribution are then essentially the same as in the traditional versions of the theory. Also the consequences of the impossibility of measuring that 'amount', i.e. 'capital', in terms independent of distribution are then essentially the same as in the traditional versions of the theory. As we recalled in para. 21, that impossibility undermines the inverse relation between interest rates and capital intensity and therefore the uniqueness, stability and overall plausibility of the resulting equilibria.[54]

No important difference is on the other hand made by the fact that in the intertemporal versions the inverse relation concerns a set of own rates (intertemporal relative prices) rather than the traditional single interest rate. A tendency of the own rates to move in the same direction can be argued and, more importantly, any contrasting movements among the own rates can be seen to be due to intra-temporal phenomena hardly relevant for intertemporal adjustments (cf. paras. [7]-[9] in Appendix I).

26. This re-emergence of the neoclassical need for a 'quantity of capital' in intertemporal equilibria goes back ultimately to the basic fact that the demand for capital goods obeys principles altogether different from those governing the demand for consumption goods (para. 12). Whereas the latter comes from preferences that are specific to the goods demanded, the former results from savers' preferences that are non-specific to the individual capital goods, and are only specific with regard to the

[54] To a statement of mine (Garegnani,1970: 422 [this volume, Part II, p. 167]) to the effect that the neoclassical explanation of distribution rests essentially on the premise that a fall of the rate of interest must increase the ratio of 'capital' to labour in the economy, Christopher Bliss reacted by writing 'If by explanation of distribution the author means equilibrium theory (say of the intertemporal economy) then he has dreamed up this condition' (1975: 117n). What we just saw in the text might now convince Bliss that dreams can indeed be prescient—of course if one regards as relevant for intertemporal "equilibrium theory" the possibility of zero wages or negative interest rates in its equilibria.

aggregates of them. This is lucidly expressed by Walras when he introduces savings in his general equilibrium as the demand for the particular commodity which he calls 'perpetual net income',[55] with a price of its own which is the reciprocal of the (effective) interest rate. That of course means that, in proportion to their value, capital goods are perfect substitutes for the saver as means of transferring income in time.[56]

The question of a 'quantity of capital' in neoclassical theory is indeed no more than an application of Jevons's 'law of indifference' concerning the single competitive price and hence a single magnitude by which we must refer to any commodity which individuals, in this case wealth holders, treat as homogeneous. Just as one chooses according to the principle of the minimum price between alternative sources of, e.g. 'corn'—so one chooses between the alternative sources of 'perpetual net income', the different capital goods, according to the minimum price of such 'future income'—i.e. the maximum of the effective net rates of return. Capital goods are no more distinct commodities for savers than physically homogeneous "corn" from different farms is for its consumers.

In the case of capital goods, this basic fact is however obscured by a second fact, which mixes the market for the single commodity 'future income' with a second layer of markets and where, furthermore, a quite different kind of substitutability emerges among capital goods. Unlike homogeneous corn where the allocation of consumers' demand among different merchants or farms is theoretically uninteresting beyond the application of Jevons's law of the tendency to a single price, the allocation of the demand for future income among potential sources of supply involves nothing less than the entire theory of production—in order to determine the rentals of the several capital goods and their ratio to the respective supply price. This gives central visibility to that allocation and substitutability in production which, however, is ultimately no more relevant for an explanation of the rate of interest, or system of own rates of interest (intertemporal relative prices), than the analogous allocation of the aggregate demand for corn among the several farmers is for the explanation of the price of corn. Just as it is only the *aggregate* demand and the supply of corn that is relevant for determining the price of corn, so it is only the demand and supply of aggregates of capital goods that is relevant for the determination of the rates of interest.

---

[55] Walras ([1954: 274 ff). Of course it is difficult to define 'perpetual income' in an intertemporal equilibrium, rather than in the traditional long-period equilibrium of Walras's system (para. 1, n. 2). However, the essential nature of savings in neoclassical theory as demand for a homogeneous commodity 'perpetual income' remains the same.

[56] Walras's point incidentally explains why competitive arbitrage tends to achieve a uniform rate of return over any (however short) period by acting on the *demand price* of the capital good, and lowering it below its supply price when the rate of return on the latter is below that of other capital goods. But the prices of capital goods, like those of any product, tend to equality with the respective supply prices in the Marshallian long period, and Walras's single price will turn out to obtain on the *supply* prices of the capital goods as Walras and the present discussion imply.

27. The presence *at some stage* of the theory of a quantity representing aggregates of capital goods is therefore as inevitable for the neoclassical determination of prices on the basis of the demand and supply decisions of individuals,[57] as is the presence of the quantity of each consumption good. Individual demand and supply decisions about capital goods are ultimately taken in terms of that 'quantity' just as the similar decisions about corn consumption are taken in terms of the quantity of corn. It is on a single commodity 'capital' and not on individual capital goods that savers' preferences operate, whether in the traditional 'fund' context, or in the intertemporal 'flow' context.

The traditional versions of the theory, with their equilibrium condition of a uniform effective net rate of return on the supply prices of the capital goods, entailed already taking care of that single commodity at the level of the endowment of factors,[58] and those authors did so by expressing the endowment of capital *directly* as a single 'quantity of capital', its allocation in a capital-goods vector being then an unknown of the system. The abandonment of that traditional long-period notion of the equilibrium—not to be confused, recall, with a stationary or steady state[59]—and of its specific condition of a uniform effective rate on capital good supply prices has meant getting rid of the single commodity 'perpetual net income' and of its bearer, 'homogeneous capital', but only at the cost of assuming away, at the level of the factor endowments, the perfect substitutability of capital goods for the saver, and Jevons's indifference law with it: no surprise, then, for the methodological problems which are raised by today's pure theory.[60]

However, those high methodological costs may have been borne in vain. They have been borne, that is, for what may turn out to have been getting rid of the obviously inconsistent notion of a 'quantity of capital' at the level of the demands and supplies of the *immediately visible* factors of production, and therefore at the level of the endowments, in order to have it re-enter the theory at the less *immediately visible* but theoretically equivalent level of investment-demand and savings-supply.

---

[57] The need for that 'quantity' is in fact strictly connected with neoclassical theory. The perfect substitutability among capital goods for wealth holders does not impose the notion of an independently measurable quantity of capital in the classical theories, where the rate of interest (profits) is not explained in terms of individual demand and supply decisions about 'factors of production' and is instead obtained, essentially, as a difference between product and wages determined separately from prices.

[58] See n. 2 above.

[59] Cf. n. 8 above.

[60] Cf. e.g. para. 13 above.

Appendix I: The Determination of the *I* and *S* Schedules

[1] In para. 7 of the text[61] we had a first check of the consistency of system (F) by counting independent relations and unknowns. The existence of economically meaningful solutions for the unknown prices and quantities of (F) in the economically relevant interval of r_b, $r_{b\,min} = r_b = r_{b\,max}$ to be presently specified, is demonstrated in the Mathematical Note at the end of this chapter. However, an intuitive account of the demonstration is necessary for a better understanding of the argument which we have conducted, and of the assumptions we have introduced.

We start by noting the lower limit of the relevant interval of values of r_b. Due to our assumption that no storage is possible for either commodity,[62] the 'intertemporal price' P_{b0}/P_{b1} can fall to zero and Eq. (6f) of para. 7 will accordingly give

$$r_{b\,min} = -1 \tag{6b}$$

The specification of the upper limits of r_b where $W = 0$ will, on the other hand, require a better acquaintance with the properties of system (F) and we shall come to it in para. [6] below.

[2] As we proceed to the intermediate range of r_b, Eqs. (2f) and (6f) of system (F) in para. 7 of the text allow us to write the second price Eq. (1f) as follows:

$$1 = l_b W + a_b P_{a0} + b_b(1 + r_b), \tag{1a}$$

where, having used Eq. (2f), P_{a0} is now in effect the *intertemporal* price P_{a0}/P_{b1} as, of course, is $P_{b0} = (1 + r_b)$.

Two implications of Eq. (1a) are of interest here.

(a) It is only for $b_b(1 + r_b) \leq 1$, i.e. for $r_b \leq (1 - b_b)/b_b$ that we may have non-negative values of *both* W and P_{a0}. Considering also $r_{b\,min}$ from Eq. (6b), we may therefore begin to restrict our attention to the interval

$$-1 \leq r_b \leq \frac{(1 - b_b)}{b_b} \tag{6c}$$

of our independent variable, where $(1 - b_b)$, and hence $(1 - b_b)/b_b$, are evidently positive whenever the method of production of b is viable (para. 3 in the text).

---

[61] Paragraphs in this Appendix are numbered in square brackets to distinguish them from those of the main text.

[62] Should b_0 be storable, its intertemporal price $P_{b0}\,/P_{b1}$ could not fall below unity, or below $(1 - \alpha_b)$ when storage for a year implies costs α_b (cf. Equations (1e″), n. 13 in the text), and r_b could not accordingly fall below zero, or $(-\alpha_b)$ respectively.

(b) Eq. (1a) above will then entail that for any r_b in the interval (6c), non-negative levels of W require P_{a0} to stay in the interval

$$0 \leq P_{a0} \leq \frac{[1 - b_b(1 + r_b)]}{a_b} \tag{1b}$$

Given, then, r_b and P_{a0} in the respective intervals (6c), (1b), Eq. (1a) will determine the corresponding non-negative level of W. Consequently, the first of Eqs. (1f) determines P_{a1}. Thus the entire series of prices and the wage will be uniquely determined by Eqs. (1f), (2f) and (6f), *once* P_{a0} *is given*, besides r_b.

To that unique series of prices and the wage, there will correspond the quantities demanded expressed by the functions D_{a0}, D_{b0}, D_{a1}, D_{b1}. The amount of total savings S in Eq. (5f) with its physical components S_a, S_b of (5f) will then be determined as well. The methods of production of the two commodities being given, the same will be the case for the amount of investment I of Eq. (4f) and its physical components I_a, I_b. Such quantities need be neither single-valued, nor continuous functions of P_{a0}.[63] It will however follow common practice and not be unduly restrictive to make the following assumption:

Assumption (i) *Given* r_b *in the interval* (6c), *the quantities demanded* D_{a0}, D_{b0}, D_{a1}, D_{b1}, *and hence the aggregate quantities demanded* A_0^D *and* B_0^D *are single-valued, continuous functions of* P_{a0} *in the interval* (1b).[64]

[3] Thus, then, given a level of r_b in the relevant interval, any level of P_{a0} in the interval (1b) will entail a ratio $\delta = A_0^D/B_0^D$ which will generally differ from the ratio $\gamma = A_0^S/B_0^S$, equality with which is imposed by Eq. (7f). As we then change P_{a0} in the interval (1b), there are three possibilities (cf. Fig. 4 in the Mathematical Note to this chapter).

(a) At one or more levels of P_{a0}, $\delta = \gamma$. Equation (7f) will be satisfied and we shall have a solution of (F) for each of those values of P_{a0}.
(b) Over the entire interval (1b) of P_{a0}, $\delta < \gamma$. This will mean that at the given level of r_b it will be impossible to use a_0 in as high a proportion to b_0 as that in which we find the two commodities in the endowment. This means then that a_0 would be a free good in an equilibrium occurring at that level of r_b, when, that is, $B_0^D = B_0^S$.
(c) Finally, over the entire relevant interval of P_{a0}, we shall have $\delta > \gamma$. This is the case symmetrical to (b), in which b_0 cannot be used in as high a

[63] E.g. we cannot exclude that at some relative price P_{a0}/P_{b0} a consumer be indifferent between two goods *within* certain limiting proportions of them: all quantities staying within those limits would then be demanded at the corresponding single price. (This question, which concerns multiplicity of quantities demanded at given prices should of course not be confused with 'income effects', which may cause multiplicity of prices for the same quantities demanded: para [5].)

[64] In fact, the rise of P_{a0} together with r_b (para. [5]) will lower the economically relevant upper limit of both r_b and P_{a0} below those of relations (6c) and (1b).

proportion to a_0 as B_0^S/A_0^S (in as low a proportion as A_0^S/B_0^S) and b_0 would be a free good in an equilibrium occurring at that particular level of r_b, which would then have to be $r_b = -1$, because of $P_{b0} = 0$.

Cases (b) and (c) would exclude an economic solution of system (F) as formulated in the text, with *equalities* in the first two relations (3f), but the simple economic rationale of the cases, i.e. the non-scarcity of either a_0, or b_0 when equality between demand and supply were to be achieved for the other, indicates that a solution could be ensured by a slight formal modification of (F)[65]. However, that would complicate the exposition and risk obscuring the main points we wish to bring out, which are altogether independent of that kind of excess supplies. We shall therefore leave aside cases (b) and (c), as on the other hand we implied already by assuming two (scarce) goods in our model, for period $t = 0$, no less than for $t = 1$. We may therefore render explicit the following assumption:

Assumption (ii) *In the interval $r_{b\,min} \leq r_b \leq r_{b\,max}$, in which $W \leq 0$, and for $r_{b\,max}$ to be defined below* (para. 6), *the commodities a_0 and b_0 can be used in the proportion A_0^S/B_0^S in which they appear in the endowment.*

We may then conclude that, for any level of r_b in the interval between $r_{b\,min}$ and the level $r_{b\,max}$ to be defined, at least one level of P_{a0} will exist satisfying Eq. (7f), and thus solving system (F).

[4] The key role of the price P_{a0} in the solution of (F) at any relevant level of r_b calls for a specification, since there are two aspects of that price which play a different role in system (F): an 'intertemporal' aspect and a 'contemporary' one. Having been expressed in terms the numéraire b_1 of Eq. (2f), P_{a0} possesses an 'intertemporal' aspect, the one which we have chosen here to measure by r_b (i.e. P_{b0}/P_{b1}), the independent variable of our system (F). P_{a0} however also possesses a 'contemporary' aspect, which may be expressed by $\pi = P_{a0}/P_{b0}$, a new variable. Indeed:

$$\frac{P_{a0}}{P_{b1}} = \frac{P_{a0}}{P_{b0}} \cdot \frac{P_{b0}}{P_{b1}}$$

i.e.

$$P_{a0} = \pi P_{b0} \tag{2f'}$$

[65] The device would consist of somewhat counterintuitively dissociating the total quantities A_0^U, B_0^U of the two commodities 'used' for consumption and investment, from the respective quantities 'demanded' A_0^D, B_0^D appearing in Eq. (7f). Provided the price of the commodity in question is zero, we could then let the quantity 'demanded' A_0^D or B_0^D exceed the respective one used A_0^U or B_0^U, by allowing for inequalities in the corresponding relations [3f], where the R.H.S. expresses B_0^U, A_0^U, respectively, and in that way satisfy Eq. (7f).

In para. [3], with r_b a given, variations of P_{a0} were in fact variations only of the contemporary relative price π. The intertemporal role of P_{a0} will instead be prominent when considering the joint variation of P_{a0} and P_{b0} with r_b, as we shall presently do in Assumption (iii) (see also para. [7]).

[5] The generally made Assumption (i), and the confirmation of the two scarce-good nature of our model by means of Assumption (ii), are sufficient to ensure the existence of a solution for (F), but not its uniqueness: income effects may cause the same ratio A_0^S/B_0^S to occur for more than one value of $\pi = P_{a0}/P_{b0}$, at a given level of r_b. We may however make the following assumption:

Assumption (iii) *The value of $\pi = P_{a0}/P_{b0}$ satisfying Eq.* (7f) *together with the remainder of system* (F) *is unique for each level of r_b in the interval $r_{b\,min} < r_b < r_b^0$, where r_b^0 is the lowest level of r_b for which $W = 0$. Further, P_{a0} will be a continuous increasing function of P_{b0} i.e. of r_b in the interval $r_{b\,min} < r_b < r_b^+$, where $r_b^+ \geq r_b^0$ is the level at which that joint rise of P_{a0} and P_{b0} will have to cease, having brought to $W = 0$ in Eq.* (1a) (para. [2] above).

By excluding more than one level of π for which the ratio of the total demands $(D_{a0} + I_a)/(D_{b0} + I_b)$ for a_0 and b_0 can satisfy Eq. (7f), the first part of Assumption (iii) excludes income effects which in $t = 0$ might make the ratio A_0^D/B_0^D decrease through decreases in the consumption ratio D_{a0}/D_{b0}, as P_{a0}/P_{b0} falls; it also excludes similar effects in $t = 1$ causing D_{a1}/D_{b1} to change so as to make I_a/I_b fall rather than rise as $\pi = P_{a0}/P_{b0}$ falls.[66] Since here we wish to exclude income effects, we may proceed and make the following:

Assumption (iii(a)) *A monotonic inverse relation is assumed between D_{a0}/D_{b0} and P_{a0}/P_{b0} as well as between D_{a1}/D_{b1} and P_{a1}/P_{b1}.*

Assumption (iii(a)) only has the purpose of clarifying that the results which we shall reach as to multiplicity and instability are altogether independent of income effects. The assumption will have no consequences on our argument beyond those following from the weaker Assumption (iii).

On the other hand, as we shall see in para. [7], the direct relation between the two intertemporal relative prices P_{a0}/P_{b1} and P_{b0}/P_{b1}, postulated in the second part of Assumption (iii), amounts to simply supposing that the change in the *intertemporal* price r_b will cause no large dislocation in the *contemporary* relative demand D_{a0}/D_{b0} and I_a/I_b, so that the relative contemporary price π need not undergo large changes in order to continue and satisfy Eq. (7f).

We shall see in para. [8] some important implications of Assumption (iii) with respect to the relations between W and r_b, and between the 'own rates' r_a and r_b.

[66] A lowering of P_{a0}/P_{b0} would tend to lower the relative price P_{a1}/P_{b1} of the good requiring more of a for its production (provided the relative labour intensities in the production of a and b do not cause the variation of the wage to more than compensate that effect) and with the proportion consumed of that good increasing, the proportion I_a/I_b would also increase.

But before coming to that, we must deal with the upper limit of r_b and thereby clarify the relation between the three levels $r_b^0, r_b^+, r_{b\,max}$ which Assumptions (ii) and (iii) have already associated with $W = 0$.

[6] We saw that the monotonic rising relation between P_{a0} and r_b (i.e. P_{b0}) of Assumption (iii) comes to an end when, for $r_b^+ = P_{b0}^+ - 1$, W becomes zero in Eq. (1a). This zero wage will then permit labour unemployment in (F), and allow for a *continuum* of solutions of (F), one for each level of labour 'demanded' L^D in the interval $0 \leq L^D \leq L$. In the resulting continuum of solutions of (F), r_b can fall from r_b^+ down to the mentioned minimum level r_b^0 and/or rise up to a highest level $r_{b\,max}$, giving $r_b^0 \leq r_b^+ \leq r_{b\,max}$[67]. It also follows that in such a sub-interval of r_b, P_{a0}

[67] It might on the other hand seem that having in common $W = 0$, such a continuum of solutions of (F) would have in common also the contemporary relative price $\pi = P_{a0}/P_{b0}$ and the rest of the price system with it, so that a single level of $r_b = r_b^+ = r_{b\,max}$, and the corresponding single set of prices, would hold over the whole *continuum* for $W = 0$.

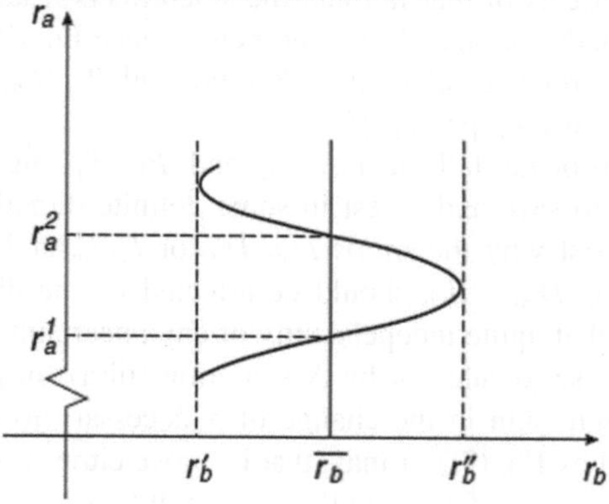

Figure B As the own rate r_b falls from r_b'' to r_b' a rise or constancy of the own interest rate r_a, as depicted in the figure, is incompatible with the monotonic increasing relation between P_{a0}/P_{b1} and P_{b0}/P_{b1} of Assumption (iii) in para. 4.

However, zero total wages $L^D W$ mean that Q_1, the value of the product in $t = 1$ (para. 9, n. 25 in the text) along the *continuum*, is given by.

$$Q_1 = S = D_{a1} P_{a1} + D_{b1}\, P_{b1}.$$

Now, if prices were not to change along that continuum, the *ratio* D_{a1}/D_{b1} would be constant, and so would then be the *ratio* I_a/I_b, though the *absolute* levels of D_{a1}, D_{b1} and therefore I_a, I_b would be falling as L^D falls (see the adjustment to the level of I of the purchasing power in $t = 1$, described in the main text: para. 9, n. 25). Since D_{a0} and D_{b0} would instead be constant also in their absolute amounts, it would follow that A_0^D/B_0^D, a weighted average of D_{a0}/D_{b0} and I_a/I_b (see the first two Eqs. (3f)), would generally be changing with L^D. This imposes a change in the contemporary price π (and hence the other prices) in order to continue to satisfy Eq. (7f).

and all remaining unknowns in (F) will no longer need be single-valued functions of r_b (see Fig. 2, in the text, para. 16). Since, on the other hand, using (2f′) of para. [4], Eq. (1a) of para. [2] becomes

$$1 = a_b \pi (1 + r_b) + b_b (1 + r_b), \quad (1a)$$

$\pi = P_{a0}/P_{b0}$ will have to change along that continuum of (F) positions, in a direction opposite to that in which r_b and hence P_{b0} vary.[68] Thus for $r_b^0 < r_b^+ < r_{b\,max}$ the increasing relation of Assumption (iii) between P_{a0} and P_{b0} (i.e. r_b) will only hold for the values of P_{a0} corresponding to what we shall call the 'main branch' of the function linking r_b with π and the remaining unknowns in (F)—the only branch, that is, in which $W > 0$.

[7] We may now come to what turns out to be perhaps the key relationship in the system, the one already considered in Assumption (iii) between the contemporary relative price $\pi = P_{a0}/P_{b0}$ and the intertemporal relative prices, represented here by r_b.

Thus, let us drop Eq. (7f) from system (F) for a moment, and see the likely effect on A_0^D/B_0^D of a fall of P_{a0}, which happened to be in strict proportion to that of P_{b0}.[69] By thus keeping constant π while r_b falls we aim to distinguish between the 'intertemporal' effects of that fall and the side-effects if any, that it may have on the relative demands for a_0 and b_0—and hence, once Eq. (7f) is re-introduced, on the contemporary relative prices $\pi = P_{a0}/P_{b0}$ and P_{a1}/P_{b1}, as well as on the other own rate of interest, r_a (para. [8]).

Now, the proportionate fall of P_{a0}/P_{b1} and P_{b0}/P_{b1} might be thought to affect the decisions to save and invest in some definite direction, but no general reason appears to exist why the *ratios* D_{a0}/D_{b0} or I_a/I_b, and therefore the ratio $A_0^D/B_0^D = (D_{a0} + Ia)/(D_{b0} + Ib)$, should be affected in one direction rather than the other. It follows that, quite independently of any uncertainty due to the income effects which we chose to rule out by Assumption (iii(a)) in para. [4], we could not expect any definite sign in the change of π necessary to keep A_0^D/B_0^D at the A_0^S/B_0^S level imposed by Eq. (7f): π may, that is, move either way, or even alternate the signs of the change as r_b falls; and the same will be true for the other contemporary relative price P_{a1}/P_{b1}, controlled by price Eqs. (1f). Therefore, unless the fall of r_b causes pronounced dislocations of relative demands in $t = 0$, a tendency can be supposed for the contemporary price π not to change drastically as r_b falls and, therefore, for the intertemporal price P_{a0}/P_{b1} to follow the other intertemporal price P_{b0}/P_{b1} (i.e. r_b) in its fall. This tendency of the two 'intertemporal' prices to fall or rise together is at the basis of our Assumption (iii).

An important and perhaps surprising implication of what we have just said should now be noted for future reference. We saw that no reason exists why as r_b

[68] It may be useful to note that r_b^0, although no greater than r_b^+, must be larger than $r_{b\,min}$. Since $P_{b0} = 0$ would entail $P_{a0} = 0$ (para. [11]), for $W = 0$ Eq. (1a) of para. [2], is only compatible with $P_{b0} > 0$, and therefore with $r_b^0 > r_{b\,min}$.

[69] Formally we replace Eq. (7f) with an equation $P_{a0}/P_{b0} =$ constant, and treat A_0^D/B_0^D as an unknown.

falls towards $r_{b\,min}$, the relative contemporary price $\pi = P_{b0}/P_{a0}$ should move in one direction rather than the other [*editor's note*: here, as well as in para. [12] below, the terms of the price ratio elsewhere in the essay defined and referred to as π are erroneously reversed, with no implications for the substance of the arguments]. However, the own interest r_b falling towards the minimum level of (-1) holding when the commodities are not storable is in fact the intertemporal price P_{b0}/P_{b1} of b_0, falling towards zero. It therefore appears that in system (F) the assumption of a zero level of the *intertemporal* price P_{b0}/P_{b1} of b_0 does *not* entail a zero level of its *contemporary* price P_{b0}/P_{a0}, contrary to what we would expect from a commodity which is becoming 'free' in the generally accepted sense—when a tendency to zero of the price of the commodity in terms of one scarce commodity (b_1 in this case) would entail a tendency to zero of its price in terms of *all* other scarce commodities (like a_0 here) whether of the same, or of another, date. We shall return on this basic point in para. [12].

[8] After seeing the grounds on which Assumption (iii) rests we may now turn to two important implications of that assumption. The first is that, as shown by Eq. (1a) of para. [2], the monotonic direct relation between P_{a0} (i.e. P_{a0}/P_{b1}) and r_b (i.e. P_{b0}/P_{b1}) entails a monotonic inverse relation between r_b and W in the interval between $r_{b\,min}$ and r_b^0. The same is true for any level in the upper interval $r_b^0 \le r_b \le r_b^+$, limitedly, however, to the 'main branch' of the functions linking r to π and the other unknowns of the system (para. [6]).

The second implication of Assumption (iii) is that the monotonic increasing relation between the intertemporal prices P_a and P_b there specified, also entails a monotonic increasing relation between r_a and r_b so that over that interval the two own rates of interest will always move in the same direction.[70]

[9] It is indeed time for some more general considerations on the relationship just referred to between own rates of interest. The considerations will refer to our simple model, but appear susceptible of generalisation. There seems indeed to be no reason why r_a should always move in the same direction as r_b when the latter changes in system (F). The relation between the two rates ensured by arbitrage is given by:

[70] Suppose that not to be so and thus r_a to fall as r_b rises in a sub-interval $r_b' < r_b < r_b''$ in the overall interval $r_{b\,min} \le r_b \le r_b^0$ (see Figure B). At least two distinct levels, r_a^1 and r_a^2, would have to correspond to any given level $\overline{r}_b$ in that sub-interval, since r_a must have initially risen from $r_{a\,min} = -1$, together with r_b, as P_{a0}/P_{b1} rose monotonically from zero together with P_{b0}/P_{b1} (Assumption (iii); and para. [11] below). However, that same monotonic relation between P_{a0} and P_{b0} entails that the two levels P_{a0}^1 and P_{a0}^2, corresponding to r_a^1 and r_a^2 respectively, would be equal because they correspond to the single value $\overline{P}_{b0} = \overline{r}_b + 1$. But then $P_{a0}^1/P_{b0} = P_{a0}^2/P_{b0}$ would have in common the same unique series of prices (para. 2), and therefore $r_a^1 = r_a^2$, contrary to our premises. The same monotonicity of the relation between P_{a0}/P_{b1} entails that r_a cannot remain constant as r_b changes: for that to happen two levels of r_b and therefore of P_{b0}, i.e. P_{b0}^2, P_{b0}^1, should correspond to the level P_{a0} holding for the given r_a.

$$1 + r_a = \frac{P_{a0}}{P_{a1}} = \frac{P_{b0}}{P_{b1}}\frac{P_{b1}}{P_{a1}}\frac{P_{a0}}{P_{b0}} = (1 + r_b)\left[\frac{P_{a0}/P_{b0}}{P_{a1}/P_{b1}}\right] \tag{6a}$$

where the factor within square brackets shows, as we would expect, that the proportion between the two rates of $t = 0$, established by arbitrage, compensates the disadvantage which those who lend in terms of the commodity whose relative price falls between time $t = 0$ and time $t = 1$, would otherwise have: thus if it is *a* that falls, the factor in question is larger than 1, and r_a is correspondingly larger than r_b, and vice versa.

The two rates might therefore *move* in an opposite direction over a limited interval of r_b[71] but only if the change in r_b were to modify considerably the variation in the relative price of the two commodities over the year: where the stress falls on 'modify' rather than 'variation', since a constancy in the price variation would allow the two rates to move, not only in the same direction, but also in strict proportion. However, the variation in question is governed by the technical conditions of production expressed in price Eqs. (1f) and its change is not therefore likely to be large unless the change in r_b affects very strongly the ratios between the three factor prices P_{a0}, P_{b0}, W and, besides, large differences exist in the proportion in which the three factors are used in producing the two goods.

[10] We have so far been mainly concerned with the determination of the two schedules at intermediate levels of r_b. Completion of the analogous determination at the 'extreme' values of $r_{b\,min} = -1$, and $r_b^0 \le r_b \le r_{b\,max}$, for $W = 0$, raises some additional problems connected with the zero levels of W or P_{b0} which those extremes imply.

We may turn first to the case of $W = 0$ along the corresponding upper range of r_b (para. [6]), and have a closer look at the supply of labour in that range. It has often been noted that there is no reason why, as the wage *approaches* zero, the supply of labour should also approach zero. If wages are the only income available to the worker for survival, the supply of labour can easily be imagined to increase, rather than decrease, as the wage gets close to zero (a quarter pound of daily bread is better than nothing.)[72] The situation only changes when the wage actually

[71] This can only happen for a part of the relevant interval of r_b, since r_a has to rise from -1 as r_b does (see the preceding note).

[72] A position which we find exemplified in Morishima (1964: 87) is to assume, at a zero wage, both a zero supply *and* the continuity of the supply schedule for labour. It might seem possible to reconcile this position with the question of 'survival' discussed in the text, by assuming a nearly horizontal segment joining the origin of the axes with a comparatively high level of labour supply for a wage close to zero (a *strictly* horizontal segment would instead be the graphic representation of the kind of continuity we are assuming). However, it is not easy to see why a worker who has been increasing his labour supply to try to survive, should abandon that purpose by progressively *decreasing* his supply when the wage is still positive: a discontinuity of supply would rather seem natural when the worker gives up hope of survival. Even more arbitrary seem to be other assumptions ensuring continuity, such as e.g. that of each individual being endowed with some quantity of each resource (Debreu, 1959: 88) i.e. of a quantity of some other resource whose price is bound to rise when that of the resource considered tends to zero, thus avoiding dependence on the latter for survival.

reaches zero, and supplying labour no longer makes any sense for the worker. It would thus seem reasonable to envisage a *discontinuity* in the supply of labour at a zero wage or close to it, where a jump to zero would presumably occur from the high level to which the supply might tend as the wage tends to zero.

Such a *discontinuity* would, however, have the undesirable consequence of eliminating the certainty of the existence of at least one economically significant solution to a system of general equilibrium: in particular, the system would no longer admit the zero wage solutions should the supply of labour happen to exceed demand at all strictly positive wages. We have therefore followed what seems to be generally supposed: i.e. a continuity of the supply of productive resources even at zero prices for their services and, therefore, that the quantity of labour made available at that price is the limit to which that quantity tends as the wage tends to zero,[73] which in the system (F) is the given supply L. This assumption—which we have in fact used already, when referring to a continuum with different levels of labour employment at a zero wage in the range $r_b^0 < r_b < r_{b\,max}$ (para [6])—and the irrational behaviour it would entail, should however be kept in mind when, in what follows, the shape of the I schedule will show the possibility of equilibria in the interval $r_b^0 \leq r_b \leq r_{b\,max}$.

[11] As we proceed now to the analogous question concerning savings, i.e. the supply of a_0 and b_0 as capital goods, it is similarly possible to envisage a state of acute scarcity for individuals whose only way to survive in $t = 1$ are stocks of (non-storable) a_0 and b_0. Savings may then well increase in physical terms as both *intertemporal* prices P_{b0}/P_{b1} and P_{a0}/P_{a1} tend to zero (on that joint tendency to zero of all intertemporal prices for commodities available in $t = 0$ cf. para. [12]), with savers discontinuously annulling their useless savings as those prices actually reach zero, and $r_b = r_a = -1$.[74] We shall however assume continuity in the supplies S_a and S_b of a_0 and b_0 as capital goods, so as to ensure the existence of at least one general equilibrium for the system. We shall therefore find at zero intertemporal prices, the levels of physical savings to which S_a and S_b tend as r_b tends to (-1).

[12] As a second preliminary to considering more closely the determination of the extreme points of the I and S schedules, we must now examine the meaning of the zero price P_{b0}/P_{b1} we assume when referring to the point in the schedules for

---

[73] We are here referring to general-equilibrium demand and supply schedules for labour, obtained from (E) by treating W as an independent variable, and using the third of relations (3e) to define the new unknown labour demanded L^D, with an adjustment in aggregate expenditure analogous to that we saw in para. 9, n. 25 in the text.

[74] The discontinuity would result from savings suddenly disappearing, at $r_b = -1$, with a_0 and b_0, being used instead entirely for consumption in $t = 0$ at the 'contemporary' price $\pi = P_{a0}/P_{b0}$, ensuring relative consumption demands D_{a0}/D_{b0} compatible with (7f). It is also possible to envisage that, through consumption loans, wage income (reaching its maximum, as r_b and r_a fall towards their minimum) be spent in advance by increasing consumptions D_{a0}, D_{b0} of both goods as their intertemporal prices relevant here fall towards zero: this could engender negative gross savings in the lower range of the S curve, and savings could become zero at some level $r_b > r_{b\,min}$.

$r_{b\,min} = -1$. This zero intertemporal price presents an interest which goes beyond its direct importance, confined as that is in system (F), to the case in which no commodity in the economy can be stored. As we noted in para. 7, where we first came across it, that zero price does not designate b_0 as a free commodity in the generally accepted sense of having a zero price also in terms of *any* other scarce commodity besides b_1. On the contrary we saw that there is no reason why b_0's *contemporary* price $\pi = P_{b0}/P_{a0}$ should be zero when P_{b0}/P_{b1} is such.

The two kinds of prices, contemporary and intertemporal, have in fact two quite different meanings. The intertemporal price P_{b0}/P_{b1} expresses the conditions at which the commodity can be transferred over time—and thus reflects merely the scarcity or abundance of savings relative to investment needs. The contemporary price $\pi = P_{b0}/P_{a0}$ reflects instead the scarcity of b_0 relative to a_0 in $t = 0$, and by setting $r_b = -1$ we did not assume anything in particular about it. This contemporary relative scarcity is largely dependent on the endowments A_0^S and B_0^S, which remain exactly the same all along the *I* and *S* schedules and up to $r_{b\,max}$.

Indeed our Assumption (ii) in para. 2, that a_0 and b_0 can always be used in the given proportion A_0^S/B_0^S, has excluded the possibility of either b_0 or a_0 having a zero *contemporary* relative price whether at $r_{b\,min}$ or at any other level of r_b. And what we just saw in para. [11] entails that both b_0 and a_0 might become *increasingly* scarce for consumption in $t = 0$, as r_b approaches its minimum level, with the corresponding *definite scarcity of* b_0 *relative to* a_0, expressed by $\pi = P_{b0}/P_{a0}$. What is *assumed* not to be scarce the moment in which we give the value of (−1) to our independent variable r_b is only the purchasing power which people seek to transfer from $t = 0$ to $t = 1$, *relative* to the only possibility to collectively do so in that economy: lending capital goods a_0 and b_0 to producers, who transform them into a_1 and b_1: but for that to happen a_0 and b_0 must be demanded *for production* and can therefore be in excess supply, independently of their scarcity in consumption in $t = 0$.

This nature of the zero price of b_0 at $r_b = -1$ comes more fully into light when we observe that arbitrage will then entail zero intertemporal prices of all commodities dated $t = 0$ in terms of any other dated $t = 1$. Were it not so anybody wishing to exchange b_0 for b_1 could do so via a_1 (if $P_{b0}/P_{a1} > 0$),[75] or by first getting a_0 and then b_1, and this either directly (if $P_{a0}/P_{b1} > 0$), or again through a_1 (if $P_{a0}/P_{a1} > 0$).

[75] This arbitrage condition like any arbitrage conditions entailed by indirect exchanges is implied when reducing the number of prices from that of all combinations of the n commodities taken two by two, down to $(n - 1)$. Thus e.g. $P_{b0}/P_{b1} = 0$ entails that in $P_{b0}/P_{b1} = (P_{b0}/P_{a1})(P_{a1}/P_{b1}) = 0$, with $P_{a1}/P_{b1} \neq 0$, we should have $P_{b0}/P_{a1} = 0$. This, so to speak, 'collective' zero intertemporal price of commodities dated $t = 0$, in terms of commodities dated $t = 1$, confirms on the other hand that capital goods a_0 and b_0 are perfect substitutes for the savers acquiring them (paras. 25–26 in the text) so that the zero intertemporal price of one entails a zero price of the other. The reader may however wonder how it will be possible to discriminate in practice between, on the one hand, producers of b_1 or a_1, who would get b_0 and a_0 for free, and owners of a_0 and b_0 who should instead give *some* of their commodity in order to get the other.

[13] We are now finally able to complete our discussion of the solutions of (F) at the lower and upper extremes of the possible levels of r_b. With respect to $r_{b\,min} = -1$, we know that, given the continuity assumed in para. [11] for the supply of physical savings, solutions of (F) will exist there, no less than for the remaining interval $r_{b\,min} \leq r_b \leq r_{b\,max}$.[76] We are therefore legitimised to extend to that point Assumption (iii) about the uniqueness of the solution of (F).

The peculiarity of the diagrammatic representation of this point is that the zero price we find there for both commodities a_0 and b_0, of which I and S physically consist, will make the two schedules converge to zero as r_b reaches (-1) (see Fig. 1 in the text, para. 10). The positive, finite contemporary relative price of the two commodities available in $t = 0$ (paras. 7 and 12) entails however that, should we choose to measure S and I by taking a_0 or b_0 as the numéraire, we would find there two non-zero separate points S and I, with S_a, S_b being both smaller or both larger than I_a, I_b, the sign of the inequality being the one indicated by the relation between S and I as r_b approaches $r_{b\,min}$ sufficiently (cf. para. 15 in the main text).

[14] As we proceed to the determination of the I and S points of the schedules at the opposite extreme, we find the continuum of (F) positions we outlined in para. [6]. That continuum, we said, will correspond to levels of labour employment L^D between zero and L, with the corresponding changes of the investment required to equip that variable amount of labour.[77]

We may look at the continuum by starting at $r_b = r_b^+$, where W reaches zero after falling monotonically from its maximum level as r_b rises from r_{bmin} up to r_b^0, and then along the 'main branch' of the function linking I, S and the other unknowns of (F) with r_b (see Assumption (iii), para. [5]). Beyond r_b^+, the I schedule will however sooner or later turn left as it will have to extend to touch the vertical axis as the investment demand falls to zero together with the amount of labour L^D to be equipped by means of that investment (see Fig. 2 in para. 16 of the text). Thus, starting from the value r_b^+, the schedule I may either rise or fall as it moves right or left, to finally reach the vertical axis on the left, having its highest and lowest points at, respectively, $r_{b\,max}$ and r_b^+, each or both of which may or may not coincide with r_b^+.[78]

---

[76] Cf. para. 3. The only difference is that for $r_b = -1$, i.e. $P_{b0} = 0$, Eq. (2f) of para. 4 gives the intertemporal price $P_{a0} = 0$.

[77] Given the possible multiplicity of solutions of (F) in the interval $r_b^0 \leq r_b \leq r_{b\,max}$, the determination of the (F) positions for $W = 0$ is most easily envisaged by the device of letting L^D (which is uniquely related to those positions) to take the role of independent variable when $W = 0$, so as to obtain the corresponding r_b and with it all the other unknowns of the (F) system for that level of L^D. In particular, this will allow tracing the multiple (F) positions which may correspond to the same level of r_b for $W = 0$.

[78] Assumption (iii) of para. [5], on the joint rise of P_{a0}/P_{b1} and P_{b0}/P_{b1} so long as $W > 0$, excludes that among the multiple solutions for $r_b^0 \leq r_b \leq r_{b\,max}$, there may be any with positive W , apart from those on the 'main branch' of the function relating $\pi = P_{a0}/P_{b0}$ and r_b.

The levels of S will similarly change as r_b varies in that interval, and the schedule may also extend either right or left as it rises or falls together with the I schedule, starting from point S^+ for r_b^+. No reason however exists why it should tend to zero as L^D tends to zero (see again Fig. 2 in the text)[79]: at the corresponding points, savings remain those effected out of the endowments A_0^S and B_0^S: wages being zero, the different levels of labour employment do not affect the income out of which savings are decided.

Appendix II: Two Notes on Hahn on 'the Neo-Ricardians'

[A] *Two Meanings of the Uniform Rate of Return on Capital and Some Mathematical Flaws in* Hahn's (1982) *Argument*

[i] What follows is not a belated commentary on, or an answer to, Hahn's (1982) article on the so-called 'neo-Ricardians'. That misleading article had essentially two aims: the first was to claim that Sraffa and his 'followers' were only concerned with a 'Special case' of neoclassical theory; the second was to answer their critique, centred on the notion of a 'quantity of capital', by contending that the notion plays no role in neoclassical theory.

Now, the first claim has been answered time ago by explaining that in the classical theory of Smith and Ricardo which Sraffa aimed to revive, the idea of a distribution of the social product based on the substitutability of 'productive factors' and therefore on the determining role of 'factor endowments' is absent; so that Sraffa's contribution cannot be based on the assumption of the capital endowments of Hahn's 'Special neoclassical case'.[80]

As for the second contention the answer is in the main text above, where it is argued in detail how a 'quantity of capital' is implied, together with its

[79] Contrary to what one might think at first, the income from which those savings come, is likely to change little as L^D changes since, with $W = 0$, only the owners of the initial stocks A_0^S and B_0^S will have an income (cf. n. 67 above)—the adjustment in the expenditure for $t = 1$ described in para. 9 of the text then taking care of the changes in the physical social product for that period as L^D changes.

[80] See para. [v] about the capital endowments of Hahn's 'Special' case. Cf. Garegnani (1990b: 113–5) for an answer to Hahn's (1982) first claim. We may also note that in (1975: 361) Hahn finds 'incomprehensible' the 'neo-Ricardian' idea that 'distribution precedes value'. However, it was in (1951: xxx-xlix) that Sraffa had advanced his interpretation of Ricardo and the old classical economists in terms of a wage determined by historical and institutional circumstances ('subsistence'), with the non-wage distributive variables accordingly resulting as a residue or surplus. This interpretation, where in an evident sense distribution (the determination of the real wage) precedes values, had indeed been expounded and variously discussed before, with, and after, Sraffa (1960), also with respect to its distinction from the alternative theory advanced by Joan Robinson (1956) and her other works.

deficiencies, in an intertemporal equilibrium. It is also contended there that a reference to that 'quantity' in neoclassical theory is rendered ultimately inevitable by the fact that capital goods are for savers perfectly substitutable means of acquiring future income and savers' decisions are accordingly taken with respect to that single 'quantity' (paras. 26–27 in the text).

[ii] What follows in this Appendix is therefore confined to two specific points intended to clarify some misunderstandings that have seriously marred the 'capital controversies' so far. The first is a widespread confusion between two quite different kinds of uniform rate of return on capital: a uniformity of own commodity interest rates, and that of effective rates of return on the supply prices of the capital goods. This confusion, causing the flaws we shall see in Hahn's (1982) mathematical argument, is an expression, I shall argue, of the obscuration of the change which has occurred in the notions of equilibrium during the last few decades and of its deeper causes: the change, that is, sometimes perceived as the 'Formalist revolution' in neoclassical theory.[81]

The second point, considered in Section B, regards instead a peculiarity implicit in the new notions of equilibrium, which Hahn again expresses in a particularly candid way when assuredly denying that the 'quantity of capital' has any relevance in neoclassical pure theory. The peculiarity consists, essentially, of regarding physical compositions of the capital endowment the economy moves away from, as equivalent, in defining non-stationary equilibria, with physical compositions the economy tends to.

[iii] In Hahn (1982) a key role is played by the distinction between a 'General' neoclassical case and a 'Special' one, where the latter is characterised by a uniformity of the rate of return on capital. The distinction echoes in fact one drawn by critics early in the capital controversies (para. [vii]), between the contemporary versions of neoclassical theory and the traditional ones based, as the latter were, on the above condition of a uniform effective rate of return on the supply prices of capital goods, and on the resulting 'adjusted' physical composition of the 'capital stock' (n. 3 in the text).

Hahn's model is the one we adopted for our chapter, and his 'General' neoclassical case coincides with our system [E][82] but for two elements. The first is the exclusion of the inequality signs, and associated zero prices, from the first three relations of our system [3e][83] (para. 3 in the text), regarding factor demands and supplies. The missing inequality signs rule out, besides the possibility that one of

[81] Cf. e.g. Hutchison (2000); Blaug (1999).

[82] Cf. Equations (22) in Hahn (1982: 364) corresponding to our equations (le) of para. 3 in the text; his Eq. (17), p. 363, for our (2e); then (25), p. 365, for the first three of our relations (3e) and, finally, Eqs. (23), p. 364, for the remaining two of relations (3e).

[83] Cf. Equations (25), in Hahn (1982: 365). Hahn does not, on the other hand, assume 'activities' of free disposal and justifying those equality signs.

the factors be non-scarce in the generally accepted sense, the less obvious possibility of 'extreme equilibria' arising from excess savings (point III in para. 14 of text).

[iv] Of more interest to us here is however a second shortcoming of Hahn's formalisation. It is his supposition that 'both goods are produced' (ibid., 364), which he does not motivate, as we did (para. 3 of the text), by the assumption that the two goods are non-storable: in fact, the whole issue of the storability of commodities, hardly separable from that of an intertemporal equilibrium, is absent in Hahn (1982). Now, in that unspecified form, Hahn's assumption is in conflict with the fact that the two goods are also capital goods, and for durable or storable capital goods, the possibility of demand prices below supply prices, and therefore temporary non-production of them, is the logical entailment of a system, like Hahn's, based on a given physical composition of the initial capital endowments[84] (e.g. the so-called 'Hahn problem' about adjustments to equilibria rests entirely on some capital goods not being produced, and their prices being therefore free to move *below* the respective supply prices so as to adjust to price expectations). The result is that when applied to ordinary and therefore durable, or storable capital goods, Hahn's 'General neoclassical case' falls into an over-determinacy which, curiously enough, is a neat replica in terms of present-day intertemporal general equilibria of the over-determinacy to be found in Walras's originary general equilibrium system.

The question here is ultimately that of the uniform effective rate of return on the *supply prices* of the capital goods. Demand prices below the respective supply prices for capital goods offering a potentially lower rate of return, is indeed the way in which arbitrage achieves a uniformity of returns on the *demand prices* of the capital goods. The moment in which such prices are equalised with the respective supply prices—in which, that is, production of all capital goods is assumed[85]—also is the moment in which we are introducing in the equations the traditional equilibrium condition of the uniformity of rates of return on the supply prices, postulated by Walras in common with all his contemporaries and successors up to recent decades. But in Walras that traditional condition was in conflict with a capital endowment given in its physical composition, and not as the abstract 'quantity of capital', susceptible of assuming any physical form, of his contemporaries and successors—thus causing what I have elsewhere referred to as 'Walras's inconsistency'.[86]

---

[84] Cf. n. 86 below. For the distinction between demand and supply prices of capital goods, cf. e.g. Walras's distinction between the 'prix de vente' and the 'prix de revient' of such goods, which Jaffé translates in his edition as 'selling prices' and 'costs of production' respectively (Walras, 1954: 271 ff.).

[85] Of course obsolete capital goods are not supposed to be produced but neither can they be present in the physically specified endowment of an economy like that of Walras (1954) and Hahn (1982) where only the dominant methods of production appear. I owe to Professor Fabio Petri having attracted my attention to the point.

[86] See Garegnani (1990a: 11–22); on the point in Walras's own texts, cf. also by the same author (1958) [*A Problem in the Theory of Distribution from Ricardo to Wicksell*, PhD dissertation, published in Part I of this volume; see in particular Sect. II, Chs. II and III] and (1960), Part II, Chs.

Now, in Hahn's intertemporal context, with price changes considered in the equilibrium equations, a uniform *effective* rate of return necessarily takes the form of rates of interest which *differ* according to the commodity in which the loan is expressed (like $r_a \neq r_b$ in our chapter). This *effectively* uniform rate of interest, and therefore of return on the *demand prices* of capital goods, is introduced in the equations when we refer to $n - 1$ discounted prices for n dated commodities, thus implying arbitrage through triangular intertemporal exchanges. It becomes therefore a uniform rate of return on the *supply prices* of the capital goods, the moment in which these goods are assumed to be produced and, accordingly, their prices are equalised with the supply prices. And this is just what is done by Hahn in his 'General' case, when he assumes that both goods are produced. The condition thus introduced cannot however be generally satisfied in his context, any more than it could in Walras's original system, since the physical composition of the capital endowment is as given in Hahn as it was in Walras.

This flaw of Hahn's treatment, we said, is curious. Walras's inconsistency had been acknowledged by Hahn in e.g. an earlier (1975) paper of his and indeed, as we shall see in para. [vii], is the very one he intends to show to affect the 'Special case' and to have been overcome in the 'General case', which we now see to be instead affected by it (the 'Special case' being affected by an over-determinacy of quite different origin, cf. para. [v]). The contradiction is strictly connected with the confusion between two kinds of uniformity of rates of return we mentioned at the beginning, and to which we can now turn.

[v] The confusion emerges as we proceed from Hahn's 'General' neoclassical case to his 'Special' case, and note a third flaw in Hahn's mathematical argument. He obtains the 'Special' case by adding to the relations of the General case that of a uniformity of the two *own interest rates*:

$$r_a = r_b \text{ and therefore } \frac{P_{a0}}{P_{a1}} - 1 = \frac{P_{b0}}{P_{b1}} - 1 \text{ or } \frac{P_{a0}}{P_{a1}} = \frac{P_{b0}}{P_{b1}}, \tag{I}$$

i.e. the condition of a constancy $P_{a0}/P_{b0} = P_{a1}/P_{b1}$ of the relative price of the goods over the two periods (see Eq. (21) in Hahn, 1982: 364).

Now, uniformity (I) of the *own commodity interest rates* is quite a different matter from the uniformity of the *effective rates of return on the supply prices of*

II and III. In Appendix G of the (1960) book [Engl. transl. published as Appendix E in *A Problem* ..., this volume, Part I], I also noted how Pareto, who in the *Cours* (1896–1897) had already been ambiguous as to whether all capital goods were being produced, finally abandoned in his *Manuel* (1909) any attempt to formalise the theory of capitalisation. (The over-determinacy of Walras's system becomes evident if we refer to the extreme case of absolute redundancy in the endowment of one capital good, with its rate of return on the supply price being accordingly zero or negative, and obviously less than that of any scarce capital goods.)

the capital goods referred to by the critics, to whom Hahn is there intending to answer (para. [vii]). However, he analyses the former *as if* it were the latter: in particular, he incorrectly attributes the over-determinacy of his 'Special' case to the cause pointed out by critics for Walras's over-determinacy, i.e. the given proportions between the stocks of the several capital goods in the endowment.[87]

That Hahn's interpretation of his own 'Special' case is incorrect can, on the other hand, be easily seen as soon as we extend from two to three years the life of the economy of his model (clearly, Hahn does not intend his distinction between 'General' and 'Special' neoclassical cases to be valid only for a two-year economy). We would then have *two* additional unknown prices P_{a2}, P_{b2}, but *three* new equations: the two additional price relations of type (1e) of para. 3 in the text, and the equation $P_{a1}/P_{a2} = P_{b1}/P_{b2}$ relating to the uniformity of the own rates in $t = 1$. Thus the total of excess equations in the 'Special' case now adds up to *two*, against which the *single* additional unknown B_0 or A_0/B_0 proposed by Hahn is of no avail. Indeed the physical composition of the initial capital stock has little to do with a constancy of relative prices, i.e. with the *kind* of uniformity of returns Hahn states in equation (I) for his 'Special' case.[88] This uniformity would depend, if anything, on the *size* rather than the *physical composition* of the capital endowment: it would be the size of that endowment, relative to that of labour and other original factors, that might ensure the incomes, and therefore the savings, of a stationary or steady-growth economy with its constant relative prices.[89]

[vi] In fact both in his interpretation of the 'Special' neoclassical case, and in his assumption that all capital goods are produced (para. [iii]), Hahn takes as one:

(a) the uniformity of the own commodity rates of interest of equation (I), due to *a constancy of relative prices over time*;

---

[87] Cf. Hahn (1982: 365–366), where it is suggested that B_0 be treated as an unknown, while keeping A_0 as a given.

[88] One may be curious about the reason why in Hahn's model letting the proportion between the two capital goods in the endowment be an unknown will instead ensure constancy of prices. That has to do with the peculiarity of a model which admits of one production cycle only. By starting from a sufficiently high stock A_0 relative to stock B_0 (see para. 6 in the text) and then lowering it sufficiently, we may generally continuously change P_{a0}/P_{b0} so that it rises from zero to infinity: i.e. from a_0 being a free good to b_0 being such. There must then be at least one proportion A_0/B_0 A_0 of the two stocks for which the curve described by the relative price P_{a0}/P_{b0}, with A_0/B_0 in the abscissae, intersects the analogous curve described by the production prices P_{a1}/P_{b1} of Eqs. (1e) of para. 3 in the text, thus giving $r_a = r_b$. However, as soon as a second yearly cycle of production is allowed for, and price equations must be satisfied also for P_{a2} and P_{b2}, the same relative prices could be maintained for a third year only if the economy happened to be stationary (or the technical conditions of production allowed for a labour theory of value).

[89] Cf. e.g. Hicks (1939: 118) and Garegnani (1960, Appendice E [in the present volume closely corresponding to Part I, *A Problem in the Theory of Distribution from Ricardo to Wicksell*, Sect. II, Appendix to Ch. VI]). This of course does not detract from the fact that a constancy of relative prices will generally imply also an adjusted physical composition of the capital stock.

(b) the traditional uniformity of the effective rate of return on the supply prices of the capital goods, *the result of an adjusted physical composition of the capital stock* (para. [i]),

where uniformity (b) is independent of (a) since, as shown for Hahn's 'General' case (para. [iv]), it is quite compatible with changes in equilibrium relative prices over time, and therefore with the divergent own commodity rates ruled out by uniformity (a).

And Hahn takes (a) as if it were (b) not only when, as we saw, he ascribes the over-determinacy caused by equation (I) and uniformity (a) to the proportions between the two stocks as if it were due to (b): he does so also when the traditional uniformity (b), being unaccompanied by (a), unlike what happened in the old theorists referred to by the critics (para. [vii]), is unwittingly introduced in a 'General case' intended to show those critics how one can do *without* that very traditional uniformity (b).

We may also note here incidentally that Hahn appears to misinterpret the divergence of own commodity rates of interest when he writes: 'The crudest empirical observations will convince one that there is no unique rate of profits to be observed in the economy: Do we conclude from *that* that competition is functioning badly? Answer: No. Consult any general equilibrium text' (1975: 361), thus apparently referring to divergences of own commodity rates. However, what empirical observation can reveal is divergent profit rates for different businesses, compared therefore in terms of money or some other *common numéraire*. But then, that divergence has nothing to do with divergences between own commodity rates, which would show by reckoning in *different numéraires* the same rate of profits (when, of course, the relative prices of those numéraires change over the year).

[vii] Unambiguous confirmation of the Hahn (1982) confusion about uniform rates, as well as of the intent we attributed in para. [iii] to his (1982) distinction between 'General' and 'Special' neoclassical cases, can in fact be obtained from the already quoted earlier (1975) paper of Hahn. He referred there to results advanced early in the capital controversies by the critics, who had pointed out how the contemporary attempt to surmount the inconsistency of the notion of a 'quantity of capital' by taking the capital endowment as a given physical vector entailed falling into the alternative inconsistency of Walras's originary general equilibrium. This was the case unless uniformity (b) was dropped, together with the entire traditional notion of equilibrium, as is done in contemporary pure theory—thus undermining, it was further argued by those critics, the persistency of the equilibria necessary for a correspondence between theoretical and observable variables.[90]

[90] See the references in n. 86 above, and Garegnani (1976: 38–39 [this volume, Part II, pp. 220–1]). The results are reported, e.g. in Harcourt (1972: 170–1), Robinson (1970: 338), Dobb (1973: 205n).

Accordingly, in (1975), Hahn begins by reporting statements by Harcourt (1975) to the effect that in the 'Walrasian model' it is not possible to have a 'theory of the rate of profits' [read: to determine a uniform rate of return on capital of type (b) above] and that

> to get a uniform rate of profit Wicksell (and others) had to work with Robinsonian leets [homogeneous capital].
>
> (Hahn, 1975: 360-361)

To this Hahn objects that the 'Walrasian model' *can* deal with 'the uniform rate of profit' by treating it as just 'an extremely specialised case' (Hahn, ibid.).

The passage is of some interest in itself because Hahn acknowledges there those early critical results of the capital controversies, and in particular: (i) the inconsistency between 'uniform rate of profit' and 'Walrasian model' and, therefore, (ii) the role of 'Robinsonian leets' (homogeneous capital) for 'Wicksell and others' in allowing for a uniform rate of profit. However, surprisingly enough, those two points are not mentioned in the (1982) paper, apparently devoted to answering the 'neo-Ricardian' critique on capital of which they evidently were central elements.[91]

What is of specific interest to us now is however the confirmation which the (1975) article gives of the confusion about uniformity of rates of return, and of the intent of the 'Special' neoclassical case. With respect to the first point Hahn describes as follows the 'specialisation' of the 'Walrasian model' yielding Wicksell's 'uniform rate of profit':

> General Equilibrium Theory is general and so can discuss the equilibrium of an economy whatever its initial conditions, e.g. outfit of goods inherited from the past. For most such specifications it will not be the case *that the equilibrium price of a good for future delivery in terms of the same good for current delivery will be the same for all goods.*
>
> (360, our italics)

But the uniformity of the rate of profits of 'Wicksell (and others)', i.e. uniformity (b) above, is quite different from 'the equilibrium price of a good for future delivery in terms of the same good for current delivery [being] the same for all goods', quite different, that is, from the uniformity (a) of own rates to which Hahn refers here.

(We may incidentally note how the above straight identification of Wicksell's uniform rate of profits with a uniformity of own rates of interest which is simply a constancy of relative prices, provides the key to what probably misled Hahn and other authors into confusing the two uniformities. In Wicksell, as in Walras, as in all theory up to recent decades, the persistence of the traditional equilibrium ensured by uniformity (b) above allowed abstracting from changes in equilibrium prices, so that uniformity (b) took form (a) and the latter can therefore be easily mistaken for (b)).

[91] Cf. para. [iv] and n. 87 above in this Appendix.

But, as we said, the (1975) article also clarifies the intent of the (1982) 'Special neoclassical case'. We find in (1975) words like the following referred to the 'capital outfit' allowing for a 'uniform rate of profit'

> that a very extreme specialisation of a general model somehow shows the latter to be inapplicable requires the very summit of incomprehension
>
> (1975: 360)

where the contention clearly is that the homogeneous capital referred to by the critics was introduced by 'Wicksell and others' in order to deal with what was only 'a very extreme specialisation' of contemporary neoclassical theory, with its given physical capital endowments. The passage makes clear, were it necessary, that the 1982 'Special neoclassical case' is simply this (1975) 'extreme specialisation' to which Hahn believes he can reconduct all neoclassical theory prior to recent decades.

We shall return in Section B below on this idea of Hahn, according to which an equilibrium with a capital stock of adjusted physical composition, and to which the economy therefore tends, is seen as just an extreme specialisation of 'equilibria' from which the economy would tend to depart.[92]

[viii] However what has been of interest for us here has been above all to trace through Hahn (1975, 1982) a widespread misunderstanding[93] which, during the capital controversies, has contributed to obscuring a point of considerable importance: namely the causes and implications of the drastic change which has occurred in mainstream pure theory in the wake of Hicks (1939). Uniformity (b), I submit, has played a central role in that change which, slow at first in gaining acceptance, rapidly established itself after the early phase of the capital controversies. For the reasons we saw, uniformity (b) had in fact to be abandoned when, after the failure of the attempts of Jevons, Böhm-Bawerk, Wicksell and others at an 'average period of production', it began to be admitted that capital could only

[92] As just mentioned, Hahn (1982) does not recall that this 'specialisation' was traditionally achieved by treating capital as a homogeneous substance so that the proportions between capital stocks were in fact unknowns, and not 'specialised data' which 'history' had happened to throw up (below, para. [xi]).

[93] On this failure to distinguish the basic form (b) of uniformity of returns on capital characterising a normal position of the economic system from Adam Smith down to recent decades, from the uniformity (a) between own rates due to price constancy and, besides, from the short period uniformity imposed by arbitrage (and to be presently considered in this Appendix), see e.g. Christopher Bliss's (1987) *New Palgrave* article dedicated to the 'Equality of Profit Rates'. Under what he calls 'the rate of profit' Bliss does not appear to distinguish between the above short-period uniformity on the demand prices of the capital goods and the uniformity on the supply prices, the one traditionally indicated as the 'uniform rate of profit'. The uniform 'rate of profit' is instead counterposed to the divergence of own commodity rates of interest which, as in Hahn, accordingly appears to be taken as one with the divergence of effective returns on the supply prices of the capital goods which the critics had indicated as a shortcoming of contemporary theory.

be consistently measured in terms of a set of quantities. This also meant abandoning the neoclassical version of the traditional notion of a normal or 'natural' position of the economy on which economic thinking had relied since its inception in order to achieve correspondence with observable variables (cf. e.g. para. 13 in the text; also below in this section).

Now, this disappearance of uniformity (b) with Hicks (1939) and subsequent work seems to have occurred without any clear recognition of its implications or even clear acknowledgement of the disappearance itself. Uniformity (b) could indeed be mistaken for the uniformity of the rate of return on the demand prices of the capital goods which was of course retained in the system by letting capital goods prices fall below their supply prices, but had altogether different implications. What appears however to have been decisive in preventing the issue from emerging has been, I submit, the confusion with uniformity (a), for which the disappearance of (b) from a non-stationary equilibrium has tended to be identified with the simultaneous disappearance of uniformity (a) owing to intertemporal pricing.

The obfuscation of condition (b) and therefore of the basic reasons of the change which pure theory has undergone with the adoption of the 'Walrasian' capital endowment as a capital goods vector in Hicks (1939)—the reasons, that is, of the 'Formalist revolution' in neoclassical theory as we saw it has been called[94]—has indeed made it possible to continue viewing that change in terms of Hicks' (1939) more explicit argument, namely the dependence of present individual decisions, and therefore of equilibrium, upon future prices: as if the persistence of the traditional equilibrium, made possible by uniformity (b), had not always been viewed as the basis for abstracting from such a dependence and from the radical difficulties it entails at the level of general theory. The introduction of dated prices, I submit, should indeed be seen as a *consequence* of the new equilibria and their 'fleeting' character[†] rather than a *cause* of the change over to them.[95]

(Before concluding on the question, it may be interesting to provide an example of how some contemporary authors find it difficult to grasp the traditional concept of a normal position, even in the neoclassical form it took in Marshall, J.B. Clark, Pigou, etc. An author like Christopher Bliss reconstructs as follows that concept in a writer as clear as Wicksell. We are given, Bliss describes (1975: 115), two economies 'in semi-stationary growth' such that 'the citizens are determined

---

[94] Cf. above, n. 81.

[†] [*Editor's note*: we have omitted the reference to Marshall's *Principles* present at this point of the text in the previously published version of the essay, quite clearly due to clerical error. See also the editor's note ‡ below, p. 287.].

[95] Such an attentive reading of the relevant part of Hicks's *Value and Capital* shows, I believe, that the difficulty Hicks was trying to overcome was not that of the change of equilibrium prices over time: but rather that of the 'quantity of capital'—as, on the other hand, he indicated by the very title of his book (on the point, cf. Garegnani, 1976: 30–36 [this volume, Part II, pp. 213–9]; Milgate, 1979: 6–9).

to hold capital goods of a specified value in terms of the *numéraire* no matter what equilibrium comes about' and such that 'in economy 2 the citizens [hold] a higher *numéraire* value of capital'. Wicksell's question then is, Bliss reports, 'how will the economies differ with regard to the total product produced'—an exercise, he then comments, which is 'extremely contrived' because 'no convincing specification of the demand for capital would lead to a totally inelastic demand for a particular *numéraire* value' (Bliss, 1975: 115). To unravel this description, we need three observations. First, if it were a question of semi-stationary economies (i.e. economies in steady growth: Bliss, 1975: 86–87) which is not the case for Wicksell (cf. e.g. 1934, Part III) then the steady growth condition would determine the amount of capital per head in the economy[96] and there would be no problem of 'citizens holding capital goods of a specified value'—(a question of a 'totally inelastic' *supply* rather than demand, unlike what Bliss writes). Second, the point of those equilibria in Wicksell was not 'to hold capital goods of a specified value… no matter what equilibrium comes about', but rather that a sizable increase in 'capital' (the single quantity, of course) would take time, and the capital in existence could be assumed constant over the period required for the equilibrium variables to emerge through a compensation of deviations (e.g. Marshall 1920: VI, ii, 4, 443–4[‡]). Third and last, surely Wicksell's priority in the alleged 'comparison' between the two economies would have been the respective rates of interest rather than 'the total product produced' (see e.g. Wicksell, 1934: 157, 162): indeed what Bliss describes as a 'comparison' between 'two economies' is simply, in Wicksell as in the other traditional neoclassicists, the construction of a (general-equilibrium) demand schedule for 'capital' (the mirror image of one for labour) to be then matched with the already mentioned supply. So Bliss's 'extremely contrived exercise' is essentially the basis of the neoclassical theory of the distribution between capital and primary factors, in the form in which it gained acceptance at the end of the nineteenth century and it dominated before recent decades: the lack of any wide resonance of the works of a Walras or Pareto at the time, when compared with those of Marshall, Jevons, Wicksteed, J. B. Clark or Pigou, etc., suggests that it was perhaps thanks to the roots it took in the shape of that 'contrived exercise' that neoclassical theory has been able to survive the 'Walrasian' form which, for the reasons we saw, it was forced to adopt with the 'Formalist revolution' of recent decades.)

[B] *Capital Endowments and 'History'*

[ix] It is not surprising that in his 1982 reply to the 'neo-Ricardians' on capital, Hahn should overlook the role of the notion of 'capital' as a single factor in

[96] Cf. n. 9 in the text and n. 89 in this Appendix.

[‡] [*Editor's note*: the page interval for this reference indicated in the previously published version, '443–543', was evidently incorrect, and has been properly rectified. The same page couple, in the unusual form '443 (543)', appeared in the reference erroneously present earlier in the text, as mentioned in the editor's note † above, p. 286.]

lending credence to the idea of a generalised substitutability between ‘factors of production’. This oversight is common to most contemporary pure theory (though not to applied theory) although it is transparent that, contrary to what would be required by the substitutability between *physical factors* postulated in the theory, alternative methods of production, or methods for alternative consumption goods, generally differ by the *kind* of capital goods employed, rather than by their proportions.[97]

What is more surprising is that in (1982) no trace should be found of the purely theoretical role acknowledged in (1975), which ‘capital’ played for ‘Wicksell (and others)’ in allowing for a ‘uniform rate of profit’ (see quotation in para. [vii]). It is owing to the latter oversight that in (1982: 354, our italics) Hahn can write.

> it seems to me impossible (as a matter of intellectual history) to maintain that the *possibility* of perfect capital (or labour) aggregation is a neo-classical doctrine

which would otherwise have raised the problem of how ‘Wicksell (and others)’ could refer to an aggregate capital (‘Robinsonian leets’) while failing to maintain its ‘possibility’. But Hahn may have been betrayed here by a lack of transparency in his compact language.

[x] Hahn however moves then from intellectual history to logic, and argues the irrelevance of the concept of a quantity of capital in neoclassical theory as follows:

> Arguing in a circle is not the problem [...]. The point is much simpler [...]. In general, the neoclassical equilibrium can be found given the vector of endowment which may have, say, 10^8 components. It would be surprising if there were a single number [a ‘quantity’ of capital *C*] which gives the same information as the 10^8 dimensional vector
>
> (1982: 369)

where the point is simple, but appears to be the opposite one: namely that a 10^8 dimensions capital endowment gives excessive information. Indeed, *C* would be required in order to express the capital endowment according to the perfect substitutability of capital goods *for savers*, the consequent uniform rate of return and adjusted physical composition of the endowment allowing for a persistence of the equilibrium sufficient for the traditional correspondence between theoretical and observable variables—along the lines Hahn had indeed acknowledged in 1975 to be those of Wicksell (para. [vii] above). And it is of course with this needed *C* that the ‘arguing in a circle’ comes in.

[xi] Hahn’s clear-cut belief in the uselessness of the notion of a quantity of capital in neoclassical theory may however be of use now for looking from a particular angle to what can be seen as a basic deficiency of the contemporary equilibria.

---

[97] Possibilities of substitution would still enter the system as the physical composition of the stock can change by means of capital replacement: but then, as argued in the main text, we are back to ‘capital’ as a single quantity and its problems through the relation between gross investment and the interest rate.

In 1975, after acknowledging that 'to get a uniform rate of profits Wicksell (and others)' resorted to 'Robinsonian leets', Hahn continued as follows:

> But all they had to do (writing before von Neumann they cannot be blamed for not doing so) is [...] simply assume that *history has given us the appropriate outfit.*
>
> (1975: 361, our italics)

Reflection however shows that the 'appropriate [capital] outfit' has nothing more to do with 'history' than have e.g. the particular outputs of consumption goods allowing for equality between prices and expenses of production: both sets of quantities clearly result from assuming a competitive process and not from an accident of history. Just as those consumption goods outputs can only be unknowns in a neoclassical demand-and-supply theory, so the same ought to be the case for the physical quantities constituting a given capital endowment. It was surely this, rather than any as yet missing von Neumann's theorems that made 'Wicksell (and others)' introduce capital as a single quantity.

Hahn's idea, that *any* physical composition of the initial capital endowment can be the basis of a neoclassical non-stationary equilibrium, seems thus to be ultimately not much better founded than that of taking as given in such a theory the outputs of consumption goods, and then arguing that it will be a 'Special' case when 'history' has yielded outputs allowing for prices equal to their production expenses. The necessary existence of stocks for capital goods may of course slow down, relative to many consumption goods, the competitive tendency to the equality between demand and supply prices, but surely it does not make of that tendency any less of an equilibrating tendency than the analogous one for consumption goods.

Mathematical Note to 'Savings, Investment and Capital in a System of General Intertemporal Equilibrium'

Michele Tucci

Note: equation numbering maintained as in the text.

THE MODEL

Let us take into consideration the following model (F):

$$\begin{cases} P_{a1} = l_a W + a_a P_{a0} + b_a P_{b0} \\ P_{b1} = l_b W + a_b P_{a0} + b_b P_{b0} \end{cases} \tag{1f}$$

$$P_{b1} = 1 \tag{2f}$$

$$\begin{cases} A_0 \geq D_{a0} + (a_a A_1 + a_b B_1) \\ B_0 \geq D_{b0} + (b_a A_1 + b_b B_1) \\ L \geq L_a A_1 + L_b B_1 \\ A_1 = D_{a1} \\ B_1 = D_{b1} \end{cases} \tag{3f}$$

If in the first relation of (3f) the inequality sign holds, then $P_{a0} = 0$; if it holds in the second one, then $P_{b0} = 0$. However, as is specified in Paragraph [3] of Appendix I, Assumption (ii), it should be noted that such cases will not be taken into consideration in the economic discussion in the text. The inclusion in the present demonstration is due to the need for clarifying the mathematical passages.

If the inequality sign holds in the third relation of (3e), then $W = 0$.

$$I = (a_a A_1 + a_b B_1) P_{a0} + (b_a A_1 + b_b B_1) P_{b0} \tag{4f}$$

$$S = \left(A_0^S - D_{a0}\right) P_{a0} + \left(B_0^S - D_{b01}\right) P_{b0} \tag{5f}$$

$$P_{b1}(r_b + 1) = P_{b0} \tag{6f}$$

$$\frac{A_0^D}{B_0^D} = \frac{A_0^S}{B_0^S} \tag{7f}$$

where P_{a0}, P_{b0}, P_{a1} and P_{b1} refer to prices, W indicates wages, S and I represent savings and investments, respectively, A_1 and B_1 correspond to quantities of produced commodities, A_0^D and B_0^D specify demands, and A_0^D and B_0^D specify demands, and $A_0^S (= A_0)$, $B_0^S (= B_0)$ and L refer to endowments. The single-valued mappings D_{a0}, D_{b0}, D_{a1} and D_{b1} designate standard Walrasian demand functions, which are characterised by the following assumptions:

1 the set of independent variables in the functions are those indicated by the first five among the symbols specified above;
2 in the non-negative orthant of the independent variables, each demand function is positive and continuous.

For the sake of simplicity, we suppose that the technical coefficients are all strictly positive. Moreover, the usual vitality conditions will hold. Finally, r_b specifies the own interest rate of commodity b over period $t = 0$. The first eleven among the symbols listed above constitute the unknowns of the model, while r_b is exogenously defined.

Let us substitute Eqs. (6f) and (2f) into the second equation of (1f), thus obtaining:

$$1 = l_b W + a_b P_{a0} + b_b (r_b + 1) \tag{8}$$

i.e. equation (1a) of Paragraph [2] of Appendix I.

Easy passages allow the following propositions to be derived from equations (1f), (2f), (6f) and (8):

(a) The quantities W and P_{a1} can be defined as functions of the single variable P_{a0}.
(b) Consider the interval $H_{r_b} = \{-1 \leq r_b \leq \max_{r_b}\}$, with $\max_{r_b} = (1 - b_b)/b_b$. Define $\beta_{r_b} = [1 - b_b(r_b + 1)]/a_b$. For every $r_b \in H_{r_b}$, we can determine an interval $H_{P_{a0}} = \{0 \leq P_{a0} \leq \beta_{r_b}\}$ such that, for every $P_{a0} \in H_{P_{a0}}$, $W \geq 0$, $P_{a1} > 0$.
(c) In the interval $H_{P_{a0}}$, the functions $W(P_{a0})$ and $P_{a1}(P_{a0})$ are continuous.
(d) If $-1 < r_b \leq \max_{r_b}$, then $P_{b0} > 0$; if $r_b = -1$, then $P_{b0} = 0$.

Due to the income correction, which is specified in Paragraph 9 of the text, the third of (3f) is always satisfied with the equality sign, except in border solutions, which are examined in connection with Assumption (iii), Paragraph [5] of Appendix I, and in Paragraphs [6], [10], [13] and [14] of the same Appendix, where there will be continuous set of solutions characterised by $W = 0$.

Let us assume that the equality sign holds in the first two relations of (3f). Substituting the last two equations of (3f) into the expressions on the right-hand side of the equality sign in the first two relations of (3f) and in Eq. (4f), we are able to define the variables A_0^D, B_0^D and I. Moreover, Eq. (5f) defines the variable S. In the interval $H_{P_{a0}}$, the four above-quoted expressions are continuous functions of the unique variable P_{a0}.

Define

$$\delta(P_{a0}) = \frac{D_{a0} + a_a D_{a1} + a_b D_{b1}}{D_{b0} + b_a D_{a1} + b_b D_{b1}} \tag{9}$$

$$\gamma = \frac{A_0^S}{B_0^S} = \text{constant} \tag{10}$$

In the interval $H_{P_{a0}}$, the function $\delta(P_{a0})$ is continuous.

Taking into consideration Eq. (7f), for every $r_b \in H_{r_b}$ one, and only one, of the following three sentences is necessarily true:

1. There exists $P_{a0}^* \in H_{P_{a0}}$ such that $\delta(P_{a0}) = \gamma$.
2. For every $P_{a0} \in H_{P_{a0}}$, $\delta(P_{a0}) < \gamma$.
3. For every $P_{a0} \in H_{P_{a0}}$, $\delta(P_{a0}) > \gamma$.

Figure 4 shows an example of case (1). Here, $P_{a0} \geq 0$ and the first two relations of (3f) are satisfied with the equality sign. Assumption (ii) in Paragraph [3] of Appendix I confines the main argument there to case (1) above. Therefore, the remaining two cases will be examined only for the sake of completeness.

In case (2), at the given level of r_b, commodity a_0, taken in the sum of both its consumption and investment uses, cannot be employed in as high a proportion to b_0 as the ratio γ in which it is found in the endowment. As a result, (F) can

Fig. 4 An example of case 1

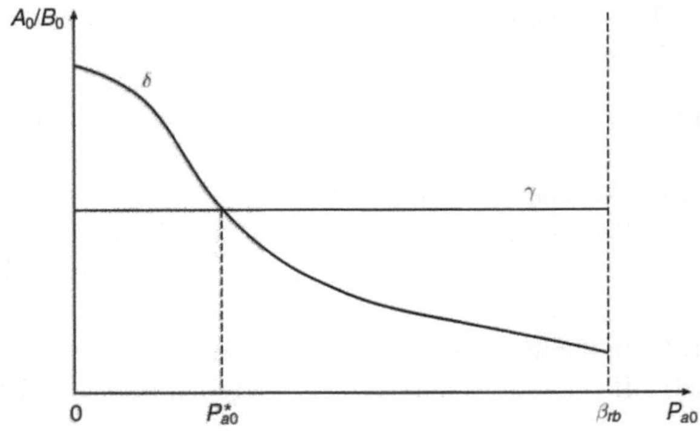

only admit solution if we allow the quantity A_0^D 'demanded' of Eq. (7f), to exceed the quantity used expressed by the R.H.S. of the first part of Eq. (3f), provided $P_{a0} = 0$ (cf. n. 65 to Appendix I).

In case (3) we have the case symmetrical to (2), where b_0 cannot be used in as high a proportion to a_0 (i.e. a_0 in as low a proportion to b_0), as the ratio in which the two commodities are found in the endowment. The inequality sign of the second relation in (3f) will allow for a solution of (F) provided $P_{b0} = 0$, i.e. if r_b is set at $r_{b\ min} = -1$. But no solution would exist if we set r_b, our independent variable, at a level $r_b > -1$—a case, however, which is of no economic importance since (F) could never, then, provide a solution of (E), where $r_b > 1$ implies $P_{b0} > 0$, and is therefore incompatible with an inequality sign in the second of relations (3e).

References

Arrow, K. J. (1989). Joan Robinson and modern economic theory: an interview. In G. R. Feiwel (Ed.), *Joan Robinson and modern economic theory* (pp. 147–185). Macmillan.

Arrow, K. J., & Hahn, F. H. (1971). *General competitive analysis*. North-Holland.

Blaug, M. (1999). The formalist revolution or what happened to orthodox economics after world War II?. In R. E. Backhouse & J. Creedy (Eds.), *From Classical economics to the theory of the firm. Essays in honour of D. P. O'Brien* (pp. 257–80). Edward Elgar.

Bliss, C. J. (1975). *Capital theory and the distribution of income*. North-Holland.

Bliss, C. J. (1987). Equal rates of profits. In J. L. Eatwell, M. Milgate, & P. Newman (Eds.), *The New Palgrave dictionary of economics* (Vol. 2, pp. 172–175). Macmillan.

Currie, M., & Steedman, I. (1990). *Wrestling with time. Problems in economic theory*. Manchester University Press.

Debreu, G. (1959). *The theory of value*. Wiley.

Dobb, M. H. (1973). *Theories of value and distribution since Adam Smith: Ideology and economic theory*. Cambridge University Press.

Garegnani, P. (1958). *A problem in the theory of distribution from Ricardo to Wicksell*, Cambridge University, Ph. D. Thesis.

Garegnani, P. (1960). *Il capitale nelle teorie della distribuzione*. Giuffrè.

Garegnani, P. (1970). Heterogeneous capital, the production function and the theory of distribution. *Review of Economic Studies, 37*(3), 407–436.

Garegnani, P. (1976). On a change in the notion of equilibrium in recent work on value and distribution. In M. Brown, K. Sato, & P. Zarembka (Eds.), *Essays in modern capital theory* (pp. 25–45). North Holland.

Garegnani, P. (1978). Notes on consumption, investment and effective demand: I. *Cambridge Journal of Economics, 2*(4), 335–353.

Garegnani, P. (1990a). Quantity of capital. In J. Eatwell, M. Milgate, & P. Newman (Eds.), *The new Palgrave: Capital theory* (pp. 1–78). Macmillan.

Garegnani, P. (1990b). Sraffa: Classical versus marginalist analysis. In K. Bharadwaj & B. Schefold (Eds.), *Essays on Piero Sraffa* (pp. 112–144). Unwin Hyman (rpt. Routledge, 2017).

Garegnani, P. (1990c). On some supposed obstacles to the tendency of market prices towards natural prices. *Political Economy—Studies in the Surplus Approach, 6*(1–2), 329–359.

Garegnani, P. (2000). Savings, investment and the quantity of capital in general intertemporal equilibrium. In H. D. Kurz (Ed.), *Critical essays on Piero Sraffa's legacy in economics* (pp. 392–445). Cambridge University Press.

Hahn, F. H. (1975). Revival of political economy: The wrong issues and the wrong argument. *The Economic Record, 51*(3), 360–364.

Hahn, F. H. (1982). The Neo-Ricardians. *Cambridge Journal of Economics, 6*(4), 353–374.

Harcourt, G. C. (1972). *Some Cambridge controversies in the theory of capital*. Cambridge University Press.

Harcourt, G. C. (1975). Decline and rise: The revival of (Classical) political economy. *Economic Record, 51*(3), 339–356.

Hicks, J. R. (1932). *The theory of wages*. Macmillan.

Hicks, J. R. (1939). *Value and capital*. Oxford University Press.

Hutchison, T. (2000). *On the methodology of economics and the formalist revolution*. Edward Elgar.

Jevons, W. S. ([1871] 1957). *The theory of political economy*. Kelley & Millman.

Keynes, J. M. (1936). *The general theory of employment, interest and money*. Macmillan.

Kirman, A. (1989). The intrinsic limits of modern economic theory: the emperor has no clothes. *Economic Journal, 99*(395) (Supplement), 126–139.

Kurz, H. D., & Salvadori, N. (1995). *Theory of production: a long period analysis*. Cambridge University Press.

Marshall, A. (1920). *Principles of economics*, 8th edition. Macmillan (reprinted and reset 1949).

Milgate, M. (1979). On the origin of the notion of "Intertemporal Equilibrium" *Economica, 46*(181), 1–10.

Morishima, M. (1964). *Equilibrium*. Clarendon Press.

Pareto, V. (1896–1897). *Cours d'économie politique*. Rouge.

Pareto, V. (1909). *Manuel d'économie politique*. Giard et Brière [Eng. trans.: A. Montesano, A. Zanni, L. Bruni, J. S. Chipman, and M. McLure (Eds), *Manual of Political Economy*. Oxford University Press, 2014].

Robinson, J. V. (1956). *The accumulation of capital*. Macmillan.

Robinson, J. V. (1970). Review of C. E. Ferguson, The neoclassical theory of production and distribution. *Economic Journal, 80*(318), 336–339.

Samuelson, P. A. (1962). Parable and realism in capital theory: The surrogate production function. *Review of Economic Studies, 29*(3), 193–206.

Sraffa, P. (1951). Introduction. In *The works and correspondence of David Ricardo*, ed. by P. Sraffa with the collaboration of M. H. Dobb,Vol. I. Cambridge University Press.

Sraffa, P. (1960). *Production of commodities by means of commodities*. Cambridge University Press.

Walras, L. (1954). *Elements of pure economics*, 4th def. ed., Jaffé's. George Allen and Unwin.

Wicksell, K. (1954). *Value, capital and rent*. George Allen & Unwin.
Wicksell, K. (1934). *Lectures on political economy* (Vol. I). George Routledge & Sons.
Wicksell, K. (1935). *Lectures on political economy* (Vol. II). George Routledge & Sons.

Part III
The Classical Approach: Value and Distribution

The Classical Theory of Wages and the Role of Demand Schedules in the Determination of Relative Prices[†]

My purpose in this paper will be twofold. First, I shall argue that the role of demand functions in determining prices depends on their role in determining distribution by means of the "relative scarcity" of the "factors of production." As a result, these functions would have no role in determining prices in the approach of Adam Smith and Ricardo who did not explain distribution in that way. These considerations will lay the ground for my second purpose: to distinguish between the notion of demand schedules for commodities and that of "effectual demand" in Smith and Ricardo, and to contend that the attempt to read in the classical authors an explanation of relative prices along the lines of modern theory is not well founded.

I. Demand and "Marginalist" Prices

The notion of demand schedule requires that the price-quantity relationship be determinate for all prices in the relevant range, and not only for the "natural" or "normal" price, which, however, is the only one that we may expect to experience under the nonaccidental conditions that are likely to emerge through a repetition of the situation. We are therefore dealing with a much stricter notion than the immediately plausible one according to which an accidental fall in the quantity supplied below its normal level is likely to be accompanied by a rise in the price, and vice versa: in this notion no attempt would be made to determine the magnitude of such a rise, considered as depending on accidental factors.

[†] Previously published in *The American Economic Review*, 73(2), 1983. All necessary permissions acquired.

P. Garegnani, *Capital Theory, the Surplus Approach, and Effective Demand*, Springer Studies in the History of Economic Thought,
https://doi.org/10.1007/978-3-031-23643-3_6

This second, weaker notion (which, as I shall contend below, is that held by the classical authors) could not be represented by a curve in the familiar diagram: the prices corresponding to quantities below (above) the normal quantity q_n would be determinate only in that they are higher (lower) than the normal price p_n. If we wished to represent this notion in such a diagram, we would find *two areas*, North-West (*NW*) and South-East (*SE*) of the normal price-quantity point *P*, where *NW* indicates where the price is likely to be found when the quantity supplied has fallen accidentally short of q_n, and *SE* indicates where it is likely to be in the opposite case. To pass from this diagram to the familiar demand curve requires the assumption that the price-quantity relations falling into those two areas are as definite as they are at the normal point *P*. This, though formally tempting, cannot be done without a theory which allows us to determine those points.

The theory which has been advanced to that effect is the dominant one in its two aspects of: (i) asserting definite tastes for each consumer such that, given his income and any set of relative prices, the quantities of goods he demands are determined; (ii) ensuring individual income levels corresponding to the full employment of their productive services or, more generally, determinable simultaneously with the demand price of the commodity and undergoing comparatively small changes as the quantity supplied changes. (The demand function is based here on the general equilibrium system, but any "partial equilibrium" notion of it rests on its general equilibrium counterpart to which we should refer in order to ascertain its properties and adequacy.).

The same analysis ensures a persistence of the demand function sufficient to correct accidental deviations from it through repetition over time. Such persistence will in fact be that of individual tastes and of the other data of the system.

It is, on the other hand, generally recognized that the same theory allows us to conclude that the demand functions will generally show a negative price-quantity relation, and thus to argue for the uniqueness and stability of the equilibrium concerned. This negative relation, I should note, requires a specific ordering between *each* price-quantity point. Even more importantly, the theory does not regard these points as results of accidental and temporary deviations of the quantity supplied from the "normal" level, but rather as determinate points likely to emerge from a repetition of the event.

If the notion of the demand function for a product depends upon the dominant theories for its rational basis, its role in determining the relative prices of the products depends on the idea, which is characteristic of these theories, that the distribution of the social product is determined by an "equilibrium" between the "demand and supply" of the services of factors of production.

In fact, let us assume, as is generally done in these theories, that constant returns to scale prevail in each industry. Let us also assume, at first, that land is free. It follows that, given the real wage, or, alternatively, the rate of profit (interest), the relative prices of all products will be determined *independently* of any demand functions. Thus the demand functions can enter into the determination of the prices of products only to the extent to which they enter into the determination of the division of the product between wages and profits. And the demand functions for products do enter the determination of distribution in modern theory, because the decreasing demand functions for services of factors are derived from them, as well as from the conditions of technical substitution.

This conclusion, according to which a demand schedule can only affect the price of the corresponding product to the extent to which it affects distribution, might at first puzzle the reader used to thinking in terms of the intersection of the demand and supply curves of the product in question. It is evident, however, that the demand curve of a product can affect its price only if the supply curve is nonhorizontal. Now, under the assumption of constant returns to scale, the supply curve will have a rising slope because the expansion of output will generally render the factors used in relatively higher proportions for the product in question more costly. Indeed the nonhorizontality of the supply curve is the *expression* of the extent to which the quantity produced, and hence the demand conditions of the commodity, affect distribution. The same nonhorizontality is, on the other hand, the *agency* through which this effect on distribution makes itself felt on the price of the commodity.

This role of consumer choice in determining prices seems, at times, to be imperfectly grasped in the literature. An example is perhaps provided by the sense of novelty that the "nonsubstitution theorems" have aroused. Thus, to take the most significant of these theorems, Samuelson (1961, p. 528) found that in an economy where production requires only labor and capital goods, "a stipulated change in the pattern of demand for end-goods" will affect neither the relative prices of such goods nor the methods of production in use, once the rate of interest (profit) is given. This proposition would have seemed less novel had it been clear that the pattern of demand can only affect relative prices.‡

II. Demand and "Classical" Prices

When this role of demand functions in the determination of the prices of products is understood, it should become clear why they are not to be found in Smith and Ricardo, who had a different theory of distribution. These authors envisaged the real wage as dependent, essentially, on institutional factors, together with the conditions affecting what might perhaps be summed up as the relative bargaining position of workers and employers.

Thus Smith attributed a central role to the notion of a culturally determined level of subsistence (*Wealth*, Vol. II, V, II, pp. 351–52) and held that the tendency towards such a level was largely explained by the "advantage" which masters have in disputes over wages, both because they are always "in a sort of tacit, but

‡ [*Editor's note*: it is evident here the missing transfer in print of a second part of the sentence, which consistency with Garegnani's argument suggests should be of the sort 'to the extent that it influences distribution'.]

constant and uniform combination, not to raise the wages of labour" and because in case of dispute they can "hold out much longer" (*Wealth*, Vol. I, I, VIII, pp. 58–9). Ricardo, for his part, also focused his explanation of the real wage on a notion of subsistence which, determined by historical no less than by biological factors, was in the given conditions the minimum acceptable by workers for any length of time. For the tendency of the "market" wage towards such a "natural" level, Ricardo, influenced by Malthus, relied on changes in population, which Smith had also considered, though more flexibly than Ricardo. Ricardo's own position was however far from rigid: he freely admitted that "with better education and improved habits" the natural wage could itself rise (compare, for example, Ricardo's spirited reaction to Malthus in *Works*, Vol. II, p. 115).

It seems therefore that what characterized these authors was not the idea of a wage determined by subsistence, even less that of a subsistence constant over time. It was, more generally, the importance attributed, in the determination of the real wage, to elements which were best studied before and independently of the determination of relative prices and of the other shares in total product. This *separate determination* found expression in the fact that these authors took the real wage as given when approaching the determination of relative prices. This in turn implied that the price system and the rate of profit could be determined independently of any demand functions for the products.

An interpretation of Smith and Ricardo as "modern economists trying to be born," holding, that is, a demand and supply analysis of wages while seeking to say something "significant and limiting about their properties" (p. 1415), has been advanced by Samuelson (1978) with his "canonical classical model." According to it, Smith and Ricardo would have determined the "equilibrium" real wage as that balancing the growth of the supply of labor with that of its demand, resulting from accumulation (p. 1416). The "demand" for labor of this interpretation would be rigid, implying, as Samuelson notices (p. 1423), either zero wages or zero profits or an indeterminate breakdown between wages and profits—which would be limiting indeed for "modern economists." But, above all, this interpretation and, particularly, the relation between the real wage and growth of population on which it is based, seems to suffer from the tendency to see functional relations of known general properties where the classical economists saw relations too complex and variable to be quantified in any exact way. Thus Smith wrote that "the liberal reward of labor," by enabling workers to provide for their children, tends to increase population (*Wealth*, Vol. I, I, VIII, p. 71), but he also brought out elements which went in the opposite direction (see, for example, *Wealth*, Vol. II, V, II, p. 353), or could go in either direction (*Wealth*, Vol. I, I, VIII, pp. 62ff.) (on this see also Spengler, 1959, p. 7). I have already mentioned the flexibility of Ricardo's position on this matter.

It might be objected that my argument concerning the classical economists has so far rested on the assumption of constant returns to scale to labor and capital and that, when this assumption is abandoned, a second route emerges through which outputs and hence, presumably, demand functions, may affect prices even when the real wage is given.

What this objection presumes is that demand functions must be introduced to determine outputs even when distribution is otherwise determined. We may here lay aside the difficulties of envisaging these functions in a classical setting (compare my earlier discussion on the determination of consumer incomes). It is the usefulness of this procedure which is questionable in the first place. As noted above, the modem analysis of demand is in fact mainly concerned with some *formal properties* of consumer tastes, specifically with the determinateness, persistence, and slope of the demand curves, and *not* with the actual *content* of these tastes (which is generally left to the sociologist or psychologist). This content, jointly with the levels of activity, distribution and techniques, is however, what determines the *position* of the demand curve and is thus the main influence on the levels of output. Now, those formal properties, basic as they are for the modern supply-and-demand analysis of distribution, were largely irrelevant for the classical economists with their different theory. It was therefore natural that these authors should, so to speak, face the content of consumer tastes *directly*, without the intermediate screen of any formal properties, whether in order to take it as given (as is generally done in modern theory) or in order to examine it, as they generally did (for example, in connection with workers' "necessaries"). In either case, the procedure was to take this content as given *when determining* the system of relative prices—leaving it for a separate analysis, like that to be conducted for the other determinants of output (real wages, levels of activity, and techniques). The very levels of output could then be taken as given in just the same way as the real wage was taken as given.

The analysis of changes in outputs and prices was thus conducted by the classical economists in what we may describe as two distinct logical stages: (i) the effect on relative prices of the change in real wages, or techniques, or outputs was examined with outputs as independent variables; (ii) the possible effects on outputs of the change in relative prices were then analysed in accordance with the circumstances of the case under consideration, jointly with any possible further effects on prices and distribution due to nonconstant returns to scale.[1] With this the classical economists distinguished between field of analysis (i), where necessary quantitative relations could be found between rates of remuneration, and between these rates and relative prices, and other fields where no such necessary relations could be established, and where actual relations had to be studied in their multiplicity and diversity according to circumstances. This procedure by separate logical stages is in fact nothing new, even for modern theory: it will, for example, be generally admitted that technical changes will generally affect consumers' tastes, but any such effect will be considered, if at all, at a stage which is logically distinct from the determination of distribution and prices, where consumers' tastes and technical conditions of production appear as data. It remains, however, true

[1] As for the dependence of prices on outputs in the case of jointly produced commodities, the relative scarcity of these commodities will tend to find an objective expression in the co-existence of processes producing the same commodities (cf. Sraffa, 1960, p. 43).

that the procedure of the classical economists renounces what was attempted by later theory, namely, a simultaneous treatment of the interrelations between most economic phenomena. This modesty of goals may however be the most appropriate one in a subject as complex as economics where, as Marshall reminds us, "the function … of analysis and deduction … is not to forge a few long chains of reasoning, but to forge rightly many short chains" (*Principles*, App. C, 3, p. 773).

III. The Classical Notion of "Effectual Demand"

In Smith and Ricardo we find the notion of "effectual demand", defined as "the demand of those who are willing to pay the natural price of the commodity" (Smith, [1776] 1910, Vol. I, I, VII, p. 49). The analysis above should make it easy to see the difference between this notion and that of demand schedule. The role of effectual demand is to explain the tendency of the actual or "market" price toward the normal price and not that of determining the latter. It does not therefore consist of a curve but of a single determinate price-quantity point. Apart from this single point, Smith needs only to suppose that when the quantity supplied falls short of effectual demand, the actual or market price will exceed the natural price, thus setting in motion forces which tend to raise the quantity supplied and bring the market price down to the natural level (and vice versa).

This classical notion of demand, which was consistent with the theoretical framework of which it was an integral part, has however been often envisaged as a rudimentary expression of the modern notion of demand function. Marshall showed the way. In his 1920 he refers to the "market" price—defined by Smith and Ricardo as the *actual* price, accidental in its absolute level and determinate only in its *order* relative to the natural price— as a "temporary equilibrium" price (see, for example, Marshall, 1920, Bk. V, Ch. V, 8, pp. 378–79). With this he attributed to Smith a *demand curve*, determinate also at points (like that of the "equilibrium" market price) other than the effectual demand point. After this first step, it was easy for Marshall to proceed and argue that the distinction between market and normal price was only one of degree, relating to the period of time over which the equilibrating process was supposed to occur, thus implicitly attributing to Smith and Ricardo also a demand-and-supply determination of the normal price (on this point, see Bharadwaj, 1978, pp. 264–65).

If, in Smith's case, the shortcomings of this interpretation could pass almost unnoticed, it was inevitable that they should crop up in the case of the more consistent version of the theory provided by Ricardo. In particular, it seemed clear that Ricardo determined prices independently of anything resembling demand schedules.

As is well known, Marshall attempted to cope with this difficulty by contending that Ricardo could avoid referring to demand and utility only by assuming what Marshall characterized as the "law of constant return", by which in the first place he meant a horizontal long-period supply curve for the industry in question (Marshall, 1920, APP. I, 2, p. 814). Marshall here overlooks or leaves aside the fact that the dependence of prices on demand functions is based on distribution and not on the laws of returns to scale to capital and labor—to which he might also be taken to refer with his "laws of return." Indeed Ricardo could have deduced a constant supply price from constant returns to scale to capital and labor only to the extent that he was not explaining the distribution of wages and profits in Marshall's way. The incorrectness of Marshall's interpretation is, on the other hand, evident from the fact that in agriculture, where clearly Ricardo did not assume "constant return" in either sense, he did not introduce demand functions any more than he had done for manufacturing.

Shove (1942) took up this argument, but was more cautious than Marshall in attributing demand functions to Ricardo. He perceived that a "step" was involved in passing from Ricardo's discussion of the "market" price to a demand function (p. 301) and saw a dilemma in Ricardo's theory of value: either introducing demand functions or remaining confined to the special case of constant supply price (p. 297). This unreal dilemma has recently been revived by Rankin (1980) who claims, p. 247, that, in Ricardo, *demand functions* do enter the determination of prices: his evidence is, however, that Ricardo has agricultural prices dependent on "demand," by which Ricardo meant "effectual demand", as is clear in the passages quoted by Rankin.

References

Bharadwaj, K. (1978). The subversion of classical analysis: Alfred Marshall's early writing on value. *Cambridge Journal of Economics,* 2(3), 253–271.

Marshall, A. ([1920] 1961). *Principles of economics* (9th (Variorum) ed., Vol. I). Macmillan.

Rankin, S. C. (1980). Supply and demand in Ricardian price theory: A re-interpretation. *Oxford Economic Papers,* 32(2), 241–262.

Ricardo, D. (1951–1973). In P. Sraffa (Ed.), *The works and correspondence of David Ricardo* (Vol. 11). Cambridge University Press.

Samuelson, P. A. ([1961] 1966). A new theorem on nonsubstitution. In J. E. Stiglitz (Ed.), *The collected scientific papers of Paul A. Samuelson* (Vol. I, pp. 520–536). M.I.T. Press.

Samuelson, P. A. (1978). The canonical classical model of political economy. *Journal of Economic Literature*, 16(4), 1415–1434

Shove, G. F. (1942). The place of Marshall's *Principles* in the development of economic theory. *Economic Journal,* 52(208), 294–329.

Smith, A. ([1776] 1910). *The wealth of nations* (Vol 2). Dent & Sons.

Spengler, J. (1959). Adam Smith's theory of economic growth, Part II. *Southern Economic Journal,* 26(1), 1–12.

Sraffa, P. (1960). *Production of commodities by means of commodities*. Cambridge University Press.

Value and Distribution in the Classical Economists and Marx[†][1]

I. Introduction

1. The theory of value and distribution is at present in a situation of unease and uncertainty: we no longer find the same general agreement about its basic elements which obtained until a few decades ago. Two main theoretical developments have undermined the dominant theory which explained distribution and relative prices by means of the "equilibrium" of the two "opposing sets of forces", demand and supply for factors of production.

The first development in order of time has been Keynes's refutation of the doctrine according to which a competitive economic system tends towards the full employment of labour, i.e. towards that equilibrium between "demand and supply" of labour, which was to determine the wage. Keynes' concentration on the short period, and the persistence in the *General Theory* of many traditional premises favoured the successive attempts to reconcile his results with orthodox long-period

The original version of the chapter has been revised: Incorrect details have been corrected.
A correction to this chapter can be found at https://doi.org/10.1007/978-3-031-23643-3_18

† Previously published in *Oxford Economic Papers*, New Series, 36(2), 1984. All necessary permissions acquired.

[1]This paper, which develops under the impact of Sraffa's Production of Commodities by Means of Commodities some propositions contained in a Ph.D. dissertation of 1955–1958 [*A Problem in the Theory of Distribution from Ricardo to Wicksell*, in this volume, Part I], is based on notes delivered at a conference on "Marx's Transformation of Values into Prices of Production" held in Siena in 1972, and used then for lectures given in Cambridge and elsewhere since 1973–4: in the meantime, references to the ideas contained in them have appeared in other works. I would like to acknowledge the benefit I derived from discussions with Piero Sraffa and from comments from many people and in particular by K. Bharadwaj, A. Campus, B. Cutilli, H. Kurz, and M. Pivetti. Financial assistance by the 'Consiglio Nazionale delle Ricerche' is gratefully acknowledged.

P. Garegnani, *Capital Theory, the Surplus Approach, and Effective Demand*, Springer Studies in the History of Economic Thought,
https://doi.org/10.1007/978-3-031-23643-3_7

analysis: but the weakening of the dominant theory which nonetheless resulted from his work can be seen both in the uneasiness which, in ever-changing forms, characterizes the renewed orthodoxy, and in the tendency of Keynes' direct followers towards a more radical departure from traditional theory.

The second development consists in the critique of the notion of capital as a "factor of production" measurable independently of distribution.[2] This critique has shown the invalidity of some propositions of the theory, like the inverse relation between the rate of interest (rate of profit) and the "quantity of capital" per worker, which are basic for the explanation of distribution in terms of demand and supply for "factors of production".

The uncertainty which has resulted from these developments finds its expression in authors who think that new theoretical approaches should be explored. It is also revealed by the nature of some of the work carried out by those who adhere to the traditional approach.[3]

It is perhaps natural that when this kind of uncertainty arises in a scientific field, there should also arise a tendency to go back into the history of the subject, and see when and how theorizing took the turn leading to the present difficulties. When we do so and look back over the two centuries of systematic economic analysis, we find that, at the cost of severe simplification, we can distinguish two successive approaches to the theory of value and distribution. The modern demand-and-supply approach had in fact been preceded by a different approach which had its centre in a notion of "social surplus". This earlier approach found its first systematic expression in Quesnay's *Tableau Économique* of 1758, became dominant with the English Classical economists from Smith to Ricardo, and was then taken over and developed by Marx at a time when the mainstream of economic analysis was already moving in a different direction.

2. The purpose of this paper will be to consider this earlier "surplus approach" to value and distribution. Sect. II will examine the premises which distinguish it from the later demand-and-supply approach. Sects. III and IV then set forth the problem of "measuring-value" which arose within it and led to Ricardo's and Marx's explanation of value in terms of the labour necessary to produce the commodities. At the end of Sect. IV, Marx's error with regard to prices of production will be seen as arising from treating as integral parts of a single method for determining the rate of profit and relative prices, what can be developed as

---

[2] This line of criticism, hints of which may be found in Sraffa's (1951), p. xlix, was first brought to light in print by Robinson (1953–1954). See also Robinson (1970), pp. 309–10 (rpt. 1973, p. 145).

[3] Thus, the attempt to avoid the difficulties besetting the theory appears to have led to an abandonment of the method based on "long-period positions" of the economic system, characterized by a uniform rate of profit. This notion had been central to the theory of competitive distribution and value since the very inception of systematic economic analysis. (See Garegnani, 1976, pp. 26–29 [this volume, Part II, pp. 210–3].)

two equivalent but distinct methods for this determination: what we shall call the "Price-equations method" and the "Surplus-equation method". The solution based on the first method will be considered in Sect. V, where it will be shown to consist of the price equations in Sraffa's *Production of Commodities by Means of Commodities*, 1960. The two solutions obtainable on the basis of the "Surplus-equation method" will then be examined, respectively, in Sect. VI, dealing with the "Integrated wage-goods sector", and in Sect. VII dealing with Sraffa's "Standard system".

II. The "Core" of the Surplus Theories

3. The notion of social surplus characteristic of the classical theories can perhaps be seen in its simplest form in Quesnay's *Tableau Économique*, where we find its first systematic expression. Quesnay saw that if the social product—which he considered to consist entirely of agricultural commodities—[4] was to repeat itself year after year without increase or diminution, a part of it had to be put back into production. Besides the necessary replacement of the means of production, this part included the subsistence of the agricultural labourers. What remained of the annual product after deducting this part constituted a "surplus", or "produit net", of which society could dispose without impairing the conditions of its survival.

The fact that the subsistence of workers was considered necessary for reproduction established a direct link between the analysis of reproduction and that of the distribution of the product among the classes into which society is divided. Thus Quesnay linked the surplus to the landowners' share of the social product. And when Smith extended Quesnay's notion of surplus by showing that surplus originated from production in general and not from agricultural production alone, profits emerged as a second component of the surplus alongside the rent of land, thus providing the basis for the English classical economists' theory of distribution up to Ricardo.

The determination of the size of the social surplus was accordingly the centre around which these theories revolved. In principle this way of determining the non-wage shares is simple. Two magnitudes are assumed to be known prior to the determination of the surplus. They are: (i) the real wage, i.e. the quantities of the several commodities constituting the wage rate,[5] (ii) the social product, i.e. the aggregate

[4]As is well known, Quesnay excluded manufactured commodities from the social product on the ground that they were a mere transformation of agricultural products.

[5]We are following the authors here discussed in assuming a single "average" or "natural" wage and thus homogeneous labour. As is well known, the possibility of reducing labour to homogeneity rests on the supposition of a constancy in the ratios between the wages for labour of different

of the commodities produced in the year. Since (iii) the technical conditions of production of the various commodities are also known prior to the determination of the surplus, a known social product implies a known number of labourers employed.[6] By multiplying the number of labourers by the known physical wages, we obtain the part of the product that goes to the labourers, which we may call "Necessary consumption", using a phrase by Ricardo (1951–73, VI, p. 108).

The surplus, i.e. the share of the product going to the classes of society other than the labourers, can then be determined by subtracting the "Necessary consumption" from the Social product, taken net of the means of production[7]; that is:

$$\begin{aligned} &\text{Social product} - \text{Necessary consumption} \\ &= \text{Shares other than wages (surplus)} \end{aligned} \tag{1}$$

an equation where "shares other than wages" is the only unknown (see also the diagram in Fig. 1).

The peculiar feature of these theories—the determination of the shares of the product other than wages as a residuum or "surplus"—thus has its logical basis in the consideration of the real wage and social product as being determinable prior to those shares. It is to the determination of the real wage and to that of the social product that we must therefore turn, however briefly, for an understanding of the view of the economic system which underlies the simple formal structure of the surplus theories.

4. We have seen how Quesnay and the Physiocrats thought that the quantity of the product retained by the agricultural labourers was fixed at the subsistence level (for example Turgot, 1766, Chap. VI). The same was true for Ricardo who, however, while holding that an increase in wages above the subsistence level would tend to be reversed by the consequent increase in population, also freely

qualities: see Ricardo, (1951–73) I, pp. 20–22 on the constancy of relative wages (see also Smith, [1776] 1910, Vol. I, Bk. I, Chap. X, p. 130). These ratios were in fact left to be studied outside what will be indicated below as "core" of these theories. (The difficulty raised by taking these ratios as known in the face of different compositions of the wages for different kinds of labour, seems to have been implicitly dealt with by taking the known *real* wage to be that of common unskilled labour and then supposing that the wages of other kinds of labour will tend to remain a constant proportion of it in terms of *value*.)

[6] We are at present assuming that each commodity can be produced by means of one method only. The consideration of alternative methods of production of the same commodity, which provides one of the two bases for the notion of a substitutability between factors of production characteristic of modern theory (cf. para. 7 below), can on the other hand only affect what has been said here by making the employment of labour associated with a given physical social product depend on the wage rate as well; under the hypothesis adopted in this paper the tendency to adopt cheaper methods will bring the economy to a definite technique, that giving the highest wage for the given rate of profit (see Garegnani, 1970, pp. 410–14 [this volume, Part II, pp. 152–6]).

[7] The assumption that the means of production are physically reproduced has the sole purpose of postponing the complications arising out of errors in Smith and Ricardo's notion of capital (para. 12 below).

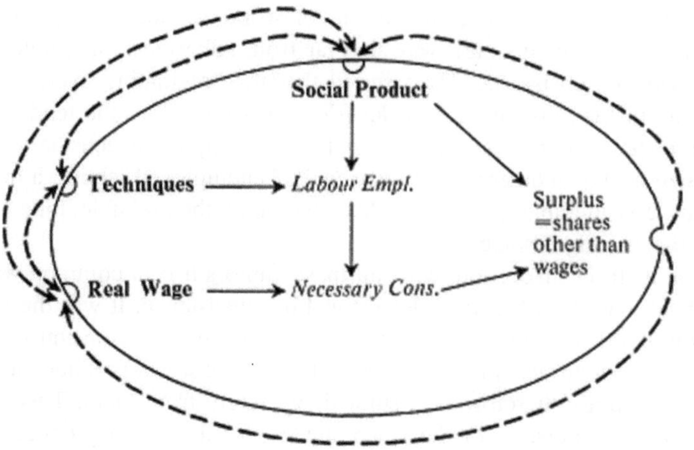

Fig. 1 A diagram of the "core" in the surplus theories. Underlining distinguishes circumstances determined outside the core. Continuous arrows point to dependent magnitudes inside the "core"; discontinuous arrows indicate influences studied outside the "core"

considered the possibility that the increase be absorbed into "subsistence" as a result of "improved habits" and thus rendered permanent (Ricardo, 1951–1973, II, p. 115). In assessing Ricardo's and Quesnay's view of the wage, it is in fact important to note that the "subsistence" they referred to was always understood as determined by historical, rather than physiological conditions. Robert Torrens, to whom Ricardo referred as having "most ably illustrated" the subject (1951–1973, I, p. 97) argued that the "habits of the country" act in this respect as a "second nature" and, accordingly, the "natural price of labour" may vary not only from country to country, but also in the same country at the "different stages of national improvement". And Ricardo' for his part, defined the natural wage as including "those comforts which custom renders absolute necessaries".[8]

Adam Smith's position regarding the "average" or "natural" wage was less clear-cut and, in some respects, more interesting than that of Ricardo. He also saw the wages as tending to an historical subsistence level, but he explained this by the "advantage" which the "masters" have in disputes over wages, rather than by any tendency of the population to grow in excess of the possibility of employment offered by accumulation. Thus, for example, Smith noted how the "masters" could "hold out" much longer than the workers in all wage disputes, since the master's "necessity" for the workman is not so "immediate" as the workman's for his master, and pointed out how "masters are always and everywhere in a sort of tacit but constant and uniform combination, not to raise wages": a "combination" against

[8] Cf. respectively Torrens (1815), quoted in Cannan (1967), pp. 191–3; Ricardo (1951–73), I, p. 94. For the social element in subsistence, see also Adam Smith's definition of "necessaries", [1776] 1910, Vol. II, Bk. V, Chap. II, pp. 351–352.

which, as Smith saw it, the combinations of workers, hindered by law, were of little avail.[9] Marx, for his part, was also far from adhering to a simple theory of wages based on subsistence. He asserted that the "regulating average wage" is given by an historically determined level of subsistence, but the tendency to this "average wage" was the result of a complex interaction between the actual wage and the size of the "industrial reserve army" of unemployed labour: a mechanism which gave considerable flexibility to his position on the probable, long-term, evolution of the "average" wage.[10]

Thus, at a closer inspection, what all these authors had in common was not, as is often held, the idea of a wage determined by subsistence. It was the more general notion of a real wage governed by conditions (often of a conventional or institutional kind) that are *distinct* from those affecting the social product and the other shares in it, and are therefore best studied separately from them. This separation between the determination of the wage and that of the social product is evident when, as in Quesnay or Ricardo, the wage is explained in terms of a customary subsistence, but the same separation between the two problems emerges in Marx and Smith, who admitted a greater influence of current economic conditions on the real wage. It is this separate determination of the real wage that is expressed in its treatment as a magnitude which is known when the determination of the other shares of the product is approached.[11]

As for the physical social product the circumstances that were seen to determine it, that is, basically, the accumulation of capital and the technical conditions

[9] In keeping with this view, pointing to the relative bargaining power of the two classes, Smith saw that in an "advancing state of the society", "masters voluntarily break through [their] natural combination ..... not to raise wages", whereas the contrary would be true in a "declining state of society" (Smith, [1776]1910, Vol. I, Bk. I, Chap. VIII, pp. 56, 61). On the idea in Hicks and Hollander (1977), in Samuelson (1978) and in Casarosa (1978), according to which Smith and/or Ricardo would have determined the "equilibrium" real wage as that balancing the growth of the supply of labour with that of its demand, resulting from accumulation, cf. Garegnani (1983), p. 311 [this volume, Part III, p. 300].

[10] Thus, for example, in Marx (1954–9), Bk. I, Chap. XXV, p. 580, Marx admits that the real wage could rise in the long run to the extent in which the corresponding "diminution of the unpaid labour... would [not] threaten the [capitalist] system itself". This position has important implications. In particular the fact that, under sufficiently general hypotheses, technical change cannot lower the rate of profit corresponding to a given real wage (cf. n. 6 above), entails the possibility of a long-term rise in the real wage which does not "threaten" the system: Marx's erroneous notion as to the possible effects of technical change on profits led him to discount this possibility. (Samuelson seems thus to move on questionable grounds when in 1971, p. 423 he reduces the question of the validity of Marx's approach to distribution to the question of "whether real wages rise or stagnate over a century". For further evidence against the idea that Marx held any simple subsistence theory of wages, cf. Baumol, 1983).

[11] As Marx observed,"the foundation of modern political economy .... is the conception of the *value of labour power* as something fixed, as a given magnitude" (Marx, 1963–71, Vol. I, p. 45, emphasis in the original).

of production,[12] were such that it was natural to suppose it was known prior to its division among the classes.

5. It is important to stress here that this *separate* determination of real wage and social product entails a structuring of the analysis which is radically different from that of the theories which were to become dominant later. The surplus theories have, so to speak, a *core* which is isolated from the rest of the analysis because the wage, the social product and the technical conditions of production appear there as already determined. It is in this "core" that we find the determination of the shares other than wages as a residual: a determination which, as we shall see in the next section, will also entail the determination of the relative prices of commodities. Further, as a natural extension of this, we shall find in the "core" an analysis of the relations between, on the one hand, the real wage, the social product and the technical conditions of production (the independent variables) and, on the other hand, the shares other than wages constituting the surplus, and the relative prices (the dependent variables).

An important point to notice is that the treatment of the real wage, the social product and the technical conditions of production as independent variables in the "core" in no way entailed denying the existence of influences of any single one of these three sets of variables over the remaining two. The interaction between these circumstances was in fact freely admitted by the classical economists and by Marx. An example is Marx's discussion of the "realization" of surplus value, in which the real wage played a key role in the determination of the size of the social product (cf. e.g. Marx, 1963–1971, Vol. II, Chap. XVII, pp. 492–96). Another example is the reverse influence which the speed of growth of the social product was generally recognized to have for a shorter or longer period on the real wage.

Moreover, the fact that those three sets of circumstances appeared as independent variables in the determination of the surplus did not prevent the classical economists from freely admitting influences of the surplus upon them: e.g. the classical economists generally admitted the influences which the level of profit could have on the real wage, via the speed of accumulation, and Marx went further by considering how a fall of the rate of profit, consequent upon a rise of the wage rate, may reverse that very rise by checking accumulation and causing technical changes, thus re-creating a sufficient level of labour unemployment (cf. para. 4 above).

What the structure of classical analysis did imply was that these interactions and reverse influences, like the influences of the other factors determining wages,

---

[12] In fact if we attempt to reduce analyses as different as those of Quesnay, Smith, Malthus or Ricardo to their common basic elements, what we find is the view that the *volume* of the social product depends on: (i) the stage reached by accumulation, which governs the number of "productive" labourers employed; (ii) the technical conditions of production which regulate the physical product per labourer and depend in turn on the stage reached by accumulation. (See Smith, [1776] 1910, Vol. I, pp. 1–2.) The *commodity composition* of the social product, on the other hand, was studied from the angle of the needs of reproduction (cf., for example, Quesnay's *Tableau Économique* or Marx's reproduction schemes in Chaps. XX–XXI of Book. II in *Capital*), or else was left to be studied case by case as the need arose.

social product and available techniques, were left to be studied outside the 'core'. The multiplicity of these influences and their variability according to circumstances was in fact understood to make it impossible to reconduct them to *necessary* quantitative relations like those, studied in the "core", between distributive variables and relative prices and between outputs or techniques and the dependent distributive variables and prices.

6. Now this separation of the analysis into distinct logical stages contrasts sharply with what we find in the later marginalist theories. In these, the determination of the wage is in fact inseparable from, and symmetrical to, that of the other shares of the product. Moreover, the demand-and-supply mechanism used in that determination implies that real wages and the other distributive variables (and hence relative values) can only be determined *simultaneously*, and simultaneously with the volume and composition of the product. Indeed, in later theory, distribution, outputs, and relative values of commodities are all determined simultaneously taking as data the tastes of consumers, the endowments of "factors of production" and the technical conditions of production. The determination of these three sets of data is then seen as falling largely outside the domain of economics. As a result, in these theories the determination of revenues other than wages and of relative prices comes to include most of economics. Instead of constituting a limited "core" of economic analysis—dealing with the necessary quantitative relationships among distributive variables and among them and prices—it becomes almost co-extensive with economics itself. The more limited scope which the theory of value has in the surplus approach[13] may however give it the greater flexibility which is required by a subject as complex as economics.[14, 15]

[13]The "core" might in fact be described as constituting the "theory of value" such as we find in the surplus theories.

[14]An important example of the greater flexibility of the "surplus theories" seems provided by the attitude to possible deficiencies of aggregate demand: while Ricardo held that no "general gluts of commodities" were possible, a different view of the problem was taken by Malthus or Marx, who also worked within the same "surplus" approach to value and distribution, and were no less consistent with it (on the necessity of "short chains of reasoning" in economics cf. Marshall, [1820] 1961, APP. C, 3, p. 773).

[15]The classical surplus theories are characterized by some authors as being concentrated on reproducible commodities, and hence "production", as opposed to the concentration on commodities of the scarcity type and hence on "exchange", which would be the hallmark of the dominant marginalist theories. Accordingly the two kinds of theory would deal with two distinct series of problems, with an opposite practical relevance in relation to time, the classical theory becoming relevant just when (in the long run) the marginalist theory becomes irrelevant (cf. e.g. Pasinetti, 1977, pp. 3, 24–6). Whereas it aptly describes some differences between the two approaches, this distinction seems not to go to the roots of the difference, which lies in the way in which *both* "production" and "exchange" are treated in each approach. The determination of the wage on the basis of the forces mentioned at para. 5 above—entailing the determination of profits as a surplus and not by the "scarcity of capital" relative to labour—also implies that the problems of exchange themselves cannot be viewed as problems of "scarcity". This remains true whether we consider a short period, or a long period, in which plant in the several industries can adapt to outputs. (For a critical view of this criterion of distinction see also Roncaglia, 1979, pp. 125–6.)

The remainder of this paper will be exclusively concerned with what has here been described as the 'core' of the surplus theories. More particularly we shall be concerned with the part of this "core" which consists of treating the real wages, as distinct from outputs or techniques, as the independent variable.

7. An effect of the above contrast in the structuring of the two theories may be seen in how modern authors, used to focusing attention on "consumers' choice" in the determination of outputs, seem often surprised by the fact that in classical theories the changes in real wages are considered separately from changes in outputs, even in outputs of wage goods. The modern focus on consumers' choice and the corresponding simultaneous determination of prices and outputs is however an integral part of the demand-and-supply mechanism for determining distribution just mentioned. Consumers' tastes for goods requiring different proportions of factors of production are in fact supposed to determine, together with the choice between alternative methods of production, the relative "scarcity" of these factors. When the explanation of distribution is different—as we saw to be the case for the classical economists—the need to study the effects of changes in wages on prices *simultaneously* with their effects on outputs is no longer evident (a similar need to study the effects of a change in the technical conditions of production simultaneously with its effects on the tastes of consumers—is for example denied in the marginalist theories using those tastes as data). It might however be insisted that if non-constant returns prevail, the output changes resulting from changes in real wages (and the consequent changes in prices and techniques adopted) will in turn affect prices and the distributive variables other than wages, and hence modify the relationships studied under the assumption of given outputs. A simultaneous determination of prices and quantities would then seem required in order to study those relationships. This line of argument presumes however the possibility of expressing the dependence of outputs upon changes in distribution by means of functional relations of the same nature as those postulated in modern theory, endowed, that is, with known properties of sufficient generality and with persistence over time. If this were in fact possible it would be natural to consider the changes in the quantities produced simultaneously with the change in distribution from which they originate. But this view was not that which the Classical economists took of the matter and, it seems, we today have even better reasons than they had for not taking it. Thus for example important changes in the real wage may have a multiplicity of effects on aggregate demand, the intensity of which will depend on the particular circumstances in which they occur and cannot, in our present state of knowledge, be reconducted to known functional relations of sufficient generality and persistence. If this is admitted, it will appear that a general determination of outputs simultaneously with relative prices is impossible, and that the basic procedure can only be that followed by the classical authors. They analysed changes in prices and outputs by what we may describe as two distinct logical stages. In the first, the effect of the change in real wage was examined while taking the outputs as given. In the second stage, the possible effect on *outputs* of the initial change was analysed in accordance with the circumstances of the case under consideration, jointly with its possible secondary effects on prices and distribution, in the case of non constant returns to scale (cf. Garegnani, 1983, pp. 311–2 [this volume, Part III, pp. 301–3]).

III. Ricardo's Measurement of the Value of Aggregates by Means of Embodied Labour

8. We have seen the rationale behind taking the Social product and the Necessary consumption as given physical aggregates when determining the shares other than wages in the surplus theories. But how are we to measure those two magnitudes in Eq. (1)? As we shall presently see, the theory cannot stop at conceiving them as physical aggregates and must proceed to their measurement in value; will these values also be given when the physical aggregates are given? It is in connection with this problem of measurement that the surplus theories of distribution meet the question of value and with it, their chief analytical difficulty. The remainder of this paper will turn on this question, which will be taken up in the comparatively advanced form it assumed in the theory of profits of Ricardo's *Principles*.[16]

Since we are concerned with aspects of the Classical problem of value which are independent of the rent of land, we shall assume that fertile land abounds and that rent can accordingly be ignored.[17] Thus, on the right hand side of Eq. (1) we shall find aggregate profits. Two observations are however necessary in order to proceed to the *rate* of profit, on which Ricardo's interest was in fact focused. The first is that in Ricardo, as in the other Classical economists, a yearly production cycle is implicitly assumed[18]; the wages are supposed to be advanced at the beginning of the cycle and are therefore a part of capital. The second observation concerns the fact that in determining the rate of profit Ricardo operated *as if* capital consisted entirely of the wages advanced for the year. In fact he saw the division of the product between wages and profits as the only factor capable of influencing

---

[16] We are thus not concerned here with the physical measurement underlying the reasoning in both Ricardo's earlier *Essay on the Influence of a Low Price of Corn on the Rate of Profit*, and Quesnay's *Tableau Économique* (on these points cf., respectively, Sraffa, 1951, pp. xxxi–xxxii and p. xxxii n. 4, and Sraffa, 1960, p. 93).

[17] We may however notice how the characteristic separation between determining the quantities produced and determining the shares of the product other than wages (para. 6 above) allowed Ricardo to isolate the share of land rent. This separation (and the implicit assumption that each worker is assisted by the same capital, whatever the land cultivated, or the intensity of its cultivation) allowed Ricardo to take as given the productivity of labour on the no-rent land or, even, that of the last labourer employed on land already under cultivation (on the latter point cf. Ricardo, 1951–73, I, p. 71).

[18] "A year is assumed in political economy as the period which includes a revolving cycle of production and consumption" (Mill, 1821, p. 185).

the rate of profit, thus ignoring the independent influence exerted by the proportion between labour and means of production.[19] In order to give an account of his theory of profit which is both consistent and sufficiently faithful, we shall assume that production requires only very simple means of production, which can be ignored.

Under the above assumptions, the annual rate of profit will be expressed by the ratio between the social surplus and the annual wages or "Necessary consumption", i.e.

$$\text{Rate of profit} = \frac{\text{Social product} - \text{Necessary consumption}}{\text{Necessary consumption}} \tag{2}$$

9. Suppose, now, that the "Necessary consumption" advanced to workers is reproduced in kind during the year and the yearly aggregate profits can accordingly be reckoned in physical terms, that is, as a *surplus product*. Even under this most favourable hypothesis it would be impossible to stop at a physical notion of the two magnitudes involved, because the surplus product and the necessary consumption would generally consist of commodities which are different, or are taken in different proportions. The ratio between the two aggregates would give the quantity of "surplus product" (a composite commodity) per unit of "necessary consumption" (a different composite commodity), but not the *rate of profit*, i.e. the ratio between the *values* of the two magnitudes.

In the *Principles* Ricardo is accordingly faced with the need to measure the Social product and the Necessary consumption in value terms and, hence, with the problem mentioned above: will these given physical aggregates also be given

[19] Cf. for example: "whether these increased productions, and the consequent demand which they occasion, shall or shall not lower profits depends *solely* on the rise of wages" (Ricardo, 1951–1973, I, p. 292, our italics; for a similar statement cf. also *ibid.*, p. 289). More generally, Ricardo failed to show any awareness that the rate of profit can change for causes other than changes in the proportion between wages and profits in the (net) social product. The origin of this error, which Ricardo shared with his contemporaries, can be traced back to Adam Smith. In a well-known passage of *Wealth of Nations* he had argued that, although it may be thought that besides wages, profits and rents, the price of a commodity also includes all that is necessary for replacing the means of production, yet since the prices of the latter are in turn made of those parts, the entire price "resolves itself either immediately or ultimately into the same three parts of rent, labour and profit" (Smith, [1776] 1910, Bk. I, Chap. VI, Vol. 1, pp. 44–45). From this view of prices, in which we find in germ the correct idea of reducing capital to wages (and rents) advanced for *various periods of time*, Smith often slipped into the altogether different idea that capital can be reduced to the wages advanced for the current year.

Marx indicated the above deficiency of Ricardo's analysis as an erroneous identification between rate of profit and rate of surplus value (cf. for example, 1963–71, II, Chap. XVII, p. 463). Marx's criticism of Ricardo seems to have been misapprehended as an accusation that Ricardo "ignores non-wage capital, at least when referring to the economy as a whole" (Steedman, 1982, p. 126). However Marx did not deny that Smith and Ricardo saw the existence of means of production (cf. for example the carefully worded passage in 1954–9, Bk. III, Chap. XLIX, p. 841 and n. 51): what he said was that Ricardo ignored the effect of changes in the proportion of labour to means of production on the rate of profit (Marx, 1963–71, Vol. II, Chap. XV, p. 373; on this point cf. also De Vivo, 1982, pp. 91–92).

when expressed as value magnitudes? If the value expression of either aggregate were to depend on the rate of profit, the determination of profits as a surplus in accordance with Eq. (1) or (2) above is threatened by circular reasoning.

Ricardo's starting point in dealing with value was Smith's theory of the "natural price". Smith had defined the natural price as the sum of the wages and profits (we are ignoring rents) which must be paid in order to produce the commodity, reckoned at their "natural" or "average" rates (Smith, [1776] 1910, Vol. I, Bk. I, Chap. VII, pp. 48–51). As for the unit in which these natural prices should be expressed, Smith had suggested a "real" or "invariable" measure of value consisting of the quantity of labour which a commodity can "command", that is, in modern terms, the wage unit (*ibid*, Chap. V, p. 26). If, however, we use Smith's measure in Eqs. (1) or (2) we are faced with exactly the difficulty we mentioned above: the *value* of the *physically given* social product will *not* be known before the rate of profit is known. Take, for example, an economy employing 3 million workers. The Necessary consumption will "command" 3 million labour-years and be a known magnitude. But the same will not be true for the Social product: with, for example, the capital consisting only of the wages advanced yearly we assumed above, the Social product will command $3(1+r)$, million labour-years, where r is the rate of profit, namely 3.3 m. if $r = 10\%$, but 6.6 m. if $r = 120\%$. We may accordingly seem to be reasoning in a circle when we follow the surplus approach and attempt to determine profits by *difference* in accordance with Eq. (2): in order to do that we need to know the size of the Social product, which is not known until we know the very rate of profit which is to be determined.[20] This dependence of the value of the product upon distribution means that, when we look at the Social product and the Necessary consumption in value terms, the constraint by which one class cannot have more without the other class having less—so evident if we could look at the product in physical terms—is no longer apparent: might not the real wage rise without affecting the rate of profit, or vice-versa? Indeed Smith himself often lost sight of the constraint and envisaged the rate of profit and the wage as determined *independently of each other*. He wrote that "the natural price varies with the natural rate of each of its component parts" (Smith, [1776] 1910, Vol. I, Bk. I, Chap. VI, p. 56) giving rise to what has been described as Smith's "adding up" theory of prices (Sraffa, 1951, p. xxxv).[21] And, after Smith, Malthus could argue that a tariff

[20]The difficulty, however, is ultimately that of expressing the capital required in production independently of distribution (cf. Garegnani, 1960, pp. 18–19 [*editor's note*: the content of these pages finds a substantial correspondence on pp. 20–1 of *A Problem in the Theory of Distribution from Ricardo to Wicksell*, this volume, Part I]. Thus, we shall see in sect. VI below how measurements in terms of commanded labour are in fact compatible with the determination of the rate of profits in accordance with Eq. (2) above.

[21]Adam Smith's "adding-up theory of prices" seems often to have been construed as anticipating the demand-and-supply explanation of value and distribution of the later marginal-ist theories, in contrast with the explanation of the same phenomena later provided by Ricardo. Thus, in 1954, p. 189, Schumpeter writes of Smith's conception of the "natural price" as "the rudimentary equilibrium theory of Chap. VII [of the *Wealth of Nations* which] ... points towards Say and, through

on corn would raise *both* the rent of land and the rate of profits, without apparently seeing the consequences these rises would be bound to have upon the real wage (e.g. Malthus, [1836] 1951, p. 398† and passim).

10. Ricardo's great merit was in fact that he saw through these "appearances" (cf. para. 11 below) and brought consistency back into economic theory. This achievement of Ricardo's *Principles* was rendered possible by relating the exchange value of the commodities to the quantity of labour necessary to produce them.

Let us in fact suppose that the proportion between wages and profits in Smith's natural prices are the same for all commodities—as they would be under our assumption at para. 8 of a capital consisting only of the advanced wages. All commodities would then exchange according to the quantity of labour required for their production. The ratio between the values of any two aggregates of commodities—or between sums or differences of such values—would accordingly be equal to the ratios between the respective quantities of labour embodied.[22] The value of Social product and of the Necessary consumption in Eq. (2) could then be "measured" in terms of the quantities of labour embodied, here indicated by P and N, and we would obtain the rate of profit r as

$$r = \frac{P - N}{N} \tag{3}$$

the latter's work, to Walras", and originates a "Smith, Mill, Marshall line" which was rival to that of Ricardo (*ibid.* 530, cf. also pp. 557–558; 567–568, 599). A similar interpretation is adopted by Maurice Dobb who, in 1973, refers to Smith's "determination of the general level [of wages and profits] by conditions of supply and demand for labour and capital respectively" (p. 50, cf. also p. 112, and passim). This view of Smith's approach to value and distribution seems to overlook that, behind Smith's vague references to the rate of profit as determined by the "competition" of capitalists, there lay, as we saw, the inconsistency of rates of wages, profits and rent determined independently of one another. And it was just this inconsistency that Ricardo and Marx criticised Smith for. The demand and supply forces of the modern theories, founded as they are, on the "substitutability" between "factors of production" (cf. above, paras. 6 and 7), are as absent in Smith as they are in Ricardo.

† [*Editor's note*: it might be of help to the reader to note that, although the content of this page of Malthus's *Principles* makes no explicit mention of tariffs, one finds in it the general premise of their alleged parallel effect on profits and rents hinted at in the text. For there, Malthus states a direct relationship between profits and the expenditure of 'consumers who are not themselves engaged in production', which would keep the value of the whole product higher than otherwise. The implication about tariffs would therefore be that the higher prices of commodities brought about by higher expenditure out of increased rents would 'make room', so to speak, for higher profits as well.]

[22] As we saw in para. 9 the rate of profit can be directly envisaged as a relative value, namely the value of the Surplus product (a composite commodity) in terms of the Necessary consumption (a second composite commodity): if all individual commodities exchange according to the quantity of labour embodied, the same will be true of these two composite commodities. When the economy is not replacing its wage capital, Eq. (3), written as $r = (P/N) - 1$, shows how the rate of profit can still be derived from a relative value: that of the Social product, relative to the Necessary consumption.

where P and N are now *known* magnitudes. Thus, if we return to our example of an economy with 3 m. workers, a doubling of the real wage and, hence, of the labour required for the production of its constituents from, for example, 1/3 to 2/3 of a labour-year, would make the rate of profit fall from $(3-1)/1=200\%$ to $(3-2)/2=50\%$. The constraint binding changes in wages and changes in the rate of profit becomes self-evident and no space is left for the illusion, generated by the appearance of price as a sum of wages and profits, that the rivalry between capital and labour "tends to increase the value of the product to such an extent that each receives a larger piece" (Marx, 1963–71, III, p. 503). In yet another quotation from Marx, relating particularly to Ricardo:

> It is the great merit of classical economy to have destroyed this false appearance and illusion, this mutual independence ... of the various social elements of wealth (Marx, 1954–1959, Bk. III, Chap. XLVIII, p. 830).

11. It may here be appropriate to notice how the nature of Ricardo's contribution in overcoming the error implicit in Smith's adding-up theory of prices may help us to comprehend Marx's often misunderstood position with respect to what he called "vulgar political economy". Ricardo had begun to overcome the difficulties which had prevented his predecessors from seeing the constraint binding wages to profits and rents: however his very success in bringing this to light had the result of exposing the class antagonisms which underlie the division of the product. In this situation, the attempt to preserve a harmonious view of society took—Marx thought—the form of turning a blind eye upon the analytical advances of Ricardo and keeping closer to the "appearances" by which the price of the product, seen as the *sum* of profits, wages and rents, may *seem* capable of accommodating the rise in one of these elements without a decrease in the others. In Marx's ironic words, already referred to above, these economists held that:

> Even if this occasionally brings them to blows, nevertheless the outcome of this competition between land, capital and labour finally shows that, although they quarrel with one another over the division, their rivalry tends to increase the value of the product to such an extent that each receives a larger piece, so that their competition, which spurs them on, is merely the expression of their harmony (Marx, 1963–1971, III, Addenda, p. 503).

The fact that these views were the result of adhering, as popular thought often does, to "appearances" explains the specific adjective "vulgar", i.e. popular, which Marx applied to these economists. Accordingly, Marx defines as "vulgar economy" that "economy" "which deals with appearances only", in contrast with "classical Political Economy ... which ... has investigated the real relations of production in bourgeois society" (Marx, 1954–1959, Bk. I, Chap. I, p. 85, n. 1). In this "vulgar economy" he includes, if not the work of Say himself, that of his followers in France and Germany (Marx, 1963–1971, III, Addenda, pp. 501–2), and that of Senior and his followers (Marx, 1954–1959, Bk. I, Chap. XXIV, pp. 592–3). Marx's frequent reference to the existence of "vulgar representations" in Smith, an author for whose scientific achievement he had the highest respect, seems on the other hand apt to bring out the specific, and not merely derogatory, meaning which he attributed to the expression "vulgar economy".

The distinction by Marx between 'vulgar' and 'classical' political economy turned thus on a second, even more basic distinction between two kinds of representation of the economic relations of bourgeois society. There are, on the one hand, the "apparent relations" or "connections", which are those perceived by the unsystematic observer and which are represented in Adam Smith's "adding up" theory of prices, when "instead of resolving exchange-value into wages, profit and rent … he constructs the exchange-value of the commodity from the values of wages, profit and rent, which are determined independently and separately" (Marx, 1963–1971, II, Chap. X, p. 217). In such an inconsistent representation of the economic system "[the] contradictory character [of capital] is totally concealed and effaced … no contradiction to labour [is evident]" (Marx, 1963–71, III, Addenda, p. 467). There are, on the other hand, the "real relations" constituting the "intrinsic", or "inner connections" of the bourgeois system. These are the relations brought to light by systematic scientific analysis. They centre on the constraint that binds changes in wages to changes in profits and rents and reveal the economic antagonism between classes (for example, Marx, 1963–1971, II, Chap. X, p. 166). Now, for Marx, these "inner connections" required, in order to be revealed, that the product be measured *independently* of its division between the three classes. Hence the role of Ricardo's measurement of values in terms of labour embodied in which, in Marx's own words, the value of the commodity "*does not depend upon its division into wages, profits and rents*" and constitutes instead "the limit … for the dividends which the labourer, capitalist and landlord will be able to draw from this value in the form of revenue—wages, profit and rent (Marx, 1954–9, Bk. III, Chap. L, p. 854, emphasis added; cf. also p. 874 and 1963–71, II, Chap. X, p. 219).[23]

[23]When faced with passages like the ones above, it seems surprising that various authors following what looks like an established tradition, should attribute to Marx's theory of value some "qualitative" role different from that which the theory had in Ricardo, i.e. that of measuring the product independently of its division (cf. Sweezy, 1946, p. 33; the idea finds an early expression in Hilferding, 1949, e.g. pp. 130–132). A recent clear-cut expression of this position may be found when it is claimed that "the idea that the theory of value developed in Vol. I of *Capital* is a (bad) theory of relative prices is … untenable" (Medio, 1977, p. 382). Medio (a participant in the Siena conference mentioned above) appears however to contradict this claim of his, when in the very next line, he admits that "the cost of production theory of price seems to be unsatisfactory [because] it contained an *apparent* element of circularity … the calculation of the rate of profit requires valuing [product, wage goods and means of production] at their equilibrium prices. The latter, however, cannot be calculated without knowing the rate of profit" (emphasis in the original). Here indeed we have a very good reason for Marx's "bad" theory of relative prices: for what means were available to Marx for breaking that "apparent circularity" if not the labour theory of value developed by Ricardo for that very purpose?

IV. Marx's "Prices of Production"

12. And for this analysis of the "inner organic connection" binding wages and profits, Marx took the road which Ricardo's theory of value had opened up for him.

As we saw (para. 8 and n. 20) when determining the rate of profit Ricardo had operated *as if* capital could be resolved entirely into the wages advanced for the year. Marx started by clearing up this confusion which Ricardo had inherited from Smith. He showed that the proportion which the means of production bear to the labour (and hence, to the wages advanced) constitutes a factor which can influence the rate of profit independently of the proportion in which the product is divided between wages and profits. Accordingly, he distinguished capital into two parts: the wages advanced or "variable capital" and the means of production or "constant capital". To simplify our exposition, we shall assume that constant capital is entirely consumed during the yearly production cycle (i.e. consists of circulating capital) and shall retain the assumption of free land. If, then, commodities exchanged according to the quantities of labour embodied, the rate of profit would be determined as

$$r = \frac{s}{c+v} \tag{4}$$

where c and v are respectively the "constant" and "variable" capitals, measured in terms of the labour necessary to produce them, whereas s, the social "surplus value", is Ricardo's $(P-N)$ and is measured by the quantity of "surplus labour", the labour exerted in the year over and above that necessary for reproducing the wages.[24]

Commodities however do not exchange according to the quantities of labour embodied. If we look at "natural" prices as resolving themselves into wages and profits, as Ricardo did, we find that these wages and profits are present in different proportions in the prices of different commodities and the latter do not, therefore, exchange in proportion to the labour necessary for their production. Ricardo had admitted this in terms of "modifications" to the rule that commodities exchange according to the labour embodied: his argument concerning profits continued however to rest ultimately on that rule.[25]

---

[24] Equation (3), by which we expressed Ricardo's determination becomes, in the new symbols, $r=s/v$ and its difference from Eq. (4), due to Marx's consideration of the organic composition of capital, may become clearer if we rewrite Eq. (4) as.

$$r = \frac{s/v}{(c/v)+1}$$

[25] Ricardo struggled with that problem until the end of his life. Cf. the paper *On Absolute and Exchangeable Value*, Ricardo 1951–73, IV, which was in fact written in the Summer of 1823, just before his death. A misunderstanding of the position of Ricardo and of Marx's criticism of it seems to occur when in Steedman (1982) it is asserted that Marx was "quite wrong ... to say that Ricardo's approach was inherently incapable of providing a theory of the rate of profit", where, as

Marx faces the question in the manuscripts posthumously published by Engels as Vol. Ill of Capital and, in the sketch of a solution he provides there, he comes within one step of a correct general solution. He even indicates the step which is yet to be taken—though, as we shall see, he failed to realize its consequences.[26]

---

the context shows, "Ricardo's approach", as distinct from Marx's, would be founded on the idea that "the general rate of profit and the prices of production *must* be determined simultaneously within the theory" (p. 124, emphasis in the original). In fact the basis of Ricardo's argument in the *Principles*, is the assumption of the *constancy* in the value of commodities "in the production of which no additional quantity of labour is required" (e.g. Ricardo, 1951–73, I, pp. 110–1). Ricardo's actual procedure seems therefore no different from Marx's in admitting that commodities do not exchange according to the quantity of labour embodied, but in determining the rate of profit as if they did so exchange—by looking, that is, for a commodity which would constitute a "medium", such that "[t]hose commodities on one side of this medium, would rise in comparative value with it, with a rise in the price of labour ... and those on the other side might fall from the same cause" (Ricardo, 1951–73, VIII, p. 193, for Marx cf. para. 14 below). Moreover Ricardo, like Marx, uses the rate of profit so determined to ascertain how far the relative prices of commodities deviate from, or change independently of, the relative quantities of labour embodied.

The main difference between Ricardo and Marx lies therefore in whether this logical order is explicitly followed and justified, as it is by Marx, or has instead to be extracted from an argument which, if taken literally, far from being a "simultaneous" determination of prices and the rate of profit, would be contradictory, since it would rest on ignoring that very dependence of relative prices on distribution which is admitted elsewhere in the argument. Now, this criticism of Ricardo is precisely the one expressed by Marx when for example he charges Ricardo with an "erroneous confusion of cost-prices and values" (Marx, 1963–71, Vol. II, Chap. X, p. 199). It would on the other hand contradict the facts to view Ricardo's procedure as a better preparation than Marx's for the later simultaneous determination of prices and profits: when the latter came, with Bortkiewicz, Seton and Sraffa (cf. n. 32 below) it grew out of Marx's equations for prices of production, rather than directly out of Ricardo's less definite procedure.

[26]We may here notice the curious misunderstanding according to which the labour theory of value is held to be incompatible with the existence of alternative techniques (cf. Morishima, 1973, p. 189; Steedman, 1977, p. 65). The dependence of labour values on the technique adopted would not in fact prevent their use in determining the rate of profit, any more than the similar dependence of physical inputs prevents them from playing the same role in price Eqs. (8) below: labour values would allow determining the rate of profit corresponding to each technique, and hence that which could be shown to rule under free competition at the given wage (cf. n. 6 above).

Here we may also notice the misconception by which Samuelson in 1974, p. 292, writes that "in a regime of values ... the technique that minimizes values at $r=0$ will minimize them for all r's, a shortcoming of the values model". A confusion occurs here between the labour theory of value, by which the several *commodities* exchange according to embodied labour—and the different conditions under which costs for the *same* commodity, produced with alternative techniques, should equal the ratio between the respective quantities of labour embodied, when the technique maximizing the net product per worker would in fact dominate at all levels of the real wage. Equal organic composition *as between commodities* does not conceptually entail equal organic composition *as between alternative techniques*, as shown for example by Samuelson's "surrogate production function", 1962, which rests entirely on labour value conditions, but clearly does not entail domination of one technique over all others.

13. There, Marx starts by asking himself why commodities do not generally exchange according to the quantities of labour necessary to produce them. The answer he gives is simple: if commodities exchanged according to that principle, those produced with capital of a higher "organic composition" (i.e. a higher proportion of "constant" to "variable" capital) would give a lower rate of profit. Thus, suppose that only corn and steel are produced in the economy and, the "rate of surplus value" s/v being for example 1, the organic composition c/v is 1 for corn and 3 for steel: steel production would give a rate of profit of 25% as against the 50% of corn production. The competitive tendency to a uniform rate of profit will then make steel exchange for more than the quantity of corn embodying the same amount of labour, so as to raise the surplus value (the difference between value of output and value of capital) in steel production and lower it in corn production until the two rates of profit become the same. It may then appear that the divergence of the price of steel in terms of corn from the ratio of the respective quantities of labour embodied, has the meaning of *redistributing* surplus value away from the surplus industries to the "deficit" industries (from the corn industry to the steel industry in our example). Marx in fact arrived at this conclusion and argued that when the redistribution has been completed, we shall find in each branch of production the same rate of profit we obtain in Eq. (4), by distributing *total* surplus value over *total* capital[27]: just as when 5 sacks of corn are re-distributed proportionally among 10 people, each will end up with $\frac{5}{10}$ of a sack, irrespective of the initial distribution. The prices of production that ensure this result will be those obtained by applying the rate of profit calculated in Eq. (4) to the capital used in each branch. In our steel and corn economy:

$$r = \frac{(s_s A_s + s_c A_c)}{(c_s A_s + c_c A_c) + (v_s A_s + v_c A_c)} \tag{5}$$

$$\left.\begin{aligned} p_s &= (c_s + v_s)(1 + r) \\ p_c &= (c_c + v_c)(1 + r) \end{aligned}\right\} \tag{6}$$

in which the prices of production p_s of steel and p_c of corn are referred to physical units of the two commodities requiring a unit of labour for their production (so that $c_s + v_s + s = c_c + v_c + s_c = 1$), and A_s, A_c indicate the quantities produced of the two commodities. The way in which r is calculated implies on the other hand that the prices p_s and p_c are expressed in terms of the composite commodity constituting the social product, taken in the quantity requiring a unit of labour for its production.[28]

This reasoning (according to which the rate of profit—the key variable of the system—is determined by Eq. (5) *as if* commodities exchanged in proportion to

[27] Cf. for example the illustration of the cotton mill in Marx (1954–9), Bk. III, Chap. IX, p. 155ff.

[28] Marx's condition that total prices should equal total values is in fact equivalent to taking as numeraire this particular composite commodity, which is also that produced with the "average" organic composition.

the quantities of labour necessary for their production, may go a long way towards explaining why Marx thought it possible to conduct his argument in Bks. I and II of *Capital* on the basis of just that assumption, postponing to Bk. III the determination of the prices of production.

14. If this is what we find in the posthumously published Chap. IX of Book III of *Capital*, Marx did not fail to notice a shortcoming in this intended solution. Competition will distribute profits in proportion to the "prices" of the constant and variable capitals, and not in proportion to their "values" (i.e. the quantities of labour embodied). He wrote accordingly "there is always the possibility of an error if the cost price of a commodity in any particular sphere is identified with the value of the means of production [and variable capital] consumed by it".[29]

Marx seems to have left the question there. Had he attempted to correct that "error", he would soon have found that the price equations modified by estimating the capitals at their prices must determine not only the prices of production but also the rate of profit: Eq. (5) would therefore have stood out as incorrect. Let us in fact modify Eqs. (6) by expressing both the constant capital, assumed here to consist of steel, and the variable capital, consisting of "corn", in terms of prices. We obtain

$$\left.\begin{aligned} p_c &= (c_c p_s + v_c p_c)(1+r) \\ p_s &= (c_s p_s + v_s p_c)(1+r) \end{aligned}\right\} \tag{7}$$

It is sufficient to divide both equations by one of the two prices, say p_c to realize that Marx's two independent price equations contain in fact only one unknown, the *relative* price p_s/p_c, and are therefore contradictory if r is to be determined by Eq. (5): in the price equations the uniform rate of profit can only be determined *simultaneously* with the relative price of the two commodities.

It is not difficult to see where lay the fault in the notion of a redistribution of surplus value which, as we saw, led Marx to Eq. (5). Unlike the 5 sacks of corn which do not change in size *relative* to the 10 people in the course of the redistribution, the size of the social surplus value does so change *relative* to capital. This surplus value is in fact the price of production of the surplus product, and cannot but *change* relative to that of social capital when, with the redistribution of surplus value, relative "prices" in general come to diverge from relative "values".[30] As we saw in para. 9 the profit rate is but the relative value of those two composite commodities and it will not be equal to the ratio between the quantities of labour embodied in them any more than the relative price of any two commodities.

---

[29] Marx (1954–9), Bk. III, Chap. IX, p. 165. As is well known Marx indicates by 'cost-price' the value (price) of the capital (constant *and* variable) used up in the production of the commodity in question. Marx continues the passage quoted above with the words "our present analysis does not necessitate a closer analysis of this point".

[30] It is curious to note how Hilferding, in his answer to Böhm-Bawerk's critique of Marx, neatly misses this point when he writes: "It is obvious that the change in distribution makes no difference in the total amount of surplus value undergoing distribution" (Hilferding, 1949, p. 160).

15. There is, however, a sense in which Marx's error was suggestive. The error can be envisaged by us as the result of treating as integral parts of a single method (for the determination of the rate of profit) what are in fact when consistently developed, two equivalent methods, each of which is sufficient to determine that rate. The first, which we may call the *Price-equations method*, is exemplified by Eqs. (7) and determines the rate of profits—or, more generally, the relation between the wage and the profit rate—*simultaneously* with relative prices. However, the basic idea of profits (the non-wage share) as a *surplus product*, which they can be seen to be whenever the economy is in a self-replacing state, inevitably leads one on to attempt some simpler method. The latter method, which we may here call the *Surplus-equation method*, is exemplified by Eq. (4) or (3) for the case in which commodities exchange according to the labour embodied. Essentially, it depends on the possibility of expressing both the surplus and the capital that appear in the equation in terms which are proportionate to their values but do not contain the unknown prices, so that the profit rate is the only unknown.

As Sects. VI and VII below indicate, this second method is also available for sufficiently general hypotheses and it appears to exhibit some advantages of simplicity and transparency over the Price-equations method.

V. The "Price-Equations Method" of Determining Profits

16. The "Price-equations method" consists of the generalization of Eqs. (6). In these equations we assumed that constant capital consists of one commodity only. When that assumption is abandoned, the constant capital of each industry has to be distinguished into as many quantities of embodied labour as there are kinds of means of production. To each of those kinds a different price of production applies: the additional unknown price thus introduced will entail an additional price equation.[31] Matters are even simpler for the variable capital: the assumption

[31] A determination of the rate of profit based on Marx's price equations was proposed as early as 1907 in Bortkiewicz (1949). In that article Bortkiewicz acknowledged a debt to Tugan Baranowsky, who had used a similar method to show that Marx was mistaken in his determination of the rate of profit. It is from the latter author that Bortkiewicz apparently derived the grouping into three sectors (means of production, subsistence goods and luxury goods) of the various industries to which Marx had separately referred when dealing with prices of production. The aggregation of the means of production into a single sector is however in contrast with the need to disaggregate constant capital, and Bortkiewicz had to refer to a single price of production, thus treating the price system as if only one capital good existed in the economy. Bortkiewicz's aggregation of constant capital also helped to hide the fact that, as we shall see below, the measurement in terms of labour embodied of the elements of capital can be replaced by a physical measurement. However, a second solution to Marx's problem of the determination of the rate of profit which did not suffer from the deficiency of the aggregation of capital goods and was based on work by Dmitriev was advanced in Bortkiewicz (1952) (cf. below, n. 39).

of a uniform real wage ensures that in all industries variable capital consists of the same composite "wage commodity": we may therefore apply to it the single price obtainable from the prices of its constituent commodities.

We may now write the price equations obtained by generalizing Eqs. (6) for the case of any number k of commodities $a, b, \ldots, k$.

Let:

a be produced during the year by L_a labourers assisted by the constant capitals A_a, B_a, ... K_a, (some of which may be zero) consisting of commodities $a, b \ldots k$; thus requiring a total quantity $A = L_a + A_a + B_a + \ldots + K_a$ of direct and indirect labour;

L_b, A_b, B_b, ... K_b, B; ...; L_k, A_k, B_k, ... K_k, K, be the analogous quantities in the production of commodities $b \ldots k$; w be the quantity of labour necessary to produce the given real wage;

λ_a, λ_b, ..., λ_g (such that $\lambda_a + \lambda_b \ldots + \lambda_g = 1$) be the quantities of labour embodied in the wage goods, g in number, constituting a unit of the "wage commodity" A, which we then choose as the numeraire.

We shall have:

$$\begin{aligned}
&\left[(A_a p_a + B_a p_b + \ldots K_a p_k) + L_a w\right](1+r) = A p_a \\
&\left[(A_b p_a + B_b p_b + \ldots K_b p_k) + L_b w\right](1+r) = B p_b \\
&\ldots\ldots\ldots\ldots \\
&\ldots\ldots\ldots\ldots \\
&\left[(A_k p_a + B_k p_b + \ldots K_k p_k) + L_k w\right](1+r) = K p_k \\
&\lambda_a p_a + \lambda_b p_b + \ldots \lambda_g p_g = 1
\end{aligned} \tag{8}$$

Equations (8) are $(k+1)$ in number and contain the same number of unknowns: the rate of profit r and the k prices of production $p_a, p_b \cdots p_k$.

It can now easily be seen that the need to distinguish the constant capital of an industry, say a, into the quantities A_a, B_a, ... K_a also makes it inessential to measure them in terms of labour embodied: the prices of production p_a, p_b,... p_k can be directly applied to the physical inputs of $a, b, \ldots k$, and the same applies to the variable capitals $(L_a w)$, $(L_b w)$, etc., consisting of the composite "wage commodity" (which, being our numeraire, has a unit price).[32] These physical measurements are clearly preferable, because they only depend on the method of production of the commodity concerned and not, in addition, on the methods of its direct and indirect means of production, like the corresponding quantities of labour embodied. Equation (8) can therefore also be read with the quantities w, A_a, B_a, etc., taken

[32] The possibility of physical measurements in Marx's equations of the prices of production, when modified by applying prices to the capitals, appears to have been first noted in print in Seton, 1957, p. 151, n. 3.

as physical quantities.[33] Henceforth we shall adopt this alternative reading of Eqs. (8).

Equations (8) are however those we find in Sraffa's *Production of Commodities by Means of Commodities*, Chap. II.[34] Sraffa's own symbols were chosen for Eqs. (8) so as to bring out the fact that his equations are the same as Marx's Eqs. (5) and (6) once these are modified by applying the prices of production to variable and constant capital. The fact that such a modification had been suggested by Marx himself has not prevented it from changing his Eqs. (5) and (6) beyond easy recognition. The essential point however is that Eqs. (8) provide a general solution for precisely the same problem which Ricardo and Marx had faced by means of the labour theory of value. The characteristic premises of the surplus approach, for which the real wage and the social product are given when determining the rate of profit and relative prices (para. 4 above) have remained unaffected and, therefore, the notion of profits as a residual and the associated view of the forces determining distribution have also remained unaffected.

17. Equations (8) are however less transparent than Ricardo's and Marx's Eqs. (3) and (4) were about the forces governing the rate of profit. The basic asymmetry between a wage independently determined and profits resulting as a residual is obscured: in Eqs. (8), to envisage profits as a difference between the value of the product and that of the wages and means of production makes no more sense than the reverse procedure of obtaining the value of the product by adding the profits, the wages and the value of the means of production together. More fundamentally the question is that these "appearances"—the very ones which had misled Smith and later authors into thinking that profits and wages could be determined independently of one another—make it more difficult to grasp the properties of the system. These "appearances", which Ricardo had overcome by measuring value in terms of embodied labour, are in fact engendered by the difficulty of viewing the effects of the interdependence of prices, and are here dispelled by the mathematical consideration of the *system* of price equations.[35] Thus, from Eqs. (8) it results that once the real wage is given, the rate of profit is determined, so that the two cannot change independently of one another. Moreover, system (8) reveals that, under sufficiently general conditions, there exists an inverse relation between the real wage and the rate of profit (below, para. 20). But a reasoning that relies on theorems which abstract from the *content* of the problems analysed cannot fully

[33] Even the numerical values of the coefficients would remain unchanged if we choose for the unit of each commodity $a, b, \dots k$, the quantity of it requiring a unit of labour for its direct and indirect production.

[34] Cf. the equations in Sraffa (1960), p. 6, which differ from Eqs. (8) above, because in Sraffa the wages are included, commodity by commodity, in the quantities of the means of production.

[35] The individual price equation may indeed misleadingly suggest, with its seeming symmetry between profits and wages, and, above all, its seeming representation of price as a sum, the idea that the two rates can be determined "independently and separately" from one another (cf. para. 9 above). Not surprisingly it is only later in the development of theory that the price equations reveal their implications as to the constraint linking the real wage and the rate of profit.

overcome the difficulty of grasping the effects of the interdependence of $k+1$ unknowns, and cannot therefore have the transparency of surplus equations like (3) or (5).[36] That transparency was in fact ultimately due to the "picture" which corresponded to those equations: that of a known product to be divided between wages and profits; with the rate of profit originating from the distribution in proportion to the amount of capital of the surplus which this product shows above the known amount of wages. This "picture" allowed a concrete mental representation of a highly abstract analysis: in the 'picture' the dependence of the rate of profit on real wages was *seen*, and the properties of the economic system associated with this key relation were under a correspondingly easier grip.[37]

Naturally, reality need not be simple, and need not allow for the existence of a surplus equation like (3) or (5), beyond the hypotheses necessary to validate the labour theory of value. But the point we wish to make is that the recovery, if at all possible, of that "picture" under the present more general assumptions, would constitute an important scientific advance. It would do so because it would entail a better grip over the economic system's known properties: and it would make it correspondingly easier to gain greater knowledge by asking further questions.[38]

---

[36] Thus, the nature of profits as a residual can be clarified by Sraffa in the first chapter of 1960 only by showing how prices just sufficient to repay the wages and replace the means of production become contradictory when a surplus product comes into existence. The fact that this indirect route had to be followed to exhibit what would have been so evident in Eqs. (3) or (5) provides an example of the loss of transparency referred to. A further and perhaps more striking example of this lack of transparency is the sense of novelty which, as late as 1961, under the name of "non-substitution theorem", greeted the proposition that, in an economy like that of Eqs. (8), the real wage is given irrespective of the "demand of consumers", when the rate of profit (rate of interest) is given (cf. Samuelson, [1961] 1966, p. 528)—a proposition which would have been obvious from Eqs. (3) and (5), or from (9) and (10) below.

[37] Of course Social product, Necessary consumption and Social capital, are, in themselves, highly abstract notions. The mind can however fit them into a "picture" and proceed to operate with them (just as the mind of a child can work with an abacus), *as if* they were concrete objects connected by the simple relations of part and whole. This mental procedure drastically differs from that which we have when entirely abstract mathematical notions must be resorted to in order to deal with variables like the prices and quantities of commodities, which, though more concrete (i.e. more directly experienced) are both numerous and interdependent.

[38] The loss of the "picture" which was associated with Eqs. (3) or (5) should in fact not be confused with the loss of a mere didactic device, which could always be made good by using appropriate, simplifying assumptions. The nature of this loss may perhaps be best illustrated by referring to the uneasiness which some physicists feel at the loss of the "pictures" of physical reality which were provided by the notions of "waves" and "particles". This uneasiness induces one physicist to hold that "as a system of calculation which gives the right answers [quantum theory] is overwhelmingly successful. But whether it tells us anything about what matter is actually like is another question" (Pippard, 1962, p. 33). And the comment of a science historian to this was "if we were forbidden to talk in terms of models at all, we should have no expectations at all, and we should then be *imprisoned … inside the range of our existing experiments*", where "model" appears here to mean something closer to what we have called "picture", than to what economists are at present in the habit of calling "model" (Hesse, 1962, pp. 56–7, our italics).

In the next section we shall indicate how, under our present assumptions, a determination of the rate of profit along the lines of the "Surplus equation method" becomes possible, provided we focus our attention on the sector of the economy where the general rate of profit is in fact determined. We shall then see, in Sect. VII, that a similar, even simpler "picture" of distribution becomes available in the shape of Sraffa's "standard system" when we envisage the rate of profit, and not the wage, as the variable which can be determined outside the "core" of the theory.

VI. The Surplus-Equation Method and the Wage-Goods Sector

18. Let us single out the price equations of the commodities a, b, ... h, consisting of the wage goods a, b, ... g, constituting the "wage commodity" (para. 16 above) and of their direct and indirect means of production $g+1$, ..., h. The definition of these commodities, h in number (with $h \leq k$), implies that in their h price-equations we find as unknowns only their h prices plus the rate of profit r. It follows that these h equations, together with the last equation in system (8), defining the wage commodity as the numeraire, will be sufficient to determine the rate of profit and the h prices independently of the remaining $(k-h)$ price equations.

This means that, once the real wage is given, the general rate of profit will depend exclusively upon the technical conditions of production of the wage goods and their direct and indirect means of production. The technical conditions of production of the others commodities—i.e. the luxury goods and the means of produdution specific to them—will only be relevant in order to determine, by means of the remaining $(k-h)$ equations of system (8), such prices for these commodities as will yield the rate of profit determined by the first h equations.[39]

19. Let us now look more closely at the part of the productive system which directly or indirectly reproduces the aggregate wages advanced to the workers for

[39]The principle according to which the rate of profit is determined by the conditions of production of wage goods, and of their direct and indirect means of production alone, is a generalization of that which Ricardo appears to have used in his *Essay on Profits* (1815), when he concluded that "it is the profits of the farmer that regulate the profits of all other trades" (1951–1973, IV, p. 4; VI, p. 104). If we in fact assume that wages consist entirely of "corn", and that this is produced by itself and labour, as is required in order to validate Ricardo's argument, then the h commodities entering directly or indirectly the wage narrow down to the single commodity 'corn'. The role of wage goods in determining the rate of profit was first pointed out, it appears, by Dmitriev (1974), p. 59 ff.. It then emerged again in the solutions of the so-called problem of "transforming" Marx's "values" into "prices of production", advanced in Bortkiewicz (1952), where the author recognised his debt to Dmitriev, and also in Bortkiewicz (1949).

the year.[40] This part of the economy constitutes what we may call the "vertically integrated sector of the wage-goods", or *integrated wage-goods sector* for short. Let us then express both the net yearly product of this sector and the wages paid in it, in terms of Smith's "labour-commanded" standard of value, i.e. in terms of the quantity of labour which those aggregates of commodities can buy. Both these two quantities will be known *before* the rate of profit and prices are known. The net product, being the yearly wages of L labourers, will evidently "command" L labour years, where L is the known number of labourers employed in the economy.[41] The wages paid in the sector, on the other hand, will be those of the L_v labourers required for the direct and indirect production of the "necessary consumption", a known magnitude, since the real wage and the technical conditions of the direct and indirect production of its constituents are known. These wages will therefore "command" L_v labour-years.

It follows that in the integrated wage-goods sector, the amount of profits in terms of "commanded labour" constitutes a "surplus value" $(L-L_v)$ which is known before the rate of profit and the relative prices are determined. This surplus value coincides numerically with Marx's own social surplus value s (since $L=v+s$ and $L_v=v$), though it differs from the latter in conception because: (i) it is the surplus value of the wage-goods sector, and not that of the entire economy; (ii) it is expressed in terms of labour commanded and not in terms of labour embodied.[42]

---

[40] For the unique determination of such a sector cf. Garegnani (1970), p. 409 [this volume, Part II, p. 150], and, more generally the notion of a "sub-system" in Sraffa (1960), p. 89. We may note that the determining role of this "sector" of the economy in no way depends on actually being able to isolate it within the real economy: the rate of profit would be determined in the same way, if the wage-goods advanced to the workers were not being reproduced. The "sector" is therefore best considered as a purely logical construction, which, like Sraffa's "standard product" to be considered in the next section, has the purpose of giving transparency to the forces regulating the rate of profit.

[41] The fact that the value of this net product, expressed in labour commanded, is independent of the rate of profit does not contradict the fact, stated in para. 9 above, that the value in labour commanded of any commodity is not independent of that rate. The constancy of the *value* of net output of the wage goods sector is in fact due to the changes in *physical size* which this net product undergoes as the real wage changes with the rate of profit. It may help the reader to note that the use made here of the labour commanded standard has no connection with that suggested by Sraffa, in *op. cit.* paras. 41–42, that is of using as numeraire a quantity of labour commanded which would vary with the rate of profit in such a way as to remain equivalent to the "Standard product".

[42] It should be noted that the net output of the integrated wage-goods sector is *physically homogeneous* with the wages paid there, since both consist of the same composite wage-commodity. The amount of profits in the sector could then be determined as the difference between two physical quantities of the wage commodity, and the rate of profit could be seen to arise from the distribution of this surplus product over the capital of the wage-good sector, reduced to wages in the manner we shall consider in the next paragraph. The commanded labour standard used in the text has however the advantage that in terms of this, the product of the integrated wage-goods sector is constant as the real wage changes either in level or in composition.

When we proceed, as we must, from the amount of profits (surplus value) to the rate of profit, the obstacle we meet is that, unlike the value of the product and of the wages, the value in "commanded labour" of the means of production of the integrated wage-goods sector is not known independently of the prices. We seem to be unable to proceed with a "surplus equation" where the rate of profit is the only unknown (above, para. 15), and to be forced to return to the price equations. This obstacle is not insuperable however. Under our present hypotheses[43] it can be overcome by the device of "reducing to labour" the means of production: as will be presently seen this device allows us to express the value in commanded labour of the means of production as a function where the rate of profit is indeed the only unknown.

The capital required for the integrated production of any commodity can in fact be regarded in either of two alternative but equivalent ways. The first is that, confined to a single yearly production cycle—between, say, moments (-1) and (0)—which we adopted for prices Eqs. (8): capital there includes the means of production, besides the wages, both kinds of capital being advanced at moment (-1): the value of the capital so conceived involves the unknown prices of the means of production. The second way of looking at capital, however, proceeds to consider the *production* of these means of production and considers it as the result of previous *stages* in the production of the final commodity: the stage between moments (-2) and (-1), in which the means of production of the commodity have been produced; the stage between (-3) and (-2) in which the means of production of those means of production have been produced, and so forth. The result of this procedure is that capital is reduced to wages with, generally (in the case of circular production, when the commodity, or one of its means of production, requires itself directly or indirectly in order to be produced) a residual of means of production which may be rendered small at will by carrying the process on through a sufficient number of stages. These wages are however conceived as having been advanced for varying periods of time; not only at moment (-1) but also at (-2), (-3), etc. The advantage of this device is that, when measured in "labour commanded", these advanced wages will be given by the quantities of "dated labour" they are the wages of. Unlike the prices of the means of production[44] in the other

---

[43] Fixed capital of constant efficiency can however be easily shown to leave the present argument unaffected (cf. n. 45 below).

[44] We are in fact expressing the prices of the means of production by means of these "advanced wages" and the profits on them for the relevant periods of time. This is made clear by the procedure for this "reduction of the commodity to dated labour", which consists of taking the price equation of the commodity and replacing the prices of means of production with the expressions given by the respective price equations. The operation is then repeated with the prices of the second layer of means of production appearing in the equation thus modified, and so forth for the further layers, which appear in succession after each round of substitutions (see for example Sraffa, 1960, pp. 34–35). When looked at from this "dated labour" angle the other view of capital appears to be the result of "collapsing" all the successive stages of production into a single year—a "collapsing" which is made possible by the availability at the beginning of the year of the products of all the intermediate stages, that is the means of production. It should however be remembered that the reduction to dated labour constitutes a mere logical device, as is shown by the fact that, when the production of a commodity is "circular", it cannot be conceived as starting with unassisted labour.

view of capital, they will therefore be *known* quantities since the methods of production of both the commodity and its means of production are known.

A simple example will show how this second view of capital can be applied to the means of production of the integrated wage-goods sector to obtain a "Surplus equation" determining the rate of profit. Consider an economy where (besides the general assumptions already made in para. 12) we suppose that wages consist only of "corn". "Corn" is produced with one "plough" per worker: the "plough", entirely consumed during the year, is in turn produced by one unassisted worker. The L_v labourers employed in the integrated wage-goods sector will therefore be distributed half in (directly) producing the "corn", and half in reproducing the "ploughs": the capital advanced for the year (reckoned, therefore, according to the first of the two views above) will consist of the wages *and* the ploughs. If we take now the second, "dated-labour" view of capital, the latter emerges instead as the wages of the two quantities of "dated labour" shown in Fig. 2a: $L_v/2$ labour years applied at moment (−2) for producing the "ploughs", which are then used in the successive "stage" of corn production—together with a further $L_v/2$ labour years applied at (−1). Expressed in "commanded labour" the wages, to which the entire capital of the integrated wage-goods sector has thus been reduced, will equal the corresponding quantities of dated labour i.e. $L_v/2$ advanced at (−2) and $L_v/2$ advanced at (−1). The rate of profit can then be seen to emerge from the distribution of the surplus value $L-L_v$, in proportion *both* to the wages advanced, and to the time by which they have been so advanced, account being taken of compound profits, that is

$$L - L_v = r\frac{L_v}{2} + 2r\frac{L_v}{2} + r^2\frac{L_v}{2} \tag{9}$$

where the term $rL_v/2$ indicates the share of surplus value allotted to the capitalists advancing the wages paid at time (−1); and the term $2rL_v/2$, together with the compound profit term $r^2L_v/2$, indicates the share allotted to those paying the wages at time (−2). The rate of profit is the only unknown in (9).

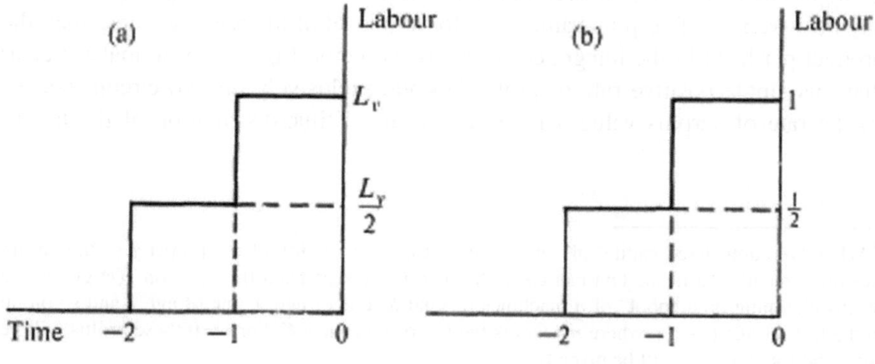

Fig. 2 The "dated labour" curve for the aggregate of wage goods paid as yearly wages (curve *a*) and the proportional distribution of labour over time in the production of the wage commodity (curve *b*)

20. It is now convenient to divide both sides of Eq. (9) by L_v obtaining

$$\frac{L - L_v}{L_v} = r\frac{1}{2} + 2r\frac{1}{2} + r^2\frac{1}{2} \tag{9a}$$

and proceed to some properties of our "surplus equation" (9a) which can be easily shown to hold beyond our present simple example.

On the left of the equality sign we find, expressed in commanded labour, the amount of surplus value per worker in the integrated wage-goods sector. This amount is identical to Marx's rate of surplus value s/v and depends purely on the level of the real wage and on the labour required for the direct and indirect production of its constituents. On the right of the equality sign we find instead a function expressing the amount of profits per worker, also expressed in commanded labour, which would be necessary in the sector in order to pay a rate of profit r. This function, which we may call "profit function" for short, depends purely on the *proportional* time distribution of the labour necessary to produce the wage commodity (see Fig. 2b): it does not therefore depend on the *level* of the real wage, but only on its *composition* and on the methods for the direct and indirect production of the wage-goods. The "profit function" has an important property which can easily be seen to hold with any kind of circulating capital, and with fixed capital of constant efficiency: it is zero when $r=0$ and then it rises monotonically with r.[45]

The solution of the "surplus equation" (9a) can now be represented in the diagram of Fig. 3a where r is measured horizontally and the rate of surplus value is measured vertically. We have there the curve Os representing the "profit function", which rises monotonically from the origin. (In the case of our example it will rise indefinitely as r rises indefinitely as in Fig. 3a; in the case of "circular production" it rises indefinitely as the rate of profit approaches a "maximum rate of profit" R as in Fig. 3c). The rate of surplus value, $(L-L_v)/L_v$, can on the other hand be represented by a horizontal line.

The level of the rate of profit which solves the equation will be that for which the "profits curve" OS cuts the surplus-value line. The fact that the "profits curve" is monotonically rising ensures that the solution will be unique and positive for any positive rate of surplus value—i.e. for any level of the real wage less than the product per head in the integrated wage goods sector. Figs. 3a or 3c make it clear that this single positive rate of profit depends exclusively on two circumstances: (i) the rate of surplus value; (ii) the proportional time-distribution of the labour

[45] When we admit fixed capital of constant efficiency the validity of the property of the "profit function" mentioned in the text can easily be seen if we start from the function $g(r)$ giving the profits obtaining on a "pool" of n machines of kind K, one of age 0, one of age 1 and so on up to the last, of age $(n-1)$, where n years is the life of machines K. For $r=0$ these profits will be zero, and for $r>0$ they will be given by.

$$g(r) = p_k\left[\frac{nr(1+r)^n}{(1+r)^n - 1} - 1\right]$$

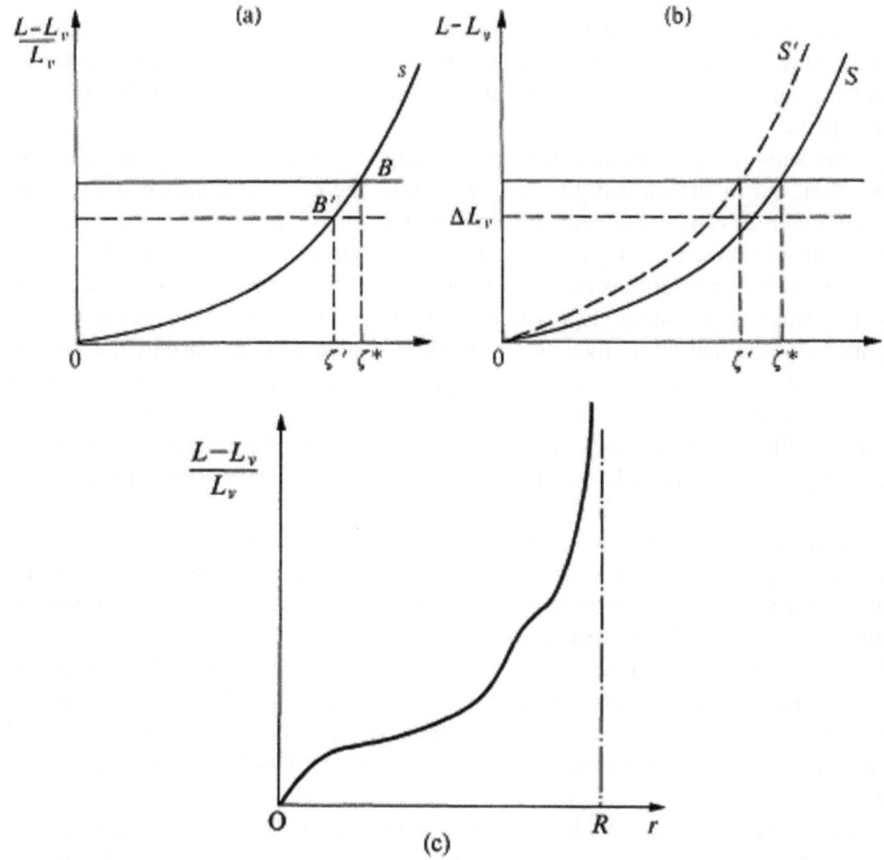

Fig. 3 Determination of the rate of profit with reference to (**a**) the rate of "surplus value", (**b**) the "surplus value" expressed in labour commanded of the integrated wage-goods sector; (**c**) indicates the shape of the "profits function" when production is "circular". [*Editor's note*: in Figs. (a) and (b) r is represented as ζ, due to typographical error in the original publication.]

necessary to produce the wage commodity, which determines the shape of the "profit function".

The fact that the "profit function" is an increasing function also makes clear a second set of properties of the system, pertaining to the relation between the

---

where p_k is the price in labour commanded of a new machine K. Now, the function in square brackets is a monotonically increasing function of r. It follows that the "profits function", in which functions of the above form will be multiplied by, or added to, those of form $[(1+r)^n - 1]$, will also be zero for $r=0$ and will then monotonically rise with r. It should also be noticed that the integrated wage-goods sector will now have to be defined so as to include among its fixed means of production only sets of machines of uniform age distribution, with the corresponding constant yearly replacement appearing in the gross output of the sector.

wage and the rate of profit. A rise in the wage, leaving its commodity composition unchanged will decrease the rate of profit. This will be so because the rate of surplus value $(L/L_v)-1$ will decrease with the rise of L_v, and will therefore intersect the unchanged "profits function" for a lower rate of profit: cf. the shift from B to B' in Fig. 3a.

The same conclusion can be seen to apply if the real wage changes in composition, but in such a way that it increases in one or more components with no decrease in any of the others. In order to see this, it is however convenient to shift our attention from Fig. 3a which relates to rates of surplus value $(L-L_v)/L_v$ to Fig. 3b which refers instead to the aggregate surplus value $(L-L_v)$ in the integrated wage-goods sector as a whole. With the assumed increment in some components of the real wage, the amount of surplus value will decrease by the amount ΔL_v of the labour required in order to produce that increment for the aggregate wages. On the other hand, for $r>0$, the curve OS of total profits in the wage-goods sector will "rotate" upwards from OS to OS' because of the profits accruing on the wages paid for the additional labour ΔL_v. Both changes will have the effect of decreasing the rate of profit.[46]

However, when the composition of the real wage changes in such a way that while the quantity of some components rises, that of others falls, and it becomes accordingly impossible to refer unambiguously to a rise or fall in the real wage—the profit curves, whether that of profits per worker (Fig. 3a), or that of total profits (Fig. 3b), can change in any way whatever. The rate of profit may then change in a direction opposite to that in which the rate of surplus value has changed—in line with what Marx saw as possible when the organic composition of social capital changed together with the real wage (cf. e.g. Marx, 1954–9, Bk. III, Chap. L, p. 869).

21. These properties, made easily visible by surplus-Eqs. (9) and (9a) are thus closer than we might perhaps have expected to Marx's conclusions on the matter. In particular, it is confirmed that the rate of profit depends on two factors only, the rate of surplus value s/v, and the proportions between means of production and labour. However, the correction of the error implicit in Eq. (5) modifies Marx's specification of the second circumstance, in terms of the "organic composition" c/v of social capital, in two important respects.

In the first place the proportion of labour to means of production on which the rate of profit depends is that of the integrated wage-goods sector, and not that of

[46] The monotonically increasing character of the profits function also implies that in Eq. (9a) a single value of L_v will correspond to any positive level of r or, in the case of circular production, to any value of r where $0=r<R$. Equation (9a) thus shows that as the rate of interest rises, the wage-rate must fall when measured in terms of *any* commodity (which, then chosen as a measure of the wage, will play the role of the "wage commodity" in that equation).

the economy as a whole as Marx thought. This in turn implies that he was mistaken in believing that changes in the relative outputs of commodities could affect the rate of profit, through variations in the proportion of labour to the means of production in the community.[47] It also implies that Marx was equally wrong when he thought that, through the same variations, changes in the technical conditions of production of "luxuries", or of their specific means of production, could affect the rate of profit.

In the second place, the proportion of labour to means of production cannot be expressed by the ratio c/v, and must instead be expressed by the proportionate distribution over time of the labour necessary to produce the wage commodity, or by the quantities of the several means of production, in the price equations. This is a consequence of the fact that it is impossible to measure capital by a single magnitude independent of distribution. This fact, which deeply affects the validity of the marginalist theories (above, para. 1), has some important consequences also here: thus if Marx had been correct the relative price of the products of two distinct processes of production would always change monotonically with r, whereas in fact such relative prices may invert their *direction* of change as r rises (falls) monotonically.[48]

VII. The "Surplus-Equation Method" and Sraffa's Standard System

22. The basis of our discussion of the surplus theories has so far been the Classical economists' premise according to which, when approaching the determination of profits and prices, the real wage should be treated as an independent variable. A different view of the wage is however suggested in Sraffa (1960). Sraffa begins by observing (p. 9) that the wage, besides a minimum consisting of the necessary subsistence, may include a share of the surplus. He proceeds to argue (*ibid.*, p. 33) that under these conditions the wage would have to be taken as given "in terms of a mere of less abstract standard" and, accordingly,

---

[47] Cf. for example Marx (1954–9), Bk. III, Chap. IX, p. 162: "There will naturally be a very great difference [in the general rate of profit], depending on whether a greater or smaller part of total capital produces a higher or lower rate of profit [i.e. whether capital has, respectively, a lower or higher organic composition]." (The deficiency of this thesis of Marx is ignored, e.g., in Mandel, 1975, p. 115 and *passim* and Rowthorn, 1976, pp. 62–63 and *passim*).

[48] There is a further aspect of Marx's views which, when appropriately modified, finds confirmation in the surplus equation of the wage-goods sector. It regards the role of prices in "re-distributing" total surplus value in proportion to the capital employed in the individual industries. This role can be detected when we look at the integrated wage-goods sector and at the prices appearing there. The same cannot however be said when we look at the economy as a whole, since in that case the amount of surplus value is not given before the prices and rate of profit are given.

[it] does not acquire a definite meaning until the prices of commodities are determined.

Then, he continues,

the position is reversed. The rate of profits, as a ratio, has a significance which is independent of any prices, and can well be 'given' before the prices are fixed.

A discussion of the view of the operation of the economic system which seems to underlie Sraffa's suggestion would bring us beyond that "core" of the theory with which we are here exclusively concerned (cf. above, para. 6). Our present interest—confined to examining Sraffa's use of the "Surplus equation method"—requires us only to consider how far the suggested change in the independent distributive variable is compatible with the surplus approach to value and distribution which is the subject of this article.

23. When within this approach to distribution we envisage changes in the rate of real wages over time, we may attribute these changes to either of two circumstances: a long-term evolution of the social conditions determining the level of subsistence, *or* the kind of economic circumstances which authors like Smith or Marx thought might keep the wage above the level of subsistence even for long periods of time (para. 4 above).[49] In the first case, the real wage will evidently have to be taken as a given magnitude in the "core" of the theory (para. 5). The same will be true in the second case only if the share of the surplus taken up by the wage depends on circumstances acting through the wages. The real wage will then appear in the "core" as the magnitude which has been determined in both level and composition by the circumstances in question: profits will continue to be determined as a pure residual, though now they will not constitute the *entire* surplus.

The share of wages in the surplus might however be alternatively determined by circumstances acting through profits, like those which Sraffa envisages when, after the passage already quoted, he writes of the rate of profit as a magnitude

susceptible of being determined ... by the level of the money rates of interest (Sraffa, 1960, p. 33).

[49] The view that the wage can exceed the level of subsistence for long periods of time seems indeed implied also in the very idea of a rising subsistence level. This rise can result only from wages remaining above the previous subsistence level for a period of time which is long enough to engender those 'habits' which may then become a 'second nature' in Torrens's phrase later adopted by Ricardo (para. 4 above) and by Marx in 1954–9, Bk. III, Chap. L, p. 845.

Then, the rate of profit will become the independent variable within the "core" and the wage, an unknown, can be treated as an "abstract" value magnitude which can be measured in terms of any standard.[50, 51]

Thus, Sraffa's replacement of the wage by the rate of profit as the independent distributive variable can be seen to result from his choice of one of the two views that can be taken of the circumstances determining the division of the surplus between wages and profits. As such it appears to be no less compatible with the surplus approach to distribution than the other view, adopted by Smith and Marx, when they saw those circumstances as acting through the wage. In either case we find the basic distinction between subsistence and surplus, and we also find the determination of the division of the surplus by means of social and economic circumstances which, whether they act through wages or through profits, are best studied outside the "core" where the unknown distributive variable is determined together with relative prices. In formal terms, what we have if we follow Sraffa is a modification of the analysis conducted in that "core": the modification consists of the addition, so to speak, of a second layer to the determination of the surplus by the difference between social product and "necessary consumption" (para. 3 above). In this second layer we have the sharing of the surplus between wages and profits, and the rate of profit appears there as a "datum" or independent variable, with the surplus wage as the unknown. The diagram (Fig. 1) may accordingly be modified as in Fig. 4.

24. The treatment of the wage as an abstract value quantity makes a very simple Surplus equation possible for the study of the relation between the wage rate—or preferably its surplus component—and the rate of profit (Sraffa, 1960, pp. 9–10). As is well-known, under the hypothesis of single-product industries a unique set of positive proportions always exists such that the net product consists of a composite commodity which requires itself as its only means of production. The unique composite commodity thus defined, which depends exclusively on the technical conditions of production, is what Sraffa calls

[50] The treatment of the wage as a residual need not however entail the treatment of the wage as an abstract value quantity. Commodities which play a primary role in workers' consumption may provide a more significant measure of the wage than is provided by other commodities. The concept of the wage as an abstract value magnitude does not, on the other hand, prevent the use of the "integrated wage-goods sector", with respect to any of the commodities in terms of which we may wish to measure the wage. With r as the independent variable in Eq. (9a), the rate of surplus value would be the unknown, giving the unique wage corresponding to the given level of r (cf. above, n. 46).

[51] E. Burmeister fails to realize this implication of Sraffa's suggestion about an exogenous determination of the rate of profit when in 1977, p. 68 n., he writes "Sraffa's measure of the real wage is flawed … [the] weights are not related in any way to human needs".

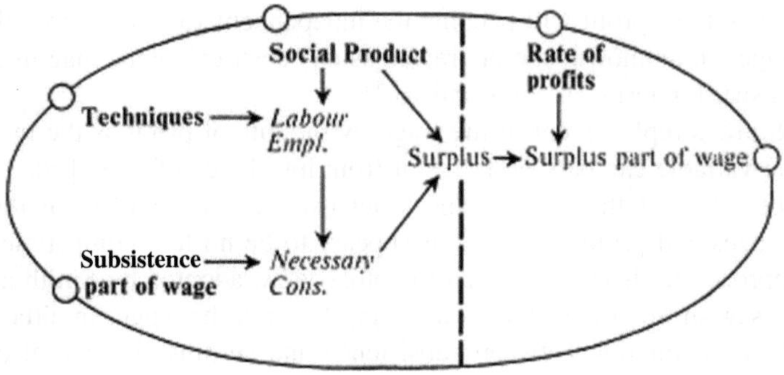

Fig. 4 A diagram of the "core" of the surplus theories when we admit that the wage may share in the surplus because of causes acting through the rate of profit (compare with Fig. 1 above).

"Standard commodity". A replica of the real economy, employing the same number of workers, but producing exclusively the Standard commodity constitutes then what Sraffa calls the "Standard system". The consideration of the wage as an abstract value quantity can then be used in order to measure the wage in terms of the Standard commodity. In the "Standard system" we shall accordingly have a physical homogeneity between all *three* magnitudes on which the relation between the wage and the rate of profit depends, namely the net product, the wages and the means of production.

Let us then take the standard net product as our unit of the standard commodity. Let us also choose as a unit of labour, the labour employed in the real economy, and hence in the Standard system, so that the wage rate w, paid *post factum*, coincides with the total wages in either. Looking at the standard system we may write

$$w = 1 - rM \tag{10}$$

where M is the amount of the standard commodity used as means of production in the standard system. If we then refer to Sraffa's "Standard ratio" R, between the standard net product and M we have $R = 1/M$ or $M = 1/R$ which when substituted in Eq. (10) gives

$$w = 1 - \frac{r}{R} \tag{10a}$$

The linear relation (10) or (10a) between r and w also applies to the real economy as soon as wages are measured in terms of the standard commodity. The price equations of the standard system are then identical to the equations of the real economy, except for the multipliers applied to the latter in order to take the industries in the proportions of the standard system.

What the standard system does, is only to provide a 'surplus equation method' of arriving at that relation, with the corresponding 'picture' of the relations of distribution (para. 17 above); in Sraffa's own words, the purpose is "to give transparency to a system and render visible what was hidden" (1960, p. 23).[52]

References

Baumol, W. J. (1983). Marx and the iron law of wages. *American Economic Review*, 73(2), Papers and Proceedings, 303–308.

Bortkiewicz, L. (1949). On the correction of Marx's fundamental theoretical construction in the third volume of *Capital*. In P. M. Sweezy (Ed.), *Karl Marx and the close of his system by Eugene von Böhm-Bawerk and Böhm-Bawerk's criticism of Marx by Rudolf Hilferding* (pp. 197–221). Kelley (first publ. 1907).

Bortkiewicz, L. (1952). Value and price in the Marxian system. *International Economic Papers* (No. 2, pp. 5–60). Macmillan (first publ. 1907).

Burmeister, E. (1977). The irrelevance of Sraffa's analysis without constant returns to scale. *Journal of Economic Literature*, 15(1), 68–70.

Casarosa, C. (1978). A new foundation of the Ricardian system. *Oxford Economic Papers*, 30(1), 38–63.

Cannan, E. (1967). *A history of the theories of production and distribution 1776 to 1848*. Kelley.

De Vivo G. (1982). Notes on Marx's critique of Ricardo. *Contributions to Political Economy*, (1), 87–99.

Dobb, M. H. (1973). *Theories of value and distribution since Adam Smith*. Cambridge University Press.

Dmitriev, V. K. (1974). *Economic essays on value, competition and utility*, Eng. transl.. Cambridge University Press (first publ. 1904).

Eatwell, J. (1975). Mr. Sraffa's standard commodity and the rate of exploitation. *Quarterly Journal of Economics*, 89(4), 543–555.

Garegnani, P. (1960). *Il capitale nelle teorie della distribuzione*. Giuffrè.

Garegnani, P. (1970). Heterogeneous capital, the production function and the theory of distribution. *Review of Economic Studies*, 37(3), 407–436.

Garegnani, P. (1976). A change in the notion of equilibrium in recent work on value and distribution. In M. Brown, K. Sato, & P. Zarembka (Eds.), *Essays in modern capital theory* (pp. 25–45). North Holland.

Garegnani, P. (1983). The classical theory of wages and the role of demand schedules in the determination of relative prices. *American Economic Review, Papers and Proceedings*, 73(2), 309–313.

[52] Sraffa's reference here is to the transparency acquired by properties of the system like those pertaining to the inverse relations between w and r, or to switches in methods of production, etc.. To refer to a 'direct link' between the use of the standard commodity and the use of the labour theory of value by Marx, "to expose the nature of (the) exploitation [of labour]" (cf. for example Eatwell, 1975, pp. 543–4) would therefore seem misleading. The basic analytical role of the labour theory of value which we saw in Sections III and IV leaves no room for its use in expressing exploitation, (which, it seems, would only consist of showing what is already clear, that is that workers do not get the entire product: cf. n. 23 above). Moreover, Sraffa's use of the standard product, though strictly analytical, is "auxiliary" (Sraffa, 1960, p. 31) and is therefore unlike that of Ricardo and Marx, who depended on the labour theory of value for their conclusions regarding the rate of profit and relative prices.

Hesse, M. D. (1962). Models and matter. In S. Toulmin (Ed.), *Quanta and reality* (pp. 49–57). Hutchinson.

Hilferding, R. (1949). Böhm-Bawerk's criticism of Marx. In P. Sweezy (Ed.). *K. Marx and the close of his system by E. Böhm-Bawerk and Böhm-Bawerk's criticism of Marx by R. Hilferding* (pp. 119–96). Kelley (first publ. 1920 ca.).

Hicks, J. & Hollander, S. (1977). Mr. Ricardo and the moderns. *Quarterly Journal of Economics,* 91(3), 351–369.

Hunt, E. K. & Schwartz, J. G. (Eds.) (1972). *A critique of economic theory.* Penguin Books.

Malthus, T. R. ([1836] 1951). *Principles of economics* (2nd ed.). Basil Blackwell.

Mandel, E. (1975). *Late capitalism.* New Left Books.

Marshall, A. ([1820] 1961). *Principles of economics,* 9th (Variorum) edition (Vol. I). Macmillan.

Marx, K. (1954–1959). *Capital* (3 Vols.). Lawrence and Wishart.

Marx, K. (1963–1971). *Theories of surplus value* (3 Vols.). Lawrence and Wishart.

Medio, A. (1977). Neoclassicals, Neo-Ricardians and Marx. In J. Schwartz (Ed.), *The subtle anatomy of capitalism* (pp. 381–411). Goodyear Publishing Company.

Mill, J. (1821). *Elements of political economy.* Longmans.

Morishima, M. (1973). *Marx's economics.* Cambridge University Press.

Pasinetti, L. L. (1977). *Lectures on the theory of production.* Macmillan, Columbia University Press.

Pippard, A. B. (1962). Particles and waves. In S. Toulmin (Ed.), *Quanta and reality* (pp. 25–33). Hutchinson.

Ricardo, D. (1951–1973). *Works* , Sraffa ed. (11 Vols.). Cambridge University Press.

Robinson, J. V. (1953–1954). The production function and the theory of capital. *Review of Economic Studies,* 21(2). 81–106.

Robinson, J. V. (1970). Capital theory up to date. *Canadian Journal of Economics/Revue Canadienne d'Économie,* 3(2), 309–17; rpt. 1973 in *Collected economic papers* (Vol. IV, pp. 144–54). Blackwell.

Roncaglia, A. (1978). *Sraffa and the theory of prices.* Wiley.

Rowthorn, B. (1976). Late capitalism. *New Left Review,* 98, 59–83.

Samuelson, P. A. ([1961]. 1966). A new theorem on nonsubstitution. In J. E. Stiglitz (Ed.), *The collected scientific papers of Paul A. Samuelson* (Vol. I, pp. 520–36). M.I.T. Press [first publ. in H. Hegeland (Ed.), *Money, growth and methodology and other essays in economics.* In honor of Johan Akerman. CWK Gleerup].

Samuelson, P. A. (1962). Parable and realism in capital theory: The surrogate production function. *Review of Economic Studies,* 29(3), 193–206.

Samuelson, P. A. (1971). Understanding the Marxian notion of exploitation: A summary of the so-called transformation problem between Marxian values and competitive prices. *Journal of Economic Literature,* 9(2), 399–431.

Samuelson, P. A. (1974). Marx as mathematical economist. In G. Horwich & P. A. Samuelson (Eds.), *Trade, stability and macroeconomics* (pp. 269–307). Academic Press.

Samuelson, P. A. (1978). The canonical classical model of political economy. *Journal of Economic Literature,* 6(4), 1415–1434.

Schumpeter, J. A. (1954). *History of economic analysis.* Oxford University Press.

Seton, F. (1957). The transformation problem. *Review of Economic Studies,* 24(3), 149–160.

Smith, A. ([1776], 1910). *The wealth of nations* (Vol. 2). Dent and Sons.

Sraffa, P. (1951). Introduction, in Ricardo (1951–73) (Vol. I, pp. xiii–lxii).

Sraffa, P. (1960). *Production of commodities by means of commodities.* Cambridge University Press.

Steedman, I. (1977). *Marx after Sraffa.* NLB.

Steedman, I. (1982). Marx on Ricardo. In I. Bradley & M. C. Howard (Eds.), *Classical and Marxian political economy* (pp. 115–156). Macmillan.

Sweezy, P. (1946). *The theory of capitalist development.* Dennis Dobson.

Torrens, R. (1815). *An essay on the external corn trade.* Hatchard.

Turgot, A. R. (1766). *Réflexions sur la production et la distribution des richesses.*

Misunderstanding Classical Economics? A Reply to Blaug †*

From Professor Blaug's (1999) article (unspecified page references are to it) there emerges the paradox that an interpretation pointing to the basic role of institutional and historical factors in the classical theory of distribution and capital accumulation is criticized as "amazingly narrow" (215), one that looks at those economists "through the lenses of the linear production model" (234). Further, the contrast between the seeming narrowness of the interpretation and the evident broad character of classical works induces Blaug to view that interpretation as one that reads "backward" into Smith's and Ricardo's texts Sraffa's theoretical alternative to neoclassical theory (215)—as if the contrary was not rather the case, with those texts being the sources to which one had to resort in order to understand Sraffa's terse *Production of Commodities* (1960). A need for clarification is therefore present.

Blaug is critical of the interpretation advanced by "Sraffian" authors (I may note in passing how such collective references may easily if unwittingly result in blurring the issues) because, in his view, the notion of social surplus they refer to, while adequate for the French physiocrats (Blaug, 1987, 439), does not provide a valid interpretation of Ricardo and the English classical economists.

A first reaction to this is one of some surprise. In his concrete work on the classical economists, Blaug has often acknowledged elements that are at the basis of Sraffa's interpretation of Smith and Ricardo. Recall his references to Ricardo's "corn model" and "fundamental theorem of distribution." Or remember his

†Previously published in *History of Political Economy*, Vol. 34, No. 1, 2002. All necessary permissions acquired.

*The original reply submitted in July 2001 has been appreciably shortened as editorially requested for the present discussion and is forthcoming as a *Quaderno di Ricerca* of the Centro Studi e Documentazione 'Piero Sraffa' ['Professor Blaug on understanding classical economics', Centro Studi e Documentazione 'Piero Sraffa', *Quaderno di Ricerca* n. 3, 2003].

P. Garegnani, *Capital Theory, the Surplus Approach, and Effective Demand*, Springer Studies in the History of Economic Thought,
https://doi.org/10.1007/978-3-031-23643-3_8

recognition of permanent labor unemployment in Ricardo (Blaug, 1958, 1973, 179), a feature basic enough to raise the question of a theoretical approach alternative to the modern one and along the lines of Sraffa's interpretation. The contradiction in Blaug comes, we shall suggest, from his seeing those classical elements in isolation, and not in the connections that make them aspects of an approach to distribution and prices basically different from the modern one: an expression, one may argue, of the difficulty of conceiving the possibility of an approach to distribution and prices other than some form of the modern one, based on demand and supply functions for "factors of production." One result is that Blaug has to repeatedly fall back on ascribing the undeniable and striking differences between Smith's or Ricardo s analyses and the modern ones, to confusions and primitivism (see below).

A preliminary observation is, however, in order here. Sraffa's interpretation was explicitly advanced for "the *old* classical economists *from Adam Smith to Ricardo*" (Sraffa, 1960, v; emphasis added); Blaug argues instead as if the interpretation he criticizes referred to a wider "British tradition of classical political economy, starting more or less with Smith in the third quarter of the eighteenth century and ending more or less with John Stuart Mill and Karl Marx in the third quarter of the nineteenth century" (215).

This is surprising from the author of a book (*Ricardian Economics*), a chapter of which was titled "The Half Way House of John Stuart Mill," and who is therefore aware of the reasons for which Sraffa may have wished to exclude Mill (for one) from his purview. However, the inconsistency may have been favored by Blaug's tendency to locate in subject matter (220) the domain of Sraffa's interpretation, which is instead focused on the logical structure of Smith's and Ricardo's theory.[1]

A Central Misreading

Blaug describes the Sraffian interpretation as one for which the classical economists addressed the question of "how an 'economic surplus' is generated, spent, and augmented from period to period," where the "economic surplus" is "the disposable part of total output that is left over after capital consumption has been made good and the workers fed" (216; see also 214). However, what was originally meant in that interpretation was more specific: it was the tracing in Adam

[1] This should of course not be confused with Sraffa providing a "rational" rather than "historical" reconstruction of the old classical economists (213). The case here is similar to that of a contemporary grammar of classical Latin, in which a Latin writer of the period should recognize the rules he consciously or unconsciously followed in expressing himself; as Blaug would agree, the grammar would constitute a *historical* reconstruction of that Latin.

Smith and Ricardo of an *approach to distribution and relative prices* alternative to any however primitive form of modern demand and supply of factors.[2]

Aware perhaps of the vagueness of his definition, Blaug focuses then on what he describes as the "hard version" of the interpretation, which he attributes in particular to my work. And it is here that a basic misreading occurs. He characterizes that version by the role of "data," which, he claims, I ascribe to real wages, outputs, and technical conditions of production in the analyses of Smith and Ricardo. But what I contended (e.g., Garegnani, 1987, 560) was different: it was that those three sets of circumstances were data *when determining the nonwage distributive variables and the relative prices*, and not data for the theory as a whole, as Blaug imputes.

The question, we shall see, is one and the same as the one above of the alternative theory of distribution in Smith and Ricardo, who determined the nonwage distributive variables on the basis of the *difference* between the (net) product and the wages of the workers producing it, governed by subsistence. Within *that* determination, the physical product and the real wage appeared therefore as givens. But since obviously no economist, least of all Smith and Ricardo, can avoid being concerned with determining product and wages, that meant that, unlike in modern theory, those magnitudes (and the technical conditions with them) were determined *separately* from the nonwage distributive variables and the prices. They only appeared as data in a purely quantitative "core" of the theory in which the relationships between prices and distributive variables enforced by free competition were seen to determine profits of capital and/or rents of land as the mentioned residual or "surplus." They were so to speak "intermediate data" and not ultimate, as Blaug interprets.

It may be immediately noted how this misreading about "data" is directly responsible for the drastic reversal in the thrust of the Sraffian interpretation we emphasized above in the opening section: the institutional and historical richness of classical works, rightly stressed by Blaug, emerges in the treatment of wages, outputs, and technical conditions—precisely what Blaug's misreading neatly excises from the interpretation.

However, the *substance* of the question of intermediate data, as distinct from its definition, also needs clarification. It consists, essentially, of a distinction between two fields of economic analysis that the classical authors had drawn instinctively (Garegnani, 1987, 562).

---

[2] This was what I argued when advancing that interpretation on the basis of Sraffa's introduction to Ricardo's *Principles* (1951–1973) in a Cambridge Ph.D. dissertation (1958) [*A Problem in the Theory of Distribution from Ricardo to Wicksell*, this volume, Part I], comparing classical and neoclassical theories on the problem of capital. For the applicability of that interpretation in particular to Smith, see *ibid.*, 13–24 [this volume, 10–14]; also Garegnani (1987), 566–67, and the bibliography therein. See also Blaug himself who, in Blaug (1987), 439, writes that the interpretation "captures much of the drift of the *Wealth of Nations*."

1. The first was the determination of the nonwage variables and prices by means of the competitive relations of the core that, whatever the language (algebraic, arithmetical, or literary) expressing them, entailed quantitative properties general and definite enough to warrant a mainly deductive analysis.
2. The second covered the rest of the theory, and in particular the determination of wages, outputs, and technical conditions. Given the multiplicity and variability of the factors felt to be involved, a determination of those circumstances by functional relations similar to those of the core—such as the demand and supply functions of later theory—would have corresponded to what F. Y. Edgeworth ([1881] 1967, 4) was aptly to describe as using "arbitrary functions representing not merely *not numerical knowledge* but *ignorance* (italics in the original)."[3]

The distinction between fields 1 and 2 thus left no space, as a matter of general theory, for a single system of quantitative relations determining prices, distribution, and outputs simultaneously. It rather meant that wages, outputs, or technical conditions were studied *separately* from the prices and nonwage distributive variables determined in the core of the theory.[4]

We have referred to the distinction between the two fields of analysis as drawn instinctively by Smith and Ricardo. We can therefore hardly expect to find the distinction explicitly stated by them (see, however, Marx on wages, below). What we find are unambiguous expressions of it, like Ricardo's table in his *Essay on Profits* (1951–73, IV, 17), where corn wages and corn outputs are independent variables in determining profit rate and rents—or like that determination of prices separate from outputs, which forced Alfred Marshall ([1920] 1961, APP. I, 2, 814; APP. L, 833–34) to attribute to Ricardo the two assumptions of "constant return" in manufacturing and an absolutely inelastic demand for the products of agriculture where constant return would obviously not have done.

Blaug, we said, objects to my interpretation by arguing that the classical economists, far from taking technical conditions, outputs, and wages as (ultimate) data, were much concerned with explaining them.

---

[3] Blaug briefly mentions the above criterion for my distinction of two parts in classical theory (217), but seems to forget it when in the article as a whole he objects to my interpretation by simply arguing that the classical economists were much concerned with explaining wages, outputs, and technical conditions, as if that had ever been denied. Indeed, had I denied that, something would have been seriously amiss in Blaug's argument too. He insists on my distinction between what is in, and what is out of, the "core" (e.g., 218–19)—but what could ever be *out* of it, if its data happened to be the ultimate ones of the theory? Perhaps in order to temper this contradiction latent in his argument, Blaug slips, at times, into taking the different tack that, by excluding wages, outputs, and techniques from the core, the interpretation takes them to have been of secondary importance for classical authors, and at the "periphery" of their interests (219, 222)—a criterion that, however, has nothing to do with that of method, on which my distinction rests.

[4] This may incidentally explain what Joseph Schumpeter (1954, 472–73) famously perceived as "the Ricardian vice" of "[bundling up] as large parts [of the general system] as possible … so that [they] should be frozen as given."

With respect to technical conditions, limits of space confine us here to considering how Blaug points to the "[Sraffians'] historical misrepresentation of technology as an exogenous variable in classical economics" (221), exemplified by their "utter indifference … to the opening three chapters of the *Wealth of Nations* on the division of labor, a subject they never discuss or even mention" (220). However, in a work of mine that Blaug cites elsewhere in his article, I had stressed that, unlike modern authors, "[c]lassical economists like Adam Smith or Karl Marx thought that the technical conditions of production … were largely determined by phenomena with which economic theory had to deal, just as with wages and outputs … (think of the analysis of the division of labour in Adam Smith)" (Garegnani, 1990, 127).

Blaug's similar charge about the classical high concern for outputs is more interesting since it brings out the need to clarify an important point in Sraffa. In the preface to his 1960 book, Sraffa famously writes,

> No changes in output and ... no changes in the proportions in which different means of production are used by an industry are considered in *this* book,

and he states that this was "the standpoint of the old classical economists" (v; emphasis added). Outputs, it may then seem, are ultimate and not intermediate data for the classical economists, since their standpoint excludes changes in such data, and therefore, in Blaug's interpretation, it excludes a determination of them within the theory. However, as the oddity of the conclusion might have led one to suspect, Sraffa's point is a quite different one: it regards that "core" of the theory with which Sraffa's (1960) book is almost exclusively concerned—and *not* the theory as a whole. Sraffa states that changes are there absent from the *logical relations* by which he determines the prices of each given position of the economy.[5] This is quite unlike what a neoclassical economist does when he considers demand functions for factors and supply functions of products, the specification of whose points by means of marginal products or marginal costs or any other means entails the consideration of *changes* in outputs and in the proportion of factors: therefore he has to include "changes" in the very logical relations (equations) that define each particular position of the economy. What Sraffa is saying is in effect that, like the old classical economists, he is determining prices *independently* of any demand and supply functions.

---

[5] It may seem that this is contradicted by Ricardo's treatment of rent (224). But his "extensive" rent results from a *difference* between coexisting outputs, and not a *change* in them, and the same is true for the "intensive" rent resulting from two productive methods coexisting on the same kind of land. In this connection Blaug also lays stress on what he describes as Ricardo's "moving equilibrium" and the latter's concern for "intertemporal" rather than "intratemporal" comparisons of value (224–26). No doubt Ricardo was much concerned with a declining rate of profit and he studied it by the method of "comparative statics," as it was later called. However, for those very *intertemporal* comparisons, each compared position had to be determined first in both its profit rate and *intratemporal* relative prices; therefore the intertemporal comparison has its logical foundation in the intratemporal ones.

Nothing "grotesque," then, in all that (223); in particular, no denial of the classical concern for capital accumulation or output changes of any sort.

Wages and Outputs: The Analysis of the Old Classical Economists

Blaug opens his section on wages by writing, "We come ... to the most disputable of all the three variables that are said to be given in classical economics" (225). That given wage might, however, have seemed less disputable had Blaug recalled the following passage: "The foundation of modern political economy [is] the conception of the value of labour power as something fixed, as a given magnitude" (Marx, 1963, 45), written by an author whom Blaug (1988, 29) describes as "thoroughly steeped in the concepts and modes of thought of Ricardo." But, of course, Marx intended that wages in the "modern political economy" of Smith and Ricardo were "given" in precisely the sense of my intermediate data: he surely did not mean to exclude from economic theory the *determination* of wages on which he had of course much to say.

Blaug proceeds, then, to contrast the alleged given wage of Sraffians with its determination by classical authors.[6] His description of a subsistence-based wage trend resulting from the population principle is essentially uncontroversial, and its determination, being prior to that of profits and prices, is in fact consistent with a wage treated as an intermediate datum as Blaug himself in effect explains (227). Where controversy may arise is on the key question of the mechanism by which Smith and Ricardo supposed divergences between the relative speeds of capital accumulation and population growth were corrected so as to achieve that wage trend. A difficulty, which does not seem to have been sufficiently attended to in the literature, emerges here in the attempt by Blaug and other authors to interpret that mechanism in terms of demand and supply along neoclassical lines.

Unlike the impression often given, the inverse relation between the wage and the rate of growth of capital on the one hand, and the direct relation between wage and population growth on the other, cannot replace or imply the neoclassical

[6] Blaug, however, ascribes to Sraffians the view that the "classical economists must have taken the real wages as a datum because the logical consistency of their theory demanded it" (229). No references are given, but clearly the wage is an (intermediate) datum in the classical economists for the reasons that Blaug himself recognizes (227)—logical consistency then taking natural care of itself, Blaug's point appears, however, to relate to the even more surprising opinion that "the degree of freedom" we find in Sraffa's equations of distribution and prices is due to his assumption of fixed coefficients of production (Blaug, 1987, 441; 1988, 22). However, the entire part 3 of Sraffa (1960), and the critical literature on "reswitching," have been concerned with the choice of technique, without in the least affecting that degree of freedom; surely a demand-and-supply determination of the wage is no direct result of the assumption of alternative techniques.

demand and supply. An inverse relation between the wage and the labor employment possible *with a given amount of capital*, that is, an elastic, proper neoclassical demand function is required for the purpose. Without it, a demand and supply mechanism along neoclassical lines, far from ensuring that wages adjust the growth of population with that of capital, would rather lead to absurd zero wages when the former growth overtakes the latter, zero quasi-rents in the opposite case, and indeterminacy when the two happened to balance. Now, no such elastic demand function can be traced in either Smith or Ricardo.[7] The nonexistence of it and of the corresponding neoclassical mechanism is made clear, for example, by Ricardo's admission of permanent labor unemployment.[8] And no confusion should here be caused by the wage-fund theory in the form it took *after* Ricardo, with, for instance, John Stuart Mill.

The mechanism by which Smith and Ricardo envisaged wages to signal balance or unbalance in the relative growths of labor and capital appears to have been an entirely different one. It can be traced in passages on wages by those authors that, significantly enough, have been endless puzzles to modern historians. Think of Smith's observations on the existence of a minimum wage, or about "combinations" of "masters" or "laborers," "tacit" or explicit, imparting "advantages" to the respective parties in the determination of what, notwithstanding all that, appear to be competitive wages. And texts of Ricardo have constituted similar puzzles (see, for example, Garegnani, 2000). Those passages may be seen to point in the direction of a real wage determined by what Marshall (1920, 1961, APP. J, 825) once described (in order to reject it) as "the relative strength of the competing parties." Especially in Smith's and Ricardo's times that "strength" could be seen to be broadly measured by the "proportion of the supply to the demand" for labour (Ricardo 1951–73, I, 94)—the two *single* quantities indicated by the word *proportion* used for their relation—which thus specified rather than contradicted what is often indicated as a "bargaining theory" of wages standing alongside a demand-and-supply theory in Smith (O'Brien, 1975, 111).[9] The relative speed of the growth of population and capital, by altering the proportion, and hence the pressure, of labor underemployment, affected the relative strength and explained

[7]The issue is the one that Samuelson (1978, 1423) describes as "showing that the canonical system is ... globally stable." An even clearer recognition of the distinct roles of the two kinds of relations comes from Knight (1956, 81). For a fuller discussion of the issue, see Garegnani (2000).

[8]Blaug ([1958] 1973, 179) notes how "Ricardo assumed the existence of Marxian unemployment." Samuelson's repeated attempts (e.g., 1978, 1428; 1988) to deny that Ricardo's admitted permanent labor unemployment for his conclusions in the chapter "On Machinery" in the *Principles* are discussed in Garegnani (2000).

[9]Indeed, the way out of these puzzles adopted by modern interpreters seems mainly to consist of tracing several conflicting theories of wages in Smith, in whose work the position of the old classical economists is more fully articulated.

changes in wages capable of adjusting population to capital accumulation, without any need to appeal to labor demand and supply functions along neoclassical lines.[10]

The absence of demand and supply functions for labor is on the other hand quite naturally associated with an absence of demand and supply functions for products—and, therefore, with a treatment of outputs fundamentally different from the modern one.

Demand for products influences normal or natural prices by affecting supply prices. And the neoclassical demand functions mainly do so through the relative demands for factors and therefore the levels of the wage and profit rates.[11] The classical theory of wages would therefore be sufficient to deprive neoclassical demand functions of their influence on prices via direct effects on wages.

On the other hand, the effects that quantities demanded could have on supply prices through increasing physical returns from the division of labor, or decreasing physical returns from scarce natural resources, were seen by the classical economists to fall largely outside the sphere of the determination of prices, and in that of capital accumulation.

Moreover, the classical theory of distribution further undercut the potential relevance of demand functions by doing without the equalities between demand and supply of productive factors determining the individual outcomes from which the demand functions for products should come.

It is only natural, then, that the notion of predefined functional relations between prices and quantities demanded of products should have remained foreign to Smith and Ricardo, where they would have had no clear general determining role on prices or, even, a definite basis in individual incomes.

The several circumstances on which outputs depend (general level of activity, technical conditions, distribution of income, individual choices, etc.) then faced the classical economists with the complexity and dependence on circumstances characteristic of the second of the two fields of analysis we distinguished earlier—and thus, essentially, led them to taking normal outputs as intermediate data in the determination of prices in the "core."

That, of course, also did without any supply functions of products: as we said returns to scale only became relevant when output changes were considered outside the core where they could be dealt with according to the circumstances of the case. In particular, there was no need to assume the "constant return" in manufactures or the rigid demand for corn that Marshall read into Ricardo's work in his attempt to reconcile it with his own demand and supply apparatus.

---

[10] A fuller discussion of the question is in Garegnani (2000); see also Garegnani (1990), 118–22.

[11] Contemporary economists have of course been reminded of this by the nonsubstitution theorem.

With this we have come full circle to see how—far from taking an "amazingly narrow" view of the classical economists (215, 233)—the "Sraffian" interpretation uncovers in their works the roots of their sociological richness. Blaug rightly stresses that richness, but he does not *explain* its presence there and its absence in modern works.

The intermediate data and the reasoning by stages that classical works entail respond, on the other hand, in a striking fashion to the need for "short chains of deductive reasoning" and for "specific experience", which Marshall (1920, 1961, APP. C, 3, 773) saw to be required by the subject matter of economics—the same need he tried to satisfy by his method of partial equilibria.

We are now also in a position to appreciate how the absence of demand and supply functions for products in Smith and Ricardo, far from being a sign of primitivism or confusion, should rather be seen as part of an alternative, consistent view of how the economy works. High among the advantages of this view—apart from freedom from the basic difficulties to be presently recalled—is its independence from the assumption of reversibility of economic changes that underlies demand and supply functions. And it is well known how that assumption, which a perceived lack of alternatives seems to have induced the majority of the profession to forget, or forgive, was worrying to Marshall. He knew well that "in Economics every event causes permanent alterations in the conditions under which future events can occur" ([1879] 1930, Pt. 2, 12): Smith, Ricardo, and their predecessors had instinctively taken good care of that.

Conclusion

Before concluding, we may briefly follow Blaug from history into theory. It is not difficult to see now that Blaug cannot be correct in commenting on how "thoroughly" Sraffa is "steeped in Walrasian general equilibrium theory" (229). Both Sraffa and Walras, it is true, deal simultaneously with prices in all sectors of the economy, but the equations they advance have little else in common. Sraffa's equations are simply the algebraic expression of what Blaug himself says classical theory focuses on, namely, "long-period … prices characterized by a uniform rate of profit on capital, … in short, what Smith called 'natural prices'" (233)—quite a different matter from Walras's equations, further characterized by the equalities between demand and supply of "productive factors."

Failure to perceive those differences becomes evident in the section on competition of Blaug's article. I strongly sympathize with his stress on the decisive importance of showing that prices and outputs "converge on an end-state" (229). That question assumes, however, a very different aspect in the two approaches, as a result, essentially, of their different explanations of the wage. In classical theory, given the stability that the wage derives from its socio-institutional determinants, the competitive tendency to uniform rates of wages, profits, and rents will generally suffice to ensure a tendency to the normal prices of the theory.[12] The problems lie on the neoclassical side, where uniqueness and stability come to depend on the shape of labor demand and supply functions. It comes therefore to depend on the difficulties besetting the conception of capital as a factor of production, difficulties that are inexistent in a classical context (as, for that matter, are the analogous difficulties caused by income effects).

Our remarks on theory have brought out, I believe, that same difficulty of recognizing the existence of an alternative theoretical approach in the old classical economists, which, we suggested at the beginning, may explain the contradictions between Blaug's criticism of Sraffa's interpretation and his acknowledgment of basic elements of it. Thus we have noticed Blaug's recognition of labor unemployment in Ricardo and his references to Ricardo's "corn model."

But perhaps the most striking contradiction is found when Blaug has to admit in Ricardo (and Smith) the very absence of demand and supply functions for products, which he describes as a "grotesque distortion" when noted by "Sraffians." The "distortion" would consist in holding "that any appeal to the forces of demand and supply in determining prices is necessarily alien to classical economics and that classical *natural prices* have nothing whatsoever in common with Marshall's long run normal prices" (Blaug, 1987, 442; emphasis added), where, as the reference to Marshall makes clear, the forces of demand and supply denied by Sraffians are the neoclassical ones and not the quite different classical concepts that we shall presently mention.

A few lines after that passage Blaug has, however, to notice that

> Ricardo (and Marx after him) propagated the *misleading idea* that demand-and-supply explanations only pertain to market prices [and, moreover, there was] Ricardo's tendency to think of demand and supply as *quantities* actually bought and sold not as *schedules* of demand and supply prices (1987, 442; emphases added).

A "confusion," Blaug concludes.[13]

The "misleading idea" is there mentioned rather incidentally and is confined to Ricardo and Marx. But, as Blaug surely knows, the notion that "demand-and-supply explanations" only pertain to market prices—that is, to deviations of the

---

[12] See Garegnani (1997) [this volume, Part III]. Differing positions on the matter are also discussed there (140, 164–65, 167–69 [in this volume, p. 354 and nn. 1–3, pp. 374–5 and nn. 36–37, pp. 380–3]). However, Blaug writes that in Sraffa "not a word is wasted on telling us how we got [to the competitive prices he supposes]" (231); Sraffa's reference to the distinction between market price and natural price (1960, 9) should, however, have been quite unambiguous in referring readers used to classical terminology to Smith's analysis of competition. Moreover, Blaug contrasts the "perfect competition" he believes I uphold with the classical notion of "free competition" (231). However, the "perfectly competitive" horizontal demand function facing the firm is a (Marshallian) descendant of Marshallian demand and supply function for the industry, and is therefore unlikely to find place in any contemporary revival of classical economics.

[13] Blaug's "quantities ... bought and sold" in this passage is clearly a slip, since they would be one and the same, and not Smith's and Ricardo's "effectual demand" and "quantity brought to market."

actual prices from natural or normal prices and not to the prices themselves—is no peculiarity at all of Ricardo and Marx: it was Adam Smith who had first treated the idea quite systematically in the whole of Chap. 7, Book 1, of the *Wealth of Nations*, titled "Of the Natural and Market Price of Commodities." And it is precisely from there that Ricardo also got his "confusion" concerning demand and supply as *single quantities*, demand being "the [effectual] demand of those who are willing to pay the natural price of the commodity" (Smith, [1776], 1910, Vol. I, Bk. I, Ch. VI: 49), supply being the "quantity brought to market."

It is then difficult to see where lies the "grotesque distortion" of maintaining that Marshall's forces of demand and supply were "alien" to Smith, Ricardo, and Marx, and in particular that they were alien to their determination of *natural prices*. Do not the texts of those authors argue just that?

Blaug also writes: "Ricardo had no theory of ... why output is made up of one set of goods rather than another. But then neither did any other premodern economist" (223), which means, I believe, that Ricardo and other "premodern economists" did not determine the composition of outputs by demand and supply functions of products. How did they treat outputs then, if not as "intermediate data"?

References

Blaug, M. ([1958], 1973). *Ricardian economics*. Greenwood Press.

Blaug, M. (1987). Classical economics. In J. Eatwell, M. Milgate P. Newman (Eds.), *The New Palgrave. A dictionary of economics* (Vol. 1, pp. 434–445). Macmillan.

Blaug, M. (1988). *Economics through the looking glass*. Institute of Economic Affairs.

Blaug, M. (1999). Misunderstanding classical economics: The Sraffian interpretation of the surplus approach. *History of Political Economy,* 31(2), 213–236.

Edgeworth, F. ([1881] 1967). *Mathematical psychics*. Kelley

Garegnani, P. (1958). *A problem in the theory of distribution from Ricardo to Wicksell*, Ph.D. Diss., Cambridge University.

Garegnani, P. (1987). Surplus approach to value and distribution. In J. Eatwell, M. Milgate & P. Newman (Eds.), *The New Palgrave. A dictionary of economics* (Vol. 4, pp. 560–74). Macmillan.

Garegnani, P. (1990). Sraffa: classical versus marginalist analysis. In K. Bharadwaj & B. Schefold (Eds.), *Essays on Piero Sraffa* (pp. 112–141). Unwin Hyman (rpt. Routledge 1992).

Garegnani, P. (1997). On some supposed obstacles to the tendency of market prices towards natural prices. In G. Caravale (Ed.), *Equilibrium and economic theory* (pp. 139–170). Routledge.

Garegnani, P. (2000). Samuelson on Sraffa's Hits and Misses. Unpublished manuscript.†

† [*Editor's note*: conceivably, the manuscript is an earlier draft of the article 'Professor Samuelson on Sraffa and the Classical Economists', *European Journal of the History of Economic Thought*, 14(2), 2007, rpt. in *The Theory of Value and Distribution in Economics. Discussions between Pierangelo Garegnani and Paul Samuelson*, ed. by H. D. Kurz, Abingdon and New York: Routledge, 2013.]

Knight, F. H. (1956). The Ricardian theory of production and distribution. In *On the history and method of economics* (pp. 37–88). University of Chicago Press.
Marshall, A. ([1879] 1930). *The pure theory of foreign trade, the pure theory of domestic values*. The London School of Economics and Political Science.
Marshall, A. ([1920] 1961). *Principles of economics*. Ninth (Variorum) ed.. Macmillan.
Marx, K. (1969). *Theories of surplus value,* Vol. I. Lawrence and Wishart.
O' Brien, D. P. (1975). *The classical economists*. Clarendon Press.
Ricardo, D. (1951–73). *The works and correspondence of David Ricardo*, ed. by P. Sraffa with the collaboration of M. H. Dobb, 11 Vols. Cambridge University Press.
Samuelson, P. A. (1978). The canonical classical model of political economy. *Journal of Economic Literature,* 16(4), 1415–1434.
Samuelson, P. A. (1988). Mathematical vindication of Ricardo on machinery. *Journal of Political Economy,* 96(2), 274–282.
Schumpeter, J. A. (1954). *History of economic analysis*. Oxford University Press.
Smith, A. ([1776] 1910). *The wealth of nations*, 2 Vols. Dent and Sons.
Sraffa, P. (1960). *Production of commodities by means of commodities*. Cambridge University Press.

On Some Supposed Obstacles to the Tendency of Market Prices Towards Natural prices

1. I had thought of taking this occasion in order to tidy up some reflections which had been stimulated many years ago by my reading of a first draft of Ian Steedman's 'Natural Prices, Differential Profit Rates and the Classical Competitive Process', which was to be published some years later in the *Manchester School* 1984. However, the time to prepare the paper I intended has not been available, and here I am with some notes only a little more developed than they were then, and without the readings I had hoped to do in the meantime. Since I have managed to convince myself that the argument holds in its essential lines, I have come to submit it for discussion.

In his article Steedman (1984) argues that Smith, Ricardo and Marx 'associated a positive (negative) deviation of a commodity's market price from its natural price, with a positive (negative) deviation of the corresponding industry's profit rate from the natural rate' (p. 123). He then asks:

> Could it not happen … that an industry whose product's market price lies *above* its natural price, purchases as produced inputs commodities whose market prices lie 'even more above' their natural price, with the result that that industry has a profit rate *below* the natural rate? (*ibid.*, emphases in the original).

This question, to which he devotes the first part of his paper, has of course an affirmative answer. Nothing prevents the compound commodity consisting of the means of production—among which we may for a moment include the real wages paid in advance at the given rate—from having a market price exceeding its natural price in a proportion larger than the output does, in which case the rate of profit will have to be below the natural rate.

† Previously published with Routledge in G. Caravale (Ed.), *Equilibrium and Economic Theory*, 1997. All necessary permissions acquired.

* Except for minor changes, this text is the same published under the same title in *Political Economy*, 6(1–2), 1990, pp. 329–59 [*editor's note*: also available online at http://www.centrosraffa.org/politicalEconomy.aspx]. I am indebted to Rosenberg Sellier for permission to reproduce that material.

P. Garegnani, *Capital Theory, the Surplus Approach, and Effective Demand*,
Springer Studies in the History of Economic Thought,
https://doi.org/10.1007/978-3-031-23643-3_9

Indeed, as far as can be seen from Steedman's own references, neither Adam Smith nor Ricardo nor Marx stated that a market price higher than the natural price is *necessarily* associated with a rate of profit higher than the natural rate. This would have been wrong, even independently of the problem raised by the means of production, because opposite signs of the deviations of market price and profit rate could also result from wages and rents exceeding their natural levels sufficiently.[1] The classical authors appear rather to have confined themselves to the less restrictive statement that it is by *raising* the market price sufficiently high, relative to wages, rents, and the means of production, that the rate of profit of the industry whose output must be increased is elevated above that obtaining in other industries.[2] Indeed, as we shall see, the very notion of an excess of the market price over the natural price has an arbitrary element attached to it because it depends on the choice of the numeraire (para. 8 below).

2. However, let us leave aside history of thought and return to analysis. More important than the possibility of a high market price going together with a low rate of profit is the question which Steedman raises in the second part of his paper: namely, whether such a possibility might not prevent the ultimate tendency of the market price towards the natural price, by causing the output of the commodity to decrease, thus sending the market price even higher.[3] We shall here argue that this question can be answered negatively.

[1] I. Steedman describes Adam Smith as stating that when 'the market price of a commodity lies e.g. below the natural price then the wage *and/or* the profit rate *and/or* the rent paid in the industry must fall below the natural rate' (1984, 124, our emphasis). Steedman admits there that Smith leaves open the *possibility* of e.g. a market price below the natural price, while the profit rate is above the natural level (rent and/or wage rates bearing the brunt of both the lower price and the higher profits). He argues however that Smith's analysis ignored the means of production and therefore the question he is specifically addressing (Steedman 1984, 125). In this connection it should, however, be remembered that Smith thought that the value of the means of production could be reduced to wages, profit and rents (Smith [1776] 1910, Bk. I, Ch.VI, 44–5). Therefore when he refers to wages, profit and rents, he could be interpreted as referring to those accruing in the *indirect*, as well as in the direct, production of the commodity in question, and thus, in fact, to the value of the means of production.

[2] See e.g. 'It is only in consequence of variations [in market prices] that capital is apportioned precisely ... to the production of the different commodities. *With the rise or fall of price, profits are elevated above, or depressed below their general level*' (Ricardo [1821] 1951, 88, our emphasis).

[3] Cf. e.g. 'If a "low" market price in a particular industry can be associated with a "high" profit rate ... then it is clear that one cannot immediately assume that the "low" market price will tend to gravitate towards the corresponding natural price' (Steedman 1984, 134; see similar passages at pp. 123–4, 127).

The reason for that result can perhaps be preliminarily surveyed in an intuitive way by noting that when e.g., for a commodity A_1, a negative deviation of the market price accompanies a positive deviation of the profit rate, then, the same opposition of signs cannot be true for at least one of the direct or indirect means of production of A_1: that having the *minimum* ratio of market to natural price.[4] For that particular means of production the profit rate deviation will have to be negative like that of the relative market price, and the associated fall of output will tend to raise its market price, leading either directly or in a finite number of stages to a fall in the rate of profit of A_1, and thus to a reversal in the initial 'perverse' rise in output.

3. Our formal argument in this chapter will be founded on *three assumptions*. The first will be a fall in the output of the industry or industries showing the *minimum* rate of profit in the economy; the second will concern the conditions under which that fall in output will result in a rise of the profit rate of the industry in question. We shall claim that the generality of those first two assumptions is hardly disputable. The third assumption will instead be more restrictive, in that it will concern a *monotonic* rise of the minimum profit rate, rather than that *eventual* rise of the rate which it will be possible to demonstrate on the basis of the first two assumptions. It will then be possible to show that when the rise of the minimum profit rate reaches the natural rate, the natural position of the economy will have been achieved. The consequences of abandoning the third assumption will then be discussed at the end of the chapter.

The layout of the chapter will be as follows. In the next section we shall introduce the postulate of given (normal) effectual demand, a basic premise of the classical treatment of market prices. There we shall also set out our definitions and assumptions about the kind of economy we shall be concerned with. In the following section (paras 9–18) we shall come to the rise of the minimum rate of profit in the economy and to the three assumptions mentioned above. The fourth section (para. 19) will instead be devoted to proving some propositions needed in order to draw the implications of that rise. In the fifth (paras. 20–5) those propositions will be used to show how, when, in its rise, the minimum rate of profit reaches the natural rate r^*, convergence to the natural position of the economy will be achieved, whatever may have been the initial deviations of the market prices of the means of production from their natural levels. In the final section we shall conclude by discussing the generality of our conclusions, and the method of argument used in the chapter. We shall then claim that, though our primary aim has been to examine and

[4] See Proposition I, para. 19 below. Assuming, as Steedman assumes in the relevant part of (1984), that all commodities are *basic*, each commodity, including that with the minimum ratio of market to natural price, must enter directly or indirectly the production of A_1.

reject the idea that divergences of market prices from natural prices for the means of production may prevent a tendency to the natural position, yet our argument may allow for some general affirmative conclusions.

Premises and Definitions

4. In the course of our argument we shall follow in the footsteps of Adam Smith and the old classical economists and take as *given,* and therefore as *constant* during the process of adjustment, the normal effectual demand of each commodity—the quantity, that is, of the commodity which would be demanded when the prices and outputs of *all* commodities were at their normal levels.[5] It should be immediately noted that this classical postulate does not imply any assumption of stationarity of the economy. It only rests on the view that the forces of competition, which may bring market prices towards the natural prices, will be acting in a way which is broadly independent of what the normal outputs (effectual demands) happen to be, or of how they happen to evolve over time. It follows that market prices are best studied *separately* from the circumstances determining the normal quantities produced and the latter may be taken as given when studying the former.

This classical postulate of given effectual demands needs to be stressed because it seems to have been frequently overlooked in recent literature, at the expense of the generality of the results obtained.[6]

5. Though the subject is beyond the aim of the present chapter some observations may here be necessary with respect to the assumption, implied in the above postulate, that the *aggregate* economic activity (on which the effectual demands of the individual commodities evidently depend) can be taken as given in analysing market prices. A first view which may be taken in that respect is that the deviations of the actual outputs from the respective effectual demands (and therefore their changes during the process of adjustment) will in general broadly compensate each other with respect to their effect on aggregate demand and its determinants. However, the classical postulate of given effectual demands does not appear to ultimately rest on any such eventual compensation of deviations. Here also what needs in effect be assumed is only the possibility of *separating* the two analyses. Thus, if we had reason to think that the effects on aggregate demand of the circumstances causing (or arising out of) certain kinds of deviation of actual from

[5] Cf. Smith ([1776] 1910, Bk. I, Ch. VII, 49). Our definition of the effectual demand of a commodity modifies that of Adam Smith by specifying that demand also in relation to the natural prices of the other commodities and to the normal outputs of all commodities. The reason for qualifying the effectual demands in the text as 'normal', will be seen in paras. 10–11 below.

[6] Cf. e.g. the argument in Nikaido (1985), which we shall consider in para. 27 below.

normal relative outputs were sufficiently important—then, it would seem, those effects could be considered in the separate analysis of the determinants of aggregate economic activity and hence of the individual effectual demands.

In this chapter, the level of aggregate demand is assumed constant in terms of the level of aggregate labour employment.

6. We may now proceed to the assumptions defining the economy we will be envisaging. We assume n commodities $A_1 \ldots A_n$, obtained, as in Steedman's paper, from single-product industries in a yearly production cycle, with wages advanced at the beginning of the year. Only one method of production will be available in each industry. All the n commodities will be 'basic products'[7] and, besides, labour will be assumed to enter all of them, directly or indirectly.

We shall also assume at first that the real wage is at its natural level and, in accordance with the premises of the classical economists, we shall take it to be given (separately determined). Our numeraire will be the composite wage commodity G, consisting of the g wage goods taken in the proportions in which they enter the natural wage rate. A quantity w^* of G will accordingly constitute the natural wage. We shall indicate the wage goods by

$$A_1, A_2, \cdots, A_g;\ \text{for}\ g \leq n$$

and call

$$g_1, g_2, \cdots, g_g$$

the quantities in which these goods appear in the physical unit of the wage commodity G. The natural wage w^* is positive and less than the maximum wage W, for which the profit rate is zero. The usual equations

$$\begin{aligned} p_1 &= \left(a_{01}w^* + a_{11}p_1 + \cdots + a_{n1}p_n\right)\left(1 + r^*\right) \\ &\cdots \\ p_n &= \left(a_{0n}w^* + a_{1n}p_1 + \cdots + a_{n_1}p_n\right)\left(1 + r^*\right) \end{aligned} \tag{1}$$

will then determine the natural profit rate r^* and the corresponding series of natural prices $p_1, \ldots p_n$, expressed in terms of the wage commodity:

$$1 = g_1 p_1 + g_2 p_2 + \cdots + g_g p_g \tag{2}$$

The market rates of profits $r_1, r_2, \ldots, r_n$ obtainable in each industry in the given 'market position'—as we may call any position of the economy other then the

[7] Sraffa (1960), 8.

'normal position'—will, on the other hand, be given by the following equations, where by $m_1, m_2, \ldots, m_n$ we shall indicate the market prices of the n commodities[8]:

$$\begin{aligned} r_1 &= \frac{m_1 - (a_{01}w^* + a_{11}p_1 + \cdots + a_{n1}p_n)}{a_{01}w^* + a_{11}p_1 + \cdots + a_{n1}p_n} \\ &\cdots \\ r_n &= \frac{m_n - (a_{0n}w^* + a_{1n}p_1 + \cdots + a_{nn}p_n)}{a_{0n}w^* + a_{1n}p_1 + \cdots + a_{nn}p_n} \end{aligned} \tag{3}$$

obtained from

$$\begin{aligned} m_1 &= (1 + r_1)\big(a_{01}w^* + a_{11}p_1 + \cdots + a_{n1}p_n\big) \\ &\cdots \\ m_n &= (1 + r_n)\big(a_{0n}w^* + a_{1n}p_1 + \cdots + a_{nn}p_n\big) \end{aligned} \tag{4}$$

and

$$1 = g_1m_1 + g_2m_2 + \cdots + g_gm_g \tag{5}$$

where, as indicated above, the market real wage has been assumed equal to the natural real wage w^*.

7. We may note that in Eqs. (3) and (4) we have expressed both the inputs and the output of each industry at the same market prices, though the inputs are bought at the beginning, and the outputs are sold at the end, of the production cycle. To this it may be objected that, to the extent to which it can be foreseen by the entrepreneurs with sufficient exactness, the appreciation (depreciation) of the product relative to the means of production during the year[9] constitutes a non-accidental element which entrepreneurs would take into account when comparing the prospective rates of profits between different industries.

It does not, however, seem that a consideration of the price changes over the production cycle is necessary at the present stage of the argument. The requirement of the correct foresight necessary to make those price changes relevant will not generally be fulfilled. And economic theory, which cannot be expected to

[8] Since the economy is not in its normal position, frictions of several kinds render free competition compatible with different *actual* prices being paid for the same commodity in different transactions occurring at the same instant of time. We shall, however, assume, as is generally done, that these different prices can be adequately represented at any given instant of time by a single 'market' price.

[9] In the case of 'continuous production' the same problem arises in the form of a change in the value of the output relative to the aggregate of intermediate products (capital) required to achieve simultaneity of the input and output flows, during the period for which those flows are reckoned. (For the notion of continuous production cf. Garegnani 1990, 25–6.)

determine actual prices, but only prices corresponding to averages of actual prices, can hardly be expected to determine the actual changes in actual prices, as distinct from providing guidance to the *sign* of those changes. Appreciation or depreciation of the capital stock of each industry relative to its product seem accordingly to be best abstracted from in a first approximation—just as we abstract from, say, the non-uniqueness of the market price in any actual situation of the economy.[10] Corrections can always be made to the conclusions thus reached, should it be likely that the price changes be sufficiently large and correctly foreseen by the entrepreneurs.[11]

8. The numeraire Eqs. (2) and (5) focus attention on the fact that the problem of the deviation of market from natural prices is a question of the deviation of *relative* market prices from *relative* natural prices. An implication of this relative nature of the deviation of market from natural prices should be noted. By definition, market and natural prices must coincide for the commodity which we use as our standard of value—and which, for the sake of clarity, we may for a moment suppose to be a single commodity, call it A_1, and not the composite commodity. This coincidence does not of course imply that output and effectual demand need coincide for A_1 any more than for any other commodity. For A_1, as for A_2, A_3, etc., an excess, say, of output over effectual demand will imply a *relative* market price which is below the relative natural price. Thus if, for example, all the other commodities happened to exchange among themselves according to their natural prices, the market prices of those commodities would all have to be uniformly higher than their natural prices, as an expression of the excess of output over effectual demand for A_1 (as well as of the corresponding shortage of the output of those commodities relative to the respective effectual demands).[12] This is evident when, as just assumed, the standard of value consists of a single commodity A_1, but the same element will be present when we refer to any composite commodity, like our commodity G above.

[10] See n. 8 above.

[11] E.g. we may note how forecasts that the relative market price of a commodity in the production of which a low rate of profit can be obtained will rise over time, and vice versa, would decrease somewhat the divergence between the market profit rates.

[12] See the assumption of constant aggregate demand made in para. 5 above.

The Rise of the Minimum Profit Rate

9. Let us then begin by considering a commodity A_h, in the production of which the rate of profit is the minimum among the market rates of profits $r_1, r_2, \ldots, r_n$ resulting from Eqs. (3).[13] Competition will ensure that capital will flow out of the industry A_h, and its output O_h will decrease, possibly after a time lag.[14] We may accordingly write

$$\frac{dO_h}{dt} < 0, \text{ if } r_h \leq r_i \, (i = 1, \cdots, n) \tag{6}$$

with the strict inequality holding for at least one couple *h, i*.

This eventual decrease in the output of the industry (or industries) showing the minimum among the rates of profits in the economy, is the first of the two basic assumptions on which our argument will be based (para. 3 above).

The effect of that decrease in output in raising the market price of A_h, relative to its means of production and wage costs—and therefore its effect in raising the rate of profit (see Eqs. (3))—cannot, however, be taken for granted. We shall see, in paras. 16–17 below, that the input–output relations and the corresponding interactions between the market price of a commodity A_h and those of the means of production and wage goods used in its production will constitute no obstacle to the rise in r_h. The obstacles to such a rise which we must consider now are instead those which may conceivably affect the 'demand' in some sense for A_h because of the fall in O_h, and because of any adjustments simultaneously occurring in the outputs and prices of the *other industries,* about which nothing will be postulated in our argument. In fact, if those changes were to lower the 'demand' for A_h *more rapidly* than O_h is lowered, then clearly we could not expect a rise in r_h.

In order to deal with such changes in 'demand' we must first try to provide a sufficiently definite notion of that 'demand'. This we shall do by means of the concept of a 'market effectual demand', as distinct from that of the 'normal effectual demand' referred to so far.

10. By *market effectual demand* D_i^m for commodity A_i ($i = 1,2,\ldots, n$) we shall mean the quantity of A_i which would be demanded for use[15] in the current

[13] In case more than one industry happened to have that same minimum level, what we shall say should be referred to that group of industries, in the form which we shall see in paras. 20–25 below.

[14] Cf. para. 29 below for the implications of the lag between production decisions and realized outputs. Cf. also the Appendix to this paper, for a discussion of what would have to be understood by changes in the output O_i when we abandon the assumption that all capital is circulating capital, and accordingly introduce the distinction between outputs changing merely because of a change in the degree of utilization of production capacity and outputs which change together with a corresponding change in the level of capacity.

[15] We exclude, that is, from market effectual demand any quantity demanded for changes in inventories.

'market' position of the economy, but at a price m_i^* of A_i which, unlike m_i, would yield the natural rate of profit r^* on the wages and the prices of the means of production estimated at their *market levels*. The price m_i^* is therefore given by the equation

$$m_i^* = \left(1 + r^*\right)\left(a_{0i}w^* + a_{1i}m_1 + \cdots a_{ii}m_i^* + \cdots + a_{ni}m_n\right) \quad (7)$$

Except, that is, for the price m_i^*, which we may for brevity call the *reference price* of A_i in the given market position of the economy, the market effectual demand for A_i will be referred to the actual prices and outputs of that position.[16]

The price m_i^* is thus neither the market price nor the natural price p_i. It is needed in order to define the market effectual demand, which in turn provides a common quantitative expression for the effects on the market of A_i of the adjustments in outputs and prices occurring in the whole economy. It will exceed, or fall short of the corresponding market price m_i, according as r_i exceeds, or falls short of, r^*. The price m_i^* will on the other hand exceed, or fall short of, the natural price p_i because of the deviation of the market prices of the wage goods and means of production from the corresponding natural prices. The *market* effectual demand D_i^m will thus differ from the corresponding *normal* effectual demand D_i^n , not only because the price m_i^* differs from the natural price p_i but also, and above all, because of the deviations from the respective normal levels of all outputs, and of the prices of the commodities other than A_i. In fact D_i^m depends on the level of those market magnitudes to the extent to which A_i is required as an input for those commodities, or has a relation of complementarity or supplementarity in consumption with them, or, also, to the extent to which those magnitudes affect the distribution of the social income and the part of it spent on A_i.

11. The usefulness of this concept of market effectual demand lies in the fact that the current behaviour of market prices will depend on the 'proportion'[17] which the current output bears to it, rather than on the proportion it bears to the normal effectual demand. The consideration of the latter proportion as governing the current behaviour of market prices and rates of profit, such as we find it in Adam Smith and the other classical authors, appears in fact to have been implicitly founded on the idea that the effects on the demand for A_i of the deviations of the actual outputs and of the prices of the other commodities from their normal levels would tend to compensate each other. That compensation cannot however be assumed. The effects in question may in principle be appreciable enough to raise questions for the tendency of actual prices and outputs to their normal levels, and must accordingly be examined.

[16] The present concept is close to that of 'actual' effectual demand put forward in Ciccone (1990, 4–5). Though intended to take into account the effects of accidental circumstances on demand, that concept is, however, still defined for a price of the commodity equal to the natural price.

[17] For the characteristic classical concept of 'proportion' between demand and supply cf. Garegnani (1987, 565).

12. It would thus seem that the same reasons for which Adam Smith could postulate that when the quantity brought to market of the commodity A_i exceeded its *normal* effectual demand D_i^n, then m_i would fall short of p_i and vice versa (Smith [1776] 1910, Bk. I, Ch. VII, 49–52) now justify us in assuming that when O_i exceeds the *market* effectual demand D_i^m, then m_i falls short of m_i^* (and vice versa).[18] Moreover, as Smith did for the corresponding magnitudes,[19] we may assume that as the proportion O_i/D_i^m rises, the ratio m_i/m_i^* falls (and vice versa).[20] These conditions for which

$$\text{if} O_i \overset{>}{\underset{<}{-}} D_i^m, \text{then } m_i \overset{<}{\underset{>}{-}} m_i^* \ (i = 1, 2, \ldots, n)$$

and

$$\frac{d\left(m_i/m_i^*\right)}{dt} \overset{>}{\underset{<}{-}} 0 \quad \text{according as} \quad \frac{d\left(O_i/D_i^m\right)}{dt} \overset{<}{\underset{>}{-}} 0 \tag{8}$$

will constitute the second basic assumption of our argument (para. 3 above)[21]—an assumption the generality of which would not seem to fall short of the corresponding one in the classical economists.

13. Equation (7) and assumption (8) entail not only that $r_i \lesseqgtr r^*$ as $O_i \gtreqless D_i^m$ but also, and most importantly, that r_i rises as O_i/D_i^m falls. The problem we left at the end of para. 9, about the effect of the fall of the output O_h of commodity A_h on the minimum rate of profit r_h, then becomes the problem of the effect of the fall in O_h on the ratio O_h/D_h^m.

The difficulty is of course that, as O_h changes, D_h^m may also change, as a result, partly, of the change in O_h (for example, to the extent in which A_h is used as an input for itself) and, partly, of what may be happening in the rest of the economy,

---

[18] It may be noted that even when A_i happens to be the numeraire, and therefore $m_i = 1$, m_i^* will not generally be unity. Also in that case, therefore, m_i/m_i^* can change as O_i/D_i^m changes.

[19] Smith writes: 'the market price will rise more or less above the natural price according as … the greatness of the deficiency [of the quantity brought to market] … happen[s] to animate more or less the eagerness of the competition', and a similar passage can be found to explain how 'the market price will sink more or less below the natural price' (Smith [1776] 1910, Bk. I, Ch. VII, 50).

[20] See the Appendix below on the conflict sometimes claimed between the classical assumption of a *rise* in the market price in situations in which supply exceeds the effectual demand and the assumption in modern theory of a *fall* in price in the presence of excess supply.

[21] This second basic assumption should be interpreted as referring to quantities *supplied* inclusive, that is, of any (algebraic) de-cumulation of inventories of the commodity, rather then to outputs only. The presentation chosen here has been preferred for reasons of exposition and is justified by the assumption about inventories which we shall discuss in para. 14 below and which will be used for our third general assumption of para. 15.

about which, as we said, nothing is assumed in our argument. We can, however, analyse the circumstances on which the market effectual demand depends, and attempt to reach some general conclusions about the sign of the changes which O_h/D_h^m will undergo because of the output and price changes mentioned above.

A main cause of the changes in D_h^m is likely to be the change in the outputs of the commodities of which A_h is an input.[22] It is particularly because of these changes that we cannot exclude the possibility that, in some circumstances, as O_h falls, the market effectual demand D_h^m may fall even faster, leading to the result of a rise, and not a fall, in the ratio O_h/D_h^m and therefore (by our second basic assumption above) to a further fall in the minimum rate r_h.[23]

However, it seems safe to assume that the market effectual demand for any basic commodity (as we have here assumed all the n commodities to be) has a positive minimum, below which it cannot fall for any length of time. Indeed, no commodity whatsoever could continue to be produced (to be produced, that is, while replacing its means of production) without giving rise directly or indirectly to a positive effectual demand for each of the basic commodities. Now, each of the n commodities in the economy will require different quantities of A_h per worker for its integrated production.[24] A *minimum market effectual demand* for A_h may accordingly be assumed to exist in the given economy, which can be no smaller than the amount of it which would be demanded if the net product of the economy (the size of which remains constant in terms of the total labour employed: above, para. 5) consisted only of the commodity requiring the minimum such amount of A_h. The market effectual demand for A_h could not indeed fall below that minimum for any length of time, unless the economy were on the way to extinction. The same minimum level of D_h^m will evidently be there if the fall in that variable were to be the result of adjustments causing distributive changes or changes in prices and outputs for commodities which are complements or supplements of A_h.

It seems therefore possible to conclude that as O_h falls and approaches that minimum level of D_h^m, then, if not before, it will not be possible for D_h^m to fall faster than O_h, and O_h/D_h^m will have to *rise* together with r_h.[25]

---

[22] Only changes in the outputs for which the commodity A_h is a *direct* input need be considered, since the case in which A_h is an *indirect* input for a third commodity will be taken care of by the changes in the output of the commodity A_j, which, while entering the production of that third commodity, requires A_h as a *direct* input.

[23] E.g. if A_h is used directly for the production of itself, an element of D_h^m will be proportional to the O_h of the subsequent year, and will therefore fall faster than O_h, if O_h falls at an increasing speed. It is then possible that O_h/D_h^m will rise as O_h falls.

[24] For this notion of integrated production cf. Sraffa's concept of a sub-system producing a net physical quantity of the specified commodity (Sraffa 1960, 89).

[25] For O_h/D_h^m to fall sufficiently there will be no need for O_h to fall below the minimum level indicated in the text. By assumption, O_h/D_h^m is initially higher than unity, and it must remain so, so long as the minimum rate r_h remains below the natural level r^*. When, on the other hand, O_h/D_h^m has become unity, thus indicating that the minimum rate r_h has become equal to r^*, the natural position of the economy will have been achieved (as we shall see in para. 19 below) and market effectual demand will coincide with normal effectual demand.

14. Our conclusion as to the fall of O_h/D_h^m when r_h is the minimum profit rate concerns an *eventual* fall of that ratio and rise in r_h. We shall presently simplify our argument by provisionally assuming that O_h/D_h^m falls (r_h rises), not only eventually, but whenever the condition that r_h is the minimum rate of profit is verified—thus in fact assuming a *monotonic* rise in the minimum profit rate in the economy (our third and last assumption: para. 3 above). In order to justify that assumption it is however necessary to consider first a complication which, were it not for the sake of a simpler exposition, we would have introduced before. In fact, our second basic assumption (8) should, strictly speaking, have been formulated in terms of the quantity supplied S_i of the commodity A_i, and not directly in terms of its output O_i, the difference $(O_i - S_i)$ being given by the algebraic accumulation of *inventories* of A_i. Indeed, a sufficiently large running down of inventories could make the supply exceed the output sufficiently to render the condition $O_i<D_i^m$ compatible with $m_i<m_i^*$ and also to make a fall of O_i/D_i^m compatible with *a fall* of r_i.

However, it should be evident that any effect of the decumulation of inventories in making S_h/D_h^m rise, and the minimum rate r_h fall, in spite of the fall of O_h/D_h^m, could be only *temporary*. Any such running down of inventories could not proceed indefinitely, because the inventories would evidently be limited. Above all, by lowering the price of the commodity, any such liquidation of inventories would enhance the fall in the output O_h which, in the end, is bound to dominate the behaviour of the ratio S_h/D_h^m, and therefore the behaviour of r_h. The same applies in the opposite case, an accumulation of inventories of A_i, which would prevent a fall of r_i despite the rise of O_i/D_i^m. Such an accumulation could proceed only for a limited time (the costs of carrying such inventories would see to that) and it would enhance the rise of O_i/D_i^m and, therefore, the eventual rise of S_i/D_i^m.

Now, this temporary character of the effects of the building up or running down of inventories is in evident contrast with the fact that any tendency to the natural position of the economy cannot but be a long-period tendency, implying as it does changes in the size of plant and in the number of firms in the industry. And, with respect to any such long-period tendencies, build-ups or run-downs of inventories are likely to be mere episodes. This observation is strengthened by the consideration that a liquidation of inventories, which could make the minimum rate of profit r_h fall further, is rendered unlikely or, in any case, likely to be very short-lived, by the fact that it would occur for a commodity the value of which, relative to that of the mass of other commodities, could be expected to rise in the longer run. We shall, however, return to the question below (para. 29), when discussing the implications of abandoning the assumption about the monotonic rise of r_h to which we must now proceed, and by which we shall provisionally rule out the above possible influence of inventories (thus making it unnecessary to change the form in which we wrote condition (8)).

15. In fact the conclusions of para. 13 above on the *temporary* nature of any rise of O_h/D_h^m and those just reached in para. 14 about the similar nature of any liquidation of inventories, preventing the rise of m_h/m_i^* despite the fall of O_h/D_h^m, allow us now to simplify the exposition by adding the third assumption mentioned above. This third, provisional, assumption is that the rise in the minimum rate of profit will be verified whenever the rate of profit in question happens to be the minimum, so that the eventual rise of the minimum rate which we demonstrated at para. 13 becomes, as we stated, a monotonic rise, though the commodity or commodities in the production of which that minimum rate can be obtained may be changing in the process.[26]

We may now see that this third provisional assumption entails a fall of O_h *fast enough* to overcome any effect of a fall of D_h^m in raising the ratio O_h/D_h^m.[27] Moreover, it allows us to concentrate attention on long-run trends by excluding the possibility that a liquidation of inventories of the commodity may lower r_h despite the fall in O_h/D_h^m. As already mentioned, the consequence of dropping this third assumption will be discussed in para. 29 below.

16. What we must now consider is how the rise of r_h may in fact occur, without meeting any obstacles in the necessary relations between profit rates and prices which are established by the existing methods of production. The rise in the market rate of profit r_h will, as we said, require a rise of m_h, *relative* to the market prices of the means of production proper, *or* to wages, *or* to both.

1. A rise in the rate of profit r_h through a rise in the price m_h relative to the prices of the *means of production* of course requires that the production of A_h should use means of production other than A_h itself. That will always be the case because A_h is not the only commodity in the economy (no problem of deviations of market from natural prices would otherwise arise) and because, all commodities being basic (para. 6 above), at least one other commodity must appear among the means of production of A_h.[28]
2. A rise in r_h through a rise in m_h relative to wage costs is on the other hand always possible, except when A_h happens either to be the only wage good, or to be produced without any direct labour,[29] in which case the rise in r_h can occur only through route (1).

---

[26] A less restrictive assumption would in fact seem sufficient for our argument in this chapter: it is that, should the minimum rate of profit of the economy ever (temporarily) fall, each minimum level then reached would lie above the previous one. Since in either form the assumption would have been dropped in the last section of the chapter, the form given in the text has been preferred because it allows of a simpler exposition. In either formulation the assumption is of course taken to be verified under that condition of absence of new disturbances which constitutes the necessary premise of the analysis of the tendency of market prices to natural or normal prices (cf. para. 29 below).

[27] It may seem that this third assumption is in conflict with what we said in note 23 about the way in which increasing speed in the fall of O_h may cause a rise in the ratio O_h/D_h^m, when A_h is a means of production of itself. However, the present assumption concerns the absolute speed of the fall in O_h, and not its variation over time.

[28] For a demonstration of this proposition see para. 19 below.

[29] Our assumption (para. 6 above) is that labour is required directly or *indirectly* in the production of every commodity. All products being here assumed to be basic, that assumption could be satisfied even if only one of the commodities required direct labour. We cannot therefore exclude the case of A_h having no wage costs (the ageing of wine is the example traditionally envisaged of a production process requiring no direct labour).

Which of the two routes, (1) or (2), the rise of r_h will mainly or exclusively take will depend partly on the technical conditions of production, and partly on what is happening to the prices of the other commodities about which, as already remarked, nothing is postulated here. (It may be interesting to note at this point how, because of our choice of the composite wage commodity as the numeraire, and of our assumption of a constant w, it is only when the rise in r_h involves a rise in m_h relative to wage costs that m_h will experience an *absolute* rise as the output of O_h falls. If the rise in r_h is exclusively due to a rise in m_h relative to its means of production, m_h will not rise, and may indeed fall as the profitability of its production rises.)

17. Since, however, A_h enters directly or indirectly into the production of commodities which in turn enter directly into the production of A_h as means of production or as wage goods, the question may be posed as to whether the effect on the other industries of the rise in the relative market price m_h of A_h may not pose some obstacle or constraint to that very relative rise in m_h and, therefore, some obstacle or constraint to the rise in r_h. The relative rise in m_h will in fact lower the rate of profit in the industries using A_h as a means of production, and therefore, were that profit rate to fall below the natural rate, it will set in motion forces tending to raise it again through rises in the relative market prices of the respective commodities. The question then arises of whether the impact of those secondary rises on the costs of A_h may not conceivably annul the initial rise in m_h, relative to the means of production and wage goods, thus annulling the initial rise of r_h.

The answer to this question lies in the fact that the rate of profit r_h which is rising is the *minimum* in the economy and we are therefore sure that that rise cannot force any profit rate elsewhere in the economy below itself. As soon as any rate of profit fell as far as r_h *because of the rise of the latter,* the process we are envisaging would raise it back jointly with r_h (cf. below, paras 20ff.). In fact the rise in r_h will not have to proceed beyond r^* where, as we shall presently see (para 19 below), all other rates will also have to be equal to r^*. Indeed, in principle, the rise in r_h could even occur while ensuring that no rate of profit ever falls below r^* elsewhere in the economy.[30]

We may thus conclude that the rise in r_h is entirely compatible with the possible secondary effects it may have on the market prices of its direct and indirect means of production. The convergence to natural prices could be prevented by a direct or indirect effect on the production expenses of A_h of its own relative price rise, if and only if some industries could 'resist' a fall in their profit rates at levels of those rates higher than the natural rate of profit r^*. The fact that such cannot be the

[30] Cf. n. 32 below.

case is at one with the assumption of free competition and the associated tendency towards a uniform rate of profit.[31]

18. As r_h continues to rise by finite increments, it will finally have to reach the level of one of the rates of profit obtaining in some other industry, say that for A_{h+1}. There are then two possibilities: either (1) r_{h+1} is already r^*, or (2) it is *less* than r^*. To see why $r_{h+1} > r^*$ is not possible, and in order to discuss possibilities (1) and (2) we shall, however, need first some propositions, to which we must now proceed.

Three Propositions on Market and Natural Prices

19. Of the three propositions to be demonstrated in this section, Proposition I and its strict complement, Proposition II, appear here only as a basis for Proposition III, which is the one central to our argument.

Proposition I

Whatever the deviations of market from natural prices, the production of a commodity A_m for which the ratio M_m of the market to the natural price is the minimum in the economy, will always yield a rate of profit which is below the natural rate.

Let us indicate by $M_1, M_2, \ldots M_n$ the ratios of market to natural prices of the n commodities

$$M_2 = \frac{m_1}{p_1},\ M_2 = \frac{m_2}{p_2}, \ldots, M_n = \frac{m_n}{p_n}$$

From the numeraire Eqs. (2) and (5) above it follows that either $M_1 = M_2 = \ldots = M_g = 1$ or, if they differ, some of them will be larger and some smaller than unity. It may however be noted that the case $M_1 = M_2 = \ldots = M_g = 1$, does not entail $M_{g+1} = \ldots = M_n = 1$, and does not therefore coincide with the 'natural position' of the economy.

It follows that the minimum such ratio, let it be the ratio M_m for the commodity A_m, need not be less than unity. It is true that if the M's of the wage goods are not all equal, then, as we saw, the M of some wage goods will have to be smaller than unity, and therefore $M_m < 1$. We cannot, however, rule out the above possibility that the M's for the wage goods be all equal, and therefore equal to unity, with

[31] Under competitive conditions no 'resistance' to a fall in the rate of profit can be effected in any industry except by means of a fall in the output and of the consequent (eventual) rise of the market price of the product relative to the means of production and/or wage goods. This is unlikely to happen and in any case cannot last at a rate of profit above the natural rate r^*.

commodities other than the wage goods having different M's, none of which happens to be less than unity. In that case the minimum M would be unity. (The case would be the one we already noticed in the example of para. 8, of an excess in the output over the effectual demand for the numeraire commodity which will have to show in a general excess of the market prices of all the other commodities relative to their natural prices.)

In order to simplify the notation, let us now indicate by a the level of the minimum ratio M_m between market and natural prices, pertaining to the commodity A_m, so that we can write:

$$a \leq 1 \tag{9}$$

Let us also indicate by b the analogous ratio as it applies to the means of production of A_m, taken as a single composite commodity, i.e.

$$b = \frac{\sum_{i=1}^{n} a_{im} m_i}{\sum_{i=1}^{n} a_{im} p_i} = \frac{\sum_{i=1}^{n} (a_{im} p_i) M_i}{\sum_{i=1}^{n} (a_{im} p_i)}$$

We can of course be sure that b, which is the above average of the M's of the means of production of A_m, with the positive weights shown, will not be less than M_m. We cannot, however, immediately exclude the possibility $a = b$, i.e. that, for the chosen commodity, having the minimum ratio M_m between market price and natural price, the direct means of production of the commodity may all have the *same* minimum ratio M_m. In that case, the commodity—call it A_1, one, then, of the several sharing the same minimum ratio M_m—would not yet be the commodity A_m we are looking for, which will instead show

$$a < b \tag{10}$$

However, we shall then be bound to find A_m among those means of production of A_1, or (should also their own means of production all exhibit the minimum ratio M_m), among the means of production of those means of production etc., within a number of steps which cannot exceed $(n - 1)$. This is so because, by hypothesis, *some* commodity exists with an M larger than the minimum, and since all commodities are basic (para 6), such a commodity will enter (indirectly) into the production of A_1.

As for the maximum number of steps $(n - 1)$ within which A_m must appear among the means of production of A_1 we know that, until all direct and indirect means of production have appeared through the several stages of the 'reduction to labour' (Sraffa 1960, 34ff.) of A_1, at least one *new* means of production other than A_1 must appear at each stage of that reduction: otherwise no new means of production could ever appear at any later stage of the same process. Thus the number of stages we may have before all means of production have appeared cannot exceed $(n - 1)$.

We may now choose as physical unit of the commodity A_m thus traced that quantity of it which is of unit value when estimated at its natural price for the given r^*. Let v be the proportion of that value taken up by the (circulating) means of production, when estimated at their *natural prices,* so that bv will be the same proportion when estimated at *market price* of the means of production, and let u be the analogous proportion taken up by wages. We can then write the market rate of profit obtainable in producing A_m as

$$r_m = \frac{a - (u + bv)}{u + bv} = \frac{a}{u + bv} - 1 \tag{11a}$$

and the natural rate of profit is

$$r^* = \frac{1 - (u + v)}{u + v} = \frac{1}{u + v} - 1 \tag{11b}$$

(where, as we saw in para. 6 above, we assume wages to be at their natural level in dealing with the market prices of Eq. (11a)).

We must now show that under conditions (9) and (10), $r_m < r^*$, i.e. that

$$\frac{a}{u + bv} - 1 < \frac{1}{u + v} - 1 \tag{12a}$$

Since both the (11) expressions are positive (*or,* if $r_m < 0$, the positivity of r^* will make the demonstration of $r_m < r^*$ unnecessary) the above can be written as

$$\frac{a}{u + bv} < \frac{1}{u + v} \tag{12b}$$

Since $(u + v)$ and $(u + bv)$ are both positive, inequality simplifies into

$$u(1 - a) > v(a - b)$$

which is always true, since $v(a - b) < 0$ by condition (10), whereas $u(1 - a) \geq 0$, by condition (9).

As we wanted to show, the production of a commodity A_m having the minimum M will always give a rate of profit below r^*.

Proposition II *The commodity, or one of the commodities, having M at its maximum level will necessarily have* $r > r^*$.

This proposition can be demonstrated by a procedure strictly analogous to the one we followed for Proposition I.[32]

[32] If now we return to the commodity A_m of Proposition I, in the production of which the rate of profit must be below the natural rate r^*, we may note that the production of at least one of the other commodities would have to yield a profit rate higher than r^*. Indeed, we cannot exclude that this will be the case with *all* commodities other than A_m. Thus, as mentioned in para. 17 of the text, we cannot exclude that, when one market rate is below r^*, all the others are above that same natural rate.

Proposition III *When none of the market rates of profit of the* n *industries lies below the natural rate, then all the rates of profits must be equal. They are therefore equal to the natural rate, and we are in the natural position of the economy with market prices equal to natural prices. The same holds true when none of the* n *rates of profits lies above the natural rate* r*.

In fact if, in the situation envisaged in Proposition III, the *M*'s were not all the same, then by Proposition I above we would be able to single out a commodity A_m such that its production would yield a rate of profit $r_m < r*$. Since by hypothesis no profit rate lies below $r*$, we must conclude that the *M*'s must all be the same. By the numeraire Eqs. (2) and (5), they must then be all equal to unity. We are therefore in the natural position of the economy, with market prices equal to the natural prices, and with a uniform rate of profit $r*$.

Strictly analogous reasoning will prove the proposition in the case in which none of the *n* rates of profit lies *above* the natural rate.

The Convergence to the Natural Position

20. We can now return to the level r_{h+1} which the rate of profit r_h has reached in its rise, and to the two cases $r_{h+1} = r*$, and $r_{h+1} < r*$, mentioned at the beginning of para. 18 above. Let us begin with the case $r_{h+1} = r*$.

The market rate r_h was the minimum *r* in the economy, and, by the nature of the process envisaged above, it must have remained so. If $r_h = r_{h+1} = r*$, then, by Proposition III, convergence to the natural position has been achieved.

21. We may proceed to the second case, where the level r_{h+1} at which r_h meets the rate of profit of the industry of A_{h+1} is below $r*$. We can then envisage the continuation of the fall of O_h and rise of r_h, this time jointly with a fall of O_{h+1}, and the rise of r_{h+1}, which is consequent upon that fall for the same reasons we saw in paras 9–18 for r_h. For the sake of simplicity, and without loss of generality, we may assume that the falls of O_h and O_{h+1} are such as to make the two rates of profit rise in step,[33] and we shall indicate by *H* the group of commodities (including A_h and A_{h+1}, so far) in the production of which the rate of profit is thus made to rise uniformly.

Everything that we said in paras 16–17 above, concerning the rise of r_h and its possibility, can now be repeated, with the slight reformulations made necessary by

[33] No difference to our conclusions would in fact be made if the two rates did not rise uniformly. The only element on which our present argument rests is that the minimum rate, whether r_h or r_{h+1}, or the two together, should monotonically rise (cf. paras. 13 above and 27 below). The assumption of a uniform rise of the two allows an easier exposition of the answer to the problems which that joint rise presents us with.

the fact that the rate of profit which is rising is the rate r_H common to the group of commodities *H,* and not that of the single commodity A_h. Thus, similarly to what we saw in para. 16, the possibility of a rise in r_H obtains because of one, or the other, or both of the following circumstances:

1. For at least one of the commodities *H,* one or more of its means of production must be commodities other than those of group *H.* This must be so because all commodities are basic and enter therefore, directly or indirectly, into the production of each of the commodities *H* (para. 6 above): evidently none of the commodities other than *H* could enter even indirectly into those of group *H,* if at least one of them did not enter *directly* into the production of at least one of commodities *H* (thus making it possible for all the commodities outside group *H* to enter *indirectly* into all those of the group: cf. the same point in the demonstration of Proposition I, para. 19 above). As a result a rise in the rate of profit r_H common to group *H* can always be achieved by raising the market prices of commodities *H* sufficiently, relative to those of the other commodities.
2. There must exist wage costs for the production of commodities *H* and, therefore, the possibility of raising the prices of commodities *H* relative to those wage costs. This will be so unless all wage goods are already included in group *H,* or no commodity of group *H* required any direct labour to be produced.

22. As in the case of the single commodity A_h, the further question then arises of whether the effect on the profits and prices of the remaining industries of the rise in the rate of profit obtained in the production of commodities *H* may not in fact ultimately undo that rise. The answer to this question is the same we gave in para. 17 above: no such obstacle can be met by the rise here required in r_H, which needs to proceed only up to r^* and is therefore compatible with any rise in the market price of the remaining commodities which may be necessary in order to keep the rate of profit obtainable in their production from falling below r_h or, indeed, below r^*.

23. It is now easy to see our way forward to the conclusion of the argument. As $r_h = r_{h+1}$ rise in step with each other, they will sooner or later meet a third profit rate r_{h+2} and there will again be two cases. Either we shall have $r_H = r_h = r_{h+1} = r_{h+2} = r^*$ and then, by Proposition III, the natural position would have been reached. Or, alternatively, $r_h < r^*$ and then, as commodity A_{h+2} joins group *H,* all three can rise together in exactly the same way we saw above, until they meet a fourth rate of profit $r_{h+3} \leq r^*$, and so on until the rate of profit r_H common to the thus enlarging group of commodities *H* finally reaches r^* and hence, by Proposition III, all the remaining rates of profit. In a finite number of steps (that of the commodities joining the group *H,* which obviously cannot be larger than the number *n* of commodities) this process will lead to the normal position of the economy.

24. The fact that nothing is here being postulated about the behaviour of outputs and prices outside the industries *H* whose profit rate is being increased may, however, seem to raise a difficulty, with which we should deal before concluding our argument.

We have assumed a monotonic fall in the output of A_h and more generally of the commodities of group *H*, in parallel with a monotonic rise in the profit rate r_h obtainable from their production. We cannot, however, exclude the possibility that, in the initial situation, the market effectual demand for A_h—whose proportion to output, as we saw, plausibly governs the sign of the deviation of the market, from the natural, profit rate (para. 12 above)—be considerably below the normal effectual demand so that the output of A_h, while larger than the 'market' demand, thus explaining $r_h < r^*$, will be below the 'normal' demand. In such a case the convergence towards the natural position will ultimately require some *rise* in the output of A_h (and thus be incompatible with a monotonic fall), and therefore also, presumably, that r_h at some stage rises above the minimum and possibly beyond r^* before falling back to it. In that special case we can see the *necessity* of a non-monotonic movement of the output and rate of profit for one of the commodities *H*, but of course the possibility of such non-monotonic movements is always there, as a profit rate may, so to speak, 'shoot' beyond r^* (e.g. as a result of a particularly rapid fall in the relative market price of its means of production) before getting back to it or to r^*.

However, the phenomenon we have then to envisage is entirely compatible with the process of convergence we have discussed. To see that this is so, it is sufficient to realize that in such cases r_h will have had to meet some other profit rate $r_{h+1} \leq r^*$ before it could 'shoot beyond' r^*. Its place in the progressive rise towards r^* will then have been taken by r_{h+1}. In fact our procedure only requires that none of the rates of profit of commodities *H*, which we accompany in their progressive rise, ever falls back below the uniform level of the group. Some rates of profits may be allowed to go ahead and even 'shoot' above r^*.

25. We may now finally drop the assumption that, during the process envisaged above, the real wage is, and stays, at its natural level w^*, and suppose instead that we have a variable 'market' real wage *W*.

However, the tendency of *w* towards w^* is a different question from that with which we have been concerned here, and has to do with the forces which allow *w* to be treated as an independent variable in classical theory. This difference in the forces involved is what has induced us to separate the two questions by supposing that the wage is and remains at its natural level during the adjustment in prices and profit rates envisaged above.

What can be of concern to us here is therefore only whether the two tendencies, that of the real wage towards its natural level, and that of the profit rate and relative prices towards their own natural levels, may not interfere with each other. From what can be seen from the side of the latter tendency—without entering, that is, into the way in which the market real wage will gravitate towards its natural level—there do not seem to be grounds for any such interference.

One could in fact argue as follows. At any given level of the market real wage w', the tendency to the general rate of profit r' corresponding to that wage, and the connected tendency to the corresponding series of $(n - 1)$ natural relative prices, will occur in the way discussed in this chapter. This should ensure that, as the general rate of profit r' itself changes by effect of the movement of the market wage w' towards the natural wage w^*, the former tendency will translate into a tendency towards the natural rate of profit r^*.[34]

Some Conclusions

26. We may now try to pull together the threads of our argument and assess the meaning of our results. The argument in this chapter has been designed to examine the obstacles which the market prices of the means of production have been thought to raise against a tendency towards the normal position of the economy. The chapter has thus been focused on showing that a fall in the output of the industries yielding the minimum rate of profit is sufficient to bring the economy to its normal or natural position, irrespective of what the market prices of their means of production may initially have been or may have become in the course of the adjustment.

27. The results thus reached may, however, extend beyond the non-existence of those particular obstacles. This may be seen by taking now an overall view of the premises and assumptions used for those results

Our argument has first of all been founded on the classical postulate of given 'normal' effectual demands. This postulate, which follows from the basic premises of the classical approach (para. 4 above), has in fact been frequently overlooked in recent literature purporting to deal with the classical tendency of actual or market prices towards prices of production.

This is a result of the difficulty many authors seem to have in coming to terms with the classical determination of outputs and its independence from the demand and supply forces of present-day mainstream theory. However, overlooking this classical postulate has imposed on that literature special assumptions about

[34] The effect of the change in real wages in changing the 'market' effectual demand for commodity A_h (or for the commodities of group H) should not, on the other hand, affect the conclusions we reached in para. 13 above about the fall in A_h ultimately entailing a fall in the ratio O_h/D_h^m. Though it cannot be excluded that the adjustments in the real wage might temporarily cause falls in the market effectual demand D_h^m for A_h, which are faster than those of the output, such a faster fall obviously could not last as the market wage got progressively closer to the natural rate.

normal outputs like that of steady growth.[35] This has in turn favoured the choice of hypotheses about the behaviour of actual prices and outputs, the arbitrary character of which seems to have escaped attention, and to have led to unwarranted conclusions about an instability in the prices of production.

Cases in point have been some two-commodity models where the normal position of the economy has been taken to be that of uniform growth. Thus in Nikaido (1985) (cf. also Lippi 1990, discussed in the Appendix to this paper) it has been assumed that, with real wages included among the means of production, the outputs of the given initial 'market position', whatever they might happen to be, will be totally absorbed by the production for the following period, except for a fixed consumption out of profits. The coefficients of production of the two commodities being given, that assumption will fully determine the outputs of the following period.

Then, if we assume that the production of commodity A_2 requires itself in a proportion to A_1 higher than the production of A_1 does, and, for the sake of simplicity, we further assume a zero consumption out of profits—then, an initial excess in the supply of A_2 relative to the quantity required for uniform growth would result in an even larger excess supply in the following period. For exactly the same reason the excess supply would be still larger the period after, and so on up to the point at which the proportion O_2/O_1 will exceed the maximum in which the two commodities can be absorbed (by assumption, that in which they are required for producing A_2). Hence Nikaido's conclusion that the 'natural position' is unstable.

It seems, however, to have escaped notice that such a conclusion would require the relative price of A_2 to be such as to provoke the above increase in the relative output of A_2, i.e. that it should lie *above* the natural level, and this should occur when the output of A_2 *exceeds* its 'market' effectual demand (which is here equal to the normal effectual demand, and bears therefore the proportion of uniform growth to the similar demand for A_1)[36]—contrary to what any competitive bidding would entail. It appears then that, when the effects of competitive bidding are correctly taken into consideration, that conclusion of instability can be neatly reversed. A relative price of A_2 below its natural level because of the initial excess

[35] As I have had occasion to point out elsewhere (Garegnani 1990, 52), the assumption of steady growth seems to have been often adopted in the belief that it would allow an analysis of the average rate of growth of the economy. This overlooks the fact that no reason exists why any such average growth of the real economy should or ever could entail a proportional increase in all sectors and employed resources.

[36] We have here assumed no consumption out of profits and therefore the demand for consumption good A_2 comes exclusively from wages. The general assumptions of Nikaido's model entail, on the other hand, a level of labour employment which, though growing from period to period, is given in any given period. The market effectual demand for A_2 will therefore be equal to aggregate real wages and thus to the *normal* effectual demand, whatever the market position of the economy (and therefore the reference price m_2*) may be. The same will then be true for A_1.

supply will result in a progressive fall in the proportion in which A_2 and A_1 are produced towards the single proportion of the natural position of steady growth assumed there, and in that position any excess supply will disappear.[37]

The above conclusion about the stability of the position of steady growth of that model will be equally true when the two commodities are 'hetero-intensive'. Under either assumption about the coefficients of production, the excess in the supply of A_2, relative to the quantity to be used as input for the production of the subsequent period, will of course result in some accumulation of inventories to be liquidated later, just as the symmetrical shortage of A_1 will have to be made good from inventories. Indeed, by the very fact that a market position *is not* a normal position of the economy, the kind of market clearing occurring in the former will generally involve some building up or running down of inventories of the commodity.[38]

28. Let us proceed now to the assumptions we made in our analysis. If we leave aside the assumptions of paras. 4–8 regarding the kind of economy with which we have been concerned, similar to those generally made in dealing with our topic,

---

[37] Nikaido's argument may perhaps emerge more clearly by using a *curve qq* where the abscissa x measures the proportion O_2/O_1 between the outputs of the two commodities A_2 and A_1 of the model, and the ordinate y, the proportion in which the two commodities are *demanded as inputs* when the output proportions are those on the abscissa. Fig. 1 depicts the case in which the production of A_2 is 'self-intensive' and therefore y rises from the minimum a_{21}/a_{11} for $x=0$, and tends to its maximum a_{22}/a_{12} as $x \to \infty$. Fig. 2 depicts the opposite case of hetero-intensity. Suppose now in Fig. 1, that the relative outputs of the initial situation happen to be x', with a relative *market* effectual demand which, for the reasons seen in note 36 above, will correspond to the proportion x^* of uniform growth and therefore of the *normal* effectual demands. There will be a positive excess demand for A_2, indicated by the horizontal difference $(x^* - x')$ (or by the vertical difference between $y^*=x^*$ and the ordinate y' of the bisectrix through the origin.) The proportion x'' in which the two commodities should be produced the following year in order to absorb the current outputs available in proportion x' can then be found as the abscissa x'' of the intersection q'' between the q curve and the horizontal line drawn from the point of ordinate $y' = x'$ on the bisectrix. As can be seen from Fig. 1, the proportion x''' would then indicate the next output proportion required to absorb the two commodities thus produced in the proportion x'', with no proportion of outputs being then any longer capable to absorb the two commodities thus produced in the proportion x^*. Similarly in the case of an initial proportion x_1 of the outputs, with an excess supply of A_2 expressed by the difference $x_1 - x^*$ (also shown vertically by $(y_1 - y^*)$, the sequence of outputs x_1, x_2, would show a similar instability. However, the leftward instability disappears as soon as we observe that, to be ever realized, the sequence x', x'', x''' would require $m_2/m_1 < p_2/p_1$, which cannot be the case with the excess demand expressed by $(x^* - x')$—just as the rightward instability would require $m_2/m_1 > p_2/p_1$, which is not possible with an excess supply $(x_1 - x^*)$. Such excess demands or supplies will instead be accompanied by relative market prices ensuring the tendency to the relative effectual demand x^*. And the same tendency will be there in the 'hetero-intensive' case of Fig. 2.

[38] This building up or running down of inventories would probably be generally considered as 'unintended'. It does not, however, seem to be easy to distinguish such 'unintended' inventory changes, clearly connected with reservation prices and, therefore, with expectations about future prices, from 'intended' inventory changes.

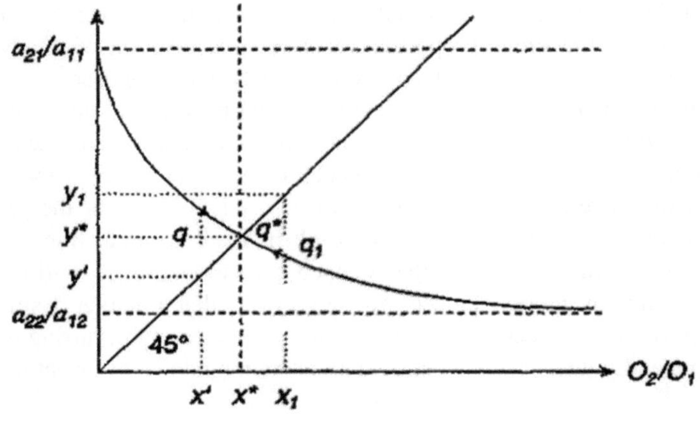

Fig. 1 Case of 'self-intensive' production of A_2 (fn. 37)

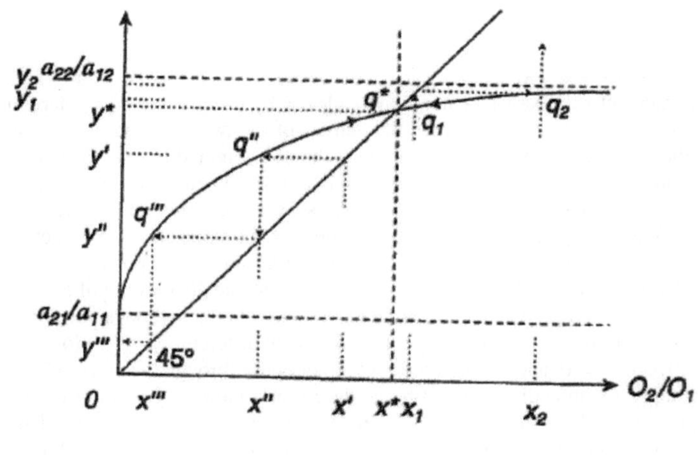

Fig. 2 Case of 'hetero-intensive' production of A_2 (fn. 37)

our conclusions have been founded on the two basic assumptions we mentioned in para. 3 above. The first has been the decrease in the output of the industry (industries) yielding the minimum rate of profit in the economy (para. 9). The second has been that a fall in the proportion which the output of the commodity A_i bears to its 'market' effectual demand, will raise its market price relative to the 'reference price' m_i*, yielding the natural rate of profit in the given 'market position' of the economy, and vice versa (para. 12).

The generality of the first of these two basic assumptions would not appear to be in doubt, since it is based on the tendency of investors to maximize their returns.[39] The second assumption, on the other hand, is a generalization of Adam Smith's postulate about the market price exceeding the natural price when the output of the commodity falls short of the normal effectual demand, and vice versa.[40] It seems therefore to be no more disputable than Adam Smith's own postulate.

29. A third assumption of a more restrictive nature has, however, also been used by us. The assumption is that, instead of *eventually* rising as demonstrated in paras. 13–14 above, the minimum rate of profit will rise straight away. As we noted (para. 15 above), that need not necessarily be true because the ratio of the output of the commodity to its market effectual demand may temporarily rise rather than fall. Also, the liquidation of inventories of some commodity of group H may temporarily depress the rate of profit in the corresponding industry, even when O_h/D_h^m is falling. In these cases the minimum rate of profit of the economy could temporarily fall.

The restrictions which this third assumption has imposed on our argument may be summed up by saying that it has excluded the possibility of any but convergent oscillations in reaching the normal position of the economy. Oscillations of constant or even widening amplitude in the profit rate of some industries had not in fact been ruled out by our demonstration of the *ultimate* rise of a profit rate which happens to be the minimum in the economy. They have been instead assumed away by the monotonic rise in the minimum rate of profit of the economy of our third assumption.

Before considering in the light of our previous analysis the sources and likelihood of any such constant or widening oscillations, we must, however, remind ourselves of a possible ambiguity concerning them, and make clear the nature of those oscillations which are the only ones we need to be concerned with. The oscillations around the normal position which can always be expected to occur in the actual economy will generally arise from the continuous occurrence of *exogenous* accidental circumstances. However, by their nature, those oscillations are excluded from an analysis of the tendency of the economy towards its normal position. If the latter tendency can be shown to exist—given an arbitrary initial deviation from that position, and in the absence of further disturbances—then there will be grounds for concluding that the continuously occurring exogenous disturbances will tend to compensate for each other over a sufficiently long-period of time, with the result that the market price will gravitate *around,* rather than *towards*, the natural price.

The only oscillations relevant to the analysis of the tendency to natural prices are therefore those of a different, endogenous kind, and that is the kind of those assumed away by our third assumption. However, it appears that the previous

[39] The implications of the possibility of a temporary rise of output in the least profitable industry because of the lag between production decisions and realized outputs (para. 9 above) will be considered presently.

[40] Cf. para. 12 above.

argument by which we could prove, in paras. 13–14 above, the *eventual* rise of the minimum rate of profit, had in fact left little room for any but convergent oscillations.

Indeed there seem to be only two possible sources of those constant or divergent oscillations which have been assumed away by our third assumption. The first is the time lag between production decisions and realized outputs, for which O_h may temporarily rise even when A_h is a minimum-profit commodity (cf. condition (6) above, about an *eventual* fall of O_h): we have implicitly excluded the effect of that lag to the extent that the monotonic rise of r_h entails a corresponding fall of O_h/D_h^m and therefore, presumably, of O_h whenever A_h is a minimum-profit commodity. Now by assuming away those effects we have also assumed away the possibility of phenomena like the 'hog cycle'. The possibility is that for which in some industries a low rate of profit may cause decisions to decrease output which, when put into effect, will reveal themselves to have been excessive, thus causing a sharp rise in the profit rate above the natural level and then, conceivably, a rise in output well beyond its normal level and thus a widening cycle.

The second conceivable source of constant or widening oscillations of individual profit rates, ruled out by our third assumption, is inventory cycles of the commodity concerned. Although for the reasons we saw in para. 14 we cannot imagine a liquidation of inventories of the commodity to cause an indefinite continuous fall in the rate of profit yielded by its production, yet the rise in relative price (and profit rate) following upon the end of that liquidation might provoke as a reaction a new liquidation of inventories, bringing the profit rate even below the minimum level previously reached, and so on and so forth.

However, with respect to this second source of oscillations, the reasons we saw at para. 14 above make it difficult to envisage the possibility of such widening inventory cycles. It would in fact seem that the effect of those cycles on the prospective rate of profits obtainable by producing the commodity would tend to be confined within narrow limits by the analogous, opposite effects on that rate due to the changes in output, and hence in supply, caused by those very cycles. Those cycles would also tend to be narrowly confined by the fact that, as the rate moves away from the normal level, the inventory change would run counter to plausible expectations about the longer-run behaviour of the relative price of the commodity.

On the other hand, with respect to the first possible source of divergent oscillations, the lag between production decisions and realized outputs relevant to the 'hog cycle' phenomenon will chiefly concern the short-period decisions regarding the outputs obtainable from existing plant (we are of course abandoning here our assumption about all capital being circulating capital). The long-period decisions concerning the size of plant will presumably have time to be revised as the effects on the relative price of the commodity of the short-period decisions gradually reveal themselves.

It seems, therefore, that when the demonstrated ultimate rise in the rate of profit (paras. 13–14) has narrowed the possibilities of instability in the prices of production down to the above cases of divergent oscillations, the conclusions about any such instability would have to be negative. Even leaving aside the considerations above, those possibilities of non-convergent endogenous oscillations would have to rest on the possibility of indefinitely repeating, on the same, or an increasing, scale, the errors made possible either by the lags between output decisions and realized outputs, or by changes in inventories of the commodity.[41] Until convincing examples are brought to the fore to the contrary, it would seem legitimate to suppose that in such cases individuals could and would learn from their experience and that any such endogenous oscillations in the markets of individual commodities[42] would tend to decrease in amplitude.[43]

30. A feature of the argument put forward in this chapter may finally be commented on. Following the method of the classical economists, we have attempted to confine the assumptions on which our argument has rested to the *signs* of the changes in the relevant variables (*a fall* in the least profitable output O_h, a *rise* in r_h as O_h/D_h^m *falls,* etc.). The importance of this lies, in the first place, in that the simplicity of those assumptions allows direct comparison with, and hence confirmation (or lack of it) by, observation. No less important, these assumptions are by their nature quite general, since nothing is there postulated about the *size* of the rates of change over time of outputs and prices.[44] They render possible, therefore, equally general conclusions. This generality and possibility of conclusive comparisons with observation are on the other hand essential for a problem as central as the tendency to the positions of the economy determined by the theory, on which tendency the validation of classical theory, as of any conceivable alternative theory, does ultimately depend.

The fact that—once some essential premises of classical theory, like that of given effectual demand, are correctly understood and taken into account—results

[41] A word may be added about the continuity which for simplicity of exposition we have here sometime assumed for the changes in prices and outputs. It does not seem that this assumption can in any way have affected our conclusions. Even in the case of an economy with only two commodities—where discontinuity might seem essential to oscillations, since when the two market rates of profit became equal in the course of their continuous change no further endogenous changes might seem possible—even in that case, as we saw, production lags, rather than discontinuity, are what is essential for oscillations. In fact continuity in the variation of the relative prices would not prevent 'overshooting', to the extent to which the changes in output when the two rates of profit are equal would respond to decisions taken when they were unequal.

[42] Oscillations in aggregate demand are of course a different question from oscillations in market prices and accordingly the former have here been excluded by means of the classical assumption of given 'normal' effectual demands (para. 4 above).

[43] Thus taking as an example the 'cobweb' of a divergent 'hog cycle' (e.g. Samuelson 1980, 381–3), it would seem difficult to imagine that producers—far from learning about their errors in excessively increasing and then decreasing their outputs, and that speculators, far from taking advantage of any such persisting, visible errors would allow them to be repeated on an ever increasing scale.

[44] Except of course for the *finiteness* of those rates of change, which has been assumed throughout the chapter.

appear to be obtainable by means of such simpler and more general assumptions, confined to the signs of the changes, seems, on the other hand, to confirm the basic correctness of the classical method.

Acknowledgements In putting together the earlier notes I have drawn benefit from comments by M. Caminati, G. Duménil, H. Kurz, D. Lévy, F. Petri, B. Schefold and, in particular, from discussions with R. Ciccone. Work on this chapter has been facilitated by research grants from the Consiglio Nazionale delle Ricerche and from the Ministero dell'Università e della Ricerca Scientifica e Tecnologica.

Appendix

A contrast seems to have sometimes been seen, between the assumption of the classical economists of a *fall* of the market price when effectual demand exceeds supply, and the modern assumption of a *rise* in price whenever there is 'excess demand'. Thus in Lippi (1990) the modern assumption is taken to entail a rise of the market price until output reaches effectual demand where, the price being then necessarily *above* its natural level, output would have to increase further, engendering cycles, which, in Lippi's view, would prevent convergence to the natural price.

However, at a closer examination, no such contrast between the classical and the modern assumptions appears to exist since the two refer in fact to *different stages* of the process of adjustment which generally follow one another, and are equally admitted in either theoretical approach. And once that is made clear, it also becomes clear that Lippi's instability results are due not, as he seems to think, to 'feedbacks' between outputs and prices ignored by the classical economists but, rather, to Lippi's own mathematical model which ignores the distinction between such two stages.

Indeed the first reaction to an unforeseen change, say a rise, in effectual demand will be a rise in price up to a level where a *temporary equality* between quantity demanded and supplied is achieved and where the rise in price will accordingly stop. We shall presently consider the temporary nature of the demand and supply there involved, but what needs to be stressed straightaway, for clarity's sake, is that their *equality* will be generally reached *before,* often long before, the more permanent equality characterizing the new long-period position: indeed a lasting increase of demand for, say, coal, cannot be expected to cause a continued *increase* in its price—as distinct from a continued price *higher than normal*—for all the years before new coal mines are opened up.

On the side of supply, this first stage of the adjustment will generally include, so far as increases in output are concerned, only those increases which might be possible in the time *before* the above temporary demand and supply equality is achieved—output increases which may even be zero. What that supply will instead generally include will be purely temporary adjustments like the running down of sellers' inventories.[45]

Temporary factors will be even more important on the demand side. Quite apart from any substitution which might conceivably be possible even in such a very short time run, and any likely effect of the price rise in reducing the purchasing power of buyers, we would generally expect delayed purchases, liquidation of buyers' inventories—and even queuing and other forms of rationing—which, when confined, as they would here be, to the very short run, would appear to be compatible with *long run* free competition.

This first stage of the adjustment is that which Marshall represented as a 'temporary equilibrium' ([1920] 1961, V, v, 4, 369), and which the classical authors *took for granted* by referring to a market price higher than the normal price, when the quantity 'brought to market' fell short of effectual demand. It is indeed a stage which quite naturally draws more attention in modern theory, since it is the *only* stage possible under the hypothesis of 'pure exchange' common in its standard expositions.[46] However also in modern theory that stage of the adjustment recedes to its proper role of a first preliminary stage when production is introduced.

A second stage has in fact to begin as soon as the first is completed. It consists of the gradual fall in the price of the commodity because of the increase in output made possible by the higher price and the longer time run which can now be considered. In this second stage the price ensuring the 'temporary' equality of demand and supply moves downwards toward its normal level, as the initial shortage of the commodity is gradually removed while output is increased towards what the classical economists called the 'effectual demand', and modern theorists describe instead as the long-period equilibrium output.

To show the form in which this second stage of the adjustment—the one which drew the almost exclusive attention of the classical economists—is equally present in modern theory, we have recalled in Fig. 3 below its standard description in terms of the sequence of the short-period equilibria of that theory. As the demand has unexpectedly risen from *dd* to *d'd'*, the price initially rises from its long period equilibrium level of p^* to the short-period equilibrium level p' (involving here *some* rise in output) along the short-period supply curve resulting from the summation of the short period marginal cost curves of existing firms (similar summations of variable and total short-period average costs, are also shown). However, as firms increase in number and (initially) in size because of the higher profitability,

---

[45] Thus, for the opposite case of a glut, Smith explains that '[w]hen the quantity brought to market exceeds the effectual demand … [t]he market price will sink more or less below the natural price, according … *as it happens to be more or less important to* [the sellers] *to get immediately rid of the commodity.* The same excess in the importation of perishable, will occasion a much greater competition than in that of durable commodities; in the importation of oranges, for example, than in that of old iron' ([1776] 1910, Bk. I, Ch. VII, p. 50, our italics).

[46] It generally is the only stage of adjustment possible also in the market for 'factors of production' envisaged in modern theory.

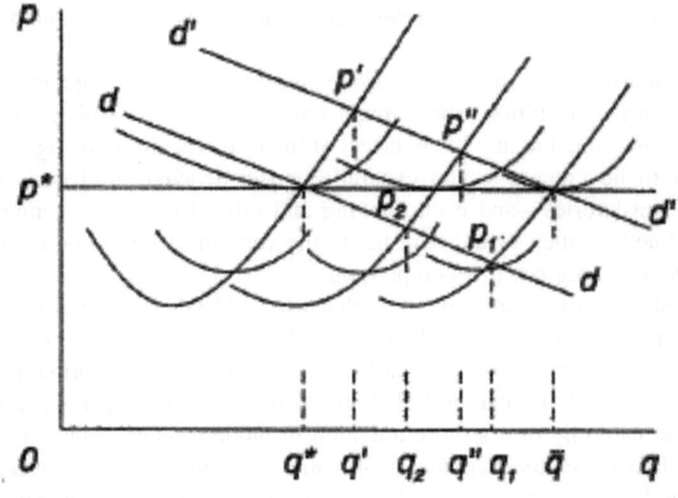

Fig. 3 Sequence of standard short-period equilibria

the short-period supply curve shifts gradually to the right and the short-period equilibrium price progressively falls to p'' … etc. down to p^*, while the output rises to q'' etc. to finally reach $\bar{q}$. (The opposite process of a fall in price from p^* to p_1 followed by a rise *to* p_2 etc., up to p^*, is also depicted for the case of an unexpected lasting fall in demand from *d'd'* to *dd*.)

No *necessity* can evidently emerge, either here or in classical theory, of the cycles around the normal price envisaged by Lippi. The reason of these different results is simple. It is that Lippi's mathematical model has put together the output increases of the *second* stage of adjustment and the price increases of the first, ignoring the temporary equality between demand and supply that separates the two stages. This has been done by *assuming* that prices continue to rise until output reaches effectual demand. Indeed in his equation [4] p. 6, Lippi supposes that the (relative) price p_t of the commodity will *continue to rise,* so long as (relative) output Q_t is below the quantity required to produce the output Q_{t+1} of the following period, the two becoming equal only when both will equal the effectual demand Q^*.[47] No trace then in Lippi's equations of the temporary demand-and-supply equality which closes the first stage of the adjustment and the associated temporary phenomena.

Lippi however comments as follows on a Ricardo passage (Ricardo [1821] 1951, 119) describing the usual Smithian gravitation of the market price back to the natural price after a rise of effectual demand and price:

---

[47] For what interests us here it would make no difference if, in Lippi's equation [4], Q^* appeared directly, replacing the quantity demanded in order to produce Q_{t+1} and thus cutting through the 'feedbacks' of outputs on demand.

> Ricardo's statement does not appear to contain any immediately apparent mistake. Nonetheless, it must be pointed out that: (i) while Q_t rises between some point [and another] to the [left of the level of effectual demand] the simultaneous rise of P_t is not mentioned; (ii) while P_t falls, between some point [and another] to the right of [the level of effectual demand] the simultaneous rise of Q_t is not mentioned. Thus, one has the impression that Ricardo's firm belief in convergence relies on his inability to keep under control the feedback determination of quantities and prices, or perhaps on taking the two directions of causation one at a time. Firstly high price causes quantity ratio to rise, but price ratio rises as well.[48] Subsequently, price falls and equilibrium is reached; by contrast, quantity ratio rises *at the some time,* and equilibrium, if reached, can only occur as the limit of an oscillatory process (1990, 64).

However Ricardo (and Marshall) realised so well the 'feedbacks' price-quantity that they explained the fading price of their second stage, by the increasing output of that stage. Hence comes the fact noted by Lippi that while the 'quantity rises between some point [and another] to the [left of the point of effectual demand] the simultaneous rise of [the price] is not mentioned' by Ricardo: that rise is not mentioned because there is a *fall* and not a *rise* of the price, and there is a fall just because of the 'feedback' of the increasing output. That 'feedback' is indeed the same which Lippi places to the *right*, and not the *left*, of the level of effectual demand (which is what under (ii) Lippi then reproaches Ricardo for not doing).

The difference between the two arguments is thus due to the *different feedbacks* assumed, and not to 'Ricardo's inability to keep under control the feedback determination etc.'. It seems then that 'Ricardo's firm belief in convergence' is a result of his keeping a *correct* control of 'the feedback determination etc.' in its normal form and that it is Lippi's opposite belief which instead contemplates a very special case—that for which, in our previous example, a rise of the effectual demand for *coal* would cause a *continued rise of coal prices* over all the years before the new mines are in production. When therefore in the conclusion of his article Lippi writes

> once … we understand that the working of the system is more complicated than in the näive classical representation … we should no longer be committed to the idea that market prices must converge (1990, p. 65),

it seems natural to observe that a naivety may also lie, at times, in a modern excessive trust on mathematical treatments requiring assumptions which are too simple to adequately represent the complications of the economic system.

[48] Thus the 'feedbacks' which Lippi accuses Ricardo of ignoring would seem to consist of the interactions between prices and quantities, and not the feedback of outputs on the demand for the commodity because of its use in production—a feedback present in Lippi's model. However, as implied in n. 47 above, consideration of that feedback would not alter our conclusions: the fact that coal is used to produce coal does not entail that the price of coal will have to continue to rise until new mines come to be exploited.

References

Ciccone, R. (1990). 'Short-run Prices in Classical and Neoclassical Analysis', unpublished paper presented at the Workshop on Convergence to Long-period Positions, Siena, 5–7 April, 1990 [*editor's note*: later published as 'Classical and neoclassical short-run prices: a comparative analysis of their intended empirical content' in G. Mongiovi and F. Petri (Eds.), *Value, Distribution and Capital. Essays in Honour of Pierangelo Garegnani* (pp. 69–92). Routledge, 1999].

Garegnani, P. (1987). Surplus Approach to Value and Distribution. In J. Eatwell, M. Milgate, & P. Newman (Eds.), *The New Palgrave: A Dictionary of Economics* (Vol. 4, pp. 560–574). Macmillan.

Garegnani, P. (1990). Quantity of Capital. In J. Eatwell, M. Milgate, & P. Newman (Eds.), *Capital Theory* (pp. 1–78). Macmillan.

Lippi, M. (1990). Production Prices and Dynamic Stability: Comment on Boggio. *Political Economy,* 6(1–2), pp. 59–68 [available online at http://www.centrosraffa.org/pe/6,1-2/6,1-2.5.%20Boggio.pdf]

Marshall, A. ([1920] 1961), *Principles of Economics*, 9th (Variorum) ed., Vol. I. Macmillan.

Nikaido, H. (1985). Dynamics of Growth and Capital Mobility in Marx's Scheme of Reproduction. *Zeitschrift f r National konomie, Journal of Economics,* 45(3), 197–218.

Ricardo, D. ([1821] 1951), *On the Principles of Political Economy and Taxation,* in *The Works and Correspondence of David Ricardo,* ed. by P. Sraffa with the collaboration of M. H. Dobb, Vol. I. Cambridge University Press.

Samuelson, P. A. (1980). *Economics*. McGraw Hill.

Smith, A. ([1776] 1910), *The Wealth of Nations,* Vol. I. Dent and Sons.

Sraffa, P. (1960). *Production of Commodities by Means of Commodities*. Cambridge University Press.

Steedman, I. (1984). Natural Prices, Differential Profit Rates and the Classical Competitive Process. *Manchester School,* 52(2), pp. 123–140.

Part IV
The Classical Approach: Aggregate Demand

Notes on Consumption, Investment and Effective Demand: I[†*]

The purpose of these Notes is to reconsider the theoretical problems raised by the question of the long-run influence of consumption on investment.

Current economic theory does not appear to provide a generally accepted answer to this question: its position on the issue is ambiguous and contradictory. Pre-Keynesian theory gave a simple answer: the level of investment is determined by the community's decisions to save, allowance always being made for frictions not dissimilar to those admitted in other parts of economic theory. In order to obtain a larger volume of investment, consumption should be discouraged. The criticism by Keynes has shown the weakness of this traditional answer. But while Keynes's different conclusions have been generally accepted for the analysis of trade cycles and other short-period phenomena, the theoretical situation remains uncertain with respect to the long period, which is our primary concern here. With

[†] Previously published in the *Cambridge Journal of Economics*, 2(4), 1978. All necessary permissions acquired.

[*] These notes are an abridged version of a paper first published in Italian in *Economia Internazionale*, 1964 and 1965. The translation has been prepared by Jan Kregel, Ian Steedman and the present author. The original paper was itself taken from the theoretical part of a study conducted in 1961 for the 'Associazione per lo Sviluppo deI Mezzogiorno' (SVIMEZ). The subject of that study was the relationship between consumption and investment in the Italian economy. The theoretical part included, besides the material of this article, an analysis of how the independence of investment from the capacity to save may assert itself in the course of a process of accumulation. This was done with particular regard to economies with a large reserve of labour which either is unemployed or utilises traditional methods of production. The theoretical part was followed by an empirical part in which a comparison between unutilised capacity and the additional outputs required, directly and indirectly, by hypothetical additional investment (for 1955–60), specified in volume and composition, seemed to suggest that the limit to investment in Italy in that period was set by the incentive to invest and not by the level of consumption, contrary to what was then often argued. The results of the study are available as a mimeographed volume from SVIMEZ (via di Porta Pinciana, 6, Rome), which I thank for permission to publish the part contained in these Notes. I also wish to thank Claudio Napoleoni, Sergio Steve, Paolo Sylos-Labini and Volrico Travaglini for their comments on the manuscripts of this work.

P. Garegnani, *Capital Theory, the Surplus Approach, and Effective Demand*,
Springer Studies in the History of Economic Thought,
https://doi.org/10.1007/978-3-031-23643-3_10

respect to long-period analysis some discussions of Keynes's theory, conducted on the assumption of flexible wages and prices—or, more realistically, on the assumption of a flexible monetary policy—have, in fact, created a climate of professional opinion by no means hostile to a reaffirmation, in less rigid terms, of the traditional theory—though they have not succeeded in restoring to that theory the confidence it once enjoyed.

Our consideration of the problem has seemed useful because the terms in which the question has been discussed so far may be significantly modified, in the present writer's view, by the recent criticisms of the notion of 'capital' as a factor of production.

The traditional doctrine, in which planned investment adjusts to planned savings, appears to be centred on the idea of an investment demand function elastic with respect to the rate of interest. This idea has not been disputed in the course of the Keynesian controversy, at least with respect to long-run conditions. Keynes himself adopted it in the form of the 'marginal efficiency of capital' and focused his criticism on the notion that the rate of interest would be flexible enough to be the equilibrator of saving and investment decisions. This particular course, followed by the Keynesian controversy, is important, we believe, for an explanation of the present theoretical uncertainty concerning problems of capital accumulation. The notion of a demand function for investible resources has, in fact, provided the main basis for attempts to confine to short-period conditions the obstacles which impede the equilibrating role of the rate of interest and has thus favoured the persistence, in part of the literature, of a confidence in the traditional theory of accumulation.

We shall argue in these Notes that this notion of an interest-elastic investment demand function has its basis in the conception of capital as a factor employable in production in proportions which will increase, relative to other factors, as the rate of interest decreases. It follows that the recent criticism of this conception of capital has an important bearing on the question of the influence of consumption on investment. We shall indeed argue that such criticism provides a firmer ground for the rejection of the long-period dependence of investment on decisions to save.

These Notes will consist of two parts. In Part I we shall investigate the premises from which traditional theory derived the assertion that there exists a tendency for effective demand to adapt to productive capacity. We shall see in section 1 how this is the question which lies behind the problem of the relation between consumption and investment. The analysis will begin, in section 2, by distinguishing between two theoretical approaches which Keynes included in what he called the 'classical school': that of Ricardo and the 'classical school' proper, on the one hand, and, on the other, that of the later marginalist theories to which Keynes was in fact referring. In Sects. 3–6 we shall then proceed to argue that it is in these latter theories only that we can find premises supporting the traditional thesis. In Sect. 7 we shall then discuss the validity of these premises, and conclude that, even if we remain within the limits of an analysis conducted in 'real' and 'static' terms—abstracting, that is, from the obstacles which the monetary system and the state of expectations may raise for an equilibrating process—economic theory does not seem to provide a sufficient basis for the idea that market forces can ensure the adjustment of decisions to invest to decisions to save in the long period.

In Part II the question will be taken up in the context of monetary theory, within which Keynes conducted his criticism of traditional theory. We shall then examine the subsequent attempts to support the traditional doctrine by means of an analysis founded on the hypothesis of flexible money wages or, alternatively, a flexible monetary policy. We shall seek to show that these attempts rest crucially on the hypothesis of a high interest elasticity of investment. At this point we shall refer back to the results of the analysis in 'real' terms conducted in Part I and conclude that even in long periods and in normal situations, investment will be independent of saving decisions, at least below the limit set by the community's saving in conditions of full utilisation of productive capacity and constancy of the level of prices.

Part I: 'Real' Analysis

1. The Tendency to a Full Utilisation of Productive Capacity

As is well known, the position of traditional theory on the relation between consumption and investment derives from the idea that the aggregate demand for output tends to the level which ensures the full utilisation of the available productive capacity. Let us in fact assume a rise in the relevant part of the curve representing the community's propensity to consume. If productive capacity always tended to be fully utilised, the increased output of consumption goods could only be obtained by decreasing the output of capital goods, i.e. by decreasing investment.[††] A closed economy will be assumed; we shall also abstract from all state economic activity other than monetary policy. Traditional theories did not, of course, ignore the possibility of 'frictions' capable of delaying the achievement of full utilisation of productive capacity; it was in terms of these 'frictions' that trade cycles were explained. But this admission did not alter the conclusion that the volume of investment, taken as an average over a normal succession of periods of prosperity and depression, would be determined by the community's decisions to save.

However, when we admit, as Keynes did, the possibility of equilibria with partial utilisation of productive capacity, the traditional thesis can no longer be maintained. An upward shift of the schedule of the propensity to consume might in fact result in an increased utilisation of productive capacity and might therefore result in a constant, or even an increased, volume of investment. The question of the effect on investment thus remains open: investment might decrease if production is

---

[†] A closed economy will be assumed; we shall also abstract from all state economic activity other than monetary policy.

close to the limit of productive capacity, but the opposite effect is also possible—and indeed probable if there are margins of unutilised productive capacity, whether they be large or small.

In the following sections we shall examine the premises from which traditional theory derived the doctrine that market forces lead to the full utilisation of productive capacity. Before proceeding to this examination, however, an observation must be made. By productive capacity we have so far meant the equipment of capital goods[‡] in existence in the economy in a given situation, together with only that part of the total supply of labour which is required for the full utilisation of this equipment. By this definition we have departed from the terms in which the controversy between Keynes and traditional theory was conducted. It was there assumed that a full utilisation of the existing capital equipment would allow for the employment of the entire labour force.

The more general notion of productive capacity we have so far used would seem to be the appropriate one in discussing long period tendencies, where unemployment of labour from below-capacity utilisation of equipment may itself generate so-called 'structural' unemployment unless it is quickly corrected; indeed this notion of capacity has been that on which the traditional thesis of the alternative between consumption and investment had to be based in order to apply it to economies with 'structural unemployment'. A difficulty however would be raised by using the general notion in the rest of this paper, for the assumptions by which such 'structural' unemployment has been reconciled with traditional theory (i.e., fundamentally, the existence of circumstances imposing a real wage higher than that which competition would enforce, and the lack of a sufficient variability in the proportions between capital and labour) would interfere with an examination of the Keynesian controversy in its own terms. We have accordingly decided to separate the two issues: our examination of the Keynesian controversy will be carried out under the assumption that existing equipment suffices to employ the entire supply of labour, whereas the applicability of our conclusions to an economy with 'structural' unemployment will be considered later, at the end of Part II of these Notes.

2. Ricardo and 'Say's Law'

As soon as we consider the question of the premises from which the traditional theories drew the conclusion about the tendency to 'full employment', it becomes necessary to distinguish clearly between the two types of theories which Keynes included in what he called the 'classical school'. According to Keynes that school included Ricardo and 'the *followers* of Ricardo … who adopted and perfected the theory of the Ricardian economics, including (for example) J. S. Mill, Marshall,

[‡] As usual, productive equipment is assumed to be appropriate to the composition of aggregate demand at its full employment level, so as to abstract from problems of disproportions among industries. In what follows the concept of 'productive equipment' will refer only to fixed capital goods; it may be supposed that circulating capital (stocks and goods in process) can adapt rapidly to changes in the level of activity.

Edgeworth and Professor Pigou' (Keynes, 1936, p. 3n). Now, the theory of Ricardo, on the one hand, and the theories of Marshall and Pigou (and more generally the theories developed in the last quarter of the past century), on the other, differ radically on the principle of full employment. While this is not the place to deal with the question at all exhaustively, we have to consider it because we shall find that we must confine our attention to the second group of theories alone.

Apart from Marshall's tendency to present his own doctrines as a continuation of Ricardian theory, what more specifically led Keynes to identify Ricardo's position with that of Marshall and Pigou in this respect, was a particular interpretation of the famous controversy between Ricardo and Malthus on the possibility of a 'general glut of commodities'. On closer examination, this interpretation appears to have been seriously misleading.

Malthus held that an accumulation of capital at the expense of 'unproductive consumption' (the consumption of classes other than the workers) would cause a rapid fall of the rate of profit and would thus eliminate the incentive to further accumulation. This fall would result from the decrease in prices due to the difficulty of finding outlets for the increased production. In Malthus's words:

> under a rapid accumulation of capital … the demand, compared with the supply of material products, would prematurely fail, and the motive to further accumulation be checked … It follows that … it is necessary that a country with great powers of production should possess a body of consumers who are not themselves engaged in production (Malthus, 1836, p. 398).

Ricardo, for his part, rejected the idea that accumulation would be limited by a lack of outlets for the increasing output, asserting that 'demand is only limited by production' (Ricardo, [1821] 1951a, p. 290).

The question under discussion between Malthus and Ricardo thus exhibits undoubted similarities with that which was under discussion, more than a century later, between Keynes and Pigou. These similarities may be expressed by saying that Malthus, like Keynes (and numerous authors who were Malthus's contemporaries or predecessors), recognised the possibility that demand could set a limit to aggregate production, whereas Ricardo, like the 'orthodox' contemporaries of Keynes, denied that possibility. But it would be an error to move from acknowledging a similarity in the *question* under discussion to asserting a similarity in the *analysis* of that question. In particular, it would be an error to attribute to Malthus and Ricardo something akin to the theoretical core of the controversy between Keynes and the orthodox economists, i.e. the question whether the rate of interest can ensure that decisions to invest will adjust to decisions to save.†

† Keynes advanced this interpretation in his essay on Malthus written in 1933: see in particular the phrases 'Malthus's complete comprehension of the effects of excess saving on output' (Keynes, 1933, p. 118); or 'The whole problem of the balance between Saving and Investment had been posed in the Preface [to the *Principles* of Malthus]' (p. 122). This interpretation is again taken up in the *General Theory*, where Ricardo is considered as the originator of the 'classical theory' and, in particular, of the 'classical theory of interest' (Keynes, 1936, Ch. 14, especially pp. 190–192). This interpretation, which remains flexible in Keynes, becomes more rigid in some Keynesian literature (cf., e.g., Klein, 1950, pp. 125–130).

The most evident deficiency of such an attribution is that both Malthus and Ricardo always identified decisions to save with decisions to invest‡: there could therefore be no disagreement between them concerning the existence of factors capable of equilibrating decisions to invest and decisions to save. In Ricardo and Malthus, as in Smith before them, the question of a possible divergence between the two magnitudes had not been posed. They took it as a *fact* that anyone who had saved would have used his savings to employ productive labourers, or would have lent it to others who would have so used it.§

When we consider the position of the classical economists in this light, it should not come as a surprise that we cannot find in Ricardo the idea that the rate of interest would be the 'balancing factor which brings the demand for saving in the shape of new investment ... into equality with the supply of saving' (Keynes, 1936, p. 165), which Keynes attributed to the 'classical school'. The rate of interest appears in Ricardo only as a phenomenon subordinate to the rate of profits and governed by the latter. No particular role is attributed to it, apart from that of distributing profits between those who lend money and those who bear the 'risk and trouble' of employing capital in production (see, for example, Ricardo, [1821] 1951a, pp. 296–298 and 363–364).

It seems that a more correct interpretation of the controversy between Ricardo and Malthus should begin by recognising that the question under discussion concerned the circumstances determining the rate of profits. Ricardo's theory of profits was being advanced against the vaguer dominant theory, which had its origins in Adam Smith and which Malthus adopted with some particular emphasis. Smith had asserted:

> When the stocks of many rich merchants are turned into the same trade, their mutual competition naturally tends to lower its profit; and when there is a like increase of stock in all the different trades carried on in the same society, the same competition must produce the same effect in them all (Smith, [1776] 1904, Bk. I, Ch. IX, p. 89; cf. also Bk. II, Ch. V, pp. 352–353)

thus seeming to suppose that the limit which the market poses to the expansion of output in a single industry also exists for the expansion of aggregate output. It was from this theory of Smith that Malthus started in his defence, against Ricardo, of 'unproductive' consumption which, he argued, was essential in order to give a

‡ See, e.g., Malthus's acceptance of Ricardo's assertion that an increase of £10,000 in the income of an individual would bring about an increase in the demand for commodities of the same value, whether this increase were saved or consumed (Malthus, 1836, pp. 322–323). The fact that Malthus, like the other classical economists, tended to identify savings and investment, has been noted by R. L. Meek (1950–51), p. 156, n. 2; Robbins (1958), p. 248 and Schumpeter (1954), p. 641, n. 41, and has been used by Corry (1959) for a more general criticism of the prevailing idea that Malthus was a precursor of Keynes.

§ Nor can we find in these authors an analysis of the possible changes in the intervals of time elapsing between the acts of purchase and sale; an analysis which would have led, by another route, to the admission of a possible divergence between planned savings and investment as they are defined today. A few decades after Ricardo's ***Principles***, this kind of analysis brought Marx to reject 'Say's law' and the Ricardian position on the subject (cf., e.g., Marx, 1969, pp. 493–499).

profitable outlet to production. In his words, unproductive consumption constituted 'a means of increasing the exchangeable value of the whole produce' and hence the rate of profits (Malthus, 1836, p. 398).

Ricardo opposed these views on profits (see Sraffa's introduction to Ricardo ([1821] 1951a), pp. xxxi–xxxiii). Arguing from the premise that, in the long run, the wage would be determined by the level of subsistence, he drew the logically consistent conclusion that the rate of profits could fall in the process of accumulation only as a result of the diminished productivity of the labour employed, on progressively less fertile lands, to produce the subsistence of an increasing population (Ricardo, 1951a, p. 292). No room was left for any permanent influence of demand on profits. Smith's argument concerning the influence of 'competition' on the rate of profits, on the other hand, consisted simply of an illegitimate extension, to an increase of aggregate output, of a proposition applicable to an increase in the output of a particular commodity. In the case of a single commodity, a part of the income generated by the additional production will be used for buying other commodities and will therefore not be available for absorbing the increased output of the commodity at an unchanged price. But this is clearly not so when a simultaneous expansion of all outputs occurs in the appropriate proportions. Since Malthus appears to have failed to add anything clear and consistent to Smith's argument,[†] their ideas on profits must have appeared to Ricardo to be the result of overlooking the necessary connection between production and income. Since Ricardo identified decisions to save with decisions to invest, to recognise the connection between production and income was the same as admitting Say's principle, that 'demand is only limited by production'.[‡]

It therefore seems possible to conclude that in Ricardo 'Say's law' was not the result of an analysis of the investment-saving process but rather the result of the *lack* of any such analysis.

[†] In Malthus's *Principles* (1st ed., 1820) it is stated that the productivity of labour on the least fertile land under cultivation does not determine the rate of profits, but only establishes a maximum above which profits cannot rise. Below this limit profits would be determined by the circumstances to which Malthus variously refers as 'principles of competition', 'principles of demand and supply', 'demand' sometimes specified by the adjectives 'effectual' or 'effective', etc. (Malthus, 1836, Ch. V). Malthus expressly refers to Smith for his ideas on the subject: 'We can know little of the laws which determine profits, unless, ... [we] have recourse to that very principle of competition brought forward by Adam Smith, which Mr Ricardo expressly rejects...' (Ricardo, 1951b, p. 269).

[‡] The question is dealt with in Ch. XXI of the *Principles*, in the form of a criticism of Smith's theory (cf. in particular pp. 289–296). Also in the 3rd edition of the *Principles* (1821), published after Malthus's *Principles*, Ricardo does not explicitly refer to Malthus's ideas on the subject. He seems to have thought that the criticism of Smith in Ch. XXI was sufficient. In his letters to Malthus and in his *Notes on Malthus* (1820), his arguments keep close to those of Ch. XXI, except when Malthus's ambiguities lead him to believe that Malthus's statements might coincide with his own (cf. Ricardo, 1951b, p. 311, n. 201).

It would perhaps be possible to go further and assert that, in this respect, Ricardo's theory of distribution is *open*, in the sense that it *neither* provides premises capable of justifying the tendency of investment to adjust to saving, *nor* depends on the existence of such a tendency.[§] This 'open' character sharply distinguishes the Ricardian theory from the subsequent marginalist theories, which saw distribution as the result of forces of demand for and supply of 'factors of production'. As we shall argue presently, these theories provide the premises from which the role of the rate of interest as the equilibrator of decisions to invest and decisions to save was originally derived. At the same time, by determining distribution in terms of the equality between demand for and supply of factors of production, these theories depend for their validity on the absence of any long-run limits to aggregate production stemming from demand.

The absence from Ricardo's work of the notion of demands for the factors, elastic with respect to their prices, deserves to be stressed here, because it makes clear how little Keynes's 'Classical school' has in common with Ricardo. We have seen that the 'Classical' proposition criticised by Keynes concerned the existence of forces leading to the full employment of labour. But 'Say's law' did not lead Ricardo to any such proposition; it only led him to deny that demand could prevent the system from achieving that level of employment which was compatible with past accumulation, whether this level allowed for the employment of the entire labour force or only a part of it. Thus Ricardo admitted the possibility of the unemployment of labour and thought that it could only be eliminated by further accumulation of capital, or by a decrease in the population. Lower wage rates could therefore reduce unemployment only through higher profits and faster accumulation, or through a slower increase of population—and not, as marginalist theories were later to maintain, by causing such changes in the methods of production, or in the relative outputs of consumption goods, as would permit the employment of the entire labour force with an unchanged 'quantity of capital'.[†]

[§] Thus Marx had no difficulty in rejecting 'Say's law' while sharing the basic elements of Ricardo's theory of value and distribution (cf. n. §, p. 392 above). The Ricardian theory of distribution, while it excludes the possibility of permanent effects of aggregate demand on the rate of profits, is not incompatible with effects of that demand on aggregate output or the speed of accumulation.

[†] Of the numerous relevant passages of the *Principles*, the following, which summarises the conclusion of his famous ch. XXXI 'On Machinery', may suffice here: 'the discovery and use of machinery may be attended with a diminution of gross produce; and whenever that is the case, it will be injurious to the labouring class, as some of their number will be thrown out of employment, and population will become redundant, compared with the funds which are to employ it' and, a few lines above, 'But with every *increase* of capital he would employ more labourers; and, therefore, a portion of the people thrown out of work in the first instance, would be subsequently employed' (Ricardo, [1821] 1951a, p. 390; our italics). An interesting expression of the contrast between the Ricardian and the marginalist theories on the employment of labour is provided by Wicksell's criticism of Ricardo's thesis on the effects of the introduction of machinery. Wicksell argues that production will not decrease because 'as soon as a number of labourers have been made superfluous by these changes, and wages have accordingly fallen, then, as Ricardo failed to see, [other] methods of production … will become more profitable...and absorb the surplus of idle labourers' (Wicksell, 1934, p. 137).

3. The Marginalist Theories

The search for premises capable of supporting the principle of a tendency to full utilisation of productive capacity must therefore turn to the theories developed in the final quarter of the last century around the twin concepts of marginal utility and marginal productivity. These theories determine the relative prices of commodities and the distribution of the social product by means of three groups of data: (a) consumers' preferences; (b) technical conditions of production; (c) the quantities of 'factors of production' available in the community. In equilibrium the relative prices of the commodities and of the services of factors of production would be such that the quantities of commodities demanded would be equal to the quantities produced and, at the same time, the quantities of factors' services required in production would be equal to the respective quantities supplied.‡ It is in *this* equality between demand for and supply of factors' services—and not in Ricardo's theory—that we find Keynes's 'classical' principle of the tendency to 'full employment' of labour and other factors.

The premises from which the marginalist authors derived—or, in Keynes's opinion, believed they could derive—the principle of a tendency to the full employment of factors are well known. They can be traced back to a particular conception of the social process of production. In this conception the elements required for production are treated as 'factors of production' which can be employed in the economic system in proportions which vary as the relative prices of their services vary. This is, in turn, the result of two characteristics of the economic system as envisaged in the marginalist theories. On the one hand, we have the 'substitutability' in consumption between goods which will generally require different proportions of the factors for their production. On the other hand we have, for any given level of technical knowledge, the possibility of producing any commodity with different proportions of the same factors; under the assumption of continuous variability of factor proportions, this leads to the well known conditions of profit maximisation in terms of the 'marginal products' of the factors. By either route we arrive at an inverse relation between the price of the service of the factor and the quantity in which the factor would be employed in equilibrium, given the quantities employed of the other factors.†

‡ This is true under the assumption that the factor is scarce, i.e. that the quantity available does not exceed the quantity which entrepreneurs would demand at a price of zero.

† The changes in the distribution of the social product which correspond to changes of the relative prices of productive services may themselves influence the quantities of the services demanded. Thus, a preference by workers for labour-intensive goods would tend to decrease the quantity of labour demanded as the wage decreases, and would therefore act in a direction contrary to the 'substitution effect' considered in the text. We have, however, ignored, here and elsewhere in the text, the circumstances which may cause an instability of the (non-monetary) equilibrium of exchange and production: we have therefore supposed that, as is usually assumed, such causes of instability do not generally raise serious difficulties in factor markets (cf. Hicks, 1946, p. 104).

The way is then open for a second proposition according to which competition among the owners of a factor will modify the price of its service until the entire supply will be employed. With this second proposition, the inverse relation between the employment of a factor and the price of its service can be legitimately envisaged as a 'demand function' which, in conjunction with a 'supply function' of the same service, will give rise to the competitive tendency to an 'equilibrium' between such demand and supply.

The reasoning leading to a negatively elastic demand for the factor was conducted on the assumption that the quantity employed of the other factors remained constant, or more generally, remained equal to their supply (assumed not to fall drastically as their remuneration rises). But this assumption can now be seen to have been justified, for the same process which is at work in the market for the variable factor, assuming an equality between the quantity demanded and supplied of the other factors, will be at work in the market for the latter factors and will secure that very equality.

These, in summary, were the forces which would lead the economic system towards the full employment of all factors. Thus Pigou in his *Theory of Unemployment*, to which Keynes would later refer as his primary example of the 'classical' analysis, stated, not without reference to the unemployment afflicting England in the period between the wars, that

> [w]ith perfectly free competition among workpeople and labour perfectly mobile ... [t]here will always be at work a strong tendency for wage-rates to be so related to demand that everybody is employed (Pigou, 1933, p. 252).

The basis of this statement was fundamentally an application to labour, and to short-period conditions, of the basic argument that the quantities demanded and supplied of the factors would tend to equality by means of changes in the relative prices of their services.

4. Savings, Investment and the Marginalist Theory of Interest

But were the above premises regarding the productive process in fact adequate for the derivation of a tendency of the economic system to the full employment of labour and of the other productive resources ? As is well known, Keynes denied this.

In the *General Theory* he starts from an examination of the idea that changes in the wage rate would lead to full employment and he distinguishes two 'postulates'. He accepts the first, according to which the wage must be equal to the marginal product of labour, *given the level of employment.* In doing so, he accepts the conception of the productive process found in traditional theory. However, he rejects the second 'postulate', which states that '[t]he utility of the wage when a given volume of labour is employed is equal to the marginal disutility of that amount of employment' (Keynes, 1936, p. 5). Market forces, that is, would not succeed in equalising the quantity demanded and supplied of labour.

The argument which Keynes uses to deny that the flexibility of the wage would lead to the full employment of labour is founded on the premise that market forces cannot ensure that investment will adjust to savings. Given that premise, one must conclude that decreases in the money wage rate—the only wage rate on which the competition of unemployed workers can act directly—cannot ensure a tendency to the full employment of labour. In fact, if entrepreneurs reacted to the decrease in wages by increasing employment, the level of real national income would rise and savings would then exceed investment.† Since the latter would not adjust to the former, aggregate demand would be insufficient to absorb the increased production at its 'supply price' and output would be decreased. Indeed, if the fall of money wages should leave the level of investment unaffected, the employment of labour would have to return to its previous level, the only one at which saving is in equilibrium with investment. The only effect of the fall of the money wage would be a proportionate fall of the price level, leaving both the real wage and the amount of employment unchanged.

A detailed consideration of Keynes's position on the effects of a fall in wages must be postponed until Part II of these Notes. We have referred to the problem here only in order to bring to light the conclusion that the marginalist notion of a demand for labour elastic with respect to the real wage rate does not suffice to support the conclusion that competition among workers will lead to full employment. The *further* condition that investment adjusts to the changes in savings consequent on changes in employment is also required.

This second condition, concerning the dependence of investment on saving, is that which was referred to above when we discussed Ricardo and Malthus. The marginalist context is, however, very different from that of those authors. The identification of decisions to save with decisions to invest, which explained Ricardo's acceptance of 'Say's law', is not to be found here. Instead we find the theory that the rate of interest is 'the factor which brings the demand for investment and the willingness to save into equilibrium with one another' [Keynes (1936), p. 175].

Keynes's tendency in the *General Theory* was to consider this theory of interest as a further, unwarranted hypothesis that marginalist authors had introduced alongside the valid hypothesis concerning the variability of the proportions of factors of production in the productive process. It appears, however, that the theory of interest is in fact strictly dependent on those marginalist hypotheses.

In order to clarify this dependence, it is convenient to start by distinguishing two propositions in that theory of interest. The first concerns the possibility of establishing an inverse relation between the volume of planned investment and the

† The concepts of national income, investment and saving used in the text are the generally accepted ones of gross national income, investment and saving. With regard to the well known ambiguity implicit in the use of the terms 'investment' and 'saving', it is sufficient to recall here that, while *realised* investment and saving are equal by definition, investment and saving may differ when we consider the quantities that would result from individual decisions *under hypothetical circumstances*, e.g. the amount of saving at a given level of real income, distributed in a *given* way, with a *given* system of relative prices, etc. The expressions 'decisions to invest' and 'decisions to save' or, alternatively, 'planned investment' and 'planned savings', will be used in the text to indicate investment and saving in this second sense.

rate of interest. The second proposition concerns the possibility of supposing that the interest rate is sufficiently sensitive to divergences between investment decisions and full employment saving to ensure its equilibrating role.

It is to the first of these two propositions that we must now turn our attention. The proposition is essential to the traditional theory, particularly when we admit, as is generally done, that, given the level of real national income, the dependence of decisions to save on the rate of interest is uncertain in both direction and intensity. If we could not suppose that—on average and under normal conditions—a decrease in the rate of interest would bring about an increase in the volume of investment, we could not suppose that there would be a rate of interest at which planned investment would be equal to full employment saving. No ground would then be left for the second proposition above (on which Keynes was to focus his criticism), concerning the tendency of the rate of interest toward such an 'equilibrium level'.

It is in this relationship between the rate of interest and planned investment that the dependence of the traditional theory of interest on marginalist premises is most clearly manifest. To understand this dependence it will first be necessary to consider why, and in what way, marginalist theorists have to introduce a special 'factor of production'—capital—conceived as the value of the capital goods used in production.

5. Capital as a Factor of Production and the Demand Function for Investible Resources

We have seen how the marginalist theory of distribution hinges on the notion of factors of production which may be employed in variable proportions in the economic system. Capital goods have to find a place among these factors. However, the application to capital goods of the notion of a factor, or factors, of production raises special problems. Capital goods, like other produced goods, have values which tend to equality with their supply prices. But free competition entails that the share of national income attributed to the owners of such goods, over and above what is necessary for their replacement, tends to be distributed in proportion to the value of those goods, so as to give rise to a uniform rate of return on all kinds of capital goods. If we consider this uniform rate of return from the viewpoint of these theories, in which each rate of remuneration is the price of the service of a factor of production, the various capital goods will *ultimately* have to appear as quantities, measured by their values, of a single factor of production, 'capital'. The net rate of return on capital goods, or rate of interest on 'capital', will then have to be determined by *ultimately* referring, in the forms considered below, to the conditions of demand and supply of this special factor.

We have so far identified a factor of production, 'capital', conceived as an amount of value which may assume the form of the specific capital goods appropriate to the situations considered. But, as an amount of value, 'capital' is not defined until we have specified the standard in which that value is to be measured.[†] Beneath the variety and, at times, the vagueness of the indications given in this respect by the marginalist theorists, there lies a common idea. The capital goods, and hence the quantity of capital they represent, result from investment; since investment is seen as the demand for savings, 'capital' emerges as something which is homogeneous with saving. Its natural unit is therefore the same as we would use for saving, i.e. some composite unit of consumption goods capable of measuring the subjective satisfactions from which (according to these theorists) consumers abstain when they save. 'Capital' thus appears as past savings which are, so to speak, 'incorporated' in the capital goods existing at a given instant of time. As a result of the productive consumption of those goods, these past savings will periodically re-emerge in a 'free' form and can be re-incorporated in capital goods of the same or of different kinds; alternatively, they can be turned back into consumption.

Marginalist theorists then proceeded to apply the argument described in Sect. 3; this special factor, measured in value terms, now being included alongside the others.[|] In particular, they thought it possible to state that, given the quantities employed of the other factors, entrepreneurs would find it profitable to use a larger 'quantity of capital' the lower the rate of interest.

The application of this principle to the theory of distribution has taken two forms, which we shall now distinguish in order to show how either route leads to the idea of a demand function for investment elastic with respect to the rate of interest.

The first approach is that of authors like J. B. Clark, Böhm-Bawerk or Wicksell, who expressly aim at a general solution of the problem of distribution. These authors refer to an equilibrium situation in which the condition of a uniform net rate of return on the various capital goods is realised. Given this condition, it

---

[†] In the case of factors of production which can be measured in physical terms, the choice of the unit of measurement is unimportant because a change of unit only implies multiplying the quantities by a *constant*. However, this is no longer true in the case of capital and other value magnitudes since the relative values of the commodities constituting alternative standards of value will themselves be different in different situations (e.g. in the situations to which the different points of the demand function for a factor of production refer).

[|] Some marginalist theorists, such as J. B. Clark and, ultimately, also Marshall and his school, seem to have thought that the case in which a factor of production, 'capital', is conceived as an amount of value, could be treated similarly to that in which all factors are measurable in physical terms. A more interesting, indirect procedure was that adopted by theorists such as Böhm-Bawerk and Wicksell, who conceived of capital as a 'subsistence fund', used in order to 'advance' the remuneration to the 'original' factors of production (land and labour) during the time elapsing before completion of the consumption goods produced by them. In any given instant, this 'fund' would be 'embodied' in the capital goods, and it would be measured by their value in terms of consumption goods. As the rate of interest decreased (the wage increased), the 'time structure' of production was supposed to change so as to require a larger 'subsistence fund' in order to employ the same quantities of the 'original factors'. (Cf. the following footnote for Walras's still different approach.)

becomes impossible to take the physical capital stock, i.e. the available quantities of the various capital goods, as given.‡ The 'capital' incorporated in such goods, i.e. their value, has instead to be taken as given. Capital is thus allowed to change its 'form'—though not its quantity—in order to acquire the physical composition compatible with equilibrium conditions. The theory of distribution then follows along the lines already indicated in Sect. 3. It may be described in terms of the forces envisaged to be at work in the capital market. We shall have a *total* demand for capital, i.e. for capital *as a stock*, as distinguished from the demand for investment, i.e. for capital *as a flow*. This 'total' demand function gives the quantity of capital which the system would employ at the various rates of interest, assuming that the markets for products and for the other factors are all in the equilibrium corresponding to the rate of interest.† Given the amount of capital available, the rate of interest will be determined together with the rest of the system (cf. Clark, 1907, Ch. 9; Böhm-Bawerk, 1891; Wicksell, 1934).

We thus find a demand function for capital elastic with respect to the rate of interest, but we do not immediately find a demand function for *investment* elastic with respect to the rate of interest. The latter is, however, implied by the former or, more exactly, the former represents, in the form of a demand for a stock, a time sequence of demands for investment through which alone that stock-demand can be manifested and can determine the rate of interest. In any given instant the available 'capital' will not in fact be a 'fluid' which may quickly assume a form compatible with the conditions corresponding to any point of the demand function for capital. On the contrary, in any given instant 'capital' is incorporated in a given set of capital goods and it can only assume the appropriate physical form *over a*

‡ A demonstration of the inconsistency between a uniform rate of return on the supply price of capital goods and the treatment of the quantities of the various kinds of capital goods as data has been given by the present author (Garegnani, 1960, Parte II, Capp. II, III and Appendice G [see, in this volume, Part I, *A problem in the Theory of Distribution from Ricardo to Wicksell*, Sect. II, Chs. II, III and Appendix E]. The problem is there considered as a criticism of Walras's theory of distribution which suffers from this very inconsistency.

† Under more general assumptions, the demand function' for capital described in the text would result from the following procedure. We take as *data*: (a) the preferences of the consumers; (b) the techniques of production; (c) the available quantities of all factors except capital; (d) the criteria determining the distribution of ownership of capital goods (the quantities of which are among the unknowns of the equations) among the individuals; (e) the criteria determining the age distribution of fixed capital. For any level of the rate of *interest—the independent variable* in this system—the equations concerning the conditions of equilibrium in the markets for the products and for the factors *other than* capital will determine, in addition to the usual unknowns of a general equilibrium system, the physical quantities of the capital goods of the different kinds in use in the assumed equilibrium position. The prices of these capital goods being also determined by the equations, the quantity of capital employed in equilibrium for the given rate of interest can easily be obtained. By repeating this procedure for other rates of interest, we obtain the corresponding points of the demand function for capital. In short, we subtract from the usual equations of general equilibrium the one requiring equality between the quantity of capital employed and the quantity available; the degree of freedom which the system acquires permits the definition of the relationship between the quantity of capital employed and the rate of interest.

period of time during which most of the capital goods in existence are consumed and the available capital becomes 'free' to be reinvested in capital goods suitable for use with other techniques or in other productive sectors.

This relation between demand for capital as a stock and demand for investment can be seen in its most simple form if it is assumed that, in each industry, production takes place in an annual cycle and all capital is circulating capital (i.e. is entirely used up in the course of one year). If the wage rate and product prices are assumed to adapt without appreciable delay to the equilibrium compatible with the new rate of interest, the investment demand function at the end of each year will be nothing other than the demand function for capital as a stock. When there is fixed capital the analogous relation between demand for investment and demand for capital as a stock will be less simple but no less strict (see Appendix below).

The theory implies that such circumstances as delayed adjustments in the markets for labour and products, or irregularity in the age distribution of fixed capital, do not fundamentally alter the terms of the question. As a result, the interest elasticity of the sequence of demands for investment would reflect, on average, the elasticity of the demand for capital as a stock. Hence the significance of a demand for capital as a stock which exhibits, in a clear form, the basic tendencies which must emerge from the multiplicity of forces acting in any given moment of time.

By contrast, this multiplicity of forces is precisely what the second way of approaching the variability of the proportions between 'capital' and labour (and other factors) may seem to be dealing with. This second approach is that of Marshall and the tradition which he originated; it underlies both the controversy between Pigou and Keynes and the subsequent related literature. It is presented, less ambitiously, as a theory of the 'short period' and at times it seems that Marshall declines to claim it as a theory of distribution at all.† Unlike the version of Clark and Böhm-Bawerk, it appears to renounce the attempt to determine an equilibrium situation characterised by a uniform rate of return on the supply prices of the capital goods. It can thus avoid referring to the 'quantity of capital' available in the community as a given magnitude. Instead, it takes as given the productive equipment existing in the various industries, on which a 'quasi rent' is obtained, depending on the level of the wage and the demand for the products. The real wage, on the other hand, is determined by the relation between the supply of and the demand for labour, the latter depending on the available productive equipment. The rate of interest results, finally, from the equilibrium between the current demand for investible resources and the current supply of savings. It is here, in the analysis of the investment-savings market, that the notion of capital as an amount of value appears in this group of theories (cf. the distinction between 'quasi rent on an old investment of capital' and 'interest on free capital', Marshall, 1920, V, ix, 3; also VI, ii, 4; VI, vi, 6).

† In a well known passage coming after he has given an example to demonstrate why entrepreneurs will invest up to the point where the 'marginal product' of capital is equal to the rate of interest, Marshall says, 'But illustrations of this kind ... cannot be made into a theory of interest, any more than into a theory of wages, without reasoning in a circle' (Marshall, 1920, VI, I, 8).

Indeed, if we were to take literally the claims of these theories, and to confine ourselves to considering the capital goods as physically specified elements of a given productive equipment (modifiable only by means of current investment), it would be difficult to see how we could ever provide any theoretical basis for the notion, plausible as it may seem, of a demand function for investment elastic with respect to the rate of interest. We should be moving on the dubious ground of wages and prices determined according to a short-period analysis of the economy as a whole (for a critique of this particular group of theories, see Kaldor, 1955–56, pp. 90–91). In the course of such an analysis we would be faced by a multiplicity of factors, each of which may influence the demand for investment. We should thus have to take account of the disproportions between available equipment and the level of demand for products in each industry; the age structure of existing equipment and the connected irregular replacement requirements, etc.. Above all, the hypothesis of a given productive equipment, whose physical composition in each industry, and distribution among industries, has not adapted to the state of demand for products, would force us to attribute a decisive role to the expectations which the entrepreneurs entertain about future changes in relative prices, demands for products, wage rates and the general level of prices. The attempt to determine the effects on investment of changes in the rate of interest on such indefinite grounds would seem liable to dissolve into casuistry concerning the influence of these changes on the expectations of entrepreneurs. And this influence would differ from situation to situation, thus making impossible any general and unambiguous conclusions concerning direction and intensity of the effects of interest on investment. Moreover, consideration of the influence of the rate of interest on the decisions of entrepreneurs regarding the techniques to be adopted for the new plant, and the product to be obtained from it,[†] would not permit any conclusion to be drawn concerning the *amount* of investment involved, if the comparison between techniques and lines of production were conducted in terms of equipments defined in *physical* and not in *value* terms.

It is therefore evident that this cannot in fact be the basis on which the theories here described assert that 'the demand for the loan of capital ... obeys a law

[†] Numerous difficulties would be encountered in specifying this influence of the rate of interest. They would result from the short-period assumptions and the consequent indefiniteness of the effects which the rate of interest will have on real wages and the system of relative prices. On the other hand, with real wages and relative prices expected to remain constant, there is no reason why, assuming perfect competition and a fall in the rate of interest, the tendency to profit maximisation should lead entrepreneurs to change the techniques of production, rather than simply to expand the scale of production to profit from the gap between the rate of profits and the rate of interest. Under the assumptions of the theory, in fact, the individual producer always has the possibility of acquiring additional quantities of labour; the limit set by the available labour force can only influence the entrepreneur's decisions through increases in wages. More generally, investment decisions taken by the entrepreneurs in the expectation that the ruling rate of wages and the relative prices will remain unchanged could hardly be realised, since they would have to be revised as soon as the effects of the change in the rate of interest on prices and wages became perceptible.

similar to that which holds for the sale of commodities … When the price rises the amount that can be sold diminishes' (Marshall, 1920, VI, I, 8). It must then be supposed implicitly that the circumstances characteristic of the short period (the disproportions in the physical composition of the available equipment, and the influence of expectations) are classified with those to which Marshall referred as 'passing events … and causes whose action is fitful and short lived', so that over a sufficiently long period of time they 'efface one another's influence' and allow the 'persistent causes' to emerge. And these 'persistent causes', to which we are thus referred as the basis for an investment demand elastic with respect to the rate of interest, are ultimately the same as those analysed by the first group of theories: i.e. the substitution between factors (through both alternative techniques of production and consumers' choices) as a result of which a fall in the rate of interest would lead to an equilibrium position such that the proportion in which 'capital' (the value magnitude) is combined with other factors is larger (Marshall, 1920, V, III, 7). The different starting point—i.e. the physically specified equipment—and the apparent realism of the second group of theories appears to have obscured but not altered the basis on which the supposed inverse relation between investment and interest, essential for both groups of theories, must rest in the last analysis.

6. The Premises of Marginalist Theory and the Tendency to the Full Utilisation of Productive Resources

Our search for the premises of the traditional thesis that aggregate demand tends to adjust to the level of production thus seems to lead us to the marginalist conception of the process of production. This conception has, in effect, provided the theoretical basis for an inverse relation between the amount of investment and the rate of interest and hence for the first of the two propositions which we distinguished above (p. 398) in the traditional theory of interest.

That relation once admitted, the marginalist approach to the theory of distribution led naturally to the second step: to suppose a sensitivity of the rate of interest to a divergence between planned investment and planned savings sufficient to tend to eliminate that divergence. This step was in fact taken when the rate of interest was considered (sometimes more explicitly, sometimes less so) as the price for the service of 'capital', determined by the conditions of demand for and supply of that factor, simultaneously with the prices for the use of the other factors.[†]

[†] We may note, in this connection, the contrast which Keynes pointed out in these economists, between the general acceptance of the notion that the rate of interest is 'the factor which brings the demand for investment and the willingness to save into equilibrium with one another' and the difficulty of finding a treatment or even an explicit statement of the notion (cf. Keynes, 1936, pp. 175ff.). These authors rarely conducted a detailed analysis of the process by which savings are turned into increments of the capital stock; they derived their position on the question largely from the idea that the prices of the productive services are determined by the equilibrium between the respective quantities demanded and supplied (cf., e.g., Marshall, 1920, VI, ii, 4).

Since the *General Theory*, it has been widely recognised that this second step hid serious and perhaps decisive difficulties for the traditional theory of distribution. As Keynes showed, money in its role as a store of value may deprive the rate of interest of a sensitivity sufficient to adjust decisions to invest to decisions to save. A more powerful equilibrator between the two kinds of decisions can then act: variations in the level of employment of labour. And the controversy concerning the validity of the traditional thesis of the tendency to full employment has in fact been centred principally on problems related to the sensitivity of the rate of interest.

The basic idea of a demand function for investible resources has not been questioned, however. Nor is it surprising that criticism of the full employment thesis took this particular course. When, in the period between the two wars, the contrast between this thesis and the fact of large unemployment in the chief capitalist economies was particularly acute, criticism of the received theory naturally turned to the more empirical and less thoroughly explored monetary side of the theory, rather than to premises of pure theory which had by then acquired unchallenged acceptance. But the question we must now ask ourselves is whether those premises were in fact as solid as Keynes himself seems to have supposed. As we shall see in the next section, this question cannot be answered affirmatively.

It thus becomes possible, and necessary, to criticise the traditional view that interest is the equilibrator between saving and investment, while remaining within the confines of that analysis of 'real forces' in which this view was supposed to have its basis. The remainder of Part I of these Notes will be devoted to this question. The other criticism which Keynes conducted in terms of a monetary economy, and the controversy which ensued from it, will then be discussed in Part II. We shall there see how the uncertainty of the conclusions of that controversy with respect to long-period tendencies will lead us back to the questions of 'real theory' discussed in Part I.

7. The Validity of the Marginalist Postulates and the Theory of Interest

We have seen in Sect. 5 how the competitive tendency to a uniform rate of profits ultimately brings the marginalist theorists to the notion of a factor of production, 'capital', measured in value terms; we also saw how the corresponding demand function finds concrete expression in a demand function for investible resources, elastic with respect to the rate of interest. What we must now discuss is the validity of these notions.

The difficulties arise from the fact that the introduction of the factor 'capital' is incompatible with the logical basis on which the marginalist schema of factors of production rests. The principle that the proportions in which the factors are employed vary with the prices of their services, so as to give rise to demand functions of these services, can in fact be deduced from the conditions of equilibrium in production only if the quantities of the factors can all be defined independently of the system of prices.

But this *cannot* be done when one of the factors is the value of the magnitude 'capital'. As the rate of interest and the wage rate vary, the switch of techniques or the change in the relative outputs of consumption goods might well change the proportions between the two factors in a direction contrary to that asserted in marginalist theory. [See the 'Symposium' in the *Quarterly Journal of Economics* (1966), and Garegnani (1970). [*Editor's note*: latter references added in the original by the editors of the host Journal; Garegnani (1970) rpt. in this volume, Part II.]

In fact, when we recognise the dependence of the value of capital goods on distribution, it becomes meaningless to compare the proportions of capital to labour required by different techniques, or in different lines of production, in the unqualified way characteristic of traditional theory, and the same applies for any comparison of the proportions in which the two factors are used in the economy at different rates of interest and wages. With respect to the first type of comparison, the *order* in which the techniques for the production of a commodity are placed with reference to their proportions of capital to labour will depend on the system of relative prices, and thus on the rate of interest or wages at which the comparison is made. As for comparisons between ratios of capital to labour in the economy, the very direction in which this ratio will change with distribution will depend on the commodity in terms of which the value of the capital goods is measured. (The assumed change in the rate of interest may indeed change the relative value of two alternative standards of value in such a way that, when using one standard we have an *increase* in the ratio of capital to labour, whereas the use of the other standard will give a *decrease* in that ratio.)

If the marginalist principle concerning the way in which the proportions of factors change with distribution is incorrect, we may ask what theoretical basis, if any, remains for the notion of demand functions for factors. In Sect. 3 we examined the relation between the price of the service of a factor and the quantity of it employed with a constant quantity of the other factor. We then considered how the *negative slope* of that function, and the analogous form of the corresponding relation for the other factor, allowed these relations to be viewed as 'demand functions' capable of determining, in conjunction with the 'supply functions' of the factors, the prices of their services. Let us now follow the same line of argument, assuming that the two factors are 'capital' and labour.

Consider first the relation between the rate of interest and the value of the capital goods in use, assuming a constant quantity of labour employed and equilibrium in the markets for the products.† The value of the capital goods employed will vary with the rate of interest for two different reasons, which we must now attempt to distinguish.

† This relationship between the value of the capital goods and the rate of interest results from the procedure indicated in n. †, p. 400 above.

In the first place, we have changes in the value of the physical capital employed to which there corresponds no physical change in capital: these changes will be due purely to a change in the value of the capital goods relative to the commodity used as the standard of value.

In the second place, we have those changes in the value of physical capital to which there correspond *physical changes* in capital, which are due either to changes in the techniques adopted for producing the commodities, or to changes in the proportions in which those commodities are produced. The traditional thesis was that these changes in physical capital would ensure a *rise* in the value of the capital goods employed as the rate of interest falls, and vice versa. However, we now know that the analysis underlying this conclusion is invalid and that there is no reason why this second kind of change should have one sign rather than the other.

When we combine the two kinds of value changes that we have just considered separately, it seems that little or nothing of general validity can be said concerning the form of the relationship between the value of physical capital and the rate of interest. If we represent the relationship on a diagram, with the rate of interest on the vertical axis, the curve may just as well slope up to the right as down to the right, and it may alternate such slopes any number of times. Moreover, the form of the curve will depend on which commodity is used as the standard of value.

It seems, then, that even if the initial hypothesis of a constancy in the quantity of labour employed were well founded, the form which the relationship between the value of the capital goods and the rate of interest could assume would make it difficult to envisage it as a 'demand function' for capital—i.e. as the basis of a demand function for investible resources, capable of determining, together with a supply function of such resources, the rate of interest.

Yet the considerations which make this true of the relation between the rate of interest and the quantity of capital also undermine the validity of the assumption of constancy in the quantity of labour employed. As we have seen above, the traditional theory assumed a mechanism which equalised the quantity demanded and supplied of labour and thus ensured that the quantity employed would remain constant—or that it would change in accordance with the supply function of labour if this had some elasticity. But this equilibrating mechanism of demand and supply can no longer be assumed: the relationship between the real wage and the labour employed with a constant quantity of capital would show the same characteristics as the relationship between the quantity of capital and the rate of interest and hence it could not be interpreted as a demand function, any more than could the first relationship.

What we have attempted to argue here throws doubt on the entire explanation of distribution in terms of demand and supply for factors of production. It does so for reasons altogether independent of any 'Keynesian' argument regarding the obstacles which money or the state of expectations may raise to the tendency towards 'equilibrium' in the markets for labour and investment. The questions in the theory of distribution which are thus opened up are the subject of the current debate on capital, and to these questions we shall have occasion to return in our

Part II. Our concern here is only that of showing the weakness of the premises underlying the notion of a demand function for investment elastic with respect to the rate of interest. Thus deprived of its theoretical foundation, that notion cannot, on the other hand, find genuine support on any purely empirical ground.†

It therefore seems possible to assert that—even if the rate of interest could be assumed to be sufficiently sensitive to divergences between planned investment and planned savings—there would not be sufficient ground for arguing that the rate of interest could ensure that decisions to invest will adapt to decisions to save: nor would there be sufficient ground for arguing that aggregate demand will adapt to the level of production compatible with the full employment of the productive resources available in the economy. We shall return to these considerations in Part II, after discussing the criticism of the traditional principle of a tendency to the full employment of labour, which Keynes raised on the different ground of monetary analysis.

Appendix

This appendix deals with the relationship between the demand for capital as a stock and the demand for investment in the case of fixed capital.

Suppose, for example, that all capital goods last for 10 years, being of constant efficiency throughout their lives and that the initial capital stock is of a uniform age structure. Each year 1/10 of the initially existing set of capital goods will be used up, 'freeing' 1/10 of the workers employed in the economy. Each year, therefore, 1/10 of the initial physical capital can be replaced in the most appropriate form, and in 10 years the replacement cycle will be completed. If the initial prices were equilibrium prices and if conditions remain unchanged, the entrepreneurs will demand each year capital goods identical to those which have been used up during the year. At the interest rate prevailing in the initial situation, there will thus be an annual demand for investment equal in value to a given fraction (lying between 1/10 and 1/5 and depending on the interest rate) of the value shown by the demand for capital function at that interest rate. If the supply of gross savings is equal to that value of investment, the equilibrium will be maintained. Suppose

† The changes in the rate of interest discussed here would imply changes in most of the variables of the system (the relative prices of the products, the levels of output, the labour employed, etc.), each of which may in turn react on the level of investment. It would therefore seem that the question of the influence of interest on investment can only be meaningfully discussed within a theoretical scheme which accounts for the relations between these variables. It seems unlikely that all these interrelationships could be accounted for in an empirical study. As it happens, the results of the numerous empirical investigations concerning the *direct* influence of the rate of interest on entrepreneurs' decisions to invest are known to be negative (cf. Andrews, 1938; Sayers, 1940; Ebersole, 1938–39; Brockie and Grey, 1956).

now that—the supplies of the other factors, technical conditions and consumers' tastes all being unchanged—the rate of interest falls and the wage rate and product prices adapt without appreciable delay to the equilibrium compatible with the new rate of interest. The entrepreneurs will then have an incentive to employ the 1/10 of the workers ('freed' each year by the using up of the physical capital) with the techniques and in the industries which are most profitable at the new rate of interest;[†] they will thus demand each year capital goods with a value equal to a given fraction, slightly greater than the previous fraction,[‡] of the value shown by the demand for capital function at the new rate of interest. Because of the form which the theory attributes to that function, the demand for investment will thus be greater than it was at the previous level of the rate of interest and will be able to absorb a greater volume of savings. By considering other possible levels of the rate of interest, one could thus define an investment demand schedule. It would no longer be identical to the demand curve for capital as it was in the case of circulating capital; it would nevertheless be a scale copy of it—but for the effect of the rate of interest on the fraction of the value, of the total stock which is represented by the value of the yearly replacement—and would indeed reproduce its fundamental property of elasticity with respect to the rate of interest.

[†] It is assumed here that the increase of wages and the changes in the prices of the products consequent on the decrease in the rate of interest are not so drastic as to drive the gross income from the operation of the not yet fully depreciated initial physical capital to zero. The demand for investment could then no longer be a scale copy of the demand for capital, since the early scrapping of existing physical capital would presumably cause an additional demand for investment. (It should be noted that this additional investment would not result specifically from the *decrease* in the rate of interest, for additional investment due to this cause could equally well result from sufficiently drastic *increases* in the rate of interest.)

[‡] At a rate of interest (profits) $r=0$, the value of a fixed capital of constant efficiency decreases linearly (i.e. by an equal fraction in each year) during its lifetime of n years. For $r>0$, however, the same value traces a step curve which will be the more concave toward the origin the higher the level of r (see for example, Sraffa, 1960, p. 71). The area below the curve constitutes a measure of the value of a stock consisting of a multiple n of pieces of that fixed capital of uniform age distribution between 0 and $n-1$. The vertical intercept will then measure the yearly replacement which will keep the stock intact year after year. The decreasing concavity of the curve as r falls makes it evident that the ratio between the value of the replacement and that of the stock will increase, as was asserted above. (This may be checked from the algebraic value of this ratio which, for $r>0$, will be given by

$$\frac{p(1+r)^n(rn-1)+1}{r(1+r)^n-1}$$

where p is the value of the replacement and n indicates the life of the fixed capital.)

References

Böhm-Bawerk, E. (1891). *The Positive Theory of Capital.* Macmillan.

Brockie, M. D., & Grey, A. L. (1956). 'The marginal efficiency of capital and investment programming', *Economic Journal,* 66(264), 662–675.

Clark, J. B. (1907). *Essentials of Economic Theory*. Macmillan.

Corry, B. A. (1959). 'Malthus and Keynes – A reconsideration', *Economic Journal,* 69(276), 717–724.

Ebersole, J. E. (1938–39). 'The influence of interest rates upon entrepreneurial decisions in business – a case study', *Harvard Business Review*, XVII(i), pp. 35–39.

Garegnani, P. (1960). *II Capitale nelle Teorie della Distribuzione*. Giuffrè.

Garegnani, P. (1970). 'Heterogeneous capital, the production punction and the theory of distribution', *Review of Economic Studies,* 37(3), 407–436.

Hicks, J. R. (1946). *Value and Capital*. Clarendon Press.

Kaldor, N. (1955–56). 'Alternative theories of distribution', *Review of Economic Studies*, 23(2), 83–100.

Keynes, J. M. (1933). *Essays in Biography*. Rupert Hart-Davis.

Keynes, J. M. (1936). *The General Theory of Employment*. Macmillan.

Klein, L. R. (1950). *The Keynesian Revolution*. Macmillan.

Malthus, T. R. ([1836] 1951). *Principles of Political Economy* (2nd ed.). Kelley.

Marshall, A. (1920). *Principles of Economics* (8th ed.). Macmillan.

Marx, K. (1969). *Theories of Surplus Value* (Vol. II). Lawrence and Wishart.

Meade, J. E. & Andrews, P. W. S. (1938). 'Summary of replies to questions on effects of interest rates', *Oxford Economic Papers*. 1, 14–31.

Meek, R. L. (1950–51). 'Thomas Joplin and the theory of interest', *Review of Economic Studies*, 18(3), 154–63.

Pigou, A. C. (1933). *Theory of Unemployment*. Macmillan.

Ricardo, D. ([1821] 1951a). *On the Principles of Political Economy and Taxation*, in *The Works and Correspondence of David Ricardo*, ed. P. Sraffa (Vol. I). Cambridge University Press.

Ricardo, D. (1951b), *Notes on Malthus*, in *The Works and Correspondence of David Ricardo*, ed. P. Sraffa (Vol. II). Cambridge University Press.

Robbins, L. (1958). *Robert Torrens and the Evolution of Classical Economics*. Macmillan.

Sayers, R. S. (1940). 'Business men and the terms of borrowing', *Oxford Economic Papers*, No. 3, 23-31.

Schumpeter, J. A. (1954). *History of Economic Analysis*. Oxford University Press.

Smith, A. ([1776] 1904). *An Inquiry into the Nature and Causes of the Wealth of Nations* (Vol. I). Methuen.

Sraffa, P. (1960). *Production of Commodities by Means of Commodities*. Cambridge University Press.

Symposium (1966). 'Symposium on paradoxes in capital theory', *Quarterly Journal of Economics,* 80(4), 503-83.

Wicksell, K. (1934). *Lectures on Political Economy* (Vol. I). Routledge.

Notes on Consumption, Investment and Effective Demand: II †*

Part II: Monetary Analysis

In Part I we looked for the premises from which traditional theory derived the assertion that aggregate demand would adjust to productive capacity. These premises were found to lie ultimately in the conception of capital as a 'factor of production' employable in increasing proportion to other factors as the rate of interest falls—the basis, as we argued, of the idea of a demand schedule for 'saving' determining the rate of interest in conjunction with the supply schedule of full employment saving. The deficiencies of that conception of capital led us to the conclusion that, contrary to what is often argued, an analysis conducted in 'real' and 'static' terms provides no basis for the belief that investment decisions can, in the long period, adjust to decisions to save.

In this second Part of the paper, the problem will be approached in terms of the 'monetary' analysis of Keynes' *General Theory* and the subsequent controversy. In Sect. 1, we shall use Wicksell's theory of the price level as an example of how traditional theories would link their 'real' analysis of distribution with their analysis of the money rate of interest. We shall then argue, in Sect. 2, that Keynes's different conclusions concerning the effects of deficiencies in aggregate demand are explained by his rejection of the orthodox theory of the interest rate, and not by the assumption of money-wage rigidity. The examination, in Sect. 3, of the deficiencies of Keynes's own critique of that theory of interest will then pave the

† Previously published in the *Cambridge Journal of Economics*, 3(3), 1979. All necessary permissions acquired.

* The first part of these Notes was published in the December 1978 issue of this *Journal*, 2(4) [this volume, Part IV].

P. Garegnani, *Capital Theory, the Surplus Approach, and Effective Demand*, Springer Studies in the History of Economic Thought,
https://doi.org/10.1007/978-3-031-23643-3_11

way for a discussion, in Sect. 4, of the subsequent attempts to rehabilitate traditional theory. We shall thus finally arrive, in Sect. 5, at those questions of 'real' theory to which the differences between the conclusions of Keynes and those of the orthodox economists are ultimately traceable, and we shall conclude the article by referring back to the results of our analysis in Part 1.

1. An example of the marginalist analysis of the market for loans: Wicksell's monetary theory

While the economic theories prevailing before Keynes's critique assumed a spontaneous tendency to the full employment of productive capacity, they nevertheless had to explain the fact that periods of prosperity alternate with periods of depression, in which there is unemployment and in which production in many sectors falls below productive capacity. The explanation of these phenomena was found in obstacles—not unlike the 'frictions' recognised in other branches of economic theory—which retarded the action of the underlying forces described by the theory, obstacles which were generally attributed to the working of the credit system. The treatment of these problems thus came to be part of a theory of money, separate from the main body of economic theory concerned with distribution and relative prices.

One kind of explanation of the alternation between periods of prosperity and of depression saw its origin in fluctuations of the psychological state of confidence, intensified by the speculative purchasing of commodities financed by bank loans when prices rise, and by the inevitable subsequent sales as soon as a downturn in prices is foreseen. This appears to have been Marshall's position. He saw the sole effective remedy for unemployment due to depression as lying in the greatest possible restriction of 'reckless inflations of credit', which are 'the chief cause of all economic malaise', in that they are followed by liquidations and bankruptcies which shake the 'general state of confidence'. In the subsequent period, marked by lack of confidence, individuals, while having the power to purchase, can choose not to exercise that power; and, in particular, they can choose not to lend capital to new firms. Unemployment results in the industries which produce investment goods; unemployment which then tends to spread to the consumer goods industries as well (Marshall, 1920, VI, xiii, 10; see also Marshall, 1923, IV, iii, 3, pp. 249–251). Thus, according to Marshall, no real limits to the possibility of employing additional capital in production are involved; the limit consists only in an overestimation of risk, which is bound to disappear as soon as the consequences of the previous wave of optimism have exhausted themselves.

By contrast, an alternative explanation of these phenomena stressed objective factors and, in particular, the discontinuous character of technical progress. This was Wicksell's approach. He wrote: 'The principal and sufficient cause of cyclical fluctuations should rather be sought in the fact that in its very nature technical or commercial advance cannot maintain the same even progress as does, in our days, the increase in needs … but is sometimes precipitate, sometimes delayed' (Wicksell, 1935, p. 211; see also Wicksell, 1907), which results, according to Wicksell, in fluctuations in the profitability of investment, to which the structure of interest rates on money loans adjusts only with a lag, causing price variations meanwhile. Here we meet Wicksell's monetary theory, to which we must now proceed. This theory constitutes perhaps the most important pre-Keynesian attempt to ground by means of a systematic analysis of the money loan market (the market in which the rate of interest is actually observed) the marginalist concept of interest as the supply-and-demand determined price of the productive factor 'capital'. Moreover, Wicksell's analysis is akin to that of the *General Theory,* in that it is focused on the source and the effects of variations in *aggregate* monetary expenditure: it will thus prove useful as a term of comparison below, when we consider the 'real' or 'monetary' nature of the hypotheses underlying the different conclusions reached by Keynes.

Fundamental to Wicksell's theory is the concept of an interest rate referred to as 'natural', 'normal' or 'real': the rate, that is, at which *'the demand for loan capital and the supply of savings* exactly agree' (Wicksell, 1935, p. 193, emphasis in the original).† The 'natural' rate, Wicksell writes, 'more or less corresponds to the expected yield on the newly created capital' or, as he puts it elsewhere, to the return on capital which becomes 'free' in the course of the period considered, and can thus be 'invested' in the most profitable physical form.‡ Since the expected

---

† Savings, the supply of which is referred to by Wicksell in the above passage, should be understood to be the planned gross savings (cf. Part I of these Notes, footnote on p. 397), given by the difference between gross income and consumption under the assumption of full employment of resources with equilibrium relative prices and distribution. (See footnote ‡ on p. 415 below for a discussion of alternative interpretations of these equilibrium prices.)

‡ Wicksell's concept of 'free' capital merits closer consideration because it highlights some difficulties which are implicit in the traditional concepts of the demand for and the supply of saving. At the time of *Geldzins und Güterpreise* (1898), Wicksell assumed that money lent to entrepreneurs for investment would, in the final analysis, be spent solely on consumption goods, to be 'advanced' as wages and rents to the 'original' factors (see, for example, Wicksell, [1898] 1965, pp. 102–103); such goods would have constituted a 'free' or 'liquid. capital. which is to be distinguished from 'invested' capital represented by capital goods. Yet this concept of investment expenditure is invalid unless one supposes an economy in which the production of consumption goods takes place in annual cycles and starts each year with land and labour unassisted by any capital goods. Under any other assumption investment expenditure will be largely upon capital goods. Then the consumption goods which the saver has 'forgone' are not produced at all when the investment process develops smoothly; the role of such 'forgoing' being only that of freeing for the production of capital goods the resources which would otherwise have been required for the production of the 'forgone' consumption goods. In this case, as Wicksell recognises in the *Lectures* (Wicksell, 1935, pp. 192–3), 'free' capital does not take any *physical* form at all; and the concept merely serves to mark the fact that, in so far as the decisions in question were *correctly foreseen in the past,* the relevant sums of money may be spent on capital goods of any type whatever

The qualification concerning the necessity that the current saving and investment decisions were correctly foreseen in the past is important: demand for, and supply of saving involve the decisions of *three* groups of people and not just of two, as might appear at first sight. The idea of a 'supply of savings' presupposes the coincidence of the savings decisions of income recipients and the decisions of producers concerning the division of aggregate supply between consumption and capital goods. Similarly, the idea of a demand for saving or investment presupposes that the producers of capital goods correctly foresee the physical composition of the investment demand.

return on 'newly created capital' will tend to coincide, under normal conditions, with the return which will be realised, the 'natural' rate of interest is the rate of interest which Wicksell had related, in the real part of his theory, to the data concerning the available quantities of factors, technical knowledge and the tastes of consumers (cf. Wicksell, 1935, pp. 205–206). It follows that the natural rate of interest is liable to vary as a result of changes in any of these data. The explanation of variations in the price level can then be found, Wicksell argues, in the slowness with which the banks adjust their lending rates of interest to variations in the natural rate.

Before proceeding with Wicksell's argument, let us stop to emphasise two aspects of it which are important for us here. The first is the assertion that the market rate of interest can differ from the 'natural' rate for non-negligible periods of time. The second is that the possibility of this is attributed to the existence of the banking system. Wicksell maintains in fact that if money loans were to take place directly, from person to person, their supply would be largely determined by money savings. The forces of demand for, and supply of savings could then act *directly* on the market for money loans and bring the rate of interest back to the level of the natural rate, as soon as the former began to diverge from the latter. Thus if, for example, there were an increase in the profitability of investment, the increased 'demand for loan capital' would encounter the limit to the supply of loans set by the flow of savings: an increase in the market rate of interest, towards the new level of the 'natural' rate, would result. The situation is quite different when there is a developed banking system. Indeed, the volume of bank loans is independent of the flow of money savings: 'By the concentration in their hands of private cash holdings ... [the banks] possess a fund for loans which is always elastic and, on certain assumptions, inexhaustible' (Wicksell, 1935, p. 194). Hence the banks can accommodate any variation in the demand for loans without changing their rates of interest and can thus sever the link between the market rate of interest and the 'natural' rate which would otherwise have operated through demand and supply in the loan market.

Yet if this direct link between the two rates is broken, Wicksell continues, another, far less rigid link will nevertheless continue to hold good and will act via the price level. Let us in fact consider an initial situation of real and monetary equilibrium, in which there occurs an increase in the profitability of investment, and suppose that the banks meet the increased demand for loans by an expansion of credit, leaving the rate of interest unchanged. As the loans come to be used for the purchase of means of production, the flow of aggregate money expenditure will increase: to an initially unchanged consumption expenditure there will be added the increased investment expenditure. This increased aggregate expenditure, meeting a virtually unchanged volume of output, will lead to an increase in money prices: the increase will at first be in the prices of investment goods, but then, when the increased money income thus generated permits increases in consumption expenditure, the prices of consumer goods will also increase—and this latter increase may be contributed to by transfers of resources from the production of consumer goods to that of investment goods (see Wicksell, 1935, p. 194).[†] If we assume that the money rates of payment to primary factors tend to increase in the same proportion as prices, the profitability of investments will continue to exceed the market rate of interest and, as long as this condition holds good, the inflationary process will continue (*ibid.*, pp. 195–197). An analogous process will take place, but in the opposite direction, when the 'natural' rate of interest falls and the banks keep the market rate unchanged (*ibid.*, p. 200). But, Wicksell concludes, it will be these very cumulative processes of inflation or deflation which will compel the banks eventually to raise, or lower, the market rate of interest towards its 'natural' level (*ibid.*, p. 201), the only level at which there will be price stability.

The theory briefly set out above brings to light the (often implicit) grounds on which the marginalist theorists maintained that the separation between savings decisions and investment decisions—or the influence of monetary factors in the loan market—could not endanger, other than temporarily, the claimed tendency to the full employment of the factors of production. At the basis of their argument there lay the postulate of the elasticity of the demand for capital with respect to the rate of interest.[‡] This elasticity, it was thought, would make it possible for the

[†] To the extent that monetary expansion transfers resources from the production of consumption goods to the production of investment goods, real accumulation will be higher than it would have been at the 'natural' rate. To this extent, the 'natural' rate itself would tend to fall and approach the market rate. Wicksell admits this effect, but considers it to be of secondary importance (evidently because of his implicit assumption of a highly elastic demand for capital) (cf. Wicksell, 1935, pp. 198–199).

[‡] In *Geldzins und Güterpreise* Wicksell seems to explain the increase in the demand for 'loan capital' that results from a decrease in the rate of interest in terms of the incentive that the growing difference between the rate of profits obtainable in production (equal to the 'natural' rate of interest) and the market rate of interest gives entrepreneurs to expand the *scale* of aggregate output (cf. Wicksell, [1898] 1965, pp. 89–90, and Wicksell, 1935, pp. 194–196).

This explanation brings us to the question hinted at above (footnote † on p. 413) concerning the relative prices and distribution underlying the schedules of the demand for and supply of saving in traditional theory. Two alternative assumptions are conceivable: (a) that relative prices and factor remunerations are those ruling in the given situation and do not change as we move along the schedules; (b) that wages, the rents of natural resources and the relative product prices are those which would obtain in the equilibrium situation corresponding to the rate of interest assumed for the loan market (see Part I of these Notes, footnote † on p. 400). According to assumption (a), used in *Geldzins,* the rate of profits obtainable in production being given, independently of the assumed rate of interest on loans, the search for maximum profits would lead, not only to changes in production methods adopted (factor proportions), but also to changes in the *scale* of every line of production. This explanation of the demand for investible funds does not, however, appear to be acceptable. Since the traditional theory assumes that labour and natural resources always tend to be fully utilised, the tendency to increase the scale of production in the aggregate could only lead to changes in the real remuneration of labour and natural resources. The investment planned to change the scale of production would thus be countermanded when, as it began to be carried out, distribution and relative prices adapt themselves to the rate of interest ruling in the loan market. The demand for investible funds will then in fact turn out to be rate of interest to adjust planned investment to planned savings through the play of demand and supply in the market for money loans. But if this first demand-and-supply mechanism were seriously hampered by monetary factors, that same elasticity would ensure that changes in the rate of interest would suffice to re-establish equilibrium in the face of variations of aggregate expenditure due to inequality between planned savings and investment. It is Wicksell's merit to provide a systematic and rigorous version of this line of thought; even if, in doing so, he shows that the link between saving and investment decisions must often be the indirect one.†

It is not surprising, therefore, that Wicksell did not find, in his analysis of the loan market, any factors which might bring into question the conclusions of the 'real' theory on the tendency to full employment of factors: variations of monetary expenditure are seen to have effects on the level of prices, but not on the levels of production and of factor employment. The rationale for this lay in two complementary elements. On the one hand, there was the idea that on the appearance of unemployment of the primary factors, competition would lead to a decrease in their monetary rates of remuneration; this made plausible the hypothesis that prices would fall in step with monetary expenditure, leaving the volume of output virtually unchanged. On the other hand, this hypothesis did not entail admitting an absurd process of unending deflation or inflation of prices: the elasticity of demand for investible funds in fact ensured the existence of a 'natural' rate of interest to which the banks would be able, and eventually compelled, to bring back the money rate of interest. It was thus natural for Wicksell to suppose that any under-utilisation of productive equipment and primary factors could only be temporary and could therefore be neglected in an analysis of value and distribution conducted at the level of general principles.‡

---

determined exclusively by the tendency to change the ratio of capital to 'original' factors, i.e. according to assumption (b), as was assumed in the argument of Part I of these Notes (cf. pp. 400–1). (Similar considerations hold for the supply of savings, which will also be influenced by changes in distribution and relative prices.)

In the *Lectures* Wicksell seems to take account of this and to modify somewhat his earlier position (cf., for example, the reference in Wicksell, 1935, p. 195, to 'increasing roundaboutness which is undoubtedly invoked by a fall in interest rates').Wicksell's reluctance to adopt this second point of view exclusively is probably due to the difficulty of admitting a rapid adjustment of distribution and relative prices to the rate of interest on loans or, alternatively, of assuming correct entrepreneurs' forecasts of such effects. But since assumption (a) is even less acceptable, it would seem that this difficulty is inseparable from the idea of supply and demand schedules for savings.

† Similar suggestions were frequent in other marginalist writers. Consider, for example, Marshall's argument in *Money, Credit and Commerce* that an influx of precious metals would initially produce a fall in the rates of interest, which would then rise again as a result of the rise in prices that that influx had brought about (Marshall, 1923, IV, iv, 2, p. 256).

‡ The possibility is mentioned in the *Lectures* that increases in money demand [*editor's note*: to be understood as monetary demand] might be satisfied, in part, by increases in output made possible by the presence of previously unemployed productive resources. Such a possibility is judged to be of secondary importance and is ignored in the rest of Wicksell's discussion (Wicksell, 1935, p. 195).

2. Keynes's Theory and the Rigidity or Money Wages

What we must now consider is why Keynes, although starting from premises not unlike those of Wicksell, arrives at radically different conclusions.

The picture which Keynes's *General Theory* draws is well known. As in Wicksell, the system of interest rates is proximately determined by monetary factors. Keynes approaches the problem of the rate of interest from the angle of the demand for and supply of the stock of money. The demand for money, or 'liquidity preference', is explained in terms not only of the two traditional 'transactions' and 'precautionary' motives, but also in terms of the 'speculative motive', which expresses the preference for money, as a means of holding wealth, of those who expect falls in the value of bonds (= increases in the rate of interest). According to Keynes, the demand for money due to this third motive must be elastic with respect to the rate of interest, since the lower is that rate, the greater is the risk that it will rise, and the smaller is the compensation for such risk provided by the interest rate (Keynes, 1936, pp. 201–202). The rate of interest is thus the price which will bring into equality, not the demand for and supply of saving, but rather the desire to hold wealth in the form of money and the quantity of money made available by the monetary authorities. It is therefore determined once 'liquidity preference' and the quantity of money are known. Planned investment, on the other hand, depends on the rate of interest in the manner shown by the 'marginal efficiency of capital schedule'. Once the rate of interest is determined, therefore, the volume of planned investment is also determined, when expressed in 'real' terms, i.e. in wage-units.[†]

There is thus no reason why the amount of investment' should coincide with the amount of saving out of full employment income. Yet equilibrium requires equality between planned investment and planned saving; if that equality is not satisfied, aggregate monetary expenditure will tend to change over time.

It is necessary to distinguish, at this point, between the case in which planned investment exceeds full employment savings and the opposite case. In the former, equilibrium would be reached, according to Keynes, via an inflationary process not unlike that found in Wicksell: because of the increase of prices and money wages, the money value of national income (and thus the 'transactions' demand for money) would increase until it caused a rise in the rate of interest great enough to eliminate the cause of the inflation (see, for example, *ibid.*, p. 202). For the analysis of the second case, however, Keynes introduces the 'propensity to consume' and, therewith, the most original part of his analysis. It is assumed that, other things being equal, when employment increases the community will increase aggregate consumption, but by less than income has increased. It is then shown

[†] Keynes reduces the different qualities of labour to homogeneity by multiplying the quantity of each by the ratio which its wage bears to that of a standard type of labour. These ratios are assumed to be constant (1936, pp. 41–2).

how, when planned investment falls short of planned saving, equality between investment and saving will be achieved through a contraction of the national product. The possibility of 'equilibria' characterised by unemployment of labour and under-capacity working of equipment is thus asserted.‡

Keynes's conclusions concerning his second case stand in sharp contrast to those which Wicksell had reached for the case in which the rate of interest was initially above the 'natural rate'. The search for the sources of this difference cannot but start from the most obvious difference between the assumptions underlying the two analyses: the high flexibility of money wages assumed by Wicksell but denied by Keynes. As we have seen, Wicksell assumed a tendency for prices and wages to fall in the same proportion as aggregate expenditure; it was precisely this process of price and wage deflation that would eventually oblige the banks to bring the rate of interest down to its 'natural' level. By contrast, Keynes assumes that any shortfall of planned investment relative to planned saving is followed by decreases in total expenditure *measured in wage-units:* he assumes, that is, that money wages do not fall or, more exactly, do not fall in the same proportion as money expenditure has fallen. Given this assumption, there must be a shrinking of output, since the entrepreneurs will not continue to produce at below normal profits. It must now be asked to what extent Keynes's thesis would remain valid were we to admit, with Wicksell, that competition amongst unemployed workers would give rise to a continuous fall in the money wage. Must we then conclude that under-employment 'equilibria' exist only during the time required for a sufficient fall in money wages?

As is well known, Keynes denied that the novelty of his conclusions turned on the hypothesis of money wage rigidity and Chapter 19 of the *General Theory* is devoted to this question. The argument develops in two stages. Keynes assumes at first that the fall in the money wage rate will cause a shift in neither the consumption function nor the marginal efficiency of capital schedule. He also assumes that it will not affect the rate of interest. In this case, the fall in wages could not lead to permanent increases of employment and real income (Keynes, 1936, pp. 261–262). Thus, Keynes concludes, the fall in wages could affect employment *only* through its effects on the propensity to consume, on the marginal efficiency of capital schedule, and on the rate of interest.

‡On the assumption given above concerning the behaviour of consumption, the aggregate demand function will intersect the aggregate supply function from above and the equilibrium can be supposed to be stable. Thus, if employment happened to be higher than is indicated by the equilibrium point, entrepreneurs would have an incentive to reduce the number of workers employed, since the aggregate expenditure in wage units would be *less* than the 'aggregate supply price' of that output. This would be so if this expenditure were that shown by the aggregate demand function, i.e. that which would obtain with a disposable income equal to the supply price; a fortiori, expenditure will be less than supply price if, as a result of the failure to realise the full supply price, the disposable income is itself less than the 'supply price'. Similarly, entrepreneurs would have an incentive to increase output whenever employment was initially below the equilibrium level.

Keynes then proceeds to the second stage of his argument and considers the effects of a fall in wages on the consumption function and on the marginal efficiency of capital schedule. He concludes that, in a closed economy, these effects will be negative, rather than positive, in their implications for employment. He therefore turns to consider the effects on the rate of interest, remarking that it is to these effects alone that reference can be made by those who claim that wage flexibility will lead to full employment. Yet if the available quantity of money contracts in step with money income, 'there is ... nothing to hope in this direction'. If the quantity of money remains approximately constant, however, Keynes continues, there will be effects on the rate of interest analogous to those which the monetary authorities can achieve by purchasing bonds on the 'open market'. In either case the quantity of money increases relative to money income: a greater quantity of money thus becomes available to meet the demand for money deriving from the 'speculative motive' and, given the speculative demand schedule, the interest rate must fall. It follows, says Keynes, that, leaving aside the disadvantages specific to this particular method of increasing the relative supply of money, decreases in money wages encounter limits to their effect on the rate of interest analogous to those specific to open market operations. Just as open market operations can have but a limited influence on long-term rates of interest when the increase in the quantity of money is moderate, whereas they can have unfavourable effects on the state of confidence when the increase is large, so a moderate fall in money wage rates will prove insufficient, whereas a large fall could shatter the state of confidence. Keynes thus concludes by asserting firmly that: 'There is, therefore, no ground for the belief that a flexible wage policy is capable of maintaining a state of continuous full employment—any more than for the belief that an open-market monetary policy is capable, unaided, of achieving this result' (Keynes, 1936, p. 267; but see also p. 27 and our own footnote ‡ on p. 421 below).

We shall have reason to return to this argument of Keynes later on and to discuss its limitations. Here we need only note that the hypothesis of money wage rigidity does not suffice to explain the difference between Keynes's conclusions and those of the traditional economists; the flexibility of prices and wages would lead to the full employment of factors *only if* the resulting decrease in the rate of interest could so affect planned investment as to make it equal to full employment savings. Keynes denied that the rate of interest could play that equilibrating role and it is *here,* in the theory of the rate of interest, that he diverges from Wicksell and the other 'orthodox' economists.

Thus two results begin to emerge from this preliminary discussion of Keynes's analysis. The first result is to confirm what we maintained in Part I of these Notes (see pp. 396–8): the source of the difference between Keynes and the orthodox economists is to be sought in the theory of the rate of interest.

The second result concerns the precise *nature* of this difference in the theory of the rate of interest. Keynes's conclusions rest, in fact, not so much on the particular theory of the rate of interest which he put forward, as on his rejection of the traditional theory, which determined the rate of interest by the demand for and the supply of savings. An interesting expression of this negative role which the theory of the rate of interest plays in the *General Theory* may perhaps be found in a seldom noted passage written by Keynes one year after that book. Referring to his own theory and to its genesis, he says:

> the initial novelty lies in my maintaining that it is not the rate of interest, but the level of incomes which ensures equality between saving and investment. The arguments which lead up to this initial conclusion are independent of my subsequent theory of the rate of interest, and in fact I reached it before I had reached the latter theory. But the result of it was to leave the rate of interest in the air. If the rate of interest is not determined by saving and investment in the same way in which price is determined by supply and demand, how is it determined? … It was only when [attempts in other directions failed] … that I hit on what I now think to be the true explanation (Keynes, 1937, p. 250).

It is then in the *critique* of the traditional theory of interest, rather than in the hypothesis of money wage rigidity, that the roots of Keynes's conclusions are to be sought. It is to that critique, contained in Chapter 14 of the *General Theory,* that we must now direct our attention. Indeed, if the critique were well founded, the hypothesis of money wage rigidity would appear to be a consequence, and not a premise of the thesis that there exists no tendency to the full employment of factors. To assume wage flexibility, in the absence of a rate of interest capable of adjusting planned investment to full employment saving, would compel us to allow for an absurd process of unending deflation of prices and wages when investment is less than full employment savings.†

3. Keynes's Critique of the Traditional Theory of Interest

Keynes's critique of the traditional theory of interest appears to contain two strands. On the one hand, there is the charge that the theory is indeterminate. To each level of utilisation of productive capacity there corresponds a different real income and hence a different supply of savings schedule: given the marginal efficiency of capital schedule, there are therefore not one but many rates of interest at which planned investment and planned saving are equal—one for each level of real income (Keynes, 1936, pp. 179–182). On the other hand, there is the thesis that the rate of interest constitutes not the price of savings but, rather, the price needed to induce individuals to hold wealth in forms other than money.

The first criticism does not seem to be well founded. Let us begin by accepting, in accord with traditional theory, the following two propositions: (a) that at each level of real income the action, in the loan market, of the demand for savings and the supply forthcoming at that real income, creates a tendency for the rate of

† Keynes's conclusions concerning the effects of money wage decreases on the propensity to consume have been questioned in terms of the so-called 'Pigou effect': the significance of the latter for our argument will be discussed below, p. 426, n. †.

interest to move towards the level at which the two schedules intersect;[†] (b) that the money wage is flexible in the presence of unemployment.

We now assume a level of investment insufficient to ensure the full employment of labour; by assumption (b) the money wage will fall. As Keynes admits in his discussion of falls in money wages, one can now suppose that the entrepreneurs react initially by increasing output in the expectation of a demand for their products which is unchanged in money terms. Under our present hypothesis, this expectation could not be entirely disappointed, since, the supply of 'real' savings being shifted to the right, there will, by assumption (a), be a tendency for the rate of interest to fall; the consequent increase in investment will make possible the maintenance, at least in part, of the initial increase in employment. Since, by assumption (b), there will be decreases in the money wage as long as there is unemployment, this process will eventually lead to the achievement of full employment. As a result the full-employment supply schedule of savings is the *only* supply of savings to which the theory under examination need refer in the determination of the equilibrium rate of interest: the dependence of the supply of savings on the level of employment does not warrant the charge of indeterminacy laid by Keynes.[‡] (Analogous conclusions would be reached if traditional theory were to maintain, with Wicksell, that the presence of the banking system makes assumption (a) unacceptable, but were to admit, at the same time, the possibility, and eventually the necessity, that the banks should bring the rate of interest to its 'natural' level.)

We may therefore confine our attention to the second strand of Keynes's criticism of the received theory of interest. This may be summarised by saying that the traditional theory of interest ignored the effects deriving from the role of money as a store of value. When this role is given due weight, Keynes states, one must recognise that the aggregate demand for money depends on the rate of interest,

---

[†] If this assumption is not accepted, the critique of the traditional theory will lie in the reasons for which the assumption is rejected and not in any indeterminacy of the theory.

[‡] Keynes himself appears at times to imply that variations in money wages could justify the traditional theory of interest when this refers to a full employment income for defining the supply schedule of saving. Thus he writes, 'the position could only be saved by some complicated assumption providing for an automatic change in the wage-unit of an amount just sufficient in its effect on liquidity-preference to establish a rate of interest which would just offset the supposed shift [of the marginal efficiency of capital], so as to leave output at the same level as before' (Keynes, 1936, pp. 179–180). But in introducing the idea of 'liquidity preference', Keynes here forces his own theory on the traditional one. More relevant to the latter would seem to be another passage: 'If, however, there is a negligible demand for cash from the speculative-motive except for a short transitional interval, an increase in the quantity of money will have to lower the rate of interest almost forthwith, in whatever degree is necessary to raise employment and the wage-unit sufficiently to cause the additional cash to be absorbed by the transactions-motive and the precautionary-motive' (*ibid.*, p. 171). Keynes is here referring to increases in the quantity of money, but the same conclusions hold for reductions in the money wage, given the quantity of money; it is then difficult to see how this position can be reconciled with the assertion that the traditional theory is indeterminate.

as well as on the total money volume of transactions. For a given money value of output, the demand for money will be greater the lower is the rate of interest: the latter will then have the role of bringing about equality between the quantity of money made available by the monetary authorities and the demand for money, not that of equating the demand for and the supply of saving (see, for example, Keynes, 1936, p. 167).

Keynes therefore confines himself, in this second criticism, to counterposing his own theory of interest to the traditional one, and the force of his argument is thus merely that of the theory which he puts forward. The idea that the demand for money depends on the rate of interest—which is quite in accord with marginalist principles when it is presented in terms of equality, at the margin, between the sacrifice of liquidity and the payment therefore—has been generally accepted in subsequent literature. The same has not occurred for the critique of the traditional theory of interest which Keynes wished to base on that idea. Indeed, we shall see in the next section how it has been argued that the rate of interest can equalise both the demand for and supply of the stock of money and the demand for and supply of savings.

These attempts to reinstate the traditional analysis were undoubtedly encouraged by the feeling that Keynes's theory of interest would not conflict with orthodox theory properly interpreted. As exemplified above by reference to Wicksell, the orthodox theory of interest was only meant to refer to long-run tendencies, destined to assert themselves against the short-term obstacles raised by a number of other factors.

When examined from this standpoint, Keynes's theory of interest appears to be unsatisfactory. The quantity of money demanded on account of the speculative motive depends, Keynes says, not on the absolute level of the rate of interest but, rather, on the extent to which that rate lies below the rates which the various holders of wealth expect in the future (see *ibid.*, p. 201). The position of the speculative demand for money schedule, and hence the rate of interest, thus come to depend on expectations about the future course of the latter. However, in the absence of their ulterior explanation, these expectations introduce a serious element of indeterminacy into the theory. Thus if it were assumed that expected rates of interest tend, albeit with a certain lag, to move parallel to the actual rate of interest, the principal reason advanced by Keynes for the interest-elasticity of the speculative demand for money—the growing divergence between expected rates and the current rate when the latter falls—would lapse. This point is reinforced when it is noted that the supply of money which is to satisfy the speculative demand can only change due to *either* changes in the money value of aggregate output *or* the policy of the monetary authorities: and it is difficult to imagine, in either case, that there will not be some effect on expected interest rates. Keynes does in fact recognise this possible instability of the expectations on which the market rate of interest would depend and he takes it into account by admitting the possibility of shifts in the speculative demand for money schedule in the face of, for example, a central bank policy of monetary expansion (see, for example, *ibid.*, pp. 197–198). Yet it is clear that, in so far as it is probable that speculative demand shifts as the supply of money changes, Keynes's analysis loses much of its force: like any other analysis in terms of demand and supply, it presupposes a sufficient mutual independence of the two schedules.

Keynes's theory appears therefore to rest on the assumption of a considerable degree of stability of the expectations concerning the rate of interest: a stability which can only be based on stable views, on the part of the owners of wealth, as to what constitutes a 'normal' level of the interest rate. This seems in fact to be Keynes's rationale for the 'speculative' demand for money. Yet when it is interpreted in this way, the inadequacy of the liquidity preference theory as a long-period analysis of the rate of interest becomes even clearer; the average value, over time, of the rate of interest on long-term loans proves to be largely determined by views about the 'normal' rate of interest, views which the theory does not explain (cf. *ibid.*, p. 201).

This deficiency of Keynes's theory was, for example, the starting point for a more direct defence of the traditional theory than that which we shall consider in the next section; the prevailing views about the normal level of the interest rate were explained by some authors in terms of a substantially correct estimation of the rate of interest needed to adjust investment to the economy's full employment level of saving (taken as an average over the long period).† This defence of traditional theory does not appear to be adequately argued, but the very fact that it could be put forward serves to indicate the *lacuna* left by Keynes in his long-period analysis of the rate of interest; a *lacuna* which had to be filled, either by a return to the traditional theory or by its more radical rejection.‡

4. The Attempts to Rehabilitate Traditional Theory

If the *General Theory* left the theory of interest at this parting of the ways, Keynes's concept of the marginal efficiency of capital made it easy to return to the traditional theory. Keynes had already considered this possibility when he affirmed that those believing in the re-equilibrating tendencies of the economic system must base their argument on the effects which falls in money wages and prices, or

† 'What this seems to point to is that [the normal rate of interest] must be determined by people's estimate of the pressure of outside forces of some kind; and it seems natural to suggest that in a free enterprise economy these forces are none other than our old friends productivity and thrift' (Robertson, 1963, p. 388).

‡ There are hints in this latter direction in the *General Theory*. Keynes, in fact, asserts the 'conventional' character of the rate of interest, and hence the capacity of the monetary authorities to control the average level of the interest rate on long-term loans, if they act with sufficient 'persistence and consistency of purpose' (cf. Keynes, 1936, p. 204). This idea which, if consistently developed, would lead to a theory of value and distribution radically different from the marginalist theory (see below, pp. 432–3) does not seem to have been taken up in the subsequent literature.

open market operations of the central bank, could have in increasing the quantity of money available for meeting the speculative demand. As was seen in Sect. 2, Keynes had denied that one could thus reach full employment. However, his arguments to this effect—based principally on the negative effects which significant falls in money wages or increases in the quantity of money would have on the 'state of confidence'—lose much of their force when the issue is, not the recovery of the economy from a situation of cyclical depression, but rather the possibility of keeping the average level of investment sufficiently close to the full employment volume of savings over a long period. In this latter context, once it is admitted (on the basis of marginalist principles) that the marginal efficiency of capital schedule is highly elastic with respect to the rate of interest, the decreases in money wages, or increases in the quantity of money, required to ensure a sufficiently high average level of employment no longer appear drastic, as they can now be spread out over a long period of time. Besides, in the long period. the psychological factors summed up in the 'state of confidence' lose much of their force by comparison with the objective factors on which the real profitability of investment is supposed to depend.

This is in fact the line of argument taken in the attempts to rehabilitate traditional theory, which we referred to in the previous section.† The dominant concern of these authors with long period tendencies‡ allowed them to ignore the negative psychological effects of falls in wages and prices, or increases in the quantity of money. That same concern explains, in part, a subtle but important shift in the interpretation of the 'speculative' demand for money. This demand is now made to depend not so much on views of what constitutes a normal level of the rate of interest, but rather on the convenience and security deriving from the holding of one's wealth in the form of money; the security in question is relative to those risks of changes in the value of bonds, entirely due to uncertainty, which would exist even when a rise in the rate of interest appeared no more probable than an

† Hicks (1937) seems to have opened up this line of argument by distinguishing between Keynes's special theory' and his 'general theory'. In the former, one would not consider the effect of changes in the money value of output on the demand for money; in the latter, admitting this influence, one would, by contrast, reach 'appreciably more orthodox' conclusions—amongst others, the possibility of increasing employment via money wage reductions, as well as by increases in the quantity of money (Hicks, 1937, pp. 467–470; and p. 465 for the effects of money wage flexibility). The argument was then taken up and rendered more explicit by Modigliani (1944); Haberler (1939), Ch. 8 and (1964), pp. 240–243; by Tobin (1955), etc. The conclusions of this line of argument have provided the theoretical basis of the numerous theories of economic growth on traditional lines (see, for example, Solow, 1956, pp. 91–93; Swan, 1956, p. 335; Meade, 1961, pp. 3–5).

‡ Thus in Modigliani (1944, p. 187) the analysis is said to be conducted 'under "static" assumptions', since its object is the 'determinants of equilibrium and not ... the explanation of business cycles'.

equal fall.[§] By this change in the interpretation of liquidity preference, a sufficient stability is attributed to the demand for money without having recourse to views about a 'normal' rate of interest, which are not explained within the theory. Moreover, one thereby avoids consideration of the possibility of a high elasticity of the demand for money, with respect to the rate of interest, at rates above the minimum level to which we shall refer below; a possibility to which Keynes had attached considerable importance[|] and which can be explained only in terms of sufficiently unanimous views of wealth holders about what constitutes the normal level of the interest rate.

Given these premises, it is not difficult to conclude that, if unemployment of labour leads to the continuous fall of money wages, one will eventually reach—subject to the exception to be considered shortly—a state of equilibrium. In this equilibrium, the ratio between the money value of output and the available quantity of money permits a level of the interest rate at which investment is equal to full employment savings.

The significance of this argument does not depend on the assumption of a high flexibility of money wages, an assumption generally held to be of doubtful applicability. If the flexibility of money wages would permit the achievement of full employment in the way just described, then the same result can be obtained with an expansionary monetary policy. As Modigliani puts it, 'It is the fact that money wages are too high relative to the quantity of money that explains why it is unprofitable to expand employment to the "full employment" level'; and the remedy can take the form of *either* a decrease in money wages *or* an increase in the quantity of money, money wages being constant (cf. Modigliani, 1944, p. 225, and Hicks, 1937, p. 465 and pp. 473–475).

We referred above to an exception to these conclusions. The authors in question in fact admit only one situation in which money wage flexibility, or an expansionary monetary policy, cannot lead the economy back to full employment. This is the so-called 'Keynesian case': a situation in which the rate of interest required to ensure full employment is negative or, at least, lower than that rate of interest which, in the view of the majority of wealth holders, would be barely sufficient to compensate for the risk and inconvenience of holding any part of their wealth in any form other than money. At this level of the interest rate the elasticity of the demand for money would tend to become infinite (cf. Modigliani, 1944, p. 222; Hicks, 1937, pp. 470–472), and decreases in money wages or increases in the quantity of money could not lead to any further fall in the rate of interest. However, these authors attribute limited importance to this possibility—and here we find, yet again, the basic marginalist idea of a demand for capital which is, under normal conditions,

---

[§] On the distinction between these two interpretations of 'liquidity preference', see Robertson (1963), pp. 382–383. For the tendency to adopt the second interpretation of 'liquidity preference' in these rehabilitations, see Hicks (1937), p. 467, and Modigliani (1944), p. 193.

[|] Cf. for example, 'opinion about the future of the rate of interest may be so unanimous that a small change in present rates may cause a mass movement into cash' (Keynes, 1936, p. 172; see also p. 203).

highly elastic with respect to the rate of interest. The inelasticity and position of the schedule of the marginal efficiency of capital which would be needed to explain a full-employment rate of interest lying below that minimum level are held to be possible only in deep depressions, when they would be due to the conditions of uncertainty and over-estimation of risks characteristic of such situations. These authors in fact maintain, agreeing here with Keynes, that a situation in which the preceding accumulation of capital has reduced the actual yield of capital almost to zero has never yet occurred (Modigliani, 1944, p. 222n; Keynes, 1936, p. 207).

The relevance of the 'Keynesian case' is thus confined to the analysis of short-period phenomena and the same is true for the importance of the psychological factors to which Keynes had referred, in Chapter 19 of the *General Theory,* in order to deny the possibility of reaching full employment through falls in money wages or increases in the quantity of money. In the former as in the latter context, the psychological state of lack of confidence characteristic of depressions would, as long as it persisted, constitute the obstacle which prevents a return to the full employment of factors, following an argument not unlike that which had been put forward by Marshall long before.†

5. Novel and Traditional Elements in Keynes's Theory: The Marginal Efficiency of Capital

The line of argument considered in the previous section thus leads to a substantial rehabilitation of traditional theory for the long period and, in particular, for accumu lation. The schema of the long-run inter-relation between 'real' and

---

† A different attempt to rehabilitate the principle of the tendency to full employment is that based on the so-called 'Pigou Effect'. When money wages and prices fall, the aggregate net credit of the private sector of the economy—equal to the total net debt of the government and the central bank (banknotes and government stock) in a closed economy—will increase in real terms. The propensity to save of wealth-holders will consequently fall until the full employment level of savings equals the level of investment forthcoming in the situation under consideration. (Cf. Pigou, 1947, pp. 249–251; Haberler, 1964, pp. 483–489; Patinkin, 1948, pp. 258–270.) This argument does not support the traditional doctrine that the level of investment is determined by the community's propensity to save and is thus of limited interest to us here. One remark concerning it may however be made. It is reasonable to suppose that the greater part of saving comes from high income recipients and that this group will also hold a large fraction of both the public debt and idle money balances. Thus what the 'Pigou Effect' implies is an increase in wealth of high income recipients (whose incomes will also increase in real terms at the expense of tax payers so long as the state pays a constant rate of interest on its debt) such as to lead them to reduce their savings by the required amount. Now—even admitting that the redistribution of wealth and income against private debtors and the redistribution of income through the government's interest payments do not impede the reduction in the propensity to save—it seems hard not to conclude that long before the community comes to accept such a redistribution of wealth, other methods of solving the problem of unemployment will have become inevitable, which will be of more direct and less uncertain effect.

monetary forces which that argument presents does not differ essentially from that which Wicksell had presented earlier. In the former, as in the latter, it is admitted that monetary factors can, temporarily, keep the market rate of interest at a level other than the full employment rate[†]—equivalent to the 'natural' rate in Wicksell's theory. In both schemata, however, the full-employment—or 'natural'—rate of interest continues to be the equilibrium one towards which the market rate of interest tends to gravitate. The divergence between the two rates would cause inflationary or deflationary tendencies, whether the latter consist principally of falls in prices and wages or mainly of unemployment of labour; these tendencies would then induce the monetary authorities, who are credited, in both arguments, with proximate control over the rate of interest, to adjust the ruling rate to its 'natural', or full employment, level.[‡]

When compared with these similarities in the conclusions, the concepts of liquidity preference and of the consumption function—the specifically Keynesian elements of the above rehabilitations of the traditional theory—are of relatively minor importance. These elements are accorded a dominant role only for the analysis of the short period and the trade cycle. In this more limited context, the effects of the rate of interest on the demand for money highlight an obstacle capable of retarding the action of the 'real forces' on the rate of interest, particularly in the case of deflation. The consumption function then allows a theoretical treatment of the effects on real income and employment of decreases in money expenditure in the presence of rigid money wages. Thus, in Hicks's words, Keynes's theory appears to be 'the Economics of Depression'; and, in this perspective, Keynes's specific contribution consisted of laying 'enormous emphasis' on the qualifications to traditional theory, the need for which had already been admitted by Marshall or by his successors (Hicks, 1937, p. 472 and p. 465).

We have clearly moved far from the meaning which Keynes himself attributed to his theory when he contrasted it with the traditional theory, which he held to be applicable only in the 'special case' of full employment. And what is most remarkable is that this reversal of meanings is achieved without rejecting the basic assumptions of the *General Theory,* but, on the contrary, by moving within its conceptual framework. This possibility of attributing contrasting meanings to Keynes's theory would therefore seem to arise from within that theory itself, and it will be of interest, at this point in our argument, to seek to identify its source.

[†] It is interesting to note how the concept of a full-employment rate of interest, though a consequence of the idea of a marginal-efficiency-of-capital, is given very little prominence in the *General Theory,* where it just crops up here and there almost accidentally (cf., e.g., Keynes, 1936, pp. 202, 236, 375).

[‡] The 'spontaneous' tendency to equilibrium in the case of wage flexibility, asserted in these arguments, still requires that the monetary authorities hold the stock of money constant and thus permit the *ratio* of the available quantity of money to the money value of the national product to rise.

To note that the theory had been formulated by Keynes on the basis of short-period assumptions, and thus left open problems concerning long-period tendencies, does not appear to go to the root of the matter. Indeed, it remains to be explained why Keynes restricted to the short period an argument whose implications would, he thought, reach far beyond the theory of cyclical phenomena.[†] Above all, we have to explain why the long-period implications which Keynes thought he could deduce have proved to be open to contradiction within his own theoretical framework.

It seems that the root of this ambivalence must rather be sought in the composite character of Keynes's theory. The *General Theory* might be said to contain two fundamentally heterogeneous strands of thought, the one superimposed on the other. A vision of the mode of operation of the economic system, which is in radical conflict with that of the dominant theory, is imposed, as if by force, upon a conceptual basis which is to a large extent still the traditional one, thus giving rise to an inherently unstable compromise. The novel part of Keynes's theory centres on the thesis that it is principally variations in the level of aggregate output that equilibrate investment and saving in a capitalist economy,[‡] a thesis which is suggested directly by an unprejudiced observation of the facts. But this thesis was in conflict with the generally accepted theory of distribution on both the latter's main flanks: that of the labour market—where Keynes had to deny that wages would be determined by the equilibrium between the demand for and supply of labour—and that of the capital market—where Keynes had similarly to deny that the rate of interest would be determined by the equilibrium between the demand for and supply of savings. Thus, in order to develop his initial idea and to get it accepted, Keynes had to work out a critique of the traditional theory of distribution and it is in the way in which he conducted that critique that the compromise referred to above finds its origin.

As was seen in Part I of these Notes, one can distinguish two successive logical stages in the traditional analysis of distribution (cf. Pt. I, pp. 405–6). In the first, from the marginalist premises concerning production and consumption one derives the idea that, given the quantities employed of all factors but one, the quantity employed of this latter factor increases as its real rate of remuneration falls. In the next step, it is maintained that, as a result of competition both amongst the entrepreneurs and amongst the owners of factors, there will be a tendency towards rates of remuneration at which the quantity employed will equal the quantity supplied for each factor. Now, in his critique, Keynes accepts the first stage of the argument: in this way he inherits the traditional part of his theory, which is epitomised by the two schedules of the marginal efficiency of capital and of the marginal

[†]For the long-period consequences that Keynes drew from his theory, consider Keynes (1936), pp. 372–373; see also the passage quoted in n. †, p. 433 below as well as, more generally, the first two sections of Ch. 24 of the *General Theory*.

[‡]In this connection see the passage from the *General Theory* quoted on p. 420 above.

product of labour. His critique has then to turn exclusively on the second stage of the argument. And at the second stage—with the conclusions from the first stage having already been admitted—the capacity of traditional theory to resist attack proved to be greater than Keynes had thought.

The traditional strand of Keynes's thought does not, of course, merely represent a remnant of received modes of thought which can readily be separated from the remainder of his theory, leaving the latter unaffected. Indeed, it is the schedules of the marginal product of labour and of the marginal efficiency of capital which determine the level of real wages and the volume of investment within the system. One may perhaps wonder how acceptable these determinations are and, above all, how consistent they are with the other parts of Keynes's theory, as soon as problems which are not strictly confined to the short period have to be confronted.[†] The fact remains, nevertheless, that it is thanks to this particular conjunction of traditional elements and short-period assumptions that Keynes is able to develop, to some extent, the novel strand of his thought, without having simultaneously to face the fundamental problems of value and distribution.

However, the price which Keynes has to pay for the traditional strand in his thought becomes clear with respect to the schedule of the marginal efficiency of

[†] In Keynes's theory the money rate of interest is made to depend on factors which are largely independent of those affecting the real wage. While this may be admissible in a short-period analysis, in which the distributive variables may be said to diverge from their long-period levels, the same could not be admitted for these latter levels without contradicting the unique, inverse relation which must obtain in the long period between the real wage and the rate of profits (and hence the average long-period rate of interest) (cf., e.g., Sraffa, 1960, Sect. 49). Doubts about Keynes's determination of the wage are strengthened when one considers that the assumption of decreasing returns on which it is based may be questioned as soon as we admit: (a) that the degree of utilisation of the existing productive equipment will generally vary with the quantity of labour employed; and (b) that, in the short period, the quantity employed of some types of labour is constant, or varies less than in proportion to the quantity of output. But if the returns to labour were constant or increasing, up to or near full utilisation of existing equipment, then a real wage equal to the marginal product of labour would imply that gross profits remain constant or fall as the level of activity increases, which is clearly contrary to experience. It will also be clear that this same determination of the wage is of no relevance when we leave a strict short-period analysis and must therefore first explain why the productive equipment is what it is rather than some other.

Keynes's use of the marginal efficiency of capital also presents difficulties. In particular, it is not clear in what sense decreasing returns to increases in the stocks of the different capital goods can be assumed, as is done by Keynes (1936, p. 136), when, there being unemployment, additional equipment could be used together with additional labour.

These deficiencies regarding the marginal productivity of labour and marginal efficiency of capital may serve to confirm the difficulties Keynes had in reconciling the innovatory and the traditional parts of his thought in the *General Theory*. They can also explain how the desire to bring consistency back into economic theory might have encouraged the attempts to confine the implications of Keynes's theory strictly to short-period analysis.

capital.[†] As was seen in Sect. 2, the conflict with traditional theory over the tendency to an equilibrium between demand and supply in the labour market is, in effect, reducible to that over the determination of the rate of interest. The critique of the traditional theory of interest becomes then the key to an acceptance of Keynes's arguments—and the concept of the marginal efficiency of capital proves to be the Achilles' heel of that very critique. Keynes sees the rate of interest as determined by monetary factors: but, as Wicksell's earlier analysis had shown, the idea of an investment demand schedule constitutes an obstacle which a monetary theory of interest cannot easily overcome. Indeed, admitting an elastic investment demand schedule leads to maintaining, on the one hand, the existence of a full-employment level of the rate of interest and, on the other, the presence of inflation, or deflation and unemployment, when the actual rate of interest is not the full employment one; the idea that the market rate of interest tends to gravitate towards its full employment level then acquires plausibility.

It thus seems that the origin of the contrasting meanings attributed to Keynes's theory is to be sought in the doubtful compatibility, from the standpoint of an analysis of long-period tendencies, between the concept of the marginal efficiency of capital and the argument that the level of output plays the leading role in equilibrating planned savings and planned investment. Once the former idea is accepted, it is difficult not to confine the importance of the latter argument to the explanation of the trade cycle and other short-period phenomena. On the other hand, the different conclusions to which Keynes was pointing can be sustained in so far as

[†] An opinion about the nature of the 'marginal efficiency of capital' different from that in the text—and from that of Keynes, who saw his notion as a version of the traditional one (cf., e.g., Keynes, 1936, pp. 139–140)—is advanced by L. Pasinetti, when he writes that such a Keynesian concept reveals a 'different origin' than marginal economic analysis (1974, p. 43). Pasinetti assumes in fact that the prospective yields of capital assets are *independent* of the rate of interest ruling in the loan market (cf., e.g., p. 37). The investment projects could then be always ordered according to a decreasing rate of profitability, independent of the interest rate, thus ensuring the existence of a decreasing relation between the interest rate, and the volume of investment.

We have, however, seen in n. ‡, p. 415 above, that there are some arguments for which the assumption of prospective yields and prices independent of the ruling interest rate does not seem acceptable. We may now add that Keynes himself allowed for the effect of the interest rate on prospective yields (e.g., Keynes, 1936, p. 143). We may also observe that the dependence of prospective yields on the ruling interest rate follows from Pasinetti's own analogy between the marginal efficiency of capital and 'Ricardo's ranking of all lands in a decreasing order of fertility' (Pasinetti, 1974, p. 43): the ordering of lands according to fertility must in fact take into account the changes in interest and prices associated with the extension of cultivation.

Now, when we admit that the prospective yields of capital assets and the ruling interest rate can, and sooner or later will, adjust to each other, it does not seem that a generalised inverse relation between the rate of interest and the volume of investment can find a theoretical basis other than the marginalist notion of an increase in the proportion of capital to other factors as the rate of interest falls. In particular, there seems to be no general reason why the construction of new plant for previously unemployed workers (to which Pasinetti refers on p. 43) should be permanently favoured by a fall of the interest rate rather than by its rise (a rise might indeed raise the long-term profitability of investment and thus provide an incentive for it).

investment is assumed to be insensitive to the rate of interest, even in the long period. But this assumption is in sharp conflict with the presuppositions of the traditional theory of distribution and cannot find a firm foundation until the critique of that theory has undermined those presuppositions.

If this is so, the conflict between the traditional thesis and that of Keynes, concerning the dependence of investment on the propensity to save, cannot be resolved solely on the terrain of monetary theory, which Keynes chose for his critique. Rather, this conflict leads us back to the questions of 'real' theory discussed in Part I of these Notes. And to the conclusions which were reached there we must now return.

6. Conclusions

Our argument in Part II has thus brought us to an alternative, the central element of which is the acceptance or the rejection of the traditional representation of capital as a productive factor, employable in the economy in quantities which increase relative to the quantities of the other factors as the rate of interest falls. If one accepts this representation and, consequently, the traditional thesis with respect to the dependence of investment on the rate of interest, it becomes difficult to reject the traditional doctrine concerning the long-period relation between the propensity to save and the level of investment; unless, that is, one assumes either capital saturation or a long-period deflationary policy on the part of the monetary authorities. By contrast, if the validity of that representation of the productive process is found wanting, the doctrine that the community's propensity to save determines the level of investment is thereby deprived of its foundation.

Now, the argument presented in Part I leads us to maintain that the second possibility is that which permits a better understanding of the facts and we may conclude that, in a long-period analysis no less than in a short-period one, the level of investment should be considered as independent of the propensity to save.

It is then necessary to distinguish between two possible situations. The first is that in which the incentive for private investment remains, for long periods of time, at such a level that aggregate demand presses on the limits of available productive capacity, in almost all major sectors of the economy. There will then tend to be a price inflation, one effect of which could be that of reducing consumption, thus making room for the high level of investment. In such conditions, a fall, or a reduced increase, in consumption—especially of those goods which draw on productive equipment which could be used for investment goods†—may have the effect of reconciling the high level of investment with greater price stability.

† In the short period, the limited adaptability of the existing productive equipment prevents any global alternative between consumption and investment. This alternative becomes increasingly important beyond the period required to set up new plant. Then, however, it applies chiefly to economies without 'structural' unemployment. Where there is unemployment, the labour required to man the new equipment need not be drawn from other productions which can accordingly continue with older equipment.

The more usual situation would, however, be a second one, in which private investment does not reach the limit set by available productive capacity. In this case a fall, or a reduced increase, in consumption could not have any *direct* effect in increasing investment, and the indirect effects could well be negative through the contraction of demand for consumer goods and the consequently reduced incentive to invest.‡

The above conclusion, like any adoption for long-period analysis of the Keynesian thesis concerning the relationship between saving and investment, inevitably implies a rejection of the traditional theory of production and distribution. It thus re-opens the problem of the long-period determination of both the volume of the social product and its distribution between profits and wages. A treatment of these problems is beyond the scope of these Notes, but before concluding we may indicate a few points which directly follow from what we have said so far.

With respect to the long-period determination of the level of social product and labour employment we may return to a question we raised in Sect. 1 of Part I. We there assumed that the productive equipment in the economy was sufficient to employ the entire supply of labour.§ As will be remembered, this was done in order to follow the Keynesian controversy without having to take care of the dominant explanation of 'structural unemployment' in terms of rigid real wages.

We might now note that rigid *real* wages, entailing, as they generally will, rigid *money* wages, could only have strengthened any negative conclusions concerning the long-period dependence of investment on the propensity to save; monetary policy alone would have to be relied on for the necessary adjustments in the interest rate. But when the ground for rejecting the idea of an aggregate demand tending to adjust to productive capacity is that advanced in these Notes, the possibility of 'structural' unemployment emerges quite independently of any rigidity of real wages. The critique of the concept of a demand for capital (investible resources) which is elastic with respect to the rate of interest is, in fact, at one and the same time a critique of the 'twin' concept of a demand for labour which is elastic with respect to the real wage rate (cf. these Notes, Pt. I, pp. 406–7 above). If that critique is well founded, no absorption of 'structural' unemployment could be hoped for from lower real wages and any consequent changes in the physical form of the given 'capital endowment'. This also implies that real wages cannot be relied on to ensure that employment possibilities will increase over time in step with the supply of labour. The factors capable of keeping long-period unemployment within

‡ '[T]he growth of capital depends not at all on a low propensity to consume but is, on the contrary, held back by it; and only in conditions of full employment is a low propensity to consume conducive to the growth of capital' (Keynes, 1936, pp. 372–373).

§ Keynes's assumption of a decreasing marginal product from the labour employed with *given productive equipment* has generally been interpreted to mean that the marginal product falls very little as long as there is some unused productive equipment and then falls sharply; a reasonably definite limit to the quantity of labour that can be employed with a given productive equipment is accordingly also implied in that notion.

socially tolerable limits are then to be sought not in any spontaneous tendency of the demand for labour to adapt to an autonomous growth of population. They have rather to be sought in the complex economic and demographic phenomena of mutual adjustment between the demand for and the supply of wage labour, which the history of the capitalistic economies has long presented for study.†

With respect then to the problem of distribution—which is also opened up by any adoption of the Keynesian thesis for long-period analysis—we may notice the relevance here of that relation, often used in these Notes, between the wage and the rate of profits, which, asserted by Ricardo, has recently been taken up again, overcoming the problems encountered by Ricardo and then by Marx for its exact formulation. This relation may in fact provide a basis for the necessary work of reconstruction. Thus, given such a relation, Keynes's suggestion that the average level of the rate of interest on long-term loans will be determined by conventional factors, ultimately subject to the policy of the monetary authorities (Keynes, 1936, pp. 203–204), would suffice to constitute the nucleus of a theory of distribution. Indeed, it seems reasonable to suppose that, as a result of competition in product markets, the average rate of profit and the average rate of interest on long-term loans will tend, over a sufficiently long period of time, to move in step with one another. If, then, the rate of interest depends on the policy of the monetary authorities, both the long-term movement of the average rate of profit‡ and, through the relation just mentioned, that of real wages are explained by that policy. This does not entail maintaining afresh that the wage bargain has no power to change real wages: the policy of the monetary authorities is not conducted in a vacuum and the movement of prices and of the money wages determined in the wage bargain will be amongst the most important considerations in the formulation of that policy.

References

Haberler, G. (1939). *Prosperity and Depression* (2nd ed.). League of Nations.

Haberler, G. (1964). *Prosperity and Depression* (5th ed.). George Allen and Unwin.

Hicks, J. R. (1937). 'Mr Keynes and the "Classics"; A suggested interpretation', *Econometrica,* 5(2), as rpt. in Haley and Fellner (eds), *Readings in the Theory of Income Distribution.* Blakiston, 1946, 461–76.

Keynes, J. M. (1936). *The General Theory of Employment.* Macmillan.

Keynes, J. M. (1937). 'Alternative theories of the rate of interest', *Economic Journal,* 47(186), 241–252.

Marshall, A. (1920). *Principles of Economics* (8th ed.). Macmillan.

Marshall, A. (1923). *Money, Credit and Commerce.* Kelley, 1965.

Meade, J. E. (1961). *A Neo-Classical Theory of Economic Growth.* George Allen and Unwin.

† The possibility of what is today called structural unemployment is in fact admitted by Keynes. Cf. e.g., the passage '[The rate of interest] may fluctuate for decades about a level which is chronically too high for full employment' (Keynes, 1936, p. 204; see also *ibid.*, p. 217).

‡ Cf. the hint in this direction given by Sraffa (1960), p. 33.

Modigliani, F. (1944). 'Liquidity preference and the theory of interest and money', *Econometrica*, 12(1), as rpt. in American Economic Association, *Readings in Monetary Theory*, III. Irwin (1951), 186–239.

Pasinetti, L. L. (1974). *Growth and Income Distribution: Essays in Economic Theory*. Cambridge University Press.

Patinkin, D. (1948). 'Price flexibility and full-employment', *American Economic Review*, 38(4), as rpt. in American Economic Association, *Readings in Monetary Theory*, III. Irwin, 1951, 252–83.

Pigou, A. C. (1947). 'Economic progress in stable environment', *Economica,* 14(55), as rpt. in American Economic Association, *Readings in Monetary Theory*, III. Irwin, 1951, 241–51.

Robertson, D. H. (1963). *Lectures on Economic Principles*. Collins (first publ. 1957–59).

Solow, R. (1956). 'A contribution to the theory of economic growth', *Quarterly Journal of Economics,* 70(1), 65–94.

Sraffa, P. (1960). *Production of Commodities by Means of Commodities*. Cambridge University Press.

Swan, T. W. (1956). 'Economic growth and capital accumulation', *Economic Record,* 32(2), 334–361.

Tobin, J. (1955). 'A dynamic aggregative model', *Journal of Political Economy,* 63(2), 103–115.

Wicksell, K. (1907). 'The enigma of business cycles', as rpt. in Wicksell, *Interest and Prices* (221–239). Kelley, 1965.

Wicksell, K. (1935). *Lectures on Political Economy* (Vol. II). Routledge.

Wicksell, K. (1898). *Interest and Prices*. Kelley, 1965.

Two Routes to Effective Demand: Comment on Kregel[†*]

I.

1. To be clear about the problems raised by Kregel (1983) we must distinguish two routes along which orthodox theory can be criticized in order to establish the "principle of effective demand", by which I shall mean the principle that aggregate demand may be insufficient to absorb the output produced from normal use of existing capacity.[1] The first route centres on the criticism of orthodox "real" theory. The second route, favoured by Kregel, centres on "liquidity preference" and the criticism of orthodox "monetary" theory. This latter route was that taken by Keynes. Let us look briefly at each.

II.

2. We start from the simplest possible scheme of orthodox "real" theory—a scheme which also has the advantage of a consistent treatment of capital. We suppose an economy where "corn" is produced in yearly production cycles by labour and capital consisting exclusively of "corn", the two being susceptible of combination in continuously variable proportions. Land is free and the capitalists are the entrepreneurs. Each capitalist entrepreneur is faced with a curve of the marginal product of labour which results when the variable quantity of labour is applied

† Previously published with Macmillan in *Distribution, Effective Demand and International Economic Relations*, ed. by J. A. Kregel, 1983. All necessary permissions acquired.

* Research assistance from the "Consiglio Nazionale delle Ricerche" and the "Ministero della Pubblica Istruzione" is gratefully acknowledged.

[1] In referring to "aggregate demand" we naturally assume away all effects of disproportions in the existing productive capacity, i.e. we assume that the capacities of the various sectors are proportionate to the composition of the aggregate demand taken at the level which we describe as ensuring "full utilization of capacity".

P. Garegnani, *Capital Theory, the Surplus Approach, and Effective Demand*, Springer Studies in the History of Economic Thought,
https://doi.org/10.1007/978-3-031-23643-3_12

with the quantity of corn-capital that the capitalist possesses. For well known reasons, the competitive capitalist will maximize his profits when he hires the number of labourers for which the marginal product, a quantity of corn, is equal to the corn-wage he finds ruling in the market. The marginal product curve then becomes what we might call the "employment curve" (not yet the "demand curve") for that individual capitalist, and indicates the number of laborers he should employ to reach his maximum profit at any real wage. These individual "employment curves" can be then added up to obtain a similar "labour-employment curve" (*LE*)-(*LE*)' for the whole economy such as that indicated in Fig. 1(a) below.

3. We may now introduce the *additional* assumption that unemployed workers may bid down the corn wage, or that capitalists, unable to hire the workers may bid it up. *Given the negative slope of the employment curve* this assumption will (a) be plausible; (b) transform the employment curve (*LE*)-(*LE*)' into a "demand curve" for labour and therefore (c) lead to the familiar demand-and-supply determination of wages and profits.

As an illustration, suppose that the wage is w' and the number of labourers employed, *OA'*, is less than *OL*, the number of labourers whom we assume to be seeking employment. If workers are assumed to bid down the wage this process will lead to w^* at which all labourers will find employment. And the opposite process of capitalists bidding will lead to the same level, w^* if the wage happened to be initially $w'' < w^*$.We can then plausibly argue that the economy of our example will gravitate around the wage w^*. This conclusion also depends, however, on the assumption that all corn-capital will be employed, an assumption which we made more acceptable in the present context by assuming that the capitalists are the entrepreneurs. But a similar decreasing "capital-employment curve" (*KE*)-(*KE*)' could have been obtained by assuming the workers to be entrepreneurs (Fig. 1(b))[2]; indeed the *negative* slope is retained for the capital-employment curve corresponding to *any* number of workers employed—and to the labour-employment curve corresponding to *any* quantity of capital employed.[3] This would ensure that even with a third party acting as entrepreneur, a tendency towards full utilization would exist for each factor *independently* of the quantity of the other employed: thus there would be a tendency towards the simultaneous full employment of *both* factors.

We could conclude that the economy defined by our hypotheses would gravitate around the wage w^* and the corresponding profit (interest) rate r^*. It is this conclusion which allows us to describe the curve (*LE*)-(*LE*)' as a "demand curve" for labour with *L-L'* as the corresponding "supply curve", so that these two curves

[2] The curve depicts the behaviour of the "net" marginal product of capital, where by "net" marginal product we refer to the marginal product diminished by 1, i.e. by the replacement of the additional unit of corn-capital.

[3] Indivisibilities in the process of production are assumed away in accordance with the hypothesis of constant returns to scale.

together determine the "equilibrium" wage w^* and profit rate r^*. The same determination can be envisaged symmetrically, in terms of the curves *(KE)-(KE)'* and *K-K'*.

4. We have so far assumed that all transactions take place directly in corn. But the above "real" analysis provided "orthodoxy" with a way out of the difficulty which is raised by money and its possible use as a store of value.

The difficulty is that when incomes are paid in money, decisions to save need not result in the accumulation of "corn-capital", as was the case when incomes were paid in corn. Money savings might indeed fail to be spent (by the saver himself, or by others) in order to buy corn, with the result that aggregate demand in money terms might fall below the level necessary to buy the entire corn output at the ruling money price of corn. Then there comes into existence an interaction between the labour market and the capital market different from that considered above (Sect. 3) and this difference must be examined before we can conclude that the economy should gravitate around w^* and r^*.

In fact when wages are paid in money, competition of unemployed workers will first affect the *money* wage rate. Now, assume that employment and output initially expand in response to the fall in money wages (unaccompanied as yet, by any fall in the money price of corn): if, then, the money savings resulting from the additional money incomes fail to find their way to the "corn-capital" market, aggregate money demand will be insufficient to absorb the increased corn output at the previously ruling money price of corn.[4] In this case the assumed flexibility of wages would abort as an equilibrating mechanism, since it would only lead to a cumulative process of deflation of the money wage and price of corn.

However, for "orthodox theory" this problem only means that the equilibrating mechanism in the capital market envisaged in the "real" theory takes on a new importance when money is considered, and that the analogous mechanism in the labour market now *asymmetrically* depends on the mechanism at work in the capital market, while the latter does not depend on the former in the same way. In fact it remains true that the decreasing shape of the capital-employment curve would ensure that the additional money savings would provide additional "corn-capital", only if these savings succeeded in lowering the rate of interest sufficiently. And, with e.g. Wicksell, orthodox theory argued that the additional savings would plausibly lower the rate of interest, *either* by exerting direct pressure on the loan market, *or*, if this direct route were closed, by the deflation of wages and prices in the manner already described. The flexibility of the money-wage will then be compatible with a sufficient stability of the money price of corn and the adjustment mechanism of the labour market envisaged in the "real" theory will come back into its own.

---

[4] If incomes had been paid directly in terms of corn, a failure of savings to be employed as corn-capital could not have affected the level of labour employment since the corn which is thus neither consumed nor lent for productive employment would still have been "invested" (whatever its final destination: consumers' stocks, or merely waste).

5. Now, as we stated in Sect. 2 above, this analysis depends critically on the negative slope of the *(LE)*-*(LE)'* and *(KE)*-*(KE)'* curves, here ensured by the principle of decreasing marginal productivity (and — if we had admitted a plurality of consumption goods, all produced with corn-capital and labour — by the principle of decreasing marginal utility).[5] If, in fact, the employment curves happened to be similar to those of Fig. 2 it would have been impossible to construe them as "demand curves", with *L*-*L'* or *K*-*K'* as the corresponding "supply curves". And even more basically it would have been impossible to assume an indefinite flexibility of wage and interest (profit) rates, because this would have led to the absurd conclusion of a wage which falls indefinitely to zero, or alternatively a wage which rises to absorb the entire social product — depending on whether the wage happens to be initially below or above w^*.

It would, on the other hand, be a misconception to contend that this would merely be a case of "unstable equilibrium", which would not as such call into question the general demand-and-supply theory of distribution described above. To counter this contention it should be sufficient to recall how Alfred Marshall qualified stable equilibrium as the only "real equilibrium" and considered positions of unstable equilibrium as "the dividing boundaries between two positions of stable equilibria": with this Marshall showed how well aware he was that "unstable" equilibrium positions would call into question the validity of a demand-and-supply explanation of prices, unless one can convincingly argue that they are exceptional and furthermore that, should they arise, they would not lead to results too much at variance with experience.[6] Indeed, if the employment curves were to be like those of Fig. 2, it would be unreasonable to describe them as "demand curves", and reasonable to look elsewhere for an explanation of the division of the product between wages and profits: to look, for example, to the kind of determination of the wage by relative class strength which we find in the classical economists like Adam Smith and Marx.

6. We need no more than this to see the first route to the establishment of the principle of effective demand. As we all know, an important aspect of the general difficulty concerning the notion of capital used in orthodox theory is that when the

---

[5] Thus, if we had supposed two consumption goods, corn and cloth, each producible with a single method in which cloth required more corn capital per worker to be produced, any fall in the interest rate would lower the price of cloth relative to corn. Then, the orthodox analysis of consumers' choices states in general that a higher proportion of labour will have to be employed in producing cloth with a consequent increase in the quantity of "corn-capital" assisting the given labour force.

[6] Marshall ([1920] 1949), APP. H, 2, p. 665 and n.). In that note Marshall went on to consider as one of "the difficulties which beset the theory of equilibrium in regard to commodities which obey the law of increasing return", the possibility that the equilibrium position corresponding to the highest price be unstable. He then felt it necessary to establish that the consequence of this would remain confined to the fact that

> the production of the commodity in question on a small scale will not remunerate the producers: so that its production cannot be commenced at all unless some passing accident has caused temporarily an urgent demand for the commodity, or has temporarily lowered the expenses of producing it (...).

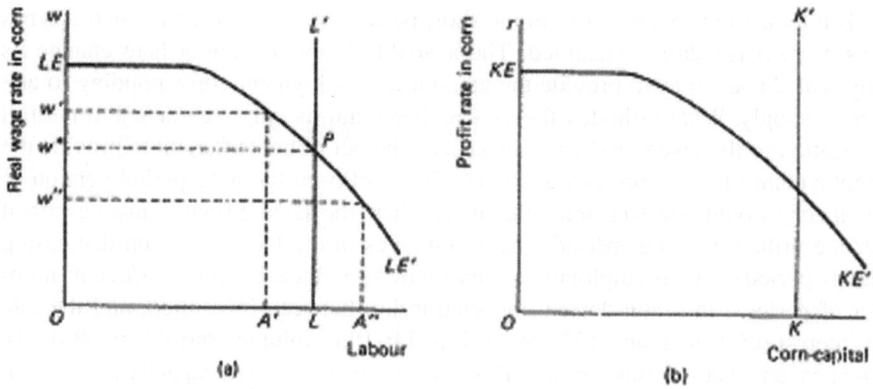

Fig. 1 (a) 'Labour-employment' and (b) 'Capital-employment' curves consistent with orthodox theory

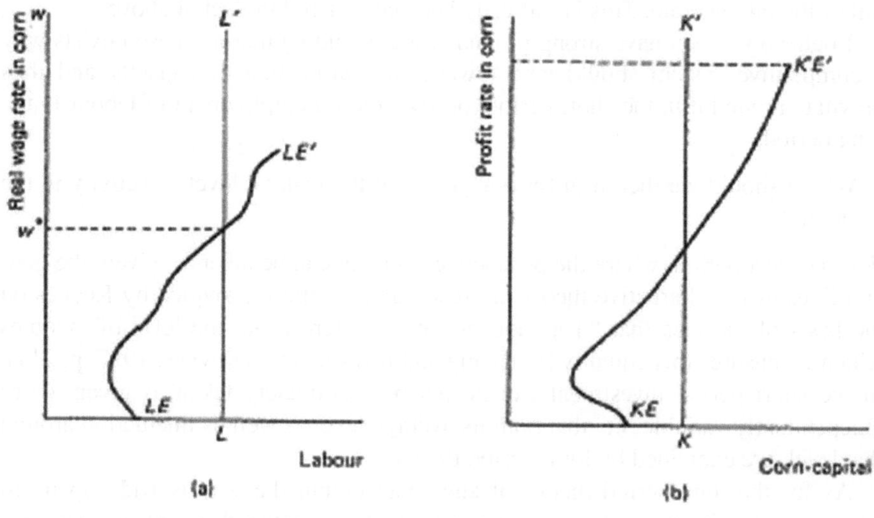

Fig. 2 (a) 'Labour-employment' and (b) 'Capital-employment' curves inconsistent with orthodox theory

theory is applied not to the *imaginary* corn economy, but to the *real* economy, with "capital" as a value magnitude, there is no reason to suppose that the employment curves should resemble those of Fig. 1, rather than those of Fig. 2.[7] For the reasons we have seen this is sufficient to deny plausibility to the traditional argument about *a long period* tendency towards the full employment of labour.

[7] Cf. Garegnani, 1970, pp. 423–4 [reasonable page reference by the editor, in place of the evidently incorrect original]; [this volume, Part II, pp. 168–9]. It should be noticed that the positive relation between w and labour employed (LE) assumed for Fig. 2(a) implies the symmetrical positive relation between r and (KE) in Fig. 2(b), provided we assume that the relation in Fig. 2(a) depends on the *proportion* L/K and not on the absolute entities L and K. The inverse relations between r and w then entails that an increase in w with an increase in L/K *is* a decrease of r with a decrease in K/L.

But let us turn to the theory in the short-period formulation with which Keynes was more particularly concerned. The available "capital" cannot here change its physical shape, so as to provide the amount of employment corresponding to any labour supply. What orthodox theory can then claim is only a tendency to the full utilization of the given productive capacity, whether or not sufficient to provide the employment of the entire labour force[8] (the validity of the long-period version of the theory would however imply that it is). Then, the same difficulty just described for the orthodox "long- period" theory emerges in the fact that a non-decreasing (long- period) capital-employment curve will be reflected, over a sufficient number of periods, in a non-decreasing relationship between investment and the rate of interest (cf. Garegnani, 1978–9, Pt. I, p. 346 [this volume, Part IV, pp. 400–1]). The consequences of this for the full utilization of productive capacity are evident if we remember that the only mechanism which can be envisaged as capable to adjust investment to full-capacity saving is that investment should increase upon a fall of the interest rate. This has already been considered in Sect. 4 above.

I believe we then have strong grounds for concluding that no reason exists why a competitive system should tend towards full utilization of capacity and thus gravitate around it in the short period, or towards full employment of labour in the long period.

7. Where should we then turn for our theory of the general level of activity in the economy?

For the short period, where the productive capacity can be taken as given, the general lines of the alternative theory are ready and are those provided by Keynes on the basis of the idea that "it is, not the rate of interest, but the level of incomes which ... ensures this equality [of saving and investment]" (Keynes, 1937, p. 211). In the short period investment can in fact be legitimately taken as given, or as independently variable, i.e. that both its average level as well as fluctuation around that level, are explained by long-period theory.

As for the long-period theory of aggregate output the way is wide open. To attempt to see its general course we must first remember that: (a) by overturning the orthodox long-period theory of output, one also overturns the orthodox long-period theory of distribution, and (b) a flexible framework for an alternative theory of distribution is available in the "surplus approach" of Marx and the Classics, already mentioned, where the division of the product between wages and profits is *not* determined by the demand-and-supply forces described above.[9]

---

[8] This assumes that a definite quantity of employment of labour can be associated with any level of productive equipment available in the economy and seems in contrast with Keynes's assumption of a regularly decreasing "marginal product" of labour applied to such equipment. This Keynesian notion has however been generally interpreted to mean that the marginal product falls very little as long as there is some unused productive equipment and then falls sharply: a reasonably definite limit to the quantity of labour that can be employed with a given productive equipment is accordingly implied.

[9] An alternative long-period theory of the level of aggregate output thus seems indissoluble from an alternative theory of distribution. It seems then difficult to agree with Joan Robinson when she writes:

In fact, the "surplus approach" to distribution does not preclude the possibility of long-period deficiencies of aggregate demand, i.e. that aggregate demand may influence the pace of accumulation. Ricardo believed in Say's law, but nothing in his theory of value and distribution warranted this belief. As we know Marx shared the basic elements of Ricardo's theory, but he had no difficulty in rejecting Say's law (cf. Garegnani, 1978–9, Pt. II, pp. 79–81 [this volume, Part IV, pp. 431–3. *Editor's note*: see Part I of the cited essay, this volume, p. 394, n. §, for even more pertinent reference]).

Possessed of this flexible "surplus approach" for long-period analysis, and of Keynes's short-period theory of capacity utilization, I believe that a satisfactory long-period theory of output does not require much more than (a) an analysis of how investment determines saving through changes in the level of *productive capacity* (and not only through changes in the *level of utilization* of productive capacity); (b) a study of the factors affecting the long-run levels of investment; and (c) a study of the relation between consumption expenditure and aggregate income. Theoretical and applied studies have already prepared much material in the last two fields.

III.

8. The route to effective demand which we have just sketched was not however open in Keynes's time[10] and accordingly was not the one he took. He believed in what the facts suggested, i.e. that the massive unemployment of the 1930s could hardly be explained by a failure of wages to fall sufficiently. Relying in part on the previous work of Richard Kahn (1931), he went on to develop what his eyes suggested by means of the concepts of the multiplier and of the consumption function. However, and here we come to the difficulty, Keynes also believed in the premises of orthodox theory and did not challenge the notion of substitution between labour and capital on which, as we saw, the orthodox theory based its conclusions concerning the tendency towards the full employment of labour. The problem therefore is: how did Keynes attempt to reconcile these two contradictory strata of his thought?

We know how he did it. After utilizing the consumption function to show how a fall in money wages could leave employment and real wages unaffected except for its effect on investment, he went on to deny that this effect could be sufficient to

---

> Economic analysis, serving for two centuries to win an understanding of the Nature and Causes of the Wealth of Nations, has been fobbed off with another bride — a Theory of Value (1956, p. v).

It would rather seem that the theory of distribution and hence, necessarily, the "theory of value" (relative prices are known when the distribution of the social product between wages, profits and rents is known) is necessary to obtain results on the Nature and Causes of the Wealth of Nations, as Adam Smith recognized when he placed it at the very beginning of his book.

[10] As is well known, the critique of "real" orthodox theory is a result of work of the 1950s and 1960s.

bring about full employment. For this crucial second step of his argument he relied basically on the joint outcome of two elements: (i) liquidity preference, i.e. the obstacle which expectations concerning the future course of the interest rate would raise to the fall in the interest rate being sufficient to bring investment into line with full-employment saving; and (ii) the effect of expectations concerning the future profitability of production making investment fluctuate. With element (ii) full employment of labour emerged as increasingly dependent upon quick adjustments of the interest rate, precisely when, by element (i), doubts were raised about the adaptability of the interest rate.

This second, Keynesian route to effective demand, with its heavy reliance upon expectations, was (at least until very recently) quite successful in getting the effective demand principle established for the short period policies which were Keynes's immediate concern. The same route has however turned out to be much less successful in getting the principle of effective demand accepted for long-run theory as Keynes clearly thought it should.

Hicks, or Modigliani, or Patinkin did not in fact find serious difficulties in accepting Keynes's concepts and arguing that in the long period the system could gravitate around a position sufficiently close to full employment — if the monetary authorities were flexible enough to compensate for any rigidity of the money wage.[11] These authors could rely on two elements: (a) the elasticity of investment with respect to the rate of interest, which Keynes had conceded with his "marginal efficiency of capital"; and (b) the decrease in the independent action that (incorrect) expectations might produce over the long run. These two elements indicate that Keynes's comparative failure in getting effective demand established in long-run analysis goes back to the fact he had not challenged the premises of the orthodox theory which had produced the conception of forces of demand and supply leading to the full employment of the "factors of production", but rather had rested on the uncertainty and incorrectness of expectations.

Keynes's acceptance of the traditional premises also helps to explain a second factor which underlies his failure to get the principle of effective demand established in long-period theory. Except for brief unsystematic statements we do not find in his work any alternative to the orthodox long-period theory of the level of aggregate output. Indeed, showing that the economy does *not* tend to full employment in the short period, is not the same thing as showing that the economy does not gravitate around a position sufficiently close to full employment in the long run. Consider Fig. 3 below. It is one thing to show that at any given point in time, t^*, the economy may have a level of aggregate output, E^*, less than the level, C, corresponding to a normal utilization of the productive capacity existing at t^*, with the correspondingly lower level of labour employment. It is quite a different thing to show that point E^* will *not* be on a curve oscillating around a line $C - FC'$ indicating the development of aggregate output over time, under the hypothesis

[11] This argument provided then the basis on which subsequent work could proceed (cf. in this respect Bharadwaj, 1983).

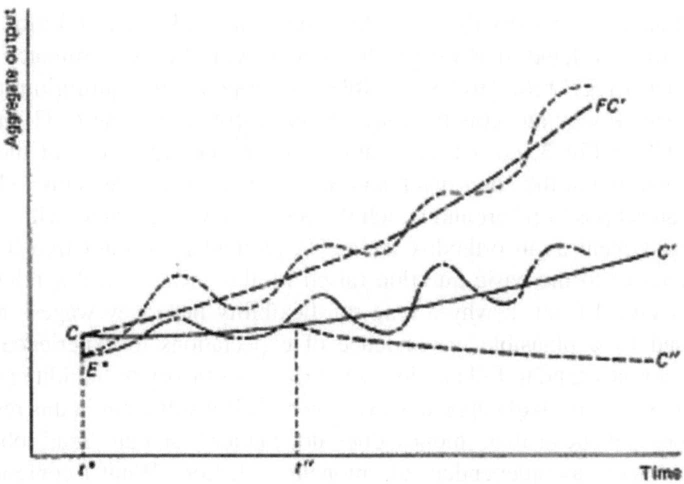

Fig. 3 Short-run deviations from normal capacity output around full-employment trend or diverging-from-full-employment trend

of continuous normal utilization of productive equipment, the growth of which is explained by the saving forthcoming from the income corresponding to this normal utilization, and invested in the physical forms allowed by the labour force and technical knowledge available. It is, in other words, a different thing to show that point E^* can in fact lie on a curve oscillating around a trend line $C - C'$ which may fall below the C–FC' line and progressively diverge from it.[12]

IV.

9. One merit of Kregel's paper is that it recognizes this distinction between establishing the principle of effective demand for short-period analysis, and establishing it for long-period analysis.

Kregel refers to "natural positions" towards which the economy will gravitate[13] — i.e., if I understand him correctly, the positions which I have elsewhere called "long-period positions" of the system, characterized, under free competition, by a uniform rate of profit (cf. Garegnani, 1976, p. 26 [this volume, Part II, p. 210]). However, he seems then to confine himself to stating that the "natural position" that the economy is at any moment gravitating around need not be full employment. He does so by contrasting the possible "multiplicity" of natural positions with the "unique full-employment equilibrium" of orthodox theory (Kregel, op. cit., p. 63).

---

[12]From each point of the trend line C–C' a new trend line, like C–C'' in Fig. 3, might have departed either downwards or upwards according to whether around time t'' the average utilization of the then available productive capacity rose above, or fell below, that implied in the line C–C'.

[13]Cf. Kregel (1983).

I would advance two strictly connected comments on Kregel's position. I do not believe on the one hand, that we can be content with the indeterminacy which is implied when Kregel refers to the possible "multiplicity" of equilibrium positions. We must *explain* why an economy may gravitate around the line *C–C'* rather than around *C–C''* in Fig. 3, i.e. we must aim at a long period theory of the level of aggregate output. On the other hand, and most importantly, it remains to be shown that the "natural position" around which the economy will gravitate will not be that of full employment as in orthodox theory. In particular I do not find in Kregel's paper an answer to the basic question raised by the "neoclassical synthesis", and all that descended from it: why a long-run flexibility in money wages and prices, accompanied by a plausible respondence of expectations to experience will not make the economy tend to full employment? Keynes's theory of liquidity preference (to which Kregel repeatedly appeals) has shown itself insufficient in this respect.

This does not mean that "money does not matter", or that "real" phenomena will again emerge as independent of "monetary" factors. What I contend is only that, Keynes's liquidity preference is not necessary to establish the principle of effective demand in the short or the long period. Money does play an essential role for effective demand in that, as we saw in Sect. 4 above, it allows the circle production-income-demand-production to break in the savings-investment link; but this, so far as I can see, has little to do with an explanation of the rate of interest by means of Keynes's liquidity preference. And above all, money is likely to play an essential role in determining such "real" phenomena as the distribution between profits and wages (cf. Garegnani, 1978–9, Pt. II, p. 81 [this volume, Part IV, p. 433]) or the growth of aggregate output.

References

Bharadwaj, K. (1983). On Effective Demand: Certain Recent Critiques. In J. A. Kregel (Ed.), *Distribution* (pp. 3–27). Macmillan.

Garegnani, P. (1970). Heterogeneous Capital, the Production Function and the Theory of Distribution. *Review of Economics Studies,* 37(3), pp. 407–436.

Garegnani, P. (1976). On a Change in the Notion of Equilibrium in Recent Work on Value and Distribution. A Comment on Samuelson. In M. Brown, K. Sato, & P. Zarembka (Eds.), *Essays in Modern Capital Theory* (pp. 25–45). North Holland.

Garegnani P. (1978–9). Notes on consumption, investment and effective demand. *Cambridge Journal of Economics*, Part I: 2(4), pp. 335–53; Part II: 3(1), pp. 63–82.

Kahn, R. F. (1931). The Relation of Home Investment to Unemployment. *Economic Journal,* 41(162), pp. 173–198.

Keynes, J. M. (1937). Alternative Theories of the Rate of Interest. *Economic Journal*, 47(186) as rpt. in *The Collected Writings of John Maynard Keynes*, Vol. XIV, *The General Theory and After*, Part II, *Defence and Development* (pp. 201–215), ed. by D. Moggridge. Macmillan, 1973.

Kregel, J. A. (1983). Effective Demand: Origin and Development of the Notion. In J. A. Kregel (Ed.), *Distribution, Effective Demand and International Economic Relations* (pp. 50–68). Macmillan.

Marshall, A., & ([1920] (1949). *Principles of Economics* (8th ed.). Macmillan.

Robinson, J. V. (1956). *The Accumulation of Capital.* Macmillan.

Some Notes for an Analysis of Accumulation †*

1. Introduction

1. If we were to ask ourselves what determines the speed of capital accumulation and of growth in an economy, we would get two different answers from today's economics. The first is the traditional one, according to which the community's decisions to save in conditions of full utilization of resources (defined so as to allow for a normal succession of booms and slumps) will determine the trend of capital accumulation. This trend of capital accumulation, taken together with the growth of population and the development of technical knowledge, will then determine the trend of aggregate output.

The second answer is less homogeneous, and includes, in fact, two different positions sharing what may be called for short the Keynesian Hypothesis.[1] This shared hypothesis is that in the long period, in which productive capacity changes,

† Previously published with Palgrave Macmillan in *Beyond the Steady State. A Revival of Growth Theory*, ed. by J. Halevi, D. Laibman and E. J. Nell, 1992. All necessary permissions acquired.

* This paper summarizes parts of a longer one delivered at a conference organized by the Centre for Advanced Economic Studies in Udine in August 1982. Other commitments have so far prevented me from preparing the longer paper for publication, and I have been flattered into thinking that the present one may be of some use as it stands. This explains the almost complete absence of references both to the previous literature and, above all, to the literature which appeared on this subject in *Political Economy. Studies in the Surplus Approach* [available on-line at http://www.centrosraffa.org/fromthearchives.aspx] after 1982. Some of the ideas in this paper had been advanced in a mimeographed volume of 1962 (Garegnani, 1962), concerning the role of aggregate demand for Italian economic development. In revising the present paper I have drawn benefit from discussions with several colleagues and, in particular, with Dr Roberto Ciccone of Rome University, Professor Heinz Kurz of the University of Graz, and Professor Franklin Serrano of the Federal University of Rio de Janeiro. Work on this paper has been made easier by research grants from the Consiglio Nazionale delle Ricerche and by the Italian Ministry of Education.

[1] Cf. Kaldor (1955–6), p. 95.

P. Garegnani, *Capital Theory, the Surplus Approach, and Effective Demand*,
Springer Studies in the History of Economic Thought,
https://doi.org/10.1007/978-3-031-23643-3_13

no less than in the short period analyzed by Keynes, it is an independently determined level of investment that generates the corresponding amount of savings, rather than an autonomous propensity to save that generates the level of investment as in the traditional answer. However, the savings can be generated by investment along two entirely different routes, and it is the route which is being postulated that separates the two Keynesian positions. The first route is by lowering the real wage thereby raising the normal rate of profits and, other things being equal, the proportion of profits in national income.[2] Since the propensity to save out of profits can be safely assumed to be higher than that out of wages, the rise in the proportion of savings to consumption will follow. The second route through which investment can generate the corresponding amount of savings is by raising the level of output together with the corresponding productive capacity, without any need to change the real wage and the normal rate of profits.[3] For brevity we shall refer here to the theoretical positions characterized by those two routes as, respectively, the 'First' and the 'Second' Keynesian Positions.

The First Keynesian Position is that which has attracted more attention, leaving the Second in the shadow. However, once some misunderstandings are cleared up, it may become apparent that the second of those two routes is that which a market economy is more likely to take in adjusting to the incentive to invest. In fact, this division in the theories of accumulation based on the Keynesian Hypothesis does not seem to have been sufficiently analysed and discussed. The purpose of this paper is to contribute to that analysis.

2. For the sake of simplicity, our analysis (Sect. 2) will be conducted on the assumption of a competitive, closed economy, with homogeneous labour and no scarce natural resources, so that the social product is divided into wages and profits only. We shall also argue as if the availability of labour did not constitute a limit to the growth of the economy. We shall assume that the real wage rate w^* and the technical conditions of production are both given, so that the corresponding normal rate of profits r^* and the system of relative prices are known.

[2] The rate of profits (interest) here referred to as 'normal' is that to which economic theory has traditionally referred when associating a level of that rate with any given level of the real wage under conditions of free competition. We shall later distinguish this notion of a 'normal' rate of profits from a second 'ex-post' notion of the rate of profits (see below).

[3] By 'productive capacity' of the economy in the given situation we shall mean, as is generally meant, the 'productive equipment' in existence, together with that part of the workforce which is required to operate it. By 'productive equipment' we mean, on the other hand, the aggregate of what has traditionally been referred to as the 'plant' of a firm or industry, that is those inputs, mostly fixed capital goods, which cannot be adjusted to the level of outputs, with the same rapidity as, e.g., the stocks of raw materials. It is here assumed, as is generally assumed, that the capacity is distributed among the sectors according to the given composition of aggregate demand at the level which would enable a normal (desired) utilization of aggregate capacity.

We shall indicate by y the ratio which the output bears to the capital, reckoned at the given prices and when capacity is utilized at the normal or 'desired' level,[4] and we shall assume that y remains constant as capacity changes. We shall assume further that the marginal net propensity to save s is constant and equal to the average propensity. None of the above assumptions appears, however, to be essential to our conclusions.[5]

3. Our argument will proceed in three steps. In the first (Sect. 2) we shall indicate how, in the long period in which productive capacity can change, investment can engender the corresponding amount of savings by varying the level of productive capacity and output, rather than by changing the real wage rate and the normal rate of profits. It will be shown there that this can occur in the long period with even more ease than it can in the short period with a given productive capacity, for which the generation of savings through changes in aggregate output was originally envisaged by Keynes. It will thus emerge that increases (decreases) in output, accompanied by increases (decreases) in productive capacity, may be the long-run normal effect of changes in effective demand, with the real wage and the normal rate of profits left to be determined by other circumstances – in particular, by the circumstances envisaged in the classical theories.[6]

This conclusion may, however, appear to contradict the interpretation sometimes given of the so-called 'Cambridge equation':

$$s_c r = g$$

which we take here in its simplest familiar form assuming zero savings of workers and a given propensity to save of capitalists s_c. In fact, that equation has sometimes been interpreted to entail a necessary link between the real wage w^* and normal rate of profits r^*, on the one hand and, on the other, the ratio g between net investment and the value of the capital stock, or 'rate of accumulation' as we shall here call it for short.[7] The next two steps in our argument will accordingly be taken up with showing why such an interpretation of the equation would not be correct.

We shall argue that the Cambridge equation faces us with an alternative. In Sect. 3 we shall examine the first branch of the alternative—that in which the

[4] The notion of normal or 'desired' level of utilization of capacity will be discussed below.

[5] The independence of our conclusions concerns in particular the assumption of a given aggregate propensity to save s which may in some cases become incompatible with the assumption of given propensities to save out of profits and wages. In fact though both the real wage w^* and the ratio y of capacity output to capital are assumed constant in our analysis in Sect. 2 below, the *proportion* in which the social product is divided between wages and profits may yet change when, in that analysis, we consider changes in the level of capacity utilization. A constant aggregate propensity to save s becomes then incompatible with constant propensities to save out of wages and profits.

[6] Cf., e.g., Garegnani (1984, pp. 294–6 [this volume, Part III, pp. 308–11]).

[7] Cf. the passages reported in para. 4 and n. 3. As for the value of capital to be put in the denominator of the rate of accumulation g, see para. 15.

equation is taken to refer to the *normal* rate of profits r^*, and to the corresponding real wage w^*. It will be shown that the 'rate of accumulation' g^* which will then have to appear on the right-hand side of the equation will need have nothing to do with the *actual* rate of accumulation $\widehat{g}$. In Sect. 4 we shall examine the second branch of the alternative – that in which we take the rate of accumulation appearing in the Cambridge equation as the *actual* rate of accumulation $\widehat{g}$. We shall show there that the 'rate of profits' $\widehat{r}$ which will then have to appear on the left-hand side of the equation, will be what we may describe as an 'ex-post' rate of profits, and will need have nothing to do with the normal rate of profits r^* and the corresponding wage rate w^*.

Either way, it will emerge that the Cambridge equation entails no necessary relation between the actual rate of accumulation, on the one hand, and the real wage and normal rate of profits, on the other. The equation will thus confirm, and not contradict, the results of Sect. 2 about the independence of the real wage and the normal rate of profits from aggregate effectual demand.

2. Spare Productive Capacity and the Generation of Savings by Investment in a Long-Period Analysis

4. The fact that a large underutilization of productive capacity cannot last indefinitely seems in fact to have led to the idea that the burden of adjusting savings to investment in the long run will have to fall largely, if not exclusively, on the distribution between wages and profits. Thus Joan Robinson wrote in her *Essays on the Theory of Economic Growth* (1962, p. 11):

> In long-run competitive equilibrium the relation of total income to the stock of capital is determined within certain limits by technical conditions .... The distribution of income, however, is strongly influenced by the amount of investment.[8]

[8] Similarly S. Marglin was more recently to write

> In the short run ... the rate of capacity utilisation changes in accordance with aggregate demand.... But in the long run ... there is no excess capacity to accommodate investment demand. Distribution must bear the brunt of adjusting aggregate demand to supply (Marglin, 1984, pp. 474–5; I owe this quotation to Professor Heinz Kurz).

To eliminate a possible ambiguity it should be added that a few lines before the passage quoted in the text, Joan Robinson had made it clear that the question of 'distribution of income' to which her passage refers is that of 'what determines the *normal* rate of profits, when the real wage is not to be taken as given' (emphasis mine). The context of the passage by Marglin also makes it clear that he understands the real wage and hence the normal rate of profits (see n. 2 above) to be the 'distribution' which is affected by investment. We should in fact distinguish the effect on the wage rate and normal rate of profits postulated in the First Keynesian Position, from any change in the amount of profits relative to capital which results merely from changes

Now, the premise concerning the temporary nature of any large excess capacity may be correct, but the conclusion that the real wage and the corresponding normal rate of profits have therefore to be influenced by the amount of investment does not follow. When it is capacity that adjusts to aggregate output, rather than output to capacity, the disappearance of excess capacity in the long period is the *result* of a low aggregate demand, and cannot therefore have acted as a constraint upon it, imposing a choice between consumption and investment and, hence, between wages and profits. And as soon as aggregate demand revives, the process of destruction of capacity will be set in reverse, and productive capacity will be recreated, leaving space for additional investment *and* consumption.

In fact, it is not difficult to show that even a small degree of excess capacity may involve a failure to obtain an appreciable increment of productive capacity in the subsequent periods, when account is taken of the cumulative, further investment output derivable from the capacity brought about by the increment in investment obtainable by using the initial excess capacity. As we shall presently see, such a potential increment of capacity grows over time like a sum at a compound rate of interest, and the rate at which it accumulates is given by the ratio of savings to capital at normal (desired) utilization of a capacity.

In the rest of this section we shall attempt to give an idea of the influence on future potential output of any failure to realize this year's potential output,[9] thus showing how in the long period in which productive capacity can change, the margins for expanding output in response to aggregate demand widen rather than narrow, contrary to what is implied in Joan Robinson's passage above.

5. Let us in fact assume an additional utilization of capacity in year 0 of a numerical value of 10, so that if the propensity to save s is 0.2, the potential increment of output would provide additional investment of the value of 2, which, given a ratio of output to capital y of 0.5, would establish a unit potential additional productive capacity (that is, we assume an additional utilization of capacity numerically given by $x = 1/ys$, engendering an additional capacity of $syx = 1$: see Table 1, p. {53}). We are here measuring utilization of capacity by the corresponding amount of net output estimated at the given prices of production, just as we are measuring capacity itself by the amount of net output obtainable from it when utilized at the normal (desired) level.

in the level of capacity utilization and may well leave the real wage and normal rate of profits unchanged (cf. the ex-post rate of profits $\hat{r}$ in para. 14).

[9] In the otherwise rich literature on potential output only Okun seems to have remarked on how the failure to use this year's potential fully will influence future potential aggregate social product (Cutilli, 1980, p. 1354). Okun in fact writes:

> To the extent that low utilization rates and accompanying low profits and personal incomes hold down investment ... the growth of potential GNP will be retarded (Okun, 1970, pp. 134–5).

But Okun also left it at that.

Table 1 XXX

Potential additional capacity C_t engendered by a use of spare capacity $1/sy$ in year 0 $C_t = C_{t-1} + yI_{t-1} = \sum_{i=0}^{t} yI_i = (1+ys)^{t-1}$	Year t	Potential additional investment resulting from the use of that additional capacity $I_t = sC_t$
	0	$s[1/sy]$
1	1	s
$1+ys$	2	$s(1+ys)$
$ys(1+ys)+(1+ys)$	3	$s(1+ys)^2$
$ys(1+ys)^2+(1+ys)^2=(1+ys)^3$	4	$s(1+ys)^3$
$ys(1+ys)^3+(1+ys)^3=(1+ys)^4$	5	$s(1+ys)^4$
...	...	...

The unit additional capacity thus obtained will on the other hand be available from the year 1 onwards and will make possible, if sufficient effective demand is obtained, an additional yearly output of a unit for ever after. It would thus make it possible, in particular, to have an additional net investment of $s=0.2$ in year 1 and therefore an additional productive capacity $s=0.1$ from year 2 onwards.[10] This will bring to a total of

$$1 + ys = 1 + 0.1 = 1.1$$

the additional capacity which would have come about by year 2, had there been a sufficient incentive to invest.

Then, in year 2 the potential additional investment could be

$$s(1 + ys) = 0.2 \cdot 1.1 = 0.22$$

and the potential additional capacity this investment would make available from year 3 onwards would be a fraction y of it, that is

$$ys(1 + ys) = 0.5 \cdot 0.22 = 0.11$$

bringing the total potential additional capacity engendered by year 3 to

$$ys(1 + ys) + (1 + ys) = (1 + ys)^2 = 1.1 + 0.11 = 1.21.$$

[10] The (potential) investment we are considering is evidently net investment since it is assumed to bring about additional (potential) productive capacity: hence our definition of s as a net propensity to save (para. 2). The assumption of the same net propensity to save out of the initial additional aggregate income resulting from increased utilization of *existing* capacity, and out of the subsequent aggregate income resulting from utilization of *new* capacity, might be questioned on the grounds that the need for the replacement of plant is likely not to increase in proportion to the degree of its utilization. If that is so, a smaller amortization would need to be deducted from the gross income obtained from an additional use of existing capacity than from the gross income out of new capacity. However, a consideration of the former net propensity to save as higher would only have strengthened our case, by rendering smaller the additional use of existing capacity necessary to set up a given new capacity in year 1.

This will in turn make it possible a potential additional investment in year 3 of

$$s(1 + ys)^2 = 0.2 \cdot 1.21 = 0.242,$$

and this investment would make available a further potential additional capacity of

$$ys(1 + ys)^2 = 0.5 \cdot 0.242 = 0.121$$

in year 4, bringing the total potential additional capacity created by year 4 to

$$(1 + ys)^2 + ys(1 + ys)^2 = (1 + ys)^3 = 1.21 + 0.121 = 1.331,$$

and so on and so forth as shown in Table 1.

A potential additional capacity of 1 engendered through an increased utilization of 10 in the year 0, could thus grow (if effectual demand were strong enough) to 1.6 after 5 years, to 2.6 after 10 years, to 17.5 after 30 years, to 118.3 after 50 years, etc. This means that a 10% underutilization of capacity for a single year would, other things being equal, forego a potential doubling of the overall initial capacity in less than 50 years.[11]

As Table 1 shows, this potential always-enlarging, never-ending process of creation of savings and productive capacity is strictly analogous to that of a sum of money increasing at a compound rate of interest. The growing sum is here the productive capacity initially brought into existence by an additional utilization of *existing* capacity, and the compound rate ys is the ratio of savings to capital when capacity is utilized at the normal or 'desired' level, or 'ratio of capacity savings' as we shall henceforth call it for short.

If we then proceed from the case of an underutilization of capacity lasting a single year to that of an underutilization of $x\%$ lasting over t years, the capacity which has failed to materialize after t years because of insufficient effective demand would have been numerically given by the sum of t annuities of x, accumulated over the t years at the compound rate ys, that is

$$\frac{syx[(1 + ys)^t - 1]}{ys} = x[(1 + ys)^t - 1] \tag{1}$$

Thus, under the hypothesis that the incentive to invest had been enough to ensure a 10% additional use of the initial productive capacity over the t years, a doubling of that capacity could have been achieved in 25 years, and a trebling in 32 years. An additional use of the initial capacity over the t years confined instead to 5% could have achieved the same doubling in 32 years and a trebling in 39 years, whereas a mere 1% additional use over the t years could have achieved them in 49 years and 56 years, respectively.

[11] It should be noted that in passing from absolute changes to per cent changes in levels of utilization of capacity and of capacity itself, we are assuming that the output/capital ratio is the same for new capacity y (investment) as for existing capacity.

Naturally these calculations can provide little more than rough indications. They ignore the complications associated with the age composition of fixed capital.[12] Above all they ignore the destruction of capital which is inevitably associated with any process of capitalistic accumulation because of bankruptcies, duplication of capacities by competing firms, etc. The rise of potential output will on the other hand depend on whether there is structural unemployment of labour as we have here supposed — or whether, additional labour being unavailable in sufficient quantity, the additional investment could take the form only of an anticipated renewal of plant, with a consequent rise in the productivity of labour in the system.[13] Our examples do, however, indicate the order of magnitude of the phenomenon.

3. The Cambridge Equation: A First Interpretation

6. The elasticity that a capitalist economy is thus shown to have in reacting to incentives for a more rapid growth by bringing about additional productive capacity, or, symmetrically, by eliminating excess capacity and erasing the visible traces of the losses in output due to a low such incentive,[14] should have already made clear that no necessity exists for a change in the real wage, and in the associated

[12] We may mention here a difficulty associated with the age distribution of fixed capital. We have assumed that the ratio y of (net) income to capital will be the same for the additional capital (investment), as for the capital already in existence (on the valuation of the latter, see para. 15). We have seen in n. 10 above the doubts this might raise because the needs of replacement of plant may, in a certain range at least, be less than proportional to the degree of its utilization. A different kind of doubt might be raised because, where fixed capital is involved, investment will consist of machines which are new and therefore more valuable than most of those which constitute existing capital – and which, for simplicity, we may here assume to be of a uniform age distribution. It might then seem to follow that, other things being equal, productive capacity will increase by *less* than in the proportion which current net investment bears to the value of existing capital and the ratio y of output to capital will have to be lower for new capital (investment) than for existing capital. This conclusion would not, however, be correct. It overlooks the fact that as a result of the net investment considered, productive capacity will ultimately increase by more than the new machines of which that net investment initially consists. In fact, the *gross* output obtainable from the new machines of which that investment initially consists will provide 'replacement' machines already in the first years of life of the original machines, before any replacement is required. The result will be that the number of machines resulting from the initial investment will change over time tending (as the age distribution of the machines brought into existence with that net investment tends to uniformity) to a fraction of the existing machines equal to the fraction which the initial investment bears to the value of capital.

[13] In such a case, the incentive for additional investment would probably go together with a stimulation to technical innovations directed to over-coming the labour shortage.

[14] Steindl noted this elasticity of the productive system as 'characteristic of capitalism' (1952, p. 10).

normal rate of profits, in order to generate (eliminate) the savings corresponding to any increased (decreased) demand for investment.

This result about the independence of the real wage and rate of profits from investment and accumulation may, however, seem to fly in the face of the Cambridge equation, which we may take here in the same simplest form we saw above,

$$s_c r = g \tag{2}$$

and where g, the rate of accumulation, is treated as an independent variable because of the Keynesian Hypothesis (para. 1 above). Since s_c can be plausibly assumed (at least as a first approximation) to be determined by institutions or slowly changing individual habits, it may then seem to follow from Eq. (2) that a theory of accumulation founded on the Keynesian Hypothesis implies that the incentive to invest underlying g will determine the real wage and the normal rate of profits.

7. This interpretation of the Cambridge equation into which some authors seem to have slipped at times,[15] appears, however, to confuse two radically different meanings of the equation. As already indicated above, the first meaning occurs when the distribution thus asserted to depend on the rate of accumulation consists of the normal rate of profits r^* and of the associated real wage rate w. In that case, as we shall see in the remainder of this section, the rate of accumulation g^* appearing on the right-hand side of Eq. (2), which we may then rewrite in the form

$$r^* s_c = g^* \tag{3}$$

[15] It is from this that Joan Robinson appears to derive the following (immediately after the quotation in para. 4):

> Whatever the ratio of net investment to the value of the. stock of capital may be, the level of prices must be such as to make the distribution of income such that net savings per unit of value of capital is equal to it. Thus, given the propensity to save from each type of income (the thriftiness conditions) the rate of profit is determined by the rate of accumulation of capital (Robinson, 1962, pp. 11–12).

and indeed a version of Eq. (2) appears in the footnote appended at the end of the passage. See also:

> In my model the rate of accumulation and the propensity to save out of profit are the independent elements that determine the rate of profits on capital; while the rate of profit, together with technical conditions, determine the real wage (Robinson, 1963, p. 409).

Similarly Richard Kahn (1959) states that the Cambridge 'identity' leaves open only two possibilities: either 'a system of ideas under which the rate of growth of capital is derived from the rate of profits' or a 'system under which the rate of profits is derived from the rate of growth' (1959, p. 144). Kahn can then conclude that under the conditions stated there, amounting to what we have here called the 'Keynesian Hypothesis', the second possibility is the only acceptable one. In fact, as we hope to show in this paper, the 'Cambridge identity' does leave open a third possibility: that the rate of growth and the rate of profits are independent of each other.

need no longer bear any relation to the actual rate of accumulation, call it $\hat{g}$, and this even when the latter is taken as an average over any sufficiently long period of time. It would in fact be more correct to refer then to g^* simply as the ratio of savings to capital when the aggregate income is that corresponding to the normal or 'desired' utilization of existing capacity – that 'ratio of capacity savings' which we have already encountered above and not as a rate of accumulation. Then, clearly, the Keynesian Hypothesis by itself will in no way entail that g^* can be treated as an independent variable in Eq. (3) and, therefore, Eq. (3) will not entail g^* determining r^* any more than r^* determining g^*.

The second meaning of the Cambridge Eq. (2) occurs when g is instead taken to refer to the actual rate of accumulation $\hat{g}$ which can indeed be taken as an independent variable in the Cambridge equation, rewritten in the form

$$\widehat{rs_c} = \hat{g} \tag{4}$$

Then, however, as we shall see in Sect. 4 below, the 'rate of profits' $\hat{r}$ determined by $\hat{g}$ need not have anything to do with the normal rate of profits r^*, and, in particular, it can change with $\hat{g}$ without in the least affecting the real wage. It will then again be illegitimate to interpret the Cambridge equation as entailing that the rate of accumulation determines the normal rate of profits and the real wage rate. That interpretation can arise only from a confusion between the two meanings of the equation, when the equation is read as if $\hat{g}$ could appear on the right-hand side with r^* appearing on the left-hand side.

8. In order to examine these two alternative meanings of the Cambridge equation, and the distinction between them, we must start by considering more closely the concept of a normal or 'desired' degree of utilization of capacity, to which we have already repeatedly referred. It is the degree of utilization of capacity desired by the entrepreneurs, and on which, therefore, they base their investment decisions about the size of a new plant relative to the output they expect to produce.

This desired level of capacity utilization, we should be careful to note, is never likely to be the technically possible maximum. There are several reasons for this fact, the relevance of which for the elasticity of aggregate output we discussed in Sect. 2 should be obvious. There may in the first place be reasons of costs, for unit costs may rise as the utilization of productive equipment gets close to its technical maximum (*e.g.*, a rise in labour costs because of night shifts).

There are, however, also other reasons which may induce entrepreneurs to keep the output made technically possible by their investment above the average output they expect to produce over the lifetime of the plant. These are reasons relating to the desire to keep the customers which a firm already has, and, if possible, enlarge their number. Productive capacity will thus generally be planned so that it can meet the peak levels, and not only the average levels, of demand,[16] when the

---

[16]The notion of 'demand' used here, although referring to the product of each individual firm, can be understood along the lines of the classical notion of effectual demand, that is a quantity demanded at the given production price of the commodity.

latter is expected to fluctuate. Further, if the average level of demand is expected to increase during the lifetime of the productive equipment, the entrepreneur, taking into account the indivisibilities of a plant, may well plan it in excess also of the peak demand expected in the earlier life of the plant, so as to be able to deal better with the increased demand in its later life. And, finally, some such excess capacity may be planned even independently of any increase in demand definitely expected during the lifetime of the plant. This may be in order not to lose opportunities of extending the sales which might unexpectedly arise during that time.[17]

9. The fact that this desired level of capacity utilization will be that on which the decisions of entrepreneurs about the size of new plant will be taken has some important implications, which we must now consider.

The profits expected from investing in a new plant will of course depend on the level of utilization expected for that plant. And that *expected* level of utilization will tend to be the 'desired' level because, by the very definition of the latter, the size of the new plant will be *designed* to make it such. The expected level of utilization will therefore tend to be independent of the levels of utilization and profits *experienced in the past.* A high past level of utilization of the plant might well result in a higher amount of investment, and a larger new plant, but there is no reason why it should imply a higher expected level of utilization of that plant. That level will remain equal to the desired level chosen by the entrepreneurs themselves when deciding their investment.[18]

10. Thus, the rate of return expected from investment will be that corresponding to the 'desired' level of utilization of the productive equipment to be set up. However, it is with respect to decisions to invest – when from the point of view of the investor, capital is 'free' to take any physical form[19] – that the concept of a rate of return or rate of profits on capital acquires relevance, as distinct from that of the quasi-rents obtainable from an already existing plant. It appears therefore that when economic theory has traditionally referred to a single 'normal' rate of profits corresponding, under competitive assumptions, and with given technical conditions. to each level of the real wage and of the other distributive variables, that single rate of profits has been that corresponding to the 'desired' level of utilization of capacity.[20] This single rate of profits is that which we have indicated as the normal rate of profits r^* corresponding to the given real wage w^*.

[17] The obvious reference for an analysis of the concept of desired level of capacity utilization is Steindl (1952, Ch. II). For the cost elements, cf. Kurz (1986).

[18] This choice of the entrepreneurs, of course, in no way implies that new plant will in fact turn out to be utilized at the desired level. As we shall show below, any long-run adjustment of capacity to output – as distinct from that of output to capacity – does entail that the new plant cannot be utilized at desired capacity, even on an average.

[19] Cf., e. g., the concept of 'free capital' used by Wicksell (1934, pp. 145, 234).

[20] Of course this will have to be done with respect to the dominant technique (cf. para. 15 and n. 28 below).

11. Equipped with this notion of desired level of capacity utilization and with the associated definition of the normal rate of profits r^*, we can now return to the first possible meaning of the Cambridge equation and examine more closely the fallacy of thinking of g^* in Eq. (3) as reflecting the actual (average) rate of accumulation and, therefore, as the independent variable determining r^*, in that equation. We shall proceed by means of an illustration.

Let us assume an initial situation in which the productive capacity of the economy happens to be utilized at the desired level. The rate of accumulation will then be g^*, equal to the 'ratio of capacity savings' (p. 451 above) and will therefore be given by the quantity $s_c r^*$, as shown by Eq. (2).[21] Let us then assume that in the year t a fall in the incentive to invest occurs, such that – after the changes we shall see, required in order to adjust capacity to that very fall – investment will become, say, one-half of what it would have been at the same date, had the previous trend of investment continued unaltered. Now, no obstacle arises against assuming, for the sake of our argument, that through an initially even smaller time rate of gross investment, entrepreneurs will, by year t', have adjusted productive capacity to the new lower trend of investment, and to the correspondingly lower level of aggregate output. When that has occurred, the rate of accumulation will necessarily be back to the ratio of capacity savings g^*.[22]

12. The above example illustrates how the rate g^* – which has to appear on the right-hand side when, as in Eq. (3), the Cambridge equation is referred to the normal rate of profits and the real wage – need have little if anything to do with the *actual* rate of accumulation $\hat{g}$, and how this remains true even when the latter is taken as an average over any number of years. In fact, in our example, $\hat{g}$ will be below g^* over any period which would include the years between t and t'.

More generally, given as in our example the real wage and the normal rate of profits r^*, and therefore the ratio of capacity savings g^*, the economy can easily accumulate at any rate $\hat{g} < g^*$ and also, within a certain range, at a rate higher than g^*. It is then clear that the rate g^*, unlike the actual rate of accumulation g^*, cannot be taken as a measure of the incentive to invest: in our example that incentive had fallen to half as measured by the amount of investment without affecting g^* at all. There is accordingly no reason why the Keynesian Hypothesis of the independence of decisions to invest from decisions to save should allow us to take g^* as independent of either s_c or r^* within Eq. (3) and, therefore. as susceptible of determining r^* in that equation.

[21] The rate $s_c r^* = g^*$ is in fact Harrod's 'warranted rate of growth'. As we shall see below, assuming desired utilization of capacity, as is done in the analysis of steady growth and in the definition of Harrod's 'warranted rate of growth', prejudges the question as to which of the two Keynesian Positions is acceptable with respect to how the economy adjusts to different intensities of the incentive to invest.

[22] We may note here that our assumption according to which, after the necessary adjustments, the time rate of investment will be half of what it would have been at the same date, had the earlier trend continued, implies that investment at the new level will itself grow at the rate g^* (and be therefore compatible with a continuing utilization of capacity at its desired level).

In fact, if we turn again to our example, in which we fully exploited the Keynesian Hypothesis by our assumption of a halving of the investment from t' onward, the rate of accumulation g^*, far from being an independent variable determining r^*, was fully determined by the latter. This was of course the result of the fact that we did *assume* the normal profit rate r^* and the real wage w^* to remain constant as the incentive to invest changed. But the point is exactly that we had no difficulty in dealing with that change, while assuming r^* to remain constant.

Indeed we can now see that if we took g^* as an independently variable rate of accumulation in Eq. (3), we would be begging the question of the determination of distribution under the Keynesian Hypothesis. We would be assuming independent changes in the rate of accumulation when the utilization of capacity is kept at the desired level, and therefore we would be *assuming* changes in the ratio of capacity savings. And the propensities to save of each class being given, together with the output/capital ratios,[23] a change in the ratio of capacity savings can be achieved only by a change in the real wage w^* and normal rate of profits r^*. This begging of the question would be there whenever we attempted to deal with the Keynesian Hypothesis in terms of a situation of steady growth and of the associated desired utilization of capacity. Indeed, in some instances, the First Keynesian Position appears to have been favoured by an unwarranted tendency to view steady growth analysis as an analysis of average actual growth.[24] We have found here one important additional reason why that view is unwarranted.

---

[23] Cf. n. 5 above.

[24] Cf. in particular the passage by Kahn in n. 15 above, where he may have been misled by the assumption of steady growth into his statement that the Cambridge equation leaves room for only two possibilities: either a determination of the rate of profits by the rate of accumulation or of the latter by the former. The case is different in Kaldor (1959); Kaldor appears to recognize that the First Keynesian Position rests on the possibility of demonstrating a tendency to the full (desired) utilization of capacity – and not simply on the fact of some long-run congruity between capacity and output, which may well result from the former adjusting to the latter, rather than the contrary, with the consequences we saw in Sect. 2. Even in Kaldor's case, however, the implications of that congruity do not appear to be fully recognized, since the latter is taken as that factual support for the theoretical argument of a long-run tendency to the full utilization of capacity, which it cannot in fact be. Cf., e.g. the following passage:

> Yet in the history of advanced capitalist societies periods of severe unemployment were exceptional and not the rule; apart from depressions, unemployment did not appear to exceed a few percent on the average since the latter half of the nineteenth century. (In the forty years, 1881–1920, in the U.K. it averaged less than five percent including both boom and depression years.) As the actual level of employment averaged 95 percent of the full employment level, this is unlikely to have been a mere coincidence (Kaldor, 1959, p. 214).

Here Kaldor assumes also a coincidence between full (desired) utilization of capacity and full employment of labour. Indeed, over a sufficiently long run labour may be not unlike productive equipment in failing to leave open traces of its underutilization. Over such long runs labour unemployment would in fact have to remain hidden in a backward sector of the economy, or disappear through emigration.

13. What becomes clear in this connection is something which was perhaps not immediately evident, namely that the possibility that investment should generate the corresponding amount of savings through changes in aggregate productive capacity (the Second Keynesian Position) is inconsistent with the assumption of an economy working over time at the desired level of capacity utilization, even only on an average taken over booms and slumps.

To see that inconsistency let us consider an economy for which, as we have assumed so far, we are given (a) the real wage and the propensities to save out of wages and profits; and (b) the initial level of productive capacity. If then the average utilization of capacity over time were to be at the desired level, the path of future capital accumulation would be completely determined.[25] Such a utilization of capacity would in fact be sufficient to determine the amount of investment of each period in the future in terms of the definite amount of savings forthcoming in that period under those conditions. It would thus rule out a determination of investment by factors other than those acting on circumstances (a) and (b) above and, therefore, given the propensities to save and the initial productive capacity, by factors other than the normal rate of profits and the real wage. That would allow for the determination of investment by the decisions to save, as in marginal theory, or for the determination of the real wage (normal rate of profits) by an independent amount of investment in the First Keynesian Position. It would not, however, allow for any independent determination of investment which would leave the real wage (normal rate of profits) unaffected, such as is envisaged in the Second Keynesian Position. It would evidently be a fluke if an independently determined average amount of investment were to coincide with the average amount of savings forthcoming over the period considered as determined, under conditions of continued desired utilization of capacity, by the given real wage and by the given initial productive capacity.

This, of course, does not mean that the Second Keynesian Position ignores the tendency of entrepreneurs to adjust capacity to output. The entrepreneurs will certainly attempt to bring about, through investment, a capacity which can be used at the desired level. And the degree of their success will depend on how well they will be able to forecast the outputs which it will be convenient for them to produce. But given the initial arbitrary level of capacity that success will show only in shifting, so to speak, backward in time the deviation of the utilization of capacity from the desired level. Even correct foresight of future output will not eliminate average utilization of capacity at levels other than the desired one. Thus, suppose the prospect emerged of a faster expansion of aggregate demand than would have been taken care of by the growth of a capacity utilized at the desired level, and therefore entirely determined by the initial capacity and distribution of income. The earlier that prospect has been perceived, the more capacity will have been adjusted by the time the expansion comes. But – supposing for simplicity that in

---

[25] This would be so except for the effects we can here ignore of different time distributions of the deviations of the utilization of capacity from the desired level.

the earlier period capacity would otherwise have been utilized at the desired level – the additional investment required to advance the desired capacity for the future faster expansion will cause a deviation from the desired level of utilization in that earlier period. Thus *either* the deviation is admitted in the later period (in the case of lack of foresight) *or* (in the case of correct foresight) it has to be admitted for the earlier period.[26]

4. The Cambridge Equation: A Second Interpretation

14. We have seen that if Eq. (2) is understood to relate to the real wage and the corresponding normal rate of profits r^*, then the ratio of capacity savings g^* appearing in the equation will need have little to do with the actual (average) rate of accumulation $\hat{g}$. Accordingly, the Keynesian Hypothesis will not entail a treatment of g^* as an independent variable in Eq. (3) and, when correctly interpreted, the Cambridge equation will in no way contradict our argument in Sect. 2 concerning the independence of distribution from accumulation.

However, we are not yet out of the difficulty we saw at the beginning of Sect. 3. If, as we did in Eq. (4), we interpret the Cambridge equation to refer to the *actual* rate of accumulation $\hat{g}$, then $\hat{g}$ will have to fall and rise as the incentive to invest does, and the Keynesian Hypothesis would justify its treatment as an independent variable in the equation. Given the saving propensity s_c, $\hat{g}$ will then determine the 'rate of profits' $\widehat{r}$ of Eq. (4), and it might again seem that distribution depends on accumulation. As we must now see, this conclusion would be misleading: the 'rate of profits' $\widehat{r}$ of Eq. (4) need in fact have little to do with the real wage and the

[26] We may mention here as a *curiosum*, what seems to be the only conceivable way of reconciling the Second Keynesian Position with an average utilization of capacity at the desired level over a number of years $n > 1$, from a year t to a year $(t+n)$. We would not only have to assume that each entrepreneur had sufficiently confident forecasts about his future most profitable output, and that such forecasts of different entrepreneurs be consistent with each other within the year to which they refer. For such output forecasts to be verified with a desired level of capacity utilization, we shall have to assume, besides, that the resulting aggregates of forecasts are 'consistent' over time. By such 'consistency' we mean that the investment $m(t+i)$, for $i = 0, 1 \ldots (w\text{-}1)$, which, given the propensity to save, is necessary in order to verify the output forecasts of the period, will be such as to ensure that capacity in the subsequent period $(t+i+1)$ be adjusted to the output forecasts of *that* period. And the Keynesian hypothesis entails that the price system buys no ground at all, even an approximate one, for such a 'consistency'. This is why the situation in which the Second Keynesian Position could be made consistent with desired utilization over time, even only for a limited time period, appears to be no more than a topical exercise.

It remains in any case true that the inconsistency between that Position and desired utilization of capacity would remain and would, so to speak, be shifted to the years preceding and to those following $(t+n)$, when the productive capacity would have to re-emerge as a given magnitude relatively to the independently determined outputs.

corresponding normal rate of profits r^*, and hence with distribution in the relevant sense.

15. We meet here the confusion we mentioned above between two different notions of the rate of profits. We have in the first place the 'normal' rate of profits which we analysed above, and which is uniquely determined once the real wage is given. It could be ideally observed within a firm using the dominant technique, on the assumption of a utilization of capacity at the desired level, and of normal prices for both inputs and outputs. This is the normal rate of profits which in Sects. 2 and 3 we could assume to remain unaffected together with the real wage, as the incentive to invest varied.

We have then, in the second place, the different notion of what, for brevity, we may here call an 'ex-post' rate of profits. This rate is the ratio between what may be reckoned to be the amount of 'net' profits realized in the economy in the year, and what may be reckoned to be the value of the capital stock during the same year. This is the 'rate of profits' $\widehat{r}$ of Eq. (4) which has to vary with the actual rate of accumulation $\hat{g}$.[27]

Significantly enough, even a definition of this second notion sufficiently exact for theoretical purposes appears to meet difficulties. The difficulties are of course those of estimating the capital goods in existence, many of which will not belong to the 'dominant technique'. Though we postponed mentioning them at the time, these difficulties already underlay the concept of a 'rate of accumulation' referred to in Sects. 1 and 3 in connection with the Cambridge equation.

In order to obtain a valuation of the capital stock in the denominator of the rate of profits $\widehat{r}$ that would first of all be independent of the ex-post amount of profits appearing in the numerator – and which will of course generally affect the current prices of capital goods as reckoned, e.g., in a Stock Exchange – we may avoid referring to the actual capital stock in use in the economy and to some current value of it. We may instead refer to the physical capital stock as it would have been, *if* all outputs had been produced with the 'dominant techniques'.[28] And we should then estimate that stock at the 'normal' prices corresponding to the given and constant real wage and normal rate of profits. This value we should also put in

[27] A seemingly analogous distinction is drawn by Joan Robinson between an 'expected rate of profit' and a 'current rate of profit,' defined as 'the ratio of current gross profits, minus depreciation, to the value of the stock of capital at current replacement costs' (Robinson, 1962, p. 29) and she asserts the importance of such a distinction in 'constructing a historical model'. However no link is there established between the 'expected rate of profit, the degree of utilization of capacity and the normal rate of profits she mentions elsewhere (see, e.g., the passage quoted in n. 8 above) or between the latter two circumstances. Indeed the concept of a normal rate of profit seems to be confused with the rate we can find in a stationary or steady growth equilibrium.

[28] By 'dominant technique' we mean that, among the several in simultaneous use in the industry, which is relevant for determining the normal price of the commodity. It will be a technique intermediate between those which are obsolete and those which on the contrary are not yet sufficiently widespread to have lowered the price of the product so as to eliminate extra profits for the entrepreneurs using it.

the denominator of our rate of accumulation $\hat{g}$. This definition of the value of capital appears to be in fact necessary if the ex-post rate of profits $\hat{r}$ is to become the 'normal' rate of profits r^* – and the actual rate of accumulation $\hat{g}$ is to become the ratio of capacity savings g^* – when capacity is utilized at the desired level.[29]

Now, when the rate of capital accumulation changes, the 'ex-post' rate of profits $\hat{r}$ has evidently to change accordingly, owing to the windfall profits or losses connected with the utilization of capacity at other than the 'desired' revel. That change, by itself, can however leave entirely unaffected the real wage and the normal rate of profits.[30]

16. A point seems now to arise naturally, and should be dealt with before drawing our conclusions. We have seen that g^*, the ratio of net savings to capital at desired capacity utilization, provides no indication of the actual rate of accumulation of the economy. It might then seem that the same reasons which prevent that ratio from being a guide to the actual rate of accumulation deprive of much of its meaning the 'normal' rate of profits, similarly reckoned for the desired level of capacity utilization and which, together with the associated real wage rate, has instead been at the centre of the conception of distribution referred to in this paper.

However that analogy would be misleading and the reason essentially lies in what we said in para. 10 above. The asymmetry, in this respect, between rate of accumulation and rate of profits is due to the fact that whereas the meaning of the rate of accumulation is that of a ratio between the corresponding aggregate quantities in the economy over a given period of time, that is not in fact so for the rate of profits. The theoretical importance of the latter lies in the first place in its influence on investment. And since entrepreneurs will generally aim to re-establish through investment the desired relation between capacity and output – then, as we saw (p. 455), the normal rate of profits will be that on which they will base their decisions to invest – a rate which, as we saw, will need bear no close relation to a ratio between aggregate actual net profits and aggregate existing capital, however the latter might be defined.[31]

No difficulty on the other hand seems to arise for taking into account, where relevant, those effects which generalized extra profits or losses resulting from

---

[29] We would not generally have such a coincidence if, for example, we included in our estimate of the capital stock the obsolete capital goods still in use, reckoned at their current prices.

[30] This concept of an ex-post rate of profits $\hat{r}$ is in fact the same to which we referred in n. 8 above as that share of profits relative to capital which is bound to change as the degree of utilization of capacity changes. We may also note here that if s_c were to change in the same direction with the rate of accumulation – owing, for example, to the tendency of firms to retain a higher proportion of profits in periods when, one year with another, the average rate of capital accumulation is high – changes in the rate of accumulation occurring with constant 'normal' distribution will affect to a correspondingly smaller extent the degree of utilization of capacity and hence the ex-post rate of profits as compared with the 'normal' rate.

[31] However, as we saw above, the nature of the normal rate of profits as the rate of return expected on investment does not mean that the normal rate of profits cannot be observed. It can be observed where entrepreneurs can observe it: under certain conditions, and in particular firms.

deviations of the utilization of capacity from the desired level may exert on the purchasing power of profit earners, or on the possibility to finance investment, or on the expectations of future demand and therefore on the *amount* of investment. These factors like all the others affecting aggregate demand, as well as the demand for particular commodities, can be taken care of in the course of the separate determination of such magnitudes (Garegnani, 1984, pp. 296–9 [this volume, Part III, pp. 311–4).

5. Conclusions

17. We have seen why, contrary to what has sometimes been supposed to follow from the Cambridge equation, the Keynesian Hypothesis in no way entails that, in a long-period analysis, autonomous investment decisions generate the corresponding amount of savings by affecting the real wage and the normal rate of profits. Through comparatively small increases (decreases) in the degree of utilization of the already existing capacity, changes in the level of investment can bring about those faster (slower) increases of productive capacity itself, which will then result in that rough correspondence between productive capacity and output which can be observed historically.[32] Indeed while waiting for a more accurate analysis of the relevant facts concerning the development of capitalist countries, it seems that once the Keynesian Hypothesis is accepted, the margins of unutilized capacity which are normal in a capitalist system make it plausible to think that, in the long period, even more than in the Keynesian short period, autonomous changes in the incentive to invest will usually generate the corresponding amount of savings through changes in output rather than through changes in the real wage rate and normal rate of profits.

There are in fact some considerations that may strengthen this provisional conclusion. A first such consideration is that an increase in the incentive to invest will generally be gradual. It will manifest itself at first in shorter slumps and longer booms rather than in drastic changes in the level of peak demand. This will make it easier to produce the additional investment goods by utilizing at first the existing capacity and then the increased capacity which has been generated by the initial increments of investment.

That of course applies to the long period in which productive capacity can change. But on the other hand, and this is the second consideration, in a short period, capacity is generally given in a highly specialized form. The short-period possibility to accommodate increased investment by lowering consumption would therefore seem in any case to be small or non-existent. That would seem to be so except in two cases. The first would be when the economy faced a general

[32] Cf. the passage by Kaldor quoted in n. 24 above.

shortage of labour whose amount was insufficient for a fuller utilization of existing capacity. The second would be when a limitation was present in the productive capacity of the wage goods industries, such that increased employment in the rest of the economy had to result in a fall of real wages. However both these cases would have their roots in disproportions – between the available aggregate capacity and labour, in the first case, and between the available capacities of different sectors, in the second – which we should ignore when discussing the general questions of aggregate output.[33]

A third consideration is that even if the increased investment were to cause a fall in real wages, such a fall would seem unlikely to last. On the one hand, the shortage of productive capacity causing that fall in real wages would probably not last for long. On the other hand, the bargaining position which was reflected in the initial level of the real wage is not at all likely to have been weakened by the increased investment. As a result, as the impossibility of maintaining the same real wage fades because new productive capacity becomes available, so real wages are likely to be brought back to their former level. Indeed the increased incentive to invest with the consequent increase in employment is likely to enhance, if anything, the bargaining position of workers and therefore to raise, rather than lower, the real wages over a long period in which productive capacity will be increasing.

A further element of elasticity in the productive system emerges, of course, if we abandon the assumption of a closed economy. Increased imports can easily make good a temporary pressure on existing capacity, caused by an unexpected increase in the incentive to invest. Then, in the long run, such increased imports could, in principle, be compensated by increased exports from the additional productive capacity which the increased investment has brought about.

It should finally be stressed that the present argument for which a long-period rise in investment needs not alter distribution in order to generate the corresponding savings, should not be taken to deny the possibility – or, indeed the likelihood – of interactions between the real wage and the normal rate of profits on the one hand, and the speed of capital accumulation on the other. We have just mentioned, e.g., the possibility that a rise in the incentive to invest and the consequent improvement in the situation of labour employment might result in a *rise* of the real wage (rather than the fall which we would expect from the First Keynesian Position). What is disputed is only the necessity of the particular effect postulated in the First Keynesian Position.

---

[33] See the definition of productive capacity given in n. 3 above.

References

Cutilli, B. (1980). Tasso di investimento e produzione potenziale. *Rassegna Economica*, XLIV(6), 1351–62.

Garegnani, P. (1962). *Il problema della domanda effettiva nello sviluppo economico italiano*, Rome: SVIMEZ [a section of this work appeared in English as 'The Problem of Effective Demand in Italian Economic Development: On the Factors that Determine the Volume of Investment', *Review of Political Economy*, 27(2), 2015, 111–33].

Garegnani, P. (1984). Value and Distribution in the Classical Economists and Marx. *Oxford Economic Papers*, 36(2), 291–325.

Kahn, R. (1959). Exercises in the Analysis of Growth. *Oxford Economic Papers*, 11(2), 143–156.

Kaldor, N. (1955–6). 'Alternative Theories of Distribution'. *Review of Economic Studies*, 23(2), 83–100.

Kaldor, N. (1959). Economic Growth and the Problem of Inflation. Part I, *Economica*, 26(103), 212–226.

Kurz, H. D. (1986). Normal Positions and Capital Utilization. *Political Economy*, 2(1), 37–54.

Marglin, S. (1984). *Growth*. Harvard University Press.

Okun, A. (1970). Potential GNP: Its Measurement and Significance, in *The Political Economy of Prosperity* (132–145). The Brookings Institution (first publ. in American Statistical Association, Proceedings of the Business and Economics Statistics Section, 1962).

Robinson, J. (1962). *Essays in the Theory of Economic Growth*. St Martin's Press.

Robinson, J. V. (1963). Findlay's Robinsonian Model of Accumulation. A Comment. *Economica*, 30(120), 408–411.

Steindl, J. (1952). *Maturity and Stagnation in American Capitalism*. Basil Blackwell.

Wicksell, K. (1934). *Lectures on Political Economy* (Vol. I). George Routledge & Sons.

Accumulation of Capital†

Two alternative answers are given by today's economists to the question of what determines the growth of an economy. The first is the traditional one, according to which the community's decisions to save in conditions of full utilization of resources ('capacity savings' for short), defined so as to allow for a normal succession of booms and slumps, will determine the trend of capital accumulation. This, taken together with the growth of population and the development of technical knowledge, would then determine the trend of aggregate output. The second answer is based instead on what has been called the 'Keynesian hypothesis' (Kaldor, 1955–6: 95). According to this hypothesis, it Is the level of investment that generates the corresponding amount of savings, Not only in the short period analysed by Keynes, but also in the long period in which productive capacity changes. (By 'Productive capacity' of the economy we mean the productive equipment in existence measured by the output which can be obtained from it when used at Its normal level, and with the appropriate employment of labour. For the notion of a 'normal' level of utilisation of capacity, see below.) This entails that in some broad sense aggregate demand, rather than propensities to save and other supply factors, is what ultimately determines the speed of growth of the economy.

As is well known, the validity of the traditional answer depends on whether or not the rate of interest can adjust investment to capacity savings. In what follows, however, we will not be concerned with the arguments for which such a role of the interest rate can be refuted together with the marginal theories of distribution of which it is an expression. Our interest will focus instead on two alternative versions of the Keynesian hypothesis. The long-run generation of savings by means of investment can in fact conceivably occur along two different routes. The first

---

† Previously published with Edward Elgar in *The Elgar Companion to Classical Political Economy*, ed. by H. D. Kurz and N. Salvadori, 1998. All necessary permissions acquired.

P. Garegnani, *Capital Theory, the Surplus Approach, and Effective Demand*,
Springer Studies in the History of Economic Thought,
https://doi.org/10.1007/978-3-031-23643-3_14

consists of a lowering of real wages (by raising money prices relative to money wages), thereby generally raising the proportion of profits in national income: a rise in the proportion of savings to consumption would follow. The second route, instead, consists of an increase of the level of aggregate output together with the corresponding productive capacity, without any need to change the real wage. For brevity we will refer here to the theoretical positions characterized by those two routes as, respectively, the distribution-based and the output-based long-period Keynesian approach.

The distribution-based approach is that which has attracted more attention, leaving the output-based approach in the shadow. However, once some misunderstandings are cleared up, it may become apparent that the latter is the approach which better represents the route a market economy is likely to take in adjusting savings to the incentive to invest.

The Long-Period Elasticity of Output

The fact that a large underutilization of productive capacity cannot be observed over sufficiently long periods of time seems to have engendered the kind of *optical illusion* we find in Joan Robinson when she writes: 'In long-run competitive equilibrium the relation of total income to the stock of capital is determined within certain limits by technical conditions (...). The distribution of income, however, is strongly influenced by the rate of investment' (Robinson, 1962: 11). Similarly, and more explicitly, Marglin says: 'In the short run… the rate of capacity utilisation changes in accordance with aggregate demand… But in the long run… there is no excess capacity to accommodate investment demand. Distribution must bear the brunt of adjusting aggregate demand to supply' (Marglin, 1984: 474–5).

Now the premise concerning the temporary nature of any large excess capacity may well be correct, but the conclusion that the real wage has therefore to fall in order to accommodate a rise in investment does not follow: capacity may adjust to output, just as output does to capacity. And when the former possibility is analysed, it becomes clear that the 'excess capacity' which could have accommodated additional aggregate demand cannot be *seen* (hence the 'optical illusion' we referred to above) only because the demand to be accommodated has *not* been there. That capacity would, however, have come into (or remained in) existence had the additional aggregate demand done the same. In other words, in the long period 'the capacity to accommodate demand' is available, but cannot be generally *observed* in the form of *excess capacity*. Then, as we will presently see, savings can be generated by the additional investment, without any fall of the real wage: so that in the long period in which productive capacity can change, the margins for expanding output in response to aggregate demand become wider rather than narrower—contrary to what is asserted by Robinson and Marglin.

We will assume a competitive, closed economy, where labour is indefinitely available and natural resources are not scarce. The real wage rate w^* and the technical conditions of production are assumed given, so that the corresponding normal rate of profits r^* and the prices expressed in the same composite commodity as w^* are also given. We will indicate by y the ratio which output bears to capital, at normal capacity utilization. For simplicity we will assume that, as output changes, y remains constant together with the marginal net propensity to save s (on the assumption of a constant y, see Garegnani, 1992 [this volume, Part IV]). Except for that on labour availability, the above assumptions could be removed without essentially altering our conclusions.

Let us now assume an additional utilization of capacity in year 0 providing for an additional output of a value of 10, so that if the propensity to save s is 0.2, the potential increment of output would have to include additional investment of the value of 2. Given a ratio $y=0.5$ of output to capital, this investment would establish a unit of additional productive capacity $\Delta C_1 = 1$ measured by the value of the net yearly output (at the given prices) it would allow for, when used at its normal (desired) level. If aggregate demand were sufficient, that additional unit of net yearly output in year 1 would entail an additional net investment of $s=0.2$ in year 1 and therefore a further additional productive capacity $ys=0.1$ from year 2 onwards. This will lead to a total of

$$\Delta C_2 = (1+ys) = 1+0.1 = 1.1,$$

the additional capacity which would have come about by year 2. Then, in year 2, the potential additional investment could be $s(1+ys)=0.2\times 1.1=0.22$, with a potential additional capacity of $ys(1+ys)=0.5\times 0.22=0.11$, bringing the total potential additional capacity engendered by year 3 to

$$\Delta C_3 = ys(1+ys) + (1+ys) = (1+ys)^2 = (1+0.10)^2 = 1.21$$

and so on and so forth, with a total additional capacity available from any year t of

$$\Delta C_t = (1+ys)^{t-1}$$

This process of creation of saving and productive capacity, which can generally be activated in response to additional aggregate demand, is in fact strictly analogous to that of a sum of money increasing at a compound rate of interest. The growing sum is here the new capacity initially brought into existence by an additional utilization of *existing* capacity, and the compound rate is ys, the ratio of saving to capital when capacity is utilized at the normal level ('ratio of capacity savings', henceforth). Thus, in our example, a 10% underutilization of capacity for a single year would forgo a potential doubling in 50 years of the initial capacity. And if we proceed to an underutilization of x percent lasting t years, the capacity which has failed to materialize after the t years will be given numerically by the cumulated sum of t annuities of x, that is:

$$\Delta C_t = \frac{syx\left[(1+ys)^t - 1\right]}{ys} = x\left[(1+ys)^t - 1\right]$$

so that if aggregate demand had been enough to ensure a 5% additional use of the initial productive capacity over the *t* years, a doubling of that capacity could have been achieved for $t=32$ years, and a trebling for $t=39$ years, while a mere 1% additional use could have achieved the same in 49 and 56 years, respectively.

Elasticity of Output and Distribution Between Wages and Profits

A first important consequence of the above argument concerns pure theory. It is that the Keynesian hypothesis need not provide us with a theory of distribution as asserted in the distribution-based Keynesian approach. The elasticity that a capitalist economy has in reacting to incentives for a more rapid growth by bringing about additional productive capacity and output, or, symmetrically, by eliminating it in the opposite case, makes clear that *no necessity* exists for a change in the real wage, and in the associated normal rate of profits (which we have in fact kept constant in our reasoning), in order to generate or to eliminate the savings corresponding to any increased or decreased demand for investment. In particular, an explanation of the distribution between wages and profits by economic and social factors along the lines envisaged by the old classical economists appears to be quite compatible with admitting the relevance of aggregate demand for the analysis of the process of accumulation.

The above result may, however, seem to fly in the face of the so-called 'Cambridge equation' which, when we assume that only capitalists save, and save with a given propensity s_c, yields the following relation:

$$s_c r = g \tag{1}$$

Since s_c is given, Eq. (1) may seem to imply that the incentive to invest, governing the yearly rate of accumulation over capital g, determines the normal rate of profits r, with the corresponding real wage w. This interpretation of the Cambridge equation, into which some authors seem to have slipped at times (see, for example, Kahn, 1959: 149 and n.), appears to confuse two radically different meanings of the equation.

The first meaning occurs when the distribution referred to is understood to consist of the real wage w^*, and, therefore, of what is traditionally referred to in economic theory as the *normal* rate of profits r^*, namely the rate of profits on capital under the assumption of *the normal (desired) level of utilization of capacity,* the one for which the methods of production introduced in the price equations (in the production functions) are defined. The rationale of such a definition is that the profit rate is a notion relevant essentially for the *investor* (whose capital has not yet been sunk into a definite physical form): and the investor will refer to the normal (desired) level of capacity utilization since, in effecting his investment, he will be able to give it the size he wishes relative to the demand he expects for his products (on this, see, for example, Ciccone, 1986; Garegnani, 1992 [this volume, Part IV]; Kurz, 1986).

Now, under this first meaning of the profit rate, the rate of accumulation over capital appearing on the right-hand side of Eq. (1), which we may then rewrite in the form

$$r^* s_c = g^*, \tag{2}$$

will be the potential rate of accumulation $g*$ *we would have* if utilization of capacity were at that normal (desired) level for which the normal rate of profits $r*$ is calculated: $g*$ would thus be equal to the 'ratio of capacity savings' defined above, and would need have little to do with the *actual* rate of accumulation. Clearly, the Keynesian hypothesis by itself will in no way entail that such $g*$ can be treated as an independent variable in Eq. (1): on the contrary, $g*$ is a *dependent* variable, determined by the propensity to save s_c and by the normal output/capital ratio y. Correspondingly, Eq. (2) cannot be seen to entail $g*$ determining $r*$, any more than it entails $r*$ determining $g*$.

The second meaning of the Cambridge Eq. (1) occurs when g is taken to refer to the *actual* rate of accumulation g, which can indeed be taken as an independent variable in the Cambridge equation, rewritten in the form

$$\hat{r} s_c = \hat{g}$$

Then, however, the 'rate of profits' $\hat{r}$ will be, so to speak, an 'ex-post profit rate' just as 'ex-post' as the level of capacity utilization which g has in fact entailed. This rate $\hat{r}$ need therefore have nothing to do with the normal rate of profits $r*$ and the real wage $w*$ (on the difficulty of even defining $\hat{r}$ and $\hat{g}$, see Garegnani, 1992: 60–61 [this volume, Part IV, pp. 459–61]). In particular, $\hat{r}$ can change together with $\hat{g}$, *without affecting* $w*$. And then it will again be illegitimate to interpret the Cambridge equation as entailing that the rate of accumulation determines the *normal* rate of profits $r*$ (that expected by the investor) and the real wage rate $w*$. That interpretation could arise only from inconsistently reading the Eq. (1) above as if it had $\hat{g}$ on the right-hand side, and $r*$ on the left-hand side.

Elasticity of Output and the Alternative Between Consumption and Growth

Our argument clearly entails that in the long period, no less than in the Keynesian short period, an increase in investment can generate the corresponding amount of savings through changes in output without any need to decrease consumption (see also Vianello, 1985). Indeed, it seems possible to argue that the margins of unutilized capacity which are normal in a capitalist system make it plausible to think that that will be the normal way in which savings will adjust to investment, so that an increase in investment will be generally accompanied by a rise in consumption (and vice versa) similar to that characteristic of the short-period multiplier.

Some considerations may in fact strengthen this conclusion. A first such consideration is that an increase in the incentive to invest will generally be gradual: it will, for example, manifest itself at first in shorter slumps and longer booms rather than in drastic changes in peak demand. This, taken together with the added elasticity provided by international trade, will make it easier to produce the additional investment goods by first utilizing the existing capacity and then making use of the increased capacity generated by that initial additional investment.

Moreover if, despite all that, the increased investment were to cause a fall in real wages and consumption, such a fall would seem unlikely to last. The shortage of productive capacity causing that fall would probably not last long, whereas the bargaining position which was reflected in the initial level of the real wage would, if anything, be likely to be strengthened by the increase in labour employment. A rise rather than a fall of the real wage might therefore be expected to accompany an increased incentive to invest and a faster growth. (It should in fact be stressed, in this connection, that our argument must not be taken to deny the possibility—or, indeed, the likelihood—of interactions between the real wage, on the one hand, and the speed of capital accumulation, on the other. What is here disputed is only the single effect postulated in the distribution-based Keynesian approach which, as just seen, might rather be the opposite of the actual effect.)

It seems, therefore, that the Keynesian hypothesis may allow rejection of the widespread idea we find in both the marginalist and the distribution-based Keynesian approaches that, initially at least, increased investment and faster growth require sacrificing consumption and that they accordingly impose lower real wages.

On the Point of View of Economic Historians

It is possible to say that some of the observations that economic historians have offered about the real experiences of growth of capitalist economies tend to confirm our analytical conclusions. Unlike economic theorists, historians have in fact often recognized the importance of demand in driving the process of growth (see Palumbo, 1994). This has been done, for example, by stressing the role of the expansion of foreign markets in enlarging production and productive investment in 18th- and 19th-century Britain (see, for example, Deane, 1965); or by observing the fact that the slower development of both domestic and external markets was the main cause of the delayed start of industrialization in other European countries such as France and Germany (Habakkuk, 1955); or by noting the strict correlation between the historical series of British growth rates in exports and in national product during the course of the nineteenth century (Kaldor, 1978: 165); or by recognizing the fundamental role of exports and public investments in the initial phase of German industrial development, when domestic demand grew only very slowly because of low incomes (Borchardt, 1973); and so on.

This does not mean, of course, that other economic historians have not reached different conclusions, more in accordance with traditional economic theory. Some authors have described the observed experiences of growth in terms of changes in supply factors: one influential example is the account of the British Industrial Revolution given by Ashton (1948). What is remarkable, however, is the fact that even some of these authors happen to offer observations on the fundamental role of demand contradicting their very theoretical premises (Matthews et al., 1982, provides an eloquent example, stressing the role of the demand for exports in different phases of British growth). This may be significant also for realizing the difficulties of the approach known as 'new economic history', which attempts to rewrite the economic history of capitalist economies by strictly applying the tools and conclusions of traditional theory.

If historical observation seems thus in general to validate the Keynesian hypothesis, it may be worthwhile trying to go further and ask whether it offers any evidence in favour of either of the above-mentioned two Keynesian approaches. The question may be addressed by considering the behaviour of the share of savings in national output during periods of fast growth (see Palumbo, 1996). Ignoring here the complications due to the international transactions and to the role of government (which, however, would not affect the substance of our argument), the inelasticity of long-period output in response to changes in the incentive to invest, claimed by the distribution-based Keynesian approach, would in fact entail, at least initially, a rise in the *share* of savings in national income when the *amount* of investment rises. The elasticity of long-period output contended in the output-based Keynesian approach may instead be conceived to leave that share unaffected, to the extent to which output and capacity rise together with investment.

Now, a near constancy of the share of gross savings in national output seems in fact to be what has been observed in various historical instances in initial periods of faster growth, and what has puzzled several historians influenced by traditional theory. A rise in the saving share is observable only after a period of faster growth of some length. This emerges in the debate on capital formation during the Industrial Revolution (see, for an account, Crafts, 1983), where the main empirical result seems to be that an increase in the investment share occurred *only decades* after a process of sustained growth had begun (the investment share nearly doubled in comparison with pre-industrial Britain only after the 1830s, the conventional date for the beginning of the Industrial Revolution being between 1760 and 1780).

Moreover, Habakkuk (1955: 161–2) notes that there was no rise in the saving share at the beginning of the growth process in the European countries that imitated British industrialization. Similarly, according to Cairncross (1963: 249), the Swedish economy witnessed a rise in the gross investment share only during the twentieth century, although 'industrialization was already in full swing and production rising rapidly long before 1900', while also for Norway the rise in the saving ratio followed rather than preceded the take-off. The same kind of evidence comes from those Asian countries which have lately experienced a process of fast industrialization and growth: the gross saving share was initially roughly constant (and very low by international standards), whereas it increased remarkably only one or two decades *after* the sustained increase in the growth rates of output had first occurred (Carrol and Weil, 1994).

This comparative constancy of the share of savings in the initial stages of episodes of fast growth seems thus to indicate a long-period elasticity of output and hence no need to change distribution to provide for savings. The later rise of the gross saving share might then perhaps be referred to a different kind of phenomenon, like the heavier dependence of a more developed economy on fixed capital and its replacement.

References

Ashton, T. S. (1948). *The industrial revolution 1760–1830.* Oxford University Press.

Borchardt, K. (1973). The industrial revolution in Germany 1700–1914. In C. M. Cipolla (Ed.), *The Fontana economic history of Europe* (Vol. 4, pp. 76–160). Fontana/Collins.

Cairncross, A. (1963). Capital formation in the take-off. In W. W. Rostow (Ed.), *The economics of take-off into sustained growth* (pp. 240–260). Palgrave Macmillan.

Carrol, C. D., & Weil, D. N. (1994). Saving and growth: A reinterpretation. *Carnegie-Rochester Conference Series on Public Policy,* 40, 133–192.

Ciccone, R. (1986). Accumulation and capacity utilization: Some critical considerations on Joan Robinson's theory of distribution. *Political Economy,* 2(1), 17–36. http://www.centrosraffa.org/fromthearchives.aspx

Crafts, N. F. R. (1983). British economic growth 1700–1831: A review of the evidence. *Economic History Review,* 36(2), 177–199.

Deane, P. (1965). *The first industrial revolution.* Cambridge University Press.

Garegnani, P. (1992). Some notes for an analysis of accumulation. In J. Halevi, D. Laibman, & E. J. Nell (Eds.), *Beyond the steady state* (pp. 47–71). Macmillan.

Habakkuk, H. J. (1955). The historical experience on the basic conditions of economic progress. In L. H. Dupriez (Ed.), *Economic progress* (pp. 149–69). Institut de Recherches Économiques et Sociales.

Kahn, R. (1959). Exercises in the analysis of growth. *Oxford Economic Papers,* 11(2), 143–156.

Kaldor, N. (1955–6). Alternative theories of distribution. *Review of Economic Studies,* 23(2), 83–100.

Kaldor, N. (1978). Capitalism and industrial development: Some lessons from Britain's experience. In *Further essays on applied economics* (pp. 154–172). Duckworth.

Kurz, H. D. (1986). "Normal" positions and capital utilization. *Political Economy,* 2(1), 37–54. http://www.centrosraffa.org/fromthearchives.aspx

Marglin, S. (1984). *Growth, distribution and prices.* Harvard University Press.

Matthews, R. C. O., Feinstein, C. H., & Odling-Smee, J. C. (1982). *British economic growth, 1856–1973.* Clarendon Press.

Palumbo, A. (1994). Alcune osservazioni sulle teorie economiche della crescita e la storia economica: Il ruolo della domanda aggregata. Materiali di discussione n. 26, Dipartimento di economia pubblica, Università di Roma "La Sapienza".

Palumbo, A. (1996). Notes on investment, saving and growth. *Contributions to Political Economy,* 15(1), 105–115.

Robinson, J. V. (1962). *Essays in the theory of economic growth*. Macmillan.

Vianello, F. (1985). The pace of accumulation. *Political Economy*, 1(1), 69–87. http://www.centrosraffa.org/fromthearchives.aspx

Part V
Classical and Marginalist Authors in the History of Economic Analysis

Sraffa's Price Equations: A Stationary Economy or 'Normal Positions'?†

Seven Points for Discussion

1. It is often argued that Sraffa's (1960) analysis relates to a stationary or steady growth economy (for example, Hicks, 1990: 100, 1985: *passim*; Samuelson, 2000: 136): even authors sympathetic to Sraffa's classical approach appear sometimes to view that assumption as being entailed by his equations, where the prices of the commodity inputs at the beginning of the production cycle are the same as those of the outputs at the end of it. Although I have not had the opportunity to give close consideration to some recent literature on the matter, certain points raised in this session induce me to submit for discussion a few reflections on the subject, one with which I have been concerned in the past (Garegnani, 1976 [this volume, Part II]).

I shall here argue for two theses. The first is that, in the context of classical theory in which Sraffa (1960) must be placed, the forces that are seen to govern the economy do not admit of a formalized dynamic *theory* based on dated prices as distinct from admitting of dynamic *models*, which can of course always be built, if relevant, in order to deal with particular questions or explore the logical implications of assumptions admitted to be special. The second thesis is that, in contemporary literature, consideration of price changes[1] within the equations determining

The original version of the chapter has been revised: Incorrect details have been corrected.
A correction to this chapter can be found at https://doi.org/10.1007/978-3-031-23643-3_18

† Previously published with Edward Elgar in *Is There Progress in Economics?*, ed. by S. Boehm, C. Gehrke, H. D. Kurz, R. Sturn, 2002. All necessary permissions acquired.

[1] The introduction of price changes referred to here should of course not be confused with the consideration of changes in prices by means of the *comparison* of two different positions of the economy.

P. Garegnani, *Capital Theory, the Surplus Approach, and Effective Demand*, Springer Studies in the History of Economic Thought,
https://doi.org/10.1007/978-3-031-23643-3_15

prices has *not* been the result of an attempt at a closer approximation to reality, but rather a purely doctrinal development intended to remedy logical deficiencies internal to the dominant theory of prices. As I have contended elsewhere and shall recall below, the consideration of price changes in the equations determining prices makes it more difficult and not more easy to relate theory and observable phenomena.[2]

I will proceed by listing, in the rest of this section, seven points summarizing my position, and I will then comment on the matter in the three sections that follow. Thus, in Sect. 2, I will focus on some lack of clarity in the claims I am discussing as to whether the prices whose changes should be considered are, in classical terms, 'market prices' or 'production prices'. We shall contend that such prices cannot but be production prices, and hence can correspond to actual prices only when the latter are averaged over a period of time allowing for a sufficient repetition of transactions. This directly contradicts any 'dating' of such prices. In Sect. 3, the argument of Sect. 2 will be used to review the meaning and importance of the traditional 'normal position'. Finally, in Sect. 4, we shall see why, even apart from the preceding general considerations, a formalized general 'dynamic' theory appears to conflict with the premises of classical theory.

2. The seven points by which I would summarize my position are as follows:

i. The thesis according to which the prices appearing in Sraffa's equations relate to a stationary or 'steady-state' economy seems to rest on a misapprehension of the analysis based on 'normal positions' which Sraffa revives—and to which both classical and neoclassical theorists constantly referred until recent decades.[3] The constancy of prices assumed in defining the normal position of the economy is an abstraction founded on the *persistence* (paras. 5–6 below) and not the *constancy* of the determining forces and is therefore compatible with ongoing changes in the economy, the study of which is in fact the main purpose of the theory.
ii. The misapprehension results from accepting the apparent argument which since Hicks's *Value and Capital* (1939) has generally been provided within the dominant theory for the shift away from the traditional notion of equilibrium and towards the 'temporary' or 'intertemporal' equilibria which that book was influential in introducing. As is well known, the argument runs in terms of a need to consider, in the definition of the equilibrium itself, the changes which prices undergo or are expected to undergo in any non-stationary economy.[4]

[2] See, for example, Marshall's passage quoted in para. 7 below about a 'dynamics in the physical sense' being impossible in economics.

[3] See Garegnani (1976: 26–9 [this volume, Part II, pp. 210–3]); see also by the same author 1960 (Appendice E) [this volume, Part I, *A Problem in the Theory of Distribution from Ricardo to Wicksell*, Sect. II, Appendix to Ch. VI].

[4] 'The current supply of commodities depends not so much upon what the current price is as upon what the entrepreneurs have expected it to be in the past' (Hicks, 1939: 117): hence the claimed need to abandon what Hicks there calls 'static theory'.

The traditional 'normal position' of the economy, defined independently of any such price changes, had accordingly to be reinterpreted as relating to a stationary or steady-state economy where normal prices would not change over time.

iii. The misapprehension is thus due to overlooking what a closer reading of Hicks (1939) is sufficient to reveal as being the real argument for the change—namely the impossibility which by then had begun to emerge of dealing with capital as a 'factor of production' within the framework of the 'normal position', contrary to what the founders of the theory had originally postulated. The misapprehension is due, that is, to overlooking that what caused introducing price changes in the definition of an equilibrium was not a preoccupation to go beyond what a logically consistent 'normal position' could reveal about reality: it was, on the contrary, the impossibility of a consistent treatment of that position. What prompted the introduction of those changes was essentially the failure of the attempt carried out over a century to reconcile the concept of capital as a 'factor of production', characteristic of the modern demand and supply theory of distribution, with the notion of a normal position of the economy always and unanimously used to ensure a sufficient correspondence between theory and observation in economics. As shown by the inconsistency of Walras' original general equilibrium system, the normal position and its basic condition of a uniform rate of return on the supply prices of the capital goods required conceiving capital as a single magnitude—which is what by the time of *Value and Capital* (1939), after his *Theory of Wages* (1932), where the single magnitude was postulated, Hicks had to admit is impossible.[5] Capital could only be conceived of as a vector of heterogeneous 'factors', making it impossible to satisfy the condition of a uniform rate of return on the supply prices of the several capital goods, and therefore to refer to normal prices *persistent enough to be determined independently of their changes*.

iv. Despite its apparent plausibility, little or no foundation seems thus attributable to an alleged need to introduce price changes and dated quantities into an analysis like Sraffa's which revives the approach to relative prices and distribution of the 'old classical economists' (Sraffa, 1960: v). This is an approach that suffers from no logical difficulty in dealing with capital as a set of distinct capital goods (Garegnani, 1960: vii–viii) and is quite consistent with the 'normal position' method. Indeed, one aim of its revival is just to do away with the neoclassical presuppositions concerning a determining role of the 'capital endowment', and the corresponding need to abandon the conception of the normal position.

[5] The argument is presented in Garegnani (1976: 34–5, 31–2 [this volume, Part II, pp. 217–8, 214–5]), where Hicks's statements concerning the fact that 'people... would often introduce in their static theory a "factor of production" capital [,] …., supposing that [it] could be treated like the static factors' (1939: 116, n.) are also reported and discussed. For the inconsistency of Walras' original general equilibrium system, see Garegnani (1960: Part II, Chs. II–III and Appendix G [this volume, Part I, Sect. II, Chs. II-III and Appendix E]).

v. The above misapprehension has on the other hand been made easier by the fact that, as I noted in 1976 (pp. 42–44 [this volume, Part II, pp. 224–6]), a criticism of the traditional normal position, parallel to that by Hicks and the subsequent neoclassical literature, has come from the Keynesian side, from Joan Robinson in particular. The motivation was different, and even opposite, in that it was designed to supersede rather than preserve the traditional demand and supply framework. It can however be argued that the criticism rested on an incorrect identification of the 'normal position' with its neoclassical representation in terms of an 'equilibrium' between demand and supply of 'productive factors', and hence with full employment of labour. It therefore overlooked the basic deficiencies of the neoclassical notion indicated above under (iii): when those deficiencies are overcome, as happens within a classical framework, we can deal with labour unemployment without in any way abandoning the notion of the normal position (as Ricardo's chapter 'On machinery' in the *Principles* or Marx's conception of the 'reserve army' of unemployed labour had made clear in their time).[6]

vi. If the doctrinal difficulties of neoclassical theory causing the abandonment of the traditional normal position are absent in classical theory, equally absent are the *endogenous* price changes on which neoclassical pure theory has come to rely in its contemporary reformulations. This is so, because the engine of those endogenous changes—the capital endowment—loses the determining role for prices it has in neoclassical equilibria.[7]

vii. In classical theory, changes in the economy and in its normal positions are instead seen to originate from circumstances analysed *outside* that 'core' of the theory which is alone susceptible of a systematically formalized treatment—outside, that is, what Sraffa defines as the 'system of production' (for example, Sraffa, 1960: 33) represented in his price equations. Thus,

[6] Cf. Garegnani (1978–79 [this volume, Part IV]; also 1989: 359). It seems to be argued sometimes as if the 'normal position' by itself entailed acceptance of Say's law (see, for example, Roncaglia, 2000: 174). In fact what is here meant by a 'normal position' of classical theory is simply the equality between 'effectual demand' and 'quantity brought to market' (Smith [1776] 1910, Vol. I, Bk. I, Ch. VII), which concerns the *relative* outputs corresponding to a *given* long-period level of activity, irrespective of whether that level is or is not influenced by aggregate demand (cf., for example, Garegnani, 1997: 141–2 [this volume, Part III, pp. 356–7]; cf. also for the compatibility between the classical analysis of distribution and prices and deficiencies of aggregate demand, Garegnani, 1978–79 [this volume, Part IV]; Roncaglia's more general position is discussed in Garegnani, 1990: 150–58).

[7] At the level of theory (as distinct from that of models: para. 1 above), Hicksian dated prices appear mainly to have been confined to the endogenous changes resulting from variations in the capital endowment. This limitation of the neoclassical 'dynamics' seems significant in revealing that its motivation lies in the difficulties which capital raises for normal prices rather than in a need to consider price changes as such, in which case demographic or technological changes would certainly be of no less importance than the changes caused by savings. (For an analogous, surprising limitation to outputs of the dynamics at times envisaged for classical theory, see n. 11 below).

for example, changes in wages may originate from broader socio-institutional and demographic elements affecting the bargaining position of workers and, unlike in a labour demand and supply setting, they cannot usefully be expressed by means of equations forming a single system with the price equations. More inductive methods taking into account historical factors are required. More generally, neither the evolution of the wage, nor that of the technical conditions or the outputs—the 'intermediate data' of the classical 'core'—can be viewed as susceptible of being expressed in terms of mathematical relations general and definite enough to provide the conceivable basis of a systematic formalized theory (as distinct from a 'model': cf. para. 1 above) running in terms of dated quantities and prices.

Which Price Changes?

3. Let us now clear the ground for a more detailed discussion of the issue by noting the apparent dependence of the claimed need to introduce changing prices on the assumption of production occurring by yearly cycles (para. 1 above): if agriculture has production cycles, industrial production is generally continuous. Though it would help us obtain a better grasp of the claim to see how it can translate in terms of continuous production, when outputs can be ascribed to inputs of the same date,[8] we shall now simply *assume* that all production occurs in yearly cycles.

Let us then proceed to ask which are the classical prices whose changes we should consider in passing from inputs to outputs: 'market prices' or 'normal prices'? The *prima facie* plausibility of the need to admit price changes between when the inputs are bought and when the outputs are sold seems to rest on referring to the prices *actually* paid for the inputs, and *actually* received for the outputs, that is, to the classical 'market prices' at the respective instants.

Then, however, the price equations would drastically change the meaning they have in Sraffa, which is that the equalization there represented uniformity between prices of commodities and normal expenses of production, that is, the revenues of producers calculated at their normal levels, would now refer to the 'market' rates of profits, wages and rents resulting from the 'market' prices of the commodity. And even assuming, as is generally done, that only a single market price exists for a commodity at each instant of time (and the same applies to the services of labour, capital goods and land used in each industry), such actual relative prices and distributive variables are essentially unknowable in classical theory except for the *sign* of their deviation from their natural or normal relative levels relevant in turn for the *sign* of the direction of their change as outputs change

[8] See Garegnani (1960: 25–9 [for corresponding arguments cf. this volume, Part I, Sect. I, pp. 24–7]).

accordingly.[9] Any attempt to determine those prices further would require special assumptions, thus again moving away from the domain of *theory* and into that of *models* (para. 1 above). We should stress that we would here be on a quite different ground from neoclassical theories, where 'temporary' equilibrium prices could be imagined to be (approximately) determined by 'temporary' demand and supply functions, which would find no basis in a context of classical 'market prices'.

It might, however, be argued that 'expected', rather than realized, 'market' prices should be considered. But even leaving aside the problems caused by the indefiniteness of expectations, it appears that expected prices cannot be used in that role in a classical context. Their use would imply a sequence, like that of Hicks's (1939) 'weeks', and therefore also the consideration of *realized* prices besides expected prices, and we would then meet the difficulty of determining market prices we have just mentioned.

4. That should clarify that, contrary to what one may naively think, the price changes we are told we should consider in a non-stationary economy cannot have anything to do with the prices which producers *actually* pay for the inputs and receive, or expect to receive, for the outputs. Indeed there would be no reason why, even in a stationary economy as generally understood, i.e. with constant *normal* prices, such day-to-day *market* prices should ever be constant.

Thus, it seems, the relative prices whose changes it is alleged we should consider would have to be the normal prices themselves, redefined by the corresponding price equations as what we may then call 'intertemporal normal prices' or 'intertemporal production prices'[10]—and their changes would be those associated with the changes in outputs, wages or technical knowledge,[11] the 'intermediate data' of the 'core' where classical prices are determined.

---

[9] See Garegnani (1997: 160–1 [this volume, Part III, pp. 379–80]).

[10] They would be determined by production equations characterized by dated prices and by a uniform effective rate of interest (profits) expressed as the own rate of interest of the numeraire (see, for example, Garegnani 2000: 397, 434; for the notion of 'effective rate of interest' see 392 n., 434 n.. [*Editor's note*: except for the first, these references do not seem to be appropriate, and should be amended as follows: replace 'p. 434' with 'pp. 434–5, n. 58'; replace 'p. 392 n.' with 'pp. 392–3, n. 2'; omit 'p. 434, n.'. In the version of Garegnani (2000) published in this volume, Part II, the (corrected) references, including the first one, are: p. 234; pp. 259–60, n. 47; p. 230, n. 2].

[11] Constant returns to scale are at times mentioned as an assumption sufficient to replace that of stationarity in order to avoid introducing dated prices in the equations of production. It is difficult, however, to see why the changes of a non-stationary economy should come from changes of outputs only and not also from changes in technical conditions or in distribution, when, of course, constant returns would be of little avail. (The fact that the outputs of a given period limit the possible outputs of subsequent periods may perhaps tempt a modem economist to envisage some dynamic analysis based on endogenous changes in outputs, with corresponding changes in relative prices because of variable returns to scale. However, even if we could leave aside the generality of capital destruction, obviously no unique functional relation could be generally established such that the output of t determines that of $t+1$. More importantly, we shall argue in para. 8 of the text that at the level of generality of the theory as distinct from that of models, changes in outputs, when relevant, can only be dealt with outside the 'core' and by the correspondingly more inductive methods.).

However, as soon as we try to deal with such changes in normal prices we meet, I believe, an intrinsic contradiction. The normal prices appearing in the price equations, whether for the commodity inputs or the outputs, could only correspond to *average prices* obtained through a sufficient repetition of transactions over time. But this repetition is precisely what is excluded by the dating of the prices, which would force us to conceive of the intertemporal price as realized at the appropriate instant of time.[12]

No reason in fact exists for prices at the specified instant t to be at their correct intertemporal level rather than at any accidental market level. In particular, there is no reason why the correct intertemporal production prices for the t, $t+1$, $t+2$ and so on outputs, should have been expected when their production cycles were started at $(t-1)$, t, $t+1$,[13] or earlier, as would be necessary (though not sufficient) for those prices to be realized. Changes in intertemporal normal prices could be perceived by, and govern the behaviour of, individual agents only as changes of *average* prices, and therefore through a *repetition* of the transactions.

Why the 'Normal Position'?

5. The above should suffice to explain why, before the progressive emergence of the doctrinal difficulties we saw under points (iii) and (v) of para. 2, all theorists shunned consideration of price changes in the general determination of prices.[14] The way they came to do so was by distinguishing two kinds of prices complementing each other. Those of the first kind were the normal prices, on which the theory could usefully focus because their changes could be ignored in determining

[12] It might perhaps be thought that we could interpret the 'date' of a production cycle as covering a number of such cycles, so as to have the dated price correspond to an average of actual or market prices. However, the same market prices would then enter the price average for the commodity as input, as for the commodity as output, except for the accidental market prices of the commodity of its earliest use (as input) and of its latest appearance (as output) in this period, depriving of significance the distinction between the two (average) prices. Nor could we replace the tendency to the normal price by the tendency to the sequence of dated prices: the accumulation of errors over time would make 'early' deviations count for more than 'later' deviations, and prevent their compensation. It has sometimes been argued that persistence is indeed a condition for approximating the actual prices of a non-stationary economy—a better approximation being then seemingly provided by a dynamic analysis with 'dated' prices. However, that thesis seems to overlook the essence of the question, which is that the dated prices have no observable correspondent (para. 4 in the text) and, more basically, that no formalized dynamic analysis appears to be possible even at the level of theory (paras. 1 and 8 in the text).

[13] The tendency to realize those prices will be the tendency to a uniform effective rate of profits (see note 11) which, with no repetition possible, would essentially have to refer to the expected prices.

[14] In neoclassical theory in particular, even if we could leave aside the question of the observable content of dated prices which arises there too, there are the well-known difficulties connected with the indefiniteness of the horizon and of the meaning of a perfect foresight about future agents with their tastes and technology.

them. The second was that of the 'actual' prices, whose changes were considered, but only as deviations from normal prices which could reasonably be held to cancel each other out, letting the corresponding normal price emerge over time as an average of the actual ones. Thus, with respect to the second kind of price, the theory's concerns were fundamentally confined to arguing the mutual compensation of their changes.

At the basis of that procedure there ultimately lay what we may describe as a 'Basic observation' about the economy: it is that prices, while differing from time to time and even from transaction to transaction, are remarkably 'persistent' in their long-run averages since their variations are *either* slow relative to the time required for a sufficient compensation of the deviations, or are 'one-off' changes, such that after a limited period of transition graduality of changes re-establishes itself.

6. That Basic observation is, it appears, what has suggested, and allowed for, an equally basic distinction between two kinds of *forces* acting on prices and, in particular, on relative prices. On the one hand, there are the forces which, in Marshall's words, consist of 'passing events, and... causes whose action is fitful and short lived' and which 'influence actual value at any time, the market value as it is often called'. On the other hand, we have the 'persistent causes' which in the long run 'dominate value completely' (Marshall, [1920] 1961: 349–50).

Now, the distinction between the two species of *prices* that we traced in para. 5 above follows naturally from this distinction between the two kinds of *forces*. In the first place the persistence of the causes of the normal price allows us to abstract from the gradual changes which the normal price might be undergoing over time.[15] This as we saw has nothing to do with denying the possibility of sharp 'one-off' changes in those determinants (for example, an important invention), or with

[15] The Basic observation should clear the doubts at times expressed about whether the speed of the adjustment to the normal price is sufficiently high relative to that of the changes in the latter to warrant the assumption of its constancy (see, for example, Caminati, 2000: 208). It is indeed hard to think that, as is sometimes suggested, contemporary technical change has altered those relative speeds and undermined the validity of the Basic observation. It would e.g. be a curious coincidence that such a striking change in economic reality should have occurred at about the time when Hicks had to admit the logical impossibility of introducing into the analysis 'a factor of production, capital, and its price interest' (n. 5 above).

We may also note that another objection frequently raised against the normal positions, their possible 'path dependence' (see, for example, Caminati, 2000), does not in fact apply to the *classical* normal position as distinct from the *neoclassical* one. The fact that the analysis of changes can be conducted outside the 'core' of the theory (para. 8 below) allows for any possible 'path dependence' of the normal position. Path dependence is a problem for the *neoclassical* normal positions, which rest on data whose changes are mostly thought not to be analysable in economic theory and are correspondingly treated as independent of the changes they cause in the system. Path dependence is indeed strictly associated with the irreversibility of economic changes, which flies in the face of a demand and supply analysis as of any analysis conducted in the mathematical terms of reversible functions.

overlooking the long-term effects of the gradual changes we are ignoring in determining the normal price (for example, the net investment in a neoclassical context, or the extension of cultivation in Ricardo); indeed, as we recalled in para. 1, the method of the normal positions has the precise purpose of studying the effects of such changes by comparisons of the position before and after the change.

In the second place, the same persistence allows the inevitable day-to-day changes of the actual prices to be represented as deviations from the normal prices compensating each other over time: this it does by permitting a repetition of transactions occurring on the basis of nearly unchanged data. The inclusion in the determination of normal price of all the factors whose action is seen to be persistent warrants the compensation.[16]

The persistence of the normal price is thus a necessary condition of the two-prices method of para. 5 for avoiding the introduction of price changes into its determination. A second condition necessary for it is of course the tendency of the actual prices to their normal levels, whichever accidental level they might be in at any given moment. Without this tendency, there is evidently no reason why the repetition of transactions allowed by the persistence of the price should permit it to emerge as a guide to an average of the actual positions. Now, if the difficulties about capital we saw in para. 2 at point (iii) have undercut the persistence of the determinants, making the introduction of price changes inevitable, the difficulties concerning the stability of the neoclassical equilibria have also favoured the abandonment of the normal position by throwing into question its second necessary condition. It is in fact beginning to emerge that this second kind of difficulty, in the most decisive part, is altogether independent of the long-known income effects, with which neoclassical theory has managed to coexist: rather, they are a second effect, besides the non-persistent character of the new equations, of the deficiencies of the neoclassical notion of capital.[17]

We may here wonder whether something similar to the Basic observation about prices, applies also to outputs. A distinction may here be relevant between the two theories. Neoclassical distribution entails a strict interrelation between prices and outputs, so the persistence of prices is thus one with persistence of the output levels. The same is not true in classical theory where the persistence of prices only excludes changes of outputs large enough to trigger appreciable decreasing returns from natural resources or appreciable increasing returns from division of labour.

[16] In 1848, Mill ([1848] 1909: 453) referred to 'the centre value towards which … the market value of a thing is constantly gravitating and any deviation from which … sets forces in motion tending to correct it … On an average of years sufficient to enable the oscillations on one side of the central line to be compensated by those on the other, the market value agrees with the natural value'. For similar passages see, for example, Ricardo ([1821] 1951): 91–2; Walras (1954): 380; Pareto (1896): 17–8, paras. 36–8; Clark (1907): 94; cf. also the passage by Marshall quoted in the text.

[17] See Garegnani (2000), in particular 443. [*Editor's note*: the content of this page shows no specific relationship to the point in the text of the present paper where the reference is made (with contrast to the 'in particular' which qualifies the reference). It therefore seems likely that the reference is incorrect. The appropriate place in Garegnani (2000) appears to be para. 10, pp. 406–8 (para. 10, pp. 244–5 in the version of the essay included in this volume, Part II).]

On the Classical Analysis of Changes

7. It is to the Basic observation rather than to any deficiencies of the mathematical tools available at the time that I believe we should turn for explaining the traditional unanimous reliance upon normal prices determined independently of their changes over time. The mathematical tools for an economic dynamics had in fact been ready since Newton's time, and Marshall, who came to economics from mathematics, just as Wicksell or Pareto did, was quite explicit on the substance of the matter in a passage I have often quoted:

> Thus, then, dynamical solutions in the physical sense of economic problems are unattainable. And if we are to adhere to physical analogies at all, we must say that statical solutions afford starting points for such rude and imperfect approaches to dynamical solutions as we may be able to attain to (Marshall, 1898: 39).[18]

To my knowledge the reasons prompting Marshall's statement have never been countered by Hicks or in the literature which followed in the wake of *Value and Capital*. The fact is of course that the doctrinal difficulties which those authors had to face at the time left them little choice but to change the notion of equilibrium, with the entailed introduction of dated prices in the determination of the system. A theoretical discontinuity as would have been involved in abandoning, with the notion of capital as a single quantity, the determining role of the 'capital endowment' and hence the demand and supply approach to distribution and relative prices, was inconceivable at the time, when that was taken to be economic theory *tout court*. Even Keynes had apparently found its abandonment inconceivable enough to place himself in the contradictions I have tried to examine elsewhere (1978–79) [this volume, Part IV]. However, the alternative provided by Sraffa's rediscovery of the classical approach exists now, and it would be paradoxical to introduce into his system a procedure based on intertemporal prices, which is one of the most striking sequels of the deficiencies he criticizes in neoclassical theory.

---

[18] An argument brought at times in defence of dated prices is the need to deal with exhaustible resources, where decisions as to the conservation of the resource by its owner would be based on such prices. The scarcity made visible by the coexistence of processes using the resource with different intensities clearly depends on the policy of conservation of the resource for future use by its owners. Now, according to the argument, owners would aim to maximize the value of the resource over time, given the interest rates expected for the future. Observation and theory alike throw doubts on that argument. Such a paramount case of exhaustible resource as oil seems to suggest that the royalty for the resource will generally respond more to 'the relative strength' of users and owners *who compete in sharing the value of the advantage which the resource gives in production*, than to an intertemporal pricing which would generally be founded on circumstances too distant in time and too uncertain and complex in their occurrence to provide the owners with more than a reservation price founded on a reasonable certainty of some future use, the royalty for which can however be only a matter of speculation.

8. Let me conclude by quickly turning to points (vi) and (vii) on my initial list of para. 2. The endogenous price changes which had to be introduced in the equilibria of contemporary theory are, we said, those originating from the changes in the capital endowment resulting from savings and investment (point vi para. 2). But in classical theory the capital endowment constitutes no part of the determinants of prices in the formalized 'core' of the theory, and no similar 'dynamic' analysis can accordingly be conducted there.

More generally the causes of price changes in classical theory, though they act *through* the 'intermediate data' consisting of the real wage, the outputs and the technical knowledge, will normally originate from outside the 'core', and the analysis of their effects will also normally require going beyond it. This means that their action will not be of a kind which can be expressed in terms of formal quantitative relations general and definite enough to be significant for a theory, as distinct from a model concerned with special assumptions or particular questions (para. 1 above). And this is true independently of the difficulties we saw as besetting the *meaning* of dated prices, and of the irrelevance in a classical context of the doctrinal difficulties they are meant to remedy.

Appendix

What we recalled in para. 8 about the separation between the determination of relative prices, on the one hand, and that of outputs or wages on the other might perhaps be interpreted in terms of what has been described as 'piecemeal theorizing' in the sense of a methodological position for which

> [n]o special set of causal factors is predominantly responsible for all major economic phenomena. In each given problem situation, the economist must isolate the major causal factors by empirical investigation and theoretical ingenuity'.[19]

It appears, however, that the above separation in classical theory has to be interpreted as the characteristic feature of an analysis, which constitutes no less of a unitary *system* because of it. The separation, that is, should be envisaged as a natural adaptation of the method of analysis to a reality in which two broadly different but strictly interacting kinds of objective forces are seen to operate in the economy. First, there are forces of competition which, by tending to realize uniform rates of profits, wages and rents, establish the purely quantitative relations of the 'core' between such rates and the prices. These forces are, however, seen to operate within a setting of institutional and historical forces forming, together with those of competition, a coherent system. The theory has then to reflect this

[19] The passage is from Hausman (1981: 183), who wrote it in a different context. It is quoted with reference to the present context in Signorino (2001: 250–1). For what appears to be a similar position, see Roncaglia (2000: 162).

system of objective forces. Outputs, wages and technical conditions are 'intermediate data' in the 'core' not because of any choice of isolating the determinants of relative prices and the non-wage variables, a choice which could then apply to different variables as the problem investigated changes. They are 'intermediate data' because the nature of the dependencies, their complexity and variability, relative to the comparatively simple and constant character of the forces of competition analysed in the 'core', is seen to require two different methods of analysis: a mainly deductive method for the purely quantitative relations of the 'core' which have sufficiently definite general properties, and more inductive and historical methods for the determination of wages, outputs or the technical conditions of production, in which the relations of the 'core' are, so to speak, immersed.

References

Caminati, M. (2000). Concorrenza, lungo periodo e cambiamento economico. In M. Pivetti (Ed.), *Piero Sraffa* (pp. 203–225). Carocci.

Clark, J. B. (1907). *Essentials of economic theory*. Macmillan.

Garegnani, P. (1960). *Il capitale nelle teorie della distribuzione*. Giuffré.

Garegnani, P. (1978–79). 'Notes on consumption, investment, and effective demand', I and II. *Cambridge Journal of Economics,* 2(4), 335–53 and 2(3), 63–82.

Garegnani, P. (1990). 'Sraffa: Classical versus marginalist analysis' and 'Reply' (to discussants). In K. Bharadway & B. Schefold (Eds.), *Essays on Piero Sraffa* (pp. 112–40 and 148–58). Unwin Hyman (rpt. Routledge, 1992)

Garegnani, P. (2000). Savings, investment and the quantity of capital in general intertemporal equilibrium. In H. D. Kurz (Ed.), *Critical essays on Piero Sraffa's legacy in economics* (pp. 392–445). Cambridge University Press.

Garegnani, P. (1976). On a change in the notion of equilibrium in recent work on value: A comment on Samuelson. In M. Brown, K. Sato, & P. Zarembka (Eds.), *Essays in modem capital theory* (pp. 25–45). North Holland.

Garegnani, P. (1989). Some notes on capital, expectations and the analysis of changes. In G. R. Feiwel (Ed.), *Joan Robinson and modern economic theory* (pp. 344–367). Macmillan.

Garegnani, P. (1997). On some supposed obstacles to the tendency of market prices towards natural prices. In G. Caravale (Ed.), *Equilibrium and economic theory* (pp. 139–170). Routledge.

Hausman, D. M. (1981). *Capital, profits and prices. An essay in the philosophy of economics*. Columbia University Press.

Hicks, J. R. (1932). *The theory of wages* (2nd ed.). St. Martin's Press.

Hicks, J. R. (1939). *Value and capital* (2nd ed.). Clarendon Press.

Hicks, J. R. (1985). Sraffa and Ricardo: A critical view. In G. A. Caravale (Ed.), *The legacy of Ricardo* (pp. 305–319). Blackwell.

Hicks, J. R. (1990). Ricardo and Sraffa. In K. Bharadwaj & B. Schefold (Eds.), *Essays on Piero Sraffa* (pp. 99–102). Unwin Hyman (rpt. Routledge, 1992).

Marshall, A. ([1920] 1961). *Principles of economics* (9th (Variorum) ed., Vol. I). Macmillan.

Marshall, A. (1898). Distribution and exchange. *Economic Journal,* 8(29), 37–59.

Mill, J. S. ([1848] 1909). *Principles of political economy with some of their applications to social philosophy*. Longmans Green.

Pareto, V. (1896). *Cours d'Économie Politique* (Tome Premier). F. Rouge.

Ricardo, D. ([1821] 1951). *On the principles of political economy and taxation*. In *The works and correspondence of David Ricardo*, ed. by Piero Sraffa with the collaboration of M. H. Dobb, Vol. I. Cambridge University Press.

Roncaglia, A. (2000). Produzione di merci a mezzo di merci: Critica dell'approccio marginalista e ricostruzione dell'approccio classico. In M. Pivetti (Ed.), *Piero Sraffa* (pp. 161–179). Carocci.

Samuelson, P. A. (2000). Sraffa's hits and misses. In H. D. Kurz (Ed.), *Critical essays on Piero Sraffa's legacy in economics* (pp. 111–52), Cambridge University Press.

Signorino, R. (2001). On the limits to the long-period method in classical economics. A note. *Review of Political Economy*, 13(2), 245–251.

Smith, A. ([1776] 1910). *An inquiry into the nature and causes of the wealth of nations* (Vol. 2). Dent and Son.

Sraffa, P. (1960). *Production of commodities by means of commodities*. Cambridge University Press.

Walras, L. (1954). *Elements of pure economics* (4th def. ed., Jaffé's Engl. ed.). George Allen & Unwin.

On a Turning Point in Sraffa's Theoretical and Interpretative Position in the Late 1920s[†*]

I. Introduction

1. Among Sraffa's manuscripts deposited in Cambridge, at Trinity College, is a document I believe to be highly interesting: about seventy pages with a title on the cover in Sraffa's own hand: 'Notes/London, Summer 1927/Physical real costs, etc.'.[1]

† Previously published in *The European Journal of the History of Economic Thought*, 12(3), 2005. All necessary permissions acquired.

* Although based on a study of the manuscripts conducted for several years over different intervals of time (cf. Garegnani, 1998 [Eng. ver. Garegnani (2003)]), this essay is strictly provisional. The reason is the difficulty in gaining sufficient control over a vast mass of relevant, but fragmented manuscripts, reflecting a highly original and long process of research in which the author had to open up his own path all along, step by step. The essential points in the present essay were presented at the Conference 'Piero Sraffa: A Centenary Estimate' organized in October 1998 in Turin by the Einaudi Foundation. The presentation there was exclusively verbal (which seems to have led to some misapprehensions and also to expectations which, I hope, will be disappointed by the present paper: see De Vivo 2001: 158). I should finally mention that the present author is among those engaged in the publication of Sraffa's manuscripts: he is however responsible alone for the views advanced in the present essay (which concerns manuscripts of a period entrusted to his case for publication). The translation from the Italian original has been conducted by Mr. Julian Bees.

[1] D3/12/3 in the Trinity catalogue, and from A4.4 to A4.28 in the Bharadwaj–Garegnani inventory. The document may at first appear to show discontinuities, but apart from the unity attributed to it by Sraffa's binding it together, a close study shows a substantial continuity between the three longest manuscripts constituting it, classified in the inventory as A4.4; A4.16; A4.21, separated by pages consisting almost entirely of bibliographies and reading notes that can be associated

P. Garegnani, *Capital Theory, the Surplus Approach, and Effective Demand*,
Springer Studies in the History of Economic Thought,
https://doi.org/10.1007/978-3-031-23643-3_16

We know that Sraffa left Italy for England[2] early in July after agreeing to hold a course on the advanced theory of value in Cambridge in the following October. The document's contents leave little doubt that it contains preparations for that course,[3] then postponed by a year to October 1928 for reasons that I think we may be able to help to elucidate. These notes are quite separate from the long, 200-page later manuscript containing the lectures in fact held in 1928–31 (D/2/4, MI/7). In what follows, I will refer to the first of these manuscripts as the 'pre-lectures', as distinct from the later 'lectures'.

In fact, if we make a close analysis of the document from the summer of 1927, compare it with the lectures of 1928, and then take into account other important manuscripts from the period—including those where we find the first formulations of the equations later developed in *Production of Commodities*—we can, so to speak, see with our own eyes how, over a period of a few months, a turning point matured in Sraffa's theoretical position, away from that of the articles of 1925 and 1926. And this turning point was one thing with what Sraffa came to see as the re-discovery of the position of the 'old Classical economists', beyond the Marshallian interpretation he had hitherto followed, attributing to them an implicit hypothesis of constant returns (constant costs).

This turning point is indeed what Sraffa (1960) himself had implied when, in the Preface to *Production of Commodities*, after denying the dependence of his argument on the assumption of constant returns, he commented:

> The temptation to presuppose constant returns is not entirely fanciful. It was experienced by the author himself when he started on these studies many years ago—and it led him in 1925 into an attempt to argue that only the case of constant returns was generally consistent with the premises of economic theory.
>
> (Sraffa, 1960: vi)

The same Preface also makes it possible to see that the earlier position must have been relinquished in the brief period elapsing between the article of 1926, where it was still present, and early in 1928 when, as Sraffa writes: 'Lord Keynes

with the main texts immediately preceding them. (I note here that the catalogue drawn up by Trinity College Library often proceeds by groups of manuscripts and, as far as is accessible to me at present from Italy, does not separate the sometimes numerous manuscripts distinguished in the inventory. As a result, the page numbering will here refer to the latter, drawn up by Krishna Bharadwaj and the present author immediately after Piero Sraffa's death (Garegnani, 1998: 151 [Eng. ver. Garegnani (2003): 623]). In the following, I will therefore give references to both classifications, with that of the Trinity catalogue first, followed by that of the inventory, which scholars consulting the manuscripts will normally find indicated in pencil on each manuscript page. (Classifications in the inventory given here with A, E or C stand, for the sake of brevity, for G.S.A; G.S.E; G.S.C).

[2] Cf. Naldi (1998).

[3] See, for example, 'I want to make clear that in this course…' (D3/12/3, A4.21.xb). See also what appears to be a brief scheme of the intended course (para. 5 below).

read a draft of the opening propositions of this paper, he recommended that, if constant returns were *not* to be assumed, an emphatic warning to that effect should be given' (*ibid.*, italics in the original) and when, therefore, constant returns were no longer assumed.

A suggestion of the content of the change or, at least, of how radical it was, can on the other hand be found in the Preface not only because of its reference to as basic a question as the assumption of constant returns but also, and even more fundamentally, in the distance taken at the very beginning of the Preface from:

> anyone accustomed to think in terms of equilibrium of demand and supply
>
> (*ibid.*).

There is, further, the statement that the standpoint adopted in the book will be that:

> of the old classical economists from Adam Smith to Ricardo [...] submerged and forgotten since the advent of the 'marginal' method
>
> (*ibid.*).

That 'submerged and forgotten' standpoint was clearly not the well-known Marshallian one on Ricardo and the Classical economists, which Sraffa had previously accepted. The turning point concerns, in fact, the rediscovery of the determination of prices and distribution, which Sraffa will trace to Ricardo in the *Introduction* to the Royal Economic Society's edition of the *Principles* (Sraffa 1951), and will be developed in *Production of Commodities* (Sraffa 1960).

2. In the next section we will recall Sraffa's theoretical position in the two articles of 1925 and 1926, with the important additional elements regarding distribution which the very pre-lectures provide us with. In the third section, we will then proceed to the difficulties Sraffa ran into when, in preparing his lectures for that autumn, he found himself forced to reexamine his earlier conclusions in favour of Marshall's method of partial equilibrium, on which he had based his argument until then.[4] Those difficulties led Sraffa to the issue of an 'ultimate standard of value', and thus to both a critique of Marshall's subjective 'real' costs, and their replacement with the concept of 'physical real costs'. And, it is in his attempts to develop the latter idea that Sraffa, we shall argue, stumbles into the turning point, which is our subject here. We will deal with that in Sect. IV, jointly with the questions it opened up for Sraffa.

In Sect. V, finally, we will consider the implications of that turning point for the interpretation of the Classical economists, as well as the traces of it that will emerge in 1928–31 in the lectures. The section will close with some reflections on the difficult situation that the evolution of his theoretical position and the awareness of the importance of his results created for him as a teacher in Cambridge.

[4] Sraffa uses Marshall's own expression of 'particular equilibria'. Here, we have preferred the less exact expression that has now entered general use.

II. The Initial Position

3. The theoretical position on value lying at the heart of the articles of 1925 and 1926 is known and well summed up in the following passage by Sraffa himself:

> In normal cases the cost of production of commodities produced competitively—as we are not entitled to take into consideration the causes which may make it rise or fall—must be regarded as constant in respect of small variations in the quantity produced. And so, as a simple way of approaching the problem of competitive value, the old and now obsolete theory which makes it dependent on the cost of production alone appears to hold its ground as the best available
>
> (Sraffa 1926: 540–1).

The argument is thus founded on the hypotheses of partial equilibria, but Sraffa writes that, if we wanted to extend the field of enquiry so as to examine the conditions of simultaneous equilibrium, we would be faced with the theory of general equilibrium: 'a well-known conception, whose complexity, however, prevents it from bearing fruit, at least in the present state of our knowledge, which does not permit of even much simpler schemata being applied to the study of real conditions' (Sraffa 1926: 541).

There are two important points here. The first is that, in this early critical position of his, Sraffa accepts the determination of price by the equilibrium between Marshallian supply and demand functions and therefore, essentially, the whole apparatus of demand and supply of the marginal theories—even if he then denies the possibility of consistently considering the influence of demand on the price of the individual commodity and, more generally, wishes to expunge the subjective elements of 'utility' and 'disutility' from that apparatus. The second point is that, by accepting the Marshallian interpretation of the 'old and now obsolete theory' of Ricardo and the Classical economists in terms of 'constant returns',[5] Sraffa implicitly attributes the same demand and supply apparatus to those authors.

4. It therefore comes as no surprise if, in the pre-lectures, Sraffa describes the determination of prices by an 'equilibrium' between demand and supply functions, as an idea of 'immense scientific importance'.[6]

Besides this general importance of the idea of a demand and supply equilibrium as such, Sraffa also attributes to it an interesting specific merit, that of having:

[5]It should be recalled that Marshall's (and Sraffa's) definition of constant returns is stricter than that of 'constant returns to scale' usually applied to production functions today. Marshallian constant returns (i.e. a horizontal supply schedule) imply also a constancy of the relative prices of the productive services in the face of changes in the output of the commodity in question (cf. below, Sect. V).

[6]D3/12/3, A4.4.ii and iv respectively. From now on our reference to the pre-lectures will be abbreviated to the Arabic numeral of the manuscript, following A4 and to the small roman numeral of the page (in the present case 4.ii and 4.iv, omitting, that is, the indications [D3/12/3] and, save when possibly unclear, [A4], common to all pre-lectures references.

> wiped out the primitive notion that there had to be somewhere or other one single, ultimate cause of value'
>
> (4.iv)[‡]

where that 'primitive notion' (also attributed, as we shall see, to Ricardo and the classical writers) is characterized, he says, by a 'philosophical as opposed to a technical outlook', its relinquishment thus being in accordance with 'the general scheme of progress in science' (4.i).

It was in two ways, Sraffa argues, that the concept of equilibrium fulfilled its role of purging economic analysis of these alien philosophical elements. The first was that, with regard to the two conflicting schools of 'cost' and 'utility', the concept had:

> the great practical advantage that, being to a certain extent compatible with both schools of thought (since it embodied their doctrines), it closed the old controversy and brought back the T.[theory of] V.[value], from the field of politics to that of economic theory
>
> (4.iv).

For the school of 'cost' Sraffa is here referring to Ricardo's 'cost value', influenced, Sraffa says, by that author's 'anti-landlords complex' whereby 'rent not entering into cost is disgraced'. The second school, that of 'utility', and with it the conflict between the two, came instead into being, Sraffa continues, when Ricardo's 'cost' theory was 'taken up by Marx and used as a weapon for the workers'. That provoked by reaction the 'immediate simultaneous success' of the utility-based theory of value of Jevons, Menger and Walras—a theory that, significantly enough, was ignored when it made its first appearance in the work of authors such as Dupuit and Gossen,[7] before Marx's work created the need to develop a substitute for labour values.

Still more important—and here we come to the second way in which the concept of equilibrium fulfilled its 'purging' role—the return 'from politics to economic theory' was not, Sraffa says, just the result of the reconciliation between the two schools by means of the 'scissors'—Marshall's well-known description of demand and supply. It was also due to the fact that the notion of equilibrium: 'put as [the] principal problem to be solved by [the] T[heory of] V[alue], not the question of the causes of the value of all commodities together, but the determinants of the value of one article considered separately, and regarded as independent from all the others' (*ibid.*). As Sraffa sums it up, the return to science was due to the fact that Marshallian equilibrium focuses attention on the: 'mechanism through which the actual price of such things as boots or candles was fixed' (4.v) and not, as had happened before, on the 'cause of value', or on 'estimating the wealth of a nation' or, in later times, on 'what we call "distribution"' (*ibid.*).

---

‡ [*Editor's note*: reference abbreviation as specified in n. 6 above.]

7 4.ii and xi; cf. also para. 15 and n. 32 below.

5. The above passages, and the problem of distribution raised in them as an influential motivation behind the search for the 'causes of value', lead us to an important question, which was left in the shadow in Sraffa's earlier articles and which the pre-lectures can now begin to clarify for us: the theory of distribution and its link to value, as Sraffa envisaged it at the time.

Sraffa argues that thanks to the hypothesis of constant returns imposed by the conditions of partial equilibrium, the price of commodities is determined exclusively by production expenses.[8] But these expenses are simply the other face of the prices of the productive factors and, therefore, of the distribution of the social product between them. How then is this distribution determined?

The question is dealt with when, after indicating the practical-political connection with distribution of the 'primitive' notion of a single 'ultimate cause of value', Sraffa writes:

> At present we have a separate theory of distribution: we do give to it a very great importance, but we recognise that besides it there is a different, but also very important question—the fixing of prices of single articles. Besides it has been found that the two questions cannot be treated simultaneously: different general assumptions and different methods of analysis are required
>
> (4.v–vi).

and he continues by explaining:

> We know that the ultimate forces which regulate the division of product of industry between factors are the same that regulate the price of hats […]: but we also recognise that the frictions, the obstacles through which those forces have to work is so great, that […] when they reach what we may call the capillary blood vessels of the economic body their action is so much different in degree as almost to be a difference in kind from what their action is in the main streams […]. Certain subtle features […] which act upon the first [the capillary blood vessels], may be neglected when considering the broad lines of the general equilibrium: while the dominating elements of the latter may […] be regarded as […] not affected by […] the microscopic changes [in the capillary blood vessels]
>
> (4.vi–vii).

The final lines indicate how Sraffa thinks that small (microscopic) variations in the quantities produced can be ignored at the level of factor demand and supply, and therefore at that of factor prices, thus justifying the hypothesis of constant returns and with it the separation between distribution and the value of individual commodities.

Sraffa's initial plan for his lectures appears in fact to have rested on this separation between the problem of distribution and that of relative prices, as is indicated

[8] In the documents of that early period, Sraffa makes a neat distinction between, on the one hand, 'production expenses', or equivalently 'money expenses of production'—a mere money value—obtained by taking factor prices as givens, and, on the other hand, 'production costs', seen as a result of either the Marshallian 'efforts and sacrifices', or Ricardo's and Marx's labour quantities, or, also, the 'utility' of alternative uses forming the basis for 'opportunity cost' in Wicksteed and other authors (cf. the passage in the pre-lectures, 4.xiii–xiv, quoted in para. 7).

by what is likely to be a programme of the lectures, sketched on the following page as follows:

> (1) Introductory
> Sketch of development of theory of value
>
> Distinction between two meanings of 'theory of value'
>
> Examples of confusions arising from failure to distinguish them
>
> Hypotheses of free competition (law of indifference): its implications; and how it is not possible to regard impediments to it as friction only.
>
> (2) Elementary statement of theory of particular equilibria
>
> (4.viii)

where we find no obvious trace of the theory of distribution. And this is indeed one of the main differences between the lectures that Sraffa is here planning on the lines of the 1925 and 1926 articles, and the lectures he will actually give, where the initial and newer part will instead introduce the basic elements of the alternative theory of distribution of the Classical economists re-discovered in the meantime through a reconstruction of their idea of the cost of commodities.

III. The Transition

6. At the time, then, Sraffa still thought of distribution in terms of demand and supply functions for productive factors ('the ultimate forces that regulate the division of product [...] are the same that regulate the price of hats'), albeit 'purged' of utility and/or 'efforts and sacrifices', and thus of the practical and political content that Sraffa saw them as still bearing in Marshall. But this explanation of distribution raised several serious difficulties for the overall position that Sraffa had reached in the articles of 1925 and 1926.

In the first place, in the passage above, Sraffa refers to a theory of distribution separate from the analysis of what determines the price of individual commodities. There is, however, a condition that must be satisfied for this separation. It is valid for only small variations in the quantity produced of an individual commodity, which, in addition, does not use significant proportions of the total endowment of any of the factors needed for its production—for variations of outputs, that is, that cannot cause appreciable changes in factor prices. So, as Sraffa notes in the pre-lectures,

> this method of reasoning [about distribution] is legitimate only in respect of one commodity at a time: we could of course apply it in succession to each of the other commodities, [...] but not to all or several commodities at the same time'
>
> (14.ii).

However, when kept within those limits, the argument is not really sufficient to support the conclusions Sraffa had aimed for in his two articles, in particular, when he wrote, as recalled above: 'And so, as a simple way of approaching the problem of competitive value, the old and now obsolete theory which makes it dependent on the cost of production alone appears to hold its ground as the best available' (Sraffa 1926: 541).

Here, the point is a general way of solving 'the problem of competitive value', and it refers therefore to commodities in general, rather than to an individual commodity taken in isolation. Moreover, the solution is referred specifically to the 'now obsolete theory which makes it dependent on the cost of production alone', evidently the theory of the Classical economists. Yet they certainly did not use their theory solely for small variations pertaining to commodities taken one at a time. In fact, as we shall see shortly, Sraffa continues the above passage of the pre-lectures by recognizing the impossibility of limiting the analysis of value to partial equilibrium.

Closely connected with this first difficulty, there is, however, a second deficiency inherent in Sraffa's early synthesis. Even admitting, as a first approximation, that the principle of constant returns can be applied in a sufficiently general way, it establishes the equality between normal prices and production expenses, where, however, factor prices—and hence the magnitude of the expenses, as distinct from their variations—lead us back to demand for goods and, hence, to the utility Sraffa wished to expunge by referring to constant returns.[9] As he notes in the pre-lectures:

> Suppose now that we found that the price of one commodity is determined exclusively by expenses of production: could we conclude […] it is 'ultimately' determined only by real costs? Of course not […] We could only say that the price of those commodities is only determined by 'the conditions of supply', i.e. by the wages, interests, rents that have to be paid for its production, and that demand price has nothing to do with its determination. But this would not in the least exclude that we might hold a theory of distribution which said that wages, interest etc. are only determined by the utility of their products (as a whole) or by monopoly, or any other general theory of value. The difference would be that utility would make its influence felt through the conditions of supply of that (or each of all) commodity, and not through its conditions of demand
>
> (21.i–ii).[10]

This fundamental point will then be taken up by Sraffa at greater length in an exam question for his students in the lectures of 1928–31:

> Is it correct to say that if all industries were operated under conditions of constant returns, the normal value of the products would be entirely determined by their cost of production, and demand would have no influence upon it?

[9]Thus, for example, the level of the wages compared with the profit rate would depend on the relative demand for the goods produced with higher proportions of labour to means of production so that the level of the supply curve for those goods, taken as horizontal, would be the higher in terms of an average commodity used as numeraire, the higher that relative demand (14i, n.).

[10]For a similar passage, cf. 20.i.

(Note that, (1) an affirmative answer would probably follow from M[arshall]'s assumptions, but (2) all those who have minimised the importance of cost in determining value, e.g. Jevons and the Austrians, have never used the argument of variability against it: and they certainly would say that their arguments are independent of the variability or constancy of costs (e.g. changes in remuneration of factors might affect values and be due to changes in demand*. This point of the relations between the theories of value and distribution is one of the most neglected by Marshall and his treatment is very unsatisfactory)

(D/2/4, MI/7: 167a–b‡).

And for the asterisk, Sraffa adds: '*Thus we fall back on the difficulty of defining 'real cost of production'. We left it aside at the beginning now it crops up again, and invalidates all our conclusions' (*ibid.*).

If the above two difficulties touch directly on Sraffa's attempt to cast utility out of price theory by means of the hypothesis of constant returns, a third more general and radical difficulty, of which the first two can be seen as specific aspects, concerns the solidity of the foundations on which the whole argument rested, namely, the method of partial equilibria. In substance, in the pre-lectures, Sraffa's attempt at a clarification and fuller comprehension of the *ceteris paribus* condition of Marshall's partial equilibrium made him increasingly sceptical as to the significance of that method, progressively dousing the enthusiasm he had shown for it in the early pages of the pre-lectures.[11] In particular, the hypotheses of partial equilibrium—in the last analysis, the assumption that, not only factor prices, but also the prices and quantities of all the commodities other than the one considered were given—emptied of much of its significance the latter's demand curve, which would depend in particular on the given prices and quantities of the commodity's substitutes (14.i). Strictly speaking, the curve would be transformed, Sraffa argues in a different manuscript, into a constant outlay curve and could only determine a price already taken implicitly as given by assuming given the rest of the system.

If the purchasing power of money is given all the prices must be given, [and,] rigorously, also the price of the commodity in question ought to be given [...]. If all prices are given, all quantities purchased must be given, since they are functions of prices. Besides, all incomes are given [...] [and] [w]e do not require anything else to know the demand curve: of course it will be a constant [...]

(D3/12/7, A7.30).[12]

7. In the notes grouped in the pre-lectures, we thus find a growing awareness in Sraffa of the limits of his previous synthesis. It is important to follow this evolution closely in order to gain a better understanding of how he arrived at the turning

‡[*Editor's note:* since on this manuscript the marking according to the Bharadwaj-Garegnani inventory is not evident, we integrate the present indication by specifying the marking according to the Trinity catalogue: D2/4 8.]

[11] It is as if the enthusiasm for a form of analysis, which he thought could be made independent of the practical and political presuppositions altering its objectivity, had led him to overestimate initially the significance of Marshall's partial equilibrium method.

[12] Cf. also 4.2, headed 'Demand curves a truism or false'.

point we are about to study, and of what that involved. A convenient thread to follow for that purpose is the distinction he makes initially between 'two meanings of the theory of value' or, on occasion, between two different 'theories of value',[13] a distinction that ends by constituting the central issue in the pre-lectures.

The distinction is essentially the one underlying the contrast already seen earlier between the problem of value as viewed by the economists of the past, and relating to questions such as the measurement of national wealth or its distribution, and the problem as seen by the moderns, who focus rather on the 'technique' of price determination for products and productive factors, the contrast being the one in which, as we may also recall, Sraffa saw an example of how science progresses from a 'philosophical' to a 'technical' viewpoint. The problems 'of the past' in fact covered issues such as whether costs (Marshall's 'efforts and sacrifices' or Ricardo's quantities of labour)—or else utility, or both determine values. These concepts, still present in the theories contemporary to Sraffa, were then seen by him as something that had lost real importance for the present, and remained only as a left-over of the 'primitive' notion, whereby there was supposed to be a single 'ultimate cause' of value. As Sraffa writes at the beginning of the pre-lectures: 'the contrast between the idea we have today of the question of value and that of Ricardo and his contemporaries is impressive' (4.iv). And, a few pages later in the programme of the lectures to be held, already quoted above (para. 5), we find among the other subjects of the introductory part: 'Distinction between the two meanings of the "theory of value"', accompanied by 'Examples of confusion arising from failure to distinguish them'.

The argument is however resumed a few pages later with what already seems to be a slightly different emphasis. If the passage from the 'classical economists who were inquiring into the prime cause [...] and ultimate standard of value' to the moderns is still seen in terms of the 'continuous progress from the philosophical and general to the technical and particular', the tendency of the moderns to ignore the 'prime causes of value' of the Classical authors is noted with the comment 'not that [those questions] have been solved, nor that they have been proved to be insoluble' (4.ix–x). Thus, after all, Sraffa seems to feel that questions of the 'ultimate cause' of value are sufficiently substantial to be 'soluble', or at least such as to make it worth showing that no solution is possible.

In fact the relative importance of the two 'theories of value' starts to be overturned some further pages along when Sraffa writes:

> How deep is the difference between the two points of view may be seen, for example, in the opposite attitude that it is legitimate to take in the two cases towards measuring value in terms of money. If we are inquiring into the general problem of the causes of value, it is no use for us to argue that the value of bread is determined by the price of corn and by the money wages of bakers, that the price of corn is determined by the money wages of labourers and by the price of agricultural implements, [...] and so on ad infinitum—this

[13] 4.viii and 21.i.

> would be a perfectly futile way of reasoning in a circle. In this general problem we must find some ultimate standard, independent from the variables we are considering, such [as] utility or disutility or labour. But if we confine our inquiry to such a question as that of how, being given all the prices and amounts consumed and produced of all other commodities, what is the mechanism through which the price of a given article is caused to be what it is, and not higher nor lower: or how an increase in its demand, *ceteris paribus*, would affect its price—the position is entirely different: there is no objection to our measuring costs and utilities in terms of money—indeed we can entirely dispense with such conceptions. We can substitute to costs of production the much simpler 'money expenses of production' and to marginal utility 'marginal demand price'
>
> (4.xiii–xiv).

Thus, the question of the 'cause' or 'ultimate standard' of value, initially described as 'primitive', now turns out to be what we have to refer to, if circular reasoning is to be avoided, as soon as we wish to go beyond the limited problems concerning the formation of an individual price, allowing us to take as given the distribution between factors and the prices of all the commodities different from that taken into consideration.

The argument is repeated, and the reversal in the importance of the two 'aspects' of the theory of value is completed later in the pre-lectures, in the course of an attempt to return to what, according to the initial programme of the lectures (see para. 5 above) was to constitute the body of them after the 'Introductory' part, namely, the 'theory of particular equilibria'. After having expounded the hypotheses on which the equilibria rest, including that 'all prices and quantities of other commodities are constant', Sraffa adds:

> But so soon as we want to analyze how the general equilibrium is reached—i.e. [...] to analyze the interactions of one commodity upon the other, how they affect each other's conditions of production and utilities, and how the remuneration of common factors of production is determined—then our ultimate standard of value is required
>
> (14ii–iii).[14]

For Sraffa, the relative weight has now clearly shifted in favour of the first of the two 'meanings' of theory of value, the 'ultimate standard of value', which is seen as necessary for solving problems such as: (i) how a general equilibrium is reached; (ii) how one commodity influences the conditions of production and utility of others; or finally, and certainly not the least important of the problems, (iii) how the remuneration of the production factors is determined.

8. At this point, it is natural to raise the question of why Sraffa, as he grew increasingly aware of the limitations of the 'second' theory of value, would turn to the 'ultimate standard of value' rather than to the general equilibrium to which he also makes frequent references in the pre-lectures and the manuscripts of the time. The question is natural, not only because, in 1926, he referred to general equilibrium when he was dealing with the limits of partial equilibrium, but also because,

---

[14] A similar clear distinction between the significance of the 'two classes of theory of value' is to be found at 20i.

at this stage, if Sraffa sees the need for the 'ultimate standard', he also sees no satisfactory version of it in the theories current at that time. Just after the phrase quoted above, which gives the clearest statement in the pre-lectures of the 'ultimate standard's importance, in a lapidary comment clearly referring to 'costs' and 'utility', he writes:

> Two standards offered: they are the same thing—words
>
> (14iii).

The answer to the question we have raised is no simple matter, above all because it is not simple to understand how an 'ultimate standard of value' as envisaged at the time could resolve the problems left open by partial equilibrium. Yet it seems that the answer should remain substantially what Sraffa himself had already offered in (1926): the complexity of general equilibrium made the whole idea sterile (see para. 3 above).

An interesting, more detailed analysis of why that conception was sterile and was accordingly rejected comes to light in the pre-lectures, when Sraffa discards the possibility of 'imagining' the marginal utility of a commodity as a function of thousands of variables (the quantities of the other commodities consumed), because of the non-observability of the resulting demand curve for the commodity. Unlike what can be argued for Marshall's partial equilibrium demand, the curve could not be referred to demand prices for the commodity that are observable at least in principle. And Sraffa adds:

> It should here be added that it is not sufficient to make utility of one commodity function of quantity of all others consumed by individual but also by community! It would be as if in astronomy we said the movement of each star depends upon all others, but we have not the faintest idea of the shape of the functions!
>
> (21x–xb, n.)

Faced with the inherent sterility of general equilibrium (to which Sraffa grants no more than the role of showing the logical consistency of reasoning carried out in terms of partial equilibria[15]) Sraffa may have come to see an 'ultimate standard' as the only direction along which he could move in order to overcome the limitations of partial equilibrium without losing the possibility of significant results.

IV. The Turning Point

9. We have seen Sraffa's concise comment on of the 'ultimate standards of value', which were suggested by his contemporaries: 'words'. Immediately after this comment, however, we find what appears to be the germ of the turning point:

[15] Cf. for example 4vi.

'However there is one reality in cost, i.e. labour' (14iii)[16] where, however, labour is not considered in the sense that we might perhaps expect, that of Ricardo's and Marx's theories of value. In fact, after two pages devoted to what is apparently a closer analysis of production expenses, we find the title, 'Physical real cost',[17] followed by some pages of closely argued criticism of Marshall's subjective 'real costs',[18] and then, again, repeated as a heading, 'Physical real cost', where it becomes clear that the expression is intended to refer to the subsistence required by the labour necessary for the direct and indirect production of the commodity in question, and not to labour itself along Ricardian or Marxian lines.

Here, however, Sraffa expresses the doubt that substitutability between wage goods may prevent unique identification of a composite 'necessary commodity' providing for workers' 'subsistence'. But he goes on to say:

> It should be remarked that if this difficulty (of no substitutes[19]) were overcome and an absolutely necessary commodity found, the difficulty of reducing to a common measure the various things[20] entering into real cost would solve by itself. In effect it would be easy to find the cost of all the other things in terms of the necessary one, and thus by going back enough in the genealogy of production (and stopping along each branch so soon as we have resolved it into our necessary commodity) we might find exactly the total amount of corn (if this were the ideal necessary commodity [...]) that has actually entered into the production of, say, this book, and covers entirely its cost of production, at the exclusion of any other commodity
>
> (16iii–iv; underlines in the original).

10. This passage is followed by a number of pages in which Sraffa returns to his criticism of the Marshallian concepts of costs. To find a resumption of the argument he began there about the 'necessary commodity', we have to turn to manuscripts that we can date to November 1927 and to the period immediately after. The first manuscript we shall consider is part of a group that Sraffa put in a

[16] In the manuscript the word 'clay' is added in parentheses after 'labour', presumably in order to indicate that labour is malleable in the way that clay is: it can be used for, and take the form of, any commodity.

[17] 16iii.

[18] Sraffa's criticism points out that Marshall's purely psychological concept of costs as a readiness to accept a sacrifice in return for utility is closely connected to the existence for the resource in question of alternative uses, the renunciation of which constitutes in fact the 'sacrifice'. This, Sraffa notes, makes it a relative, not an 'ultimate' concept of cost: and Sraffa wonders: 'What happens then if, as it is necessary in a quest of an ultimate standard, we go so far as to consider the whole of the commodities produced, and the efforts incurred at one and the same time? Shall we not then entirely miss any alternative use, since ex hypothesis we have included them all into our consideration?' (16ii).

[19] This is clearly an abbreviation for the 'difficulties caused by the existence of substitutes for the subsistence goods'.

[20] 'Things' replaces a crossed out 'factors', which was Sraffa's first choice of word.

folder marked 'Winter 1927–28'.[21] The manuscript takes up the idea of the 'necessary commodity' measuring costs, and makes a start by 'reducing' the commodities to one or more of them. The procedure rests on some algebraic relationships whose form we shall examine in detail in para. 12 below, and which we will call here simply as 'the equations' (as Sraffa does in his manuscripts). They express the relationship between a product and its means of production, where the latter include the subsistence of the workers directly involved in the commodity's production. The reduction, e.g. of A, the quantity produced of commodity a, to a quantity of commodity c, which we may suppose to be the 'necessary commodity', is effected by repeatedly replacing each of the direct and then indirect means of production of a different from c, with the respective 'equation' so that, in the end, the production of a is explained as if it only required c, in the way indicated in the passage quoted from the pre-lectures for the 'necessary commodity'.

Thus, on the first page of the document we mentioned, we find what seems to be the reduction to itself of commodity a, one of two commodities, a and b, constituting an economic system with no surplus, and which, to borrow Sraffa's (1960: 4) later expression, finds itself in a 'self replacing state', the quantities produced being equal to the quantities consumed in production. This first attempt, to which we will return below, is abandoned, and the page in which we find it is crossed out with a pen stroke. The attempt at reducing a product to quantities of a single commodity is however resumed on the following page, this time with a three-commodity system allowing for a surplus. This second attempt is then pursued for the remaining six pages, through the imaginable labyrinth of algebraic expressions, before being again apparently abandoned.

11. The above document is not interesting, however, solely because of the attempt to carry out the reduction to a 'necessary commodity' contemplated in the pre-lectures. Also, and above all, its interest lies in that the attempt is developed in such a way as to make it almost inevitable that Sraffa should promptly come upon a different kind of physical real costs and should then proceed, in other manuscripts of the same period, along a different path—the one that will lead in time to the price equations (or 'production equations' in Sraffa's expression in *Production of Commodities*).

Thus, on the first, cancelled page of the above manuscript, the 'equations' are written as follows:

$$\begin{aligned} A &= a_1 + b_1 \\ B &= a_2 + b_2 \end{aligned} \tag{1}$$

where A clearly indicates the quantity of the commodity a produced using quantities a_1 and b_1 of, respectively, a and b—and similarly for B. As we have said, Sraffa assumes here replacement of the resources consumed in production, but no surplus. He can therefore write the further two equations:

[21] D3/12/6, CXVI.1i–vii.

$$A = \sum a = a_1 + a_2$$
$$B = \sum b = b_1 + b_2 \quad (2)$$

Now, before trying to reduce a to itself, Sraffa notes that from the first of relations (1) follows:

$$A - a_1 = b_1$$

and from the first of Eqs. (2):

$$A - a_1 = a_2$$

so that, if the conditions for the replacement of the means of production are to be satisfied, the further condition written on the same page of the manuscript:

$$a_2 = b_1 \quad (3)$$

must also hold in the sense, evidently, that the quantity a_2 of a will have to exchange with the quantity b_1 of b, i.e. in the symbols we shall see below:

$V_{a/b} = \frac{b_1}{a_2}$ for the price of a in terms of b, as well as the reciprocal

$V_{b/a} = \frac{a_2}{b_1}$ for b in terms of a.

Thus, in a further manuscript from another folder also dated 'Winter 1927–28', we find equations similar to Eqs. (1), but for more than two commodities on which Sraffa now comments:

> These are homogeneous linear equations. They have infinite sets of solutions, but the solutions of each set are proportional [...]. These proportions we call ratios of absolute values. They are purely numerical relations between the things *A*, *B*...
>
> (D3/12/5, A6.1i).

A way of representing 'physical real costs'—what is *physically necessary* for the commodity's production—more direct than the 'necessary commodity' has been found, and the attempt to achieve a 'reduction' to such a commodity is apparently abandoned.

12. By now the reader will surely have wondered at the peculiarity of 'equations' such as Eqs. (1) and (3), the same found in numerous other of Sraffa's manuscripts of the same period, where heterogeneous physical quantities are added up or represented as equal. This has naturally been cause of some perplexity in the literature.[22]

In the same connection a brief Sraffa manuscript dated '26.6.28' and titled 'Ramsey'[23] has also attracted attention, since it appears to have been written after a meeting with the Cambridge mathematician Frank Ramsey, a close friend of Keynes. After a report on the possibility to solve the price equations for an

[22] Cf. De Vivo (2003: 9–11), Gilibert (2004: 28).

[23] D3/12/2, A1.26. Sraffa's diary shows that the date fixed for the meeting with Ramsey was 28 June 1928.

economy without surplus,‡ and the probable uniqueness of the result, we read: 'Equations without surplus: each quantity must be expressed by two letters, one being the number of units, the other the unit of the commodity otherwise, if I use only one letter, this would stand for heterogeneous things and the sum would be meaningless'.[24]

The temptation has been strong to conclude that in relations like Eqs. (1) and (3) Sraffa, no mathematical expert, had committed a simple error, which was then corrected by Ramsey. Yet the passage on homogeneous and linear equations we found above and that can be dated to before the meeting with Ramsey indicates that Sraffa was not so lacking in mathematical notions, and that would seem sufficient to cast serious doubts on the idea of a straightforward error. In my view, and for the reasons we shall presently see, those doubts would be more than justified.

In looking at relations like Eqs. (1) and (3), it is in fact important to remember the nature of circular reasoning that, in common with the economic literature of his time, Sraffa had attributed to the determination of price in terms of the expenses of production[25]: we saw that in the passages quoted from the pre-lectures (see para. 7 above). It is not surprising therefore that, when he got to his 'equations', in a document of November 1927 Sraffa should argue:

> When I say that the value of a product is 'determined' by the physical volume of commodities used upon its production, it should not be understood that it is determined by the value of those commodities. This *would be a vicious circle* […]. What I say is simply that the numerical proportions between amount of factors and […] of product is by definition, the absolute value of the product
>
> (D3/12/11, E2.90; our italics; the underlining is instead by Sraffa).

And, in a substantial sense, Sraffa is of course right. Commodity values are determined by the parameters of the equations as normally written, and these parameters are physical quantities of commodities. Thus, for example, as we noted, relation (3) above, $a_1 = b_2$, equalizing two heterogeneous quantities, can be easily and directly read as an expression of the exchange ratio between the two commodities imposed by replacement. This easy determination is due to the simplicity of the two-commodities case, but it may have made clear to Sraffa that the same must have been true in some sense in the more general case.

All this does not of course remove the fact that, while 'the equations' taken in that form may give an intuitive form to the logical conditions that the 'numerical ratios' of equivalence between heterogeneous commodities A, B, a_1, b_1, a_2, b_2 must satisfy to ensure replacement of the means of production, yet they cannot generally be solved for those ratios by the received methods.

‡ [*Editor's note*: actually, the first part of the paper opens, in Sraffa's writing, with reference to 'Equations with surplus'.]

24 The word 'unit' here seems to have been interpreted by those commentators as a slip of the pen for 'price'.

25 Compare for example Dobb (1937: 9–10), 'A principle of value is not adequate which merely expresses value in terms of some one or other particular value'.

Now, a striking document of the period shows that Sraffa was quite aware of the normal way of writing 'the equation' and was consciously choosing the form of Eqs. (1) or (3)—and all this almost certainly before the mentioned meeting with Ramsey. The document (D3/12/6; CXVI.4i–xiv) is in fact in a folder dated 'Winter 1927–28', well before the meeting, which, as we said, occurred in June, 1928. There (*ibid.*, CXVI.4ii), Sraffa writes the expressions:

$$\begin{aligned} A + A_s &= (5a_1 + 6b_1 + 3c_1)r \\ B + B_s &= (4a_2 + 2b_2 + 6c_2)r \\ C + C_s &= (7a_3 + 2b_3 + 3c_3)r \end{aligned} \tag{4}$$

for a three-commodity economy with a physical surplus of them, which, as specified in the manuscript (*ibid.*), are each in the uniform proportion (r – 1) to their respective initial stocks. In Eqs. (4), where the 'equations' clearly ask to be read as 'the quantity produced ($A+A_s$) of a requires for its production 5 units of a, 6 of b, 3 of c and similarly for ($B+B_s$) etc.' heterogeneous quantities are again 'summed' as in Eqs. (1). But Sraffa writes immediately afterwards[26]:

> If this were unsatisfactory, we could put the equations in a form which shows explicitly that our real unknowns are values, and rate of surplus. This may be done thus. Suppose we want to know all the values in terms of B or any other one. Call $V_{a/b}$ the value of A in terms of B, etc. We have:
>
> $$\begin{aligned} V_{\frac{a}{b}}(A + A_s) &= \left(V_{\frac{a}{b}} a_1 + b_1 + V_{\frac{c}{b}} c_1\right) r \\ (B + B_s) &= \left(V_{\frac{a}{b}} a_2 + b_2 + V_{\frac{c}{b}} c_2\right) r \\ V_{c/b}(C + C_s) &= \left(V_{a/b} a_3 + b_3 + V_{c/b} c_3\right) r \end{aligned} \tag{5}$$
>
> The unknowns are $V_{a/b}$, $V_{c/b}$, r, same number as equations
>
> (*ibid.*, CXVI.4iii).

Here, Sraffa clearly makes a conscious choice between two ways of presenting or writing 'the equations' in which the second way shows 'explicitly', as he puts it, the 'real unknowns'. Sraffa thus knows that he *implies* these 'real unknowns' in the first way of writing the 'equations' and clearly he prefers it because, to his own eyes, it makes immediately clear the fact that values are determined by the physically heterogeneous quantities that must be equalized in exchange and that, therefore, there is no question–begging reasoning by which values are determined by other values. In fact, except for expert mathematicians who may have an intuitive grasp of the logical process entailed in equations such as Eqs. (5), the comprehension of the non-circularity of that price determination is entrusted to a counting of equations, or, more generally, to the 'black box' of a purely technical–mathematical analysis, in which the concrete economic reason of their determining role

[26] From the handwriting it transpires that the digits 5, 6, 3, etc. have been inserted in the 'equations' (4) after the rest of them had been written.

remains obscure, or even unknown, at least until the equations are explicated in further economic analysis (such as, for example, that of the Standard commodity and Standard system, or, more generally, that of Chapters III–VI of *Production of Commodities*).

We must realize that Sraffa is struggling to express even for his own understanding the basic result he has just arrived at thanks to the concept of 'physical real costs', namely that, essentially, the physical conditions of production of the commodities and the need to allow production to be repeated are sufficient to determine relative prices quite independently of what are generally understood as 'demand and supply forces'. This was an idea totally new for his contemporaries, and for Sraffa himself, steeped as they were in the complexities of the post-classical demand and supply analysis—which had paradoxically resulted in obscuring, and then forgetting, what had begun to emerge with Ricardo and the Classical economists. And Sraffa has to grasp and express this idea against the common sense notion of the time that an explanation of prices solely in terms of production expenses would involve circular reasoning.

Returning now to Ramsey's role in the question, there is, of course, a margin of uncertainty in dating the above manuscript to the Winter of 1927–8, months before the meeting of June 1928. By association of subject matter, or simply by mistake, a later manuscript can have been put, or have slipped, into that folder dated 'Winter 1927–28'. But, even if it were of a later date, the document would support our central argument—Sraffa would still be writing for himself the 'equations' in a way that he clearly continued to find significant, despite the defects that Ramsey had stressed to him.

In light of the above, it seems possible to conclude that the note relating to the meeting with Ramsey does not have the meaning one is at first tempted to attribute to it of correction, that is, of a straightforward mistake by Sraffa. The note may, for example, have concerned Ramsey's reaction to a presentation of 'the equations' made to him in the form Sraffa preferred, or also here reported the Ramsey's reply to a doubt expressed by Sraffa as to the best way to represent the logical process involved.

13. We have seen how Sraffa counter-posed physical 'real costs' to Marshall's subjective 'real costs'. Now, Marshall's 'ultimate standard of value', like that based on utility alone, could only lead to alternative interpretations of the results of a supply and demand system, which was essentially common to both, and which, as we have seen, Sraffa had hitherto accepted, once freed from the subjective slant given by these particular interpretations. But, unlike those 'ultimate standards', the physical real costs that he finally arrived at brought him to a determination of relative prices (or relative costs), which was alternative to the dominant one based on demand and supply functions, and was apparently unexpected for Sraffa himself. If the result was enthusiastically welcomed by Sraffa, who seems to have immediately perceived its revolutionary importance, at first it seems to have left him disconcerted and searching for the relationship between that way of arriving at relative prices and the one in terms of demand and supply he had hitherto accepted.

The situation finds a fascinating reflection in two manuscripts, part of a group in a folder marked in Sraffa's handwriting with a generic dating: 'After 1927'. I think the points we shall see make it possible to ascribe them to the first of the periods that Sraffa devoted to what would later become *Production of Commodities*, the one from the Autumn of 1927 to the early 1930s (the remaining two being, as is well known, the early 1940's and then the second half of the 1950's). Significantly enough, the first of the two manuscripts is headed: 'Why I neglect increasing and decreasing returns in equations'. In it, Sraffa writes:

> The reply is that these equations cannot possibly answer as to how or why prices change. They only explain why, at a given moment (?),[27] prices of different things bear to one another the proportions which they do. [They do not explain] variations of one commodity at different times [...]. No system of equations, whether it considers variable returns or not, could tell this if time does not enter as a variable. Take a pair of Marshall's D[emand] and S[upply] curves. They tell that, given the conditions, the price will be AB: to this effect it is quite indifferent whether the supply curve is SS_1 or $S_{11}S_{111}$ [a small diagram is drawn here in a corner of the page with the usual Marshallian cross, and the ordinate AB as the equilibrium price resulting from a decreasing supply curve, SS_1, and also a rising one, $S_{11}S_{111}$]. It may be thought this is relevant to a case in which 'there is a change in demand'. The real point is that it is believed that Marshall's curves provide 'forces' which, in case the price falls below or above AB by 'chance', will restore it to AB. Now I am not assuming any forces: I simply say that, if the values will in reality be as given by the equations certain conditions will be satisfied: if not, they will not be satisfied
>
> (D3/12/7, A7.29i)

In the same manuscript, under a new heading, 'Man from the moon', Sraffa writes:

> The significance of the equations is simply this: that if a man fell from the moon on the earth, and noted the amount of things consumed in each factory [...] during a year he could deduce at which values the commodities must be sold, if the rate of interest must be uniform and the process of production repeated. In short, the equations show that the conditions of exchange are entirely determined by the conditions of production
>
> (*ibid.*, A7.29iii)

where the new mid-page title and, above all, the clarity as to the nature of the result could indicate a later addition to the manuscript:[28] a fact which would be significant in itself as an indicator of the gradualness with which Sraffa came to grasp the significance of his own results.

The second manuscript on the other hand takes us back to the uncertainties of the first part of the previous document. It is headed: 'Difference (simultaneous) versus Change (succession in time)', and we read with reference presumably to the results of the 'equations':

[27] This question mark and the further one that Sraffa inserts at Point (1) of the second manuscript to be presently quoted in the text give graphic expression to Sraffa's search for the meaning of his results and to the necessity for Sraffa to open up for himself the path he follows.

[28] The issue of the possible later date for this second part of the manuscript was brought to my attention by my colleague, Roberto Ciccone.

> The general confusion in all theories of value [...] must be explained by the failure to distinguish between two entirely distinct types of questions and the universal attempt of solving them both by one single theory.
>
> The two questions are:
>
> (1) what determines the (difference in the?) values at which various commodities are exchanged in a given market on a given instant?
> (2) what determines the changes in the values of commodities at different times? (e.g. of one commodity)
>
> (*ibid.*, A7.38i; underlines and question marks in the original)

and after seeking radical differences between the two points of view, in the uniformity of prices, wages and profits in the first, and changes in these magnitudes in the second, he continues:

> Therefore it is possible that the two problems have to be solved in different ways: and that of two opposite general theories of value, one may be true in respect of one question and the other in respect of the second [...] The first problem gives rise to a geometrical theory, the second to a mechanical one [...]. The first problem must be solved by the theory of value. The second, I think, can only be solved by the theory of industrial fluctuations [...] Marshall's theory of value, with its increasing and diminishing costs and marg[inal] utility, scissors, pillars and forces, can only be understood as an attempt to solve the first question in terms of the second
>
> (*ibid.*, A7.38ii–iii).

In these two documents, Sraffa seems to be surprised by the fact that he can determine prices without the supply and demand apparatus and the consequent hypotheses on returns. He hunts then in several directions for the reasons of his result, here essentially in terms of a distinction between 'differences' and 'changes', which, as we will shortly see, he will soon recognize was unfounded, at least in the form in which he outlines it at this time. Accordingly, the idea in the first manuscript appears to be that returns are relevant for 'changes', which, as such, can take place only in 'time', while 'the equations' he arrived at are 'timeless'. Hence the idea, also found in the second manuscript, that 'the equations' could express only a given situation and hence explain, in some sense, only 'differences' between 'simultaneous values' (in fact, relative values, as the first document puts it more appropriately), while Marshall's supply and demand with variable or constant returns concern 'forces', which explain changes or, alternatively, lead back to an equilibrium after accidental deviations from it. The two procedures or theories seem to be viewed at times as complementary by Sraffa—one 'geometrical' to explain 'differences' and the other 'mechanical' to explain 'changes' or the tendency to equilibrium; the first being more properly called a 'theory of value', the second a 'theory of industrial fluctuations'.

In reality, in the second manuscript, Sraffa realizes already that the distinction between 'the equations' for 'differences' versus Marshall's demand and supply for 'variations' is unfounded. Referring to the 'common substance', which he has just said should explain 'differences' between prices, he continues: 'This way of putting the distinction is confusing. If the "common substance" is drawn in for the first [problem] it is clear that as it explains the equality [between simultaneous values] in the first case it will explain the difference in the second' (*ibid.*, A7.38iv).

Yet the effort at clarification in these manuscripts brings Sraffa quite close to grasping another implication of the results he has arrived at—besides, that is, the fact that 'the equations', no less than Marshall's demand and supply, suppose 'forces': those forces, which, under the title 'Man from the moon', he had called 'conditions of production'. This further implication emerges when in the second of the two manuscripts Sraffa writes:

> [Marshall's] machinery of supply and demand [...] seems to be directed to answer questions such as 'what will happen to price if a tariff be imposed? or a bounty or tax? or change in tastes? or invention?' *The point is—can such questions be answered in a general way, i.e. assuming the 'initial' movement to be entirely arbitrary ? or is it not necessary to know how it has arisen?*
>
> (*ibid.*, A7.38iii–iv; our italics)

Only Marshall's ambiguities could leave any doubt as to the question in marginalist terms where, in reality, each change in demand could only result from a change in some data in the system of general equilibrium, which would then also define the eventual corresponding changes in the supply functions. Yet, where, with 'the equations', the prices are no longer supposed to be determined by demand and supply functions, but by other forces summed up as conditions of production, Sraffa's observation becomes of fundamental importance and will be resolved by the separation between the determination of prices and the determination of outputs, i.e. with the given outputs that we find in *Production of Commodities* and, in fact, already in the equations, like Eqs. (1), (2), (3), (4) and (5) above, that Sraffa is at this point developing.

It is not surprising, then, that in the first of the two manuscripts there emerges already what we shall find in the Preface of *Production of Commodities* more than thirty years later:

> I am afraid it will be difficult to make it clear that we are considering what has actually happened in the markets, and not what might have happened had things been different. It will therefore be useful to explain that the reader may assume that constant returns prevail
>
> (*ibid.*, A7.29ii)

where 'what might have happened' consists of all the points of the supply and demand functions other than those for the equilibrium, and which had him to state in that Preface: 'No changes in output and [...] no changes in the proportions in which different means of production are used by an industry are considered, so that no question arises as to the variation or constancy of returns' (Sraffa 1960: v).

14. In fact, Sraffa's disorientation at first in grasping the relationship between the theory of value he started out from, and that he arrived at, seems to have been, initially, even more radical than might directly emerge from the manuscripts we have just considered. There, he is sufficiently clear that what comes out of the solution of the equations are prices that we expect to be realized in the markets as

'normal' or 'production' prices. But manuscripts that are in all probability of an earlier date show considerable uncertainty in that respect.[29]

As we have seen, Sraffa arrived at 'the equations' when he was looking for an 'ultimate standard of value' envisaged as 'physical real costs' in contrast with Marshall's subjective real costs. To start with, he saw the results obtained from 'the equations' as 'costs' and, therefore, as the 'absolute values' we saw in two of the passages we quoted above—something distinct, at least in principle, from observable prices. Thus, under the title 'Natural value', Sraffa writes:

> When A. Smith etc. said 'natural' he did not in the least mean the 'normal' or the 'average' nor the 'long run' value. He meant that physical, truly natural relation between commodities, that is determined by the equations, and that is not disturbed by the process of securing a greater share in the product. 'Exchange value' was the result of natural value disturbed permanently by the scramble for the surplus
>
> (D3/12/11, E2.73; underlining in the original)

where, clearly, the effect of the uniform rate of profit or, more generally, of the distribution of the surplus, on relative prices is seen as a factor for difference and disturbance with regard to the 'absolute values' representing the true costs of the commodity for the community. This is confirmed in another manuscript where we read:

> Ratio of solutions are "absolute values". It is not contended that they are actual exchange values (this depends on institutions), which is [sic] indeterminate
>
> (D3/12/6, CXVI.3i).

The same ambivalence as to the meaning to be given to the unknowns determined by 'the equations', emerges as regards whether and how the values obtained for an economy without surplus should be modified when a surplus is present. We have seen how, in the manuscript titled 'Natural value', the implication is that relative costs should not be influenced by the 'scramble for the surplus': the problem surfaces again in the manuscript we have just quoted with the question: 'How to "justify" or explain the equal percentage added to initial stock of each industry' (*ibid.*, CXVI.3vii).

Sraffa's answer is not, as one might perhaps naturally expect, that it is a condition directly imposed by free competition on the markets. Rather, it is sought in the necessity of ensuring that capital is not removed from branches of the economy which would otherwise finish up with a lower rate of profit and would prevent the system from reproducing itself on an unchanged scale—even if, as Sraffa

[29] The two manuscripts from which we quoted in para. 13 are we said, in a folder dated 'After 27' by Sraffa. Those we shall presently refer to are in two bundles (E.2 and CXVI in the Bharadwaj–Garegnani inventory), both of which are instead dated November 1927.

notes in the manuscript, in this way 'we are allowing to come back through the window the [notion of cost as] 'inducement' we had excluded from the door'.[30]

V. The Interpretation of the Classical Economists and the Cambridge Lectures

15. We have so far considered Sraffa's development of the idea of 'physical real costs' in those years, from the viewpoint of his own theoretical position, but the same development could not fail to have drastic implications for his interpretation

---

[30] D3/12/6, CXVI.3viii. Thus it appears that Sraffa came to his 1927 'equations' in strict continuity with the work he had done for his 1925 and 1926 articles. There is little sign, in fact, that Sraffa's

> shift of emphasis (in 1926–7) from his critique to Marshall to his 'equations' was mainly due to his (re-)reading of Marx
>
> (De Vivo 2003: 6);

or, more generally, that:

> [at the beginning of 1927] when he started preparing his lectures on the 'Advanced theory of value' for Cambridge Sraffa began a more extensive study of the classical economists, and in particular of Marx
>
> (*ibid.*: 5).

and that it was in the course of this study, and under the direct influence of Marx that he developed the 'equations' (*ibid.*: 6). As we saw the signs are rather that Sraffa's original intention was to lecture on the material of the 1925 and 1926 articles, after an introduction on the more general theoretical context in which he had located it (see para. 5 above). The dates from November 1927 onwards of the corresponding reading notes testify that the intensive study of Marx and the classical authors came after, and not before the 'equations' arrived at in the Autumn of 1927.

Indeed, as we saw, the 'equations' emerged from counter–posing to Marshall's subjective real costs, the objective concept of 'physical' real costs, begetting at first the notion of the 'necessary commodity': all this without any specific reference to Marx and to his schemes of simple reproduction of *Capital*, volume II, in which De Vivo (2003: 9–10) and Gilibert (2004: 28) attempt to trace their origin. The affinity between the 'equations' and Marx's schemes, lying in the common reference to output proportions ensuring replacement, seems on the other hand quite sufficient by itself, to explain the Sraffa annotations about those schemes on which Gilibert (2004: 28) and De Vivo (2003: 9) base their thesis.

An important implication of the above should also be noted. Sraffa's consideration of November 1927 that the 'ultimate' result of his work would be:

> a restatement of Marx, by substituting to his Hegelian metaphysics and terminology our own modern metaphysics and terminology
>
> (D3/12/4, A5.14.i, quoted by De Vivo 2003: 7)

made together with the decision, noted down in those same weeks, of writing a book (para. 21 below) can hardly be seen as expression of a project connected with the Cambridge lectures as such, as De Vivo (2003: 4 and n. 4) seems to contend. The project emerges rather as a natural, direct expression of the Autumn 1927 breakthrough, and of Sraffa's awareness of the novelty and importance of his results.

of the Classical authors in whose work (in particular that of the Physiocrats) that general idea of costs clearly had its origin. As we recalled, Sraffa had accepted the Marshallian interpretation of Ricardo and the Classical economists in terms of constant returns and, therefore, of equilibria between demand and supply. The discovery that 'physical real costs' implied a determination of relative prices which would not introduce any demand and supply functions, could not but revolutionize his interpretation of those authors by revealing a theory of relative prices and distribution more radically alternative to the dominant one than Sraffa had until then supposed. And we must stress that, contrary to what has been contended by some commentators,[31] the evidence is that the change in the interpretation was not the gradual result of a deliberately planned inquiry: it was as rapid and unexpected as the achievement of the 'equations' in the way we described above.

The reliance on physical real costs rather than the subjective real costs and/or utility, claimed as 'ultimate standards' of value by Marshall and the other marginalist authors, thus came to replace, for Sraffa, the assumption of constant returns as the true discriminating criterion between Classical theory and the subsequent theories. As he wrote in a manuscript of a few lines headed 'Evolution of the

[31] Thus Kurz and Salvadori in their otherwise suggestive (2005) write

> At the beginning of his academic career Sraffa appears to have adopted by and large the received Marshall's interpretation of the classical economists as early and rude types of demand and supply theorists with the demand side still in its infancy. However, he gradually came to see that this interpretation implied a travesty of facts […]. The radical change of his view of the classical authors received some support from his reading, in 1927 and 1928, of the French translation of [Marx's *Theories of Surplus Value*]
> (Kurz and Salvadori 2005: 416).

The change in the interpretation of the classical authors does not however appear to have been gradual, but to have rather been a matter of months, if not weeks, early in the Autumn of 1927, as Sraffa arrived at 'the equations'. It thus seems misleading to refer to a Sraffa who 'in the late 1920's deliberately sought to elaborate an objectivist alternative to contemporary theory' (*ibid.*: 414) or who, in a similarly deliberate way, set himself 'three huge tasks' consisting of the tracing of the essence of classical theory, of the reconstruction of it and, thirdly, of finding its differences from dominant theory (Gehrke and Kurz 2006: 102–3). The basic solutions to these problems occurred, in a sense, all at once to Sraffa, the moment in which he came upon what Kurz and Salvadori describe as his 'objectivist alternative' (Kurz and Salvadori 2005: 414; cf. also Kurz and Salvadori 2004). In this connection it might indeed be noted that if Sraffa's question had then been to achieve 'objectivism', rather than that of having stumbled on an alternative theory of relative prices and distribution, based on the notion of surplus, he would probably have thought to have conquered that 'objectivism' already in his 1925–26 synthesis, when he was determining prices independently of a demand, which, in any case, he held to be definable with no recourse to subjective utility.

On the other hand we stressed already (n. 30 above) how, from the argument conducted, and the literature referred to in the pre-lectures, on the way to the 'necessary commodity' and hence to 'the equations', the change in question emerges as a strictly autonomous development of Sraffa's previous position. No trace seems visible there of specific external influences, whether from new readings of Marx—or, also, from particular natural sciences, in the way which is being suggested by Kurz and Salvadori (2005: 424–31) and Gehrke and Kurz (2006: 97–98).

concept of cost': 'the trend has been from meaning by cost the means necessary to enable production to be made, to meaning the incentive required to induce somebody to overcome the sacrifice involved in production' (D3/12/4; A5.6; underlining in the original).

The evolution of the cost concept had been, that is, from the things objectively necessary for production (means of production and workers' subsistence) to the incentives subjectively required to induce a supply of those means (undertaking the efforts and 'sacrifices' of labour and 'waiting'). As Sraffa explains:

> It was only Petty & the Physiocrats who had the right notion of cost as 'the loaf of bread'. Then somebody started measuring it in labour, as every day's labour requires the same amount of food. Then they proceeded to regard cost as actually an amount of labour. The[n] A. Smith interpreted labour as 'the toil and trouble' which is the 'real cost' […] and the 'hardship'. Then this was by Ricardo brought back to labour, but not far back enough, and Marx went only as far back as Ricardo. Then Senior invented Abstinence. And Cairnes unified all the costs (work, abstinence & risk) as sacrifice
>
> (D3/12/4, A5.4i)

—and, again, in another manuscript making the point more freely and expressively:

> This [the concepts of subjective costs and/or utility as ultimate standards] was an enormous breach with the tradition of Pol[itical] E[conomy]; in fact, this has meant the destruction of the classical P[olitical] E[conomy] and the substitution for it, under the old name, of the Calculus of Pleasure & Pain […].
>
> When the Jevonsians turned back to write their own history, they found with pride (it ought to have been with disma[y]) that they had no forerunners amongst P[olitical] E.[conomists]; their forerunners were mainly two or three cranks, an engineer Dupuit, a mathem[atician] Cournot, a Prussian civil servant Gossen, who had only cultivated P[olitical] E[conomy] as a hobby. […][32]
>
> They had not the slightest knowledge of the works of the Classical economists. They drew it out of their fancy. In fact, no competent P[olitical] E[cono]mist, with a conscience of his tradition, would have degnato [in Italian in the text: deemed worthy] to entertain those views
>
> (*ibid.*, A5.2i).[33]

The fundamental importance that Sraffa attributed to the concept of objective (physical) 'real costs' in contrast to subjective 'real costs' and/or utility will be less

[32] In the manuscript, Sraffa specifies: 'I do not mean by this that cranks can never find new theories: on the contrary when a big breach with tradition is required, their intervention is usually necessary. What I mean to prove is that there has actually been a breach with tradition, and the intervention of the cranks is an element of the evidence' (*ibid.*, A5.2ib; underlining in the original).

[33] The document continues: 'What had happened in the meantime, to change so much the mind of the economists, and induce them to scrap all that had been done up to that time? (It was in fact scrapping the whole: Jevons, Preface, and Cannan, Theories, 379–383, […]. Socialism has been the cause of all this. In fact, classical P[olitical] E[conomy], with its surplus to be arbitrarily divided, leads straight to Socialism' (*ibid.*, A5.2ii).

surprising for today's economists, who are used to seeing these problems in different forms, when we recall that the idea of physical real costs to be found in Petty and Quesnay is one and the same thing as the central concept characterizing the alternative classical theory that Sraffa was now in the process of rediscovering: the concept that is of a 'surplus' produced over and above the materials used and the workers' subsistence, with the corresponding determination by difference of rents (Quesnay) and/or profits (Smith and Ricardo). As we have seen, it is indeed the concept that quite naturally enters Sraffa's manuscripts of the period concerning 'the equations', which are always distinguished according to whether they refer to an economy with or without 'surplus'.

16. It is above all through this Classical conception of costs and the resulting notion of surplus that what Sraffa is developing in his manuscripts filters into the more than 200 pages of notes that he wrote for the lectures on the 'Advanced theory of value', as they were then held for the three academic years from 1928 to 1931 (D2/4). It is not the task of this essay to examine the lectures, or even to make a systematic treatment of the traces we find there of the 1927 turning point. We will do no more than indicate some of the salient characteristics of these traces.

The most obvious novelty with regard to the articles of 1925 and 1926 and to Sraffa's initial project for his lectures (see para. 5 above) lies in a first section of the lectures taking about one-third of the whole of the notes. This first part is devoted to the alternative between, on the one hand, subjective costs and/or utility, and on the other hand, the 'physical real costs' of the pre-lectures, which, however, are now generally indicated as objective costs or simply 'costs'.[34] The remaining two–thirds of the lectures consist then of material referring largely to the 1925 and 1926 articles.

The apparent purpose of the first part of the lectures is to show the inconsistency of Marshall's compromise of a twofold 'ultimate standard of value': utility, on the one hand, and costs in the form of 'efforts and sacrifices' on the other, where in equilibrium the two would have to be equal. In his lectures Sraffa argues then that the notion of 'costs' was developed by the Classical economists as a completely different objective concept referring to workers' subsistence and the other material means of production. These objective costs would not have been commensurable with utility as the ultimate standard of value, subsequently

[34] In a manuscript titled 'Principio' [Beginning] contained in a file dated November 1927, which may refer to a revised program for the Cambridge lectures (or perhaps to an outline for the opening of the projected book mentioned in para. 21 below) Sraffa writes: 'I shall begin by giving a short 'estratto' [extract] of what I believe is the essence of the classical theories of value, i.e. of those which include W. Petty, Cantillon, Physiocrats, A. Smith, Ricardo and Marx […] Then I shall go over these theories very cursorily, dealing with them, not at all exclusively but examining only those points which are relevant to my present purpose. So, of the Physiocrats, I shall not talk of […] the physiocratia, but only of one of its basic points' (*ibid.*, A5.11).

developed in contrast with the Classical costs. For the commensurability it logically needed, the Marshallian compromise had therefore to refer to subjective costs consisting, as we have seen, of the incentive necessary to induce the owners to allow their resources to be used in production. If this makes the costs commensurable with utility, it also transforms them, Sraffa argues, into nothing more than the negative utility of the alternative uses, which are given up in order to use the resources in the production in question. The Marshallian compromise is therefore no compromise at all, since it in fact leaves utility as the sole 'ultimate standard of value'. The real alternative as to the 'ultimate standard' is therefore the one between utility on the one hand and the Classical objective costs on the other.

As to which of the two should be chosen, Sraffa does not explicitly take sides in the lectures. Thus, for example, after distinguishing between the Classical notion of costs and the Marshallian one that he is about to trace back to utility alone, he observes: 'between these two notions of real cost it is not so much a question of one of them being right and the other wrong, as of one being relevant for dealing with one set of questions, and the other for an entirely different sort of questions' (D2/4, MI.7: 24–5).

Sraffa is allowed this agnosticism because, in concluding this first part, and moving on to the rest of the lectures, he argues:

> Of course, the next part of our analysis would have been made easier, if first we had found that there is one clear and definite conception of cost of production, about which all economists agree. But we shall see that, in the detailed application of the notion of cost to the theory of value, we are able to carry our analysis a fairly long way before we are faced by the sort of difficulties which may compel us to make up our mind about what exactly we mean by cost. And this is due chiefly to the fact that for the purpose of many questions arising in the determination of the price of any one particular commodity, the notion of expenses of production will be sufficient for most purposes without being necessary to decide[35] whether it is (1) merely a shadow of 'real costs' or sacrifices behind it or (2) another name for the utility of the product (opportunity cost) or (3) itself the ultimate real costs (not as a sum of money, but a sum of things consumed in production)
>
> (*ibid.*, MI.7: 61)

where the big novelty, announced with little fanfare, lies in the third possibility.

This argument that one can go 'a fairly long way' in the theory of value without dealing with what costs are, may however seem to echo the initial position in the pre-lectures, where the question of the causes of value was contrasted with that of the exchange 'of commodities between each other' (D3/12/3, A4.4v). But to pose the problem is also to realize how far Sraffa had travelled in the meantime as indicated already by the fact that this whole part of the lectures was nowhere to be found in the pre-lectures (see para. 5 above).

---

[35] In the rest of the passage, we have followed the alternative version that Sraffa inserts in the margin of his text, rather than the text itself, which says simply that there is no necessity of deciding 'what [the notion of expenses of production] is based upon, and whether it has any foundation at all'. (For an example of how the difficulties mentioned in the passage quoted in the text, cf. the quotation from the lectures above [*editor's note*: the latter sentence and the reference in it are evidently incomplete, possibly a residue of earlier drafts]).

The initial position in the pre-lectures had in fact been that of excluding from economic theory proper the question of the 'causes of value', whether costs or utility, as a 'primitive' and political—philosophical issue, all this in favour of a theory of value based on a notion of equilibrium independent of that issue. Here, instead, in this first part of the lectures, the discussion is pursued within the very framework set by the two 'causes of value'—it centres, that is, on the very aspect of the theory of value that Sraffa was there hoping to expunge (see above [Sect. III, *editor*]).

Indeed the vision is now that of two alternative theories of value distinguished according to the respective idea of the 'causes' of value, namely utility, or costs, the latter being now more precisely defined in the classical objective sense. The theory of value or more exactly the two alternative theories of value are now seen to be susceptible of a common treatment independent of the contrasting 'causes of value' to which they appeal but this only for part of the argument: Sraffa states that a point will come (basically with the theory of distribution: para. 6 above) at which one will be faced 'by the sort of difficulties which will compel us to make up our mind about what exactly we mean by cost'.

As a matter of fact, that 'fairly long way' common to both approaches—which will turn out to be largely that of the two articles of 1925 and 1926—is hardly compatible with the critique of partial equilibrium to which Sraffa had arrived at end of the pre-lectures and, it would seem, with the results that he had been achieving or was achieving in the manuscripts discussed above. In particular, as will be shortly confirmed by the lectures themselves, those results were throwing into doubt that pillar of partial equilibrium, which consists of the supply curve of a commodity. But, as will be argued in para. 19 below, this conflict between lectures and manuscripts may in part be the consequence of the compromise Sraffa had to strike because, beyond what he says about Classical costs and surplus in the first part of the lectures, he clearly felt that that new material emerging in the manuscripts was still in too fluid a state to be handled in lectures. However, in that first part of the lectures, Sraffa had allowed the central elements of an alternative theory to emerge, and in this way he had placed, so to say, a lien on all the rest of the lectures. However, the novelty was too radical and was presented with too little emphasis to allow his Cambridge students of the time to understand and perhaps even really notice it.

17. In fact the notion of surplus, which is completely missing in the pre-lectures, is introduced very concisely, but with great conceptual clarity as part of the objective conception of costs, when, e.g. Sraffa writes:

> This view [of wages as necessary subsistence for workers and not as inducement to the 'sacrifice' of working] leads to a conception of wages [...] during the productive process: they come thus to be identified with capital or at least with an important part of capital. Profits (and rent of course) are a part of the product and precisely *the excess of the product over the initial stock*
>
> (D2/4, MI.7: 24, our italics).

The contrast with the parallelism between wages and profits which the doctrine of subjective costs ('efforts and sacrifices') had attempted to establish, could not have been stated more sharply.

Or, again:

> For Quesnay […] the cost is […] an element of the productive process, which must be exactly measured in order to compare it with the product and thus determine whether the product contains *a surplus over and above cost*
>
> (*ibid.*, MI.7: 25–6, our italics),

and more generally:

> the notion of the surplus product plays an important part in classical economics. A. Smith adopted this notion of surplus and with it the idea of cost of the Physiocrats
>
> (*ibid.*, MI.7: 27).

Accordingly, in the theory of wages, which Sraffa traces in the Classical economists, we find the basic elements which, in their independence of supply and demand functions for labour, are in fact the ultimate foundation for the notion of surplus. 'Ricardo's theory regarded as the fundamental problem […] the distribution between the landlord and the other classes; when this was done the division of their share between capital and labour would take place on *entirely different principles*' (*ibid.*, MI.7: 7–8, our italics). This passage clearly excludes Marshallian labour demand and supply functions from any role in what is there called the 'division' between capital and labour. It would indeed be difficult to see such a determination of wages and profits as based on 'entirely different principles' from those applied for the classical rents, of which those Marshallian labour demand and supply functions are in fact intended to be a generalization.

18. As hinted above, there are in the lectures, besides the conception of surplus, also signs of a second central feature distinguishing the Classical approach which Sraffa is re-discovering, from the demand and supply of marginal theories. It is the negative one of the lack of any notion of supply functions for commodities. This is a direct consequence of determining prices and outputs in the way we saw in the winter-1927 manuscripts, independent of supply and demand functions, and a result, ultimately, of the different theory of distribution. Thus, in the margin of one passage of the Lectures, Sraffa notes:

> The interdependence of cost and quantity produced is quite a modern idea. All the classical economists ignore it altogether […]. It was only with the introduction of the concept of marginal utility that a possible quantitative connection between value and utility was perceived […] and in consequence of it […] variations of costs as a function of quantity produced were connected with the determination of value
>
> (*ibid.*, MI.7: 66–7)

and he adds, again in the margin:

> so much so that it cannot even be said that they assume constant costs to operate throughout as their argument implies, since they don't take the question into consideration at all
>
> (*ibid.*, MI.7: 66)

a striking change with regard to his Marshallian interpretation of the Classical economists of 1926 and 1927. Even if a residue of the Marshallian approach may perhaps be still detected in that phrase 'as their argument implies', in denying the existence of a supply function in the Classics, Sraffa is in effect saying that they took the quantities produced as given when determining prices. And this is in line also with his observation noted in para. 13 above, according to which the behaviour of costs as outputs vary is said to require specific consideration as to how and why outputs change.

In effect, if the Classical economists ignore the inter-dependence of prices and outputs while at the same time not assuming constant returns, their procedure can only have consisted of determining prices for the quantities produced in the situation under consideration, i.e. of taking outputs as given when determining prices. This is confirmed and reinforced by the consideration that when the behaviour of costs is likely to differ with the causes of the change in outputs (and information in this respect is not already included in the equation system determining prices: see para. 13 above), what is natural is to proceed by separating the determination of costs and prices from that of outputs, i.e. determining prices for given outputs and then consider how those prices are likely to change in response to the specific output changes envisaged. And this procedure is precisely the one Sraffa was in fact following when taking the quantities produced as given in 'the equations' of his manuscripts.

19. We have considered the new theoretical position Sraffa arrived at, but, as indicated already by Sraffa's caution in the lectures, we should not run too far ahead. He arrived at that new position in the sense of the initial break–through of the discovery that 'physical real costs' are sufficient to determine exchange relations independently of any demand and supply functions. It is the theoretical break–through that enabled Sraffa to say in his Preface to *Production of Commodities* that the 'central propositions' [in the book] had taken shape in the late 1920s and that, as early as 1928, 'Lord Keynes read a draft of the propositions with which this work opens'. But what we saw in para. 12–15 has shown us how, precisely because of its novelty, the new position needed all the development that Sraffa will put into it in subsequent years.

The structure and content of the Lectures of 1928–31 appear, however, to be a reflection not only of the above need for completion, but also of the very special situation in which Sraffa came to find himself as lecturer in Cambridge. Clearly, by character he was anything but an improviser and would find it impossible to hold lectures on material of which he felt not to be in full command. And, still more important perhaps, the fundamental break with contemporary theory, which he knew to be inherent in the theoretical position he had arrived at, was such as to make him even more careful. That break did not allow elements of the new position to be advanced before the whole of it had been brought to a certain degree of maturity. The approximations, inexactness or even inconsistencies, which may be a tolerable blemish when the terrain is that generally shared in the profession, can cause grave if not irreparable damage when the terrain is a new, unfamiliar one, as in Sraffa's case, in view also of the miscomprehensions and resistances, which that analysis would inevitably have encountered, if only for its distance from the positions that the profession had long occupied.

It should therefore not come as a surprise that, in the Lectures, there is, for example, no mention at all of 'the equations' that Sraffa was developing in those months or years, and that the expressions of the new position were limited to those of the kind we saw emerge through the Classical concept of objective costs as opposed to Marshall's subjective ones. Thus, as we said, in the remaining two–thirds of the lectures, we find materials coming largely from the two earlier articles, the same that Sraffa was now questioning in his manuscripts, but which was also that for which he had felt ready to lecture in Cambridge when invited by Keynes to do so in 1926.

20. This will also help to explain, among other things, why Sraffa found holding lectures in Cambridge painful enough to free himself of it as soon as he could: it may, that is, explain that difficulty quite irrespective of what may or may not have been the elements of character often attributed to him. (After all, he did not seem to find it particularly burdensome to give lectures in Perugia or Cagliari, nor, in those years, to give papers at King's College seminars on Italian politics, or the Florentine bankers,[36] nor was he particularly reluctant to hold lectures in Cambridge on subjects like the European banking system or, later, on 'Industry'—or even, as we shall presently see, on any other subjects, but the theory of value).

Something new and unexpected had in fact occurred with regard to the situation in which he had agreed to hold lectures on the theory of value, and it concerned the specific subject on which he was called upon to lecture.[37] The unexpected fact was the discovery of a theoretical approach, which was radically new for his contemporaries, and which because of this, he felt he should not prematurely expose to criticism. If the conquest, or rather re–conquest, of that theoretical position had roused his enthusiasm, it had also thrown into a crisis the synthesis he believed to have reached in 1925 and 1926, and possibly the developments of it he was projecting at the time. He thus found himself in the position that, on the one hand, he could not lecture on what he was intensely working on and, on the other, that the alternative he was apparently left with, was to lecture on what he had earlier committed himself to, i.e. on theories and concepts on whose validity, or at least significance, he had now come to have radical doubts. It would indeed be surprising if anybody enjoyed giving lectures in these circumstances. And, after some first attempts at communication, similar difficulties seem to have emerged for theoretical discussions even with his closest colleagues, whenever the exchanges went beyond a critical discussion of their work or of his own *past* work.

21. Thus, at a more immediate level, it is hardly surprising that Sraffa asked the university to let him postpone the lectures announced for October 1927. The subject matter for his lectures had been plunged into a crisis. Time was needed to attempt re–structuring the lectures, as he finally managed to by October 1928, with that first part, which, as we said, laid down a lien on what came after and in some way allowed Sraffa to reconcile the lectures he was giving with the new theoretical

[36] See the manuscripts [D2/5; MI.2], [D2/2; MI.3], [D2/6; MI.4], [D2/3; MI.5].

[37] See the documents quoted in para. 21 below.

landscape he was exploring. Moreover, all his interests and energy were now focused on the latter task, and on clarifying the results he had just arrived at. It could only be burdensome to give instead the necessary attention and time to preparing lectures on materials on whose validity, as we said, he could only be in doubt and which, in any case, must have seemed pale and lifeless by comparison with that on which he was working.

A sign of these two reasons for postponing the lectures is in fact readable in the letter that Sraffa wrote on 11 January 1928 to the General Board of the university, to apply for a second delay after the one he had obtained the previous October. He explains his request in the following way:

> This is partly due to the fact that now that I have prepared a certain number of lectures, I am convinced that the subject I have chosen is quite unsuitable. It is also partly due to the fact that I have been engaged on a piece of research which has so much occupied my mind as to interfere with everything else.
>
> [B9/1/16 in Trinity catalogue]

Qualifying as 'unsuitable' for his lectures, the subject he had earlier accepted to lecture on and which was that of the articles on which he had worked for years, successfully enough to be invited to Cambridge to lecture on it, will seem less startling when it is realized that the subject was exactly the one in which what we have called 'the new fact' had occurred. As for the research that had occupied his mind so much 'as to interfere with everything else', it was certainly a question of the fervour and excitement that is palpable in many of the manuscripts of the period, some of which we have quoted here.

The same factors behind Sraffa's procrastinations can be read even more significantly in the rough copy of a letter, which, at about the same time, on 14 January 1928 [B9/1/11 in Trinity catalogue], he planned to send to Pigou for the same purpose, while promising o give the lectures the following October. Here, he explains that his commitment is now 'independent of the program of work which I mentioned to you', and moreover that it is a commitment specific to holding the lectures on the theory of value or also—he, however, revealingly writes—'if I could not in the near future overcome the difficulties which have prevented my lecturing on that subject at present, on some subject *unconnected with it*' (my italics). What we have seen in this article may explain, on the one hand, what was the 'program of work' about which he had evidently talked with Pigou. On the other hand, the draft letter also casts a clear light on 'the difficulties which have prevented my lecturing on that subject at present'. These clearly had little to do with a general repugnance to lecturing: Sraffa offers to lecture on any other topic provided, he significantly says, it is 'unconnected' with the theory of value.[38]

[38] The letter to the board is quoted in Marcuzzo (2004: 126–7). The draft of the letter to Pigou is mentioned both in her paper and in Nerio Naldi (2004), whom I thank for drawing my attention to the two documents.

As for Sraffa's fervour and excitement for his work at this time, Keynes noted it down with his characteristic self-confident humour, when he wrote to his wife on 27 November 1927:

> Sraffa is in so much intellectual ferment and excitement about his ideas since I said that I thought there was something in them that he walks very fast up and down his room all day thinking about them. It is impossible for him to write them down, because as soon as he thinks about them, he has to start walking again. He is now inclined to give up his Christmas visit to Italy so that he can be able to continue in these courses for several weeks more.[39]

It is in these weeks—it is important to note—that Sraffa decides he will have to write a book.[40] Today, we can see that while striding back and forth in his room, he was also writing quite a lot and not about things of little import.

22. We can now conclude by mentioning an important manuscript whose tone shows in all its vivacity Sraffa's sense of discovery at this other world of economic theory, which he now understands to have been that of the Classical economists:

> in the middle of the 19th century a man succeeds, either by accident or by superhuman effort, in getting again hold of the classical theory: he improves it, and draws its practical consequences from it
>
> (D3/12/4, A5.14iii).

It seems clear that the man in question is Marx. (With these lines, we may incidentally note, Sraffa permits himself some immodesty in his inner dialogue: if it was so difficult to grasp Classical theory again only thirty years after Ricardo's death, how much more so a century after? Or did Sraffa think he had chanced on it 'by accident'?)

Now, this document and similar ones[41] seem to have been interpreted as the expression of a long-term strategy envisaged by Sraffa to rehabilitate Marx. What we have said above should be sufficient to show that this is far off the mark. It may be closer to reality to say that, before his theoretical break-through, Sraffa certainly had a good knowledge of Marx. He sympathized with his political and philosophical theses and also with some aspects of his ideas in economic theory, but entertained doubts about the strictly economical, rather than political–philosophical value of other aspects, including the labour theory of value (see the quotations in paras. 2, 4 and 11). It is only after his independent re-discovery of what he saw to be Classical economics, done along his very particular, personal path of a critique of Marshall's 'real costs', and the counter position to them of 'physical real costs' inspired by Quesnay and the Classical authors in a general sense, and after the

---

[39] For this letter, see Nerio Naldi's (2004: 101n.).

[40] See the manuscript D3/12/11, E2.49 contained in a block of notes dated November 1927 and headed 'Impostazione del libro [Outline of the book]'. Other notes from the period alluding to the book can be found in, for example, D3/12/4, A5.5; D3/12/9, E6.8 dated respectively November and Winter 1927.

[41] See, for example, D3/12/16; A3.12i.

resulting 'equations', that Sraffa came to recognize a new Marx as economic theorist, the one that arouses his admiration in the passage quoted above, and stimulates him to dive into reading (or re-reading) his works,[42] to come then, for example, in (1951), to the conclusion that the labour theory of value had in fact had a basic analytical role: that of expressing independently of distribution the aggregates on which a theory founded on the notion of social surplus naturally operates.[43]

---

[42] See, for example, apart from those quoted above, the further manuscripts D3/12/4, A5.2; *ibid.*, A5.7; D3/12/11, E.2.76; *ibid.*, E2.81; *ibid.*, E2.82; *ibid.*, E2.84; *ibid.*, E2.86; D3/12/10, E3.6; *ibid.*, E3.7; *ibid.*, E3.10; *ibid.*, E3.11; all of them manuscripts datable from November to December 1927.

[43] Thus Porta (2001) follows De Vivo (2000) in associating with the Cambridge lectures as such, Sraffa's intention of writing a book whose 'ultimate result' would be 'a restatement of Marx in 'our own modern metaphysics and terminology' (n. 30 above). Porta then writes:

> Sraffa's ambitions are very clear. The lectures [...] at Cambridge are to be made the occasion for a book' in which Marx must provide the guide both in method and in context
> (Porta 2001: 253).

And he proceeds to argue that 'behind the scenes' already at the time of the 1925 and 1926 articles, Sraffa's 'much larger ambition'(*ibid.*: 257) was to establish on Marx's lines both economic analysis in general and, through the interpretation of Ricardo he was to advance in (1951), the very history of political economy. However, as we saw in n. 30 above, the November 1927 manuscript to which Porta refers, far from revealing a project dating from the middle 1920's, appears to be rather the straightforward result of the theoretical break-through of that Autumn, and of Sraffa's consequent rediscovery of Marx and classical economics. [*Editor's note*: the above reference to n. 30 of the present article appears to be incongruous. The manuscript quoted in Porta (2001: 253) is D3/12/11, item 55 (E2.49 in the Bharadwaj–Garegnani inventory), of which no mention is made in n. 30 above. That manuscript is instead referred to in n. 40 above.] Indeed Porta's concern for Sraffa's ideological positions seems at times to get the upper hand upon demonstrating the putative errors, which that ideology would have caused in Sraffa's interpretation. Thus in his (1986) essay, referred to in (2001), and dealing with Sraffa's alleged central error of attributing to Ricardo a surplus procedure peculiar to Marx, Porta does not seem to ask himself the basic question of how could Ricardo have arrived in 1813–14 at his novel theory of profits, except by that very surplus procedure which he denies to the classical author (cf. Garegnani, 1983).

The latter point seems in fact to be at present granted also by Hollander (2000) who however sees now Sraffa's surplus founded interpretation as 'truncated' of the 'demand and supply' entering the system of the classical economists through the determination of the wage (2000: 197, 203). In common with Porta, he then proceeds to an examination of the manuscripts in order to trace the ideological reasons for Sraffa's alleged 'going astray' in his interpretation of Ricardo (2000: 193). Hollander might however have devoted more attention to his own allegation, and to some basic differences between the demand and supply of labour in Ricardo and the 'old' classical authors, on the one hand, and the homonymous neoclassical functions which he wishes instead to attribute to Ricardo on the other. It is the differences shown, for example, by the admission of permanent labour unemployment contained in Adam Smith (recognized by Hollander himself 1973: 245) and of course, in Ricardo's chapter 'On Machinery' and elsewhere in the *Principles*. (On classical labour demand and supply, and, in particular, on the frequent confusion between, on the one hand the classical relationships between the wage and the *growths of population and employment* and, on the other hand, the neoclassical labour supply and demand functions relating the wage to the labour supplied and employed *in a given position of the economy*, cf. Garegnani, 2002: 248–9 [this volume, Part III, pp. 346–8]).

References

De Vivo, G. (2000). Produzione di merci a mezzo di merci: Note sul percorso intellettuale di Sraffa. In M. Pivetti (Ed.), *Piero Sraffa. Contributi per una biografia intellettuale* (pp. 265–95). Carocci. (Eng. transl. De Vivo, 2003.)

De Vivo, G. (2001). Some notes on the Sraffa papers. In T. Cozzi & R. Marchionatti (Eds.), *Piero Sraffa's political economy* (pp. 157–164). Routledge.

De Vivo, G. (2003). Sraffa's path to production of commodities by means of commodities. An interpretation. *Contributions to Political Economy,* 22, 1–25.

Dobb, M. (1937). *Political economy and capitalism*. Routledge.

Garegnani, P. (2003). On Piero Sraffa's manuscripts (Eng. ver. of Garegnani, 1998). In H. D. Kurz & N. Salvadori (Eds.), *The Legacy of Piero Sraffa* (Vol. II, pp. 623–625). Edward Elgar.

Garegnani, P. (1983). Ricardo's early theory of profits and its rational foundation: A reply to Professor Hollander. *Cambridge Journal of Economics,* 7(2), 175–178.

Garegnani, P. (1998). Sui manoscritti di Piero Sraffa. *Rivista Italiana degli Economisti,* III(1), 151–155.

Garegnani, P. (2002). Misunderstanding classical economics? A reply to Blaug. *History of Political Economy,* 34(1), 241–254.

Gehrke, C., & Kurz, H. D. (2006). Sraffa on von Bortkiewicz: Reconstructing the classical theory of value and distribution. *History of Political Economy,* 38(1), 91–149.

Gilibert, G. (2004). The equations unveiled: Sraffa's price equations in the making. *Contributions to Political Economy,* 22, 27–40.

Hollander, S. (1973). *The economics of Adam Smith*. University of Toronto Press.

Hollander, S. (2000). Sraffa and the interpretation of Ricardo: The Marxian dimension. *History of Political Economy,* 32(2), 187–232.

Kurz, H. D., & Salvadori, N. (2004). Man from the moon. On Sraffa's objectivism. *Économies et Sociétés,* 35, 1545–57. Rpt. In H. D. Kurz & N. Salvadori (Eds.), *Interpreting classical economics. Studies in long-period analysis* (pp. 120–130). Routledge, 2007.

Kurz, H. D., & Salvadori, N. (2005). Representing the production and circulation of commodities in material terms: On Sraffa's objectivism. *Review of Political Economy,* 17(3), 413–441.

Marcuzzo, M. C. (2004). Sraffa all'Università di Cambridge. In *Atti del Convegno Internazionale 'Piero Sraffa'* (pp. 123–155). Accademia dei Lincei.

Naldi, N. (2004). 'Piero Sraffa: Emigrazione e attività scientifica fra gli anni Venti e gli anni Quaranta. In *Atti del Convegno Internazionale 'Piero Sraffa'* (pp. 81–121). Accademia dei Lincei.

Naldi, N. (1998). Some notes on Piero Sraffa's biography, 1917–1927. *Review of Political Economy,* 10(4), 493–515.

Porta, P. L. (2001). Sraffa's Ricardo after fifty years: A preliminary estimate. In E. L. Forget & S. Peart (Eds.), *Reflections on the classical canon in economics. Essays in honor of Samuel Hollander* (pp. 241–269). Routledge.

Porta, P. L. (1986). Understanding the significance of Piero Sraffa's standard commodity: A note on the Marxian notion of surplus. *History of Political Economy,* 18(3), 449–454.

Sraffa, P. (1951). Introduction to the *Principles*. In P. Sraffa with the collaboration of M. H. Dobb (Eds.), *The works and correspondence of David Ricardo* (Vol. I, pp. xiii–lxii). Cambridge University Press.

Sraffa, P. (1925). Sulle relazioni tra costo e quantità prodotta. *Annali di Economia,* 2(1), 277–328.

Sraffa, P. (1926). The laws of return under competitive conditions. *Economic Journal,* 36(144), 535–550.

Sraffa, P. (1960). *Production of commodities by means of commodities*. Cambridge University Press.

On Sraffa's Contribution to Economic Theory[†*]

1. It is not only during the last few decades that Sraffa has acquired an important place in discussions of economic theory. An article on the laws of variable returns published as early as 1926 (Sraffa, 1926) when he was 28, in which he was already pointing towards a criticism of the demand and supply theory of value, attracted much attention as soon as it appeared. At that time however the interest focused on some remarks on the theory of the firm, which were to be developed later by Joan Robinson in her theory of imperfect competition. The work by Sraffa which is at the heart of the discussion today belongs mainly to the period since 1951. I am referring to the *Works* of Ricardo (1951–73) which Sraffa edited for the Royal Economic Society, and to his book, *Production of Commodities by Means of Commodities* (1960). These works relate to two connected themes which are important (more important, perhaps, than is immediately apparent) for an understanding of the present situation of economic theory. The two themes are the criticism of the dominant demand-and-supply theory of distribution and relative prices, and the revival of a different approach to these problems: that of the British classical economists down to Ricardo. An attempt, however brief, at reporting Sraffa's contribution therefore requires some preliminary words about the dominant and the classical approaches to distribution, and the criticism levelled against the former.

2. I have referred to the 'modern' theory of distribution and relative prices, and to Sraffa's role in the criticism of it. By that I mean the theory based on the 'marginal' method that has held almost undisputed sway over economic thought since the last quarter of the nineteenth century. At its basis lies the idea of a

---

[†]Previously published with Macmillan in *Joan Robinson and Modern Economic Theory*, ed. by G. R. Feiwel, 1989. All necessary permissions acquired.

[*]With some modifications regarding the arrangement and presentation of the material, this text is the same as that published in Italian, together with texts by other authors, in the weekly paper *Rinascita* of 4 August 1978, on the occasion of Sraffa's eightieth birthday. It was therefore intended for a public consisting mainly of non-economists.

P. Garegnani, *Capital Theory, the Surplus Approach, and Effective Demand*, Springer Studies in the History of Economic Thought,
https://doi.org/10.1007/978-3-031-23643-3_17

substitutability between factors of production, traditionally founded upon the twin concepts of 'marginal utility' (i.e. the increment of satisfaction derived from a unit-increment of the consumption of a particular good) and 'marginal productivity' (i.e. the increment in output with a unit- increment of the 'factor of production' applied). By correlating a decrease (whether 'smooth' or 'by steps' is irrelevant here) in marginal utility and marginal productivity with an increase in the use of the good and of the factor of production respectively, this theory has sought a rational foundation capable of sustaining the notion of 'demand functions' for factors of production (traditionally: labour, capital and land). These 'demand functions' are then assumed to determine the remunerations of the factors by their intersection with the corresponding 'supply' functions. This intersection or 'equilibrium' of the demand for, and supply of, factors of production can be then shown to entail similar equilibria on the markets for the products, thereby determining the relative prices and outputs of the latter. In the words of the author who, more than anybody else among the initiators of the theory, contributed to its extraordinary success, Alfred Marshall:

> The normal value of everything, whether it be a particular kind of labour or capital or anything else, rests, like the keystone of an arch, balanced in equilibrium, between the contending pressures of its two opposite sides; the forces of demand press on one side, and those of supply on the other (Marshall, [1920] 1961, VI, II, 1, 526).

The practical implications of this theory for our view of the economy and of its management are, of course, far-reaching. Thus, for example, the theory underpins the generally accepted idea according to which competitive prices tend to reflect the 'scarcity' of 'factors of production' and products, and to guarantee a maximum of satisfactions for the community in some exactly definable sense.

3. Now, marginal theory, with its complex analytical structure, has been increasingly called into question as a result chiefly of two theoretical developments of the last four or five decades. The first development goes back to the late thirties and is a result of Keynes's work, and of the experience of the great economic crisis of those years. The idea was then admitted that, at least in the short period, there would be no spontaneous tendency to that equality between the quantity of labour demanded and supplied on which the theory relied for its determination of wages, profits and prices.

However, Keynes's criticism did not question the basic premises of orthodox theory and in particular the idea of a regular 'substitutability' between factors of production ensuring an inverse relation between the quantity of these employed and their relative rates of remuneration. On the contrary, Keynes explicitly accepted those premises. It was the second of the two theoretical developments referred to above that went on to question these premises. This was done, essentially, by criticizing the concept of capital as a factor or set of factors of production characteristic of the theory. This criticism has already shown the invalidity of some central propositions of the theory—such as that which postulates a direct relationship between 'capital intensity' and real-wage rates. It has also shown that a production technique which has been abandoned because of a rise in wages may profitably 'return' after wages have undergone a further rise: the phenomenon which has become known as the 'reswitching of techniques'. Of course, the latter possibility directly contradicts the proposition according to which wage rises lead to the introduction or expansion of more capital-intensive processes, thereby reducing the level of labour employment compatible with a given endowment of capital. And it was this proposition that was supposed to provide the rational basis for declining 'demand curves' of labour and the other factors of production and hence 'stable equilibria', thus supplying the foundation for an attempt to explain the distribution of the social product in terms of the marginalist supply and demand.

4. However, if we are to understand the place which Sraffa's work occupies in today's economic theory, it is not enough to refer to the criticism of marginal theory. We must also take a step back in the history of economic thought. As mentioned already, marginal theory was preceded by the theoretical approach which had been progressively worked out up to the time of the French Physiocrats and was then developed by the classical economists, particularly Ricardo. The analytical problems we shall presently mention (para. 5) were important in favouring the abandonment of this earlier approach, but no doubt important was also the theoretical support which the socialist movement was able to derive from Ricardo's work, especially in England, and already before the time of Marx.

In that earlier theoretical approach, the wage was not seen to be determined by an equilibrium between counterposed forces of demand and supply for factors of production. It was rather seen to be regulated by socioeconomic forces such as the historically determined level of subsistence (François Quesnay, Ricardo) or, more generally, the relative bargaining position of the social classes involved (Adam Smith, Marx). As a result the wage could be explained *independently* of the other forms of income: that is to say, it could be taken as a known quantity when determining the other forms of income, and especially the profits on capital.

Incomes other than wages could accordingly be calculated as what remained of the social product after deducting the known amount allotted to the workers: that is, income other than wages appeared as a 'surplus' over and above that amount—regardless of whether this surplus was determined in value form, as a 'surplus-value' or in physical terms, as a 'surplus-product'.

5. We now have the main elements for attempting to situate Sraffa's contribution. The importance of his work for today's economic theory seems to me to rest essentially on the three following elements: (i) his rediscovery of the theoretical approach characteristic of the classical economists; (ii) his solution to a number of analytical difficulties that were not resolved by Ricardo and Marx; (iii) his criticism of marginal theory.

For the first of these three elements, we should refer, apart from *Production of Commodities,* to the critical edition of Ricardo's work which absorbed the middle years of Sraffa's life (cf. Ricardo, 1951–73: for this classic among critical editions in all subjects, the Swedish Academy of Sciences awarded him the gold medal for the economic sciences, an honour which he shares only with Keynes and Myrdal). It was in fact in his 1951 *Introduction* to the first volume of that edition, and especially in the pages of it dealing with Ricardo's need to measure the product in terms independent of its distribution, that Sraffa succeeded in bringing back to light the approach peculiar to the classical theories (Sraffa, 1951, xxx–xxxvii). As he himself was later to say, this approach had been 'submerged and forgotten' (Sraffa, 1960, v). It had been submerged and forgotten beneath a thick layer of interpretations depicting Adam Smith and Ricardo as primitive precursors of subsequent marginal theories. There may indeed be a sense in which this first aspect of Sraffa's work is the most fundamental one since it provides the basis on which the remaining two stand.

As regards the second element, we should turn to *Production of Commodities by Means of Commodities* (1960). Here we find Sraffa's solution to the problem of determining the rate of profits and the relative prices of commodities, a solution based on more general hypotheses than those under which commodities would exchange in accordance with the labour necessary in order to produce them. These latter hypotheses were those to which the solution put forward by Ricardo and Marx had remained confined, because of the difficulties of the general case which they did not succeed in fully overcoming, and which were to play the role already mentioned in the abandonment of the classical approach.

Finally, with regard to the third main element of Sraffa's contribution, the same book rigorously sets out the propositions concerning that 'reswitching of techniques' which we already mentioned, and whose implications for a criticism of marginalism were then to be developed further by other writers.

These three main elements of Sraffa's contribution may help to clarify an issue which has been frequently aired in discussions both in Italy and elsewhere: the relationship between Sraffa's work and that of Marx. The question is a complex one which does not lend itself to a short answer. A first thing which may be said is that the conception which some people appear to have concerning that relationship is to my mind seriously misleading. In order to reach a correct understanding of the matter we should first try to understand the relationship between Marx and the classical economists, particularly Ricardo.

As I have argued elsewhere (Garegnani, 1984, 305–9 [this volume, Part III, pp. 320–4]), this relationship should be seen in terms of a strict continuity at the level of economic analysis. This constitutes no contradiction of the obvious fact that unlike Ricardo and the classical economists, Marx sought to show that the capitalist mode of production is no more permanent than the modes which had preceded it—the fact, that is, that Marx aimed at a 'critique of political economy'. There is no contradiction between the two things because it is normal that one author operating within a given theoretical approach should reach conclusions which were not reached by his predecessors, and which, for that matter, may then be either confirmed or disproved by the work of his successors. This is just the way in which a theoretical approach develops, so long as it is alive. This, I believe, is exactly the kind of relationship which Marx saw, and we can see, between his 'critique of political economy' and the work of Ricardo. Thus Marx deduced the transitory character of capitalism from a kernel of analysis whose content is what he often called the 'inner' or 'intrinsic' connections of the bourgeois system and, in particular, the antagonistic relation between wages and profits (cf. e.g. Marx, 1968, 164–6; 216–22). Now, as Marx himself repeatedly stated, these 'inner connections' were discovered by the classical economists, and especially by Ricardo, in connection with his theory of the rate of profits. And it was precisely this theory of profits which Marx took up and developed for his 'critique'.

Once this continuity between the classical economists and Marx is correctly understood, it becomes easy, I believe, to grasp the true relation between Sraffa and Marx. A resumption of the classical approach had naturally to start from the highest points of analytical development which that approach had achieved in the past—and in many respects these points are those at which we find that approach in Marx's work.

7. Once the relation between Marx and Sraffa is understood in these terms we are in better condition to deal with one aspect upon which the current discussion on the relation between Marx and Sraffa has sometimes insisted. A criticism of Marx has sometimes been seen to be implicit in the fact that we do not find in Sraffa the labour theory of value. It appears, however, that this point simply brings us back to the second of the three aspects of Sraffa's work we mentioned above: namely, the solution he provided for the problem of value for more general hypotheses than those under which Ricardo and Marx had solved it. Solving this problem and abandoning the labour theory of value as understood by Ricardo and by Marx are, in reality, two sides of the same coin. As should not need recalling, any living theoretical approach does develop, that is, it modifies some of its propositions.

In fact the idea according to which Sraffa would have exposed the invalidity of Marx's economic theory, since we do not find there Marx's labour theory of value, can only be understood, I believe, by recalling the ethical or sociological meanings ascribed to the labour theory of value by that Marxist tradition which had its beginnings at the end of the nineteenth century, following upon the criticism of Marx and of the labour theory of value by marginalist authors. I have argued elsewhere (cf. Garegnani, 1981, 71–3; 76–88 [Eng. ver. 2018, 631–2; 634–41]‡) that these meanings of the labour theory of value were not in fact present in Marx. They were developed later, largely as an answer to the marginalist criticism, and appear to have reflected the obfuscation which, by that time, had spread over the approach of the classical economists. That obfuscation appears in particular to have prevented an understanding of the analytical role which the labour theory of value played in allowing Ricardo and Marx to overcome the basic error by which Adam Smith had overlooked the constraint which binds the real wage and

‡ [*Editor's note*: Garegnani (2018), published several years after the author's departure, is the English version of Garegnani (1981), revised by the author and prepared for publication by Professor Fabio Petri. Since the revision (still in progress at the time of Garegnani's death, as specified by Petri in the initial note) did not modify either the contents or the structure of the essay, the references to the English version here provided exactly match the original references to the Italian version.]

the rate of profits, given the technical conditions of production. It is significant that this role of the labour theory of value (which was a discovery of Ricardo, and not of Marx) should have been brought back to light by Sraffa himself, in his Introduction to Ricardo's *Principles* (Sraffa, 1951, xxxii–xxxiii). In this way, far from criticizing Marx for his use of that theory, Sraffa in fact made an effective defence of it in the analytical sense in which it had been used by Ricardo and by Marx. It should be recalled in this connection how Marx himself had always been contemptuous of any attempt to draw ethical or sociological conclusions from the labour theory of value (cf. e.g. Marx, 1970, 62n).

8. This having been said, it is important to remember that Sraffa only laid the premises for a resumption of the classical approach to distribution and relative prices. He did this by clarifying anew the basic elements of that approach, and by providing a solution to the problems of value theory that had been left open by Ricardo and Marx. It would therefore be a mistake to seek in *Production of Commodities* what is not actually there: to seek, that is, an explanation of capital accumulation, or even (except for some hints) an analysis of the way in which social relations determine the division of the product between wages and profits. As indicated above, so far as these problems are concerned, Sraffa appears to refer us to the places where they have received the most advanced treatment in the framework of this theoretical approach, and therefore to all the work which has to be done in order to develop the ideas of the classical economists in conformity with the present state of economic reality and of economic knowledge.

9. Another basic issue, which has been aired in current discussions in Italy and elsewhere, concerns the relation that can be established between the analysis of Sraffa and that of Keynes. I can attempt to say something on this issue here only after reformulating it in terms of the relationship which in my opinion exists between Keynes and the resumption of the classical theoretical approach which has been initiated by Sraffa. For, in his published writings, Sraffa has only marginally concerned himself with Keynes.

Looking at things in this more general light, we are immediately struck by Keynes's complex relationship to marginal theory. True, Marshall's variant of this theory constituted the entire horizon within which Keynes received his training and beyond which, in a sense, he never went. In this respect, Sraffa's work is of a profoundly different character, being directed from the very beginning to a criticism and replacement of marginal theory. Yet, at the same time, Keynes dealt a serious blow to that theory when he disputed the tendency to an equality between the supply of, and the demand for, labour. This second element could not fail to draw Keynes close to those, like Sraffa, who criticized such a theory.

In my view, however, this negative, critical element is not the only, or even the main contribution which the contemporary resumption of classical theory can draw from Keynes's work. As I said, this resumption inevitably has in Marx's analysis one of its main starting points. Now, unlike what is true in subsequent marginal theory—indeed, unlike in Ricardo himself—the idea that aggregate demand tends to adjust to the productive capacity of the economy is quite foreign to Marx's analysis. As is well known, Marx's theory of crises clearly raises the very problems of 'effective demand' which are posed by Keynes. Keynes's 'multiplier' principle, which does a great deal to explain the mechanism by which slumps come about, may provide us with a highly valuable element for developing the analysis of the link between economic cycles and the process of accumulation. As a matter of fact, the principles of the 'multiplier' and of 'effective demand' are entirely independent of other Keynesian concepts bearing the traces of marginal theory (like the concept of a regular inverse relation between investment and the interest rate), which are also those that allowed marginal theory to achieve some success over the last thirty years in its attempt to reabsorb Keynes's criticism.

References

Garegnani, P. (1981). La teoria del valore: Marx e la tradizione marxista. In *Marx e gli economisti classici* (pp. 55–88). Einaudi.
Garegnani, P. (1984). Value and distribution in the classical economists and Marx. *Oxford Economic Papers, New Series,* 36(2), 291–325.
Garegnani, P. (2018). On the labour theory of value in Marx and in the Marxist tradition. *Review of Political Economy*, 30(4), 618–42 (Eng. ver. of Garegnani, 1981).
Marshall, A. ([1920] 1961). *Principles of economics* (9th edn, Vol. I). Macmillan.
Marx, K. (1968). *Theories of surplus value*. Lawrence & Wishart.
Marx, K. (1970). *Capital. A critique of political economy* (Vol. I). Progress Publishers.
Ricardo, D. (1815), *An essay on the influence of a law price of corn on the profits of stock,* in Ricardo (1951–73), Vol. IV.
Ricardo, D. (1951–73). *The works and correspondence of David Ricardo*, edited by P. Sraffa with the collaboration of M. H. Dobb (11 Vols.). Cambridge University Press.
Sraffa, P. (1926). The laws of returns under competitive conditions. *Economic Journal,* 36(144), 535–550.
Sraffa, P. (1951). Introduction to the *Principles*. In Ricardo (1951–73) (Vol. I, pp. xiii–lxii).
Sraffa, P. (1960). *Production of commodities by means of commodities*. Cambridge University Press.

Correction to: Capital Theory, the Surplus Approach, and Effective Demand

Correction to:
P. Garegnani, *Capital Theory, the Surplus Approach, and Effective Demand*, Springer Studies in the History of Economic Thought,
https://doi.org/10.1007/978-3-031-23643-3

The original version of the book was inadvertently published with incorrect information in chapters 1, 2, 7, and 15, the corrections are given below:

- p. 41, fn. 100: replace subscript "L" with 1: Q1
- p. 160 end of the last line end dot inserted after "etc."
- p. 477, fn. †: replace "There Is" with "Is There"; replace "Bohem" with "Boehm"
- On p. 338 a mistake appears in the diagram here reproduced, as already present in the original publication, which consists of the word "Substance" instead of the correct "Subsistence". The book and the chapters have been updated with the changes.

The updated version of these chapters can be found at
https://doi.org/10.1007/978-3-031-23643-3_1
https://doi.org/10.1007/978-3-031-23643-3_2
https://doi.org/10.1007/978-3-031-23643-3_7
https://doi.org/10.1007/978-3-031-23643-3_15

P. Garegnani, *Capital Theory, the Surplus Approach, and Effective Demand*, Springer Studies in the History of Economic Thought,
https://doi.org/10.1007/978-3-031-23643-3_18

MIX
Papier aus verantwortungsvollen Quellen
Paper from responsible sources
FSC® C105338

FSC
www.fsc.org

If you have any concerns about our products,
you can contact us on
ProductSafety@springernature.com

In case Publisher is established outside the EU,
the EU authorized representative is:
Springer Nature Customer Service Center GmbH
Europaplatz 3, 69115 Heidelberg, Germany

Printed by Libri Plureos GmbH
in Hamburg, Germany